新概念英汉小词典

《新概念英汉小词典》编委会

主　编：严　明

副主编：沈米成　胡中华

编　者：（以姓氏笔画为序）

马安根　王　勇　牛春明

申丽娅　吕慧芳　刘惠芳

杜　丽　范冬梅　姜晓芳

秦　亮　高山雁　董小丽

吉林出版集团有限责任公司　外语教育出版公司

Foreign Language Education Books,Jilin Publishing Group

图书在版编目(CIP)数据

新概念英汉小词典 / 严明主编.—长春：吉林出版集团有限责任公司，2008.01

ISBN 978-7-80762-277-2

Ⅰ.①新… Ⅱ.①严… Ⅲ.①英语—词典②词典—英、汉 Ⅳ.①H316

中国版本图书馆 CIP 数据核字(2007)第 198333 号

新概念英汉小词典

主　　编：严　明
责任编辑：潘莉莉
封面设计：苏毅强
开　　本：850×1168　1/64
字　　数：600 千字
印　　张：12.125
版　　次：2008 年 1 月第 1 版
印　　次：2012 年 1 月第 5 次印刷

出　　版：吉林出版集团有限责任公司
发　　行：吉林出版集团外语教育有限公司
地　　址：长春市泰来街 1825 号
邮编：130011
电　　话：总编办：0431-86012683
发行部：0431-86012675　0431-86012826(Fax)
网　　址：www.360hours.com
印　　刷：河北新华第一印刷有限责任公司

ISBN 978-7-80762-277-2　定价：13.80 元

前　言

本词典遵循以下几个原则:一、简明:根据中学英语教学的实际情况,参照新《英语课程标准》,精选了初高中阶段常用的3,600余个单词,重点讲解常用释义,并附有说明用法的简明例句。二、实用:考虑到使用者的实际情况,本书设置常用短语、词汇拓展和用法工具箱等小栏目,及时解决读者在学习中遇到的问题。三、清新:版面设计整齐清晰,各个小栏目均采用不同的版式设计,力求使读者一目了然。

本词典由著名英语辞书专家、教授刘庆双博士等策划,教育部大学英语教学指导委员会委员、大学英语四、六级考试委员会委员、著名英语教授严明博士领衔主编,保证其准确性和权威性,特此致谢。

编　者

体例说明

§ **单词**

本词典共收单词 3,600 余条，均按英语字母顺序排列。

两个拼法相同，但字义各异的单词，分别在该单词的右上角上加注 1、2……，分立词目。

例 **arm**[1]，…… **n.** ❶臂，……

arm[2]，…… **v.** ❶用武器装备，……

§ **发音**

1. 本词典采用 K. K. 音标和 IPA 音标来标注读音，置于〔 〕之内，并用 ‖ 隔开。

2. 有些单词在发音时分强读和弱读，本词典均予以标注。

例 **have** 〔(强)hæv ‖ hæv；(弱)həv ‖ həv〕

3. 因词性不同而读音有别时按释义中的词性分别标出。

§ **词形变化**

名词的复数形式(用[名复])；形容词、副词的比较级变化(比较级用[比]，最高级用[最])；动词的变化(过去式用[过去式])过去分词(用[过去分词])

§ **词性**

单词的词性用下列英文缩写标明

n. ——名词 { C——可数名词；U——不可数名词 }　　P——用复数形式

v. ——动词 { **vi.** ——不及物动词；**vt.** ——及物动词 }

a. ——形容词　　**ad.** ——副词

prep. ——介词　　**art.** ——冠词

conj.——连词　　　　int.——感叹词
pron.——代词　　　　v. aux.——助动词
abbr.——缩略词

§ **释义**

1. 为了加深单词释义的理解和使用，重点释义均附以例句。

2. 释义按其常用性用❶、❷、❸标示。

3. 大体相同的若干释义列在一条内。

4. 补充说明词义的用法放在[　]内；英美用法和学科用语放在【　】内。

例　**ability** 〔ə'bɪlətɪ‖ə'bɪlɪtɪ〕 **n.** 能力；能耐，本领[＋to-v]
　　director ……❹【主美】【音】指挥

§ **附加小功能**

1. 常用短语：列出以该词为中心词的常用短语，必要时给出例句。

2. 词汇拓展：给出该主词条为词根的衍生词、复合词。

3. 用法工具箱：给出与该主词条有关的语法知识、近义词辨析等相关内容。

4. 反义词：以〔**反义**〕标示。
　同义词：以〔**同义**〕标示。

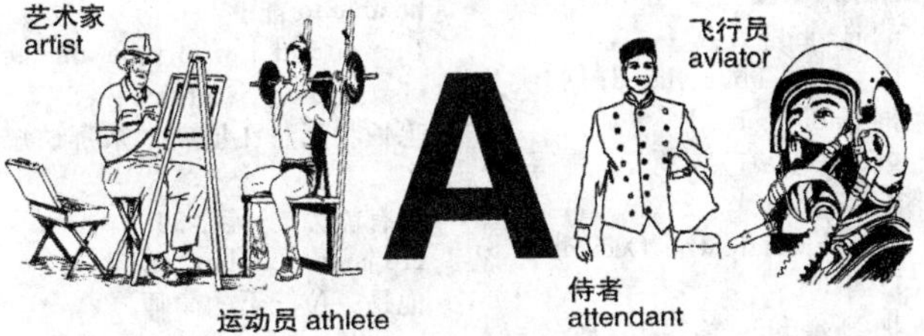

A〔(强) e‖eɪ;(弱)ə‖ə〕，以元音音素开始的单词前用 an〔(强)æn‖ən;(弱)æn‖ən〕

art. ❶一,一个(用在单数可数名词之前)

a pen

一支笔

an egg

一个鸡蛋

❷泛指一类人或物

A dog is a lovely animal.

狗是可爱的动物。

❸每一(个)

He comes here twice a week.

他每星期来这儿两次。

❹同一,相同

We are of an age.

我们同龄。

Your shoes and mine are of a size.

你和我穿同样尺码的鞋。

❺某一(指说话者不认识的人)

A Mr. Smith wishes to speak to you.

有一位史密斯先生要跟您说话。

❻为……的作品(用于艺术家名字之前)

I want a Rembrandt.

我想要伦伯朗的作品。

❼像……一样的人

He is a Shakespeare of China.

他是中国的莎士比亚。

abandon〔əˈbændən‖əˈbændən〕[过去式] abandoned;[过去分词] abandoned

vt. 放弃,遗弃

The crew abandoned the ship.

船员们放弃了这条船。

He abandoned his wife and went away with all their money.

他遗弃了他的太太,带走了所

有的钱。

A

abbreviate 〔əˈbrivɪˌet ‖ əˈbriːvɪeɪt〕

［过去式］abbreviated；［过去分词］abbreviated

vt. 缩写，缩短，简化，简写成，缩写为

to abbreviate the December to Dec.

把 December 简写为 Dec.

abbreviation 〔əˌbrivɪˈeʃən ‖ əˌbriːvɪˈeɪʃən〕

n. 缩写，节略；缩写词，略语

Jan. is the abbreviation for January.

Jan. 是 January 的缩写。

ability 〔əˈbɪlətɪ ‖ əˈbɪlɪtɪ〕

n. ［C］［U］❶能力；能耐，本领［+to-v］

She did the work to the best of her ability.

她已尽力去做那件工作了。

Man has the ability to speak.

人有说话的能力。

❷才能；专门技能［P］

The acting abilities of both are well-known.

两人的表演才能都是众所周知的。

able 〔ˈebl̩ ‖ ˈeɪbl〕

a. ❶能够［+to-v］

常用短语

be able to 能够

I am afraid I won't be able to visit you on Saturday.

恐怕我无法在星期六来拜访您了。

❷有能力的；能干的

He is an able lawyer.

他是一位能干的律师。

aboard 〔əˈbord ‖ əˈbɔːd〕

ad. 在船（或飞机、车）上；上船（或飞机、车）

It's time to go aboard.

现在是上车的时候了。

prep. 在（船、飞机、车）上；进入，上（船、飞机、车）

Let's go aboard the ship.

咱们上船吧。

about 〔əˈbaʊt ‖ əˈbaʊt〕

prep. ❶关于，对于

My mother often spoke to me about you.

家母常和我谈起你。

❷在……的附近；在……的周围

She sat up and looked about her.

她坐了起来，环顾四周。

❸在……的身边，手头

I had no money about me.

我身边没有带钱。

ad. ❶在四周；到处

She likes to walk about.
她喜爱四处走走。
❷在附近，在近处
There were few people about.
附近几乎无人。
❸大约；几乎
John is about the same age as Tom.
约翰和汤姆的年龄相仿。

常用短语

be about to do 即将，正要
He is about to go.
他正要走。
What/How about … (表示劝诱)……怎么样？/(事情)……怎么样了？
How about a cup of coffee?
来杯咖啡如何？
What about your new plan?
你的新计划怎么样了？

above 〔ə'bʌv ‖ ə'bʌv〕
prep. ❶在……上面
The moon is above the trees.
月亮挂在树梢上。
❷在……之上，超过
They are children above 6 years old.
他们是6岁以上的孩子。
❸高于；优于；胜过
In the company, Dick ranks above Tom.
在公司里，迪克的地位比汤姆高。
ad. ❶在上面；向上面
There are snowy peaks above.
上面是白雪皑皑的群峰。

on 是［接触于……之上］
on the table
在桌子上
above 是［离……上有一点距离］
The plane was flying above the clouds.
飞机在云上飞行。

用法工具箱

❷(级别，数目等)更高；更大；更多
Men and women of 18 and above are eligible to vote.
年龄在18岁以上的男女有投票表决权。
❸在上文
See the examples given above.
见上述例子。
a. 上文的，前述的
n. 上文；上述事实
In addition to all of the above, she won the Pulitzer Prize in 1980.
除上述外，她还在1980年获得

普利策奖。

A

abroad 〔ə'brɔd ‖ ə'brɔːd〕

ad. ❶在国外；到国外

My son is still living abroad.

我的儿子仍住在国外。

❷在外面；到外面

They usually walk abroad in warm days.

在暖和天气他们通常去户外散步。

n.（用在 from 后）异国，海外[U]

They just returned from abroad.

他们刚从国外回来。

absence 〔'æbsn̩s ‖ 'æbsəns〕

n. ❶不在，缺席[C][U][(+from)]

〔**反义**〕presence 出席；到场

❷缺少，缺乏[U][(+of)]

常用短语

absence of mind 心不在焉

absent 〔'æbsn̩t ‖ 'æbsənt〕

a. ❶缺席的，不在场的

Three members of the class were absent this morning.

今天早晨该班有 3 人缺席。

❷缺少的，不存在的

Snow is absent in his country.

他的国家不下雪。

❸茫茫然的，心不在焉的

He had an absent look on his face.

他脸上露出心不在焉的神色。

absolute 〔'æbsəˌluːt ‖ 'æbsəluːt〕

a. ❶纯粹的；完全的

His story was an absolute lie.

他的所述是十足的谎言。

❷绝对的

There's no absolute standard for it.

它没有绝对的标准。

❸专制的

An absolute ruler can do just as he pleases.

一个专制的统治者可以为所欲为。

词汇拓展

absolutely *ad.*

❶绝对地，断然

❷（回答）正是那样

accent 〔'æksɛnt ‖ 'æksənt〕

n. [C]❶重音；重音符号

❷口音，腔调

Judging by her accent, she must be a Southerner.

从她的口音判断，她准是南方人。

accept 〔ək'sɛpt ‖ ək'sept〕

[过去式] accepted；[过去分词] accepted

vt. ❶接受，领受；答应，同意

He has accepted our invitation.
他已经接受了我们的邀请。
❷承认,认可[(+as)][+that]
The astronaut accepts danger as being part of the job.
宇航员承认他们的工作包括危险。
❸相信[+that]
He wouldn't accept that smoking did harm to health.
他不相信吸烟有害健康。

accident 〔ˈæksədənt ‖ ˈæksɪdənt〕
n. ❶事故;灾祸[C]
He died in an automobile accident years ago.
他数年前死于车祸。
❷意外事情;偶然因素,机遇[C][U]
The discovery was a happy accident.
这一发现出人意料,令人高兴。

常用短语

by accident 偶然
I met him in the train by accident.
我偶然在火车上遇到他。

according 〔əˈkɔrdɪŋ ‖ əˈkɔːdɪŋ〕
ad. according to +名词
❶根据;按照
❷取决于
❸据……所载;据……所说
According to the report, he is alive.
据报道,他还活着。
They are arranged according to their size.
它们按照大小顺序排列。

account 〔əˈkaunt ‖ əˈkaʊnt〕
[过去式] accounted; [过去分词] accounted
n. ❶ 账,账目,账单[C]
The accounts show we have spent more than we received.
账目显示我们已经入不敷出了。
❷账户;客户 [C]
The company is our best account.
这家公司是我们的最佳客户。
a bank account
银行户头
❸记述,描述;报道[C][(+of)]
The policeman gave an account of the traffic accident.
警察叙述了交通事故的经过。
❹解释,说明[C][(+of)]
❺估价;价值,重要性 [U]
He is a man of little account.
他是个无足轻重的人。

常用短语

on account of 因为;由于

He retired on account of poor health.
他因健康欠佳而退休了。
on no account 决不
On no account will I do it.
我决不会做。
take into account 考虑到;体谅
You must take it into account.
你必须把这事考虑一下。
vi. ❶报账
❷解释,说明;对……负责[(+for)]
He could not account for his absence from school.
他无法说清楚为什么旷课。

across 〔ə'krɔs ‖ ə'krɔːs〕
prep. ❶横越,穿过
We walked across the street.
我们穿过马路。
❷在……那边
He stared at the Englishman across the table.
他一直盯着坐在桌子对面的那个英国人。
❸与……相交叉
The two lines cut across each other.
两条线相互交叉。
ad. ❶横过
We got into the boat and rowed across.
我们上了船,将船划到对岸。
❷宽
The river is two miles across.
河宽两英里。
❸在对面;向对面
Can you jump across?
你能跳过去吗?
常用短语
come /run across 偶然遇见(某人),突然想起(某事)
I came across him on the street.
我在街上偶然遇见他。

act 〔ækt ‖ ækt〕
[过去式] acted;[过去分词] acted
vt. ❶扮演
He acted Othello at the Royal Theater that evening.
那天晚上他在皇家剧院扮演奥赛罗。
❷装出;举动像
He acted the wise man who knew everything and never made mistakes.
他假装成是无所不知,从不出错的聪明人。
vi. ❶行动
We should act immediately.
我们应该立即行动。
❷起作用,见效[(+on/upon)]
❸假装;演戏,表演

The actress acts very well.
这位女演员的表演非常出色。
❹扮演，充当[(＋as)]
John acted as chairman in his absence.
他不在时，约翰充当主席。
❺举止，表现
n. [C]❶行为；行动
Helping a blind man is an act of kindness.
帮助盲人是慈善的行为。
❷【戏】(常大写)幕；节目
She was magnificent in the First Act of *Carmen*.
她在《卡门》的第一幕中演得好极了。
❸(常大写)法案，法令
Would you tell us something about the new Education Act?
请你给我们讲讲新的《教育法》好吗？

act 和 action
act 指个人的行为，action 指整体的行为。
如，an act of kindness
慈善的行为
a man of action
实践家

用法工具箱

action ['ækʃən ‖ 'ækʃən]
n. ❶行动；行为；活动[C][U]
The quick action of the firemen saved the building from being burned down.
消防队员行动及时，该建筑物方免遭焚毁。
❷作用[U]
The action of water on rock should be taken into account.
应考虑到水对岩石的作用。
❸情节
All the action in the play takes place at one railroad station.
该剧的整个情节均发生在一个火车站上。

active ['æktɪv ‖ 'æktɪv]
a. ❶活跃的；活泼的
Mrs. Brown is over 80 and not very active now.
布朗太太已八十多岁，现在不大活动了。
❷积极的；勤奋的
He became an active social reformer.
他成了一位积极的社会改革家。
❸在活动中的；在进展中的
Mount Vesuvius is an active volcano.
维苏威是一座活火山。

A

词汇拓展

actively *ad.* 活跃地,积极地

activity 〔æk'tɪvətɪ ‖ æk'tɪvɪtɪ〕

[名复]activities

n. ❶活动;活动力

mental activity

脑力活动

❷(某一团体的)特殊活动;带消遣性的活动

campus activity

校内活动

actor 〔'æktɚ ‖ 'æktə〕

n. [C]男演员;演员

He was considered the best actor in London.

他当时被看成是伦敦最出色的演员。

〔反义〕actress 女演员

actual 〔'æktʃuəl ‖ 'æktʃuəl〕

a. 实际的,事实上的

What he told us was an actual happening.

他告诉我们的是一件真实事情。

词汇拓展

actually *ad.* 实际地,真实地

A. D.

abbr. =Anno Domini 公元

add 〔æd ‖ æd〕

[过去式]added;[过去分词]added

vt. ❶添加;增加

The fire is going out, will you add some wood?

火快熄了,请你加些木柴好吗?

❷将……相加[(+up/together)]

If we add these marks up, we'll get a total of 90.

如果我们把这些分数加起来,总数就有 90 分了。

❸补充说

"I felt very sorry for her," Bob added.

"我为她感到非常惋惜,"鲍勃又说道。

vi. ❶增加[(+to)]

The snowstorm added to our difficulties.

暴风雪增加了我们的困难。

❷做加法;加起来

The little girl has begun to learn to add and subtract.

这个小女孩已在学做加减法了。

addition 〔ə'dɪʃən ‖ ə'dɪʃən〕

n. ❶加,附加[U][(+to)]

❷【数】加法[U]

❸增加的人(或物)[(+to)]

He had an addition to his family last year.
去年他家又多了一口人。

常用短语

in addition 另外
I paid 3,000 dollars in addition.
我加付 3,000 美金。

in addition to 除……之外(还)
He earns 10,000 yen in addition to his salary.
除了薪水之外,他还赚了10,000日元。

address 〔ə'drɛs ‖ ə'dres〕
[过去式] addressed; [过去分词] addressed
n. ❶住址,地址[C]
What's your home address?
你的家庭住址呢?
❷演说,致辞[C]
The mayor gave a television address yesterday evening.
市长昨晚作了电视讲话。
❸称呼,头衔[C](通常用 addresses)
vt. ❶在……上写收件人姓名地址
She addressed the parcel wrongly because of anxiousness.
因为着急,她把包裹上收件人的地址写错了。
❷(在大会上)向……作正式讲话,向……发表演说
He is going to address the meeting.
他将向大会作演说。
❸对……说话
He is addressing the chairman.
他正在跟主席说话。

admire 〔əd'maɪr ‖ əd'maɪə〕
[过去式] admired; [过去分词] admired
vt. ❶钦佩;欣赏[(+for)]
We admire her for her diplomatic tact.
我们佩服她的外交技巧。
❷称赞,夸奖
He admired her new hat.
他称赞她的新帽子。

admit 〔əd'mɪt ‖ əd'mɪt〕
[过去式] admitted; [过去分词] admitted
vt. ❶承认
You must admit the task to be difficult.
你得承认这个任务是艰巨的。
❷准许进入;准许……进入(或加入)[(+into/to)]
He was admitted to the school.
他获准进入那所学校就读。
❸容许;可容纳
The theater admits 1,000 people.

A

该剧院可容纳 1,000 人。

vi. ❶ 承认[(+to)]

I must admit to feeling ashamed of my conduct.

我得承认因自己的行为而感到羞惭。

❷容许，有余地[(+of)]

This matter admits of no delay.

这事不容耽搁。

adopt 〔ə'dɑpt ‖ ə'dɒpt〕

[过去式]adopted;[过去分词]adopted

vt. ❶ 采取;采纳;吸收

After much consideration, the president decided to adopt her suggestion.

总统再三考虑之后，决定采纳她的建议。

❷过继，收养[(+as)]

Mr. Kern adopted the orphan as his own son.

克恩先生将那孤儿收养为自己的儿子。

词汇拓展

adoption *n.* 采用;收养

adult 〔ə'dʌlt ‖ 'ædʌlt〕

a. ❶成年的;成年人的

He'd spent all his adult life in the army.

他的成年生活全是在军队里度过的。

❷成熟的

Dick is a rather adult child.

迪克少年老成。

❸【美】限于成年人(观看)的(指电影等);【婉】色情的

an adult bookstore

卖黄色书刊的书店

n. [C] ❶成年人

In this sense, children and adults have equal rights.

从这个意义上说，儿童和大人享有同样的权利。

❷已长大的动物(或植物)

an adult deer

成年的鹿

advance 〔əd'væns ‖ əd'vɑːns〕

[过去式]advanced;[过去分词]advanced

vt. ❶使向前移动;推进，促进

The president has done his best to advance the national interest.

总统已尽了最大努力来增进国家的利益。

❷将……提前

The date of the meeting was advanced by 4 days.

会议提前 4 天召开。

vi. ❶前进;向前移动

She advanced on him silently.
她悄悄地向他走去。
❷进展;进步
We had greatly advanced in our knowledge of the world.
我们在世界知识方面大有长进。
n. ❶前进
The advance of the enemy troops was halted by a heavy snow.
一场大雪阻止了敌军的进攻。
❷发展 [C]
Remarkable advances have been made in space science.
太空科学已有了长足的发展。
❸增长;增高;擢升 [C]
Her colleagues were all surprised at her rapid advance in the company.
她的飞速升迁令公司同人均感惊奇。

常用短语

in advance ❶在前面 ❷预先
Please let me know the time of your arrival in advance.
请事先告诉我你到达的时间。
in advance of 在……的前面;在……的前沿
His policy was in advance of his times.
他的政策走在时代的前端。

advantage [əd'væntɪdʒ ‖ əd'vɑːntɪdʒ]
n. ❶有利条件,优点,优势[C][U]
He had the advantage of a good education.
他具备受过良好教育的优势。
❷利益,好处[C][U]
What is the advantage of using nuclear power?
使用核能有何好处?

常用短语

take advantage of ❶利用
Don't take advantage of others' weakness.
不要利用别人的弱点。
❷欺骗;占……的便宜

adventure [əd'ventʃɚ ‖ əd'ventʃə]
n. ❶冒险,冒险精神[U]
He is a man full of adventure.
他是一个充满冒险精神的人。
❷冒险活动(或经历)[C]
They set out on a daring space adventure.
他们着手进行一项大胆的太空探险。
❸激动人心的活动(或经历)[C]
The storm made our hike a real adventure.

A

暴风雨使得我们的徒步旅行成了一次真正令人难忘的经历。

词汇拓展

adventurous *a.* 喜欢冒险的
adventurer *n.* 冒险家

advertisement
〔ˌædvəˈtaɪzmənt ‖ ædvəˈtaɪzmənt〕
n. 略作 ad. 广告，宣传
Advertisement helps to sell goods.
广告有助于推销商品。

advice 〔ədˈvaɪs ‖ ədˈvaɪs〕
n. ❶劝告，忠告[U]
I want your advice, sir. I don't know what to do.
先生，我需要您的指点。我不知该怎么办才好。
❷消息，报告[P]
Advices from abroad indicate that war is about to begin.
来自国外的消息表明战争即将开始。

advise 〔ədˈvaɪz ‖ ədˈvaɪz〕
[过去式]advised;[过去分词]advised
vt. ❶劝告，忠告
We advised her that she (should) wait.
我们劝她等。
❷通知，告知[(+of)]
Please advise us of any change in your plan.
你们的计划倘有变更，请告诉我们。

affair 〔əˈfɛr ‖ əˈfeə〕
n. [C]❶事情，事，事件
How are your affairs going on?
你的情况怎么样?
❷事务，业务；事态[P]
The premier deals with important affairs of state.
总理处理国家重要事务。
❸恋爱事件，风流韵事

affect 〔əˈfɛkt ‖ əˈfekt〕
[过去式] affected;[过去分词] affected
vt. ❶影响；对……发生作用
The amount of rain affects the growth of crops.
雨量影响作物的生长。
❷使感动，使震动
She was deeply affected by the news of her father's death.
她父亲去世的消息使她深受震动。
❸(病)侵袭；罹患
Her kidneys had become affected.
她的肾脏受到了感染。

afford 〔əˈfɔrd ‖ əˈfɔːd〕
[过去式] afforded;[过去分词]

afforded

vt. ❶(常与 can, could, be able to 连用)买得起;有足够的……(去做……)

They did not consider whether they could afford the time or not.

他们没有考虑是否抽得出时间。

❷【书】提供,给予

Dancing affords us pleasure.

跳舞给我们带来快乐。

afraid [ə'fred ‖ ə'freɪd]

a. ❶害怕的,怕的[(+of)][+to-v][+(that)]

She was afraid that she might lose her job.

她担心会丢掉工作。

I am afraid to do it.

我不敢去做。

I am afraid of doing it.

我害怕做。

❷(用于提出异议,告诉不好的消息等场合,使语气婉转)恐怕,遗憾[+(that)]

I'm afraid (that) your wife had an accident.

很遗憾,你妻子出事了。

Africa ['æfrɪkə ‖ 'æfrɪkə]

n. 非洲

African ['æfrɪkən ‖ 'æfrɪkən]

n. 非洲人

a. 非洲的;非洲人的

after ['æftɚ ‖ 'ɑːftə]

prep. ❶在……以后

After graduation he went abroad.

毕业后他去了国外。

❷在……后面;随……之后

I'll come after you.

我随后去。

❸低于;次于

A captain comes after a major.

上尉军衔低于少校。

❹仿照,模仿

Read after me.

跟着我读。

conj. 在……之后

I will tell you after they leave.

他们走后我再告诉你。

ad. ❶以后,之后

They arrived shortly after.

不久以后他们抵达了。

❷在后面,随后

Tom went on Monday, and Mary left the day after.

汤姆星期一走的,玛丽第二天就离开了。

a. 以后的

His health was declining in after years.

在以后的岁月,他的健康不断衰退。

A

常用短语

after all 终究

The plan failed after all.

这个计划最终失败。

afternoon 〔ˌæftəˈnun ‖ ɑːftəˈnuːn〕

n. 下午,午后[C][U]

〈在 this, that, tomorrow 等词后面不用 in〉

It will rain in the afternoon.

下午可能下雨。

Please come this afternoon.

请今天下午来。

常用短语

Good afternoon. 午安。(午后问候语)

again 〔əˈgɛn ‖ əˈgen〕

ad. ❶再,再一次

Could you say that again?

请你再说一遍好吗?

❷重回;恢复原状

Henry was glad to be home again.

亨利很高兴又回到家里。

❸再者;此外

Then again, I doubt whether he will come.

再说,我怀疑他是否会来。

常用短语

again and again 再三地

now and again 常常

once again 再一次

against 〔əˈgɛnst ‖ əˈgenst〕

prep. ❶反对;违反

I am for peace and against war.

我赞成和平,反对战争。

❷逆;对着

I swam against the stream.

我逆流游泳。

❸倚;靠

His desk is against the wall.

他的办公桌靠墙放着。

❹以……为背景

The building is beautiful against the sky.

这座建筑物在天空的映衬下很美。

❺防备;预防

He saved money against old age.

他存钱以养老。

age 〔edʒ ‖ eɪdʒ〕

n. ❶年龄[C] [U]

What's the age of that old building?

那座古老的建筑有多久的历史了?

❷(人生的)某一时期[U]

I used to play tennis there when I was your age.

当我在你这个年纪的时候,我常在那里打网球。

❸老年[U]
❹很长时间[P]
I haven't seen you for ages.
我好久没见到你了。

agency 〔ˈedʒənsɪ ‖ ˈeɪdʒənsɪ〕
n. ❶代办处,经销处,代理机构[C]
a detective agency
私人侦探所
❷专业行政机构,局,署,处,社[C]
❸中介;代理[(+of)]
Through the agency of relatives he got the position.
通过亲戚的介绍,他得到了那个职位。

ago 〔əˈgo ‖ əˈgəʊ〕
ad. 在……以前
I lived in Shanghai 10 years ago.
我 10 年前住在上海。

> ago 是从现在往前;before 是从过去往前。
> 如,I visited him two days ago, but he had gone to London 5 days before.
> 我两天前去看他,可他 5 天前已经去伦敦了。
>
> **用法工具箱**

agree 〔əˈgri ‖ əˈgriː〕
[过去式] agreed;[过去分词]agreed
v. 意见一致,同意,赞同

常用短语

agree to… (对提案等)赞成
He agreed to the plan.
他赞成这个计划。
agree with… (对人的意见)赞成
I agreed with him.
我同意他的意见。
agree on… (对事情)意见一致
We agreed on the plan.
我们对此计划意见一致。

agriculture 〔ˈægrɪˌkʌltʃɚ ‖ ˈægrɪˌkʌltʃə〕
n. [U]农业,农耕

ahead 〔əˈhɛd ‖ əˈhed〕
ad. ❶在前;向前
The school is two kilometers ahead.
学校就在前面两公里的地方。
❷预先,事前
You'd better plan ahead.
你最好事先计划一下。
❸领先,占先
Two people were ahead of us, and travelling fast.
有两个人在我们前面,走得很快。

A

aid 〔ed ‖ eɪd〕
［过去式］aided；［过去分词］aided
vt. ❶帮助，救助，支持
She made no effort to aid Sophia.
她根本不去帮助索菲娅。
❷有助于
A good dictionary can aid language learning.
一部好词典有助于语言学习。
n. ❶帮助，救助，援助［U］
He should be able to read this without the aid of a dictionary.
他应当能够不用字典就读懂这个。
❷有辅助作用的事物［C］
a visual aid
视觉教具

aim 〔em ‖ eɪm〕
［过去式］aimed；［过去分词］aimed
vt. ❶把……瞄准；把……对准掷向［（＋at）］
He aimed the gun at the door.
他把枪对准那扇门。
❷将……针对；以……用于［（＋at）］
This anti-smoking campaign is mainly aimed at young teenagers.
这场反吸烟运动主要是针对青少年的。
vi. ❶瞄准，对准［（＋at）］
The hunter aimed at the lion and fired.
猎人瞄准了狮子开火。
❷致力，意欲，旨在［（＋at/for）］［＋to-v］
My brother aims to be a novelist.
我兄弟立志当小说家。
n. ❶ 瞄准；瞄准的方向
❷目标，目的［C］［（＋of）］
Our aim now is to set up a factory.
我们现在的目的是创办一座工厂。

air 〔ɛr ‖ eə〕
n. ❶空气；大气［U］
❷天空，空中［U］
The air was full of butterflies.
天空中飞舞着许许多多的蝴蝶。
❸样子，神态［C］
He came into the room with an air of importance.
他带着一副了不起的神情走进室内。

常用短语

by air 通过航空途径；乘飞机
in the air ❶在空中；向空中 ❷

在传播中流行；可感觉到的

on the air 在广播

put on airs 摆架子

up in the air 悬而未决的

airline 〔'εrˌlaɪn ‖ 'eəlaɪn〕

n. ❶(飞机的)航线[C]

❷航空公司[P]

airmail 〔'εrˌmel ‖ 'eəmeɪl〕

n. 航空邮件，航空信

airplane 〔'εrˌplen ‖ 'eəpleɪn〕

n. 【美】飞机[C]

战斗机 fighter plane

客机 passengerplane

直升机 helicopter

预警飞机 early warning plane

airport 〔'εrˌpɔrt ‖ 'eəpɔːt〕

n. 机场；航空站[C]

They landed at a small airport.

他们在一座小型的机场降落。

airsick 〔'εrˌsɪk ‖ 'eəˌsɪk〕

a. 晕机的

alarm 〔ə'lɑrm ‖ ə'lɑːm〕

n. ❶警报；警报器[C]

The doorkeeper gave the alarm as soon as he saw the smoke.

守门人一看见冒烟就发出警报。

❷闹钟[C](＝an alarm clock)

❸惊慌，恐惧，担忧[U]

"What's up?" he asked in alarm.

"出什么事了？"他惊恐地问道。

album 〔'ælbəm ‖ 'ælbəm〕

n. 相簿；集邮簿[C]

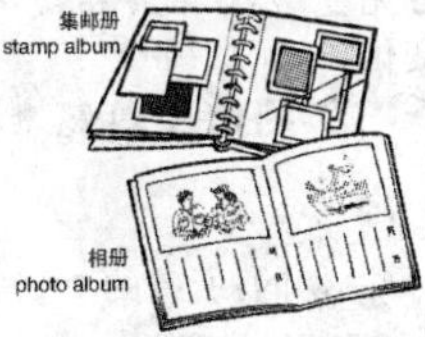

a photograph album

影集唱片集，唱片套册

a record album

唱片专集

alcohol 〔'ælkəˌhɔl ‖ 'ælkəhɒl〕

n. ❶酒精[C][U]

❷含酒精饮料；酒[U]

He decided to keep off alcohol after the accident.

发生那次事故后，他决定不再饮酒。

alike 〔ə'laɪk ‖ ə'laɪk〕

a. 相同的，相像的

They look very much alike.

他们长得很像。

alive 〔ə'laɪv ‖ ə'laɪv〕

a. 活着的；现存的

Is that dog alive or dead?

A

那条狗是活的还是死的?

❶alive 不可置于名词之前,它只能作表语。
如,The fish is still alive.
那条鱼还活着。
❷无比较级和最高级的变化。

用法工具箱

all 〔ɔl ‖ ɔːl〕

a. ❶一切的,所有的

All men are mortal.

凡是人都会死。

❷整个的,全部的

The child played all day long.

这孩子一整天都在玩。

pron. 全体,一切,全部

I know that all is well with her.

我知道她一切都好。

常用短语

all along 始终

all in all 总的说来

all over ❶全部结束❷浑身;到处

all right ❶安全的;(健康)良好的 ❷正确的 ❸行

all together 一道

not at all 别客气

allow 〔əˈlau ‖ əˈlaʊ〕

[过去式]allowed;[过去分词]allowed

vt. ❶允许,准许

Swimming is not allowed at this beach.

这片海滩禁止游泳。

❷准……进;准……出

He doesn't allow cats in the room.

他不允许猫进入房内。

常用短语

allow for 考虑

We should allow for every possible delay.

我们必须考虑到任何可能的延误。

allow of 容许有……的可能

The situation allows of no delay.

情况不容许有任何延误。

almost 〔ˈɔlˌmost ‖ ˈɔːlməʊst〕

ad. 几乎,差不多

It was almost dark when they got there.

他们抵达那里时,天几乎黑了。

alone 〔əˈlon ‖ əˈləʊn〕

a. ❶单独的,独自

She watches TV when she is alone.

独自一人时,她便看电视。

❷只有,仅;单单

The rent alone is $300.

单房租就 300 美元。

ad. ❶单独地

For years Mary lived alone in New York.

玛丽孤身一人在纽约生活了好几年。

❷独自地

I can do it alone.

我可以独自办理此事。

常用短语

let alone 更不用说

He can't speak English, let alone German.

他连英语都不会说，更不用说德语了。

let/leave…alone 任其……不管

Leave me alone.

不要管我。

along 〔əˈlɔŋ ‖ əˈlɒŋ〕

prep. 沿着；顺着

I was driving along a muddy path.

我沿着泥泞的小路开车。

ad. ❶ 向前

He sang loudly as he walked along.

他边向前走边大声唱着歌。

❷一起；带着[(+with)]

Come along with us.

跟我们一道去吧。

❸来到；去到

I'll be along in a minute.

我一会儿就来。

常用短语

get along 过生活，进展

How are you getting along?

你过得如何？

aloud 〔əˈlaʊd ‖ əˈlaʊd〕

ad. ❶出声地

❷大声地

read aloud

朗读

alphabet 〔ˈælfəˌbɛt ‖ ˈælfəbɪt〕

n. ❶字母系统，字母表，全套字母[C]

The English alphabet has 26 letters.

英语共有26个字母。

❷初步，入门

alphabet of radio

无线电初步

already 〔ɔlˈrɛdɪ ‖ ɔːlˈredɪ〕

ad. 已经；先前

I have had lunch already.

我已用过午餐了。

> already 用于肯定句，疑问句中 already 表示惊讶、意外。
>
> Have you done it already?
>
> 你已经做好了吗？（好快）
>
> **用法工具箱**

A

also 〔ˈɔlso ‖ ˈɔːlsəʊ〕
ad. ❶也，亦；还
John is also 19 years old.
约翰也是 19 岁。
❷同样地
Since you've accepted the invitation, I'll also accept it.
既然你已接受邀请，那我也接受邀请。

alternative 〔ɔlˈtɝnətɪv ‖ ɔːlˈtɜːnətɪv〕
a. ❶两者（或若干）中择一的；非此即彼的
I offered the alternative suggestions of spending the vacation in the mountains or by the sea.
我提议这次假期要么上山玩，要么到海边。
❷替代的；供选择的
an alternative plan
替代计划
n. ❶选择，二择一[(+of)]
You have the alternative of speaking or keeping quiet.
你要么发言，要么保持肃静。
❷供选择的东西(或办法等)[C]

although 〔ɔlˈðo ‖ ɔːlˈðəʊ〕
conj. ❶虽然；尽管
Although he was ill, he worked hard.
他虽然生病，但仍努力工作。
❷然而
I did not know that then, although I learned it later.
当时我不知道那件事，但我后来知道了。

altogether 〔ˌɔltəˈgɛðɚ ‖ ˌɔːltəˈgeðə〕
ad. ❶完全，全然
I am altogether on your side in this matter.
在这个问题上我完全支持你。
❷全部，合计
He bought altogether 500 hectares of land.
他总共买了 500 公顷土地。
❸总之，总而言之
Altogether, exports are looking up.
总的说来，出口贸易在好转。

always 〔ˈɔlwez ‖ ˈɔːlweɪz〕
ad. ❶总是，经常
They always make fun of Mr. Smith.
他们总是嘲弄史密斯先生。
❷永远，一直
Labor Day is always the first Monday of September.
劳工节一直是 9 月的第一个礼拜一。
❸(动词用进行式)老是，一再
I'm always misplacing my glas-

ses.
我老是将眼镜乱放而找不到。

am〔(强)æm ‖ æm;(弱)əm ‖ əm〕
［过去式］was;［过去分词］been
vi.(用于第一人称单数现在式)是
I am a college student.
我是个大学生。
v. aux.(与 v-ing 连用构成现在进行式;与 v-ed 连用构成被动态)
I am always encouraged to speak English.
人们总是鼓励我讲英语。

A. M. , a. m.
abbr.【拉】=ante meridiem (=before noon) 午前
at 7 a. m.
上午 7 点
〔反义〕p. m. 下午

amateur〔ˈæməˌtʃur ‖ ˈæmətə〕
n.［C］❶(科学,艺术,运动等的)业余爱好者
You are a professional, but I am an amateur.
你是专业的,而我是业余的。
❷外行;粗通(某一行)的人

ambassador〔æmˈbæsədɚ ‖ æmˈbæsədə〕
n. 大使;使节［(+to)］［C］
the Japanese ambassador to France
日本驻法大使

ambition〔æmˈbɪʃən ‖ æmˈbɪʃən〕
n. ❶雄心,抱负［C］［U］
Her son was filled with ambition to become a great inventor.
她儿子一心想成为伟大的发明家。
❷野心;追求的目标［C］
Her ambition was to become a film star.
她一心追求的是做电影明星。

ambulance〔ˈæmbjələns ‖ ˈæmbjuləns〕
n.［C］救护车

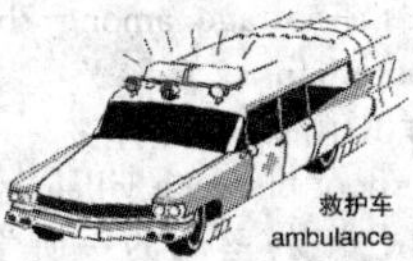

救护车
ambulance

America〔əˈmɛrɪkə ‖ əˈmerɪkə〕

美国国旗
national flag of America

美国地图
map of America

A

n. ❶美国
❷美洲

American 〔ə'merɪkən ‖ ə'merɪkən〕
a. 美国的;美洲的
n. 美国人;美洲人

among 〔ə'mʌŋ ‖ ə'mʌŋ〕
prep. 在……之中;在……中间
Tom has always been popular among his classmates.
汤姆在同学中一直很受欢迎。

among 和 between:通常 among 用于三个以上的之间;between 用于两者之间。
如,a cottage among the mountains
群山中的一间小屋
a shool between villages
(两个)村落间的一所学校

用法工具箱

amount 〔ə'maʊnt ‖ ə'maʊnt〕
[过去式]amounted;[过去分词]amounted
n. [C][(+of)]
❶ 总数;总额
What is the amount we owe them?
我们总共欠他们多少钱?
❷数量
They need a small amount of fuel.
他们需要少量的燃料。
vi. [(+to)]❶合计,共计
The total cost of repairs amounted to $100.
修理费用总计100美元。
❷相当于
Keeping what belongs to another amounts to stealing.
将他人之物占为己有等于偷。

amuse 〔ə'mjuz ‖ ə'mjuːz〕
[过去式]amused;[过去分词]amused
vt. ❶使欢乐,逗……高兴;使发笑
A clown's job is to amuse the spectators.
小丑的工作就是娱乐观众。
❷给……提供娱乐,消遣
It was too rainy to play outside, so she amused herself with a book.
雨大,不适合在外面玩,所以她看书消遣。

amusement 〔ə'mjuzmənt ‖ ə'mjuːzmənt〕
n. ❶乐趣;兴味 [U]

❷娱乐，消遣；娱乐活动[C][U]

analysis 〔ə'næləsɪs ‖ ə'næləsɪs〕
n. ❶分析；分解；解析[C][U]
❷【美】精神分析[U]

ancestor 〔'ænsɛstɚ ‖ 'ænsestə〕
n. [C]❶祖宗，祖先
❷原型；先驱

ancient 〔'enʃənt ‖ 'eɪnʃənt〕
a. ❶古代的
We were impressed by the ruins of an ancient building.
我们对一处古建筑废墟印象颇深。
❷古老的；古旧的，旧的
He drives an ancient car.
他开着一辆老式汽车。

and 〔(强)ænd ‖ ænd；(弱)ənd ‖ ənd〕
conj. ❶和，及，与，同；又
They sang and danced all night.
他们通宵唱歌跳舞。
❷然后
She went to the United States in 1960 and has lived there ever since.
她于1960年去了美国，此后就一直住在那里。
❸而且
You must stop, and at once, this sort of behavior.
你必须停止此种行为，而且必须立即停止。
❹就；所以，因此
❺而，但是

并举三个以上的单词时，只在最后一个单词前加and，其他用逗号连接：
John，Tom，Bill and Ted 约翰、汤姆、比尔以及特德
并举人称代词时，通常按照第二人称、第三人称、第一人称的顺序：
You，he and I are good friends.
你、我和他是好朋友。
连接相同的单词，表示反复强调：
for days and days 连着好几天
miles and miles 好几英里
better and better 越来越好
more and more interesting 越来越有趣

用法工具箱

A

angel 〔'endʒəl || 'eɪndʒəl〕
n. [C]❶天使
❷天使般的人
Be an angel and bring me a cup of coffee.
请做点好事给我拿杯咖啡来。
❸守护神

anger 〔'æŋgɚ || 'æŋgə〕
n. 怒，生气[U]
Tom shouted in anger.
汤姆气愤地叫喊着。

angle 〔'æŋgl̩ || 'æŋgl〕
n. [C]角；角度
We need to look at the issue from a different angle.
我们需要从一个不同的角度来看这个问题。

angry 〔'æŋgrɪ || 'æŋgrɪ〕
a. ❶发怒的，生气的[(+at/with/about)]
The old woman often gets angry about trivial things.
老太太常因琐屑小事发火。
❷因为……而生气[+that][+to-v]
He'll be angry to find that nothing has been done.
看到什么也没有做，他准会生气。

animal 〔'ænəml̩ || 'ænɪməl〕
n. [C]动物
Human beings are social animals.
人是社会性的动物。

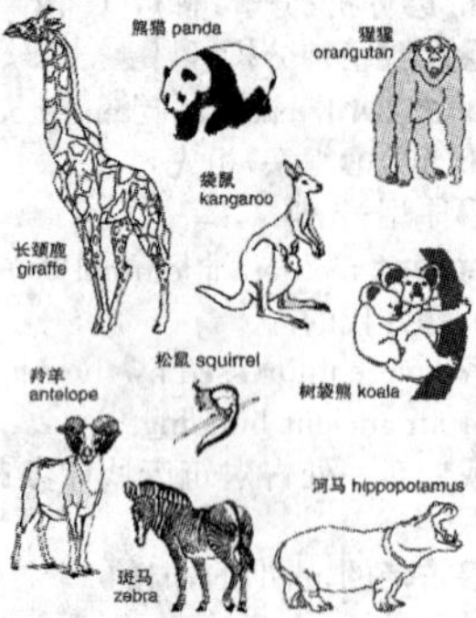

ankle 〔'æŋkl̩ || 'æŋkl〕
n. [C]踝，足踝

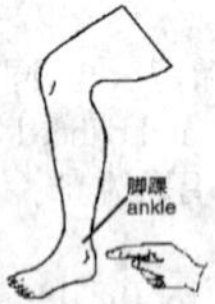

anniversary 〔ˌænə'vɝsərɪ || ˌænɪ'vɜːsərɪ〕
n. [C]❶周年纪念；周年纪念日
❷结婚周年；结婚周年日

announce 〔ə'naʊns || ə'naʊns〕
[过去式]announced；[过去分词]announced

A

vt. ❶宣布,发布[+that]

They announced that she would give one extra song.

他们宣布说她将再唱一首歌。

❷通报……的到达;通知……已准备好

The servant announced Mr. and Mrs. Hunter.

仆人通报亨特夫妇驾到。

词汇拓展

announcement *n.* 发表,通告
announcer *n.* 广播员,发表者

annoy 〔ə'nɔɪ ‖ ə'nɔɪ〕

[过去式]annoyed;[过去分词] annoyed

vt. ❶惹恼,使生气;使烦恼[(+by/at/with)]

His mother was annoyed with him for being so rude to their neighbors.

他母亲因为他对邻居如此粗暴无礼而生他的气。

❷打搅,困扰

These flies are annoying me.

这些苍蝇一直在打搅我。

词汇拓展

annoyance *n.* 烦恼、可厌的人或事

annual 〔'ænjuəl ‖ 'ænjuəl〕

a. ❶一年的;一年一次的

Employees are entitled to an annual paid leave of 15 days.

职员一年可享受15天带薪的假期。

❷每年的;全年的

Mr. Watson's annual income is $20,000.

沃森先生全年的收入为20,000美元。

another 〔ə'nʌðɚ ‖ ə'nʌðə〕

a. ❶又一,再一

He drank another glass of beer.

他又喝了一杯啤酒。

❷另一;另外的

That's another matter.

那是另外一回事。

pron. ❶又一个,再一个

The little boy finished his cake and asked for another.

小男孩吃完自己的蛋糕后,要求再吃一块。

❷另一个

I don't like this one, please show me another.

我不喜欢这个,请给我另一个。

常用短语

one after another 相继地,依次地,一个一个地

They came one after another.

A

他们相继到来。

one another 互相

We should help one another.

我们应该互相帮助。

answer 〔'ænsɚ ‖ 'ɑːnsə〕

[过去式]answered;[过去分词] answered

n. [C][(+to)]

❶回答;答复;复信

I'm waiting for an answer to my letter.

我正在等候回信。

❷反应

He said good night to her but she gave no answer.

他向她道晚安,而她却毫无反应。

vt. ❶回答;答复

Ann asked many questions and I did my best to answer them.

安问了许多问题,我尽可能地回答。

❷接(电话);应(门)

Who answered the telephone?

谁接的电话?

vi. ❶ 回答;答复

I knocked at the door but no one answered.

我敲了门,但无人应答。

❷答辩

How would you answer the criticism made of your work?

你对针对你的工作提出的批评作何辩解?

ant 〔ænt ‖ ænt〕

n. 蚂蚁[C]

anxiety 〔æŋ'zaɪətɪ ‖ æŋ'zaɪətɪ〕

n. ❶焦虑,挂念[C][U][(+about/for)]

The mother was filled with anxiety about her daughter's health.

母亲为女儿的健康忧心忡忡。

❷焦虑的原因;令人焦虑之事[C][(+to)]

That is a great anxiety to me.

那是一件使我深感焦虑的事情。

❸渴望[C][(+for)][+to-v]

Their anxiety to go was obvious.

他们想去的急切心情是显而易见的。

anxious 〔'æŋkʃəs ‖ 'æŋkʃəs〕

a. ❶焦虑的,挂念的[(+about/at/for)]

I'm anxious about her safety.

我对她的安全担心。

❷令人焦虑的

The week of the flood was an anxious time for all of us.

闹水灾的那一星期是我们大家

都焦虑不安的日子。
❸渴望的[(+for)][+to-v][+that]
We're anxious for your safe return.
我们盼望你平安归来。

any 〔'ɛnɪ ‖ 'enɪ〕
a. ❶任一,每一
He wanted a job, any sort of a job.
他需要一个工作,任何工作都行。
❷(一般用于疑问句、否定句、if从句中)若干,一些;一点,丝毫
If there is any trouble, do let me know.
如遇到麻烦,务必告诉我。
❸尽可能多的;所有的
Send me any data you can find.
把你能找到的所有资料送来给我。
pron. ❶ 任何一个;任何人
Richard is taller than any of us.
理查德比我们当中任何人都高。
❷若干;一点
Give me some if there is/are any.
如有,给我一些。
ad. (用于疑问句、否定句、if从句中)少许,稍微
Don't go any closer.
别再走近。
Correct errors, if any.
如果有错,就改正。

anybody 〔'ɛnɪˌbɑdɪ ‖ 'enɪˌbɒdɪ〕
pron. ❶(用于疑问句或否定句时)谁,任何人
I didn't meet anybody.
我没遇见任何人。
❷(用于肯定句时)无论谁,无论哪个人
Anybody may come.
谁来都行。
n. 【口】(常用于疑问句、否定句或if从句)有名气的人,重要的人[U]
If you want to be anybody, do your best.
如果你想成为重要人物,你就要全力以赴。

anyhow 〔'ɛnɪˌhaʊ ‖ 'enɪhaʊ〕
ad. ❶无论如何,不管怎么说
It may snow, but anyhow I will go to town.
可能要下雪,但我无论如何要进城。
❷不管从什么角度(或用什么方法),总之
He couldn't convince her anyhow.
他怎么想办法也不能使她信

服。

A

anyone 〔ˈɛnɪˌwʌn ‖ ˈenɪwʌn〕

pron. ❶(用于疑问句或否定句)谁,任何人

I didn't meet anyone.

我没遇见任何人。

❷(用于肯定句时)无论谁,无论哪个人

Anyone thinks so.

人人都这么想。

anything 〔ˈɛnɪˌθɪŋ ‖ ˈenɪˌθɪŋ〕

pron. ❶(用于疑问句或否定句)任何东西,任何事情

Do you know anything about him?

你知道关于他的什么事吗?

❷(用于肯定句时)无论任何东西,无论任何事情

I' ll do anything for you.

我会为你做任何事。

anywhere 〔ˈɛnɪˌhwɛr ‖ ˈenɪhweə〕

ad. 在任何地方,往任何地方

I can sleep anywhere.

我在哪儿都能睡。

apartment 〔əˈpɑrtmənt ‖ əˈpɑːtmənt〕

n. [C]【美】(一户)公寓房间

They live in the apartment above ours.

他们住在我们楼上的一套公寓房间里。

apologize 〔əˈpɑləˌdʒaɪz ‖ əˈpɒlədʒaɪz〕

[过去式]apologized;[过去分词]apologized

vi. 道歉;认错,赔不是[(+to/for)]

He apologized to her for not going to her party.

他因为没有出席她举行的宴会而向她表示歉意。

apology 〔əˈpɑlədʒɪ ‖ əˈpɒlədʒɪ〕

n. [C]❶ 道歉;赔罪[(+to/for)]

I owe you an apology for my rudeness last night.

昨天晚上我太粗暴,应该向你道歉。

❷辩解;辩护

Her open letter was really an apology for her way of life.

她的公开信实际上是对她生活方式的辩护。

apparent 〔əˈpærənt ‖ əˈpærənt〕

a. ❶表面上的,外观的;未必真实的

The apparent cause of his illness was excessive drinking, but the real cause was his deep grief at his wife's death.

他生病的表面原因是饮酒过

度，但实际原因是丧妻之痛。
❷明显的，显而易见的；明白无误的[(+to)][+that]
It was apparent that he was in no condition to travel.
他的健康状况显然不宜旅行。

appear 〔ə'pɪr ‖ ə'pɪə〕
[过去式]appeared；[过去分词]appeared
vi. ❶出现；显露
Gradually a smile appeared on her face.
她脸上渐渐地露出笑容。
❷似乎，看来好像[(+to-v)][+(that)]
It appears (that) they are right.
看来他们是对的。
❸出庭，到案
She will appear in court next Friday.
下星期五她将出庭。

appearance 〔ə'pɪrəns ‖ ə'pɪərəns〕
n. ❶ 出现；显露[C]
John's appearance in the doorway was welcomed with shouts.
约翰出现在门口时，大家高喊着欢迎他。
❷露面；来到；演出[C]
The singer made her first appearance in a concert in Boston.
这位歌唱家第一次演出是在波士顿的一个音乐会上。
❸出版[C]
❹出庭，到案[C]
❺外貌，外观；外表[C][U]
The appearance of the old house completely changed.
那所旧房子的外观全变了。

applause 〔ə'plɔz ‖ ə'plɔːz〕
n. [U]❶鼓掌欢迎，喝彩
❷称赞，嘉许

apple 〔'æpl̩ ‖ 'æpl〕
n. 苹果[C]
An apple a day keeps the doctor away.
一日一苹果，医生不登门。

application 〔ˌæplə'keʃən ‖ ˌæplɪ'keɪʃən〕
n. ❶应用，适用；运用[C][U][(+of/to)]
That rule has no application to this case.
那条规则不适用于这种情况。
❷申请，请求；申请书[C][U][(+to/for)][+to-v]
He sent in his application to the office.
他向公司提出申请。
❸用功，专心[U]
The work demands close appli-

A

cation.
这项工作要求思想高度集中。

apply 〔ə'plaɪ ‖ ə'plaɪ〕
[过去式]applied；[过去分词]applied
vt. ❶涂，敷；将……铺在表面[(＋to)]
The nurse applied a bandage to the wound.
护士将伤口包上绷带。
❷应用；实施[(＋to)]
We should apply both theories to the language classroom.
我们应把两种理论都运用到语言教室中去。
❸使起作用；使适用[(＋to)]
This rule can not be applied to every case.
这条规则并不是在每种情况下都能适用的。
❹把……用(于)[(＋to)]
❺(后常接 oneself)使致力(于)，使专心从事[(＋to)]
vi. 申请，请求[(＋for/to)][＋to-v]
He has applied for a post in England.
他已申请在英国供职。

appoint 〔ə'pɔɪnt ‖ ə'pɔɪnt〕
[过去式]appointed；[过去分词]appointed
vt. ❶任命，指派[(＋as/to)]
They appointed him (to be) manager.
他们任命他为经理。
❷约定，指定；安排
Our visitors arrived at the appointed time.
我们的来宾在约定的时间到达了。

appointment 〔ə'pɔɪntmənt ‖ ə'pɔɪntmənt〕
n. ❶(尤指正式的)约会[C][(＋with)][＋to-v]
I have an appointment with them in the evening.
今晚我与他们有个约会。
❷(会面的)约定[U]
❸任命，委派[U][(＋as/of)]
The appointment of a new judge was reported in the newspaper.
报上报道了任命一位新法官的消息。

appreciate 〔ə'priʃɪˌet ‖ ə'priːʃieɪt〕
[过去式]appreciated；[过去分词]appreciated
vt. ❶欣赏，赏识
Her talent for music was not appreciated.
她的音乐才能无人赏识。

A

❷感谢,感激

They deeply appreciated his kindness.

他们对他的好意深表感谢。

April 〔'eprəl ‖ 'eɪprəl〕

n. 略作 Apr. 4月

an April fool

在愚人节受愚弄的人

Arabia 〔ə'rebiə ‖ ə'reɪbjə〕

n. 阿拉伯(半岛)

are 〔(强)ɑr ‖ ɑː;(弱)ɚ ‖ ə〕

[过去式]were;[过去分词]been;[现在分词]being

vi. ❶(用于第二人称单复数现在式,第一、三人称复数现在式)是

You are a pupil.

你是学生。

❷(与 v-ing 连用构成现在进行时;与 v-ed 连用构成被动态)

They are asked to practice every day.

要求他们每天练习。

area 〔'ɛrɪə ‖ 'eərɪə〕

n. ❶面积[C][U]

The city covers an area of 15 square kilometers.

该城市的面积为15平方公里。

❷地区,区域[C]

❸场地,区[C]

There is a parking area over there.

那儿有一个停车场。

❹领域,范围,方面[C]

Maths is my special area.

数学是我的专业。

arithmetic 〔ə'rɪθməˌtɪk ‖ ə'rɪθmətɪk〕

n. [U]❶算术,计算

❷算术知识(或技巧)

arm¹ 〔ɑrm ‖ ɑːm〕

n. [C]❶臂

The baby fell asleep in her mother's arms.

婴儿在母亲的怀抱里睡着了。

❷臂状物;(椅子的)扶手;(起重机等的)臂,杆;大树枝

He is sitting on the arm of a chair.

他正坐在椅子扶手上。

常用短语

arm in arm 臂挽臂地

with folded arms 抱着胳膊

arm² 〔ɑrm ‖ ɑːm〕

[过去式]armed;[过去分词]armed

vt. ❶用武器装备[(+with)]

The robber was armed with a rifle.

强盗有步枪装备。

❷提供,配备[(+with)]

We set out armed with warm

A

clothes.
我们动身时带了御寒的衣服。

armchair 〔'ɑrmˌtʃɛr ‖ 'ɑːmˌtʃeə〕
n. 扶手椅[C]

army 〔'ɑrmɪ ‖ 'ɑːmɪ〕
n. [C] ❶军队
There they formed an army of about 2,000 men.
他们在那里组建了一支2,000人的军队。
❷陆军;军团
John is in the army.
约翰服务于陆军。

around 〔ə'raʊnd ‖ ə'raʊnd〕
ad. ❶到处,四处
Just drive me around.
开车带我四处走走就行了。
❷周围,附近
Let me see if he is around.
我看看他是否在附近。
❸向相反方向
She turned around to see who was calling her.
她转身看谁在叫她。
❹环绕;循环地
prep. ❶围绕,环绕
They sat around the table.
他们围桌而坐。
❷在……四处
Ann travelled around Europe for a few months.
安在欧洲各地旅游了数月。
❸在……附近
She liked to work around her own home.
她喜爱在她自己家的附近工作。
❹大约,将近,左右
I'll be there around 9 o'clock.
我9点左右的时候会到达那里。

arrange 〔ə'rendʒ ‖ ə'reɪndʒ〕
[过去式] arranged; [过去分词] arranged
vt. ❶ 整理;布置
She arranged the flowers in a vase.
她把花瓶里的花插好。
❷安排;筹备[+to-v][+that][+wh-]
It was arranged that they should leave the following spring.

已安排他们于第二年春天离开。

vi. 作安排，作准备[(＋about/for)]

Bill arranged for this man to come whenever needed.

比尔安排这人随叫随到。

arrangement [ə'rendʒmənt ‖ ə'reɪndʒmənt]

n. ❶安排；准备工作[P][(＋for)]

We made arrangements for departure.

我们做好了出发的准备。

❷约定，非正式协议；调停[C][U][(＋about/with)][＋to-v]

We came to an arrangement with him.

我们跟他达成了协议。

❸整理；布置；排列[C][U]

flower arrangement

插花

arrest [ə'rɛst ‖ ə'rest]

[过去式]arrested；[过去分词]arrested

vt. 逮捕；拘留

You could get arrested for doing that.

你干那种事可能要遭逮捕。

n. 逮捕；拘留[C][U]

The police made several arrests.

警方逮捕了好几个人。

arrival [ə'raɪvl̩ ‖ ə'raɪvəl]

n. 到达；到来；达到[U]

She is waiting for his arrival.

她正等他来。

arrive [ə'raɪv ‖ ə'raɪv]

[过去式]arrived；[过去分词]arrived

vi. ❶到达；到来

The delegation arrived in London last Monday.

代表团上星期一抵达伦敦。

❷(邮件，物品等)被送来

The books will arrive tomorrow.

这些书明天到。

❸(时间等)到来；(婴儿)出生

The baby arrived yesterday morning.

孩子是昨天上午出生的。

> arrive in 和 arrive at：到达比较小的地方用 arrive at；到达比较大的地方用 arrive in
>
> 如，He arrived at bridge.
>
> 他到了桥上。
>
> They arrived in Paris.
>
> 他们到达了巴黎。
>
> **用法工具箱**

A

arrow 〔ˈæro ‖ ˈærəʊ〕
n. [C] ❶箭
He shot an arrow at the hare.
他对准野兔射了一箭。
❷(指示方向等的)箭号，箭头

art 〔ɑrt ‖ ɑːt〕
n. ❶艺术；美术[U]
She teaches art history.
她教授艺术史。
❷艺术品；美术品[U]
There has never been an exhibition of African Art held in my small native town.
在我的家乡小镇上从没举办过非洲美术品展览。
❸人文科学；文科[P]
She received a bachelor's degree in arts in 1974.
她于1974年获文科学士学位。
❹(包括绘画、音乐、建筑等的)艺术学科[P]

article 〔ˈɑrtɪkl̩ ‖ ˈɑːtɪkl〕
n. [C] ❶(物品的)一件；物品；商品
She had several articles of clothing in her bag.
她手提包内有几件衣物。
❷文章；论文
He has written an article for the magazine.
他已给该刊撰写了一篇文章。
❸条款，条文
Article 15 of the constitution deals with this problem.
宪法的第15条谈此问题。
❹冠词

artificial 〔ˌɑrtəˈfɪʃəl ‖ ˌɑːtɪˈfɪʃəl〕
a. ❶人工的，人造的；假的
an artificial flower
人造花
❷矫揉造作的，不自然的
an artificial smile
不自然的笑

artist 〔ˈɑrtɪst ‖ ˈɑːtɪst〕
n. 艺术家；美术家(尤指画家)

as 〔(强)æz ‖ æz；(弱)əz ‖ əz〕
ad. ❶跟……一样地，同样地
Sam is as rich as Alexander.
山姆像亚历山大一样富有。
❷如同；例如
Such animals as foxes and squirrels have bushy tails.

有些动物，如狐和松鼠，有蓬松的尾巴。

prep. ❶作为，以……的身份

She works as an interpreter in that company.

她在该公司里担任翻译员。

❷当做

She didn't think much of him as a painter.

她对他作为一位画家评价不高。

❸像；如同

The old woman was dressed as a young lady.

这位老妇人打扮得像一位年轻人。

conj. ❶像……一样；依照；像

You ought to do as Paul tells you.

你应按照保罗吩咐的做。

❷当……时

As she left the room she remembered that book.

她离开房间时想起了那本书。

❸随着

As the sun rose, the fog dispersed.

太阳一出来，雾随之消失。

❹因为

As it rained, I stayed at home.

因为下雨，所以我待在家里。

❺虽然

Young as he is, he works hard.

他虽年轻，但工作努力。

pron. ❶（与 such, the same, as 等词连用，引导关系从句）与……相同的事物（或人）

He has earned as much money as I have.

他赚的钱和我赚的一样多。

❷（引导从句，对前述内容作补充）本情况，该事实

She has married again, as was expected.

她已再婚，这是意料中的事。

常用短语

as for （用于句首）至于；说到

As for me, it doesn't matter.

至于我，我没有关系。

as if /as though 犹如；好似

It looks as if he were ill.

他看来好像病了。

as long as 达……之久

He had stayed in London for as long as 20 years.

他曾在伦敦住了长达 20 年之久。

as to 至于；关于

He said nothing as to money.

他没说一句有关钱的话。

as well as 又，也，还

They owned two cows as well as a horse.

他们有两头奶牛和一匹马。

倍数的表示方法

A is as…as B

A跟B一样的……

He is as tall as I.

他跟我一样高。

A is half as…as B

A是B一半的……

This pencil is half as long as that one.

这只铅笔是那只铅笔一半那么长。

A is … times as…as…B

A是B……倍的……

Mt. Ali is 4 times as high as this mountain.

阿里山的高度是这座山的4倍。

用法工具箱

ash 〔æʃ || æʃ〕[名复]ashes

n. ❶灰,灰烬[U][P]

The cabin burnt to ashes.

小木屋烧成灰烬。

❷骨灰,遗骸[P]

❸废墟[P]

The castle was left in ashes.

这个城堡成了一片废墟。

ashamed 〔əˈʃemd || əˈʃeɪmd〕

a. ❶羞愧的,感到难为情的[(+of)][+to-v][+that]

She was ashamed of having failed in the examination.

她因考试不及格而感到羞愧。

❷耻于……的,因难为情而不愿……的[+to-v]

She was ashamed to tell anyone that she had fallen in love with him.

她羞于告诉任何人自己爱上了他。

Asia 〔ˈeʃə || ˈeɪʃə〕

n. 亚洲

Asian 〔ˈeʃən || ˈeɪʃən〕

n. 亚洲人[C]

Many Asians work in the Arab oil states.

许多亚洲人在阿拉伯产油国工作。

a. 亚洲的;亚洲人的

aside 〔əˈsaɪd || əˈsaɪd〕

ad. ❶在旁边;到(或向)旁边

He stepped aside.

他走到一旁。

❷(暂时地)离开;撇开

Put your trouble aside.

忘掉你的麻烦。

ask 〔æsk || ɑːsk〕

[过去式]asked;[过去分词]asked

vt. ❶问；询问
She asked him his name.
她问他叫什么。
❷请求；要求[＋to-v][＋that]
He asked that they (should) be allowed to use a dictionary.
他要求准许他们用词典。
❸索(价)；要求得到[(＋for/of)]
They asked too much of her.
他们对她要求过高。
vi. ❶问；询问；问候[(＋about)]
Tell George my parents ask about him.
转告乔治我父母问他好。
❷要求；请求[(＋for)]
She asked for a cup of tea.
她要一杯茶。

asleep 〔ə'slip ‖ ə'sliːp〕
a. 睡着的
The baby is asleep in the bed.
那个婴儿在床上睡着了。

常用短语

fall asleep 入睡
I fell asleep while watching TV.
我看着电视就睡着了。

aspect 〔'æspɛkt ‖ 'æspekt〕
n. 方面，观点[C][(＋of)]
We love the valley in all its aspects.
我们爱这山谷的一切。

assign 〔ə'saɪn ‖ ə'saɪn〕
[过去式]assigned；[过去分词]assigned
vt. ❶分配，分派
Each overseas teacher was assigned a flat.
每位外籍教师都分配到一套房间。
❷派定，指定，选派[(＋to/for)]
Jack was assigned to the assembly shop of the factory.
杰克被分配到厂里的装配间工作。

词汇拓展

assignment *n.* (分派的)任务，工作，分配，作业

assist 〔ə'sɪst ‖ ə'sɪst〕
[过去式]assisted；[过去分词]assisted
vt. 帮助，协助[(＋with/in)]
We asked him to assist us in designing a new bridge.
我们请他帮助我们设计一座新桥。
vi. 帮助，协助[(＋with/in)]
He assisted in designing the new bridge.

他协助设计那座新桥。

A

astronomy 〔ə'strɑnəmɪ ‖ əs'trɒnəmɪ〕

n. 天文学[U]

at 〔(强)æt ‖ æt;(弱)ət ‖ ət〕

prep. ❶ 在……地点

They were already waiting at the gate when I got there.

当我到达那里时,他们已等候在门口了。

❷在……时刻

Jane will meet her boyfriend at Christmas.

简将在圣诞节和她男友见面。

❸向,朝,对着

Don't shout at me.

别对我叫喊。

❹在……方面

❺因为,由于

I was surprised at the news.

听到那个消息我很吃惊。

❻(状态,从事)正在……

He is at home.

他在家。

He is at table.

他正在用餐。

❼以(某种价格、速度等)

I bought it at a low price.

我以低价买进。

The car ran at 40 miles an hour.

车子以每小时 40 英里的速度行驶。

常用短语

at last 最后

at least 至少

at once 立刻

Atlantic 〔ət'læntɪk ‖ ət'læntɪk〕

n. 大西洋

a. 大西洋的

atmosphere 〔'ætməsˌfɪr ‖ 'ætməsfɪə〕

n. ❶大气

❷(某特定场所的)空气

The atmosphere of the city is very much polluted.

那个城市的空气受到严重污染。

❸气氛

The talk was conducted in a friendly atmosphere.

会谈是在热情友好的气氛中进行的。

atom 〔'ætəm ‖ 'ætəm〕

n. [C]❶原子

❷微小物;微量,一点儿

He couldn't produce an atom of evidence.

他一点证据也拿不出。

atomic 〔ə'tɑmɪk ‖ ə'tɒmɪk〕

a. 原子的,原子能的

attack 〔əˈtæk ‖ əˈtæk〕

［过去式］attacked；［过去分词］attacked

vt. ❶进攻，袭击

The enemy attacked our airport all night.

敌人彻夜攻击我们的机场。

❷抨击，责难

The governor was attacked by the press for failing to keep a campaign promise.

州长因没能履行一项竞选时的承诺而受到新闻界抨击。

vi. 进攻，袭击

n. 攻击，抨击［C］［U］［（＋on/against）］

The planes began their attack on the city.

飞机开始攻击这个城市。

attend 〔əˈtɛnd ‖ əˈtend〕

［过去式］attended；［过去分词］attended

vt. ❶出席，参加

He did not attend the meeting yesterday.

昨天他没有参加会议。

❷上（大学等），前往

The school was attended entirely by local children.

到这个学校读书的全是当地的孩子。

❸照料；护理；侍候

There was no one to attend him but Tina.

除了蒂娜，再无人照顾他了。

vi. ❶ 出席，参加［（＋at）］

❷照料，处理［（＋to）］

I'll attend to the matter.

我来处理此事。

❸护理；侍候［（＋on/upon）］

❹注意，倾听；致力于［（＋to）］

She didn't attend to what I was saying.

她并不注意听我所说的话。

attention 〔əˈtɛnʃən ‖ əˈtenʃən〕

n. ❶ 注意；注意力；专心［U］

Let me have your attention!

请注意听我讲话！

❷照料；检修［U］

❸照顾；治疗

She gave her aging parents much attention.

她悉心照料年迈的双亲。

❹立正姿势（或口令）［U］

attitude 〔ˈætəˌtjud ‖ ˈætɪtjuːd〕

n. 态度，意见，看法［（＋about/to/toward）］

Leigh takes a maternal attitude toward the Chinese girl.

利像母亲一般对待这个中国女孩。

attract 〔əˈtrækt ‖ əˈtrækt〕

［过去式］attracted；［过去分词］attracted

vt. ❶吸；吸引

The garden city attracts many tourists.

那个花园城市吸引了许多游客。

❷引起(注意，兴趣等)

❸引起……的注意(或兴趣等)；引诱

Jim was attracted to the Italian girl.

吉姆对那位意大利女孩产生了好感。

attractive 〔ə'træktɪv ‖ ə'træktɪv〕

a. 有吸引力的；引人注目的；妩媚动人的

She is an attractive girl.

她是个迷人的姑娘。

audience 〔'ɔdɪəns ‖ 'ɔːdɪəns〕

n. ［C］❶听众，观众；读者群

His books have a large audience.

他的书有广大的读者。

❷爱好者

❸谒见；会见

He was granted an audience with the king.

他获准会见国王。

August 〔'ɔgəst ‖ 'ɔːgəst〕

n. 略作 Aug. 8 月

Australia 〔ɔ'streljə ‖ ɒs'treɪljə〕

n. 澳大利亚

澳大利亚国旗
national flag of Australia

澳大利亚地图
map of Australia

author 〔'ɔθɚ ‖ 'ɔːθə〕

n. ［C］❶作者；作家

Mark Twain is his favorite author.

马克·吐温是他最喜爱的作家。

❷(作家的)著作

Many American authors have been translated into Chinese.

许多美国作家的著作已译成中文。

authority 〔ə'θɑrətɪ ‖ ə'θɒrɪtɪ〕

n. ❶权，权力；职权［U］［(＋for)］［＋to-v］

Who gave you authority to do this?

谁给你权力这样做的？

❷当权者，管理机构［C］

❸官方，当局［P］

The authorities did not interfere with us.

当局不干涉我们。

❹权威人士；专家，泰斗[C][(+on)]
He is an authority on international law.
他是一位国际法权威。

automobile 〔ˈɔtəməˌbil ‖ ˈɔːtəməbiːl〕
n. 【美】汽车；摩托车[C]
He rode away in an automobile.
他开车走了。

autumn 〔ˈɔtəm ‖ ˈɔːtəm〕
n. 秋季，秋天[C][U]
American people use the word "fall" to mean autumn.
美国人用"fall"这个词来表示秋天。

avenue 〔ˈævəˌnu ‖ ˈævɪnjuː〕
n. [C]❶大街，大道
Fifth Avenue is a good place for window shopping.
(纽约市)第五大道是逛街的好去处。
❷林荫大道

average 〔ˈævərɪdʒ ‖ ˈævərɪdʒ〕
[过去式] averaged；[过去分词]averaged
n. ❶平均，平均数[C]
An average of two students are absent each day.
每天平均有两个学生缺席。
❷一般，普通；中等[C][U]
a. ❶平均的
The average age of the boys in this class is 15.
这个班级中男生的平均年龄为15岁。
❷一般的，普通的；中等的
It was an average piece of work.
那是一件普通的产品。
vi. 平均为
The rainfall there averages 300 mm a year.
那儿的年降雨量平均每年为300毫米。

avoid 〔əˈvɔɪd ‖ əˈvɔɪd〕
[过去式]avoided；[过去分词]avoided
vt. ❶避开，躲开
I avoided him as much as possible.
我尽量避开他。
❷避免[(+n. /v-ing)]
They all avoided mentioning

that name.
他们都避免提及那个名字。

awake 〔ə'wek ‖ ə'weɪk〕
[过去式]awoke, awaked; [过去分词]awoke, awaked
vt. 唤醒,使醒过来
I was awaked by the noise.
我被噪音吵醒。
vi. 醒来
I awoke in the middle of the night.
我在半夜中醒来。
a. 醒着的;清醒的
I was awake all night.
我整夜没合眼。

award 〔ə'wɔrd ‖ ə'wɔːd〕
[过去式]awarded; [过去分词]awarded
vt. 授予,给予
He was awarded the first prize.
他被授予一等奖。
n. [C]❶ 奖,奖品;奖状
He won the second award.
他得了二等奖。
❷奖学金

aware 〔ə'wɛr ‖ ə'weə〕
a. ❶知道的,察觉的[(+of)][+that][+wh-]
I am well aware that this is a tough job.
我深知这是一件棘手的工作。
❷(与副词连用)有……方面知识(或意识)的
He is an artistically aware young man.
他是个懂艺术的青年。

常用短语

be aware of 意识到
I wasn't aware of my danger.
我不知道自己处于危险之中。

away 〔ə'we ‖ ə'weɪ〕
ad. ❶离开[(+from)]
He hasn't been away from home before.
以前他从没有离开过家。
❷(用在名词后)隔开……远;尚有……时间
The hotel is only two miles away.
旅馆离这里只有两英里。
❸不在;外出
Harry is still away.
哈里还是不在。
❹消失;(用)光;完,……掉
The snow melted away.
雪融化了。

蝴蝶
butterfly

生物学家
biologist

B

军号
bugle

佛教
Buddhism

baby〔'bebɪ ‖ 'beɪbɪ〕

n.［C］❶婴儿

She has a 5-month-old baby.

她有一个 5 个月大的婴儿。

❷幼畜；幼兽；雏鸟

back〔bæk ‖ bæk〕

n. ❶背脊，背部［C］

Someone patted me on the back.

有人在我背上轻轻地拍了一下。

❷后部［(＋of)］

Grandpa and grandma sat in the back of the car.

爷爷和奶奶坐在汽车后排的座位上。

❸后面，背面［(＋of)］

❹椅背［(＋of)］

❺(书报等的)末尾［(＋of)］

There is an appendix at the back of the book.

该书末尾处有一附录。

❻(足球等的)后卫；后卫球员［C］

ad. ❶在原处；回原处

Joan and I walked back to the college.

我和琼步行回到学校。

❷向后；后退地

Please go back 3 steps.

请退后 3 步。

❸以前；追溯

A few years back you could see nothing but barren land there.

数年前人们在那儿所能看到的只是荒野。

a. ❶后面的，后部的

He sat in the back seat of the car.

他坐在车子后面的座位上。

❷过去的；过期的

I bought some back issues of science magazines yesterday.

昨天我买了几本过期的科学杂志。

常用短语

B

at the back of 在……后面
There is a big tree at the back of my house.
我房子后面有棵大树。
back and forth 前后来回
The swing moved back and forth.
秋千来回摆动。
back to back 背靠背

background 〔ˈbækˌgraʊnd ‖ ˈbækgraʊnd〕
n. ❶背景(与前景 foreground 相对)[C]
I took a picture of her with the mountain in the background.
我以那座山为背景给她拍了张照片。
❷(事件等的)背景;出身背景;(包括学历在内的)经历[C][U]
He is a young man with a college background.
他是个有大学学历的年轻人。

backward 〔ˈbækwɚd ‖ ˈbækwəd〕
a. ❶向后的,反向的,返回的
He made a backward step.
他向后退了一步。
❷落后的,发展迟缓的
It is not a backward country.
它不是落后的国家。
ad. ❶向后;倒
She looked backward over her shoulder.
她回头往后看。
❷背向前地
It is dangerous to walk backward.
倒着走是危险的。

bad 〔bæd ‖ bæd〕
[比]worse 〔wɝs ‖ wɜːs〕;[最]worst 〔wɝst ‖ wɜːst〕
a. ❶坏的,不好的;拙劣的;令人不悦的
The weather was really bad.
天气真糟。
❷不健全的;有病的;疼痛的
I felt bad all day.
我一整天觉得不舒服。
❸有害的[(+for)]
Reading in dim light is bad for the eyes.
在暗淡的光线下看书有损视力。
❹(食物)腐坏的;腐烂的
The meat went bad.
这块肉坏了。
❺不适合的;不适当的
❻好极了的;棒极了的

badminton 〔ˈbædmɪntən ‖ ˈbædmɪntən〕

n. 羽毛球

bag 〔bæg ‖ bæg〕
n. [C]❶袋;提袋
handbag
手提包
paperbag
纸袋
❷钱包;(女用)手提包
❸一袋之量[(+of)]
We brought home two bags of potatoes.
我们带了两袋马铃薯回家。

baggage 〔'bægɪdʒ ‖ 'bægɪdʒ〕
n.【美】行李[U]【英】luggage
He carried two pieces of baggage.
他拿了两件行李。

balance 〔'bæləns ‖ 'bæləns〕
[过去式] balanced;[过去分词] balanced
n. ❶平衡,均衡[U]
I lost my balance and fell.
我身体失去平衡,摔了一跤。
❷天平,秤[C]
In what way is a laboratory balance different from a balance found in a store?
实验室的天平与商店里的秤在什么方面有所不同?
vt. 使平衡;保持……的平衡
In order to balance their trade, they would have to buy less goods in the United States.
为了平衡贸易,他们将不得不减少在美国购货。

ball[1] 〔bɔl ‖ bɔːl〕
n. [C]球;球状体
The two boys were kicking a ball on the grass.
两个男孩在草地上踢球。

ball[2] 〔bɔl ‖ bɔːl〕
n. ❶舞会[C]
The ladies were all dressed beautifully at the ball.
舞会上女士们全都穿得很漂亮。
❷【口】快乐的时光
We had a ball in LasVegas.
我们在拉斯维加斯玩得很开心。

balloon 〔bə'lun ‖ bə'luːn〕
n. [C]❶气球,热气球
❷(用作玩具的)气球

bamboo 〔bæm'bu ‖ ˌbæm'buː〕
n. ❶竹,竹子[C][U]
❷竹材[U]

B

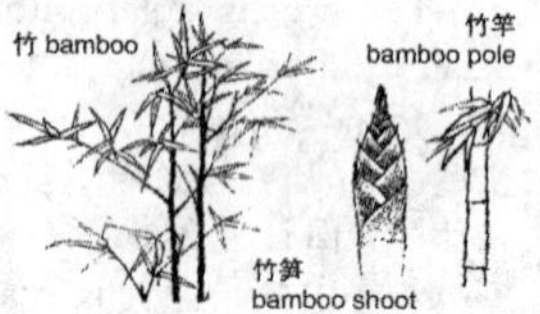

banana 〔bəˈnænə ‖ bəˈnɑːnə〕

n. ❶香蕉[C]

Laying on the table were some apples and two bunches of bananas.

桌上放着几只苹果和两串香蕉。

❷香蕉味;草黄色

band[1] 〔bænd ‖ bænd〕

n. [C]❶带,细绳;箍

❷【机】传送带,传动带

❸(无线电的)波段,频带

❹条纹;嵌条

The blue pitcher has yellow bands around the neck.

那把蓝色水壶的柄上有一圈圈的黄色条纹。

band[2] 〔bænd ‖ bænd〕

n. [C]❶(一)伙(人),(一)帮,(一)群

We were set upon by a band of robbers.

我们遭到了一帮强盗的袭击。

❷乐团,乐队;管乐队

The band played several marches.

乐队演奏了几首进行曲。

bandage 〔ˈbændɪdʒ ‖ ˈbændɪdʒ〕

n. 绷带[C]

bank[1] 〔bæŋk ‖ bæŋk〕

n. [C] ❶银行

I keep my money in a savings bank.

我的钱存在一家储蓄银行里。

❷(医用器官等的)储存所;库

The hospital has its own blood bank.

这家医院有自己的血库。

bank[2] 〔bæŋk ‖ bæŋk〕

n. [C] ❶堤;岸

They stood on the river bank to fish.

他们站在河岸边钓鱼。

❷田埂

bar 〔bɑr ‖ bɑː〕

n. [C]❶棒,条;(长方或椭圆形的)条状物

Here is a bar of soap.

这儿有一条肥皂。

❷闩,横杠

❸酒吧;小吃店;柜台

There are several bars in the hotel.

这家旅馆有好几个酒吧。

barber 〔ˈbɑrbɚ ‖ ˈbɑːbə〕
n. 理发师[C]
I had a shave at the barber's.
我在理发店剃须修面。

bare 〔bɛr ‖ beə〕
a. ❶裸的
The child was bare to the waist.
那孩子打赤膊。
❷光秃秃的
The trees are bare in winter.
树到冬天叶子都掉光了。
❸空的
a bare cupboard
空橱柜
❹勉强的；仅仅的
All they had were the bare necessities of life.
他们所有的仅仅是生活必需品而已。
❺没有……的[(+of)]
The little room was almost bare of furniture.
这个小房间几乎没有什么家具。

barely 〔ˈbɛrlɪ ‖ ˈbeəlɪ〕
ad. ❶仅仅，勉强；几乎没有
He has barely enough money to live on.
他的钱仅够勉强维持生计。
❷贫乏地；光秃秃地
The room was furnished barely but neatly.
房间陈设十分简陋，但很整洁。
❸公开地，露骨地
The facts are presented barely, without any comments.
事实原原本本摆了出来，没有加任何评论。

bargain 〔ˈbɑrgɪn ‖ ˈbɑːgɪn〕
[过去式]bargained；[过去分词]bargained
n. [C] ❶协议，买卖，交易[(+with)][+that]
I made a bargain with him.
我和他做了笔交易。
❷特价商品，便宜货
These toys are a real bargain at such low prices.
这些玩具价钱这么低，确实便宜。
vi. ❶讨价还价[(+with/over/about)]
She bargained with the fishmonger over the price.
她与鱼贩讲价钱。
❷达成协议
They bargained on a two-year term.
他们讲定以两年为期。
vt. ❶讨价还价后卖掉
❷经谈判后使得

They finally bargained out the obstacles to an agreement.
他们通过谈判终于排除了达成协议的障碍。

B

base 〔bes ‖ beɪs〕
n. [C] ❶基，底，基部
The machine rests on a wide base of steel.
这个机器由一个很大的钢制底座支撑。
❷基础；基料
❸基地，总部
Our company's base is in Taipei, but we have branches all over the island.
我们公司的总部在台北，但是全岛都有分公司。

baseball 〔'bes'bɔl ‖ 'beɪsbɔːl〕
n. ❶棒球运动[U]
❷棒球[C]

basic 〔'besɪk ‖ 'beɪsɪk〕
a. 基础的，基本的；初步的[(+to)]
These poor people lack the basic necessities of life.
这些穷人缺乏生活的基本必需品。

basin 〔'besn̩ ‖ 'beɪsn〕
n. [C] ❶盆；脸盆；食物盆
❷盆地，凹地

basket 〔'bæskɪt ‖ 'bɑːskɪt〕
n. [C] ❶篮，篓，筐
❷一篮（或篓、筐）的量[(+of)]
Mary came up to me, carrying a basket of apples.
玛丽提着一篮苹果向我走来。

basketball 〔'bæskɪtˌbɔl ‖ 'bɑːskɪtbɔːl〕
n. ❶篮球运动[U]
❷篮球[C]
Let's play basketball.
咱们玩篮球吧。

bat 〔bæt ‖ bæt〕
n. 蝙蝠[C]

bath 〔bæθ ‖ bɑːθ〕
n. [C]❶浴缸，澡盆
❷(一次)沐浴，洗澡
I am going to take a bath.
我打算洗个澡。
❸洗涤液；(一缸)洗浴水
The bath is too hot.

洗澡水太烫了。

bathe〔beð ‖ beɪð〕

［过去式］bathed；［过去分词］bathed

vt. ❶给……洗澡

Will you help me bathe the baby?

你能帮我替孩子洗澡吗？

❷弄湿；上药水

The nurse bathed his wound with iodine.

护士在他的伤口上涂碘酒。

❸使沉浸其中［(+in/with)］

Her eyes were bathed in tears.

她眼泪汪汪。

vi. ❶【美】洗澡；日光浴

She is bathing for the baby.

她在给婴儿洗澡。

❷沉浸

He bathed in luscious strains.

他沉浸在悦耳的乐曲中。

bathroom〔ˈbæθˌrum ‖ ˈbɑːθrʊm〕

n.［C］❶浴室

❷【美】【婉】化妆室；厕所

battery〔ˈbætərɪ ‖ ˈbætərɪ〕

n. 电池；蓄电池［C］

battle〔ˈbætḷ ‖ ˈbætl〕

n. 战斗；战役［C］〈指局部战斗，全面战争是 war〉

win / lose a battle

战胜/战败

B. C.

abbr. = before Christ 公元前……年(基督之前……年)

〔反义〕A. D. 公元后

be〔(强)bi ‖ biː；(弱)bɪ ‖ bi〕

v. aux. ❶(与动词的现在分词连用，构成各种进行时态)正在……，在……

I won't be free this afternoon. I'll be seeing a friend off.

我今天下午没空，我要给朋友送行。

❷(与及物动词的过去分词连用，构成被动语态)被……

The problem was solved long ago.

问题早解决了。

❸(与动词不定式连用，表示命令，职责，义务，意图，约定，可能性等)应该做……；必须做……；会做……

He is to go abroad tomorrow.

他明天要出国。

原形	现在式	过去式	过去分词	现在分词
be	am are is	was were was	been	being

vi. ❶是

At that time he was the chair of

B

the department.
当时他是系主任。
❷(表示时间,度,量,价值等)是;值;等于
The watch is 100 dollars.
这表值 100 美元。
❸(常用命令语气或不定式)要;得;成为;变成
Be quiet, please.
请安静。
❹(与 there 连用)有
There is a chair in the room.
房间里有把椅子。

beach 〔bitʃ ‖ biːtʃ〕
n. [C]❶海滩;海滨度假地
They are vacationing at the beach.
他们正在海滨度假。
❷湖滨,江滨

> beach , coast and shore:
> beach 倾斜度小,有沙有石的海滨。
> coast 陆地的沿岸
> shore 湖,海,河的岸
>
> **用法工具箱**

bear[1] 〔bɛr ‖ bɛə〕
[过去式] bore;[过去分词] borne, born
vt. ❶支持,承受;承担
Mrs. Ann Bader bears all expenses.
安妮·巴德太太承担一切费用。
❷忍受;经得起[+to-v][+v-ing][+that]
He could not bear that his friends would laugh at him.
他受不了朋友们竟也嘲笑他。
❸写有,印有,带有
Her face bore signs of tears.
她的脸上带着泪痕。
❹生(小孩);开(花);结(果)

bear[2] 〔bɛr ‖ bɛə〕
n. [C]❶熊;似熊的动物
a polar bear
北极熊
❷鲁莽的人;笨拙的人

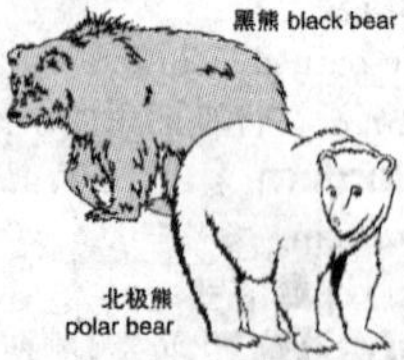

beast 〔bist ‖ biːst〕
n. [C] ❶兽,野兽
The lion is the king of beasts.
狮子为万兽之王。
❷粗暴(或凶残,蠢笨,卑劣)的

人，畜生

beat 〔bit ‖ biːt〕

［过去式］beat；［过去分词］beat, beaten

vt. ❶打，击，敲；冲击

He beat his brother for lying.

他因为他弟弟说谎而揍他。

❷打败，胜过

I think Jack can beat all the runners in the country.

我认为杰克可以胜过这个国家的所有赛跑选手。

vi. ❶打，击，敲［(＋at/on/upon/against)］

The rain was beating against the windows.

雨打在窗户上。

❷拍打；扑动，跳动

His heart beats violently.

他的心剧烈地跳着。

beautiful 〔ˈbjutəfəl ‖ ˈbjuːtəfəl〕

［比］more beautiful；［最］most beautiful

a. ❶美丽的，漂亮的

She has a beautiful face.

她有一张漂亮的脸蛋。

❷出色的，完美的

That's a beautiful shot.

那一枪打得真准。

〔反义〕ugly 丑陋的

because 〔bɪˈkɔz ‖ bɪˈkɔːz〕

conj. ❶因为

He is absent because he is ill.

他因病缺席。

❷(用在表示否定意义的句中)不因……而

Don't despise others because they are poor.

不要因为别人穷就瞧不起人家。

常用短语

because of 因为

He was absent because of sickness.

他因为生病缺课。

become 〔bɪˈkʌm ‖ bɪˈkʌm〕

［过去式］became；［过去分词］become

vi. 变成，成为；变得，开始变得

He became a great man.

他成了伟人。

vt. 适合；同……相称

This color becomes you.

这颜色适合你。

bed 〔bed ‖ bed〕

n. ❶床；睡眠处［C］［U］

Joe sat on the bed.

乔坐在床上。

❷睡觉；就寝时间［U］

It's too early for bed.

睡觉还太早。

❸(河)床；(海，湖的)底；底部

B

[C]
a river bed
河床

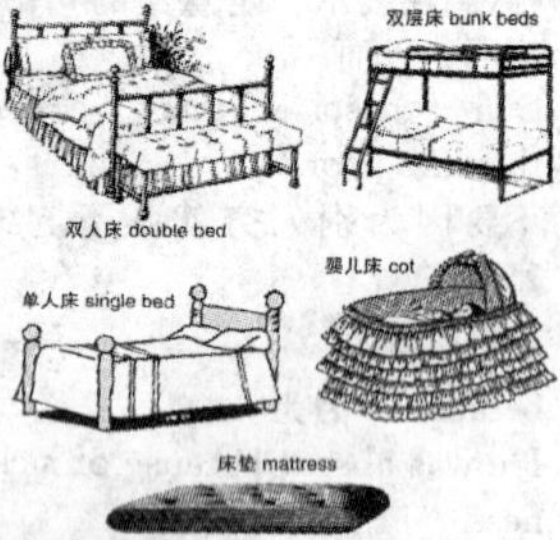

常用短语

be ill in bed 因病在床
get out of bed 起床
go to bed 就寝，睡觉
put to bed 使入睡

bedroom 〔ˈbedˌrum ‖ ˈbedrʊm〕
n. 卧室，寝室[C]
There are 3 bedrooms in my house.
我家里有 3 间卧室。

bee 〔bi ‖ biː〕
n. 蜜蜂，蜂[C]
He is as busy as a bee.
他忙得团团转。

beef 〔bif ‖ biːf〕
n. 牛肉[U]
He loves beef steak.
他爱吃牛排。

been 〔bɪn ‖ biːn〕
（be 的过去分词）❶ have/has +been 现在完成式
Where has he been?
他去哪儿了？
❷had+been 过去完成式
I had been sick two days before.
两天前我病了。
❸have/has been in…
曾经住在
He has been in London.
他曾在伦敦待过。
❹have/has been to …
曾经去过，刚刚去过
Have you ever been to the United States?
你去过美国吗？
I have been to the post office.
我刚去过邮局。

beer 〔bɪr ‖ bɪə〕
n. ❶啤酒[C][U]
a glass of beer
一杯啤酒
❷一瓶（杯，罐）
Order two beers.
叫两杯啤酒来。

before 〔bɪˈfor ‖ bɪˈfɔː〕
prep. ❶在……以前（时间）
Only two days remained before

the examination.
考前只剩下两天了。
❷(指顺序，重要性等)在……之前，先于
Your name comes before mine.
你的名字在我之前。
❸在……前面；在……面前
He made a speech before a large number of audience.
他在一大群听众面前演说。
ad. 以前；曾经
He was never late before.
过去他从不迟到。
conj. ❶在……之前
Check it carefully before you hand it in.
交来之前仔细核对一下。
❷与其……宁可……
I'd die before I told.
我宁死也决不会说出来。
❸否则，要不然
Get out before I call the police.
滚开，否则我叫警察了。

beg 〔bɛg ‖ bɛg〕
vt. vi. ❶乞讨
From whom did he beg the money?
他向谁讨到这钱的？
❷请求，恳求[＋to-v][＋that]
I beg that neither of you will say anything more.
我请求你们谁也别再说什么了。
❸(礼貌用语)请(原谅)，请(允许)[＋to-v]
I beg to suggest a different plan.
请允许我提出一个不同的计划。
I beg your pardon.
(因自己犯错) 对不起，请原谅。
(没听清)请再说一遍。

begin 〔bɪ'gɪn ‖ bɪ'gɪn〕
[过去式]began；[过去分词]begun
vt. 开始，着手；动手[＋v-ing][＋to-v]
When did you begin learning English?
你何时开始学英语的？
I began to study /studying at 7 o'clock.
我 7 点钟开始学习。
vi. ❶开始；开始进行
The concert began at 8 p.m.
音乐会晚上 8 时开始。
❷始于；源于
The campaign began last year.
这场运动始于去年。

常用短语

to begin with 首先
To begin with, you should ask

B

for his help.
首先你应该请求他的帮助。
begin with… **由……开始**
The concert began with a piano solo.
音乐会以一首钢琴独奏曲开始。

beginning 〔bɪˈgɪnɪŋ ‖ bɪˈgɪnɪŋ〕
n. 开始，起始；起源，发端[C][U]
from beginning to end
自始至终
the beginning of April
四月初

behave 〔bɪˈhev ‖ bɪˈheɪv〕
[过去式]behaved；[过去分词]behaved
vi. 表现，行为举止
She behaved well.
她举止得体。
vt. （后接 oneself）使检点，使守规矩
Behave yourself!
规矩点！

behavio(u)r 〔bɪˈhevjɚ ‖ bɪˈheɪvjə〕
n. 行为，举止；态度[U]
He was on his best behavior.
他表现极好。

behind 〔bɪˈhaɪnd ‖ bɪˈhaɪnd〕
prep. ❶在……的背后；在……的后面；向……的背后
There is a garden behind the house.
屋后有个花园。
❷落后于，不如
George always falls behind his schedule.
乔治老是不能按时完成计划。
❸迟于；晚于
She arrived at the office 10 minutes behind her usual time.
她到办公室时比往常晚了10分钟。
ad. ❶在背后；向背后
Mary drove. Her 10-year-old daughter sat behind.
玛丽开车，她10岁的女儿坐在后面。
❷(留)在原处；(遗留)在后
Both of them stayed behind.
他们两个留下未走。
❸迟；落后
We are lagging far behind.
我们大大落后了。

常用短语

leave… behind **留下……，忘了带……**
I left my umbrella behind.
我忘了带伞。

being 〔ˈbiɪŋ ‖ ˈbiːɪŋ〕
n. ❶存在；生存；生命[U]

When did the universe come into being?
宇宙是何时形成的?
❷生物;人[C]
Has anybody ever seen any beings from outer space?
有人见到过外星人吗?
human being
人类

belief 〔bɪ'lif ‖ bɪ'liːf〕
n. ❶相信;信任,信赖[U][(+in)][+(that)]
My father had no much belief in doctors of traditional Chinese medicine.
我父亲不太相信中医。
❷信念,看法[U][+that]
My belief is that the visiting team will lose.
我看客队会输。
❸信仰[C][(+in)]

believe 〔bɪ'liv ‖ bɪ'liːv〕
[过去式]believed;[过去分词]believed
vt. ❶相信;信任
I don't believe a single word he says.
他的话我一句也不信。
❷认为;猜想,料想
We believe Mr. Smith to be innocent.
我们认为史密斯先生是无辜的。

常用短语

believe in… 相信……的存在
believe in God 相信上帝的存在

bell 〔bɛl ‖ bel〕
n. 钟;铃;钟声;铃声[C]
The church bells are ringing.
教堂的钟声响了。

belong 〔bə'lɔŋ ‖ bɪ'lɒŋ〕
[过去式]belonged;[过去分词]belonged
vi. ❶(在分类上)属,应归入;(在关系方面)属(于)
They belong to the younger generation.
他们属于年轻的一代。
❷合得来;成为集体的一分子
I belong to the Tennis Club.
我是网球俱乐部成员。

常用短语

belong to ❶(在所有权等方面)属 ❷是……的成员

below 〔bə'lo ‖ bɪ'ləʊ〕
ad. ❶在下面;在下方
From the hill top we could see the plains below.
从山顶上我们可以看到山下的大平原。
❷在下级;在某一级以下

I mean officers of the rank of major and below.
我是说少校及少校以下的军官们。
❸在水面(或地面)下
The miners are working below.
矿工们在矿井下干活。
❹在本页下面(或下面一页)
prep. ❶(指位置)在……下面;到……下
Her skirt came below her knees.
她的裙子长过膝。

> below 和 under: below 是相对 above 而言的,表"在下方"。under 是相对 over而言的,表"正下方"。
> 如,under the bridge 在桥下
> below the bridge 在桥下方
>
> **用法工具箱**

❷(指数量,价格,程度,年龄等)在……以下
The cost of the whole work was below 2,000 dollars.
办理此事的全部费用在2,000美元以下。
❸(指地位等)低于
His position in the company is below hers.
他在公司里职位比她低。

belt 〔bɛlt ‖ belt〕
n. [C] ❶腰带;带;带状物
There is a belt of trees between the two fields.
那两块地之间有一片狭长树林。
Fasten your safety belt, please.
请系紧安全带。
❷地带,地区
Iowa is in the corn belt.
衣阿华州地处玉米带。

bench 〔bɛntʃ ‖ bentʃ〕
n. 长凳;长椅[C]
The old man sat on the park bench.

那位老人坐在公园的长椅上。

bend 〔bɛnd ‖ bend〕

[过去式] bent;[过去分词] bent

vt. ❶使弯曲,折弯

He bent the iron bar as if it had been made of rubber.

他将铁棍折弯,仿佛那是用橡胶做成的。

❷使致力(于)[(+on/to)]

The boys bent their attention on making model ships.

男孩们聚精会神地制作船舶模型。

❸使屈服(于)[(+to)]

She tried to bend her husband to her wishes.

她设法使丈夫顺从她的愿望。

vi. ❶弯曲;转弯

The road bends to the right.

公路向右弯曲。

❷俯[(+down/over)]

The nurse bent down and kissed the child.

护士弯下身子吻了孩子一下。

n. [C] ❶弯,曲;俯

❷(道路等的)转弯处

There is a sharp bend in the road here.

这段路上有一处急转弯。

benefit 〔'bɛnəfɪt ‖ 'benɪfɪt〕

[过去式]benefited;[过去分词] benefited

n. 利益,好处;优势[C][U]

The new hospital will be a great benefit to the town.

新建成的医院将给全城带来莫大好处。

常用短语

for the benefit of… 为了……的利益

vt. 对……有益,有益于

The sea air will benefit you.

海边的空气对你有益。

vi. 得益,受惠[(+by/from)]

We benefited greatly by this frank talk.

这次坦率的谈话使我们获益匪浅。

I benefited from his advice.

我获益于他的忠告。

beside 〔bɪ'saɪd ‖ bɪ'saɪd〕

prep. ❶在……近旁;在旁边

He sat down beside Emma.

他在埃玛身旁坐下。

❷和……相比

She seems dull beside that girl.

与那个女孩相比,她显得乏味。

❸和……无关;离(题)

That's beside the point.

那件事与此不相干。

besides 〔bɪ'saɪdz ‖ bɪ'saɪdz〕

B

ad. 此外，而且，加之

It's too late to go out now. Besides, it's beginning to rain.

现在出去太晚了，而且天开始下雨了。

〔同义〕in addition

prep. 在……之外，除……之外

What has he done, besides reading the paper?

除了看报，他还做了什么？

I want nothing besides this.

除此以外我什么都不要。

best〔best ‖ best〕

a.（good 和 well 的最高级）

❶最好的；最熟练的；道德最高尚的

She's my best friend.

她是我的至交。

❷最大的；主要的

It took the best part of a day to get there.

花了大半天时间才到达那里。

ad.（well 的最高级）

最好地；最适当地；最有效地

He read it best.

他读得最好。

I think Friday would suit me best.

我想星期五对我最适合。

〔反义〕worst 最坏的；最差地

词汇拓展

best-known *a.*（well-known 的最高级）最著名的

n. ❶最好；最佳；最好（或最能干，最有名望等）的人；最好的事物

She always wants the best.

她总是要最好的。

Even the best of us makes mistakes.

甚至我们当中最能干的人也会出错。

They wore their best to the party.

他们盛装赴宴。

❷（常用 one's best）（某人的）最大努力；最佳状况

I will try my best. 我会尽最大努力。

常用短语

at one's best 最佳情形；全盛状态；巅峰

The cherry blossoms are at their best.

樱花现在正盛开。

do one's (level) best 全力以赴

I'll do my best to complete the work.

我会尽最大努力完成这项工作。

in one's (Sunday) best 穿着节日盛装

make the best of 充分利用

Make the best of your time.

充分利用你的时间。

better 〔ˈbetɚ ‖ ˈbetə〕

a. (good 和 well 的比较级)

❶较佳的;更好的

We're hoping for better weather tomorrow.

我们希望明天天气转好。

❷健康状况有所好转的;健康恢复的

Are you feeling any better?

你觉得好一些了吗?

ad. (well 的比较级)更好地;更适当地

She speaks English much better than I do.

她英语说得比我好多了。

Try to do better next time.

下次争取做得更好些。

〔**反义**〕worse 较差的;较差地

between 〔bəˈtwin ‖ bɪˈtwiːn〕

prep. ❶(指时间,空间,顺序等)在……之间

They planted a lot of trees between the two buildings.

他们在两座建筑物之间栽了许多树。

He returned between 3 and 4.

他在 3 点到 4 点之间回来的。

❷(指数量,距离,程度等)介乎……之间

He is a man between 60 and 70.

他的年龄约在 60 到 70 之间。

❸为……所分享(或分担)

We didn't have much money between us.

我们的钱放在一起也不多。

> between 用于"两者"之间,among 用于"三者"之间。
>
> 如,a house between the two trees
>
> 两棵树之间的房子
>
> a house among the trees
>
> 树林中的房子
>
> **用法工具箱**

beyond 〔bɪˈjɑnd ‖ bɪˈjɒnd〕

ad. 在更远处;往更远处;再往后;在那边

The dog came to the front door, but not beyond.

狗走到前门,但没有再向前走。

prep. ❶越过;在……的那一边;向……的那一边

Beyond the mountains is a thick

forest.
山那边是一片浓密的森林。
❷迟于，晚于
Don't stay there beyond the visiting hours.
待在那儿别超过会客时间。
❸(指程度)深于；(指范围)越出；不可及
The question is beyond my power.
这问题太难了，我答不上来。

Bible 〔ˈbaɪbḷ ‖ ˈbaɪbl〕
n. (基督教和天主教的)《圣经》(the Bible 亦称 the Holy Bible)

bicycle 〔ˈbaɪsɪkḷ ‖ ˈbaɪsɪkl〕
n. 自行车[C] (口语中是 bike)
ride on a bicycle
骑自行车

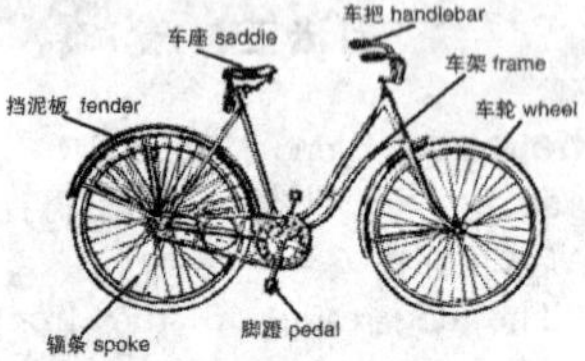

big 〔bɪg ‖ bɪg〕
[比]bigger；[最] biggest
a. ❶(在面积、体积、数量、程度等方面)大的，巨大的
How big the birthday cake is!
这生日蛋糕好大呀！
Big Ben
英国国会大厦钟楼上的大钟
❷长大了的；年龄较大的
No arguing. You're big boys now.
别争吵啦，你们都是大孩子了。
❸重大的；主要的；伟大的
a big event
大事件

bill 〔bɪl ‖ bɪl〕
n. [C] ❶账单[(＋for)]
The store sent me a bill for $50.
那家商店寄给我一张 50 美元的账单。
❷【美】钞票
❸议案，法案
The House of Commons has not yet passed the bill.
下议院尚未通过该议案。

billion 〔ˈbɪljən ‖ ˈbɪljən〕
n. ❶(美国，法国)十亿
❷(英国，德国)万亿
❸大量，无数[P][(＋of)]

billionaire 〔ˌbɪljəˈnɛr ‖ ˌbɪljəˈneə〕
n. 亿万富翁

bird 〔bɝd ‖ bɜːd〕
n. 鸟；禽[C]

[有关鸟的谚语]
A bird in the hand is worth two in the bush.
一鸟在手胜过两鸟在林(到手的东西才是可靠的)。
The early bird catches the worm.
早起的鸟才捕得到虫(凡事趁早)。
Kill two birds with one stone.
一石两鸟(一举两得)。

用法工具箱

birth [bɜ˞θ ‖ bɜːθ]

n. ❶出生,诞生[C][U]

The exact date of his birth is not known.

他出生的确切日期无人知道。

❷血统,家世,出身[U]

He is a man of German birth.

他是个德国血统的男子。

常用短语

give birth to 生(孩子)

She gave birth to twins.

她生下一对双胞胎。

birthday [ˈbɜ˞θˌde ‖ ˈbɜːθdeɪ]

n. [C]❶生日

For her birthday I bought her a piano.

我买了一架钢琴作为她的生日礼物。

birthday cake

生日蛋糕

birthday party

生日聚会

birthday present

生日礼物

❷【喻】诞生的日子;开始的日子

July 4, 1776 is the birthday of the United States of America.

1776 年 7 月 4 日是美利坚合众国诞生的日子。

bit [bɪt ‖ bɪt]

n. [C] ❶(一)小片,(一)小块,(一)小段

The dog was pulling the newspaper to bits.
狗把报纸撕成了碎片。
❷少量,一点点[(＋of)]
She is out to do a bit of shopping.
她出去买点东西。
❸一会儿,片刻[(＋of)]
Please wait a bit.
请稍等片刻。

常用短语

bit by bit 渐渐地
a bit (of) 有点,稍微;一小块的,一片的
Give me a bit of bread.
给我一片儿面包。
I feel a bit tired.
我觉得有点累。

bite 〔baɪt ‖ baɪt〕
[过去式]bit;[过去分词] bitten
vt. vi. ❶咬;啃
My younger sister's dog bit me yesterday.
我妹妹的狗昨天咬了我。
❷(蚊子,跳蚤等)叮,蜇(蜂等蜇人用 sting)
n. 咬,叮;一口之量[C]
The dog gave the mailman a nasty bite.
这条狗将邮差猛咬一口。

bitter 〔ˈbɪtɚ ‖ ˈbɪtə〕
[比]more bitter;[最]most bitter,bitterest
a. ❶有苦味的,苦的
The medicine tastes bitter.
此药苦口。
❷痛苦的,难堪的
They learned a bitter lesson.
他们接受了惨痛的教训。
❸极冷的,严寒刺骨的
The wind is bitter.
寒风刺骨。
❹充满仇恨的;极为不满的;激烈的;尖刻的
one's bitter days
艰苦的日子
bitter words
恶言

词汇拓展

bitterness *n.* 苦味,悲痛,酷烈
bitterly *ad.* 伤心地,愤怒地;极其,非常

black 〔blæk ‖ blæk〕
[比]blacker;[最]blackest
a. ❶黑色的;漆黑的;黑暗的
It was a cold, black night.
那是个寒冷而漆黑的夜晚。
❷(关于)黑人的(1960 年起代替有种族歧视的 Negro)
❸(咖啡)不加牛奶(或奶油)的
Do you want your coffee black?

你的咖啡中不加牛奶吗?

n. ❶黑色[U]

The black shows up against the white.

在白色的衬托下,黑色很显目。

❷(有时大写)黑人;美国黑人[C]

He was the first black to be elected as Mayor.

他是第一位被选为市长的黑人。

常用短语

black and blue 遍体鳞伤

black and white 白纸黑字

blackboard 〔ˈblækˌbord ‖ ˈblækbɔːd〕

n. 黑板[C]

Write your name on the blackboard.

把你的名字写到黑板上。

blacksmith 〔ˈblækˌsmɪθ ‖ ˈblækˌsmɪθ〕

n. [C]❶铁匠,锻工

❷马蹄铁匠

smith 表"金属工匠",如 goldsmith 金匠 silversmith 银匠

用法工具箱

blank 〔blæŋk ‖ blæŋk〕

[比]blanker;[最]blankest

a. ❶空白的

He handed me a blank check.

他递给我一张空白支票。

❷无表情的,茫然的

There was a blank look on his face.

他脸上没有表情。

n. 空白,空白处;空白表格[C]

Fill in the blanks.

填写空白处。

blanket 〔ˈblæŋkɪt ‖ ˈblæŋkɪt〕

n. [C]❶毛毯,毯子

❷毯状物;(厚厚的)覆盖层[(+of)]

The valley was covered with a blanket of snow.

山谷白雪如毯。

bleed 〔blid ‖ bliːd〕

[过去式]bled;[过去分词]bled

vi. 出血,流血

He was bleeding badly.

他流了很多血。

bless 〔blɛs ‖ bles〕

[过去式]blessed, blest;[过去分词]blessed, blest

vt. ❶为……祝福,为……祈神赐福

❷保佑,庇护

Goodbye, and may God bless

B

you.
再见，愿上帝保佑你。
❸赞美；感谢，对……感激
They blessed her for her kindness.
他们感谢她的好意。
❹使有幸得到[(+with)]
He was blessed with great talent.
他天资非常聪颖，真是幸运。

blind 〔blaɪnd ‖ blaɪnd〕
a. ❶瞎的，盲的
He is blind in one eye.
他一只眼睛失明。
❷视而不见的；不愿承认的
We must not be blind to the suffering of others.
我们不能对他人的痛苦视而不见。
❸盲目的，未加思考的；漫无目的的
He made a blind guess.
他胡猜了一通。

block 〔blɑk ‖ blɒk〕
n. [C] ❶块[(+of)]；积木[P]
a block of rock
一块岩石
❷【美】(四面围有街道的)街区
The clothes store is 3 blocks away.
那家服装店距此有 3 个街区。
❸阻塞(物)，障碍(物)
There is a block in the pipe and the water can't flow away.
管子里有阻塞物，水流不出去。
traffic block
交通阻塞

blood 〔blʌd ‖ blʌd〕
n. ❶血，血液[U]
Lots of people donated blood.
许多人献血。
❷血统，家族关系[U]
They are not of the same blood.
他们并非同宗。

词汇拓展

bloody *a.* 血腥的，血污的

blouse 〔blaʊs ‖ blaʊz〕
n. [C] ❶(妇女，儿童等的)短上衣，短衫
❷(肚间束带的)工作服

blow 〔blo ‖ bləʊ〕
[过去式] blew；[过去分词] blown

vi. ❶吹，刮
A breeze blew over the garden.
一阵微风吹过花园。
❷吹动；随风飘动
The flags were blowing in the wind.
旗帜在随风飘扬。
❸吹响，鸣响；吹奏
We heard the bugles blowing.
我们听到号角在吹响。
vt. ❶吹
The wind blew her hair.
风吹动她的头发。
❷吹动；吹掉；(风)刮走
The storm blew down several large trees.
暴风雨刮倒了几棵大树。
❸吹响；吹奏
Who is blowing the horn?
谁在吹号角？

blue 〔blu ‖ bluː〕
[比]bluer；[最]bluest
a. ❶蓝色的；天蓝色的；青色的
The sky was bright blue.
天空一片蔚蓝。
❷【口】沮丧的，忧郁的；(脸色)发青的
Kathy felt blue all day.
凯茜整天沮丧着。
n. ❶蓝色；天蓝色[C][U]
She was dressed in blue.
她穿着蓝色衣服。
❷(源自美国黑人的)布鲁斯乐曲[P]
He used to like the blues very much.
他过去非常喜爱布鲁斯乐曲。

board 〔bord ‖ bɔːd〕
n. ❶木板；板[C]
He sawed the board in half.
他将木板锯成两块。
❷牌子；布告牌；黑板；(棋)盘[C]
❸膳食；伙食[U]
We will provide room and board for them.
我们将提供他们的食宿。
❹委员会；理事会；董事会；(政府的)部，局，会[C]
He has recently joined the board of the company.
他最近加入了该公司的董事会。

常用短语

on board 在(船，车，飞机)上
As soon as we went on board, our ship left port.
我们一上船，船就出港了。

boast 〔bost ‖ bəust〕
[过去式]boasted；[过去分词]boasted
vi. 自吹自擂；夸耀[(＋about/of)]

He is always boasting of his son.
他总是夸耀他的儿子。
vt. (指物)以有……自豪;拥有
Our school library boasts quite a few rare books.
我们学校图书馆以藏有好多本珍贵的书而自豪。
n. [C]❶自吹,牛皮,大话
That brother of yours is full of boasts.
你那个宝贝兄弟满口大话。
❷引以为荣的事物
It is his boast that he has never been late for work.
他为自己上班从未迟到过感到自豪。

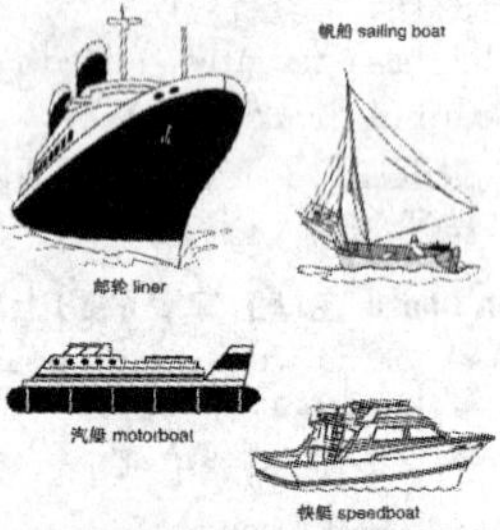

boat 〔bot ‖ bəʊt〕
n. 小船,汽船,小舟[C]
We crossed the river in a boat.
我们乘一条小船过了河。

常用短语

in the same boat 处境相同

body 〔ˈbɑdɪ ‖ ˈbɒdɪ〕
n. ❶(人,动物的)身体;肉体[C]
He has a strong body.
他身体强健。
❷(文章、书籍等的)正文;主要部分
the body of letter
信函的正文
❸团体;组织;法人[C]
a public body
公共团体
❹物体;天体[C]
❺(人、动物等的)尸体[C]

常用短语

in a body 全体一致地
keep body and soul together 勉强活下去

boil 〔bɔɪl ‖ bɔɪl〕
[过去式] boiled; [过去分词] boiled
vi. vt. ❶(水等)沸腾,开,滚
The water is boiling.
水开了。
❷煮熟
She boiled two eggs hard.
她把两个蛋煮老了。

bold 〔bold ‖ bəʊld〕

[比]bolder;[最]boldest

a. ❶英勇的,无畏的;大胆的

The young man is a bold warrior.

这个年轻人是个很英勇的武士。

❷放肆的,厚颜无耻的

How bold you are!

你的脸皮好厚。

❸显著的,轮廓清晰的,(字等)粗笔画的,黑体的

His drawings were done in a few bold lines.

他的画以几笔粗线挥就。

bomb 〔bɑm ‖ bɒm〕

n. 炸弹[C]

An atomic bomb was dropped on Hiroshima in 1945.

1945 年一颗原子弹被投到广岛。

bone 〔bon ‖ bəʊn〕

n. 骨,骨头[C]

Doris suffered a broken bone in her foot.

多丽丝的一只脚骨折了。

book 〔bʊk ‖ bʊk〕

[过去式]booked;[过去分词]booked

n.[C] ❶书,书本,书籍

She has written several books on the subject.

她已经写了几部有关这方面的书了。

❷(长篇作品的)卷,篇,部

the books of the Bible

《圣经》的各卷

vt. 预订;预雇;预约

Mary has booked a flight from New York to London.

玛丽已预订了从纽约到伦敦的飞机票。

bookcase 〔ˈbʊkˌkes ‖ ˈbʊkkeɪs〕

n. 书架;书橱[C]

There are many books in my bookcase.

我的书架上有很多书。

bookmaker 〔ˈbʊkˌmekɚ ‖ ˈbʊkˌmeɪkə〕

n. ❶著作者

❷编辑人;出版者

bookmark 〔ˈbʊkˌmɑrk ‖ ˈbʊkˌmɑːk〕

n. 书签

bookseller 〔ˈbʊkˌsɛlɚ ‖ ˈbʊkˌselə〕

n. ❶(小)书店

❷书店主

bookshop 〔ˈbʊkˌʃɑp ‖ ˈbʊkʃɒp〕

n. 【主英】书店

bookstall 〔ˈbʊkstɔl ‖ ˈbʊkstɔːl〕

n. ❶书摊

❷【英】报摊

B

bookstore 〔ˈbʊkˌstɔr ‖ ˈbʊkstɔː〕

n. 【美】书店

A new bookstore was open near my workplace.

在我工作场所附近新开了一家书店。

bookworm 〔ˈbʊkˌwɝm ‖ ˈbʊkwɜːm〕

n. ❶书蛀虫

❷喜爱读书者；书呆子

boot 〔but ‖ buːt〕

n. (长筒)靴[C][P]

She was in a pair of white boots.

她穿着一双白色马靴。

border 〔ˈbɔrdɚ ‖ ˈbɔːdə〕

n. [C] ❶边缘，边沿

He sat on the border of the stream.

他坐在溪畔。

❷饰边，滚边

The handkerchief has a lace border.

这块手帕有花边。

❸边界，边境，国界[(+ between/with)]

They were near the border between France and Germany.

他们在法德边界附近。

born 〔bɔrn ‖ bɔːn〕

a. ❶出生的，诞生的；生成的

The baby was born last Friday.

孩子是上星期五生的。

❷天生的，生来就有的

She was considered a born movie star.

她被看成是天生的电影明星。

borrow 〔ˈbɑro ‖ ˈbɒrəʊ〕

[过去式] borrowed; [过去分词] borrowed

vt. ❶借，借入[(+from)]

How much have you borrowed from him?

你向他借了多少钱？

❷借用；采用[(+from)]

Some of his ideas were borrowed from other sources.

他的某些见解是从别处借用的。

boss 〔bɔs ‖ bɒs〕

n. [C] ❶老板；上司；主人，工头，领班

Who's the boss in this office?

这间办公室的主管是谁？

❷有权势者，首领，(政党等的)领袖

He is a political boss.

他是政界首脑人物。

both 〔boθ ‖ bəʊθ〕

a. 两……(都)，两个……(都)

I want both (the) books.

两本书我都要。

❶加在可数名词复数前面。
❷定冠词 the,指示代词和所有格放在 both 和名词之间。
Both his parents are well.
他的父母都健在。
❸not＋both 表示部分否定。
I don't know both his parents.
他的双亲我并不都认识。

用法工具箱

ad. 并;又;两者皆(常用于 both…and…句型)
Both Tom and John came.
汤姆和约翰都来了。
上句的否定句是:
Neither Tom nor John came.
汤姆和约翰都没来。
pron. 两者(都);两个(都);双方(都),〈用于否定句时同形容词形式一样构成部分否定,二者均否定用 not＋either 或 neither〉
I don't know both of them.
他们两个我并不都认识。
I don't know either of them. ＝I know neither of them.
他们两个我都不认识。
Why not buy both?
为什么不把两件都买下?

bother 〔ˈbɑðɚ ‖ ˈbɒðə〕
[过去式]bothered;[过去分词]bothered
vt. 烦扰,打搅,使困惑,使不安
I can't bother him with my little affairs.
我不能因自己那点小事去打扰他。
vi. ❶烦恼,担心[(＋with/about)]
Don't bother about that trifling matter.
别为那件小事烦恼。
❷麻烦,费心[(＋with/about)][＋to-v][＋v-ing]
You needn't bother to come to my office.
你不必特地来我办公室。

bottle 〔ˈbɑtl̩ ‖ ˈbɒtl〕
n. [C]❶瓶子
❷一瓶的容量[(＋of)]
He can drink two bottles of wine at a time.
他一次能喝两瓶酒。

bottom 〔ˈbɑtəm ‖ ˈbɒtəm〕
n. ❶底;底部;下端
The bottom of the cup is bro-

ken.
这个杯子的底破了。
❷最底下的部分，底层[U]
The apples at the bottom of the basket are smaller.
篮子底部的苹果较小。
the bottom of a hill
山底
the bottom of a page
页底

常用短语

from the bottom of one's heart
衷心地
I wish you happy from the bottom of my heart.
我衷心祝你幸福。

bow[1]〔bo ‖ bəʊ〕

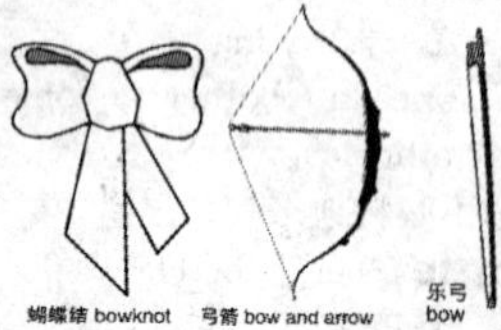

n. [C] 弓
Believe it or not, she can draw a strong bow.
信不信由你，她能拉强弓。

bow[2]〔bau ‖ baʊ〕
[过去式] bowed; [过去分词] bowed
n. [C] 鞠躬，欠身，低头
He made his bow to my father.
他向我父亲鞠躬。
vi. 鞠躬，欠身[(+to/before)]
He bowed to his teacher.
他向老师敬礼。
They bowed politely before the Queen.
他们在女王面前恭恭敬敬地鞠躬。
vt. ❶低(头)，欠(身)
He bowed his head in shame.
他惭愧地低下头来。
❷鞠躬(或欠身)表示
She bowed her thanks.
她鞠躬致谢。

bowl〔bol ‖ bəʊl〕
n. [C] ❶碗
❷一碗的容量
Would you like another bowl of soup?
请再喝一碗汤好吗？

box〔bɑks ‖ bɒks〕
[名复] boxes
n. [C] ❶箱；盒；匣
a mail box
信箱
a lunch box
便当盒
❷一箱(或一盒等)的容量[(+of)]

Mother brought home a box of chocolates.
母亲带了一盒巧克力糖回家。
❸【英】公用电话亭
❹(戏院等处的)包厢;(餐馆的)分隔式雅座
❺【口】电视机
What's on the box now?
此刻电视上演什么节目?

boxer 〔'bɑksɚ ‖ 'bɒksə〕
n. 拳击手,拳师,拳击选手[C]

boxing 〔'bɑksɪŋ ‖ 'bɒksɪŋ〕
n. 拳击;拳术[U]

拳击比赛 boxing match

boy 〔bɔɪ ‖ bɔɪ〕
n. [C] ❶少年,男孩
Don't cry. You're a big boy now.
别哭啦,你已是个大孩子了。
boyfriend
男朋友
boyhood
少年时代
❷儿子;小儿子
We have one boy and three girls.
我们有一个儿子和三个女儿。

brain 〔bren ‖ breɪn〕
n. ❶脑,脑袋[C]
❷智力,头脑[U][P]
I suppose she has more brains than any of us.
我认为她比我们都聪明。
❸【口】聪明人,智者[C]
❹智囊[P]
She was the brains of the organization.
她是这个组织的智囊。
❺计算机

brake 〔brek ‖ breɪk〕
n. 刹车,制动器[C]
The brake didn't work.
刹车不灵了。

branch 〔bræntʃ ‖ brɑːntʃ〕
n. [C]❶树枝;枝
Many birds are on the branch.
很多鸟栖息在树上。
❷支族;支流;支线;支路
The river has 3 main branches.
这条河有3条主要的支流。
❸分公司;分店;分局;分部;部门
The bank has branches all over the country.
该银行在全国各地均有分行。

B

❹(语系的)分支;(学科的)分科[(+of)]
English is a branch of the Germanic family of languages.
英语是日耳曼语系的一个分支。

brand 〔brænd ‖ brænd〕
n. 商标;牌子[C][(+of)]
Do you like this brand of tea?
你喜欢这个牌子的茶吗?

brass 〔bræs ‖ brɑːs〕
n. ❶黄铜;黄铜色[U]
❷黄铜制品,铜器[C]
The brasses need to be cleaned.
这些黄铜器需要擦一擦。

brave 〔brev ‖ breɪv〕
[比]braver;[最]bravest
a. 勇敢的,英勇的
He was as brave as a lion.
他勇猛如雄狮。

词汇拓展

bravery *n.* 勇敢,勇气

bread 〔brɛd ‖ bred〕
n. [U]❶面包
a slice (two slices) of bread
一(两)片面包
a loaf of bread
一条面包
❷食物;(必需的)营养
Peace alone could not bring bread to the masses.
和平自身并不能给大众带来必需的食品。
❸生计
How did you earn your daily bread when you were there?
你在那里的时候靠什么为生?

break 〔brek ‖ breɪk〕
[过去式]broke;[过去分词]broken
vt. ❶打破;折断;使碎裂
He fell down and broke his ankle.
他跌断了脚踝。
❷毁坏,弄坏;砸破
They broke down the door with a big and heavy log.
他们用一根粗大的木头将门砸开。
❸破坏(约束);违反
He has never broken his promise.
他从不食言。
❹打破(记录);超过
Who broke his record?
谁打破了他的记录?
vi. ❶破碎;破裂;断裂
The plate broke into pieces when it fell on the floor.
盘子落在地上摔碎了。

❷破掉，被损坏

My watch has broken.

我的表坏了。

❸猛闯，突破；强行逃脱

The man broke away from his guards.

这个人从看守处逃脱了。

❹中断，中止

常用短语

break down（机器）出故障；破坏；弄坏

My car broke down on the way.

我的车子在路上抛锚了。

They broke down the door.

他们把门撞破了。

break into… 闯入（建筑物），突然……起来

A robber broke into his house.

强盗闯入他的住宅。

He broke into tears.

他突然哭了起来。

break off… 突然停止

They broke off talking.

他们突然停止说话。

break out… 发生（战争，地震等）

A fire broke out last night.

昨夜发生火灾。

break up… 解散

The meeting broke up at 9：00 last evening.

昨晚 9 点散会。

break with… 与……绝交；断绝关系

I broke with all my friends.

我同所有的朋友绝交了。

breakfast 〔ˈbrɛkfəst ‖ ˈbrekfəst〕

n. 早餐，早饭[C][U]

This hotel serves excellent breakfasts.

这家旅馆供应非常好的早餐。

breakfast 早餐
lunch 午餐
tea 下午茶
coffee break 喝咖啡休息（上下午各一次）
supper 晚餐（一般晚餐是一天中的正餐）

用法工具箱

breast〔brɛst ‖ brest〕

n. [C] ❶乳房

She is giving the breast to her baby.

她正在哺乳她的婴儿。

❷胸部；胸膛；胸脯

breast pocket

胸前的口袋

B

breath 〔breθ ‖ breθ〕
n. ❶呼吸，气息[U]
After all that running, he was short of breath.
那样跑了一阵之后，他气喘吁吁了。
❷(呼吸的)一次，一口气
When he walked out of the room, he drew a deep breath.
他走出房间，深深地吸了一口气。
be out of breath
气喘吁吁
take breath
歇一口气
hold one's breath
屏息
❸微风
There was not a breath of air in the hot auditorium.
在那个闷热的礼堂里没有一丝微风。

词汇拓展
breathless *a.* 气喘吁吁的；屏息的

breathe 〔brið ‖ bri:ð〕
[过去式]breathed；[过去分词]breathed
vi. 呼吸；呼气；吸气
The animal was still breathing, so we knew it was still alive.
那头动物仍在呼吸，所以我们知道它还活着。
vt. 呼吸；呼出；吸入
All mammals breathe air.
哺乳类动物全都呼吸空气。

brick 〔brɪk ‖ brɪk〕
n. ❶砖；砖块[C][U]
The house is built of brick.
这幢房子是用砖建造的。
lay red bricks
砌红砖
a brick wall
一堵砖墙
❷砖块状物
I bought a brick of ice cream for my daughter.
我给女儿买了块冰淇淋。

bride 〔braɪd ‖ braɪd〕
n. 新娘；即将做新娘的女子[C]

bridegroom 〔ˈbraɪdgrum ‖ ˈbraɪdgru:m〕
n. 新郎[C]

bridge 〔brɪdʒ ‖ brɪdʒ〕
n. ❶桥，桥梁[C]
Have you ever visited the Golden Gate Bridge in San Francisco?
你观光过旧金山的金门大桥吗？
❷桥牌[U]

bright 〔braɪt ‖ braɪt〕
[比]brighter；[最]brightest
a. ❶明亮的；发亮的；晴朗的

The bright sun was shining.
阳光普照。
❷(颜色)鲜亮的,鲜明的
The box was painted bright red.
盒子被漆成鲜红色。
❸聪颖的;机灵的
He was very bright.
他很聪明。
ad. 明亮地
The fire shines bright.
火光明亮地照耀着。

brilliant 〔ˈbrɪljənt ‖ ˈbrɪljənt〕
[比]more brilliant;[最]most brilliant
a. ❶光辉的;明亮的;灿烂的;色彩艳丽的
The moon was brilliant.
月光明亮极了。
❷杰出的,优秀的;辉煌的;出色的
He came up with a brilliant idea.
他想出了一个绝妙的主意。
❸才华横溢的;技艺高超的;英明的
She is a brilliant swimmer.
她是个技艺超群的游泳健儿。
❹极为顺利的

词汇拓展

brilliance *n.* 光辉
brilliantly *ad.* 炫耀地

bring 〔brɪŋ ‖ brɪŋ〕
[过去式]brought;[过去分词]brought
vt. ❶带来,拿来
Please bring the book with you.
请把书带来。

bring 表示将人或物带到说话人所在的地方;take 表示将人或物带离说话人所在之处;fetch 表示“去拿来”。
试比较:Bring me sugar.
给我拿糖来。
Don't take the book out of the reading room.
别把书带出阅览室。
Fetch me some water.
去给我拿些水来。

用法工具箱

❷使生成,引起,导致
The success brought him great satisfaction.
成功给他带来极大的满足。

常用短语

bring about 引起
His carelessness brought about the accident.
他的粗心导致了这场意外的发

B

生。

bring up 养育

He was brought up by his uncle.

他由叔叔抚养。

Britain 〔ˈbrɪtən ‖ ˈbrɪtən〕

n. 大不列颠；英国

〔同义〕England

> 大不列颠岛是英国的主岛名称，包括苏格兰、威尔士、英格兰。
>
> **用法工具箱**

British 〔ˈbrɪtɪʃ ‖ ˈbrɪtɪʃ〕

a. ❶大不列颠的；英国的

❷英国人的；英国的

n. （总称）英国人[the]

The British drink a lot of tea.

英国人喝很多茶。

broad 〔brɔd ‖ brɔːd〕

[比]broader；[最]broadest

a. ❶宽的，阔的

a broad river

宽阔的河

broad shoulders

宽肩膀

❷（置于表长度的名词之后）宽度，……宽的

The river is about 20 feet broad.

河宽约 20 英尺。

〔同义〕wide 宽的

〔反义〕narrow 狭窄的

broadcast 〔ˈbrɔdˌkæst ‖ ˈbrɔːdkɑːst〕

[过去式]broadcast，broadcasted；[过去分词]broadcast，broadcasted

vt. ❶广播，播送

The program is broadcast every Monday evening.

这档节目每星期一晚上播出。

❷广为散播，传布

She broadcast the secret to her colleagues.

她向同事们传播这一秘密。

n. 广播；广播节目

These broadcasts will be heard in most parts of the country.

这些广播节目国内大部分地区都能听到。

broken 〔ˈbrokən ‖ ˈbrəʊkən〕

（break 的过去分词）

a. ❶破碎的；损坏的

Let's sweep away the broken glass.

让我们把这些碎玻璃扫走。

❷被破坏的；遭违背的

After a broken promise, it is hard to count on a person.

一次失约，再要人相信你就难了。

❸不连续的；中断的
She said she had a broken sleep last night.
她说昨夜她睡得不熟，常常醒。

brook〔bruk ‖ bruk〕
n. 小河，小溪

brother〔ˈbrʌðə ‖ ˈbrʌðə〕
n. [C] ❶兄弟；兄，弟
my elder brother
我哥哥
my younger brother
我弟弟
❷（复数常用 brethren〔ˈbrɛðrɪn ‖ ˈbreðrɪn〕）教友；同行业的人
❸同胞；同事，伙伴

brown〔braun ‖ braun〕
[比]browner；[最]brownest
a. ❶褐色的，棕色的
Tom often wears a pair of brown shoes.
汤姆常穿一双褐色皮鞋。
❷皮肤黝黑的
Both of us are very brown after the holiday.
度假后我们两人的皮肤都变黑了。

brush〔brʌʃ ‖ brʌʃ〕
[过去式]brushed；[过去分词]brushed
n. [C] ❶（常构成复合词）刷，刷子
a hairbrush
发刷
a shoebrush
鞋刷
a toothbrush
牙刷
❷毛笔，画笔
I paint with a brush.
我用画笔作画。

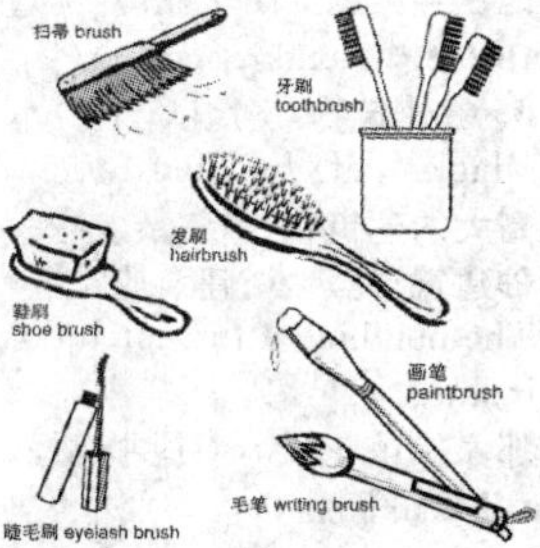

❸刷状物
vt. ❶刷；（用毛笔）写；（用画笔）画
I'm going to brush my teeth.
我要去刷牙了。
❷擦掉，拂去，推开
The maid brushed the crumbs off the table.
女佣拂去桌上的面包屑。

bug〔bʌg ‖ bʌg〕
n. [C]❶【美】虫子，臭虫
❷【计算机】（程序中的）错误

B

build 〔bɪld ‖ bɪld〕
[过去式]built;[过去分词]built
vt. ❶建筑;造
The house is built of wood.
这幢房子是用木头建造的。
❷创建;发展;增进[(+up)]
He built up his business in the United States.
他在美国创立了事业。

building 〔'bɪldɪŋ ‖ 'bɪldɪŋ〕
n. ❶建筑物,房屋[C]
a high (tall) building
高大的建筑物
❷建筑;建筑术;建筑业[U]
The building of the hotel took 7 months.
那家旅馆花了 7 个月才建好。

bull 〔bul ‖ bul〕

n. [C]❶(未阉割过的)公牛
〈ox 是阉割过的公牛,供食用或拉车用;cow 是母牛,尤指乳牛。〉
❷(象,鲸,海豹等的)雄兽
❸彪形大汉,壮汉

bullet 〔'bulɪt ‖ 'bulɪt〕
n. 子弹,枪弹,弹丸[C]
He was wounded by a bullet.
他被枪弹击伤。

burden 〔'bɝdn̩ ‖ 'bɜːdn〕
[过去式]burdened;[过去分词]burdened
n. 重负,重担;负担,沉重的责任[C]
The old man bent with a heavy burden on his back.
老人因背着重负而弯腰。
vt. 加重压于,加负担于,烦扰[(+with)]
The government burdened the nation with heavy taxes.
政府使国民负担重税。

burn 〔bɝn ‖ bɜːn〕
[过去式]burned, burnt;[过去分词]burned, burnt
vi. ❶发热;发光
The sun burns bright in the sky.
太阳在天空明亮地照耀着。
❷燃烧;着火
Dry wood burns easily.
干柴易燃。
❸烧毁;烧焦;烫伤
I smell something burning.
我闻到什么东西烧焦的味道。
vt. ❶烧毁
The whole city was burned to the ground.
整座城市都被烧成了灰烬。

❷烧伤;烧坏;烧焦;烫伤
The soup was so hot that it burned my mouth.
这汤很热,烫伤了我的嘴。

burst 〔bɝst ‖ bɜːst〕
[过去式]burst, bursted;[过去分词]burst, bursted
vi. vt. ❶爆炸;破裂
The balloon burst.
气球爆炸了。
❷冲,闯
Her door was thrust open, and Mrs. Page burst in.
她的门被猛地推开,佩奇太太冲了进来。

常用短语

burst into 突然……起来
She burst into tears when hearing the news.
当听到这个消息,她突然哭起来。
burst out 突然发生
The child burst out crying.
这个孩子突然哭起来。

bury 〔ˈbɛrɪ ‖ ˈberɪ〕
[过去式]buried;[过去分词]buried
vt. ❶埋葬,安葬
Where is she buried?
她被埋在哪里?
❷埋藏,掩藏
The pirates buried their treasure.
海盗埋藏了他们的财宝。
❸使沉浸,使专心
They buried themselves in their work.
他们埋头于工作。

词汇拓展

burial *n.* 埋葬

bus 〔bʌs ‖ bʌs〕
n. 巴士;公共汽车[C]
get on a bus
上公共汽车
get off a bus
下公共汽车
〈坐计程车或汽车时,上车是 get in;下车是 get out of〉

公共汽车 bus

business 〔ˈbɪznɪs ‖ ˈbɪznɪs〕
n. ❶生意,交易;商业;营业;行业[C][U]
Mr. Jones is in the business of selling cars.
琼斯先生从事汽车销售。
❷商店;商行;公司;企业[C]

She started a new business not long ago.
不久前她新开了一家公司。
❸职责,本分;分内事;权利[U]

〈与 business 有关的成语〉
Business is business.
公事公办。
Mind your own business.
= That's none of your business. 莫管闲事。
Everybody's business is nobody's business.
众人的事没人管。(三个和尚没水喝。)

用法工具箱

busy ['bɪzɪ ‖ 'bɪzɪ]
[比]busier;[最]busiest
a. ❶忙碌的,繁忙的[(+with/at/over)][(+in)][+v-ing]
He is busy with work.
他忙着工作。
❷充满活动的;热闹的
Yesterday I had a busy afternoon.
昨天下午我很忙。
❸【美】(尤指电话线)正被占用的,不通的
Sorry,her phone is busy.
抱歉,她的电话正在使用中。

but [(强)bʌt ‖ bʌt;(弱)bət ‖ bət]
conj. ❶但是,可是,然而
It is hot here in summer, but it is not cold in winter.
这里夏天热,但冬天不冷。
She looks very young, but she is already in her 30's.
她看上去很年轻,可是她已三十多岁了。
❷(通常用 not…but…)而是
Our purpose is not to do it for you but to teach you to do it by yourself.
我们的目的不是替你做这件事,而是教会你自己做。
❸(用于含 doubt,question 等词的否定句中,相当于 that)对于
No one believe but he will succeed.
没人相信他会成功。
I am not sure but he will come.
我不能确定他是否会来。
❹(在 no,not 等否定词之后)若……必……
It never rains but it pours.
雨不下则已,下必倾盆大雨。(祸不单行)
prep. (用于 nothing,nobody,who,all 等词后面)除……以外
No one saw it but me.
除了我没有人看到。

ad. 只,仅仅,才

It took her but a few days to learn it.

只不过几天时间她就学会了。

常用短语

but for 要不是

But for your help (=if it were not for your help), I would fail.

如果没你的帮助,我就失败了。

nothing but…不过,仅

That's nothing but a joke.

那只是个笑话而已。

not only…but also… 不但……而且……

not that…but that… 不是因为……而是因为……

Not that I dislike the work, but that I have no time.

不是因为我讨厌这个工作,而是因为我没时间。

butcher 〔ˈbʊtʃɚ ‖ ˈbʊtʃə〕

n. 肉贩,肉店老板,屠夫[C]

I bought it at the butcher's (shop).

我在肉店买的。

butter 〔ˈbʌtɚ ‖ ˈbʌtə〕

n. 奶油;像奶油的食品;酱[C]

I spread butter on the bread.

我在面包上涂了奶油。

butterfly 〔ˈbʌtɚˌflaɪ ‖ ˈbʌtəflaɪ〕

n. 蝴蝶[C]

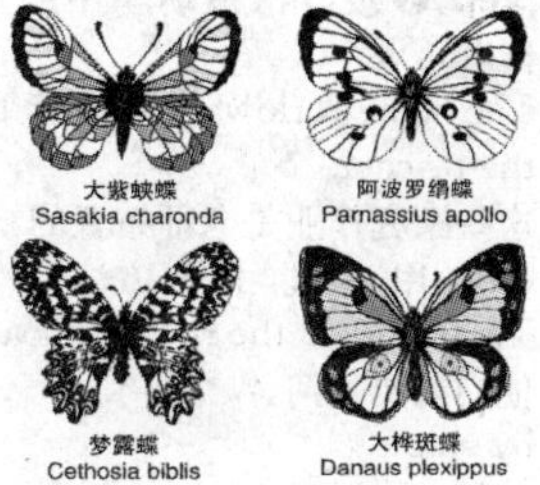

button 〔ˈbʌtn̩ ‖ ˈbʌtn〕

n. ❶纽扣,扣子[C]

I sewed a button on the coat.

我在外衣上缝了颗纽扣。

❷按钮

I pushed the button to turn on the light.

我按电钮把灯打开。

buy 〔baɪ ‖ baɪ〕

[过去式]bought; [过去分词] bought

vt. 买,购买

Mother bought me a pair of jeans.

母亲给我买了一条牛仔裤。

〈买 B(物)给 A(人): buy A B= buy B for A〉

He bought me this book. =He bought this book for me.

他给我买的这本书。

by 〔baɪ ‖ baɪ〕

B

prep. ❶被，由(被动句中的动作者)
The homework was assigned by the teacher.
这些家庭作业是老师布置的。
❷靠，用，通过(手段，方法)
They crossed the river by boat.
他们乘船过河。
by ship
坐船
by car
坐车
by plane
乘飞机
by train
坐火车
by land
由陆路
by sea
由海路
❸经由；沿
He entered the room by the window.
他由窗户进入房间。
❹在……旁边，靠近；在……手边
He sat by the stove.
他坐在暖炉旁。
❺根据，按照
Don't judge a man by his clothes.
不要以衣取人。
What time is it by your watch?
你的表几点钟？
❻(表程度)相差
He is taller than I by two inches.
他比我高两英寸。
I missed the train by a minute.
我差一分钟没赶上火车。
❼以……计，按
We hired the boat by the hour.
我们按钟点租船。
Butter is sold by the pound.
奶油是论磅出售的。
❽不迟于；在……之前
He will be back by 3 o'clock.
他将在3点以前回来。
❾(表连续或反复)逐个；逐批
Study English step by step.
逐步学习英文。
❿由于
I met him by chance.
我偶尔遇到他。
ad. ❶经过；过去
A truck went by.
一辆卡车开过。
❷在旁边
When I filled out the form she was standing by all the time.
我填写表格时，她一直站在我身旁。

bye-bye 〔ˈbaɪˈbaɪ ‖ ˈbaɪˈbaɪ〕
int. (原为儿语)再见！

骆驼
camel

咖啡
coffee

照相机
camera

仙人掌
cactus

划艇运动
canoeing

cabbage 〔'kæbɪdʒ ‖ 'kæbɪdʒ〕

n. 甘蓝菜，卷心菜[C][U]

卷心菜
cabbage

He grows cabbage in his farm.
他在农场里种卷心菜。

cabin 〔'kæbɪn ‖ 'kæbɪn〕

n. [C]❶(船的)客舱；(飞机的)驾驶舱；客舱
the first-class cabin
一等舱
❷小屋
My uncle lived in a log cabin.
我叔父住在一个小木屋里。

cable 〔'kebḷ ‖ 'keɪbl〕

n. ❶缆；索；钢索[C][U]
The truck used a cable to pull the car.
卡车用钢索拖曳汽车。
❷电缆[C]
❸越洋电报[C]
I received a cable from New York.
我收到一封从纽约来的电报。
❹有线电视[U]

cafe 〔kæ'fe ‖ 'kæfeɪ; kæ'feɪ〕

n. [C]❶小餐馆，饮食摊
❷咖啡厅
We went into the cafe for coffee and dessert.
我们到咖啡厅喝了杯咖啡，吃了些点心。
❸【美】酒馆，酒吧，夜总会

cage 〔kedʒ ‖ keɪdʒ〕

n. 鸟笼，兽笼[C]
The old man made a cage for birds.
那个老人做了一只鸟笼。

cake 〔kek ‖ keɪk〕

n. ❶蛋糕，糕饼[C][U]

My wife baked a chocolate cake for my birthday.
我妻子做了一个巧克力蛋糕庆贺我的生日。
〈当泛指饼时，是不可数名词〉
I am fond of cake.
我喜欢饼。
〈表示个别饼时，为可数名词〉
I bought 6 cakes.
我买了 6 块饼。
❷饼状食物；块状物[C]
a cake of soap
一块肥皂
a cake of ice
一块冰

常用短语

a piece of cake 轻松/愉快的事

calculate 〔ˈkælkjəˌlet ‖ ˈkælkjʊˌleɪt〕
[过去式]calculated；[过去分词]calculated
vt. ❶计算；估计；预测；推测
The teacher calculated the average mark of the class.
老师计算班上的平均分数。
She calculated that it would take less time to go there by car.
她估计开车去那里会省点儿时间。
❷(用被动式)计划，打算
The remarks were calculated to win his confidence.
这话是打算赢取他的信任的。

词汇拓展

calculator *n.* 计算机
calculation *n.* 计算，推测，打算

calendar 〔ˈkæləndɚ ‖ ˈkælɪndə〕
n. [C]❶日历；历书
❷历法
Today is her birthday according to the solar calendar.
按照阳历，今天是她的生日。

calf 〔kæf ‖ kɑːf〕
[名复]calves
n. ❶小牛[C]
❷(鲸、象等的)崽[C]

call 〔kɔl ‖ kɔːl〕
[过去式]called；[过去分词]called
vt. ❶(大声)叫喊[(+out)]
"Come on," she called out.
"快，"她喊道。
❷呼唤；召唤；召集
He called the waitress over.
他将服务小姐叫了过去。
❸打电话给
Call me at the office this afternoon.
午后打电话到我办公室来。
vi. ❶(大声)叫喊
He called to me from the other

side of the street.
他从街对面喊我。
❷打电话
Did anyone call today?
今天有人打过电话来吗?
❸顺便到……,拜访[(+at/in/on)]
I promised to call on her after the examination.
我答应考试后去看望她。

常用短语

call after ❶追在……的后面叫喊❷以……的名字为……命名
call at 到……短暂访问
I'll call at her house later.
我稍后到她家拜访。
call back
❶收回,叫回
They called him back from America.
他们把他从美国叫回来。
❷回电
I'll call you back later.
等一下我再打电话给你。
call for
❶需要
The task calls for a lot of time.
这工作需要很多时间。
❷接(人)
I'll call for you at 3.
3点我去接你。
call off 取消
He called off the party.
他取消了舞会。
call on 拜访
I'll call on him later.
我稍后去拜访他。

calm 〔kɑm ‖ kɑːm〕
[比]calmer;[最]calmest;[过去式]calmed;[过去分词]calmed
a. ❶镇静的,沉着的
You must try to be calm.
你必须设法保持冷静。
❷无风(浪)的;平静的
The high wind passed and the sea was calm again.
大风过后,大海又风平浪静。
n. ❶安静;镇定
❷平静;无风
There was a calm on the sea.
海面上风平浪静。
vt. 使镇定;使平静
We calmed the old lady down.
我们使老太太平静下来。
vi. 镇定下来;平静下来
Calm down, sir. What's the trouble?
冷静点,先生。出了什么事?

camel 〔'kæml̩ ‖ 'kæməl〕
n. ❶骆驼[C]
A camel is called a ship of the desert.
骆驼被称为沙漠之舟。
❷驼色,浅黄褐色[U]

camera 〔ˈkæmərə ‖ ˈkæmərə〕

n. 照相机；电影摄影机；电视摄像机[C]

I'll take my camera.

我会带相机去。

camp 〔kæmp ‖ kæmp〕

n. 野营；营地；兵营；帐篷[C][U]

The travellers set up a camp near the river.

旅游者在河边架起了帐篷。

campaign 〔kæmˈpen ‖ kæmˈpeɪn〕

n. [C] ❶战役

The campaign to seize the city was a failure.

攻占这个城市的战役失败了。

❷运动，活动[(＋for/against)][＋to-v]

The City Hall is planning to start a campaign against smoking.

市政府计划发起禁烟运动。

can[1] 〔kæn ‖ kæn〕

[过去式]could〔kʊd ‖ kʊd〕

v. aux. ❶(表示能力，功能)能，会

The classroom can seat 30 students.

这教室能坐 30 位学生。

❷(表示可能性)可能，可能会

I think the work can be completed ahead of time.

我认为这项工作能提前完成。

❸(表示允许，请求)可以

You can't take the book out of the room.

你不可以将这本书拿到室外。

用法工具箱

现在 He can swim. = He is able to swim.

他会游泳。

过去 He could swim. = He was able to swim.

他会游泳。

未来 He will be able to swim in a week.

他在一周之内就能游泳。

现在完成 No one has ever been able to do it.

从来没有人能做那件事。

否定 cannot 或 can't

I cannot swim.

我不会游泳。

常用短语

as…as one can 尽可能地
I ran as fast as I could.
我尽快地跑。

cannot help doing 不能不
I cannot help laughing.
我禁不住笑了出来。

can² 〔kæn ‖ kæn〕
n. [C]❶(食物)罐头
❷一罐[(+of)]
Add 3 cans of water to make the orange juice.
加进 3 罐水调橘子汁。

Canada 〔ˈkænədə ‖ ˈkænədə〕
n. 加拿大(国名)
〈在北美洲,英联邦国家之一,首都 Ottawa (渥太华)〉

Canadian 〔kəˈnedɪən ‖ kəˈneɪdɪən〕
a. 加拿大的;加拿大人的
n. 加拿大人

canal 〔kəˈnæl ‖ kəˈnæl〕
n. [C]运河;河渠,水道;灌溉水渠;管,道
Coal used to be sent here by canal.
煤过去常经过运河送来。
the Suez Canal
苏伊士运河

cancel 〔ˈkænsḷ ‖ ˈkænsl〕
[过去式]canceled, cancelled;[过去分词]canceled, cancelled
vt. 删去;取消;废除;中止
The game was canceled because of the rain.
比赛因下雨取消了。

cancer 〔ˈkænsɚ ‖ ˈkænsə〕
n. ❶癌,恶性肿瘤;癌症[C][U]
He died of stomach cancer.
他死于胃癌。
❷(社会等的)弊端,痼疾,病根[C]

candidate 〔ˈkændəˌdet ‖ ˈkændɪdɪt〕
n. [C] ❶候选人;候补者[(+for)]
He is a candidate for President.
他是总统候选人。
❷应试者,攻读学位者[(+for)]
There are 6 hundred candidates for the entrance examination.
有 600 人参加入学考试。
❸求职应征者[(+for)]
Mary was the strongest candidate for the job.
在求职应征者中玛丽具备最好的条件。

candle 〔ˈkændḷ ‖ ˈkændl〕
n. ❶蜡烛[C]

He blew out the candle and went to bed.
他吹灭蜡烛，上床睡觉。
❷烛形物[C]
❸烛光[U]

candy 〔'kændɪ ‖ 'kændɪ〕[名复] candies
n. ❶【美】糖果[C][U]
You ate too much candy. It's bad for your teeth.
你糖吃得太多了。这对你的牙齿不好。
❷【英】冰糖[U]

cap 〔kæp ‖ kæp〕
n. [C] ❶无边便帽；制服帽；(表示职业，等级等的)帽子
〈有边的帽子是 hat〉

❷盖，罩，套
Put the cap back on the toothpaste.
把盖子重新拧在牙膏管上。

capable 〔'kepəbḷ ‖ 'keɪpəbl〕
a. ❶有……的能力的，能够(做)……的[(+of)]
She is capable of judging works of art.
她有鉴赏艺术品的能力。
❷有能力的，能干的，有才华的
He is a very capable administrator.
他是个十分能干的行政人员。
❸有……的可能性，做得出……的[(+of)]
This passage is capable of various interpretations.
这段话可以有多种解释。

capacity 〔kə'pæsətɪ ‖ kə'pæsɪtɪ〕
n. ❶容量，容积[U]
The theater has a seating capacity of 800.
这个剧场可容纳 800 名观众。
❷能量，生产力[U]
The auto plant now has an annual capacity of 12,000 cars.
这家汽车厂现在每年能生产 12,000辆汽车。
❸能力，才能，接受能力，理解力[C][U][(+for)]
He has a great capacity for learning languages.
他学语言的能力很强。

cape 〔kep ‖ keɪp〕
n. 岬，海角[C]

capital 〔'kæpətl̩ ‖ 'kæpɪtl〕
n. ❶首都；首府；省会[C]
Dublin is the capital of Ireland.
都柏林是爱尔兰的首都。
❷资本；本钱[U]
The corporation has enough capital to build another factory.
这家公司有足够的资金来兴建另一家工厂。
❸大写字母[C]
❹资本家，资方[U]

captain 〔'kæptɪn ‖ 'kæptən〕
n. [C]❶陆军上尉；海军上校；【美】空军上尉
❷船长；舰长；(飞机的)机长
The captain refused to leave his sinking ship.
船长拒绝离开正在下沉的船。
❸(运动队的)队长；领队
Richard is the captain of the football team.
理查德是这个橄榄球队的队长。
❹(团体的)首领

capture 〔'kæptʃɚ ‖ 'kæptʃə〕
[过去式]captured；[过去分词]captured
vt. ❶捕获；俘虏
The police have not captured the mugger yet.
警方还没有捕获那个行凶抢劫者。
❷引起(注意)；迷住
The singer captured the hearts of audience.
这位歌唱家令听众倾倒。
n. ❶俘获，捕获；占领；获得[U]
The soldier played death to escape capture by the enemy.
那个士兵躺下装死，以免被敌人俘虏。
❷俘虏，捕获物；战利品；奖品[C]
❸吸引[U]

car 〔kɑr ‖ kɑː〕
n. [C]❶汽车
Can you drive a car?
你会开车吗？
❷有轨电车
❸火车车厢

card 〔kɑrd ‖ kɑːd〕
n. ❶纸牌，纸牌游戏[P]
He came over to chat and play cards.
他过来聊天，打牌。
❷卡片；名片；请帖[C]
I just want to talk to him. Here is my card.
我只是想跟他谈谈。这是我的

名片。

care 〔kɛr ‖ keə〕

［过去式］cared；［过去分词］cared

n. ❶看护；保护，照料；管理；关怀[U]

C

Is he in the doctor's care?

他有医生治疗护理吗？

The baby needs a lot of care.

这婴孩需要精心照料。

❷忧虑，烦恼；心事[C][U]

He is now free from all care.

他如今无忧无虑。

❸小心，谨慎[U]

Do it with great care.

要非常小心地做它。

常用短语

care of (略为 c/o)由……转交

Mr. Tom Green, c/o Mr. John Smith

请约翰·史密斯先生转交汤姆·格林先生。

take care of ❶照顾

have children to take care of

有孩子要照顾

❷处理

equipment that takes care of industrial waste

处理工业废物的装置

vi. ❶关心；担心；在乎，介意[(＋about)]

Do you care if I go?

如果我去的话，你不介意吧？

He cares a great deal about it.

他对那事很放心不下。

❷关怀，照顾[(＋for)]

Who cares for the sick?

谁照顾病人？

❸喜欢，愿意，想要[(＋for)]

I don't care for coffee.

我不喜欢喝咖啡。

vt. ❶ 对……介意，对……计较[＋wh-]

I don't care what they say.

我不在乎他们说什么。

❷喜欢，愿意，想要[＋to-v]

I don't care to go out.

我不想出去。

career 〔kəˈrɪr ‖ kəˈrɪə〕

n. ❶(终身的)职业[C]

He wasn't interested in her stage career.

他对她的演戏职业不感兴趣。

a career woman

职业妇女

❷经历；生涯；历程[C]

He found it both interesting and instructive to learn about the careers of great men.

他觉得了解伟人的生平既有趣又有教益。

careful 〔ˈkɛrfəl ‖ ˈkeəful〕

a. ❶仔细的；小心的[(＋of/about/with)][＋to-v][＋v-ing][＋wh-][＋(that)]
John was careful not to say anything about this to her.
约翰小心翼翼，避免向她提及此事。
He is careful of money.
他爱惜钱。
❷周到的，彻底的，精心的
The doctor gave him a careful examination.
医生对他作了彻底的检查。
〔反义〕careless 粗心的

careless 〔ˈkɛrlɪs ‖ ˈkeəlɪs〕
a. ❶粗心的，疏忽的；草率的
He made a careless mistake.
他犯了一个疏忽性的错误。
❷随便的；自然的
He sat into a chair with careless ease.
他随便往椅子里舒舒服服一坐。
❸漫不经心的；淡漠的[(＋of/about)]
She's careless about her clothes.
她对穿着一点都不讲究。
❹无忧无虑的

carpenter 〔ˈkɑrpəntə ‖ ˈkɑːpɪntə〕
n. 木工，木匠[C]

carpet 〔ˈkɑrpɪt ‖ ˈkɑːpɪt〕
n. [C]❶地毯
The floor is covered with a carpet.
地板上铺着地毯。
❷地毯状覆盖物
A carpet of leaves covered the ground.
一层厚厚的落叶覆盖在地上。

carriage 〔ˈkærɪdʒ ‖ ˈkærɪdʒ〕
n. [C]❶四轮马车

carriage 马车

carriage/coach 私人马车

coach/stagecoach 驿马车

❷【英】(火车)客车厢
the first-class carriage
头等车厢

carrot 〔ˈkærət ‖ ˈkærət〕
n. 胡萝卜[C][U]

Generally speaking, children

dislike carrot.
大多数小孩子都不喜欢胡萝卜。

carry 〔ˈkærɪ ‖ ˈkærɪ〕
［过去式］carried；［过去分词］carried
vt. ❶（用手、肩等）挑，抱，背，提，扛，搬
David carried his suitcase.
大卫提着他的手提箱。
❷运送，运载；搬运
The city subways carry hundreds of thousands of passengers a day.
市内的地铁每天运载数十万乘客。
❸传达（消息）；传染（疾病）
This disease is carried by mosquitoes.
这种疾病是由蚊虫传染的。
❹支撑，支持

常用短语

carry away❶**拿走**❷**使激动**
carry on 继续
They carried on the discussion.
他们继续讨论。
carry out 实现
He carried out his promise.
他履行了诺言。

case[1] 〔kes ‖ keɪs〕
n. ❶事实，实情［C］
He thought he had already solved the problem, but that was not the case.
他以为他已经解决了这个问题，可是实际情况并非如此。
❷事例，实例［C］
Here is a case in point.
这里有一个很好的例子。
❸案件；诉讼［C］
The case was tried last Wednesday.
上星期三审判了该案件。
❹个案；病例，病症；患者

常用短语

case in point 恰当的例子
in any case 无论如何
In any case you must not tell a lie.
无论如何你不可说谎。
in case ❶**假使**
In case he gives me a call, tell him that I will call him back.
如果他来电话给我，告诉他我会回他的电话。
❷**免得**
Please remind me of it again tomorrow in case I forget.
请你明天再提醒我一下，免得我忘记。
in case of 如果发生（用于不好的事情）

In case of fire, ring the alarm bell.
如遇火警，即按警铃。
in no case 决不
in that case 既然那样
in this case 既然这样

case[2] 〔kes ‖ keɪs〕
n. 箱，盒；套，壳；容器[C]
a jewel case
珠宝箱
a pencil case
铅笔盒

cash 〔kæʃ ‖ kæʃ〕
n. [U] ❶现金，现款
I have no cash on me. Can I pay you later?
我没带现金，能否以后付给你？
❷【口】钱

castle 〔ˈkæsl̩ ‖ ˈkɑːsl〕
n. 城堡[C]

常用短语

build castle in the air 建空中楼阁；做白日梦
He is building castle in the air.
他正做白日梦。

cat 〔kæt ‖ kæt〕
n. 猫[C]
When the cat is away, the mice will play.
老猫不在家，耗子成精了。

catalogue 〔ˈkætl̩ɔg ‖ ˈkætəlɔːg〕
n. [C] ❶(图书，商品等的)目录；目录册，目录簿
❷【美】大学概况一览表
vt. 登记，记载

catch 〔kætʃ ‖ kætʃ〕
[过去式] caught；[过去分词] caught
vt. ❶接住，抓住
I will throw the ball and you catch it.
我扔球你接。
❷逮住，捕获
The policeman caught the thief.
警察逮住了小偷。
❸撞见，偶然发现
The police caught him stealing a car.
他正在偷汽车时被警察撞见。
❹赶上
I got up early so that I could catch the first train.
我很早就起来，以便赶上第一班火车。
❺染上(疾病)，感染；着(火)
I've caught a cold.
我感冒了。
❻钩住，卡住，夹住[(+on/in)]
I caught my skirt on a nail.
钉子钩住了我的裙子。

C

cattle 〔ˈkætl̩ ‖ ˈkætl〕

n. ❶牛

The cattle are in the shed.

牛在栏内。

❷牲口，家畜

cause 〔kɔz ‖ kɔːz〕

n. ❶原因；起因[C][(+of)]

What was the cause of the accident?

造成这一事故的原因是什么？

❷理由，根据；动机[U][(+for)][+to-v]

You have no cause to complain.

你没有理由抱怨。

caution 〔ˈkɔʃən ‖ ˈkɔːʃən〕

n. ❶小心，谨慎[U]

Dad always drives with caution.

爸爸开车一直十分小心。

❷警告，告诫[C]

The policeman let the driver off with a caution.

警察向司机提出警告后就让他走了。

cave 〔kev ‖ keɪv〕

n. [C] ❶洞穴，洞窟

Our forefathers once lived in caves.

我们的祖先曾在洞穴居住。

❷塌落(处)

cease 〔sis ‖ siːs〕

[过去式]ceased；[过去分词]ceased

vi. 停止，终止

The experiments have ceased.

试验已经停止。

vt. 停止，结束[+to-v][+v-ing]

The general ordered his troops to cease fire.

那位将军命令他的军队停火。

ceiling 〔ˈsilɪŋ ‖ ˈsiːlɪŋ〕

n. 天花板；顶棚[C]

There is a fly on the ceiling.

天花板上有一只苍蝇。

celebrate 〔ˈsɛləˌbret ‖ ˈselɪbreɪt〕

[过去式]celebrated；[过去分词]celebrated

vt. ❶庆祝

They celebrated his birthday.

他们给他庆祝了生日。

❷颂扬，赞美

They celebrated his brave deed.

他们赞美他的勇敢行为。

词汇拓展

celebration *n.* 庆祝,庆典

cell 〔sɛl ‖ sel〕

n. [C] ❶单人牢房,小囚房

The prisoner was locked in a cell.

那囚犯被关在单人牢房内。

❷【生】细胞

cement 〔sə'mɛnt ‖ sɪ'ment〕

n. 水泥[U]

cemetery 〔'sɛməˌtɛrɪ ‖ 'semɪtrɪ〕

n. 公墓,墓地[C]

〈附属于教会的是 churchyard〉

cent 〔sɛnt ‖ sent〕

n. [C] ❶(美、加等国的货币单位,为 dollar 的 1%)分

❷一分值的硬币

central 〔'sɛntrəl ‖ 'sentrəl〕

a. ❶中心的,中央的

The railroad station is in the central part of the city.

火车站在该城的中心。

❷地处中心的,便利的,近的

The head office is in the central part of the city.

总公司位于市中心。

❸主要的,核心的;重要的[(+to)]

What's the central idea of the article?

这篇文章的中心思想是什么?

centre,【美】**center** 〔'sɛntɚ ‖ 'sentə〕

n. [C] ❶中心;中央,中心点

Alice stood in the center of a large group.

艾丽斯站在一大群人的中央。

❷中枢,核心

Our city is the industry center of the country.

我们的城市是全国的工业中心。

middle 指在时间或长的东西中间,centre 指地点、圆或球体的中心。试比较:

in the middle of the night

在半夜

in the middle of the road

在路中央

in the centre of the town

在城镇的中心地带

in the centre of a circle

圆心

用法工具箱

century 〔'sɛntʃərɪ ‖ 'sentʃərɪ〕

n. 世纪;一百年[C]
We live in the twenty-first century.
我们生活在21世纪。

ceremony [ˈsɛrəˌmonɪ ‖ ˈserɪmənɪ]
n. ❶仪式,典礼[C]
The wedding ceremony was held on April fifteenth.
婚礼在4月15日举行。
❷礼仪,礼节;(社交上的)形式[U]
❸虚礼,客套[U]
There need be no ceremony between us.
我们之间不必客套。

certain [ˈsɝtn̩ ‖ ˈsəːtn]
a. ❶确凿的,无疑的;可靠的
❷确信的,有把握的;一定会的[(+ of/about)][+ that][+ wh-][+to-v]
They are certain to succeed.
=They are certain of success.
=They are certain that they will succeed.
他们确信会成功。
❸某,一位姓……的(人)
A certain person called on you yesterday.
昨天有个人来拜访过你。
❹某种(或一定)程度的
a man of a certain age
已有相当岁数的男人

certainly [ˈsɝtn̩lɪ ‖ ˈsəːtnlɪ]
ad. ❶无疑地;必定;确实
She will certainly come.
她一定会来。
❷(用于回答)当然;可以;没问题
"May I use your telephone?"
能用你的电话吗?
"Certainly."
当然可以。

chain [tʃen ‖ tʃeɪn]
n. [C]❶链,链条;项圈
The dog was fastened to a post by a chain.
那条狗被链条拴在柱子上。
❷一连串,一系列;连锁,连续[(+of)]
The traffic accident led to a chain of events.
交通事故引起了一连串的事件。
❸连锁店,联号(chain store)

chair [tʃɛr ‖ tʃeə]
n.(通常指单人用的,有靠背的)椅子[C]
Mary sat in a chair reading a novel.
玛丽坐在椅子上读小说。

chairman [ˈtʃɛrmən ‖ ˈtʃeəmən]

n.[C] ❶主席;议长;委员长;董事长
〈称呼主席时为 Mr. Chairman〉
❷(大学的)系主任

chalk 〔tʃɔk ‖ tʃɔːk〕
n. 粉笔[C][U]
a piece of chalk
一支粉笔

表示种类时可用复数,如:some colored chalks 数支彩色粉笔
用法工具箱

challenge 〔ˈtʃælɪndʒ ‖ ˈtʃælɪndʒ〕
[过去式]challenged;[过去分词]challenged
n. 挑战;邀请比赛[C][+to-v]
He received a letter of challenge to a TV debate.
他接到电视辩论的挑战书。
vt. ❶向……挑战[(+to)]
I challenged him to show his proof.
我要他拿出证据。
❷对……提出异议;怀疑;反对
He challenged my view on that matter.
他就我对那件事的看法提出异议。

champion 〔ˈtʃæmpɪən ‖ ˈtʃæmpjən〕
n.[C] ❶(竞赛的)优胜者,冠军,第一名
❷出类拔萃的人(或物)
He is a champion at writing novels.
他是写小说的好手。
❸提倡者,拥护者;战士,斗士[(+of)]
He is a champion of equal opportunities for all races.
他是一个为各种族机会均等而奋斗的人。

chance 〔tʃæns ‖ tʃɑːns〕
n. ❶偶然;运气;侥幸[U]
He left everything to chance.
他一切都听凭运气。
❷可能性,希望[C][U][(+of)][+(that)]
We have a good chance of winning the game.
我们很可能赢得这场比赛。
❸机会,良机,际遇[C][(+of)][+to-v]
I didn't get many chances to talk to her recently.
近来我不太有机会与她会话。

常用短语

by chance 偶然
I found the jewel by chance.

我偶然发现这块宝石。

change 〔tʃendʒ ‖ tʃeɪndʒ〕
[过去式]changed;[过去分词]changed
vt. ❶(使)改变;更改;使变化[(+from…to…)][(+into)]
Heat changes water into steam.
热将水变成蒸汽。
❷换;交换,互换
Let's change seats.
咱们交换座位吧。
❸换(衣服);给(婴孩)换尿布或衣服;给(床)换床单
She changed the baby often.
她不时地给婴孩换尿布。
vi. ❶变;改变;更改;变化[(+from…to…)]
In fall the leaves change from green to brown.
秋天,树叶由绿色变成褐色。
❷更衣[(+out of/into)]
He changed into a new suit.
他换上一套新的西装。
❸换车
In New York, you'll change for Boston.
你在纽约换车去波士顿。
n. ❶变化;变更;变迁[C][U]
Many changes have taken place since then.
自那以来,发生了许多变化。
❷改变一下
I think a change might do you good.
我想换换环境也许对你有好处。
❸零钱;找零[U]
"Here's your change," said the saleswoman.
"这是你的找零,"女店员说道。

channel 〔'tʃænl̩ ‖ 'tʃænl〕
n. [C] ❶水道,航道
❷海峡
the English Channel
英吉利海峡
❸频道,波段
channel 6
(电视)第六频道

chapter 〔'tʃæptɚ ‖ 'tʃæptə〕
n. (书籍的)章,回[C]
Please read chapters of the book.
请阅读该书的第一章。

character 〔'kærɪktɚ ‖ 'kærɪktə〕
n. ❶(人的)性格;(事物的)性质;特性[C][U]
He has a changeable character.
他性格多变。
❷品质;骨气;特色[U]
A person of character would not cheat.
品德高尚的人是不会欺诈的。

❸(小说、戏剧等的)人物,角色[C]
They are the two main characters in the play.
他们是该剧中的两个主角。

charge 〔tʃɑrdʒ ‖ tʃɑːdʒ〕
[过去式]charged;[过去分词]charged
vt. ❶索价;对……索费;课(税)[(+for)]
How much do you charge for a room with a bath?
一间带浴室的房间要多少钱?
❷向……冲去,袭击
They charged the enemy 3 times.
他们向敌人发过3次突击。
❸控告,指控[(+with)]
The police charged him with theft.
警察指控他盗窃。
vi. ❶索价;收费[(+for)]
The store doesn't charge for delivery.
该店免费送货。
❷冲锋,向前冲[(+at)]
The lion charged at those little animals.
狮子向那些小动物冲了过去。
❸充电
n. ❶费用,价钱,索价[C][(+for)]
The charge for admission is $5.
入场费5美元。
❷掌管;照顾;责任[U]
The nurse is in charge of the patients.
护士负责照顾病人。
❸控告,指控[C][(+against/of)]
He was arrested on the charge of robbery.
他因被控犯有抢劫罪而被捕。

常用短语

charge for 为……收费
in charge 负责
in charge of ❶主管 ❷照料
take charge of 负责
under the charge of 由……掌管

cheap 〔tʃip ‖ tʃiːp〕
[比]cheaper;[最]cheapest
a. ❶便宜的,价廉的
Eggs are very cheap now.
现在鸡蛋很便宜。
❷劣质的,廉价品的
The coat may be expensive but looks cheap.
那件大衣也许很贵,但是看起来很粗劣。
❸容易得到的,不费力的
Talk is cheap.

说空话是不费力的。
〔反义〕expensive 昂贵的
〔同义〕inexpensive 廉价的

cheat〔tʃit ‖ tʃiːt〕
[过去式]cheated；[过去分词]cheated
vt. ❶欺骗；骗取，诈取[(＋of/out of)]
They cheated the old woman of her house and money.
他们骗取了老妇人的房屋和钱财。
❷哄骗[(＋into)]
The salesman cheated me into buying a fake.
那个推销员骗我买了假货。
vi. 行骗；作弊[(＋at/on/in)]
He never cheated in exams.
他考试从不作弊。

check〔tʃɛk ‖ tʃek〕
[过去式]checked；[过去分词]checked
n. ❶检查，检验，核对[C][(＋of/on)]
The plumber made a careful check of the pipes.
那个装修水管的工人仔细地检查了水管。
❷停止；制止，抑制；阻止者(或物)
The strike caused a check in production.
罢工使生产陷于停顿状态。
❸【美】支票[C]
He wrote his mother a check, but the check was bounced.
他开了一张支票给他的母亲，但是支票被退票了。
vt. ❶检查，检验，核对；在……上打钩儿
I have checked your answers and none of them are correct.
我检查了你的答案，没有一个是对的。
❷制止，控制；停止
Sophia checked the sobs with an immense effort.
索菲娅尽了很大努力止住了哭泣。

常用短语

check back ❶查看以往记录❷再联系
check out ❶结账离开❷检查❸通过能力测试
check up ❶核对 ❷调查
check (up) with ❶与……相符❷与……联系
hold/keep in check 抑制

cheek〔tʃik ‖ tʃiːk〕
n. 脸颊；腮帮子[C]
The little girl has rosy cheeks.
那个小女孩脸颊红润。

cheerful 〔ˈtʃɪrfəl ‖ ˈtʃɪəfl〕
a. ❶兴高采烈的;情绪好的
She is a smiling, cheerful girl.
她是个满面笑容,兴高采烈的女孩子。
❷使人感到愉快的
This is a cheerful, sunny room.
这个房间阳光充足,令人愉快。
❸乐意的;由衷的
My little brother is a very cheerful helper.
我的小弟弟很乐于帮忙。

cheese 〔tʃiz ‖ tʃi:z〕
n. 乳酪,干酪[C][U]
I'm fond of French cheeses.
我喜欢法国乳酪。

chemical 〔ˈkɛmɪkl̩ ‖ ˈkemɪkəl〕
a. 化学的,化学上的,化学上用的
He devoted his life to chemical research.
他一生从事化学研究。
n. 化学制品;化学药品[C][P]
He is experimenting with a new chemical.
他正在实验一种新的化学制品。

chemist 〔ˈkɛmɪst ‖ ˈkemɪst〕
n. ❶化学家
❷【英】药剂师,药商

chemistry 〔ˈkɛmɪstrɪ ‖ ˈkemɪstrɪ〕
n. [U]❶化学,化学性质
He is knowledgeable about the chemistry of metals.
他对金属的化学性质了如指掌。
❷化学作用

cherry 〔ˈtʃɛrɪ ‖ ˈtʃerɪ〕
n. 樱桃,樱桃树[C]
The girls are picking cherries.
姑娘们正在摘樱桃。

chess 〔tʃɛs ‖ tʃes〕
n. 国际象棋[U]
play chess
下国际象棋

chest 〔tʃɛst ‖ tʃest〕
n. [C]❶胸,胸膛(包含胸的内部)
He has a severe pain in the chest.
他胸部痛得很厉害。
〈仅指胸的外部是 breast〉
❷箱子,盒子,(有盖子的坚固)

容器

chicken 〔ˈtʃɪkɪn ‖ ˈtʃɪkɪn〕

n. ❶(小)鸡；小鸡[C]

Don't count your chickens before they are hatched.

不要没孵出小鸡就先数小鸡。[谚语](别指望过早；别打如意算盘)

❷鸡肉[U]

The chicken is tender.

这鸡肉很嫩。

chief 〔tʃif ‖ tʃiːf〕

n. ❶首领；领袖；长官[C]

The President is also the chief of the armed forces.

总统也是三军的统帅。

❷酋长；族长[C]

an Indian chief

印第安酋长

a. ❶等级最高的，为首的

Tom was appointed chief engineer of the project.

汤姆被委任为该项工程的总工程师。

❷最重要的，主要的

The chief reason for going to school is to learn.

上学的主要原因是为了学习。

child 〔tʃaɪld ‖ tʃaɪld〕[名复] children〔ˈtʃɪldrən ‖ ˈtʃɪldrən〕

n. 小孩，儿童，幼儿[C]

You are not a child any longer.

你不再是个孩子了。

childhood 〔ˈtʃaɪldˌhʊd ‖ ˈtʃaɪldˌhʊd〕

n. 幼年时期，童年时期[C][U]

Her early childhood had been very happy.

她的童年生活的初期曾是很幸福的。

chimney 〔ˈtʃɪmnɪ ‖ ˈtʃɪmnɪ〕

n. 烟囱[C]

He believes Santa Claus comes in through the chimney.

他相信圣诞老人从烟囱进来。

China 〔ˈtʃaɪnə ‖ ˈtʃaɪnə〕

n. 中国

china 〔ˈtʃaɪnə ‖ ˈtʃaɪnə〕

n. 瓷器；陶瓷器

Chinese 〔tʃaɪˈniz ‖ ˌtʃaɪˈniːz〕

a. ❶中国的，中国人的

❷中国话的；中文的

Chinese characters

汉字

n. ❶中国人

A young Chinese lent me his bi-

cycle.
一位年轻的中国人将他的自行车借给我。
❷中国话，汉语；中文[U]

chocolate 〔ˈtʃɑkəlɪt ‖ ˈtʃɒkəlɪt〕
n. ❶巧克力[U]，巧克力糖[C]
She bought a box of chocolates at the corner store.
她在街头的小店购得一盒巧克力。
❷巧克力饮料(牛奶)[C][U]
What about a cup of hot chocolate?
想喝一杯热巧克力牛奶吗？
❸巧克力色[U]
a. ❶巧克力口味的
❷巧克力色的

choice 〔tʃɔɪs ‖ tʃɔɪs〕
n. ❶选择，抉择[C]
We each had to make a choice.
我们每人都必须做选择。
I will go with him—I have no choice.
我将跟他走——我没有选择的余地。
❷被选中的人(或物)[C]
This tie was my choice.
这条领带是我选的。

常用短语

have no choice 别无选择
make choice of 选定

choice…用于任意的选择，如，
Take your choice of the ties.
选择你所喜爱的领带吧。
alternative…用于两者或三者之间选择
You have the alternative of leaving or staying.
你或去或留，二者之中选其一吧。

用法工具箱

choose 〔tʃuz ‖ tʃuːz〕
[过去式]chose；[过去分词]chosen
vt. ❶选择；挑选
He chose George as his assistant.
他选择乔治作为他的助手。
❷决定(要……)；宁愿，愿意[＋to-v][＋that][＋wh-]
He chose not to reply.
他决定不回答。
vi. ❶选择，挑选[(＋from/between)]
You have to choose between A and B.
你必须在A和B之间选择。

❷决定；愿意，随意
I can go anywhere I choose.
我愿去哪儿就可以去哪儿。

Christmas 〔ˈkrɪsməs ‖ ˈkrɪsməs〕
n. ❶圣诞节[U]
Merry Christmas and Happy New Year!
恭祝圣诞，并贺新禧！
❷圣诞节时期[C]
The past few Christmases were very quiet.
过去的几个圣诞节假期过得很平静。

church 〔tʃɝtʃ ‖ tʃɜːtʃ〕
n. ❶教堂，礼拜堂[C]
Is there any church nearby?
附近有教堂吗？
❷礼拜仪式[U]
He never went to church.
他从未去教堂做过礼拜。
❸教会；教会全体成员

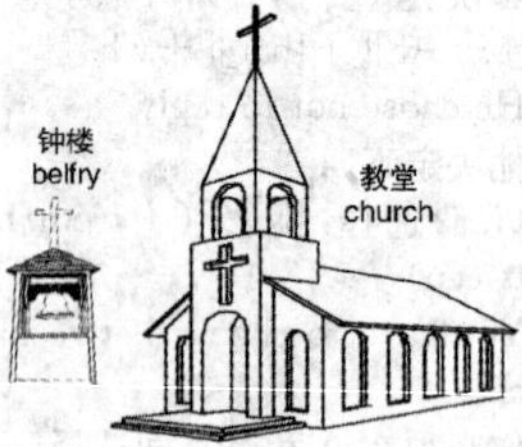

cigarette 〔ˌsɪgəˈrɛt ‖ ˌsɪgəˈret〕
n. 香烟，纸烟[C]
How about a cigarette?
来支香烟吧。

cinema 〔ˈsɪnəmə ‖ ˈsɪnɪmə〕
n.【主英】电影院[C]
Let's go to the cinema.
咱们去看电影吧！
〔同义〕movie theater

circle 〔ˈsɝkl̩ ‖ ˈsɜːkl〕
[过去式]circled；[过去分词]circled
n. [C]❶圆；圆圈
The students sit in a circle on the floor.
学生们在地板上坐成一圈。
❷圆形的东西，环状物
There is a circle of flowers around the statue.
塑像周围鲜花环绕。
❸(具有共同兴趣、利益的人们所形成的)圈子；(活动等的)范围；……界
I have a circle of friends here.
在这里我有一群朋友。
vt. ❶画圆圈；圈出；围着
Circle the correct answers.
圈出正确的答案。
❷环绕……移动(或运转)
vi. 盘旋，旋转；环行
Birds were circling overhead.

鸟儿在头顶上盘旋飞翔。

circus [ˈsɝkəs ‖ ˈsɜːkəs]

n. 马戏团；马戏表演 [C]

The circus traveled from town to town.

马戏团旅行了一个又一个城市。

citizen [ˈsɪtəzn̩ ‖ ˈsɪtɪzn]

n. [C] ❶市民，(城市)居民 ❷公民

The United States gives its citizens certain rights.

美国给予它的公民某些权利。

city [ˈsɪtɪ ‖ ˈsɪtɪ] [名复] cities

n. ❶城市，都市，市 [C]

We live in New York City.

我们住在纽约(市)。

❷全体市民，全城居民

The whole city turned out to cheer the Pope.

全城居民倾巢而出欢迎教皇。

civil [ˈsɪvl̩ ‖ ˈsɪvɪl]

a. ❶市民的，国民的，公民的；民用的

Martin Luther King was the leader of the civil rights movement.

马丁·路德·金是民权运动的领袖。

❷一般平民的，民间的

❸【律】民事的；法定的

civil court

民事法庭

civilization [ˌsɪvl̩əˈzeʃən ‖ ˌsɪvɪlaɪˈzeɪʃən]

n. 文明；文明阶段；文明国家；文明世界 [U]

the modern civilization

现代文明

clap [klæp ‖ klæp]

[过去式] clapped; [过去分词] clapped

vt. ❶拍(手)，鼓(掌)；为……鼓掌

They clapped their hands.

他们鼓掌。

❷轻拍，击 [(+on)]

vi. ❶拍手，鼓掌

The audience clapped after his speech.

他演说完毕之后，观众鼓掌喝彩。

❷砰然出声，(门，盖子等)啪地关上

class [klæs ‖ klɑːs]

n. ❶(社会的)阶级；社会等级 [C]

the upper/middle/lower class

上等/中等/下等阶级

❷班级；年级 [C]

He is first in English in his class.

他的英文是全班第一。

❸(一节)课；上课 [C][U]

Talking is not allowed during

class.
上课时不准说话。

classify 〔ˈklæsəˌfaɪ ‖ ˈklæsɪfaɪ〕
[过去式]classified;[过去分词]classified
vt. 将……分类;将……分等级
I classified my books by subjects.
我把书按科目分类。

classmate 〔ˈklæsˌmet ‖ ˈklɑːsmeɪt〕
n. 同班同学[C]

classroom 〔ˈklæsˌrum ‖ ˈklɑːsrʊm〕
n. 教室[C]
All the students are in the classroom.
所有的学生都在教室里。

clay 〔kle ‖ kleɪ〕
n. [U]❶黏土;泥土
We make bricks from clay.
我们用泥土制砖。
❷(上帝造人的)泥土;(人的)躯体,肉体

clean 〔klin ‖ kliːn〕
[比]cleaner;[最]cleanest;[过去式]cleaned;[过去分词]cleaned
a. ❶清洁的;未被污染的
The room is very clean.
房内极其干净。
❷清白的;无前科的
He has clean record.
他的历史清白。
❸干净利落的;熟练的
He made a clean jump over the bar.
他灵巧地跳过栅栏。
vt. 把……弄干净,去除……的污垢(或痕迹等)
She was cleaning the bedroom when he called her.
他给她打电话时,她正在打扫卧室。

clear 〔klɪr ‖ klɪə〕
[比]clearer;[最]clearest
a. ❶清澈的,透明的;(皮肤)洁净的
We could see fish in the clear water.
我们看到清澈的水中有鱼。
❷明亮的;晴朗的
The night was clear and the stars were out.
夜空晴朗,星星都出来了。
❸清楚的;清晰的;明了的
Professor Smith gave a clear explanation of the experiment.
史密斯教授对这次实验做了清晰的讲解。
❹显然的,明显的
It is clear that you are right.
显然你是对的。
❺无障碍的;清除了……的

When you finished working, make your desk clear.
你做完功课时，要把桌子收拾干净。
ad. ❶清晰地，明了地
He spoke loud and clear.
他讲话声音大而且清楚。
❷完全地；一直地
The ship sank clear to the bottom of the sea.
那艘船一直沉到海底。

clerk 〔klɝk ‖ klɑːk〕
n. [C]❶办事员，职员；书记；记账员
She got a job as a bank clerk.
她得到一份银行职员的工作。
❷【美】店员，销售员

clever 〔ˈklɛvɚ ‖ ˈklevə〕
[比]cleverer；[最]cleverest
a. ❶聪明的，伶俐的
She thought him to be very clever.
她原以为他很聪明。
❷灵巧的，熟练的，擅长的
My brother is a clever carpenter.
我的兄弟是个灵巧的木匠。
〔**同义**〕bright，smart，intelligent 聪明的；机智的
〔**反义**〕foolish，stupid 愚蠢的

cliff 〔klɪf ‖ klɪf〕
n. (尤指海边的)悬崖，峭壁[C]

climate 〔ˈklaɪmɪt ‖ ˈklaɪmɪt〕
n. ❶气候[C][U]
He could not stand the terrible English climate.
他忍受不了糟糕的英国气候。
❷风土；具有某种气候的区域[C]
She is not used to living in a cold climate.
她不习惯寒带生活。
❸(某一社会，时代的)风气，趋势；气氛[C][U]
After the revolution, the climate of the country remained tense.
革命以后，那个国家的气氛依然紧张。

weather…每天的天气或特定的某天、某地的天气变化，如，
We had fine weather that day.
那天天气很好。
climate…某一地区的气候，如，
The island has a warm climate.
那个岛气候温暖。

用法工具箱

climb 〔klaɪm ‖ klaɪm〕
[过去式]climbed;[过去分词]climbed
vt. ❶爬,攀登;登上
We started to climb the hill.
我们开始爬山。
❷(植物)沿着……攀缘而上
vi. ❶爬,攀登
They climbed out through the window.
他们从窗户爬了出来。
❷徐徐上升;(物价等)逐渐上升,增值
The price of grain climbed back.
粮价逐渐回升了。
The plane was climbing.
飞机正徐徐上升。
❸(植物)攀缘向上;(道路等)倾斜向上
The ivy climbed up the wall.
常春藤沿着墙攀缘而上。

clock 〔klɑk ‖ klɒk〕
n. ❶时钟[C]
The clock struck 10.
时钟敲响10点。
❷【口】(汽车等的)里程计;(车辆的)速度计
〈手表是 watch; clock 是座钟,挂钟〉

close[1] 〔kloz ‖ kləʊz〕
[过去式]closed;[过去分词]closed
vt. ❶关闭;盖上;合上
She closed the door softly.
她轻轻地关上门。
❷封闭,歇业,打烊
The street has been closed for two days.
这条街已被封闭两天了。
The store is closed today.
这商店今天歇业。
❸结束
He closed his speech with a joke.
他以一则笑话结束了他的演讲。
vi. ❶关闭;盖上;合上
The door closes quietly.
这门关起来不发出什么声音。
❷(商店等)关门,打烊
The post office closes at 6.
邮局6点关门。
❸结束
At 11 the conference closed.
11时大会结束。

close[2] 〔klos ‖ kləʊs〕
[比]closer;[最]closest
a. ❶近的,接近的[(+to)]
His old house is close to the

factory.
他的老房子靠近该厂。
❷(关系)密切的，亲密的
She is a close friend of theirs.
她是他们的挚友。
ad. ❶接近，靠近地[(＋to)]
They live close to the museum.
他们住在靠近博物馆的地方。
❷紧密地，紧紧地
Anna followed close behind.
安娜紧随在后。

closet 〔ˈklɑzɪt ‖ ˈklɒzɪt〕
n. 壁橱；碗橱；衣橱 [C]
Please hang your overcoat in the closet.
请把你的大衣挂在衣橱里。

cloth 〔klɔθ ‖ klɒθ〕
n. ❶布；(棉，毛，合成纤维等)织物；衣料[U]
5 yards of cloth
5 码布
❷(作某种特殊用途的，常用于复合词)布块；桌巾；餐巾[C]
a dust cloth
抹布

clothes 〔kloz ‖ kləʊðz〕
n. 衣服；服装
I bought a suit of clothes.
我买了一套衣服。
Fine clothes make the man.
[谚语]人靠衣装。

clothing 〔ˈkloðɪŋ ‖ ˈkləʊðɪŋ〕
n. (总称)衣服，衣着
The staff at this hotel wear uniform clothing.
这家宾馆的员工穿统一的制服。
food , clothing, shelter and transport
衣食住行

cloud 〔klaʊd ‖ klaʊd〕
n. ❶云[C][U]
The sky became suddenly covered with dark clouds.
天空突然变得乌云密布。
❷(尘埃，烟等)云状物[C][(＋of)]
a cloud of dust
一片扬尘

词汇拓展

cloudy *a.* 阴天的，多云的

club 〔klʌb ‖ klʌb〕
n. [C]❶(运动，娱乐等的)俱乐部；会；社
Alice belongs to the swimming club.
艾丽斯是那个游泳俱乐部的会员。

❷夜总会
❸棍棒
He hit me with a club.
他用棍子打我。
❹(纸牌中的)梅花

C

coach 〔kotʃ ‖ kəutʃ〕
n. ❶【美】巴士,公共汽车;【英】长途汽车
❷(普通)旅客车厢
I had to cross a number of coaches to reach the dining car.
我得穿过好几节车厢才能到达餐车。
❸(旧时的)四轮大马车,公共马车
❹(运动队的)教练;(协助应付考试的)家庭教师
Our football team has got a very experienced coach.
我们的足球队有了一个很有经验的教练。

coal 〔kol ‖ kəul〕
n. ❶煤[U]
❷(燃烧中的)煤块[C]
❸木炭[U]

coast 〔kost ‖ kəust〕
n. 海岸;沿海地区[C]
They live in a town along the coast.
他们住在一个沿海的城市里。

coat 〔kot ‖ kəut〕
n. [C] ❶外套,大衣;(西装的)上衣
Martha was wearing a heavy coat.
玛莎穿着一件厚大衣。
❷(动物的)皮毛;(植物的)表皮
The dog has a long coat.
这条狗长着一身长长的毛。
❸(油漆等的)涂层[(+of)]
a coat of paint
一层漆

cock 〔kɑk ‖ kɒk〕
n. 公鸡〈母鸡是 hen〉[C]

code 〔kod ‖ kəud〕
n. ❶法典,法规[C]
❷规则,规范;礼教习俗[C]
❸代号,代码;电码;口令[C][U]
the Morse code
摩尔斯电码
❹【计算机】以特定程序设计语言所撰写出来的一段程序

coffee 〔ˈkɔfɪ ‖ ˈkɒfɪ〕
n. ❶咖啡[U]
How about having some coffee?
要不要喝点咖啡?
❷(一杯)咖啡[C][常用于口语中]

Two coffees, please.
请来两杯咖啡。

coin 〔kɔɪn ‖ kɔɪn〕
n. 硬币,钱币[C][U]
Bill collects foreign coins.
比尔收集外国硬币。

cold 〔kold ‖ kəʊld〕
a. ❶冷的,寒冷的
It was bitterly cold that night.
那个夜晚,天气十分寒冷。
❷冷淡的,不友善的;冷酷的
He is always cold to strangers.
他对陌生人总是很冷漠。
❸(食物)未热过的;热过后变凉的;冰冻的
Would you like a cold drink?
你要不要喝杯冷饮?
n. ❶寒冷[U]
He was shivering with cold.
他冷得发抖。
❷伤风,感冒[C]
I have got a cold recently.
近来我感冒了。

collar 〔ˈkɑlɚ ‖ ˈkɒlə〕
n. 衣领[C]
I seized him by the collar.
我一把抓住他的衣领。

collect 〔kəˈlɛkt ‖ kəˈlekt〕
[过去式]collected;[过去分词]collected
vt. ❶收集,采集;使集合
Why do you collect stamps?
你为何集邮?
❷领取(信件等);接走
He has gone to collect his daughter.
他去接女儿了。
vi. 聚集,堆积
Water collects in hollows.
水在坑洼处聚集。

collection 〔kəˈlɛkʃən ‖ kəˈlekʃən〕
n. ❶收集,采集;收取[C][U]
❷收藏品,搜集的东西[C]
I have a stamp collection.
我收集了一些邮票。
❸募捐;募集的钱[C]

college 〔ˈkɑlɪdʒ ‖ ˈkɒlɪdʒ〕
n. ❶大学;学院[C][U]
She studies at a medical college in New York.
她在纽约的一所医学院学习。
❷(英国大学中各自独立的)学院[C]
❸职业学校,专科学校[C]

colo(u)r 〔ˈkʌlɚ ‖ ˈkʌlə〕
n. ❶色,色彩;颜色;彩色[C][U]
This is a color television.
这是一台彩色电视机。

❷脸色，血色
Color was coming back to his face.
他脸上的血色在好转。
❸肤色；有色人种的肤色[C][U]
Equal employment shall be accorded to all qualified individuals without regard to color or sex.
所有符合条件者不分肤色或性别均应享有平等的就业机会。
❹颜料，染料[P]
oil color
油画颜料
water color
水彩画颜料

词汇拓展

colored *a.* 着色的，有色人种的
colorful *a.* 富有色彩的

column [ˈkɑləm ‖ ˈkɒləm]
n. [C] ❶圆柱，圆柱状物
The three columns carry the roof.
三根圆柱支撑屋顶。
❷(报纸的)栏，段
He always read the sports column in the Times.
他总是阅读《泰晤士报》的体育专栏。

comb [kom ‖ kəʊm]
n. [C] ❶梳子；(羊毛等的)毛刷，马鬃刷
❷鸡冠；鸡冠状的东西；浪峰

combine [kəmˈbaɪn ‖ kəmˈbaɪn]
[过去式] combined; [过去分词] combined
vt. 使结合；使联合
Combine the blue paint and yellow paint.
将蓝颜料和黄颜料混在一起。

come [kʌm ‖ kʌm]
[过去式] came; [过去分词] come
vi. ❶来；来到
Could you come (to) see me tomorrow?
你明天能来看我吗？
❷(往对方的方向或说话者与对方一起)去
Will you come with me to the store?
你和我一道去商店吗？
❸到达(某处)；达到(某一个阶段)
Three years later, he came to power.
三年后他上台掌权了。

come 和 go 互为反义词，come 表示“向说话人或听话人所处的地方移动”“朝我来，跟我来，或到我想象我会到的地方”；go 表示“离开说话人或听话人所处的地方”“离开我或离开我想象我会在的地方”，如，

I'm going to the hospital this afternoon. Would you like to come with me?

我今天下午想去医院，你跟我一起去吗？

“Hello, Roy. Are you coming to the party tomorrow?”(i. e. “I'm going to be there.”)

喂，罗伊，明天舞会你会来吗？（言外之意“我会在那里”）

Last summer I went to Hangzhou for a vacation.

去年夏天我去杭州度的假。

用法工具箱

常用短语

come about 发生

How did the accident come about?

这意外事件是怎么发生的？

come across 偶然碰到

I came across her on the street.

我在街上遇到她。

come back ❶回来

Come back soon.

要马上回来。

❷记起

His words often came back to me.

我常常想起他的话。

come by ❶从旁边走过去❷得到

How did you come by such a large amount of money?

你怎么弄到这么一大笔钱？

comedy 〔ˈkɑmədɪ ‖ ˈkɒmɪdɪ〕

n. 喜剧[C][U]

comfort 〔ˈkʌmfɚt ‖ ˈkʌmfət〕

[过去式] comforted；[过去分词] comforted

n. ❶安逸，舒适[U]

❷使人舒服的设备，方便的东西[P]

She longed for the comforts of home.

她渴望获得使家居舒适的各种设备。

❸安慰，慰问[U]

We could give him no comfort.
我们无法给他安慰。
vt. ❶安慰，慰问
They tried to comfort her, but what could they say?
他们想要安慰她，但能说什么呢？
❷使安逸舒适

comfortable 〔'kʌmfɚtəbl̩ || 'kʌmfətəbl〕
a. ❶使人舒服的，舒适的
Make yourself comfortable.
请不要客气。
❷宽裕的；丰富的

command 〔kə'mænd || kə'mɑːnd〕
［过去式］commanded；［过去分词］commanded
vt. ❶命令［＋that］
I command that he go at once.
我命令他立即就去。
❷指挥，统率；控制
He was told to command his temper.
有人叫他控制脾气。
❸拥有，掌握
vi. 指挥；控制；命令
n. ❶命令［C］
give a command
下令
withdraw a command
撤回命令
❷控制，控制权；指挥，指挥权［U］
He has a hundred men under his command.
他指挥100个人。
❸司令部，指挥部［C］
❹掌握；运用能力［U］
She has a good command of spoken English.
她的英语口语很熟练。

commander 〔kə'mændɚ || kə'mɑːndə〕
n. 指挥官，司令官［C］

committee 〔kə'mɪtɪ || kə'mɪtɪ〕
n. 委员会
The committee consists of 20 members.
这个委员会由20位成员组成。
The committee differ in opinion.
委员们的意见不一致。

当表示委员会这个集体时，谓语动词用单数；当表示委员会成员时，谓语动词用复数。
用法工具箱

common 〔'kɑmən || 'kɒmən〕

[比]commoner, more common;[最]commonest, most common

a. ❶普通的;常见的

Smith is a very common last name in England.

在英国史密斯是很常见的姓。

❷共同的,共有的[(+to)]

Common interests bind us together.

共同的利益使我们结合在一起。

These problems are common to all societies.

这些问题是所有社会的通病。

❸公共的,公众的

We all must work for the common good.

我们大家必须为公共的利益而工作。

常用短语

in common 共同的;共有的

We have many things in common.

我们有相似之处。

communicate [kəˈmjunəˌket ‖ kəˈmjuːnɪkeɪt]

[过去式]communicated;[过去分词]communicated

vt. ❶传达;传递;传播[(+to)]

Did she communicate my wishes to you?

她有没有把我的祝福转告给你?

❷传染,使感染[(+to)]

He communicated cold to the rest of his family.

他把感冒传染给了家人。

vi. ❶交流思想(或感情,信息等);交际,交往

We learn a language in order to communicate.

我们学习语言是为了交流思想。

❷通讯,通话[(+with)]

He had no way to communicate with his brother.

他没有办法与他兄弟联系。

❸连接,相通[(+with)]

My bedroom communicates with my little brother's.

我的卧室和我弟弟的相连。

communication

[kəˌmjunəˈkeʃən ‖ kəˌmjuːnɪˈkeɪʃən]

n. ❶传达;交流,交往;通信;传染[U]

The satellite has become an important means of communication.

卫星已成为一个重要的通讯工具。

❷讯息;情报[C]

❸通讯(交通)设施[P]
Our city has excellent communications with all parts of the country.
我们的城市具有完备的交通网与全国各地联系。

C

communism 〔ˈkɑmjuˌnɪzəm ‖ ˈkɒmjʊnɪzəm〕
n. [U] ❶共产主义
❷(大写)共产主义政体;共产主义社会

communist 〔ˈkɑmjuˌnɪst ‖ ˈkɒmjʊnɪst〕
n. [C] ❶共产主义者
❷(常大写)共产党员
❸【美】(常大写)从事左翼活动的人

companion 〔kəmˈpænjən ‖ kəmˈpænjən〕
n. [C] ❶同伴,伴侣;朋友
Are you alone or with a companion?
你单独一人还是与朋友在一起?
❷(受雇服侍老人或病人的)职业伴侣(通常为女性)

company 〔ˈkʌmpənɪ ‖ ˈkʌmpənɪ〕
n. ❶公司,商号[C]
Tom works for a computer company.
汤姆在一家计算机公司上班。
❷陪伴;友情[U]
❸伴侣(们);同伴(们),朋友(们)[C]
People are judged by the company they keep.
根据某人结交的朋友便能判断其人了。
〈公司名称通常缩写为 Co.〉

compare 〔kəmˈpɛr ‖ kəmˈpeə〕
[过去式]compared;[过去分词]compared
vt. ❶比较,对照
Compare the two and take the better one.
比较两者,选择较佳者。
❷比喻为,比做[(+to/with)]
He compared books to friends.
他把书比做朋友。
vi. (可与……)相比,匹敌[(+with)][用于否定句或疑问句]
No one compares with him in English.
英文方面没人能与他相比。
n. (常用于惯用语)比较[U]
This view is beyond comparison.
这景色无与伦比。

compass 〔ˈkʌmpəs ‖ ˈkʌmpəs〕
n. ❶罗盘,指南针[C]
The compass was first used in

sailing.
罗盘首先用在航海上。
❷(制图用的)圆规[P]

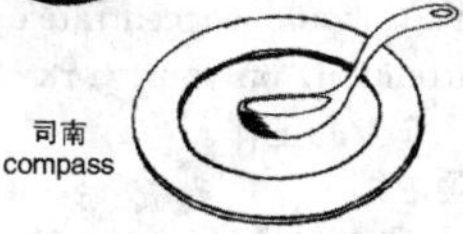

competition 〔ˌkɑmpəˈtɪʃən ‖ ˌkɒmpɪˈtɪʃən〕
n. ❶竞争,角逐[U][(+with/between/for)]
There is serious competition between the two girls.
这两个女孩子竞争得很厉害。
❷比赛,竞赛;赛会[C]
He entered skiing competition.
他参加了滑雪比赛。

complete 〔kəmˈplit ‖ kəmˈpliːt〕
[比]more complete;[最]most complete;[过去式]completed;[过去分词]completed
a. ❶完整的;全部的
Is this a complete list?
这是份完整的清单吗?
❷完成的;结束的
We can't go out until our homework is complete.
我们把作业做完才能出去。
❸完全的,彻底的
A more complete study of the subject is needed.
对这个问题需要做更加彻底的研究。

词汇拓展

completely *ad.* 完全地
completeness *n.* 完全
completion *n.* 完成

vt. ❶使齐全;使完整
Complete the sentences in the exercise by filling in the blanks.
在空白处填充使练习中各句成为完整句。
❷完成;结束
By the end of August we had completed the work.
我们到8月底就完成了这项工作。

complicated 〔ˈkɑmpləˌketɪd ‖ ˈkɒmplɪkeɪtɪd〕
[比]more complicated;[最]most complicated
a. 复杂的;难懂的;结构复杂的
complicated problems
难题

composition 〔ˌkɑmpəˈzɪʃən ‖

ˌkɒmpəˈzɪʃən〕

n. ❶写作;作曲[U]

❷作品;作文;(大型)乐曲[C]

compound 〔ˈkɑmpaʊnd ‖ ˈkɒmpaʊnd〕

n.[C] ❶混合物;化合物;复合物

❷复合字,复合句

a. ❶合成的,复合的,混合的

❷【文】复合的,合成的

computer 〔kəmˈpjutɚ ‖ kəmˈpjuːtə〕

n.[C] ❶计算机,电子计算机

The entire operation is done by computer.

整个运算是由计算机完成的。

❷计算者

comrade 〔ˈkɑmræd ‖ ˈkɒmrɪd〕

n.[C] ❶ 伙伴,同事

❷(共产党的)同志

conceal 〔kənˈsil ‖ kənˈsiːl〕

[过去式]concealed;[过去分词]concealed

vt. 隐蔽,隐藏;隐瞒[(+from)][+wh-]

She tried to conceal what she had done to them.

她试图隐瞒对他们所做的事。

常用短语

conceal something from somebody 对某人隐瞒某事

concentrate 〔ˈkɑnsn̩ˌtret ‖ ˈkɒnsentreɪt〕

[过去式]concentrated;[过去分词]concentrated

vt. ❶集中;聚集,集结[(+on/upon)]

You should concentrate (your attention) on your work.

你应专心工作。

❷浓缩

vi. ❶集中;聚集,集结

❷全神贯注;全力以赴[(+on/upon)]

词汇拓展

concentration *n.* 集中

concept 〔ˈkɑnsɛpt ‖ ˈkɒnsept〕

n. 概念,观念,思想[C]

concern 〔kənˈsɝn ‖ kənˈsəːn〕

[过去式]concerned;[过去分词]concerned

vt. ❶(不用被动式)关于

The matter concerns all of us.

这件事跟我们全体都有关系。

❷使担心;使不安

The boy's poor health concerned his parents.

那个男孩健康状况不佳,使他的父母亲忧虑。

❸使关心[(+about/with)]
He was very concerned about her.
他对她非常关心。

常用短语

as/so far as … be concerned 就……而言
As far as English is concerned, he is first in our class.
就英语而言,他是全班第一。

n. ❶关心的事,重要的事[C]
That's no concern of mine.
那不关我的事。
❷担心,挂念;关怀[C][U]
Andrew expressed his concern.
安德鲁表示了他的关切。
❸公司,企业[C]

concert [ˈkɑnsɜ˞t ‖ ˈkɒnsət]
n. 音乐会,演奏会[C]
They came into town to hear a concert.
他们进城来听音乐会。

常用短语

(英) concert hall = (美) music hall 音乐厅

conclude [kənˈklud ‖ kənˈkluːd]
[过去式]concluded;[过去分词]concluded
vt. ❶结束
We concluded our meeting at 9 o'clock.
我们9点钟结束了会议。
❷推断出,断定
What can you conclude from these observations?
你从这些观察中能得出什么结论?
vi. ❶结束,终了
The meeting concluded after two hours.
两小时后会议结束了。
❷作出(最后)决定

conclusion [kənˈkluʒən ‖ kənˈkluːʒən]
n. ❶结论;推论;决定[C]
They drew different conclusions from the facts.
他们从这些事实中引出了不同的结论。
❷结尾,结局[C]
❸终结,结束[U]
The debate did not come to a conclusion until midnight.
辩论直到午夜才结束。

condition [kənˈdɪʃən ‖ kənˈdɪʃən]
n. ❶情况;(健康等)状态[C][U]
What's the patient's condition?
病人的情况如何?

C

❷环境;形势[P]
The miners there worked in dreadful conditions.
那里的矿工们在极其恶劣的环境中工作。
❸条件[C][(+ for/of)][+ that]
I'll do it on condition that you pay for everything.
我可以做此事,条件是你得支付一切费用。

conduct 〔kən'dʌkt ‖ kən'dʌkt〕
vt. ❶引导,带领
He conducted me to my seat.
他把我带到座位上。
〔同义〕lead ;guide 引导
❷实施;处理;经营,管理
He conducted experiment carefully.
他小心地做实验。
❸为人,表现
❹指挥(军队,乐队等)

confidence 〔'kɑnfədəns ‖ 'kɒnfɪdəns〕
n. ❶ 自信,信心,把握[U][(+ in)][+to-v][+that]
He lacks confidence in himself.
他缺少自信。
❷信赖,信任[U][(+in)]
We have confidence in the new mayor.
我们信任这位新市长。
❸(向知心人吐露的)秘密,私房话[C]
He told his best friend a confidence.
他对最好的朋友吐露了秘密。

词汇拓展
confident *a.* 自信的
confidential *a.* 秘密的

confuse 〔kən'fjuz ‖ kən'fjuːz〕
[过去式]confused;[过去分词]confused
vt. ❶把……弄糊涂,使困惑
His sudden appearance confused me.
他的突然出现使我迷惑。
❷把……混同,混淆[(+with)]
You confused Australia with Austria.
你把澳大利亚和奥地利搞混了。
❸搞乱,使混乱
His granddaughter confused the papers on his desk.
他的孙女把他书桌上的文件弄乱了。

congratulate 〔kən'grætʃəˌlet ‖ kən'grætjʊˌleɪt〕
[过去式]congratulated;[过去分词]congratulated

vt. ❶祝贺；恭喜[(+ on/upon)]
❷(后接 oneself)自我庆幸[(+on)]

congratulation 〔kənˌgrætʃəˈleʃən ‖ kənˌgrætjuˈleɪʃən〕
n. ❶祝贺，庆贺[U][P][(+on/upon)]
Congratulations on your happy marriage!
祝贺你们喜结良缘！
❷祝贺词[P][(+on/upon)]

connect 〔kəˈnɛkt ‖ kəˈnekt〕
[过去式]connected；[过去分词]connected
vt. ❶连接，连结
This railway connects London and Edinburgh.
这条铁路连接伦敦与爱丁堡。
❷联想[(+with)]
We connect the word "blue" with the color of the sky.
我们由"蓝"这个字会联想到晴空的颜色。
❸给……接通电话[(+with)]
Connect me with Taipei, please.
请给我接通台北。
❹联系；结合[(+with)]
vi. ❶连接，连结[(+by/with/to)]
This wire connects with that one.
这根电线与那根连接。
❷(交通工具)衔接，联运[(+with)]

词汇拓展
connection *n.* 联系，连接

conquer 〔ˈkɑŋkɚ ‖ ˈkɒŋkə〕
[过去式]conquered；[过去分词]conquered
vt. ❶攻克，攻取
The city was conquered overnight.
那座城市在夜里被攻克。
❷战胜；克服；征服；成功地登上
I finally conquered my fear of heights.
我终于克服了我的惧高心理。
❸赢得(观众，听众等)赞誉
The singer conquered the hearts of his audience.
那位歌唱家赢得了观众的心。

词汇拓展
conqueror *n.* 征服者

conscious 〔ˈkɑnʃəs ‖ ˈkɒnʃəs〕
a. ❶神志清醒的，有知觉的
She may become conscious be-

C

fore morning.
她天亮前可能恢复知觉。
❷意识到的,觉察到的[(+of)][+that]
I suddenly became conscious that someone was looking at me.
我突然意识到有人在看着我。
❸故意的,蓄意的
We can speak Chinese without conscious effort.
我们不需要刻意努力就能说中国话。

词汇拓展

consciousness *n.* 意识,察觉

consider 〔kən'sɪdɚ ‖ kən'sɪdə〕
[过去式]considered;[过去分词]considered
vt. ❶考虑,细想[+v-ing][+wh-]
I've begun to consider what to do next.
我已在考虑下一步该怎么办。
❷考虑到[+that][+wh-]
Have you considered that he is only a little boy?
你有没有考虑到他仅仅是个小孩儿?
❸认为;把……视为[+that]
We consider that the defendant is not guilty.
我们认为被告无罪。
vi. 考虑,细想
He paused for a moment to consider.
他停下来想了一会儿。

consist 〔kən'sɪst ‖ kən'sɪst〕
[过去式]consisted;[过去分词]consisted
vi. ❶ 组成,构成[(+of)]
A university consists of teachers, administrators and students.
大学由教师、行政人员和学生组成。
❷在于,存在于[(+in)]
Happiness consists in good health.
幸福寓于健康之中。
❸一致,符合[(+with)]
The information consists with his account.
消息与他的叙述相符合。

constant 〔 'kɑnstənt ‖ 'kɒnstənt〕
a. ❶固定的,不变的
The birth rate in this city is almost constant.
这个城市的出生率几乎是不变的。
❷不停的,接连不断的,持续的

He hates his wife's constant nagging.
他讨厌他妻子唠叨不休。

词汇拓展

constantly *ad.* 时常地，持续不断地

construct 〔kən'strʌkt || kən'strʌkt〕
[过去式]constructed；[过去分词]constructed
vt. 建造，构成
They constructed the bridge in a year.
他们在一年之内就建好了那座桥。

construction 〔kən'strʌkʃən || kən'strʌkʃən〕
n. ❶建造，建设；建造术[U]
They are busy with the construction of a new building.
他们忙于建造新建筑物。
❷建筑物，建造物[C]

contain 〔kən'ten || kən'teɪn〕
[过去式]contained；[过去分词]contained
vt. ❶ 包含；容纳
The jar contains 10 glasses of water.
这只大口瓶能装10杯水。
❷控制，遏制
I could not contain my laughter.
我无法控制自己不笑出声来。
❸相当于
A gallon contains four quarts.
一加仑相当于四夸脱。

content 〔'kɑntɛnt || 'kɒntent〕
n. ❶内容，要旨[U]
The play lacks content.
这出戏缺乏实质性内容。
❷含量，容量
❸容纳的东西；具体内容[P]
Show me the contents of your suitcase.
给我看看你手提箱里的东西。

content 是用于像"演说内容"那样无形的东西；contents 则用于像"手提包里的东西"那样有形的东西

用法工具箱

contest 〔'kɑntɛst || 'kɒntest〕
n. [C] ❶争夺，竞争
❷竞赛，比赛
a speech contest
演讲比赛
a beauty contest
选美比赛
❸争论，争辩

continent 〔ˈkɑntənənt ‖ ˈkɒntɪnənt〕
n. 大陆，陆地；大洲[C]

continue 〔kənˈtɪnjʊ ‖ kənˈtɪnjuː〕
[过去式] continued；[过去分词] continued
vi. ❶继续，持续；延伸
The forest continues for miles.
森林绵延数英里。
❷留，仍旧
The weather continues cold.
天气还是冷。
vt. ❶使继续；使延伸[＋v-ing][＋to-v]
I was allowed to continue using the library.
我获准继续使用该图书馆。
❷继续说
"Don't worry about Jack," she continued.
"不必担心杰克，"她继续说道。

continuous 〔kənˈtɪnjʊəs ‖ kənˈtɪnjʊəs〕
a. ❶连续的，不断的
❷【数】连续的

contract 〔ˈkɑntrækt ‖ ˈkɒntrækt〕
n. [C]❶ 契约；合同
❷契约书；合约书

contrary 〔ˈkɑntrerɪ ‖ ˈkɒntrərɪ〕
a. 相反的，对立的[(＋to)]
My opinion is contrary to yours.
我的看法与你的相反。
n. ❶相反；相反的事物[the]
on the contrary
恰恰相反，正相反
❷反面；对立面，对立的一方[C]

control 〔kənˈtrol ‖ kənˈtrəʊl〕
[过去式] controlled；[过去分词] controlled
vt. ❶控制；支配；管理
She is skillful enough to control the machine now.
现在她已有了足够的技术可以操纵这台机器了。
❷克制；抑制
You must learn to control your temper.
你必须学会克制着不发脾气。
n. ❶支配；控制；调节；抑制[U][(＋of/over)]
They have no control over him.
他们控制不了他。
❷管制措施[C][U]

convenient 〔kənˈvinjənt ‖ kənˈviːnjənt〕
a. ❶ 合宜的；方便的；便利的[(＋for/to)]
Please come whenever it is convenient to you.
方便的时候，请随时来。
❷近而方便的[(＋for/to)]

词汇拓展

convenience *n.* 方便，便利的事物

conversation 〔ˌkɑnvə˞ˈseʃən ‖ ˌkɒnvəˈseɪʃən〕

n. ❶会话，谈话；非正式会谈[C][U][(+with)]

He got into conversation with his neighbor.

他开始与邻居交谈起来。

❷谈话技巧，谈吐[U]

convey 〔kənˈve ‖ kənˈveɪ〕

[过去式]conveyed；[过去分词]conveyed

vt. ❶运送，搬运，转运

The truck conveyed the furniture.

这辆货车运送家具。

❷传播(声音等)

❸传达，传递，表达

Words can't convey my feeling.

语言不能表达我的感情。

convince 〔kənˈvɪns ‖ kənˈvɪns〕

[过去式]convinced；[过去分词]convinced

vt. 使确信，使信服；说服[(+of)]

He convinced me of his innocence.

他使我相信他是无辜的。

cook 〔kʊk ‖ kʊk〕

[过去式]cooked；[过去分词]cooked

vt. vi. 烹调，煮

She cooked him some potatoes. = She cooked some potatoes for him.

她为他煮了一些马铃薯。

n. 厨师[C]

cookie 〔ˈkʊkɪ ‖ ˈkʊkɪ〕

n. 【美】甜饼干，(苏格兰)一种小面包[C]

cool 〔kul ‖ kuːl〕

[比]cooler；[最]coolest；[过去式]cooled；[过去分词]cooled

a. ❶凉快的

The hall is nice and cool.

大厅既漂亮又凉爽。

cold…对 hot(热的)而言的"寒冷的，冷的"，如，

a cold winter

寒冷的冬天

chilly… 冷得使人战栗，如，

I feel chilly.

我觉得冷。

cool…对 warm(温暖的)而言的，"凉爽的，不冷不热的"

用法工具箱

C

❷冷静的，沉着的

Be cool. Everything will be all right.

冷静一点，一切都会没问题的。

❸冷淡的[(+to/towards)]

They seemed rather cool towards the new comer.

对这位新来的人，他们似乎很冷淡。

❹【口】很棒的，极好的

vt. ❶使凉快；使冷却

The rain has cooled the air.

这雨使天气变得凉快了。

❷使(情绪等)平静下来

cooperate 〔koˈɑpəˌret ‖ kəʊˈɒpəreɪt〕

[过去式]cooperated；[过去分词]cooperated

vi. 合作，协作[(+with/in)][+to-v]

Let's all cooperate to get the work done quickly.

让我们一起同心协力把这工作快点儿做完。

cooperation 〔koˌɑpəˈreʃən ‖ kəʊˈɒpəreɪʃən〕

n. 合作，协力[U]

copy 〔ˈkɑpɪ ‖ ˈkɒpɪ〕

[过去式]copied；[过去分词]copied

n. ❶抄本，副本；复制品；(电影)拷贝[C]

I will send you a copy of the letter.

我将把信件的副本寄给你。

❷(相同书，报，杂志等的)份，本，册[C]

We have no copies of the book on hand.

这书我们现在手头一本也没有。

vt. ❶抄写；复制；临摹

He's busy copying the letters.

他忙于抄写信件。

❷模仿，仿效

"Good morning," he said, copying his father's voice.

他模仿他父亲的嗓音说道："早安"。

❸抄袭[(+from)]

vi. ❶抄写；复制；临摹

He copied carefully from the model.

他仔细地照那个模式仿制。

❷模仿

❸抄袭[(+from)]

corn 〔kɔrn ‖ kɔːn〕

n. ❶【英】小麦；谷物[U]

❷【美】【澳】【加】玉米[U]

❸谷粒；(胡椒等的)籽[C]

corner 〔ˈkɔrnɚ ‖ ˈkɔːnə〕

n. [C]❶角；街角

A brown cabinet sits in a corner of the room.
房间的一角立着一只棕色的橱柜。
❷(书本等的)包角
❸(遥远的)地区;偏僻处[P]
People arrived from all corners of the world.
人们纷纷从世界各处抵达。

常用短语

at/ on the corner 在拐角处
in the corner 在角落里

corporation 〔ˌkɔrpəˈreʃən ‖ ˌkɔːpəˈreɪʃən〕
n. [C]❶法人;社团法人
❷【美】股份(有限)公司
He landed a job in a large American corporation.
他在一家美国大公司谋得一个职位。

correct 〔kəˈrɛkt ‖ kəˈrekt〕
[比] more correct; [最] most correct;[过去式]corrected;[过去分词]corrected
a. ❶正确的,对的
Your answer is not correct.
你的答案不对。
❷恰当的;端正的;符合一般准则的
vt. ❶改正;纠正;矫正;校准
Would you help me correct my pronunciation?
你能帮我矫正发音吗?
❷惩治;责备
You should correct the children when they are rude.
孩子无礼时,你应该治治他们。

词汇拓展

correction *n.* 修正
correctness *n.* 正确,适当

corridor 〔ˈkɔrədɚ ‖ ˈkɒrɪdɔː〕
n. [C]❶走廊,回廊,通道
❷狭长通道;空中走廊

cost 〔kɔst ‖ kɒst〕
[过去式]cost;[过去分词]cost
n. ❶费用;成本[C]
We must reduce the production cost.
我们必须降低生产成本。
❷代价;损失[C][U]
❸【律】诉讼费用[P]
vt. [以"物或事"作主语,不可用被动语态]❶花费
The car cost him around ten thousand dollars.
这车花去他一万美元左右。
❷使付出(时间,劳力,代价等),使丧失
The error cost the company one million pounds.
这个错误使公司损失了一百万

C

英镑。
❸【英】(不用被动语态)使花许多钱

cottage 〔ˈkɑtɪdʒ ‖ ˈkɒtɪdʒ〕
n. 农舍,小屋[C]
My uncle lived in a small cottage by the river.
我叔叔住在河边的一间小农舍里。

cotton 〔ˈkɑtn̩ ‖ ˈkɒtn〕
n. [U] ❶棉,棉花,棉属植物
The shirt is made of cotton.
这件衬衫是棉质的。
❷棉纱,棉线
She sewed the buttons on with cotton.
她用棉线把纽扣缝上。
❸棉布

cough 〔kɔf ‖ kɒf〕
n. ❶咳嗽[C]
❷咳嗽病
The old lady had a bad cough.
老太太咳得很厉害。
❸咳嗽声[C]

could 〔kʊd ‖ kʊd〕
v. aux. ❶can 的过去式
She could play the violin when she was 5.
她 5 岁时便能拉小提琴了。
❷(用于假设语气,表示与事实相反的设想)能,可以
I wish I could go to France.
但愿我能去法国。
❸(表示可能性)可能
That could be my train.
那可能是我要乘的火车。
❹(用于婉转语气)能,可以

council 〔ˈkaʊnsl̩ ‖ ˈkaʊnsɪl〕
n. ❶会议;政务会;协调会[C]
❷顾问班子;地方议会[C]

count 〔kaʊnt ‖ kaʊnt〕
[过去式]counted;[过去分词]counted
vt. ❶计算,数
They are counting the books they collected.
他们正在数收集来的书。
❷将……计算在内
There are 10 people, not counting the guide.
不包括向导,共有 10 人。
❸认为;看做
You should count yourself fortunate in having good health.
你身体健康,这就算幸运了。
vi. ❶数,计数[(+to/up to)]
❷有重要意义,有价值
In sport what really counts is not the winning but the playing.
就运动而言,重要的不是赢,而是参与。

counter 〔ˈkaʊntɚ ‖ ˈkaʊntə〕
n. 柜台；柜台式长桌［C］

country 〔ˈkʌntrɪ ‖ ˈkʌntrɪ〕
n. ❶国家；国土［C］
He didn't know much about foreign countries.
他对外国知之甚少。
❷祖国；故乡［C］
She loves her country very much.
她十分热爱祖国。
❸全体国民
All the country will vote tomorrow.
明天全国投票。
❹乡下，郊外
a. 乡下的；乡村风味的；乡气的
Emily is a country music fan.
埃米莉是位乡村音乐迷。

couple 〔ˈkʌpḷ ‖ ˈkʌpl〕
n.［C］❶（一）对，（一）双［（＋of）］
I ate a couple of eggs at breakfast.
我早餐吃了两个蛋。
❷夫妇；未婚夫妻；一对舞伴
The young couple decided to start their tour immediately.
那对年轻夫妇决定立即开始旅游。
❸【口】几个，三两个［（＋of）］
They walked a couple of miles.
他们步行了几英里。

courage 〔ˈkɝɪdʒ ‖ ˈkʌrɪdʒ〕
n. 胆量，勇气，英勇［U］［＋to-v］
He didn't have the courage to tell his mother that he had failed in the exam.
他没有勇气告诉母亲他考试不及格。

> courage 是指精神上的，面对苦境的勇气；bravery 是指行动上的勇敢。
>
> **用法工具箱**

course 〔kɔrs ‖ kɔːs〕
n. ❶路线；方向［C］
Our course was straight to the south.
我们的方向是一直向南。
❷过程；进程［U］
It was one of those ideas that change the course of history.
这便是那些能改变历史演进的观点之一。
❸（竞赛的）跑道；场地［C］
❹课程，科目［C］
❺一道菜［C］

常用短语

in the course of 在……期间；

在……过程中

of course 当然

court 〔kɔrt ‖ kɔːt〕

n. ❶法庭，法院；（开）庭[C][U]

The court found him guilty.

法庭判他有罪。

❷（网球等的）场地[C][U]

He met her on the tennis court.

他与她在网球场上相遇。

❸庭院，院子[C]

❹宫廷；王宫[C]

courtyard 〔ˈkɔrtˌjɑrd ‖ ˈkɔːtjɑːd〕

n. 庭院；天井[C]

cousin 〔ˈkʌzn̩ ‖ ˈkʌzn〕

n. [C] ❶堂（或表）兄弟；堂（或表）姐妹

❷亲戚；远亲

cover 〔ˈkʌvɚ ‖ ˈkʌvə〕

[过去式]covered；[过去分词]covered

vt. ❶遮盖；覆盖[（＋with）]

Mary covered her face with her hands.

玛丽用双手捂住脸。

The highway was covered with snow.

公路被雪覆盖着。

❷掩饰；隐匿

She try to laugh to cover her anxiety.

她试图以笑来掩饰她的焦虑。

❸（不用被动语态）行过（路程）

How far can we cover a day?

我们一天能走多远？

❹用枪掩护；把枪口对准（某人）

n. ❶遮盖物；盖子；套子[C]

❷（书的）封面，封底[C]

On the front cover of the magazine is a picture of a boy.

杂志的封面是一张男孩的照片。

❸掩护（物）；掩蔽处[U]

This is only the cover for their unlawful activity.

这仅仅是他们非法活动的掩护而已。

cow 〔kaʊ ‖ kaʊ〕

n. [C] ❶母牛

❷（象，鲸，犀等大型动物的）母兽

coward 〔ˈkaʊɚd ‖ ˈkaʊəd〕

n. 懦夫，胆怯者[C]

cowboy 〔ˈkaʊˌbɔɪ ‖ ˈkaʊˌbɔɪ〕

n. [C] ❶牧童，牧牛人
❷(美国西部的)牛仔

crawl 〔krɔl ‖ krɔːl〕
[过去式]crawled；[过去分词] crawled
vi. ❶爬，爬行，蠕动
He watched the baby crawl across the room.
他看着婴儿从房间这边爬到那边。
❷缓慢地移动，徐徐行进
It was rush hour and we crawled along at 15 miles an hour.
遇上了高峰时间，我们的车子以每小时 15 英里的速度缓慢行驶。

crazy 〔'krezɪ ‖ 'kreɪzɪ〕
a. ❶疯狂的；蠢的；古怪的[＋to-v]
You're crazy to go out in this stormy weather.
在这种暴风雨的天气外出，你真疯了。
❷【口】着迷的，热衷的[(＋about/for/on)]
John's crazy about that girl.
约翰狂热地爱上了那个女孩。

cream 〔krim ‖ kriːm〕
n. ❶奶油；乳脂[U]
Butter is made from cream.
奶油是从乳脂中提取而成的。
❷含奶油的食品；乳脂状的食品[C][U]
❸膏状物；化妆用乳霜；药用乳膏[C][U]
cold cream
冷霜，面霜
shoe cream
鞋油

create 〔krɪ'et ‖ krɪ'eɪt〕
[过去式]created；[过去分词] created
vt. ❶创造；创作；设计
An artist should create beautiful things.
一个艺术家应该创造美好的东西。
❷创建；创设
❸引起，生成
Tourism creates jobs.
旅游业为人们提供就业机会。

词汇拓展

creation *n.* 创造，创作，作品
creative *a.* 创造的，有创造力的

creature 〔'kritʃɚ ‖ 'kriːtʃə〕
n. [C] ❶生物；动物
Worms are very simple creatures.
蠕虫是很简单的生物。
❷家畜

❸(含有怜爱或轻蔑的意思)人,家伙
She's a beautiful creature.
她是个美人。

crime 〔kraɪm ‖ kraɪm〕
n. ❶罪,罪行[C]
He committed a high crime.
他犯下了重大罪行。
❷犯罪,犯罪活动[U]
❸违反道德的行为,罪过[C]
It's a crime to waste food.
浪费食物是有罪的。

crisis 〔ˈkraɪsɪs ‖ ˈkraɪsɪs〕
n. [C]❶(尤指政治或经济)危机;紧急关头;转折点
We are now in a food crisis.
我们正面临粮食危机。
❷病情危险期
The sick man has passed the crisis.
这个病人已经过了危险期。
❸(戏剧,小说等情节中的)关子(最紧要,最吸引人的地方)

crocodile 〔ˈkrɑkəˌdaɪl ‖ ˈkrɒkədaɪl〕

鳄鱼 crocodile

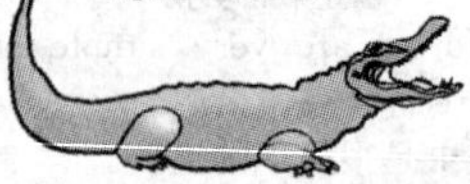

n. ❶【动】鳄鱼[C]
❷鳄鱼皮革[U]

crop 〔krɑp ‖ krɒp〕
n. [C]❶作物,庄稼[P]
Rice is one of the main crops in China.
大米是中国的主要作物之一。
❷一熟,一次收获(量),收成
They get two crops of rice a year.
他们一年收获两季稻。
〔同义〕harvest 收获

cross 〔krɔs ‖ krɔːs〕
[过去式]crossed;[过去分词]crossed
n. [C]❶十字形;十字形记号
This island is in the shape of a cross.
该岛呈十字形。
❷十字架
Jean wears a tiny golden cross.
琼戴着一只小小的金十字架。
vt. ❶越过,渡过
They crossed the river by boat.
他们乘舟渡河。
❷使交叉;与……相交
Don't cross your legs when you sit, please.
坐时请不要交叉双腿。
❸(为祈福等)画十字于
She crossed herself as she stood

before the altar.
她立在祭坛前用手在胸前画了个十字。
vi. 横穿，横渡
They crossed through the great desert.
他们横穿过大沙漠。
a. 交叉的；横贯的
She turned into a cross street.
她转身走进一条横马路。

crossing 〔ˈkrɔsɪŋ ‖ ˈkrɔːsɪŋ〕
n. ❶横渡，横穿［C］［U］
❷交叉；交叉点，十字路口［C］
There are traffic lights at the crossing.
十字路口有交通信号灯。

crowd 〔kraʊd ‖ kraʊd〕
［过去式］crowded；［过去分词］crowded
n. ❶人群，大众［C］
There was a crowd of people in front of the town hall.
市政大厅前有一群人。
❷一堆，许多［C］
I saw a crowd of magazines and papers on her desk.
我看见她桌上放着一堆杂志和报纸。
vt. 挤满，将……塞进
Passengers crowded the platform.
月台挤满了乘客。
He crowded more books onto the shelf.
他向书架上又塞了一些书。
vi. ❶挤，拥挤
People crowded into the cinema crazily.
人们疯狂地挤进电影院。
❷聚集

crown 〔kraʊn ‖ kraʊn〕
n. ［C］王冠，（常大写）王位，王权，君主
Kings and Queens wear crowns at official ceremonies.
国王和女王出席官方仪式时戴王冠。

cruel 〔ˈkruəl ‖ ˈkruːəl〕
a. ❶残忍的，残酷的［（＋to）］
He is cruel to animals.
他对动物很残忍。
❷令人痛苦的；刻毒伤人的；惨痛的
The death of their beloved son was a cruel blow.
他们的爱子的死是一个痛苦的打击。

cry 〔kraɪ ‖ kraɪ〕
［过去式］cried；［过去分词］cried
vi. ❶哭
He cried over his wife's death.

他为妻子的去世而哭泣。
❷叫喊；调用[(+out)][(+for)]
A girl cried for help at midnight.
一个女孩在深夜大声呼救。
vt. ❶哭出
❷大声地说；叫喊
"Tom, where are you?" she cried.
"汤姆，你在哪里？"她大声喊道。
n. ❶叫喊；调用[C][(+of/for)]
With a cry of delight, he found the puppy.
他找到了小狗，高兴得叫喊起来。
❷(一阵)哭
She had a long cry when her favorite doll broke.
她心爱的洋娃娃损坏了，为此她哭了好长一阵子。

cucumber 〔ˈkjukʌmbɚ ‖ ˈkjuːkʌmbə〕
n. 黄瓜，胡瓜[C]

culture 〔ˈkʌltʃɚ ‖ ˈkʌltʃə〕
n. ❶文化[C][U]
He has studied the cultures of various western countries.
他研究了西方各国家的文化。
❷教养；陶冶；修养[U]
He is a man of culture.
他是一个有修养的人。

cup 〔kʌp ‖ kʌp〕
n. ❶杯子[C]
〈玻璃制的杯子是 glass〉

❷一杯(的容量)[C][(+of)]
I'd like to have a cup of tea.
我想喝杯茶。
❸杯状物[C]
❹奖杯[C]
John won the silver cup for the high jump.
约翰赢得跳高项目的银杯。

cupboard 〔ˈkʌbɚd ‖ ˈkʌbəd〕
n. [C]❶食橱；碗柜
❷橱柜，壁橱

cure 〔kjur ‖ kjʊə〕
[过去式]cured；[过去分词]cured
vt. ❶治愈[(+of)]
The doctor cured me of cold.
医生治好了我的感冒。
❷消除(弊病等)；纠正[(+of)]

Nothing cured him of the bad habit.
什么也改不了他的恶习。
n. ❶治疗；痊愈[C][U]
❷疗法；药；(处理社会问题等的)对策[C][(+for)]
There's no known cure for a cold.
治疗感冒尚无良方。

curious 〔'kjʊrɪəs ‖ 'kjʊərɪəs〕
a. ❶好奇的，渴望知道的；爱探究的[(+as to/about)][+to-v][+wh-]
The boy was curious about everything he saw.
那男孩对所见的一切都感到好奇。
❷奇怪的；稀奇古怪的，难以理解的
I heard a curious noise last night.
昨晚我听见一个奇怪的响声。

curtain 〔'kɝtn̩ ‖ 'kɜːtn〕
n. [C] ❶帘；窗帘；门帘；帷幔

Please draw the curtains.
请把窗帘拉上。
❷(舞台上的)幕；启幕；落幕
The curtain rises.
戏开演了。

custom 〔'kʌstəm ‖ 'kʌstəm〕
n. ❶(社会，团体的)习俗，惯例，(个人的)习惯[C][U]
The celebration of Christmas is a custom.
庆祝圣诞节是一种风俗。
❷(常大写)海关[the P]
Did you have any trouble with the Customs?
你通过海关有麻烦吗？

cut 〔kʌt ‖ kʌt〕
[过去式]cut；[过去分词]cut
vt. ❶切；割；剪；削；砍
Please cut the cake into 10 pieces.
请把蛋糕切成10块。
❷削减；缩短
He cut his costs by half.
他削减掉一半的开支。
❸剪辑(影片)；裁剪
Who cut the suit for you?
谁替你裁剪的这套服装？
❹切断(电路等)[(+off)]
vi. ❶切；割；剪；削；砍
The knife cuts easily.
这刀很锋利。

❷伤人感情;刺痛,割痛

The cold wind cut through his thin clothes.

寒风穿透他的单薄衣衫。

❸(拍摄电影时)停拍

常用短语

cut down ❶削减 ❷缩短

Dad decided to cut down on smoking because it is dangerous to health.

因为吸烟有害健康,爸爸决定减少抽烟。

cut in ❶插话 ❷超车

cut off ❶切断;中断 ❷使死亡

The electricity was cut off because of the storm.

因为风暴的缘故,电源被切断了。

cycle 〔'saɪkl̩ ‖ 'saɪkl〕

n. [C] ❶周期;循环;一转

The four seasons of the year make a cycle.

一年四季成为一个循环。

❷自行车;摩托车

dad〔dæd ‖ dæd〕

n.【口】爸爸，爹爹[C]

〈也称 daddy〉

daily〔ˈdelɪ ‖ ˈdeɪlɪ〕

a. 每日的；日常的

These workers are paid on a daily basis.

这些工人领的是日薪。

ad. 每日

My father goes out for a walk daily.

我父亲每天出去散步。

n. 日报[C]

A new daily will appear soon in our town.

一种新的日报不久将在我市问世。

damage〔ˈdæmɪdʒ ‖ ˈdæmɪdʒ〕

[过去式]damaged；[过去分词] damaged

n. ❶损害；损失[U]

The earthquake caused great damage.

地震造成了极大的损害。

❷赔偿金[P]

She has not got any damages.

她没有得到任何赔偿金。

vt. 损害，毁坏

A lot of houses were damaged by the flood.

许多房子被洪水毁坏了。

damp〔dæmp ‖ dæmp〕

a. 有湿气的；潮湿的

"It's damp and cold."

"天气又湿又冷。"

"I think it's going to rain."

"我看要下雨。"

〔同义〕wet 湿的

〔反义〕dry 干的

dance〔dæns ‖ dɑːns〕

[过去式]danced；[过去分词] danced

vi. ❶跳舞，舞蹈

The villagers danced in the open.

村民们在露天跳舞。

❷手舞足蹈

n. ❶跳舞，舞蹈［C］

❷舞会［C］

We went to a dance last night.

我们昨夜去参加舞会了。

词汇拓展

dancer *n.* 舞者

舞蹈
dance

danger〔'dendʒɚ || 'deɪndʒə〕

n. ❶ 危险［U］［(＋of/to)］

He is in danger of losing his job if he goes on like this.

他再这样下去会丢掉工作的。

❷危险(物)；威胁［C］［(＋of/to)］

They regard overpopulation as a danger to society.

他们把人口过剩看成是对社会的威胁。

dangerous〔'dendʒərəs || 'deɪndʒərəs〕

a. 危险的；不安全的；招致危险的［＋to-v］

It is dangerous to swim here.

在这儿游泳危险。

dare〔dɛr || deə〕

［过去式］dared；［过去分词］dared

v. aux. 敢；竟敢

How dare you ask me such a question?

你怎敢问我这样的问题？

vt. ❶敢；胆敢［＋to-v］

He did not dare to leave his car there.

他不敢把车停放在那里。

❷挑逗，激

I dare you to cheat me.

谅你也不敢欺骗我。

❸敢于面对，敢冒(险)

She dared the anger of her father.

她不怕惹她父亲发火。

dark〔dɑrk || dɑːk〕

［比］darker；［最］darkest

a. ❶暗；黑暗的

It's getting dark.

天快黑了。

❷(颜色)深的，浅黑的；(皮肤等)微黑的

There are dark clouds in the sky.
天空乌云密布。
❸隐藏的，隐秘的
He kept it dark.
他隐瞒那事。
n. ❶黑暗，暗处
She could see nothing in the dark.
她在黑暗中什么也看不见。
❷黑夜；黄昏，傍晚[U]

常用短语

in the dark ❶在黑暗中 ❷不知道 ❸秘密地

darling [ˈdɑrlɪŋ || ˈdɑːlɪŋ]
n. [C]❶ 心爱的人，宠儿
❷(用作称呼)亲爱的(人)
Darling, would you please wait a second?
亲爱的，请稍等片刻。

date [det || deɪt]
n. [C] ❶日期，日子
What ' s the date today? = What day of the month is it today?
今天几号？[What day is it today? 是问星期几]
❷年代，时期
out of date
过时的；落伍的
up to date
最新的
❸约会
I'll have a date tonight.
今晚我有个约会。

> 日期的写法：July 4, 1998 或 4(th) July, 1998 在非正式写法中，也可简单并列数字：7/25/98 或 25/7/98 表示 1998 年 7 月 25 日
>
> **用法工具箱**

daughter [ˈdɔtɚ || ˈdɔːtə]
n. 女儿[C]
daughter-in-law 媳妇

dawn [dɔn || dɔːn]
n. [C][U]❶黎明，拂晓
We must get up at dawn.
我们必须天一亮就起来。
❷开端；曙光，端倪[(+of)]
the dawn of civilization
文明的开端

day [de || deɪ]
n. ❶ 一天(24 小时)，日[C]
"What day is it today?"
"今天星期几？"
"It's Monday."
"今天星期一。"
❷白昼，白天；黎明[C][U]

D

He is seldom at home during the day.
他白天很少在家。
〔反义〕night 黑夜
❸工作日[C]
We work an 8-hour day.
我们一天工作 8 小时。
❹时代,时期[P]
❺(常与 his,their 等连用)成名时期,全盛时期
Everybody has his day.
人人都有全盛时期。

D

常用短语

day off 休息日
I have a day off in a week.
我一周休息一天。
day after day 日复一日
It rained day after day.
天天下雨。
day and night 日日夜夜地
He worked day and night.
他日夜工作。
day by day 一天天
It's getting colder day by day.
天气一天天冷起来。
every other day 每隔一天
one day (过去)某一天;(将来)有一天
some day 总有一天
the day after tomorrow 后天
the day before yesterday 前天
the good old days 过去的好时光

dead 〔dɛd ‖ ded〕
a. ❶死的;枯的
It is a dead volcano.
那是座死火山。
❷已废的,不用的
❸无效的,失效的
Our radio receiver went dead.
我们的无线电接收机失灵了。
❹完全的,全然的
There was a dead calm after the announcement.
宣布后紧接着是一片寂静。
ad. 突然地,完全地
The deer stopped dead in her tracks.
这头鹿突然停住了。

deaf 〔dɛf ‖ def〕
a. ❶聋的
She is deaf in one ear.
她一只耳朵是聋的。
❷不愿听的[(+to)]
He was deaf to her warning.
他不听她的警告。

deal 〔dil ‖ diːl〕
[过去式]dealt;[过去分词]dealt
vi. ❶经营;交易[(+in/with)]
[经营物品时用 in,与人交易用 with]
This store deals in silk.

这家店经营丝绸。
❷论及；讨论[(＋with/in)]
❸处理，对付；对待[(＋with)]
He knows how to deal with children.
他知道怎么对付孩子。
n. ❶交易[C]
It was probably the best business deal I ever did.
那也许是我曾经做过的最好的一笔生意。
❷数量，大量[(＋of)]
He had given this question a great deal of thought.
他对这个问题做过许多思考。

dear 〔dɪr ‖ dɪə〕
[比]dearer；[最]dearest
a. ❶亲爱的；可爱的
She spoke of me as her dearest friend.
她说我是她最亲爱的朋友。
❷(常大写)(信头称谓)亲爱的，尊敬的
Dear Mr. Smith
亲爱的/尊敬的史密斯先生
❸珍贵的，宝贵的，珍视的[(＋to)]
Money is very dear to him.
他很看重钱。
int. 哎呀
Oh dear! I forgot to post the letter.
哎呀！我忘了寄信。

death 〔dɛθ ‖ deθ〕
n. ❶死，死亡[C][U]
It was a matter of life and death to them.
对他们来说，这是生死攸关的事情。
❷致死的原因[C][(＋of)]
Drinking was the death of him.
他因饮酒而死。
❸(常大写)死神[U]

debate 〔dɪˈbet ‖ dɪˈbeɪt〕
[过去式]debated；[过去分词]debated
n. ❶辩论，讨论，争论[U]
close a debate
结束辩论
❷辩论会[C]
vt. ❶辩论，讨论，争论
They debated the problem.
他们讨论了该问题。
❷与……辩论
vi. 辩论，讨论，争论
They were debating on his plan.
他们正讨论他的计划。

debt 〔dɛt ‖ det〕
n. ❶债，借款[C]
He has a lot of old debts to meet.

他有许多旧债要偿还。

❷恩义，情义[C]

The debt that he owed her could never be paid.

他欠她的情永远也还不了。

❸负债[U]

It's much easier to get into debt than to get out of debt.

借债容易还债难。

decade [ˈdɛked ‖ ˈdekeɪd]

n. 十，十年

The world will greatly change in the next few decades.

世界在未来的几十年间将有巨大的变化。

December [dɪˈsɛmbɚ ‖ dɪˈsembə]

n. 略作 Dec. 十二月

Dec.-表示"十"之意。从三月（古罗马历之年始）算起的第十个月

用法工具箱

decide [dɪˈsaɪd ‖ dɪˈsaɪd]

[过去式]decided；[过去分词]decided

vt. 决定；决意[＋wh-][＋to-v][＋(that)]

They decided that John must stay there.

他们决定约翰必须留在那里。

vi. 决定[(＋on/for/against)]

She decided on going there.

她决定去那里。

decision [dɪˈsɪʒən ‖ dɪˈsɪʒən]

n. ❶决定，决心；判断；结论[C][U]

It was a sudden decision.

这是一个突然的决定。

❷果断，决心[U]

My father lacks decision.

我父亲缺乏果断。

declaration [ˌdɛkləˈreʃən ‖ ˌdekləˈreɪʃən]

n. 宣布，宣告；宣言，声明[C][U]

a declaration of war

宣战(书)

the Declaration of Independence

(1776 年 7 月 14 日发表的美国)独立宣言

declare [dɪˈklɛr ‖ dɪˈkleə]

[过去式]declared；[过去分词]declared

vt. ❶宣布，宣告；声明

The U. S. declared her independence in 1776.

美国在 1776 年宣告独立。

❷宣称；断言

He declared himself innocent.

他声称自己是无辜的。

decrease[1] 〔dɪˈkris ‖ dɪˈkriːs〕

[过去式]decreased; [过去分词]decreased

vi. 减;减少,减小

The population began to decrease.

人口开始减少。

vt. 减;减少,减小

The driver was decreasing the speed of the train.

司机正减慢火车的速度。

decrease[2] 〔ˈdikris ‖ ˈdɪkriːs〕

n. 减少,减小;减少额,减小量[C][U][(+in/of)]

There has been a decrease in the number of students this year.

今年学生人数已减少。

deed 〔did ‖ diːd〕

n. 行为,行动[C] [do 的名词形式]

Deeds are fruits, words are but leaves.

言语是绿叶,行为结硕果。

deep 〔dip ‖ diːp〕

[比]deeper; [最]deepest

a. ❶深的,(用于数字以后)有……深的

The snow is 3 feet deep.

雪有 3 英尺深。

❷(颜色)深的,浓的,(声音)深沉的

She gave a deep sigh.

她深深地叹了口气。

ad. 深深地

The explorers went deep into the jungle.

探险家们进入丛林深处。

词汇拓展

deeply *ad.* 深深地[用于比喻]

deer 〔dɪr ‖ dɪə〕

n. 鹿[C]

〈雄鹿是 stag, buck, 雌鹿是 hind, doe, 幼鹿是 fawn〉

defeat 〔dɪˈfit ‖ dɪˈfiːt〕

[过去式]defeated; [过去分词]defeated

vt. ❶战胜,击败

The French defeated the Eng-

lish troops.
法国人打败了英国军队。
❷使失败,挫败
Our hopes were defeated.
我们的希望落空了。
n. 失败,战败,挫折[C][U]
The aggressors were doomed to defeat.
侵略者注定要失败。

defend 〔dɪˈfɛnd‖dɪˈfend〕
[过去式]defended;[过去分词]defended
vt. ❶防御;保卫;保护
We shall defend our city, whatever the cost may be.
不管代价如何,我们要捍卫我们的城市。
❷【律】为……辩护;作……的辩护律师
She defended herself successfully in court.
她在法庭上成功地为自己作了辩护。
❸为(论文等)答辩

defense,【英】**defence** 〔dɪˈfɛns‖dɪˈfens〕
n. ❶【主美】防御,保卫,防护[U]
The shooting was in pure self-defense.
开枪纯粹是为了自卫。
❷防御物;防御措施[C][(+against)]
The forest will act as a defense against desert dust.
森林能起防御沙漠风沙的作用。
❸防御工事[P]
The defenses of the city must be strengthened.
这个城市的防御工事必须加强。

definite 〔ˈdɛfənɪt‖ˈdefɪnɪt〕
a. ❶明确的,确切的
She made no definite answer.
她没有作明确的回答。
❷一定的,肯定的
It's definite that he'll be late again.
他肯定又要迟到。
❸限定的

definition 〔ˌdɛfəˈnɪʃən‖ˌdefɪˈnɪʃən〕
n. ❶下定义;定义;释义[C][U]
❷限定;定界;规定[C][U]
❸明确性;鲜明性

degree 〔dɪˈgri‖dɪˈgriː〕
n. ❶度,度数[C]
Water freezes at zero degrees Centigrade.
水在零摄氏度结冰。

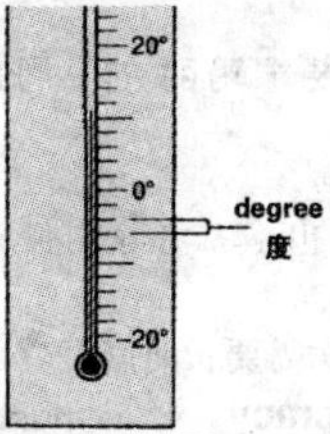

❷程度；等级[C][U]
Our teacher has a high degree of responsibility.
我们的老师有高度的责任感。
❸学位；学衔[C][(＋in)]
He has just got his M. A. degree.
他刚拿到文科硕士学位。

delay 〔dɪˈle ‖ dɪˈleɪ〕
[过去式]delayed；[过去分词]delayed
vt. ❶延缓；使延期
❷耽搁；延误
The accident delayed the train for two hours.
事故使火车耽搁了两小时。
vi. 拖延；耽搁
I'm sorry that I've delayed so long.
我很抱歉拖了这么久。
n. 延迟；耽搁[C][U]
My doctor advised me to give up smoking without delay.
我的医生劝我立即戒烟。

delicious 〔dɪˈlɪʃəs ‖ dɪˈlɪʃəs〕
a. ❶美味的；香喷喷的
The fried chicken is delicious.
这炸鸡味道鲜美。
❷妙的，有趣的
He has bags of delicious stories.
他有许多好听的故事。

delight 〔dɪˈlaɪt ‖ dɪˈlaɪt〕
[过去式]delighted；[过去分词]delighted
n. ❶欣喜，愉快[U]
To our delight, our football team won.
令我们高兴的是，我们的足球队赢了。
❷乐事，乐趣[C]
He enjoyed the delights of New York's night life.
他享受纽约夜生活的乐趣。
vt. 使高兴
I'm delighted that you are back.
你回来了，我很高兴。
vi. 高兴；喜爱；取乐（尤指不愉快的事）[(＋in)]
She delights in scandal.
她对丑闻津津乐道。

deliver 〔dɪˈlɪvɚ ‖ dɪˈlɪvə〕
[过去式]delivered；[过去分词]

D

delivered

vt. ❶投递;传送;运送

The mailman delivered the letters on time.

那个邮差准时地投递信件。

❷发表;讲;宣布

He delivered an important report at the meeting.

他在会上作了重要报告。

❸给……接生;生(婴儿)

She delivered twins last night.

昨天晚上她生了一对双胞胎。

❹解救;解脱;释放[(＋from)]

They delivered the blacks from slavery.

他们使黑人摆脱了奴隶制度。

demand〔dɪˈmænd‖dɪˈmɑːnd〕

[过去式]demanded;[过去分词]demanded

n. ❶要求,请求[C]

They rejected the union's demand.

他们拒绝了工会的要求。

❷需要,需求[U]

The supply of vegetables falls short of demand this year.

今年蔬菜供不应求。

vt. ❶要求,请求[＋to-v][＋that][(＋of)]

The boss demanded that Mary (should) finish it within a week.

老板要求玛丽在一周内完成它。

❷需要

This illness demands a long rest.

这种病需要长时间静养。

democracy〔dəˈmɑkrəsɪ‖dɪˈmɒkrəsɪ〕

n. ❶民主;民主主义;民主制度;民主政体[U]

❷民主国家[C]

A true democracy allows free speech.

真正的民主国家允许言论自由。

❸民众

❹民主精神,民主作风[U]

The principal's democracy made him popular among teachers and students.

校长的民主作风使他受到师生的欢迎。

dense〔dɛns‖dens〕

[比]denser;[最]densest

a. ❶密集的,稠密的

a dense forest

密林

❷(烟,雾等)浓厚的

a dense fog

浓雾

deny 〔dɪˈnaɪ ‖ dɪˈnaɪ〕
［过去式］denied；［过去分词］denied
vt. ❶否定，否认［＋v-ing］［＋(that)］
There is no denying that…
事实不可否认……
❷拒绝给予（应给之物）；拒绝……的要求
Women were then denied the right to vote.
那时妇女被拒给选举权。

depart 〔dɪˈpɑrt ‖ dɪˈpɑːt〕
［过去式］departed；［过去分词］departed
vi.【书】起程，出发；离开，离去
The train departed at 6：15.
火车在6点15分离开。

词汇拓展

departure *n.* 出发

department 〔dɪˈpɑrtmənt ‖ dɪˈpɑːtmənt〕
n. ❶（行政，企业等的）部；司；局；处；科；部门［C］
She's the head of the personnel department.
她是人事部门的负责人。
department store
百货公司，百货商店
❷（大学的）系［C］
the English Department
英文系

depend 〔dɪˈpɛnd ‖ dɪˈpend〕
［过去式］depended；［过去分词］depended
vi. ❶相信；信赖［(＋on/upon)］
I knew he wasn't to be depended upon.
我知道他不可信赖。
❷依靠，依赖［(＋on/upon)］
Health depends on good food, fresh air and enough sleep.
健康依靠的是良好的食物、新鲜的空气和充足的睡眠。
❸依……而定；取决于［(＋on/upon)］
It depends on the weather.
这取决于天气。

常用短语

depend on/upon 依靠；信赖

dependent 〔dɪˈpɛndənt ‖ dɪˈpendənt〕
a. ❶依靠的；依赖的［(＋on/upon)］
A child is dependent on its parents.
小孩子依赖其父母。
❷取决于……的［(on/upon)］
Skill is dependent on practice.

技能要靠练习。

词汇拓展

dependence *n.* 依赖，信赖

depth 〔dεpθ ‖ depθ〕
n. ❶深度，厚度[C][U]
The young man dived to a depth of 40 feet.
那个青年人潜到40英尺的深度。
❷(色泽)浓度；(音的)低沉；(知识等的)深奥；(感情等的)深厚[U]
We have expressed the depth of our gratitude to them.
我们向他们表示了深切的谢意。
❸深处；深渊[P]
Scientists used to believe that there was no life in the depths of the ocean.
科学家过去认为海洋深处没有生物。

descendant 〔dɪˈsεndənt ‖ dɪˈsendənt〕
n. 后裔，子孙[C][(+of)]
〔反义〕ancestor 祖先

describe 〔dɪˈskraɪb ‖ dɪˈskraɪb〕
[过去式]described；[过去分词] described
vt. ❶描写，描绘，叙述
Words cannot describe the beauty of the scene.
语言难以描述那景色之美丽。
❷形容，把……说成[(+as)]
He describes himself as a doctor.
他声称自己是医生。

description 〔dɪˈskrɪpʃən ‖ dɪˈskrɪpʃən〕
n. ❶描写；叙述；形容[C][U]
He gives a full description of the accident.
他对那个意外事件作了详细的描述。
❷(物品)说明书[C]

desert 〔ˈdεzɚt ‖ ˈdezət〕
n. 沙漠；荒野[C][U]
the Sahara Desert
撒哈拉沙漠

deserve 〔dɪˈzɝv ‖ dɪˈzɜːv〕
[过去式]deserved；[过去分词] deserved
vt. 应受，该得[+to-v]
They deserved to be punished.
他们应该受罚。

design 〔dɪˈzaɪn ‖ dɪˈzaɪn〕
[过去式]designed；[过去分词] designed
vt. ❶设计；构思；绘制
Who designed the dress?

谁设计了这件衣服?
❷打算将……用作
The experiment is designed to test the new drug.
实验的目的是试验新药。
❸计划;谋划
n. ❶图样,图纸[C][U]
❷设计术;制图术[U]
She attended a school of dress design.
她就读于一所服装设计学校。
❸图案;花纹[C]
I like the design of that rug.
我喜欢那块地毯的图案。
❹意图;计划;目的[C]
The design was to build a new library.
计划是建造一个新图书馆。

词汇拓展

designer *n.* 设计者

desire 〔dɪˈzaɪr ‖ dɪˈzaɪə〕
[过去式]desired;[过去分词]desired
vt. 渴望;要求[+to-v][+that]
He desired us to leave soon.
他希望我们尽快离开。
n. ❶欲望,渴望[C][U][(+for)][+to-v]
I have no desire to discuss the question.
我不想讨论这个问题。
❷渴望的东西;渴望的人
He brought me my heart's desire.
他给我带来了我心里渴望的东西。

desk 〔dɛsk ‖ desk〕
n. [C]❶书桌;办公桌;写字台
He was sitting at his desk when I went in.
我走进去时他坐在桌前。
❷柜台;服务台

destroy 〔dɪˈstrɔɪ ‖ dɪˈstrɔɪ〕
[过去式]destroyed;[过去分词]destroyed
vt. ❶毁坏,破坏
A fire destroyed the house.
一场火毁坏了那座房屋。
❷杀死,消灭
❸打破(希望,计划);使失败
What he said destroyed our last hope.
他所说的话摧毁了我们最后的希望。

detail 〔ˈditel ‖ ˈdiːteɪl〕
n. ❶细节;详情;琐事;枝节[C]
He can probably tell us all the details we want.
他也许能告诉我们所需的全部

详情。

❷述；细部；局部[U]

She began to tell me the plot in great detail.

她开始告诉我该阴谋的细节。

常用短语

in detail 详细地

detective 〔dɪˈtɛktɪv ‖ dɪˈtektɪv〕

n. 侦探；私家侦探[C]

a. ❶侦探的

❷侦查用的；探测用的

determination 〔dɪˌtɝməˈneʃən ‖ dɪˌtɜːmɪˈneɪʃən〕

n. ❶坚定；果断，决断力[U]

My father was a man of determination.

我父亲是一个果断的人。

❷决心，确定[U][＋to-v]

She has the determination to overcome all the difficulties.

她有决心克服一切困难。

determine 〔dɪˈtɝmɪn ‖ dɪˈtɜːmɪn〕

[过去式]determined；[过去分词]determined

vt. ❶决定[＋to-v][＋(that)]

She determined to go that afternoon.

她决定就在那天下午走。

❷使决定，使下决心

My mom's encouragement determined me to go on with my study.

我母亲的鼓励使我决心继续学业。

develop 〔dɪˈvɛləp ‖ dɪˈveləp〕

[过去式]developed；[过去分词]developed

vt. ❶使成长；使发达；发展

Swimming develops the muscles.

游泳能使肌肉发达。

❷详尽阐述；展开

❸开发

The builders are developing that part of the city.

建筑商正在开发这座城市的那个地区。

❹逐渐生成；逐渐养成；患(病)

Try to develop good reading habits.

要养成良好的阅读习惯。

❺【摄】使显影，冲洗(底片)

vi. ❶生长；成长；形成

Plants develop from seeds.

植物由种子发育而成。

❷进步；进化

❸发展

Her friendship with David developed slowly.

她与戴维的友谊发展缓慢。

development 〔dɪˈvɛləpmənt ‖

dɪˈveləpmənt〕
n. 生长；发展；开发[C][U]
physical development
身体发育

devote〔dɪˈvot ‖ dɪˈvəʊt〕
[过去式]devoted；[过去分词] devoted
vt. ❶将……奉献（给）[(＋to)]
He devoted himself to writing.
他专心写作。
❷把……专用（于）[(＋to)]

dew〔dju ‖ djuː〕
n. 露，露水，（泪，汗等的）珠，滴[U]

dial〔ˈdaɪəl ‖ ˈdaɪəl〕
[过去式]dialed；[过去分词]dialed
n. [C] ❶表盘；钟盘
❷（电话机的）拨号盘
vt. vi. 拨（电话号码）；打电话给
He dialed 110 at once.
他立刻打电话给 110。

dialect〔ˈdaɪəlɛkt ‖ ˈdaɪəlekt〕
n. 方言，土话[C][U]
the Scottish dialect
苏格兰方言

dialogue〔ˈdaɪəˌlɔg ‖ ˈdaɪəlɔːg〕
n. [C][U] ❶对话；会话，（国家等之间的）对话，意见交换
❷（戏剧、小说等中的）对话，对白，对话体
The novel is written in dialogue.
这部小说是用对话体写的。

diamond〔ˈdaɪəmənd ‖ ˈdaɪəmənd〕
n. ❶钻石，金刚钻[C][U]
She wore her diamonds to the party.
她戴着钻石首饰去参加宴会。
❷菱形[C]
❸（纸牌）方块，一张方块牌[C]

diary〔ˈdaɪərɪ ‖ ˈdaɪərɪ〕
n. [C] ❶日记，日志；日记簿
He keeps a diary in English.
他用英语写日记。
❷日程安排登记簿

dictation〔dɪkˈteʃən ‖ dɪkˈteɪʃən〕
n. ❶口述；听写[U]
The teacher gave dictation to the class.
老师叫全班听写。
❷口授（或听写）的文字[C]

dictionary〔ˈdɪkʃənˌɛrɪ ‖ ˈdɪkʃənərɪ〕
n. 字典，辞典[C]
Look it up in your dictionary.
在你的字典上查它。

die〔daɪ ‖ daɪ〕

[过去式]died;[过去分词]died

vi. ❶死[(＋of/from)]

He died in battle.

他战死疆场。

> 因意外事故而死用 be killed: He was killed in an accident.
> 他死于意外事故。
> die of 用于因癌症、饥饿、衰老而死的场合,如:die of cancer (hunger, old age); die from 用于因伤而死的场合,如:die from wound
>
> **用法工具箱**

❷(草木等)枯萎,凋谢

❸(机器)突然停转

The engine died.

机器熄火了。

❹变弱;平息;消失;熄灭[(＋away/down/out)]

常用短语

die away 逐渐止息;逐渐消失

The noise outside died away.

外面的噪音渐渐消失。

die down 变弱

The storm died down.

暴风雨平静了。

die out 消失

vt. 死于(……状态)[＋a…death]

He died a hero's death.

他英勇牺牲。

die a happy death 善终

diet [ˈdaɪət ‖ ˈdaɪət]

n. ❶日常的饮食[C][U]

My diet is made up of rice and vegetables.

我日常的饮食包括米饭和蔬菜。

❷(适合某种疾病的)特种饮食[C]

No chocolate, please. I'm on a diet.

请不要放巧克力,我在节食。

常用短语

go/be on a diet 节食

difference [ˈdɪfərəns ‖ ˈdɪfərəns]

n. ❶差别,差异[C][(＋between)]

Whether it rains or not makes no difference to me.

下不下雨对我来说都一样。

❷差,差距;差额[(＋between/in)]

The difference in temperature between the day and the night there is 30 degrees.

那里白天与黑夜的温差是30度。

❸争论;不和[P]

That is the root cause of all our differences.

那是我们一切分歧的根源。

常用短语

make no difference 没有关系;没什么影响

different 〔ˈdɪfərənt ‖ ˈdɪfərənt〕

a. ❶不同的[(+ from/than/to)]

Their school is different from ours.

他们的学校与我们的不同。

❷各种的

The delegates come from different parts of the world.

代表们来自世界各地。

词汇拓展

differently *ad.* 不同地

difficult 〔ˈdɪfəˌkʌlt ‖ ˈdɪfɪkəlt〕

a. ❶难,困难的[+to-v]

It's very difficult to swim across the Yangtze River.

游过长江很难。

❷难相处的,不随和的

Mary was a very difficult child.

玛丽过去是一个很难相处的孩子。

❸艰难的,难熬的

The most difficult days are over.

最困难的日子已经过去了。

〔同义〕hard 困难的

difficulty 〔ˈdɪfəˌkʌltɪ ‖ ˈdɪfɪkəltɪ〕

n. ❶困难,艰难[U][(+in)]

I had no difficulty in getting in touch with him.

我和他取得联系没有什么困难。

❷难事,难处,难题[C]

There are a lot of difficulties that have to be overcome.

有许多困难必须克服。

❸(尤指财务上的)困境;危难[P]

The new government is in financial difficulties.

新政府财政困难。

常用短语

be in difficulties 陷入困境

with difficulty 好不容易才……

without difficulty 轻易,毫不困难(= with ease=easily)

dig 〔dɪg ‖ dɪg〕

[过去式]dug;[过去分词]dug

vt. ❶掘(土);挖(洞,沟等),掘取(甘薯等)

D

They are digging a tunnel through the hill.
他们正在挖一条贯通这座山的隧道。
They dug worms for fishing bait.
他们掘蚯蚓做钓饵。
❷发掘，探究
The truth was dug out.
真相被发掘出来。

D

常用短语

dig out ❶发掘到 ❷发现；找出

dignity 〔'dɪgnətɪ ‖ 'dɪgnɪtɪ〕
n. ❶尊严；庄严[U]
❷尊贵；高尚[U]
A man's dignity depends not upon his wealth but upon his character.
人高尚与否不取决于他的财富，而取决于他的品格。
❸高位，显职[C]

diligent 〔'dɪlədʒənt ‖ 'dɪlɪdʒənt〕
a. ❶勤勉的，勤奋的
The Chinese people are a diligent people.
中华民族是一个勤劳的民族。
❷费尽心血的
〔反义〕lazy 懒惰的

dinner 〔'dɪnɚ ‖ 'dɪnə〕
n. ❶晚餐；正餐[C][U]
Mother is busy in preparing dinner.
妈妈正忙着做晚饭。
❷宴会，晚宴[C]
A dinner is to be given in honor of the new president.
将为新校长举行晚宴。
a dinner party
晚宴
a dinner table
餐桌

dip 〔dɪp ‖ dɪp〕
[过去式]dipped；[过去分词]dipped
vt. vi. 浸一下
She dipped her finger in the water to see if it's hot.
她把手指浸入水中，看水热不热。
The gull dipped in the ocean.
海鸥掠过海面。

diploma 〔dɪ'plomə ‖ dɪ'pləumə〕
n. [C] ❶毕业文凭，学位证书
❷执照，特许证
❸文书，公文，奖状

direct 〔də'rɛkt ‖ dɪ'rekt〕
[比]more direct；[最]most direct；[过去式]directed；[过去分词]directed
vt. ❶将(注意力，谈话等)指向[(＋to/at)]
His remarks were not directed

at you.
他的话不是针对你的。
❷指挥；主持；管理
She personally directs the operations of the company.
她亲自指挥公司的运作。
❸命令；指示
His boss directed him to cancel the meeting.
他的老板指示他取消这次会议。
❹导演；指挥（演奏）
❺给……指路；指点［（＋to）］
vi. 指导，指挥
a. ❶径直的，笔直的，直接的
He took a direct flight to New York.
他直飞纽约。
She is in direct contact with the general manager.
她与总经理直接联系。
❷直截了当的；率直的
He avoided a direct answer.
他避免直接回答。
ad. 笔直地；直接地；直达地
He went direct to the airport.
他直接去机场。

direction 〔dəˈrɛkʃən ‖ dɪˈrekʃən〕
n. ❶方向；方位［C］［U］
He drove in the direction of the farm.
他向该农场方向驶去。
❷指导；指挥；管理［U］
Our company is under good direction.
我们公司管理有方。
❸指示；用法说明［P］
Read the directions on the bottle carefully.
请仔细阅读瓶上的说明。

directly 〔dəˈrɛktlɪ ‖ dɪˈrektlɪ〕
ad. ❶直接地；笔直地，坦率地，直截了当地
He is not directly responsible.
他没有直接责任。
❷即刻，马上
He took the medicine directly.
他即刻服了药。

director 〔dəˈrɛktɚ ‖ dɪˈrektə〕
n.［C］❶主管；署长；局长；处长；主任
❷董事；经理
❸（电影等的）导演
❹【主美】【音】指挥

dirt 〔dɝt ‖ dəːt〕
n.［U］❶污物；烂泥；灰尘
Wash that dirt off your hands.
把你手上的脏东西洗掉。
❷泥，土
❸无价值的东西
He treats her like dirt.

他待她如敝屣。

❹色情描写;下流话

dirty ['dɝtɪ ‖ 'dɜːtɪ]

[比]dirtier;[最]dirtiest

a. ❶脏的,污秽的

His mother scolded him for getting his clothes dirty.

他的妈妈因他弄脏了衣服而责骂他。

❷猥亵的,下流的

They were drinking and telling dirty jokes.

他们一边喝酒,一边说着黄色笑话。

disadvantage [ˌdɪsəd'væntɪdʒ ‖ ˌdɪsəd'væntɪdʒ]

n. [C][U]❶不利条件

His lack of education was a disadvantage when he looked for a job.

他缺少教育,这在找工作时是一个不利条件。

❷不利;损失,损害

Not studying will be to your disadvantage.

不学习将对你不利。

disagree [ˌdɪsə'gri ‖ ˌdɪsə'griː]

[过去式]disagreed;[过去分词]disagreed

vi. ❶不一致,不符[(+with)],意见不合;有分歧[(+with/on)]

Our answers to the problem disagreed.

我们对这个问题的回答不一致。

We disagreed on which movie to see.

我们对看哪一部电影意见不一致。

❷(食物,天气等)不适宜,有害[(+with)]

The climate disagreed with me.

我不适应这里的气候。

disappear [ˌdɪsə'pɪr ‖ ˌdɪsə'pɪə]

[过去式]disappeared;[过去分词]disappeared

vi. ❶消失,不见;突然离开

All at once Phil disappeared.

菲尔突然不见了。

❷不复存在,灭绝

The dinosaurs disappeared long ago.

恐龙很久以前就绝种了。

disappoint [ˌdɪsə'pɔɪnt ‖ ˌdɪsə'pɔɪnt]

[过去式]disappointed;[过去分词]disappointed

vt. ❶使失望

He was disappointed that other guests were not coming.

其他客人没有来,他感到失望。

❷使(希望等)破灭,挫败
This disappointed his plans.
这件事打乱了他的计划。

discipline 〔ˈdɪsəplɪn ‖ ˈdɪsɪplɪn〕
n. ❶纪律,教养;训练,修养[U]
Discipline is necessary for young people.
训练对年轻人是必要的。
❷惩戒,惩罚[U]
❸【宗】教规,戒律[U]
❹学科[C]

discourage 〔dɪsˈkɝɪdʒ ‖ dɪsˈkʌrɪdʒ〕
[过去式]discouraged;[过去分词]discouraged
vt. 使泄气,使沮丧
〔反义〕encourage 鼓励

常用短语

discourage… from… 使某人打消念头
The doctor's advice discouraged him from smoking.
医生的忠告使他不敢再抽烟。

discover 〔dɪˈskʌvɚ ‖ dɪˈskʌvə〕
[过去式]discovered;[过去分词]discovered
vt. ❶发现
Who discovered America in 1492?
是谁在1492年发现了美洲大陆的?
❷发觉;找到
The lost bike was discovered at the bus stop.
丢了的自行车在公共汽车站那儿找到了。
〔同义〕find out 发现

discovery 〔dɪˈskʌvərɪ ‖ dɪsˈkʌvərɪ〕
n. ❶发现[C][U][(+of)][+that]
Dr. Fleming's discovery of penicillin occurred in 1928.
弗莱明医生发现青霉素是在1928年。
❷被发现的事物[C]
New scientific discoveries are being made every day.
科学上,每天都有新的发现。

discuss 〔dɪˈskʌs ‖ dɪˈskʌs〕
[过去式]discussed;[过去分词]discussed
vt. 讨论,商谈;论述,详述[(+with)][+wh-]
They discussed how to promote cooperation between the two countries.
他们讨论如何促进两国之间的合作。

discussion 〔dɪˈskʌʃən ‖ dɪˈskʌʃən〕

n. 讨论，商讨；谈论[C][U][(+about/on/over)]
We had a discussion on language and communication.
我们就语言和交际问题进行了讨论。

disease 〔dɪ'ziz ‖ dɪ'ziːz〕
n. 病，疾病[C][U]
a heart disease
心脏病

dish 〔dɪʃ ‖ dɪʃ〕
n. [C] ❶碟，盘[指盛数份食物的大盘；各人使用的扁平的碟是 plate]
Mary put the peaches in a white dish.
玛丽将桃子装在一个白盘子里。

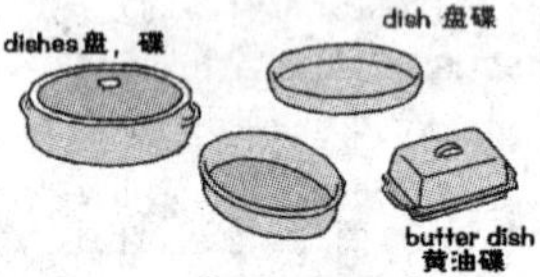

❷一盘菜；菜肴
Fried eggs are my favorite dish.
煎蛋是我最喜爱的菜。
❸(用过的所有)餐具[the P]
I'll do the dishes tonight.
今晚我洗餐具。

disk, disc 〔dɪsk ‖ dɪsk〕
n. 圆盘；唱片；【计算机】磁盘[C]

比赛用的圆盘是 a discus(铁饼)；飞行于空中的圆盘是 a flying saucer(飞碟，不明飞行物)

用法工具箱

dislike 〔dɪs'laɪk ‖ dɪs'laɪk〕
[过去式]disliked；[过去分词]disliked
vt. 不喜爱，厌恶[+v-ing]
People dislike being stared at.
人们不喜欢被人盯着看。
n. 不喜爱，厌恶[C][U]
Everybody has his likes and dislikes.
人人都有所好和所恶。

常用短语

have a dislike of/for 不喜欢；讨厌
take a dislike to 开始讨厌

dismiss 〔dɪs'mɪs ‖ dɪs'mɪs〕
[过去式]dismissed；[过去分词]dismissed
vt. ❶解散，遣散
The school was dismissed at noon.
学校在中午放学。

❷免……的职；解雇；开除

Twenty men were dismissed.

20人被解雇。

词汇拓展

dismissal *n.* 解雇，解散

display 〔dɪ'sple ‖ dɪ'spleɪ〕

[过去式]displayed；[过去分词] displayed

vt. ❶陈列；展出

The cakes were displayed in the shop window.

糕点陈列在橱窗中。

❷显；表现；显露

He displayed interest in music.

他对音乐有兴趣。

❸炫耀，夸示

n. ❶展览，陈列；表演[C][U]

Children enjoy a fireworks display.

孩子们喜爱看烟火。

❷陈列品，展览品[C]

❸显示，表现，炫耀[C][U]

He made a display of his learning.

他夸耀自己有学问。

常用短语

on display 展览

distance 〔'dɪstəns ‖ 'dɪstəns〕

n. ❶ 距离；路程[C][U][(+ to/from/between)]

It is a long distance from New York to Hong Kong.

纽约离香港很远。

❷远处

They saw a few houses in the distance.

他们看到远处有几所房子。

❸冷淡，疏远[C][U]

Her father advised her to keep her distance from that fellow.

她父亲劝她疏远那家伙。

常用短语

at a distance 有相当的距离；不很近

The picture looks beautiful at a distance.

这幅画远距离看很美。

in the distance 在远处

There is a mountain in the distance.

远处有座山。

keep one's distance from 疏远；与……保持距离

keep somebody at a distance 对某人保持疏远

distant 〔'dɪstənt ‖ 'dɪstənt〕

a. ❶远的；久远的；远离的[(+ from)]

The sun is distant from the earth.

D

太阳距地球很遥远。

❷非近亲的，远亲的

He is my distant relative.

他是我的远房亲戚。

❸冷淡的，疏远的

She's always very distant with Ann.

她对安总是很冷淡。

D

distinguish 〔dɪ'stɪŋgwɪʃ ‖ dɪ'stɪŋgwɪʃ〕

[过去式]distinguished；[过去分词]distinguished

vt. ❶区别；识别[(＋from)]

He can distinguish a genuine antique from a reproduction.

他能区别真正的古董与复制品。

❷(凭感觉器官)辨认出

I can distinguish my roommates by their footsteps.

我能根据室友的脚步声辨认出他们。

vi. 区别；识别；辨别[(＋between)]

It is certainly important to distinguish between right and wrong.

明辨是非当然要紧。

常用短语

distinguish from 区分；辨别

district 〔'dɪstrɪkt ‖ 'dɪstrɪkt〕

n. [C] ❶区，辖区，行政区

❷地区，区域，地带

The city has several shopping districts.

这个城市有几个商店区。

distrust 〔dɪs'trʌst ‖ dɪs'trʌst〕

[过去式]distrusted；[过去分词]distrusted

vt. 不信任；怀疑

〔反义〕trust 相信

n. 不信任；怀疑

He has a distrust of science.

他不相信科学。

disturb 〔dɪ'stɝb ‖ dɪ'stɜːb〕

[过去式]disturbed；[过去分词]disturbed

vt. ❶妨碍，打扰

I am sorry to disturb you so early.

对不起，我这么早打扰你。

❷扰乱，搞乱

They were charged with disturbing the public peace.

他们被指控扰乱公共治安。

❸使心神不宁

She was disturbed to hear you had been injured in the accident.

听到你在事故中受了伤她感到不安。

vi. 打扰，妨碍

dive〔daɪv ‖ daɪv〕

[过去式]dived, dove;[过去分词]dived

vi. ❶跳水[(+in/off/into/from)]

He dived from the diving board.

他从跳板上跳水。

❷潜水[(+down/for)]

She dived for pearls.

她潜水采珍珠。

n. [C]跳水，潜水，俯冲，扑向，急剧下降

divide〔dəˈvaɪd ‖ dɪˈvaɪd〕

[过去式]divided;[过去分词]divided

vt. ❶分，划分[(+into/from)]

The teacher divided our class into 4 groups.

老师把我们班分成4个小组。

❷分发；分享[(+between/among/with)]

The children divided up the candy among themselves.

孩子们把糖果分吃了。

❸分配[(+between)]

❹【数】除[(+by/into)]

12 divided by 4 equals 3.

12除以4等于3。

vi. ❶分开

We divided into two groups.

我们分成两组。

❷分裂；意见分歧

The Board of Directors divided on the new project.

董事会对这个新计划意见不同。

do[1]〔du ‖ duː〕

[过去式]did;[过去分词]done

vt. ❶做，干，制作；实行

I have nothing to do.

我无事可做。

❷(因受词而含有特殊意义)

do the dishes

洗碗

do one's hair

梳头

do a puzzle

解谜

do sb. a favour

给人帮忙

vi. ❶做，行动

Do as you are required.

按要求去做。

❷进行，进展[+well/badly]

My son does well in school.

我儿子学业顺利。

常用短语

do away with 废除；去掉

They did away with the law.

他们废除了这项法律。

do well ❶进展良好 ❷最好还

是……

do with ❶相处 ❷忍受 ❸处理；对待

do without ❶没有……也行 ❷设法对付过去；将就

do^{2}〔du ‖ du:〕

［否］don't〔dont ‖ dəʊnt〕；doesn't〔ˈdʌzn̩t ‖ ˈdʌznt〕；didn't〔ˈdɪdn̩t ‖ ˈdɪdnt〕

v. aux. ❶（构成疑问句，否定句本身没有词义；或用来构成附加疑问句）

You don't like pop music, do you?

你不喜欢流行音乐，对吗？

❷（构成强调句）

Do come, please.

请一定来。

❸（构成倒装句）

Little did he think he would win.

他根本没料到他会赢。

❹（代替动词）

"Do you like it?"

"你喜欢吗？"

"Yes, I do."

"是的，我喜欢。"

dock〔dɑk ‖ dɒk〕

n. ❶码头；港区

❷船渠；船坞

doctor〔ˈdɑktɚ ‖ ˈdɒktə〕

n.［C］❶医生，医师，大夫

You must see a doctor.

你一定得去看医生。

> doctor 各科医生；physician 内科医生；surgeon 外科医生
>
> **用法工具箱**

❷博士

Mr. Smith is a Doctor of laws.

史密斯先生是法学博士。

> bachelor 学士，a Bachelor of Arts（文学士）；master 硕士，a Master of Science（理科硕士）
>
> **用法工具箱**

document〔ˈdɑkjəmənt ‖ ˈdɒkjʊmənt〕

n.［C］❶公文，文件

❷证件，单据

does〔dʌz ‖ dʌz〕

（do 的第三人称单数现在式）

dog〔dɔg ‖ dɒg〕

n. 狗［C］

He keeps a dog to guard the house.

他养一条狗看家。

doll 〔dɑl ‖ dɒl〕
n. [C] ❶玩偶,洋娃娃
The little girl is playing with a doll.
小女孩正在玩洋娃娃。
❷美貌却不聪明的女人

dollar 〔ˈdɑlɚ ‖ ˈdɒlə〕
n. [C] ❶(美,加等国)元
They spent over one million dollars on the campaign.
他们花了一百多万美元竞选。
❷一元纸币;一元硬币

done 〔dʌn ‖ dʌn〕
(do 的过去分词)

donkey 〔ˈdɑŋkɪ ‖ ˈdɒŋkɪ〕
n. [C] ❶驴
❷傻瓜,蠢驴
❸顽固的人,犟驴

don't 〔dont ‖ dəunt〕
=do not

door 〔dor ‖ dɔː〕
n. [C] ❶门,门口;出入口
He left the door open.
他把门开着。
A salesman was standing at the door.
一个推销员站在门口。
❷家,户,门面
She lived 5 doors from Jane.
她住的地方与简隔 5 家。

常用短语

out of doors 在露天;在户外

doorbell 〔ˈdorˌbɛl ‖ ˈdɔːbel〕
n. 门铃[C]

dormitory 〔ˈdɔrməˌtorɪ ‖ ˈdɔːmɪtərɪ〕
n. [C] ❶大寝室,团体寝室
❷【美】(学院等的)学生宿舍

double 〔ˈdʌbḷ ‖ ˈdʌbl〕
a. ❶两倍的;加倍的
I'll give you double pay for working overtime.
你加班我付你双倍工钱。
❷两人用的,双人的
We reserved a double room.
我们订了一间双人房。
❸(意义,标准等)双重的
The date had a double significance.
那个日子有双重意义。

ad. 双倍地;加倍地

Be double careful when you cross the street.

你过街时要加倍小心。

n. 两倍(数或量),加倍[U]

His pay is the double of mine.

他的工资是我的两倍。

doubt 〔daut ‖ daut〕

D

[过去式]doubted;[过去分词]doubted

vt. 怀疑;不相信;不能肯定[+whether/if][+that]

I doubt whether Tom has taken my watch.

我不太相信汤姆拿了我的手表。

〈肯定句通常接 whether/ if;否定、疑问句后接 that〉

I doubted whether/if the story was true.

我怀疑这故事是否真实。

I don't doubt that he will help me.

我相信他会帮助我。

vi. 怀疑[(+of/about)]

They doubted of the feasibility of the project.

他们对这个计划的可行性表示怀疑。

n. ❶怀疑,不相信[C][U][(+about)][+whether/if]

❷疑问,不确实[U]

The outcome of the election remains in doubt.

选举的结果仍然不能肯定。

❸疑虑[P]

We are trying to dispel his doubts.

我们正试图消除他的疑虑。

doubt…不以为是真的;不信 I doubt him. 我怀疑他说的话(他的为人)。suspect…猜疑;觉得可疑 I suspect him. 我觉得他可疑。

用法工具箱

常用短语

in doubt 不能肯定的;可怀疑的

no doubt 无疑地;的确;可能

without (a) doubt 无疑地

dove 〔dʌv ‖ dʌv〕

n. 鸽(常被视为和平的象征)[C]

A dove is cooing.
鸽子在咕咕叫。

down 〔daʊn ‖ daʊn〕

ad. ❶(动) 向下
Sit down, please.
请坐。
❷(静) 在下面
The sun was already down.
太阳已经下山了。
❸向南方;在南方
The ship sailed down south.
船向南航行。
❹(程度,数量等)减少,减弱

prep. ❶往……下方;在……下方;位于较低处
Their house is half-way down the hill.
他们的房子坐落在半山腰。
❷在……尽头;沿着
Walk directly down the road and you'll get to the square.
沿这条路一直走,你能到广场。
❸往……的下游;位于……的下游
They floated down the river.
他们沿河向下游漂去。

downstairs 〔'daʊn'stɛrz ‖ ˌdaʊn'steəz〕

ad. 在楼下;往楼下
He went downstairs to lunch.
他下楼吃午餐。

downtown 〔'daʊn'taʊn ‖ ˌdaʊn'taʊn〕

ad. 在(或往)城市的商业区
They went downtown to see a film.
他们进城去看电影。
n. 城市商业区,闹区[C]

dozen 〔'dʌzn̩ ‖ 'dʌzn〕

n. ❶ 一打,十二个[C]
These eggs are $2 a dozen.
这些鸡蛋一打卖两美元。
❷几十,许多[P][(+of)]

Dr.

abbr. = Doctor〈冠于姓、姓名之前〉
Dr. Hu (shih)
胡适博士

dragon 〔'drægən ‖ 'drægən〕

n. 龙[C]

龙 dragon

drama 〔'dræmə ‖ 'drɑːmə〕

n. (一出)戏,戏剧;剧本[C]

draw 〔drɔ ‖ drɔː〕

［过去式］drew；［过去分词］drawn

vt. ❶画，绘制，描写

He drew a picture on the wall.

他在墙上画画。

❷拉，拖；拉长，拖长

The cart was drawn by two horses.

大车由两匹马拉着。

❸拔（出）；汲取；引出［（＋from）］

He drew the cork from the bottle.

他把瓶口的软木塞拔了出来。

❹吸引；招来

Her beauty drew everybody's attention.

她的美貌吸引了每个人的注意。

vi. ❶画图

She draws well.

她很会画画。

❷渐渐移动；行驶

The car drew near.

汽车开近了。

drawer 〔ˈdrɔr ‖ ˈdrɔː(r)〕

n. 抽屉［C］

I put it in the left-hand drawer.

我将它放在左手的抽屉内。

drawing 〔ˈdrɔɪŋ ‖ ˈdrɔːɪŋ〕

n. ❶描绘，素描；制图［U］

❷图画；图形［C］

〈用颜料绘的画是 painting；素描，线条画是 drawing〉

dream 〔drim ‖ driːm〕

［过去式］dreamed，dreamt；［过去分词］dreamed，dreamt

n. ❶梦［C］

I had a bad dream last night.

昨天夜里我做了一个噩梦。

❷白日梦；幻想，空想［C］

Sophie lives in a dream.

索菲生活在梦幻之中。

❸理想，愿望［C］

He realized the dream of his lifetime.

他实现了他毕生的愿望。

vt. 做(梦)［＋a…dream］；梦见［＋that］

She dreamed that she could fly.

她梦见她会飞。

vi. ❶做梦；梦见，梦到［（＋of/about）］

I dreamed about my native village.

我梦见我的家乡。

❷梦想；向往［（＋of/about）］

He dreamed of becoming a movie star when he was young.

他年轻时梦想成为电影明星。

常用短语

dream of/about ❶梦见❷梦想；渴望

dress 〔drɛs ‖ dres〕

［过去式］dressed；［过去分词］dressed

vt. ❶ 给……穿衣；打扮；替……做衣服

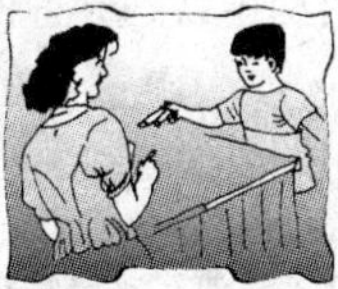

The mother is dressing her baby.

母亲正为婴孩穿衣。

❷使穿着

She is dressed in black today.

今天她穿一身黑。

vi. ❶穿衣；打扮

The girl dresses fashionably.

那个女孩穿着时髦。

❷穿晚礼服

She is dressing for the party.

她在穿礼服准备去参加晚会。

n. ❶女装；连衣裙［C］

All the pretty women wore their smartest dresses.

所有漂亮的女士都穿着自己最漂亮的连衣裙。

❷衣服；(特定的)服装(如民族服装，礼服等)［U］

Few people wore evening dress.

几乎没有人穿晚礼服。

常用短语

dress up (使)穿上盛装

drill〔drɪl ‖ drɪl〕

［过去式］drilled；［过去分词］drilled

n. ❶钻，钻头；钻床；钻机［C］

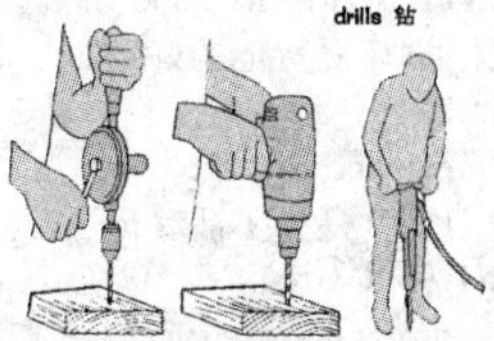

I made a hole with a drill.

我用锥子钻了个孔。

❷操练；训练［U］

vt. ❶钻(孔)；在……上钻孔

❷操练，训练［(+in)］

He drills us in English conversation.

他训练我们学习英语会话。

drink 〔drɪŋk ‖ drɪŋk〕

［过去式］drank；［过去分词］drunk

vt. ❶饮，喝

A horse is drinking water in the stream.

马在溪中饮水。

drink 以 water, tea, wine, milk, coffee 等饮料为受词;喝汤用 eat soup。

用法工具箱

❷举杯祝贺

We all drank his good luck.

我们举杯祝贺他的好运。

vi. ❶饮,喝

We eat and drink to live.

我们饮食是为了活着。

❷干杯[(+to)]

We drank to our success.

我们为我们的成功而干杯。

n. ❶饮料[C][U]

They sell soft drinks only.

他们只卖不含酒精的饮料。

❷酒[U]

He made up his mind never to touch a drop of drink.

他决心不再喝酒。

❸(饮料或酒的)一杯,一口[C]

driver ['draɪvɚ ‖ 'draɪvə]

n. [C]驾驶员,司机;赶车者;马车夫

drop [drɑp ‖ drɒp]

[过去式]dropped;[过去分词]dropped

n. ❶(一)滴[C]

a drop of water

一滴水

❷落下;下降;(水)落差

The drop in prices was quite unexpected.

价格的下跌是完全没有料到的。

vt. ❶使滴下

She dropped some lemon juice into her tea.

她在茶里滴了几滴柠檬汁。

❷丢下,扔下;降低

I dropped the letter into the mailbox.

我将信投入信箱。

vi. ❶滴下;落下;掉下

A flower pot dropped from his window.

一个花盆从他家窗子落下。

❷(价格,温度等)下降;(声音,风等)变弱

The temperature has dropped.

气温已下降。

❸(顺便)访问

I'd like to drop in and see you sometime next week.

我想在下周什么时候顺便来看看你。

drought [draʊt ‖ draʊt]

n. [C][U]❶干旱

❷旱灾,长期干旱

drug 〔drʌg ‖ drʌg〕
n. [C] ❶药品，药材
Why not try this new drug?
为什么不试一试这种新药?
❷麻醉药品；毒品
Few teenagers in our city take drugs.
我们城市极少有青少年吸毒。

drugstore 〔ˈdrʌgˌstor ‖ ˈdrʌgstɔː〕
n.【美】(常兼售化妆品、杂志等杂货的)药房，杂货店[C]

drum 〔drʌm ‖ drʌm〕
n. 鼓[C]
He is beating a drum.
他正在打鼓。

drunk 〔drʌŋk ‖ drʌŋk〕
(drink 的过去分词)
a. ❶喝醉(酒)的
He got drunk.
他喝醉了。
❷陶醉的，兴奋的[(＋with)]

dry 〔draɪ ‖ draɪ〕
[比]drier；[最]driest；[过去式]dried；[过去分词]dried
a. ❶干的；干燥的
The paint is not yet dry.
油漆还未干。
❷干旱的
This state has a dry climate in winter.
该州冬天气候干燥。
〔反义〕wet 潮湿的
vt. ❶把……弄干；使干燥
She dried her tears with a handkerchief.
她用手帕擦干了眼泪。
❷晒干；风干
They sat in front of the fire to dry their wet clothes.
他们坐在炉火前以烘干他们的湿衣服。
vi. 干，变干
Clothes dry slowly in the rainy season.
衣服在雨季不易干。

duck 〔dʌk ‖ dʌk〕
n. 鸭[C]

due 〔dju ‖ djuː〕
a. ❶应支付的；欠款的；欠的[(＋to)]
The money is due to me, but I haven't got it yet.
那笔钱是应付给我的，而我至今还未拿到。
❷到期的
The bank loan is due this month.

银行贷款本月到期。

❸(车船)预定应到的;预期的;约定的[+to-v]

The train is due at 3∶30.

火车应于3点半到达。

❹因为,由于[(+to)]

Due to the storm they didn't go.

由于暴风雨他们没走。

常用短语

due to 由于

dull 〔dʌl ‖ dʌl〕

[比]duller;[最]dullest

a. ❶乏味的,沉闷的,单调的,令人生厌的

The story is dull.

这个故事乏味得很。

❷愚钝的,笨的;迟钝的,不敏感的

All work and no play makes Jack a dull boy.

只有工作没有娱乐使杰克脑筋迟钝。

(过度工作有害身心。)[谚语]

❸钝的,不锋利的

a dull knife

不锋利的小刀

❹不活跃的,呆滞的

dumb 〔dʌm ‖ dʌm〕

a. ❶哑的,不能说话的

He is dumb and deaf.

他又聋又哑。

❷沉默寡言的;不愿说话的;(因吃惊等)说不出话的

She was struck dumb with fear.

她害怕得说不出话。

during 〔'djurɪŋ ‖ 'djuərɪŋ〕

prep. ❶在……的整个期间

Don't speak during the meal.

吃饭时别说话。

❷在……期间的某一时候

They met and fell in love with each other during the Second World War.

他们在第二次世界大战期间相遇并相爱。

during 有两种含义:特定期间的某一时间 during the afternoon;特定期间中的整个时间 during the afternoon

during 和 for:during 后面接表特定期间的词,如:during the week 在这一周中(整个一周)for 后面接表不特定期间或时间的词,如:for a week 一周的时间

用法工具箱

dusk 〔dʌsk ‖ dʌsk〕

n. [U] ❶薄暮，黄昏

He worked from dawn till dusk.

他从早工作到晚。

❷幽暗

We could see nothing in the dusk of the hall.

大厅里一片昏暗，我们什么也看不见。

dust 〔dʌst ‖ dʌst〕

n. 灰尘，尘土[U]

His clothes were covered with dust.

他衣服上全是灰尘。

dustbin 〔ˈdʌstˌbɪn ‖ ˈdʌstbɪn〕

n. 垃圾箱

Throw the broken bottle in the dustbin.

把这个破瓶子扔到垃圾箱里。

dustman 〔ˈdʌstmən ‖ ˈdʌstmən〕

n. 清洁工人；垃圾工

Dutch 〔dʌtʃ ‖ dʌtʃ〕

n. ❶荷兰语[U]

❷(总称)荷兰人[the]

a. 荷兰的；荷兰人的；荷兰语的

常用短语

go Dutch 各自付账；平摊费用

duty 〔ˈdjutɪ ‖ ˈdjuːtɪ〕

n. ❶责任；义务；本分[C][U]

It is our duty to defend our country.

保卫国家是我们的义务。

❷税[C][U]

Customs duties are paid on imported goods.

对进口货物征收关税。

❸职责；职务[P]

One of my duties is to file the letters.

我的职责之一是将信件归档。

常用短语

off duty 下班

on duty 值班；上班

dying 〔ˈdaɪɪŋ ‖ ˈdaɪɪŋ〕

a. ❶垂死的；行将结束的；快熄灭的

❷死亡的

❸临终时说(或给)的

dynasty 〔ˈdaɪnəstɪ ‖ ˈdaɪnəstɪ〕

n. 王朝；朝代[C]

E

E

each 〔itʃ ‖ iːtʃ〕

a.（两个或两个以上人或物中的）各；各自的；每

Each boy gets a present.

每个男孩得到一份礼物。

pron.（视作单数）各个；每个

Each did his share.

各人都做了自己的一份工作。

ad. 各个（地）；各自（地）；每一个（都）

The apples are 50 cents each.

苹果每只售价 50 美分。

Each child was given a gift at Christmas Eve.

圣诞夜每个孩子都得到了礼物。

常用短语

each other 相互，彼此

Tom and Mary love each other.

汤姆和玛丽彼此相爱。

> each other 用于两者之间，one another 用于三者以上之间。
>
> **用法工具箱**

eager 〔ˈigɚ ‖ ˈiːgə〕

a. ❶热心的，热切的

He looked around the circle of eager faces.

他看了看四周热切的脸庞。

❷渴望的，急切的［（＋for）］［＋to-v］［＋（that）］

She is eager for success.

她渴望成功。

词汇拓展

eagerly *ad.* 热心地

eagerness *n.* 热心

eagle 〔ˈigl̩ ‖ ˈiːgl〕

n. 鹰[C]

ear 〔ɪr ‖ ɪə〕

n. ❶耳[C]

The sound of music is pleasant to the ear.

音乐声很动听。

❷听觉;听力

You don't have to shout; we have good ears.

你不必大叫大嚷;我们的听力很好。

❸音感;辨音力[(+for)]

She has a good ear for music.

她对音乐很有鉴赏力。

earache 〔ˈɪrˌek ‖ ˈɪəreɪk〕

n. 耳痛

early 〔ˈɝlɪ ‖ ˈɜːlɪ〕

a. ❶早的;提早的;早产的,早熟的

They were much earlier than I expected.

他们比我期待的早多了。

❷早期的,早先的,在前的

In his early years, he was a keen basketball player.

他早年热衷于打篮球。

❸不久的,很快的

We look forward to an early reply.

我们期望早日得到答复。

ad. ❶早;提早

Please come to see me early tomorrow morning.

请明天一早来见我。

❷在开始阶段,在初期

early 是指较通常或指定的时间早;soon 是现在或指定的时间之后"不久,立刻"

I arrived early and had to wait for others, but soon after two o'clock they appeared.

我早到,必须等其他人,但两点过后不久,他们都到了。

用法工具箱

earn 〔ɝn ‖ ɜːn〕

[过去式]earned;[过去分词]

earned

vt. ❶赚得，挣得

How much do you earn a week?

你一周赚多少钱？

❷博得，赢得

He earned reputation for diligence.

他因勤勉而获得好名声。

❸使得到，使赢得

His achievements earned him respect and admiration.

他的成就赢得人们的尊敬和仰慕。

earphone〔ˈɪrˌfon ‖ ˈɪəfəʊn〕

n. 耳机；听筒

earth〔ɝθ ‖ ɜːθ〕

n. ❶（常大写）地球[the]

How far is the Earth from the sun?

地球离太阳多远？

❷陆地；地面，地上[U]

The balloon burst and fell to earth.

气球炸了，落到地上。

❸土壤，泥土[U]

The farmer examined a handful of earth.

那个农夫察看了一把泥土。

❹接地；地线

常用短语

on earth ❶究竟（附于疑问句，最高级之后，以加强语气）

What on earth is it?

它究竟是什么？

❷世界上，人世间

He is the greatest man on earth.

他是世界上最伟大的人。

earthquake〔ˈɝθˌkwek ‖ ˈɜːθkweɪk〕

n.[C] ❶地震

❷（社会等的）大动荡

easily〔ˈizɪlɪ ‖ ˈiːzɪlɪ〕

ad. 容易地，轻易地

He swam across the river easily.

他轻易地游过河。

east〔ist ‖ iːst〕

n. ❶东，东方[the]

China faces the Pacific on the east.

中国东临太平洋。

❷（一国或一地区的）东部；美国东部；东方国家，亚洲国家[the East]

Japan is in the east of Asia.

日本位于亚洲东部。

在英语中，“东南西北”通常为 north，south，east and west，顺序与汉语不同。

用法工具箱

a. 东的，东方的，朝东的，(风等)来自东方的

The east wall of the house is painted red.

这房子的东墙被涂成红色。

an east wind

东风

ad. 向东方；在东方；来自东方

He walked east.

他向东走去。

eastern 〔ˈistɚn ‖ ˈiːstən〕

a. ❶ 东的；东方的；朝东的，(风)从东吹来的

❷(常大写)东洋的，东方的

China is one of the Eastern countries.

中国是一个东方国家。

easy 〔ˈizɪ ‖ ˈiːzɪ〕

[比]easier；[最]easiest

a. ❶容易的；不费力的[＋to-v]

This new dancing looked easy.

这种新式舞看起来很容易。

〔反义〕difficult 难的

❷安逸的，安乐的；宽裕的

The rich young woman has an easy life.

那位富有的年轻女人过着舒适的生活。

ad. 不费力地；从容地

Change does not come easy.

改变现状并非易事。

Take it easy!

放松点！别着急！

eat 〔it ‖ iːt〕

[过去式]ate；[过去分词]eaten

vt. 吃；喝

He ate his breakfast quickly.

他匆匆地吃了早餐。

vi. 进食；用膳

Where shall we eat today?

今天我们去哪里吃饭？

echo 〔ˈɛko ‖ ˈekəʊ〕

[过去式]echoed；[过去分词]echoed

n. ❶回声；回响[C]

This wall is famous for producing echoes.

这墙壁因能发出回声而出名。

❷(舆论等的)反应；共鸣[C]

His words aroused no echo in their hearts.

他的话未能在他们心中引起共鸣。

vi. ❶发出回声，生成回响[(＋with/to)]

The hall echoed with the audience's laughter.

大厅里回响着观众们的笑声。

❷重复他人的话(或行动等)

economic 〔ˌikəˈnɑmɪk ‖ ˌiːkəˈnɒmɪk〕

a. ❶经济上的；经济学的

They bought an old house for economic reasons.
出于经济上的原因他们买了一所旧房子。
❷合算的，有利可图的

economics 〔ˌikəˈnɑmɪks ‖ ˌiːkəˈnɒmɪks〕
n. ❶经济学
❷（国民的）经济情况；经济

economy 〔ɪˈkɑnəmɪ ‖ ɪˈkɒnəmɪ〕
n. ❶节约，节省[C][U]
The employees of the firm practiced economy in doing everything.
该公司的雇员做任何事都厉行节约。
❷经济；经济情况；经济结构[C][U]
The nation's economy is growing rapidly.
这个国家的经济在快速增长。
❸（客机的）经济舱（＝economy class）

E

edge 〔ɛdʒ ‖ edʒ〕
n. ❶边，棱；边缘[C][U]
They lived in a house on the edge of a forest.
他们住在森林边缘的一所房子里。
❷刃，刀口[C]
He sharpened the edge of his knife on a grindstone.
他在磨石上磨快了他的刀刃。

edition 〔ɪˈdɪʃən ‖ ɪˈdɪʃən〕
n. （发行物的）版；版本[C]
a new edition
新版
the first edition
初版
a revised edition
修订版
a cheap edition
简装版

editor 〔ˈɛdɪtɚ ‖ ˈedɪtə〕
n. [C]❶编辑；（报刊专栏等的）主笔
the chief editor
总编辑；主编
❷编者；校订者
❸社论撰写人
❹（影片等的）剪辑者

education 〔ˌɛdʒəˈkeʃən ‖ ˌedjʊˈkeɪʃən〕
n. ❶教育；培养；训练[C][U]
The government's policy on higher education is a success.
政府的高等教育政策很成功。
❷受到的教育
She has had a good education.
她受过良好的教育。
❸教育学[U]

词汇拓展

educational *a.* 教育的

effect 〔ə'fɛkt ‖ ɪ'fekt〕

n. ❶结果[C][U][(＋on/upon/of)]

Study the cause and effect of the matter.

要研究问题的因果关系。

〔反义〕cause 原因

❷效果，效力；作用；影响[C][U][(＋on/upon)]

This had a great effect upon the future of both mother and son.

这对母子俩的将来影响很大。

常用短语

come/go into effect 生效；被实施

take effect 见效；生效

effective 〔ə'fɛktɪv ‖ ɪ'fektɪv〕

a. ❶有效的[(＋against/in)][＋to-v]

Window screens are effective in keeping out mosquitoes.

纱窗能有效地挡住蚊子。

❷(法律等)生效的，起作用的

A bill passed by congress becomes effective as soon as the President signs it.

国会通过的法案一经总统签署立即生效。

efficient 〔ə'fɪʃənt ‖ ɪ'fɪʃənt〕

a. 效率高的；有能力的，能胜任的

There must be a more efficient way.

一定有更有效的办法。

an efficient lawyer

能胜任的律师

词汇拓展

efficiency *n.* 效率

efficiently *ad.* 有效地

effort 〔'ɛfət ‖ 'efət〕

n. ❶努力，尽力[C][U]

I decided to make one more effort.

我决定再作一次努力。

❷努力的成果；成就[C]

His recent novel is a fine literary effort.

他新近的小说是一部文学佳作。

词汇拓展

effortless *a.* 不费力的

egg 〔ɛg ‖ eg〕

n. 蛋；鸡蛋，卵；卵细胞[C][U]

a boiled egg 煮熟的蛋

the white of an egg 蛋白

Egypt 〔'idʒəpt ‖ 'iːdʒɪpt〕

n. 埃及〈首都 Cairo(开罗)〉

eight [et ‖ eɪt]

a. 八的;八个的

n. ❶八(个,人,时,岁)

❷八个一组;八人的划船队

eighteen [e'tin ‖ 'eɪ'tiːn]

a. 十八个的

I need 18 people.

我需要 18 个人。

n. 十八(个,人,时,岁)

eighteenth [e'tinθ ‖ ˌeɪ'tiːnθ]

a. ❶(与 the 连用)第十八的,第十八个的

❷十八分之一的

n. (与 the 连用)第十八(个);月的第十八日;十八分之一[C]

eighth [etθ ‖ eɪtθ]

a. ❶(与 the 连用)第八的,第八个的

❷八分之一的

n. ❶(与 the 连用)第八(个);月的第八日[C]

❷八分之一

eightieth ['etɪɪθ ‖ 'eɪtɪɪθ]

a. 第八十的;八十分之一的

n. 第八十;八十分之一

eighty ['etɪ ‖ 'eɪtɪ]

a. 八十(个,人,岁)的

n. 八十(个,人,时,岁);80 年代;80 到 89 岁[the P]

in the eighties

在(世纪的)80 年代

She is in her eighties.

她八十多岁了。

either ['iðɚ ‖ 'iːðə]

a. ❶(两者之中)任一的

You may go by either road.

你两条路都可以走。

❷(两者之中)每一方的;每一的

She studied history and philosophy, but she had little interest in either subject.

她学过历史和哲学,但对这两门课都没有多少兴趣。

pron. (两者之中)任何一个

I don't agree with either of you on these issues.

在这些问题上,你们两个我都不同意。

conj. (通常与 or 连用)或者

Either you or your father must see this young man today.

你或是你的父亲今天必须见这位年轻人。

> either…or 句型中谓语动词采取就近原则,与后面的主语一致。
>
> Either he or I am right.
>
> 不是他对,就是我对。
>
> **用法工具箱**

ad. (用在否定句中)也,而且;根本
If you don't go, I won't either.
你若不去,我也不去。

> 肯定句中用 too:
> I won't go either.
> 我也不去。
> I'll go too.
> 我也去。
>
> **用法工具箱**

elbow 〔'ɛlˌbo ‖ 'elbəʊ〕
n. [C] ❶肘;(衣服的)肘部
〈肘 elbow;腕 wrist;膝 knee;踝 ankle〉

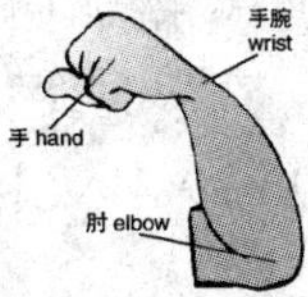

❷肘状物;(路,河等的)急弯;弯头;弯管;(椅子等的)扶手

elder 〔'ɛldɚ ‖ 'eldə〕
a. 年龄较大的(常作定语)
Her elder daughter is at college.
她的长女在上大学。
my elder brother
我哥哥〈美语中常说 my older brother 或 my big brother〉
n. ❶年龄较大者
You are my elder by 5 years.
你比我大 5 岁。
❷长者,前辈[P]
In some things you must trust your elders.
有些事你得信赖你的长者。

eldest 〔'ɛldɪst ‖ 'eldɪst〕
a. (old 的最高级之一)最年长的(常作定语)
my eldest son
我的长子
〔**反义**〕youngest 最年幼的

elect 〔ɪ'lɛkt ‖ ɪ'lekt〕
[过去式]elected;[过去分词]elected
vt. 选举;推选
They elected Tom as their representative.
他们选举汤姆作为他们的代表。

electric 〔ɪ'lɛktrɪk ‖ ɪ'lektrɪk〕
a. ❶电的;导电的;发电的
I got an electric shock from the wire.
我被这根电线电击了一下。
❷用电的;电动的
The child likes electric toys.
这个孩子喜欢电动玩具。

electricity 〔ɪˌlɛkˈtrɪsətɪ ‖ ˌɪlekˈtrɪsɪtɪ〕
n. [U] ❶电；电流；电力
❷电学

electronics 〔ɪˌlɛkˈtrɑnɪks ‖ ɪˌlekˈtrɒnɪks〕
n. 电子学

elegant 〔ˈɛləgənt ‖ ˈelɪgənt〕
a. ❶雅致的，优美的，漂亮的
Her writing was elegant.
她的文章优美。
❷讲究的，精致的
elegant dress
雅致的衣服

词汇拓展

elegance *n.* 高雅，优美

element 〔ˈɛləmənt ‖ ˈelɪmənt〕
n. ❶【化】元素[C]
Carbon is an element, while carbon dioxide is a compound.
碳是元素，而二氧化碳是化合物。
❷要素，成分[C]
Honesty, industry and kindness are elements of a good life.
诚实、勤奋和善良是正派生活的要素。

elementary 〔ˌɛləˈmɛntərɪ ‖ ˌeləˈmentərɪ〕
a. ❶基本的
❷初级的，基础的
an elementary school (= a primary school)
小学

elephant 〔ˈɛləfənt ‖ ˈelɪfənt〕
n. 【动】象[C]

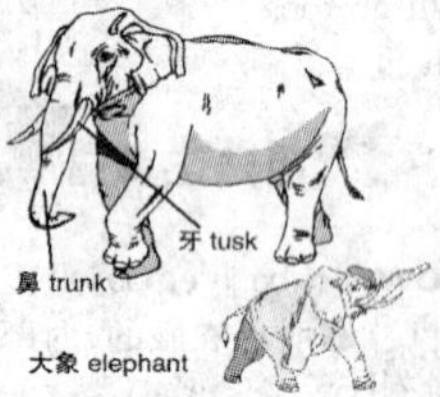

elevator 〔ˈɛləˌvetɚ ‖ ˈelɪveɪtə〕
n.【美】电梯；升降机[C]

eleven 〔ɪˈlɛvən ‖ ɪˈlevn〕
a. 十一的，十一个的
He is 11 years old.
他 11 岁了。
n. 十一，十一个
〈足球、板球等十一人组成的球队称做 an eleven〉

eleventh 〔ɪˈlɛvənθ ‖ ɪˈlevnθ〕
a. ❶（与 the 连用）第十一的，第十一个的
❷十一分之一的
n. ❶（与 the 连用）第十一（个）；月的第十一日

❷十一分之一

else〔ɛls ‖ els〕

ad. ❶(用于疑问词，不定代词后)其他，另外

I'm going to take you somewhere else.

我要带你去别处。

Who else is going?

还有谁要去？

It is somebody else's book.

这是别人的书。

❷(常与 or 连用)否则，要不然

Drink this，(or) else you will be sick.

把这喝下去，否则你会生病的。

elsewhere〔ˈɛlsˌhwɛr ‖ ˈelshweə〕

ad. 在别处；往别处；到别处

Look elsewhere.

在别的地方找找看。

embarrass〔ɪmˈbærəs ‖ ɪmˈbærəs〕

[过去式]embarrassed；[过去分词]embarrassed

vt. 使窘；使不好意思，使局促不安[(+with/by)]

He embarrassed me with a difficult question.

他出难题使我受窘。

词汇拓展

embarrassing *a.* 令人困窘的，令人为难的

embarrassment *n.* 困窘，困惑

embassy〔ˈɛmbəsɪ ‖ ˈembəsɪ〕

n. (常大写)大使馆[C]

emergency〔ɪˈmɝdʒənsɪ ‖ ɪˈmɜːdʒənsɪ〕

n. 紧急情况；突然事件；非常时刻[C][U]

In an emergency，call 110.

遇到紧急情况，请打 110。

emergency exit

太平门

emotion〔ɪˈmoʃən ‖ ɪˈməʊʃən〕

n. ❶感情，情感[C]

Love，hatred and grief are emotions.

爱、恨和悲都是情感。

❷激动[U]

We listened to his speech with emotion.

我们激动地听着他的演讲。

词汇拓展

emotional *a.* 情绪的，敏感的，激动的

emperor〔ˈɛmpərɚ ‖ ˈempərə〕

n. 皇帝[C]

emphasis 〔ˈɛmfəsɪs ‖ ˈemfəsɪs〕

n. 强调，重视，重点[C][U][(＋on/upon)]

They put emphasis on quality rather than on quantity.

他们重质不重量。

emphasize 〔ˈɛmfəˌsaɪz ‖ ˈemfəsaɪz〕

[过去式]emphasized；[过去分词]emphasized

vt. 强调，着重

He emphasized the need for practical English.

他强调使用英语的必要。

empire 〔ˈɛmpaɪr ‖ ˈempaɪə〕

n. 帝国[C]

employ 〔ɪmˈplɔɪ ‖ ɪmˈplɔɪ〕

[过去式]employed；[过去分词]employed

vt. ❶雇用

The mill will employ 1,000 workers.

这家工厂将雇用1,000名工人。

❷使用，利用

How do you employ your spare time?

你是怎样利用你的空余时间的?

❸(常与oneself连用或用被动式)使忙于，使从事于[(＋in)]

The children were employed in painting.

孩子们忙于画画儿。

employment 〔ɪmˈplɔɪmənt ‖ ɪmˈplɔɪmənt〕

n. ❶雇用；受雇[U]

A large office requires the employment of many people.

一个大事务所需要雇用许多人。

❷职业，工作[U]

He found employment as a mechanic.

他找到了一份机修工的工作。

词汇拓展

unemployment *n.* 失业

employee 〔ɪmˈplɔii ‖ ɪmˈplɔiː〕

n. 受雇者，雇工，雇员，从业员工[C][(＋of)]

employer 〔ɪmˈplɔɪɚ ‖ ɪmˈplɔɪə〕

n. 雇主，雇用者[C]

empty 〔ˈɛmptɪ ‖ ˈemptɪ〕

[比]emptier；[最]emptiest

a. ❶空的；未占用的；没有人居住的

The streets are almost empty at night.

晚上街上几乎空无一人。

❷无，没有，缺少[(＋of)]

What he said are empty of sincerity.
他所说的话没有诚意。
❸空洞的,无意义的;徒劳的
He didn't want to retire and lead an empty life.
他不想退休过空虚的生活。

enable 〔ɪn'ebl̩ ‖ ɪ'neɪbl〕
[过去式]enabled;[过去分词]enabled
vt. ❶使能够;赋予……能力
Training will enable you to find work.
培训将使你找到工作。
❷使成为可能
The program will enable a large increase in student numbers.
这一计划能使学生的人数大量增加。

encounter 〔ɪn'kaʊntɚ ‖ ɪn'kaʊntə〕
[过去式]encountered;[过去分词]encountered
vt. ❶遭遇(敌人);遇到(困难,危险等)
I encountered great difficulties in learning English grammar.
我在学习英文文法时遇到了很大困难。
❷意外地遇见(朋友等)
The first person she encountered was Cyril Scott.
她遇到的第一个人是西瑞尔·史考特。

encourage 〔ɪn'kɝɪdʒ ‖ ɪn'kʌrɪdʒ〕
[过去式]encouraged;[过去分词]encouraged
vt. ❶鼓励;怂恿
She encouraged him to talk to her.
她鼓励他与她会话。
❷促进,助长;激发
Don't encourage her laziness by doing things for her.
别替她做事,这会助长她的懒惰。
〔反义〕discourage 使……泄气

encouragement 〔ɪn'kɝɪdʒmənt ‖ ɪn'kʌrɪdʒmənt〕
n. ❶鼓励;奖励;促进[U]
❷鼓励的话(或行为);刺激[C]

end 〔ɛnd ‖ end〕
[过去式]ended;[过去分词]ended
n. [C]❶末端;尽头;最后部分,末尾
My companion waited for me at the end of the street.
我的同伴在街道尽头等我。
❷残片;残余[P]
cigarette ends

烟蒂

❸目的；目标

I used the scientific method to attain this end.

我用科学的方法来达到这一目的。

vt. 结束；终止；了结

I hoped that this might end my suffering.

我希望这能结束我的痛苦。

vi. 结束；终止

The book ends in tragedy.

这本书以悲剧结尾。

endure 〔ɪn'djʊr ‖ ɪn'djʊə〕

［过去式］endured；［过去分词］endured

vt. ❶忍耐，忍受

The old man had to endure toothache.

这位老人不得不忍受牙痛。

❷（常与 cannot 等否定词连用）容忍

I cannot endure her rudeness any longer.

我再也不能忍受她的无礼了。

vi. ❶忍耐，忍受

❷持久，持续

I can't endure to see/seeing you so discouraged.

我不忍看到你如此颓丧。

enemy 〔'ɛnəmɪ ‖ 'enəmɪ〕

n. ❶敌人，仇敌［C］

Don't make an enemy of him.

不要与他为敌。

❷敌军［the］

The enemy was/were attacking the town.

敌军正在攻打该城。

a. 敌人的，敌方的

Enemy aircraft were detected by our radar.

敌机被我方雷达发现。

energetic 〔ˌɛnɚ'dʒɛtɪk ‖ ˌenə'dʒetɪk〕

a. 精力旺盛的；精神饱满的

He is always energetic.

他总是精力充沛。

energy 〔'ɛnɚdʒɪ ‖ 'enədʒɪ〕

n. ❶活力，干劲［U］

They are working with energy.

他们正在干劲十足地工作。

❷精力，能力［P］

They devoted all their energies to the job.

他们把自己的全部精力投入这项工作。

❸【物】能，能量［U］

engage 〔ɪn'gedʒ ‖ ɪn'geɪdʒ〕

［过去式］engaged；［过去分词］engaged

vt. ❶吸引（某人的兴趣）；占用（时间，精力等）

The book engaged my full attention.
这本书把我完全吸引住了。
❷雇，聘[(＋as)]
He engaged Mary as a secretary.
他聘玛丽当秘书。
❸预订(房间，座位等)
❹使订婚
David is engaged to Ann.
大卫与安订了婚。
❺使从事，使忙于
He is engaged in business.
他从事商务。
❻保证
I engage (myself) to be there.
我保证会去那儿。
vi. ❶从事，参加[(＋in/upon)]
They engage in the study of music.
他们从事音乐研究。
❷保证；答应

常用短语

be engaged in 忙于
engage in 从事

engagement 〔ɪn'gedʒmənt ‖ ɪn'geɪdʒmənt〕
n. ❶订婚；婚约[C]
an engagement ring
订婚戒指
❷诺言，保证[C]
❸需偿付的款项[P]

engine 〔'ɛndʒən ‖ 'endʒɪn〕
n. [C] ❶发动机，引擎
❷机车，火车头

engineer 〔ˌɛndʒə'nɪr ‖ ˌendʒɪ'nɪə〕
n. [C] ❶工程师，技师
❷机械工；轮机手

England 〔'ɪŋglənd ‖ 'ɪŋglənd〕
n. 英格兰

> 英国的正式名称是 the United Kingdom of Great Britain and Northern Ireland，简称 U. K. ，用 England 一词泛指英国是不严格的泛指用法。
>
> **用法工具箱**

English 〔'ɪŋglɪʃ ‖ 'ɪŋglɪʃ〕
a. ❶英格兰(人)的；英国(人)的
Jane is English.
简是英国人。
❷英语的
He does not speak English, but he knows quite a few English words.
他不会说英语，但他认识许多英文单词。

n. ❶英语,(学科之一的)英文[U]
She speaks English.
她讲英语。
❷(总称)英国人;英格兰人[the]
He likes the English.
他喜欢英国人。

enjoy 〔ɪn'dʒɔɪ ‖ ɪn'dʒɔɪ〕
[过去式]enjoyed;[过去分词]enjoyed
vt. ❶欣赏;享受;喜爱[+v-ing]
I enjoyed reading these books very much.
我很喜欢读这些书。
❷【书】享有(利益,权利,声誉等)
We enjoy free medical care.
我们享受免费医疗。
❸使过得快活;使得到乐趣[(+oneself)]
Are you enjoying yourself?
你玩得高兴吗?

enjoyable 〔ɪn'dʒɔɪəbl̩ ‖ ɪn'dʒɔɪəbl〕
a. 使人快乐的;有乐趣的

enlarge 〔ɪn'lɑrdʒ ‖ ɪn'lɑːdʒ〕
[过去式]enlarged;[过去分词]enlarged
vt. ❶扩大;扩展
an enlarged edition
增订版
❷放大(照片)
I will have this picture enlarged.
我要将这张照片放大。

enough 〔ə'nʌf ‖ ɪ'nʌf〕
a. 足够的,充足的
We have enough chairs for everyone.
我们有足够的椅子让大家坐。
n. 足够,充分[+to-v][(+for)]
We earned enough to buy a new house.
我们挣的钱足够买一幢新房子。
ad. ❶足够地;充分地
They cannot walk fast enough.
他们走得不够快。
❷相当地,尚
The situation is serious enough.
情况相当严重。

enter 〔'ɛntɚ ‖ 'entə〕
[过去式]entered;[过去分词]entered
vt. ❶进入
He entered the classroom.
他进了教室。
❷参加;加入

The United States did not enter the war until April 19, 1917.
美国直到 1917 年 4 月 19 日才参战。
❸使参加;使进入
They entered their child at a private school.
他们让他们的孩子在一所私立学校就读。
vi. ❶进入
He rose as she entered.
他在她进来时站起身来。
❷参加,加入[(+for)]
He decided not to enter for the race.
他决定不报名参加比赛。

enterprise 〔ˈɛntɚˌpraɪz ‖ ˈentəpraɪz〕
n. ❶(有一定冒险性的)事业[C]
❷冒险精神;进取心,事业心[U]
Tom is a man of great enterprise.
汤姆很有进取精神。
❸企业,公司[C]
This enterprise is doing a good business.
这家企业生意兴隆。

entertain 〔ˌɛntɚˈten ‖ ˌentəˈteɪn〕
[过去式]entertained;[过去分词]entertained
vt. ❶使欢乐,使娱乐
We were all entertained by his humorous stories.
他的幽默故事使我们大家都很开心。
❷招待,款待[(+with/at/to)]
They often entertained their friends at weekends.
他们常在周末招待朋友。
❸怀着,抱着;持有(信心等)
I have never entertained any illusions about him.
我从来没有对他抱过幻想。
vi. 款待,请客

entertainment 〔ˌɛntɚˈtenmənt ‖ ˌentəˈteɪnmənt〕
n. ❶招待,款待[U]
We are delighted by entertainment of our friends.
我们乐于款待朋友。
❷游艺,演艺;余兴[C][U]
She played the piano for our entertainment.
她弹钢琴为我们助兴。
❸娱乐,消遣[C][U]
This law applies to all places of public entertainment.
这一法律适用于一切公共娱乐场所。

❹怀有(希望,怀疑等)[U][(＋of)]

entire 〔ɪn'taɪr ‖ ɪn'taɪə〕

a. ❶全部的,整个的

It took us an entire week to finish painting the house.

我们花了整整一星期的时间才把房子粉刷好。

❷全然的,完全的

I am in entire agreement with you.

我完全同意你。

entrance 〔'ɛntrəns ‖ 'entrəns〕

n. ❶入口,门口[C][(＋to)]

We used the back entrance to the building.

我们是从大楼的后门入口走进去的。

〔反义〕exit 出口

❷入学,入会,入场

Entrance into college was a great event in my life.

进入大学是我一生中的一件大事。

❸进入的权利;入学许可[U]

They were refused entrance to the theater.

他们被拒于戏院大门之外。

envelope 〔'ɛnvəˌlop ‖ 'envələup〕

n. [C] ❶信封;封皮;封套

❷外壳,壳层

environment 〔ɪn'vaɪrəmənt ‖ ɪn'vaɪərənmənt〕

n. ❶环境;四周状况[C]

His home environment was good.

他的家庭环境很好。

❷自然环境;生态环境[the]

envy 〔'ɛnvɪ ‖ 'envɪ〕

[过去式]envied;[过去分词]envied

n. ❶妒忌;羡慕[U][(＋at/out of/towards)]

She said it out of envy.

她出于忌妒说了这番话。

❷妒忌的对象;羡慕的目标[the][(＋of)]

His talent is the envy of his colleagues.

他的同事都羡慕他的才能。

vt. 妒忌;羡慕

I envy you your good luck.

我羡慕你的好运。

equal 〔'ikwəl ‖ 'iːkwəl〕

a. ❶相等的;相当的;均等的[(＋to/in)]

A dime is equal to 10 cents.

一角的硬币相当于10美分。

❷胜任的;能对付的[(＋to)]

I'm not equal to the task.

我不能胜任这项任务。

❸平等的
All men are created equal.
所有的人生来都是平等的。
n. [C][U] ❶(地位等)相同的人,平等的人
In spelling she had no equal.
在拼写方面她没有对手。
❷相等的事物;相等的数量
3 multiplied by 5 is the equal to 10 plus 5.
3 乘以 5 与 10 加 5 相等。

equator 〔ɪˈkwetɚ ‖ ɪˈkweɪtə〕
n. 赤道[the]

equipment 〔ɪˈkwɪpmənt ‖ ɪˈkwɪpmənt〕
n. 配备,装备,设备;器械;用具[U]

era 〔ˈɪrə ‖ ˈɪərə〕
n. [C] ❶时代;年代;历史时期 ❷纪元

error 〔ˈɛrə ‖ ˈerə〕
n. ❶错误,失误,差错[C][U]
There's an error in your calculation.
你的计算中有个错误。
❷犯错误,出错[U]
Are all men liable to error?
人人都可能犯错误吗?
❸过失,罪过,不正行为[C]

escape 〔ɪˈskep ‖ ɪˈskeɪp〕
[过去式]escaped;[过去分词]escaped
vi. ❶逃跑;逃脱[(+from)]
The soldier escaped from the enemy's prison.
这个士兵从敌人的监狱里逃了出来。
❷避免[(+from/out of)]
He traveled extensively to escape from boredom.
他到处旅游以解烦闷。
vt. ❶逃避;逃脱;避免[+v-ing]
We were lucky to escape being punished.
我们很幸运,没有受罚。
❷没有被……注意到;被……忘掉
The matter has quite escaped my memory.
这件事我完全记不得了。
n. ❶逃跑;逃脱[C][U]
He made his escape in disguise.
他化装后逃走了。
❷漏出[C][U]
Can you smell an escape of gas?
你能闻到漏出的煤气味吗?
❸逃避(现实);解闷
She read detective stories as an escape.
她看侦探小说解闷。

especially 〔əˈspɛʃəlɪ ‖ ɪˈspeʃəlɪ〕

E

ad. ❶特别；尤其；格外；主要
I liked all the children，Tom especially.
我喜欢所有的孩子，特别是汤姆。
❷特地；专门地
The dictionary is compiled especially for beginners.
这本字典是专门为初学者编写的。

establish〔ə'stæblɪʃ ‖ ɪ'stæblɪʃ〕
［过去式］established；［过去分词］established
vt. ❶创建；设立；创办
Our hospital was established in 1950.
我们的医院建于 1950 年。
❷确立；使得到承认；使立足于［（＋as/in）］
She established her fame as an actress.
她已成为大名鼎鼎的演员。
❸确定；证实；表明
The new evidence establishes the suspect's guilt.
新证据证实嫌疑犯有罪。

estimate〔'ɛstəmɪt ‖ 'estɪmeɪt〕
［过去式］estimated；［过去分词］estimated
vt. ❶估计，估量［（＋at）］［＋that］
The police estimated the number of demonstrators at about 5,000.
警方估计示威者的人数为 5 千左右。
❷评价；判断
n.［C］❶估计；估价；估计数
The expert's estimate is that the painting is worth ＄3,000.
专家估计这幅画值 3,000 美元。
❷评价；判断；看法
My estimate of the situation is not so optimistic.
我对形势的估计不那么乐观。

etc；et cetera〔ˌɛt'sɛtərə ‖ et'setərə〕
ad.（拉丁语）等等，及其他人（或事物）
The flower show featured roses，peonies，etc.
花展主要展出玫瑰、牡丹等等。

Europe〔'jʊrəp ‖ 'jʊərəp〕
n. 欧洲

European〔ˌjʊrə'piən ‖ ˌjʊərə'piːən〕
n. 欧洲人
a. 欧洲的

eve〔iv ‖ iːv〕
n. ❶（通常大写）（节日等的）前夜，前夕［U］

Christmas Eve
圣诞前夜
New Year's Eve
除夕
❷(重大事件发生的)前一刻,前夕[the][(+of)]

even ['ivən || 'iːvən]

a. ❶平的,平坦的,平滑的
The road wasn't even.
这条路不平。
❷一致的;同样的;齐的[(+with)]
The snow was even with the window.
雪积得跟窗子一样高。
❸对等的;均等的,相等的
The score is now even.
现在得分相等。
❹【数】偶数的

ad. ❶(加强语气)甚至;连
Even Mrs. Smith could not help laughing.
甚至史密斯太太也忍不住笑了起来。
❷(用于比较级前)甚至更,还
This book is even more useful than that one.
这本书比那本更加有用。
❸实际上;甚至可以说
He is ready, even eager to go.
他乐意甚至可以说渴望前去。

常用短语

even if/though 即使;虽然
Even if it rains, I will go.
即使下雨,我也要去。

evening ['ivnɪŋ || 'iːvnɪŋ]

n. ❶傍晚;晚上[C][U]
I'll do my homework in the evening.
我将在晚上做作业。
❷晚会;晚上娱乐时间[C]
Please come to our English evening on Saturday.
请参加我们星期六的英语晚会。
❸后期;末期;衰落期
He was still very active in the evening of his life.
他在晚年时仍很活跃。

event [ɪ'vɛnt || ɪ'vent]

n. ❶事件,大事[C]
Winning the scholarship was a great event in the boy's life.
赢得这项奖学金是这个男孩一生中的一件大事。
❷(比赛)项目[C]
Which events have you entered for?
你参加了哪些比赛项目?

ever ['ɛvə || 'evə]

ad. ❶(多用于疑问句、否定句和表示条件和比较的附属子

句)在任何时候;从来;至今
If you ever see George, give him my kind regards.
如果你见到乔治,请代我向他致以亲切的问候。
❷永远,始终;总是
He is ever ready to help you.
他总是乐意帮助你的。
❸(用于疑问副词或代名词之后,加强语气)究竟,到底
Who ever can it be?
那究竟会是谁呢?

E

常用短语

for ever (and a day) 永远
I'll remember him for ever.
我会永远记住他。
ever after/afterwards 从此以后一直
ever so 非常
He is ever so rich.
他非常富有。

every [ˈɛvrɪ ‖ ˈevrɪ]
a. ❶每一,每个;一切的,全部的
Mr. Miller searched every room in the house.
米勒先生搜查了这栋房子里的所有房间。
❷每隔……的
She visits her parents every few days.
她每隔几天看望她父母亲一次。
❸一切可能的,充分的
You have every reason to try it once more.
你有充分的理由再试一次。
❹(用于否定句)不是每个都
Not every man can be a writer. =Every man cannot be a writer.
不是每个人都能成为作家。

常用短语

every now and then 时常;有时
every other 每隔一……

everybody [ˈɛvrɪˌbɑdɪ ‖ ˈevrɪbɒdɪ]
pron. 每个人,人人,各人
Everybody admires him.
人人都羡慕他。

everyday [ˈɛvrɪˈde ‖ ˈevrɪdeɪ]
a. 每天的,日常的,平常的
everyday life
日常生活
an everyday occurrence
平凡事件

everyone [ˈɛvrɪˌwʌn ‖ ˈevrɪwʌn]
= everybody
pron. 每人,人人

everything [ˈɛvrɪˌθɪŋ ‖ ˈevrɪθɪŋ]
pron. ❶每件事物,事事,一切

事物
He knows everything about Paris.
他对巴黎了如指掌。
❷(仅用于补语中)最重要的东西[(+to)]
He is everything to me.
他是我的一切。

everywhere 〔ˈɛvrɪˌhwɛr ‖ ˈevrɪhweə〕
ad. 到处,处处;无论何处
I looked everywhere for you.
我到处找你。

evidence 〔ˈɛvədəns ‖ ˈevɪdəns〕
n. ❶证据;证词;证人;物证[U]
He was punished for giving false evidence.
他因作伪证而受到惩罚。
❷迹象[C][U][(+of)][+that]
There are evidences that somebody has been living here.
有迹象显示有人一直住在这里。

evil 〔ˈivl̩ ‖ ˈiːvl〕
a. ❶邪恶的;罪恶的
The man was punished for his evil acts.
这个人因为他的恶劣行径而受到惩罚。
❷不幸的,倒霉的
I received evil news.
我接到噩耗。
n. ❶邪恶,罪恶[U]
Some people return good for evil.
有些人以德报怨。
❷坏事;谗言
❸祸害,不幸
Money is thought to be the root cause of all evils.
金钱被认为是万恶之源。

exact 〔ɪgˈzækt ‖ ɪgˈzækt〕
a. ❶确切的,精确的
It was difficult to tell her exact age.
很难说出她的确切年龄。
❷精确无误的,精密的
The scholar is an exact thinker.
这位学者思维严谨。

exactly 〔ɪgˈzæktlɪ ‖ ɪgˈzæktlɪ〕
ad. ❶确切地,精确地;完全地
He arrived at the office exactly at 8 o'clock.
他 8 点整到的办公室。
❷恰好地,正好地
That's exactly what I want to say.
那正是我要说的。
❸(用于答语)一点不错
"Do you mean he is to blame?"

"你是说他该负责?"
"Exactly."
"正是。"

exaggerate 〔ɪg'zædʒəˌret ‖ ɪg'zædʒəreɪt〕
[过去式]exaggerated;[过去分词]exaggerated
vt. 夸张,夸大;对……言过其实
He exaggerated the size of the fish he caught.
他夸大了他所抓到的鱼的大小。

examination 〔ɪgˌzæmə'neʃən ‖ ɪgzæmɪ'neɪʃən〕
n. 试验,考试
He took the entrance examination for the college.
他参加该学院的入学考试。

examine 〔ɪg'zæmɪn ‖ ɪg'zæmɪn〕
[过去式]examined;[过去分词]examined
vt. ❶检查;细查;诊察
The doctor examined the boy and found there was nothing with him.
医生检查了男孩的身体,发现他是健康的。
❷审问;盘问
The lawyer examined the witness.
律师讯问了证人。
❸测验[(+in/on)]
The teacher examined the students in physics.
教师考学生物理。

词汇拓展

examiner *n.* 主考者
examinee *n.* 应试者

example 〔ɪg'zæmpl ‖ ɪg'zɑːmpl〕
n. [C] ❶例子;样本;样品[(+of)]
This dictionary has many examples of how verbs are used.
这本词典有许多关于动词用法的例句。
❷范例;榜样;楷模[(+to)]
Their courage was an example to all of us.
他们的勇气是我们大家学习的榜样。

常用短语

for example 例如
set an example 树立榜样

excellent 〔'ɛkslənt ‖ 'eksələnt〕
a. 出色的;杰出的;优等的
He is excellent in mathematics.
他的数学非常好。

except 〔ɪk'sɛpt ‖ ɪk'sept〕
prep. 除……之外

We go there every day except Sunday.
除了星期天，我们每天都去那儿。
conj. ❶除了
She did nothing except complain while she was here.
她在这里时除了抱怨还是抱怨。
❷要不是；但是
I would go except it's too far.
我想去的，只是路太远。

常用短语

except for 除了……以外
He is a good man except for his hot temper.
他是个好人，只不过脾气暴躁而已。

exchange 〔ɪks'tʃendʒ ‖ ɪks'tʃeɪndʒ〕
[过去式]exchanged；[过去分词]exchanged
vt. 交换；调换；兑换[(＋for/with)]
I'd like to exchange some pounds for dollars.
我想把一些英镑兑换成美金。
n. ❶交换；交流；交易[C][U]
An exchange of opinions is helpful.
相互交换意见是有益的。
❷兑；兑换；汇率[U]
What is the rate of exchange between the pound and the *Renminbi*?
英镑与人民币的兑换率是多少？

excited 〔ɪk'saɪtɪd ‖ ɪk'saɪtɪd〕
a. ❶兴奋的；激动的[(＋about/at/over)][＋to-v]
He was very excited at the news.
听到这个消息他很兴奋。
❷活跃的

exciting 〔ɪk'saɪtɪŋ ‖ ɪk'saɪtɪŋ〕
a. 令人兴奋的；令人激动的
He told us an exciting story.
他告诉了我们一个很刺激的故事。

excuse1 〔ɪk'skjuz ‖ ɪk'skjuːz〕
vt. ❶原谅[(＋for)]
Please excuse the offence this time: I will not do it again.
请原谅这次冒犯：我以后再也不会了。
❷辩解；成为……的理由；试图开脱
She excused her absence by saying that she was ill.
她为她的缺席申辩，说是病了。

常用短语

Excuse me. 对不起，请原谅

[在感到对对方有所冒犯或告辞时说的话]

excuse² [ɪkˈskjus ‖ ɪkˈskjuːs]

n. ❶ 辩解

❷理由;借口

There is no excuse for this chaotic state of affairs.

事情弄得如此之乱,已经没有什么理由可说了。

exercise [ˈɛksəˌsaɪz ‖ ˈeksəsaɪz]

n. ❶运动,锻炼[U]

Swimming is one of the healthiest forms of exercise.

游泳是最有益于健康的运动方式之一。

做运动
do exercise

❷练习;习题[C]

Do the vocabulary exercises at the end of the chapter.

做这一章末尾的词汇练习。

exhibition [ˌɛksəˈbɪʃən ‖ ˌeksɪˈbɪʃən]

n. 展览;展览会,展示会[(+of)]

They went to the exhibition of Chinese paintings at the museum.

他们去博物馆参观中国画展。

exhibition 展览会

an art exhibition 美术展览

exist [ɪgˈzɪst ‖ ɪgˈzɪst]

[过去式]existed;[过去分词]existed

vi. ❶存在

That word doesn't exist in English.

英语中没有那个词。

❷生存;生活[(+on)]

She existed only on milk.

她只靠牛奶生存。

existence [ɪgˈzɪstəns ‖ ɪgˈzɪstəns]

n. ❶存在,实有[U]

His existence was ignored.

他的存在被忽视了。

❷生存[U]

a struggle for existence

争取生存的斗争

expect [ɪkˈspɛkt ‖ ɪkˈspekt]

[过去式]expected;[过去分词]expected

vt. ❶预计……可能发生(或来

到)；估计；预料；预期[＋that][＋to-v]
He expected to finish the work by March.
他预期3月份完成这项工作。
❷期待；等待；盼望
That's just what we expected.
那正是我们所期望的。
❸认为理应得到；指望；要求[(＋from/of)]
Don't expect too much of him.
别对他期望过高。
❹想；认为[＋that]

expedition 〔ˌekspɪˈdɪʃən ‖ ˌekspɪˈdɪʃən〕
n. ❶远征；探险；考察[C]
They did an expedition to the Himalayas.
他们到喜马拉雅山去考察了一次。
❷远征队；探险队；考察队[C]
He was on an expedition to explore the Antarctic.
他参加探险队远征南极。

expense 〔ɪkˈspens ‖ ɪkˈspens〕
n. ❶费用；价钱；支出；消耗
I don't think we can afford the expense.
我认为我们负担不了这个费用。
❷开支；经费[P]
He said the office expenses were too big.
他认为办公室的花费太大了。
❸牺牲；损失，代价[U]

expensive 〔ɪkˈspensɪv ‖ ɪkˈspensɪv〕
a. 高价的；昂贵的；花钱的[＋to-v]

experience 〔ɪkˈspɪrɪəns ‖ ɪkˈspɪərɪəns〕
[过去式]experienced；[过去分词]experienced
n. ❶经验，体验[U][(＋of/in)]
She had no experience of life at all.
她毫无生活经验。
❷(一次)经历，感受[C]
Please tell us about your experiences in Africa.
请跟我们谈谈你在非洲的经历。
vt. ❶经历；体验
The city experienced over 2,000 such incidents last year.
去年这座城市发生过2,000次以上这类事件。
❷感受；遭受
He experienced a pang of sadness.
他感到一阵悲痛。

E

experiment[1] 〔ɪk'sperəmənt ‖ ɪk'sperɪmənt〕

[过去式]experimented;[过去分词]experimented

n. 实验;试验[C][U]

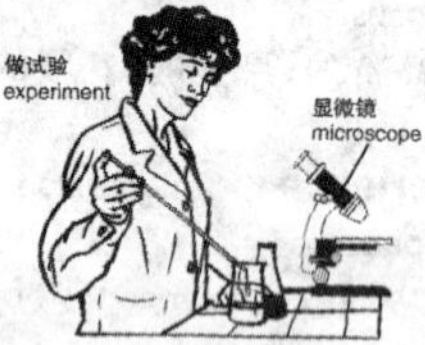

Some people learn by experiment and others learn by experience.

一些人通过实验学习,另一些人则从经验中学习。

experiment[2] 〔ɪk'sperəmɛnt ‖ ɪk'sperɪment〕

vi. 进行实验,试验[(+on/with)]

He is experimenting with drugs to cure hepatitis.

他正在试验治疗肝炎的药。

expert 〔'ɛkspɝt ‖ 'ekspɜːt〕

n. [C] 专家;能手;熟练者[(+at/in/on)]

She is an expert in training animals.

她是驯兽专家。

a. ❶熟练的,老练的;有经验的

He became an expert language teacher.

他成了一个有经验的语言教师。

❷专家的,内行的;专门的

Expert opinions are favorable to the project.

专家的意见是赞成这一工程。

explain 〔ɪk'splen ‖ ɪk'spleɪn〕

[过去式]explained;[过去分词]explained

vt. ❶解释;说明;阐明[(+to)][+wh-][+that]

He explained that he had been cheated.

他解释说他是上当受骗了。

❷为……辩解;说明……的理由(或原因)[+wh-]

He made up a story to explain why he was absent.

他编造了一个借口为他的缺席辩解。

vi. 解释;说明;辩解

I've got to explain about it.

我得解释一下这件事。

explanation 〔ˌɛksplə'neʃən ‖ ˌeksplə'neɪʃən〕

n. 说明,解释[C][U]

I could not get a satisfactory explanation.

我得不到一个满意的解释。

explode 〔ɪk'splod ‖ ɪk'spləʊd〕
［过去式］exploded；［过去分词］exploded
vt. ❶使爆炸；使爆发；使突发
The terrorists exploded a bomb in a store.
恐怖分子在一家商店引爆了一枚炸弹。
❷推翻；驳倒；戳穿
The rumor has been exploded.
谎言被戳穿了。
❸【语】发爆破音
vi. ❶爆炸；爆破
❷爆发，突发，迸发［(＋in/into/with)］
The boss exploded with anger when he saw the sales report.
当老板看到销售报告时，他勃然大怒。
❸激增，迅速扩大
The city's population has exploded in the last few years.
在最近几年里这个城市的人口急剧增加。

exploit 〔ɪk'splɔɪt ‖ ɪk'splɔɪt〕
［过去式］exploited；［过去分词］exploited
vt. ❶剥削
❷开发，开采，开拓
Japan has little natural resources to be exploited.
日本缺乏可供开发的自然资源。

explore 〔ɪk'splɔr ‖ ɪk'splɔː〕
［过去式］explored；［过去分词］explored
vt. ❶探测；探勘；在……探险
They explored this desert region in 1923.
他们于1923年在这片荒漠地区探险。
❷探究，探索
The conference explored the possibility of closer trade links.
大会探讨了进一步加强贸易联系的可能性。
vi. 探索；考察；探勘；探险

export 〔ɪk'spɔrt ‖ ɪk'spɔːt〕
［过去式］exported；［过去分词］exported
vt. 输出，出口
The United States exports soybean.
美国出口大豆。

express 〔ɪk'sprɛs ‖ ɪk'spres〕
［过去式］expressed；［过去分词］expressed
vt. 表达，陈述；表示［＋wh-］
Really, I hardly know how to express my gratitude.
我真不知道如何表达我的感激之情。

n. ❶快车[C]
the 7 : 00 a. m. express to Shanghai
上午 7 点开往上海的快车
❷快递;快运[U]
Send the parcel by express.
以快递寄出这包裹。
a. ❶快递的,快运的
Please send this parcel by express delivery.
请用快递寄送这个包裹。
❷明确的,明白表示的
The doctor gave express orders that the patient was to have no visitors.
医生明确嘱咐,那个病人不能会客。
❸快的,直达的
We took an express bus home.
我们乘特快公共汽车回家。

expression [ɪkˈsprɛʃən ‖ ɪkˈspreʃən]
n. ❶表达;表示[C][U]
That's an interesting expression.
那是很有趣的措辞。
❷表情;脸色;声调[C][U]
He had a weary expression.
他面露疲惫之色。

extra [ˈɛkstrə ‖ ˈekstrə]
a. 额外的;外加的,另外收费的
I don't suppose they wanted any extra help.
我想他们不需要额外帮助。
extra work
额外的工作

extremely [ɪkˈstrimlɪ ‖ ɪksˈtriːmlɪ]
ad. 极端地;极其;非常
It was an extremely difficult and dangerous task.
这是一项极其困难和危险的任务。

eye [aɪ ‖ aɪ]
n. [C] ❶眼睛
She has blue eyes.
她长着一双蓝眼睛。

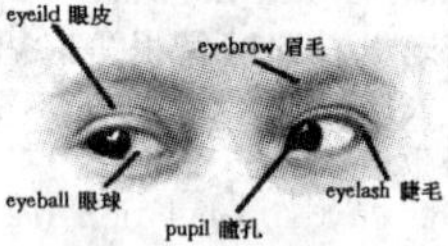

❷视力;视觉;观察力,眼光
He has a sharp eye for mistakes.
他一眼就能看出错误。
❸目光;眼神[P]
He couldn't take his eyes off her.
他无法把自己的目光从她身上移开。
❹见解;观点[P]
The Chinese are very kind in

the eyes of foreigners.
在外国人眼里，中国人是很友善的。

eyebrow 〔ˈaɪˌbraʊ ‖ ˈaɪbraʊ〕
n. 眉，眉毛[C]
Her eyebrows are thick and look very beautiful.
她的眉毛浓，并且很好看。

eyeglass 〔ˈaɪˌglæs ‖ ˈaɪglɑːs〕
n. [C] ❶单片眼镜；镜片 ❷眼镜[P]
The eyeglasses the old professor wears are very thick.
这位老教授的眼镜的镜片很厚。

eyelid 〔ˈaɪlɪd ‖ ˈaɪlɪd〕
n. 眼皮，眼睑[C]

eyesight 〔ˈaɪˌsaɪt ‖ ˈaɪˌsaɪt〕
n. 视力，目力；视野，视界[U]
His eyesight grew so bad that he couldn't see anything without eyeglasses.
他的视力变得很糟，没有眼镜什么也看不见。
His house is within eyesight.
他的家就在附近。

E

F

face 〔fes ‖ feɪs〕

［过去式］faced;［过去分词］faced

n. ❶脸,面孔[C]

His face is thin and very tanned.

他的面孔瘦削,晒得黑黑的。

> 五官:
> eyebrow 眉毛
> hair 头发
> eye 眼睛
> cheek 颊
> chin 腭
> forehead 前额
> nose 鼻子
> mouth 嘴
>
> **用法工具箱**

❷面容,表情[C]

The children's faces were brightened up when they saw their parents.

当看到他们的父母时,孩子们面露喜色。

❸表面;票面;正面[C]

He laid the cards face down on the table.

他将纸牌正面朝下放在桌上。

❹面子,尊严;威信[U]

vt. ❶面向;正对;使面对

The building faces the big river.

这房子面向着大河。

❷面临;勇敢地对付;正视

Face the facts, sir!

正视事实吧,先生!

vi. 朝;向

Their house faces east.

他们的房子朝东。

常用短语

face to face 面对面地

He sat face to face with me.
他和我面对面地坐着。

in the face of ❶面对 ❷纵然

He kept cool in the face of danger.
他面对危险却保持冷静。

He preserved in the face of difficulties.
他不顾困难坚持着。

fact 〔fækt ‖ fækt〕

n. ❶事实[C][+(that)]

The fact that he has fully recovered makes me feel good.
他已痊愈，真令我高兴。

❷实际，实情，真相[U]

Our conclusion is based entirely on fact.
我们的结论完全是实事求是的。

His facts are open to question.
他的论据易引起疑问。

常用短语

in fact =**as a matter of fact** 事实上

factory 〔ˈfæktrɪ ‖ ˈfæktərɪ〕

n. 工厂，制造厂[C]

They are factory workers.
他们是工厂工人。

fade 〔fed ‖ feɪd〕

[过去式] faded; [过去分词] faded

vi. ❶凋谢，枯萎

The flowers faded for want of water.
花儿因缺水而凋谢了。

❷(颜色，光，声等)褪去，变微弱，逐渐消失[(+away)]

The color fades when exposed to light.
这颜色曝光后会褪色。

The sound of the footsteps faded away.
脚步声渐渐消失了。

fail 〔fel ‖ feɪl〕

[过去式] failed; [过去分词] failed

vi. ❶ 失败

Our plan has failed.
我们的计划失败了。

❷不及格

She failed in the examination.
她这次考试不及格。

❸失灵；失去作用

The engine failed.
引擎出故障了。

❹(指健康)衰退；变弱；消失

My eyesight is failing.
我的视力渐渐衰退。

❺缺乏，不足；(作物)歉收

The water supply has failed.
饮水供应不足。

vt. ❶失败；不能；忘记；忽视

[+to-v]
He did very well, but failed to break the record.
他做得很出色,但未破纪录。
❷没有通过(考试),评定(学生)不及格
The professor failed almost half of the class.
该教授给班上几乎一半人评了不及格。

failure ['feljə ‖ 'feɪljə]
n. ❶失败[U][(+in)]
All his experiment ended in failure.
他所有的试验均告失败。
❷失败者;不及格者;失败的尝试(或经验)[C]
The new restaurant was a failure and soon closed.
那家新饭店经营无方,不久便关了门。
❸缺乏,不足;衰退;故障[C][U]
the failure of crops
歉收
the failure of one's sight
视力衰退

fair [fɛr ‖ feə]
a. ❶公正的;公平的;诚实的
A judge must be fair.
法官必须公正。
❷尚可的,一般的;相当的
His knowledge of English is fair.
他的英语水平尚可。
❸(皮肤)白皙的;(头发)金色的;(人)白肤金发的
She had fair hair and skin.
她有金色的头发,白皙的皮肤。
❹(天气)晴朗的
The weather will be fair tomorrow.
明天将是好天气。
n. ❶(定期)集市,庙会
He brought his piglets to the fair.
他把小猪带到集市去卖。
❷商品展览会;博览会
A book fair is to be held next month.
下个月将举行书展。

fairly ['fɛrlɪ ‖ 'feəlɪ]
ad. ❶公平地,公正地;正当地
That salesman deals fairly with his customers.
那个销售员与他的顾客做生意很公平。
❷颇为,相当地
She is a fairly good dancer.
她是一个相当不错的舞蹈演员。
❸完全地;简直

He was fairly beside himself with joy.
他简直欣喜若狂。

faith 〔feθ ‖ feɪθ〕
n. ❶信念；信任，完全信赖[U][(+in)][+that]
He always puts his faith in the future.
他对未来总是抱有信心。
❷保证，诺言；约定[U]
You should keep faith with him.
你应对他守信用。
❸信仰；宗教信仰；信条[C][U][(+in)]
People of every faith attended the mayor's funeral.
信仰不同宗教的人士出席了市长的葬礼。

faithful 〔ˈfeθfəl ‖ ˈfeɪθfəl〕
a. ❶忠实的；忠诚的；忠贞的[(+to)]
a faithful dog
忠实的狗
❷如实的；准确可靠的
〔反义〕unfaithful 不忠诚的

fall 〔fɔl ‖ fɔːl〕
[过去式]fell；[过去分词]fallen
n. ❶落下；跌倒[C][(+from)]
The fall from his horse broke his arm.
他从马上跌落摔坏了胳膊。
❷降落；降落量[C]
During the afternoon, there was a sudden heavy fall of snow.
下午突然下起了大雪。
❸下降；减少[C][(+in)]
We are expecting a fall in stock prices.
我们预料股市价格将要下跌。
❹【美】秋天[the]
〔同义〕[英]autumn
❺瀑布[P]
〔同义〕waterfall
vi. ❶落下；降落
Leaves fall from the trees.
叶子从树上落下。
❷跌落；跌倒[(+over/down)]
She slipped and fell over.
她滑了一下跌倒了。
❸下降；减退；减弱
Production costs fell by 30%.
生产成本下降了30%。
❹变成；成为
fall sick
生病
fall in love with her
爱上她
❺(城市，阵地等)陷落
The city fell to the enemy.

F

这城市已落入敌人手中。

❻(黑夜)降临，降落；(目光，重音)落在

Night has fallen.

夜幕降临了。

false 〔fɔls ‖ fɔːls〕

a. ❶不正确的，谬误的；不真实的，假的

What you're saying is false.

你所说的是假的。

❷不诚实的；虚妄的

He was accused of giving false witness.

他被指控作伪证。

❸不忠实的，无信义的[(＋to)]

Better an open enemy than a false friend.

明枪易躲，暗箭难防。

❹假的；伪造的；人造的

false hair

假发

〈伪币是 counterfeit money〉

fame 〔fem ‖ feɪm〕

n. 声誉，名望，名声[U]

He cares very little for fame and gain.

他对名利很淡薄。

familiar 〔fəˈmɪljɚ ‖ fəˈmɪljə〕

a. ❶ 众所周知的；熟悉的；常见的；普通的[(＋to)]

His name is familiar to all of us.

他的名字我们大家都熟知。

❷(某人)熟悉(某事)的，通晓……的[(＋with)]

I am of course familiar with your work.

我当然熟悉你的工作。

❸亲近的，亲密的[(＋with)]

I am familiar with her family.

我和她的家人很亲密。

family 〔ˈfæməlɪ ‖ ˈfæmɪlɪ〕

n. [C]❶家，家庭；家人，家族

> 表全体家族时谓语动词用单数；表家族成员时用复数
>
> My family is large.
>
> 我的家是个大家庭。
>
> His family are all well.
>
> 他的家人都无恙。
>
> **用法工具箱**

❷【动】【植】科；【化】【数】【天】族；【语】语族

The lion belongs to the cat family.

狮子属于猫科。

famous 〔ˈfeməs ‖ ˈfeɪməs〕

a. 著名的，出名的

The city is famous for its silk.

该市以出产丝绸而闻名于世。

fan[1]〔fæn ‖ fæn〕

n. 扇子；风扇；鼓风机[C]

She cooled herself with a fan.

她用扇子纳凉。

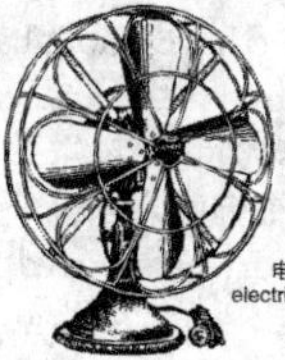

fan[2]〔fæn ‖ fæn〕

n. （运动、电影等）狂热爱好者，迷[C]

Both the father and the son are football fans.

父子都是足球迷。

fancy〔ˈfænsɪ ‖ ˈfænsɪ〕

[比]fancier；[最]fanciest；[过去式]fancied；[过去分词]fancied

n. ❶爱好；迷恋[C][(+to)]

He took a fancy to the girl next door.

他迷恋上了邻家的女孩子。

❷想象；想象力；幻想[C][U]

She has a lively fancy.

她想象力丰富。

❸想法；怪念头[C]

vt. ❶【口】想象，设想[+v-ing]

Fancy sitting in the sun all day!

想一想整天坐在太阳底下的滋味吧！

❷猜想[+that]

I fancy (that) he's pretty happy.

我猜想他很幸福。

❸【口】喜爱，爱好；想要[+v-ing]

I have a fancy for chess.

我喜欢下棋。

a. ❶别致的；花哨的；花式的

Both of them like fancy clothes.

他俩都喜欢穿新奇的服装。

❷需要高度技巧的

He is good at fancy diving.

他擅长花式跳水。

❸想象出来的；异想天开的；凭空想出的

far〔fɑr ‖ fɑː〕

[比]farther，further；[最]farthest，furthest

a. ❶远的；遥远的；久远的

Manchester is farther from London than Oxford is.

曼彻斯特比牛津离伦敦远。

❷较远的；那一边的；对面的

He lived on the far side of the hill.

他住在山的那一边。

❸（政治立场）极端的

F

He belongs to the far left.
他属于极左派。
ad. ❶远；遥远地；久远地
It happened far back in the past.
这事发生在久远的过去。
❷到很深的程度；到很远的距离[(+into)]
He often works far into the night.
他常常工作到深夜。
❸到很大程度；很；极
It turned out far better than I had expected.
结果比我预料的好得多。
〈farther 和 farthest 表示距离；further 和 furthest 表示程度〉

常用短语

as far as ❶远到……
I walked as far as the station.
我走到车站。
❷就……而言
As far as I know, he is a good person.
就我所知，他是个好人。
by far (修饰比较级，最高级，强调数量，程度等)……得多；最……
He is by far the cleverest boy in the class.
他显然是班上最聪明的男孩。
far from 完全不
He is far from rich.
他一点也不富有。

fare 〔fɛr ‖ feə〕
n. ❶(交通工具的)票价，车(船)费[C]
She didn't have enough money for the bus fare.
她的钱不够付车费。
❷(出租车等的)乘客[C]
The taxi-driver stopped to pick up a fare.
出租车司机停下车来搭载一名乘客。
❸伙食，食物；饮食[U]

farewell 〔ˌfɛrˈwɛl ‖ ˌfeəˈwel〕
int. 再会！别了！
Farewell! I hope we meet in New York next time.
再见！希望下次我们能在纽约相见。
n. ❶告别；告别的话[C][U]
They waved farewell to their friends on board the ship.
他们对船上的朋友挥手告别。
❷送别会；(欢送退休艺人的)送别演出[C]
a. 告别的
farewell present
饯别礼物

farm 〔fɑrm ‖ fɑːm〕

n. [C] ❶农场;饲养场;畜牧场
He works on a farm.
他在一个农场工作。
❷农庄住宅;农家

farmer [ˈfɑrmɚ ‖ ˈfɑːmə]
n. 农夫;农场主;农场经营者[C]

farmhouse [ˈfɑrmˌhaus ‖ ˌfɑːmhaus]
n. 农舍;农家[C]

farther [ˈfɑrðɚ ‖ ˈfɑːðə]
ad. ❶(距离,时间)更远地,再往前地
I can't go any farther.
我不能再往前走了。
❷(程度上)进一步地;此外[作此意时常用 further]
a. (距离,时间)更远的,再往前的,较远的
The farther hill is 10 miles away.
更远的山在10英里以外。

farthest [ˈfɑrðɪst ‖ ˈfɑːðɪst]
a. (距离、时间上)最远的
ad. (距离、时间上)最远地;最大限度地

fascinate [ˈfæsəˌnet ‖ ˈfæsɪneɪt]
[过去式]fascinated;[过去分词]fascinated
vt. ❶迷住,使神魂颠倒;强烈地吸引[(+by/with)]
I was fascinated by her beauty.
我被她的美貌迷住了。
❷使呆住
The frog was fascinated by the snake.
青蛙见到蛇吓得不敢动。

词汇拓展

fascination *n.* 迷人,迷惑

fashion [ˈfæʃən ‖ ˈfæʃən]
n. ❶(服饰等的)流行式样;时尚,风气[C][U]
I don't like the fashion of that coat.
我不喜欢那件上衣的式样。
❷(尤指女性的)时装[U]
❸样子,方式[U]
He greeted us warmly in his usual friendly fashion.
他以他惯有的友好方式热烈欢迎我们。

fast [fæst ‖ fɑːst]
[比]faster;[最]fastest
a. ❶快的;迅速的;速度快的
He is a fast reader.
他读书速度很快。
❷完成得快的
He did a fast job.
他很快就干完了。
❸牢的;紧的;稳固的

F

He kept a fast hold on the rope.
他紧紧抓牢绳子。
❹(钟，表)偏快的，快……(时间)的
My watch is a little fast.
我的表稍快了点。
ad. ❶快，迅速
Don't drive so fast.
别开得这么快。
❷紧紧地，牢固地
Hold fast to this rope, and I will pull you up.
抓紧绳子，我把你拉上来。

F

fasten 〔'fæsn̩ ‖ 'fɑːsn〕
[过去式]fastened;[过去分词]fastened
vt. ❶扎牢；系紧；闩住；钉牢[(+up/together)]
The little boy has learnt to fasten shoelaces.
这个小男孩已学会系鞋带了。
❷把(目光，注意等)集中于[(+on/upon)]
The old lady fastened her eyes on the stranger.
那位老太太始终注视着那个陌生人。

fat 〔fæt ‖ fæt〕
[比]fatter;[最]fattest
a. ❶肥胖的
Aunt Sarah is very fat.
萨拉阿姨很胖。
❷(肉)肥的，多脂肪的
The doctor told him to stay away from fat foods.
医生要他不要吃油腻的食品。
n. ❶(动、植物)脂肪[U]
❷油脂[U]
I don't like food cooked in deep fat.
我不喜欢油炸的食品。

fate 〔fet ‖ feɪt〕
n. 命运；天命，天数[U]
We still don't know the fate of the plane's passengers.
我们仍然不知道那架飞机上旅客的命运如何。

father 〔'fɑðɚ ‖ 'fɑːðə〕
n.[C] ❶父亲，父
You have been like a father to me.
你一直像父亲一样待我。
❷创始人；设计者；发明者[(+of)]
George Washington is called the father of his country.
乔治·华盛顿被称为国父。
❸祖先；前辈[P]
They still follow the old tradition of their fathers.
他们仍然继承着他们祖先的老

规矩。
❹(大写)神父
❺(大写)上帝;圣父[the/our]

fault 〔fɔlt ‖ fɔːlt〕
n. ❶缺点,毛病,缺陷[C]
Every man has his faults.
金无足赤,人无完人。
❷错误[C]
The teacher found many faults in spelling and grammar in my composition.
老师在我作文中发现许多拼写和文法错误。
❸(过失的)责任,咎[U]
The fault is entirely mine.
责任全在于我。

favo(u)r 〔ˈfevɚ ‖ ˈfeɪvə〕
[过去式]favored;[过去分词]favored
n. ❶赞成,赞同[U]
They will look with favor on your proposal.
他们将会赞同你的建议。
❷偏爱;偏袒[U]
A mother shouldn't show too much favor to one of her children.
做母亲的不应过分偏爱某一个孩子。
❸善意的行为;恩惠[C]
You did me a great favor.
你帮了我一个大忙。

常用短语

in favor of 支持,赞成;有利于
I am in favor of the suggestion.
我赞成这个建议。
I spoke in favor of Mr. Brown.
我帮布朗先生说话。
vt. ❶支持,拥护;赞同
We favor John's plan.
我们赞成约翰的计划。
❷偏爱;偏袒
The mother favored her eldest son.
母亲偏袒大儿子。
❸有利于,有助于
The weather favored our voyage.
天气对我们的航行有利。

favorite 〔ˈfevərɪt ‖ ˈfeɪvərɪt〕
n. [C] ❶特别喜爱的人(或物);受宠的人,亲信
Lester, the second son, was his father's favorite.
二儿子莱斯特是他父亲的宠儿。
❷最有希望获胜者(尤指马)
a. 特别喜爱的
Pepsi is my favorite drink.
百事可乐是我最喜欢的饮料。

fear 〔fɪr ‖ fɪə〕
[过去式]feared;[过去分词]

F

feared

n. ❶害怕，恐惧[(+of)][+that]

She has a great fear of water.
她很怕水。

❷可能性[U][(+of)][+that]

There is no fear that he'll be late.
他不会迟到的。

❸担心，忧虑[C][+that]

My worst fears were quickly realized.
我最大的忧虑很快成了现实。

❹(尤指对神的)敬畏

vt. ❶害怕，畏惧；担心[+(that)]

She feared that she might not find him in his room.
她担心可能在他的房间里找不到他。

❷【书】恐怕；猜想

I fear I do not know the answer to that.
我恐怕回答不出那个问题。

vi. 害怕；感到忧虑[(+for)]

She feared for her daughter's safety.
她担心女儿的安全。

feather ['fɛðɚ ‖ 'feðə]

n. 羽毛[C]

Feathers are very light, so that we say "as light as a feather".
羽毛非常轻，因此我们说"轻如鸿毛"。

feature ['fitʃɚ ‖ 'fi:tʃə]

n. [C] ❶特征，特色[(+of)]

This is a key feature of our society.
这是我们社会的一个主要特点。

❷面貌，相貌[P]

He could recall her features very distinctly.
他能够很清晰地回想起她的容貌。

❸(报纸等的)特写，特别报道，专栏

The local newspaper ran a feature on child labor.
地方报纸登载一篇有关童工劳动的特写。

❹(电影的)正片，故事片

February ['fɛbruˌɛrɪ ‖ 'februərɪ]

n. 略作 Feb. 二月

fee [fi ‖ fi:]

n. (付给律师，医生等的)酬金，服务费[C]

an entrance fee to the zoo
动物园的入场费

feed [fid ‖ fi:d]

[过去式]fed；[过去分词]fed

n. ❶(动物或婴儿的)一餐[C]

She gave her baby four feeds a day.
她每天给婴儿喂四顿。
❷饲料；牧草[C][U]
Corn is used as animal feed.
玉米被用作牲口饲料。
vt. ❶喂（养）；饲（养）[（＋on/with）]
I fed the dog on meat.
我用肉喂狗。
Feed the baby first.
先给孩子喂奶。
❷进（料）；投入；供给；提供[（＋with）]
This moving belt feeds the machine with raw material.
这条传送带供给机器所需要的原料。
❸养（家庭）
He has to feed a big family.
他必须养活一个大家庭。
vi. 吃；以……为食物；以……为能源[（＋on）]
Sheep feed on grass.
羊吃的是草。

feel [fil ‖ fiːl]
[过去式]felt；[过去分词]felt
vt. ❶摸，触；试探
I can't feel where the light switch is.
我摸不出电灯开关在哪里。
❷感觉；感知；经受
I felt the house shook.
我感觉房子震动。
❸认为，以为；相信[＋that]
I felt that she was very weak.
我觉得她很虚弱。
vi. ❶有感觉；觉得
I feel exactly like you.
我的感觉与你完全一样。
❷摸索；摸索着寻找
He felt in his pocket for the key.
他在口袋里摸着找钥匙。
❸（客体）给人某种感觉；（摸上去）给人（某种）手感
Ice feels cold.
冰摸上去是冷的。
n. ❶触觉；手感
The silk has a soft smooth feel.
这丝绸摸上去柔软光滑。
❷触，摸
Let me have a feel.
让我摸一摸。
❸感觉，气氛
There is a feel of winter.
有一种冬天的感觉。

feeling [ˈfilɪŋ ‖ ˈfiːlɪŋ]
n. ❶感觉，触觉[U]
The cold made him lose feeling in his fingers.
他的手指被冻麻了。

F

❷(……的)感觉,(……的)意识[C]
The news brought a feeling of relief.
这消息给人们带来了宽慰感。
❸看法;感想;预感[+that]
I have a feeling that we are being followed.
我觉得有人跟踪我们。
❹感情[C][U]

fellow 〔ˈfɛlo ‖ ˈfeləu〕
n. [C] ❶【口】男人;家伙;人
A fellow must eat.
人总得吃饭。
❷(大学的)研究员;(学术团体)会员
❸伙伴;同事
They are my fellows at school.
他们是我的同学。
a. 同伴的;同事的;同类的
He recalled his fellow traveler with pleasure.
他愉快地回忆起他的旅伴。

female 〔ˈfimel ‖ ˈfiːmeɪl〕
a. ❶女(性)的
Sewing is considered a female occupation.
缝纫被认为是女性的职业。
❷雌的
The hunter shot a female deer.
猎人射中一只雌鹿。
n. [C] ❶女人
❷雌性动物
This litter produced two males and two females.
这一窝产下了两只雄仔和两只雌仔。
❸【植】雌性植物

fence 〔fɛns ‖ fens〕
n. ❶栅栏;篱笆[C]
He built a fence around the garden.
他在花园周围筑了篱笆。
❷击剑术
He is a master of fence.
他精于剑术。

festival 〔ˈfɛstəvl̩ ‖ ˈfestəvəl〕
n. ❶节日,喜庆日[C]
the Spring festival
春节
❷(定期举行的)音乐节,戏剧节[C]

fetch 〔fɛtʃ ‖ fetʃ〕
[过去式]fetched;[过去分词]fetched
vt. ❶(去)拿来;去拿……给
Fetch your supper yourself, Robert.
罗伯特,你自己去拿晚餐吧。
❷去请……来,接……去
Yes, I've come to fetch you.
是的,我来接你。

fever [ˈfivɚ ‖ ˈfiːvə]

n. ❶发烧，发热；热度[C][U]

He had a slight fever.

他有点儿发烧。

❷热病[U]

❸狂热，高度兴奋[U][(+of)]

Everyone was in a fever of excitement.

所有的人都兴奋之极。

few [fju ‖ fjuː]

[比]fewer；[最]fewest

a. ❶很少数的；几乎没有的[否定的意味]

There are fewer boys than girls in my class.

我班上男生比女生少。

❷(与 a 连用)有些，几个[肯定的意味]

He has a few friends in this city.

他在这个城市里有几个朋友。

pron. ❶很少数；几乎没有[否定]

Few of my acquaintances like Sarah.

我的熟人中几乎没有人喜欢萨拉。

❷(与 a 或 the 连用)一些，几个[肯定]

Only a few of my friends were informed about it.

这件事儿只有我的几个朋友知道。

常用短语

quite a few 相当多

fiction [ˈfɪkʃən ‖ ˈfɪkʃən]

n. ❶(总称)小说[U]

❷虚构，捏造，想象[U]

The story is pure fiction.

这个故事纯属虚构。

field [fild ‖ fiːld]

n. ❶原野；田地；牧场[C]

They were working in the cotton fields.

他们在棉田里干活。

❷运动场，田赛场地；矿区，井田；(飞机)场，(战)场；(广阔的一大片)地[C]

He made a fortune in the gold

F

fields of South Africa.
他在南非的金矿区发了大财。
❸(知识)领域;专业;(活动)范畴[C]
He is a prominent scholar in the field of Linguistics.
他是语言学领域的杰出学者。

fierce 〔fɪrs ‖ fɪəs〕
[比]fiercer;[最]fiercest
a. ❶ 凶猛的;残酷的;好斗的
My grandfather became fierce when he lost his temper.
我的祖父发脾气的时候变得很粗暴。
❷狂热的;强烈的;极度的
After he got well, Bob made a fierce effort to catch up with his classmates.
鲍勃痊愈后拼命用功,以期赶上班里的同学。
❸猛烈的,激烈的
After a fierce battle the enemy was forced to retreat.
激战之后,敌人被迫撤退了。

fifteen 〔fɪf'tin ‖ fɪf'tiːn〕
a. 十五的;十五个的
n. 十五;十五个

fifteenth 〔ˌfɪf'tinθ ‖ fɪf'tiːnθ〕
a. ❶ (与 the 连用)第十五的,第十五个的
❷十五分之一的
n.[C] ❶ (与 the 连用)第十五(个);月的第十五日
❷十五分之一

fifth 〔fɪfθ ‖ fɪfθ〕
a. ❶第五的
He is already the fifth person who asked me the question.
他已经是第五个问我这个问题的人了。
❷五分之一的
n. ❶第五
❷五分之一
Three fifths of the students are women in our class.
在我们班上,五分之三的学生是女生。

fiftieth 〔'fɪftɪɪz ‖ 'fɪftɪɪθ〕
a. 第五十的;五十分之一的
n. 第五十;五十分之一

fifty 〔'fɪftɪ ‖ 'fɪftɪ〕
a. 五十的;五十个的
n. ❶五十;五十个
He is a man in his fifties.
他是一个五十来岁的人。
❷五十年代;五十几岁[P]
in the early fifties
50 年代初
She is in her fifties.
她五十几岁了。

fight 〔faɪt ‖ faɪt〕
［过去式］fought；［过去分词］fought
vi. ❶打仗；搏斗；打架；奋斗
You have to fight for your rights.
你必须为你的权利而奋斗。
❷争吵［(＋over/about)］
He and his wife are always fighting over trifling matters.
他和他妻子总是为琐事争吵。
vt. ❶与……作战；与……斗争
They fought their oppressors with all kinds of weapons.
他们用各种武器对抗压迫他们的人。
❷打(仗)；进行(战斗，决斗等)
The battle was fought in the mountains.
这一仗是在山里打的。
n. ❶战斗；搏斗；打架［C］
Who won the fight?
谁赢得了这场战斗？
❷争吵；争论［C］
Their fights were always over money.
他们的争吵总是为了钱的问题。
❸战斗力；斗志［U］
He has plenty of fight in him.
他斗志旺盛。

figure 〔ˈfɪgjɚ ‖ ˈfɪgə〕
［过去式］figured；［过去分词］figured
n.［C］❶外形；体形；人影
I saw a figure in the darkness.
我看到暗处有一个人影。
❷体态；风姿
She has an attractive figure.
她有迷人的曲线。
❸人物；名人
He has become a figure known to everyone.
他已成了一个知名人物。
❹数字
❺图形
vt. ❶计算
Please help me to figure my expenses.
请帮我算一下我的开支。
❷认为，以为，相信；估计［＋that］；料到
How do you figure that?
你如何料到的？

file 〔faɪl ‖ faɪl〕
n. ［C］❶文件夹，公文箱
❷文件，案卷，卷宗［(＋on)］
He read all the files on the case.
他阅读了有关这个案件的全部卷宗。

❸纵列
I saw a file of passengers coming down the steps.
我看见旅客鱼贯着走下阶梯。
〔反义〕rank 横列

fill 〔fɪl ‖ fɪl〕
[过去式] filled; [过去分词] filled
vt. ❶装满；填满；使充满[(＋with)]
When I had read the story, I was filled with horror.
我读完这个故事之后，心里充满了恐惧。
❷任(职)；填(缺)
Jack is the best man to fill the vacancy.
杰克是填补这一空缺的最佳人选。
❸满足
His generous donation filled our need for additional funds.
他的慷慨捐赠满足了我们对额外资金的需求。
vi. 被充满；鼓胀
Her eyes filled with tears.
她热泪盈眶。

film 〔fɪlm ‖ fɪlm〕
n. ❶软片；胶卷[C][U]
I'll buy a faster film for my camera.
我要买一卷快速胶卷。
❷电影[C]
Who stars in that film?
那部影片是谁主演的?
❸薄层；薄膜，薄皮[C]
The mirror is covered with a film of dust.
镜子上蒙了一层灰尘。

final 〔ˈfaɪnḷ ‖ ˈfaɪnl〕
a. ❶最后的；最终的
This is your final chance.
这是你的最后一次机会。
❷决定性的；确定于的，不可更改的
The headmaster has the final say.
校长说了算数。
n. [C] ❶决赛[P]
At the finals, they lost to Germany.
在决赛中他们输给了德国。
❷期末考试[P]
He failed his finals.
他期末考试没通过。

finally 〔ˈfaɪnəḷɪ ‖ ˈfaɪnəlɪ〕
ad. ❶最后，终于
❷决定性地

finance 〔ˈfaɪnæns ‖ faɪˈnæns〕
n. ❶财政；金融；财政学[U]
the Ministry of Finance
财政部
❷财源；资金；(国家的)收入；财务情况[P]

The country's finances have improved.
这个国家财政状况改善了。

find〔faɪnd‖faɪnd〕
[过去式]found;[过去分词]found
vt. ❶找到,寻得;发现;碰上
Newton found that all masses attract each other.
牛顿发现所有的物质之间都相互吸引。
He was found dead in the room.
有人发现他死在了房间里。
❷发现……处于某种状态
You will find it a difficult book.
你会觉得这是一本难以读懂的书。
❸裁决;判定
He was found guilty.
他被判有罪。

常用短语

find out 查明,找出
He found out a new method.
他找出了新方法。

fine[1]〔faɪn‖faɪn〕
a. ❶美好的,优秀的;杰出的
She is really a fine artist.
她真是一位杰出的艺术家。
❷纤细的;尖细的
This pen has a fine point.
这支笔的笔尖细。
❸(天气)晴朗的
It turned out fine again.
天又转晴了。
❹健康的;舒适的
ad.【口】很好地;妙
They are doing fine in school.
他们在学校学习得很好。

fine[2]〔faɪn‖faɪn〕
[过去式]fined;[过去分词]fined
n. 罚金,罚款[C]
The driver paid a fifty-dollar fine for speeding.
司机因超速行驶付了50美元的罚金。
vt. 处……以罚金
The judge fined him heavily.
法官重罚了他。

finger〔'fɪŋgə‖'fɪŋgə〕
n. 手指;大拇指以外的手指[C]
He burnt his finger when he lit a cigar.
他点雪茄烟时烫了手指头。

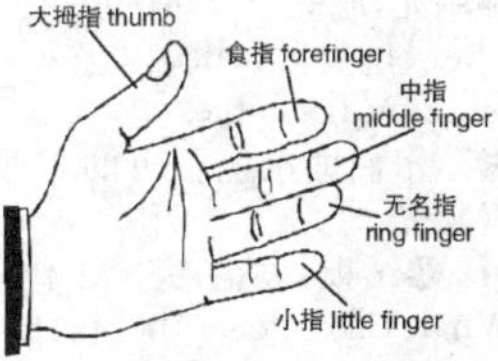

F

the thumb 大拇指
the index finger/the fore-finger 食指
the middle finger 中指
the third finger 无名指
the ring finger 左手的无名指
the little finger 小拇指

用法工具箱

finish 〔'fɪnɪʃ || 'fɪnɪʃ〕

［过去式］finished；［过去分词］finished

vt. ❶结束；完成

When does he finish his college course?

他什么时候大学毕业？

❷对……做最后加工，润饰

We'll finish our new home today and move in tomorrow.

我们今天对新居做最后修饰，明天就搬进去。

❸用完；吃完［(＋off/up)］

The boys finished up everything on the table.

男孩子们把桌上所有的东西吃得精光。

vi. ❶结束，终止；完成工作

What time does the performance finish?

表演什么时候结束？

❷(在竞赛中)获得名次

He finished third in the race.

他赛跑获得第三名。

常用短语

finish with

❶完成

Have you finished with the paper?

你看完了报纸了吗？

❷与……断绝关系

I have now finished with her.

我现在已经和她绝交了。

n. ❶结束；(比赛等的)最后阶段；终结［C］

The soldiers fought to the finish.

士兵们坚持战斗到底。

❷(家具等)抛光，末油漆

The finish on the table was scratched by a knife.

桌面上的漆被刀子划了。

fire 〔faɪr || 'faɪə〕

n. ❶火［U］

There is no smoke without fire.

无火不起烟(无风不起浪)。

❷炉火；篝火［C］

The old men sat round the fire chatting.

老人们围坐在炉火旁聊天。

❸射击；炮火；火力［U］

We opened fire at the enemy.

我们向敌人开了火。

❹火灾[C][U]

A fire broke out last night.

昨晚发生了火灾。

常用短语

catch fire 着火

The house caught fire.

这房子失了火。

firefly 〔ˈfaɪrˌflaɪ ‖ ˈfaɪəflaɪ〕

n. 萤火虫[C]

fireman 〔ˈfaɪrmən ‖ ˈfaɪəmən〕

n. 消防队员，救火队员[C]

firework 〔ˈfaɪrˌwɝk ‖ ˈfaɪəwɜːk〕

n. ❶烟火具(爆竹、花炮等)[C]

❷烟火；烟火大会[P]

firm[1] 〔fɝm ‖ fɜːm〕

a. ❶稳固的；牢固的；结实的

I don't think the chair is firm enough to stand on.

我觉得这椅子不够稳固，不能站人。

❷坚定的，坚决的；坚挺的

My brother has a firm belief in the value of cold baths.

我的兄弟坚信，洗冷水澡有益于健康。

❸坚实的

ad. 稳固地；牢固地

She holds firm to her belief in God.

她坚信上帝的存在。

firm[2] 〔fɝm ‖ fɜːm〕

n. 商号，商行，公司[C]

He has set up a firm of his own.

他自己开了一家公司。

first 〔fɝst ‖ fɜːst〕

a. ❶第一的；第一流的；(地位等)最高的

Sunday is the first day of the week.

星期日是每周的第一天。

❷最早的；最先的；最前面的

He took the first bus to town.

他乘最早的一班公共汽车进城。

n. ❶第一；第一个

He was the first to be there.

他第一个到那里。

❷第一名；优等

He will be a safe first.

他将会稳拿冠军。

ad. ❶先，首先；第一

I must finish my homework first.

我首先得做完家庭作业。

❷首次；最初

They first met in 1980.

他们在 1980 年第一次见面。

❸宁愿

He said he would resign first.

他说他宁愿辞职。

常用短语

at first 起先

F

No one listened to him at first.
起初没人注意听他说。
first of all 首先
Do your own duty first of all.
首先要尽你自己的义务。
for the first time 第一次
I took plane for the first time.
我生平第一次坐飞机。
(复合) first name 名(相对姓而言)
first hand 直接的,第一手的
first rate 第一流的

fish 〔fɪʃ ‖ fɪʃ〕
n. ❶鱼;鱼类[C]

They have a large collection of fishes.
他们收集了大量的各种鱼类。
❷鱼肉[U]
We'll have fish for dinner.
我们晚餐吃鱼。

fist 〔fɪst ‖ fɪst〕
n. 拳;拳头[C]
Ann hit him with her fist.
安用拳头打他。

fit 〔fɪt ‖ fɪt〕
[比] fitter; [最] fittest; [过去式] fitted, fit; [过去分词] fitted, fit
vt. ❶(衣服)合……身;与……相称
This dress doesn't fit me.
这件衣服不适合我穿。
❷适合于;使适合[(+for)]
We must fit the action to the word.
我们必须言行一致。
❸安装
Can you fit the electric fire for me?
你能替我装上电炉吗?
vi. ❶(衣服)合身;适合
Does this shirt fit?
这件衬衫合身吗?
❷符合;配合
a. ❶适合的;适当的;恰当的

[(+for)][+to-v]
Grass is fit for cows.
草适合给牛吃。
❷健康的;强健的
You look very fit, Mike.
麦克,你看上去很健康。
❸相称的;能胜任的[(+for)][+to-v]
He is not fit to be a lawyer.
他不适合当律师。

five 〔faɪv‖faɪv〕
a. 五的;五个的
n. ❶五;五个
❷【美】【口】五美元钞票

fix 〔fɪks‖fɪks〕
[过去式]fixed;[过去分词]fixed
vt. ❶使固定;缚紧,钉牢;牢记
He fixed the post in the ground.
他把柱子固定在地上。
❷确定;决定[(+up)][+wh-][+to-v]
You have to fix visits up with the museum.
你得和博物馆联系安排好参观事宜。
❸修理;校准;整理;收拾
We are going to have the TV fixed.
我们要请人把电视修好。

flag 〔flæg‖flæg〕
n. 旗[C]

国旗 national flag

The ship carried the national flag of Greece.
那条船挂着希腊国旗。

flame 〔flem‖fleɪm〕
n. ❶火焰;火舌[C][U]
The factory was in flames.
工厂失火了。
❷光辉,光芒[C]
❸热情;激情
A flame of anger lighted in his heart.
他怒火中烧。

flash 〔flæʃ‖flæʃ〕
[过去式]flashed;[过去分词]flashed
vt. ❶使闪光;使闪烁[(+at)]
Why is that driver flashing his lights at me?
那个司机为何用灯照我?
❷(向……)闪现出[(+at)]
I flashed a warning glance at them.

我向他们投去警告性的一瞥。
❸反照,反射[(+back)]
❹闪出;亮出;夸示
She liked flashing her diamond necklace.
她喜欢炫耀自己的钻石项链。
vi. ❶闪光,闪烁
The stars flashed in the night sky.
夜空中群星闪烁。
❷(想法等)掠过,闪现
A thought flashed through my mind.
我脑子里闪过一个想法。
❸飞驰,掠过
A car flashed by.
一辆汽车疾驰而过。
n. ❶闪烁,闪光[C]
There was a flash of lightning a moment ago.
刚才有一道闪电。
❷灯号的一闪;旗号的一挥[C]
❸【摄】闪光摄影术;闪光灯[C][U]
Did you bring your flash?
你有没有带闪光灯?

flat¹〔flæt ‖ flæt〕
a. ❶平的,平坦的
Of course, no one now believes that the earth is flat.
当然如今无人相信地球是平的。
❷(容器等)浅的
a flat plate 浅盘
❸(轮胎)泄了气的
Our car had a flat tire.
我们的汽车有一只轮胎漏了气。
n. [C]❶平面,平坦部分
I hit the table with the flat of my hand.
我用手掌击桌。
❷沼泽地;浅滩[P]
We dug clams in the flats at low tide.
退潮时我们在浅滩挖蛤蜊。
❸泄了气的轮胎

flat²〔flæt ‖ flæt〕
n.【英】(在同一层楼上的)(一套)公寓房间,公寓大楼[C][P][美]apartment

flight〔flaɪt ‖ flaɪt〕
n. ❶飞翔,飞行[C][U]
He made a round-the-world flight.
他做了一次环球飞行。
❷(飞机的)班次;(某班次的)飞机;搭机旅行;飞机的航程[C]
He completed the flight in 25 hours and 50 minutes.
他用25小时50分钟飞完了全程。
❸楼梯(或阶梯)的一段[C]

float 〔flot ‖ fləʊt〕

［过去式］floated；［过去分词］floated

vi. ❶浮

Wood floats on the water.

木头浮在水面上。

❷漂浮，浮动；飘动

The empty boat was floating on the sea.

那艘空船在海上漂浮。

❸漂泊

The orphan floated from town to town.

那个孤儿在各个城市游荡。

vt. ❶使浮起

The divers tried to float the sunken ship.

潜水员想使沉船浮起。

❷使漂浮，使浮动；使飘动

They floated the canoe out into the middle of the river.

他们将独木舟漂浮到河中间。

n. ［C］漂游物；木筏；（钓鱼用的）浮标；浮筒

flood 〔flʌd ‖ flʌd〕

n. ［C］❶洪水，水灾［P］

In 1975, the floods in that area made 233, 000 people homeless.

1975 年该地区的洪水使得 233,000 人无家可归。

❷一大批，大量［（＋of）］

He received a flood of grateful telegrams and letters.

他收到大量表示感谢的电报和信件。

floor 〔flɔr ‖ flɔː〕

n. ❶地板，地面［C］

The floor of this room is made of wood.

这个房间的地板是木头的。

❷（楼房的）层［C］

I live on the third floor.

我住在三楼。

英、美在楼层表达上不同：

〈英〉the ground floor〈美〉the first floor 一层

〈英〉the first floor〈美〉the second floor 二层

〈英〉the second floor〈美〉the third floor 三层

用法工具箱

flour 〔flaʊr ‖ ˈflaʊə〕

n. 面粉；（任何谷类磨成的）粉［C］

flow 〔flo ‖ fləʊ〕

［过去式］flowed；［过去分词］flowed

vi. ❶(河水等)流动
The river Thames flows into the North Sea.
泰晤士河流入北海。
❷涨(潮),泛滥;涌出
After the concert the people flowed out of the hall.
音乐会之后,人们从音乐厅里涌出来。
❸(头发,衣服)垂下;随风飘动
Her hair flowed over her shoulders.
她的头发垂在肩上。

F

flower 〔'flaʊɚ ‖ 'flaʊə〕
n. ❶花;花卉;开花植物[C]

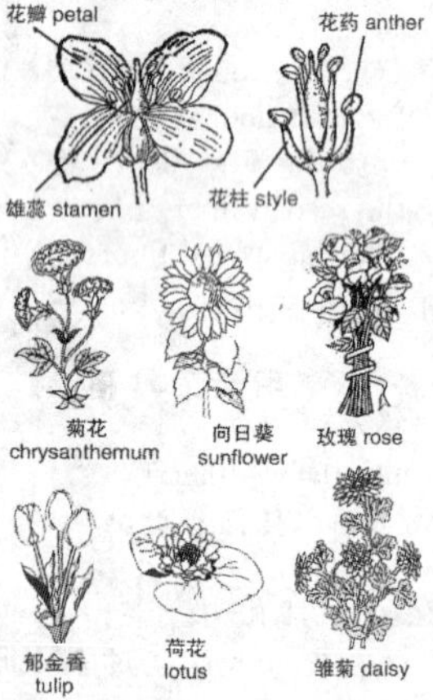

In spring many flowers bloom.
春天百花盛开。
❷开花;盛时[U]
The roses were in flower.
玫瑰花盛开着。

fluent 〔'fluənt ‖ 'flu:ənt〕
a. ❶流利的,流畅的[(+in)]
She's fluent in Polish.
她的波兰语很流利。
❷(河水等)畅流的;液态的

词汇拓展

fluently *ad.* 流利地

fly[1] 〔flaɪ ‖ flaɪ〕
[过去式]flew;[过去分词]flown
vi. ❶飞;飞行
Several seagulls flew across the sky.
几只海鸥飞过天空。
The pilot has flown for years.
这位飞行员已驾驶飞机多年。
❷乘飞机旅行
I'll fly to London tomorrow.
我明天搭飞机去伦敦。
❸(旗帜等)飘扬;飞舞
The flag was flying.
旗帜飘扬。
❹飞跑,飞奔;(时间)飞逝
I flew to see him.

我飞快地跑去见他。
Time flies.
光阴似箭。
vt. ❶驾驶(飞机)
He flew a bomber during the war.
战时他驾驶过轰炸机。
❷乘(航空公司)飞机
I always fly the United Airlines.
我总是乘坐联合航空公司的飞机。
❸空运(乘客等)
Food and medicine were flown to the area.
食物和药品被空运到该区。

fly² 〔flaɪ ‖ flaɪ〕
n. 苍蝇

focus 〔ˈfokəs ‖ ˈfəʊkəs〕
[过去式] focused, focussed; [过去分词] focused, focussed
n. ❶焦点,焦距;聚光点[C]
Rays meet in a focus.
光线聚集于焦点。
❷(注意,活动等的)中心,集中点;重点[the][(+of)]
the focus of the trouble
纷争的焦点
vt. ❶使聚焦,调节(镜头等)的焦距[(+on)]
He focused the camera on her.
他调整照相机的镜头对准她。
❷使集中[(+on)]
He focused his attention on it.
他集中注意力于那件事上。

fog 〔fɑg ‖ fɒg〕
n. 雾;雾气

浓雾 dense fog

foggy 〔ˈfɑgɪ ‖ ˈfɒgɪ〕
a. ❶有雾的;多雾的
❷模糊的;蒙眬的

fold 〔fold ‖ fəʊld〕
[过去式] folded; [过去分词] folded
vt. ❶折叠;对折[(+up)]
She folded up the letter and put it in her pocket.
她把信折起来放进口袋。
❷交叠,交叉;合拢
Fold your arms and sit up straight!
两臂交叉,坐直!
❸包;笼罩[(+up)]
He folded the pills in a piece of paper.

他用纸包住药丸。

folk 〔fok ‖ fəuk〕

n. ❶人们；(可用作称呼)各位[P]

They are the best folks on earth.

他们是世上最好的人。

❷【口】家属，亲属；双亲[P]

I write regularly to my folks.

我定期写信回家。

a. 民间的，民众的，通俗的

It is often used as folk medicine to cure snake-bites.

它常被用作民间药物来治疗蛇咬伤。

F

follow 〔ˈfɑlo ‖ ˈfɒləu〕

[过去式]followed；[过去分词]followed

vt. ❶跟随

My dog follows me to school.

我的狗跟着我去上学。

❷接在……之后

Night follows day.

黑夜接着白天。

❸沿着……行进

Follow this road to the bridge.

沿这条路一直走到桥边。

❹追赶；追逐；追求

We are being followed.

我们正被人跟踪。

❺听从；采用；信奉

Follow my advice.

听从我的劝告。

❻听懂；领会

I don't quite follow you.

我不大懂你的话。

vi. ❶跟随

He leads; we follow.

他带路；我们跟随。

❷结果生成

He is wrong, but it does not follow that you are right.

他错了，但并不能由此推断你是对的。

常用短语

as follows 如下

They requested as follows.

他们要求如下。

It follows that… 其结果是……

Because a man is rich, it doesnot follow that he is happy.

人并不因为有钱就幸福。

following 〔ˈfɑloɪŋ ‖ ˈfɒləuɪŋ〕

a. ❶接着的，其次的

In the following year the war came to an end.

第二年战争结束了。

❷下面的，下述的

Translated the following sentences into Chinese.

把下列句子译成中文。

n. 下列事物(或人员)[the]

The following is (are) important.
以下所述是重要的。

fond 〔fɑnd ‖ fɒnd〕
[比]fonder;[最]fondest
a. ❶喜欢的;爱好的[(+of)]
Tom is fond of music.
汤姆喜爱音乐。
❷溺爱的;温柔的,多情的
The fond father smiled with pleasure.
慈爱的父亲高兴地微笑了。

food 〔fud ‖ fuːd〕
n. ❶食物,食品[C][U]
Many sweet foods are on sale in the store.
这家商店在促销多种甜食。
❷(精神)食粮,材料,资料[U]
Books are food for the mind.
书是心灵的食粮。

fool 〔ful ‖ fuːl〕
[过去式]fooled;[过去分词]fooled
n. [C] ❶蠢人,傻瓜;白痴
Do you take me for a fool?
你是不是把我当傻瓜?
❷(从前宫廷内养的供人娱乐的)弄臣,小丑

常用短语

make a fool of somebody 愚弄某人,欺骗某人
Don't make a fool of him.
别愚弄他。
vt. 愚弄;欺骗
Tom fooled a lot of people into believing him.
汤姆骗得很多人相信他。

foolish 〔'fulɪʃ ‖ 'fuːlɪʃ〕
a. 愚蠢的,傻的,荒谬的,可笑的,发窘的
You are foolish to say so. = It is foolish of you to say so. 你这样说是愚蠢的。

foot 〔fut ‖ fʊt〕
n. ❶脚,足[C]

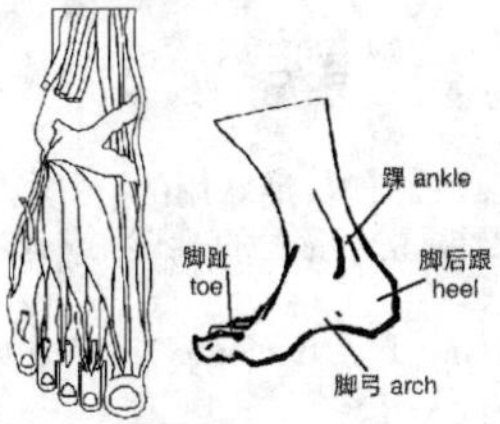

❷最下部,底部[the][(+of)]
The village is at the foot of the mountain.
村子在山脚下。
the foot of a page
页底
❸英尺[C]
The building is 60 feet high.
这幢房子有 60 英尺高。

F

常用短语

on foot 步行

He goes to shool on foot.

他步行上学。

football 〔ˈfutˌbɔl ‖ ˈfutbɔːl〕

n. ❶橄榄球;足球[U]

He is on the college football team.

他是大学橄榄球队的队员。

❷(橄榄球,足球用的)球[C]

❸被踢来踢去的难题(或人物)[C]

This has become a financial football.

这已成为财政上的难题。

for 〔fɔr ‖ fɔː〕

prep. ❶为,为了

They fought for national independence.

他们为民族独立而战。

❷代替;代表

We used boxes for chairs.

我们把箱子当椅子坐。

❸因为,由于

I am sorry for what I said to you.

我后悔不该对你讲那些话。

❹在(指定时间),(表示时间,距离等)达,计

I lived here for 5 years.

我在这儿住了5年了。

❺关于;在……方面

He has ear for music.

他懂得欣赏音乐。

❻以……为代价;以……交换

He exchanged his horse for a cow.

他用他的马换了一头牛。

I bought it for 10 dollars.

我用10美元买下它。

❼当做,作为

I know it for a fact.

我知道那是事实。

〔同义〕as 作为

❽赞成;支持;倾向于

Are you for or against the plan?

你对这个计划是赞成还是反对啊?

〔反义〕against 反对

❾朝……方向去;往,向

He left for New York.

他动身前往纽约。

❿就……而言

He is young for his age.

就他的年龄而言他是年轻的。

conj. 因为，由于

We must start early, for it will take two hours to drive to the airport.

我们得早点动身，因为开车去机场得花两个小时。

> because 表示强烈的因果关系；since，as 语气较弱；for 用来补充说明理由。
>
> **用法工具箱**

forbid 〔fɚ'bɪd || fə'bɪd〕

［过去式］forbade，forbad；［过去分词］forbidden

vt. ❶禁止，不许［＋v-ing］

The new law forbids smoking in offices.

新法律禁止在办公室抽烟。

❷阻止，妨碍

The typhoon forbade sea voyages.

台风来了，无法航海。

force 〔fɔrs || fɔːs〕

［过去式］forced；［过去分词］forced

n. ❶力，力量；力气［U］

The moral force is on our side.

道义的力量在我们一边。

❷武力，暴力［U］

The robber used force to get into the house.

强盗使用暴力强行进入住宅。

❸【物】力；力的强度［C］［U］

What is the force of gravity at sea level?

海平面的地球引力为多大？

❹军事力量；军队［P］

the Air Forces

空军

vt. ❶强迫，迫使

The policemen forced the criminals to give up their arms.

警察迫使罪犯放下武器。

❷用力推进；强行攻占（或夺取）；强行打开

We forced our way in.

我们挤了进去。

❸勉强作出（或发出）

She forced a smile.

她强作笑容。

forehead 〔'fɑrɪd || 'fɒrɪd〕

n. ［C］❶额，前额

❷前部

foreign 〔'fɔrən || 'fɒrɪn〕

a. ❶外国的

He likes collecting foreign stamps.

他喜欢收集外国邮票。

❷陌生的；不属于本身的；不适

合的[(＋to)]
Deception was foreign to his nature.
欺骗并不是他本性。

foreigner〔'fɔrənɚ ‖ 'fɔːrɪnə〕
n. 外国人[C]

forest〔'fɔrɪst ‖ 'fɒrɪst〕
n. 森林[C][U]
This is an oak forest.
这是片橡树林。

forever〔fɚ'ɛvɚ ‖ fə'revə〕
ad. ❶永远
Nobody lives forever.
没有人会长生不老。
❷(与进行式连用)老是做某事,不断地做某事
Some students in my class are forever talking.
我班上有些学生老是在说话。

F

forget〔fɚ'gɛt ‖ fə'get〕
[过去式]forgot;[过去分词]forgotten, forgot
vt. ❶忘记[＋to-v][＋v-ing][＋that][＋wh-]
I forgot posting the letter.
我忘了信已寄出。
❷忘记带(或买等)
I forgot my keys.
我忘了带钥匙了。
❸不再把……放在心上
Let's forget our disagreements.
我们不要再提我们之间的争吵了。
vi. 忘记[(＋about)]
I forgot about the food cooking on the stove.
我忘记炉子上做的饭了。
〔反义〕remember 记得

forgive〔fɚ'gɪv ‖ fə'gɪv〕
[过去式]forgave;[过去分词]forgiven
vt. ❶原谅,宽恕[(＋for)]
We forgave him for his rudeness.
我们原谅了他的无礼。
❷豁免
I'll forgive you the debt.
你欠的债我不要你还了。

fork〔fɔrk ‖ fɔːk〕
n. [C] ❶叉;耙
❷餐叉
The Chinese use chopsticks instead of knives and forks.
中国人不用刀叉,用筷子。
❸(路、河、树木等的)分岔,岔口,岔路;岔流
The villager told me to take the left fork of the road.
村民指点我走左边的岔路。

form〔fɔrm ‖ fɔːm〕
[过去式]formed;[过去分词]formed

n. ❶形状；外形[C][U]
Churches are often built in the form of a cross.
教堂常常建成十字形。
❷种类，类型[C][(+of)]
It was a form of blackmail.
那是一种敲诈。
❸(艺术作品的)表现形式，体裁[U]
He adopted the prose form.
他采用散文形式。
❹表格[C]
I filled in the application form.
我填写申请书的表格。
vt. ❶形成；构成；塑造；构(词)；造(句)
The design is formed with triangles.
该图案由若干三角形组成。
❷组织；成立
We formed a club.
我们成立了一个俱乐部。
❸养成
He forms the habit of getting up early.
他养成早起的习惯。
vi. ❶(物体)成形；被形成
Clouds are forming on the top of the hill.
山顶上形成了云。
❷排(队)，列(队)
The girls formed into three lines.
女孩子排成三行。
❸(计划，主意等)开始形成；生成，产生
An idea formed in her mind.
她脑子里生成了一个主意。

formal [ˈfɔrml̩ ‖ ˈfɔːməl]
[比] more formal; [最] most formal
a. ❶正式的；礼节上的，拘泥形式的，拘谨的，刻板的
the formal invitation to the evening feast
参加晚宴的正式邀请
formal manners
礼节形式上的
❷表面的，外形的
His obedience is merely formal.
他的服从只是表面上的。

former [ˈfɔrmɚ ‖ ˈfɔːmə]
a. ❶从前的，早前的，旧时的
In former days there was a race course here.
从前这儿有个赛马场。
❷在前的；(两者中)前者的
When she is offered ice cream or pie, she always chooses the former.
当有冰淇淋或派给她吃时，她总是挑选前者。

F

❸前任的;一度的
The guide showed us the old home of former President Theodore Roosevelt.
导游带我们看了前总统西奥多·罗斯福的故居。

formerly〔ˈfɔrmɚlɪ‖ˈfɔːməlɪ〕
ad. 以前,从前
Formerly this harbor was prosperous.
从前这个港口很繁荣。

fortieth〔ˈfɔrtɪəθ‖ˈfɔːtɪɪθ〕
a. ❶第四十的
❷四十分之一的
n. ❶第四十
❷四十分之一

F

fortunate〔ˈfɔrtʃənət‖ˈfɔːtʃənɪt〕
a. 幸运的,侥幸的[+to-v][(+in)][+that]
I am fortunate to have/ in having a good wife.
我很幸运有个好妻子。
〔反义〕unfortunate 不幸的

fortune〔ˈfɔrtʃən‖ˈfɔːtʃən〕
n. ❶财产,财富;巨款[C][U]
He received a large fortune when his uncle died.
他在叔父去世时得到了一大笔财产。
❷好运,幸运[U][+to-v]
He did not deserve such fortune.
他不配得到这种好运气。
❸命运[C]
She told my fortune by reading my palm.
她靠看手相给我算命。

forty〔ˈfɔrtɪ‖ˈfɔːtɪ〕
a. 四十的;四十个的
n. 四十;四十个

forward〔ˈfɔrwɚd‖ˈfɔːwəd〕
ad. ❶向前
He hurried forward to meet her.
他赶紧走上前去迎接她。
❷将来;今后
They never met from that day forward.
从那天以后他们就再也未能相见。
❸提前
The meeting had been put forward an hour.
会议提前一小时举行。
a. ❶前面的
We can see the forward part of the ship.
我们可以看见船的前部。
❷早的;提前的;早熟的
The spring flowers are rather forward this year.

今年春天的花儿开得相当早。

常用短语

look forward to 期待，盼望

I am looking forward to seeing you.

我盼望见到你。

found 〔faʊnd ‖ faʊnd〕

［过去式］founded；［过去分词］founded

vt. ❶创建；建造

The pilgrims founded a colony in Plymouth.

清教徒们在普利茅斯创建了一个殖民地。

❷创立，创办

They founded a college.

他们创办了一所大学。

❸将……创建在［（＋on/upon）］

His theory is founded on facts.

他的理论创建在事实的基础之上。

founder 〔ˈfaʊndɚ ‖ ˈfaʊndə〕

n. 创立者；奠基者；缔造者［C］

fountain 〔ˈfaʊntn̩ ‖ ˈfaʊntɪn〕

n. 泉水；喷泉；水源［C］

a fountain in the wood

森林中的泉水；喷水池

The fountain is playing.

喷泉正喷着水。

four 〔fɔr ‖ fɔː〕

a. 四的；四个的

n. 四；四个

fourteen 〔ˌfɔrˈtin ‖ ˌfɔːˈtiːn〕

a. 十四的；十四个的；十四人的

n. ❶十四

❷十四（个，点，人，岁）

fourteenth 〔ˌfɔrˈtinθ ‖ ˌfɔːˈtiːnθ〕

a. ❶（与 the 连用）第十四的；第十四个的

❷十四分之一的

n. ［C］❶（与 the 连用）第十四（个）；月的第十四日

❷十四分之一

fourth 〔fɔrθ ‖ fɔːθ〕

a. ❶（与 the 连用）第四的；第四个的

❷四分之一的

n. ［C］❶（与 the 连用）第四（个）；月的第四日

❷四分之一

fox 〔fɑks ‖ fɒks〕

F

n. ❶狐[C]
❷狐皮[U]
❸狡猾的人[C]

France〔fræns‖frɑːns〕
n. 法兰西,法国

F

frank〔fræŋk‖fræŋk〕
a. 坦白的;直率的;真诚的[(+with)]
I'll be frank with you.
坦白跟你说吧。

frankly〔'fræŋklɪ‖'fræŋklɪ〕
ad. 率直地;坦白地,坦率地说
Frankly speaking (To be frank with you), I cannot agree with you.
坦白地说,我不能同意你。

free〔fri‖friː〕
[过去式]freed;[过去分词]freed
a. ❶自由的;不受控制的
The prisoner was set free.
那个囚犯被释放了。
❷不受约束的[+to-v]
You are free to criticize my work.
你可以随意地批评我的工作。
❸免费的
They enjoy free medical care.
他们享受免费医疗。
❹空闲的
I am free this afternoon.
我今天下午有空。
ad. ❶免费地
Children are admitted free.
孩子们免费入场。
❷无约束地
Don't let the dogs run free.
别让狗到处乱跑。
❸松开着;脱开着
The horse broke free.
马挣脱了缰绳。
vt. 使自由;解放[(+from)]
Three people were freed from the wreckage.
有三人被救出残骸。

freedom〔'fridəm‖'friːdəm〕
n. ❶自由;独立自主[C][U][(+of)][+to-v]
freedom of action
行动自由
❷(使用,行动等的)自由权[the][(+of)]
You have the freedom of my

house and gardens.
你可以随意地到我家和花园来玩。
❸免除,解脱[U][(+from)]
freedom from hunger
免于饥饿

freeze 〔friz ‖ fri:z〕
[过去式]froze;[过去分词]frozen
vi. ❶结冰,凝固[(+up)]
When the thermometer is at 0 degree centigrade, water will freeze.
当温度计降至0摄氏度时,水便会结冰。
❷冻牢,凝住
The pond is frozen over.
水池结满了冰。
❸(用 it 作主词)冰冻,严寒
It froze hard last night.
昨夜有严重冰冻。
❹感到极冷;冻僵
I'm freezing!
我冻僵了!
vt. ❶使结冰,使凝固,使冻住[(+up)]
The cold weather froze the lake.
寒冷的天气把湖冻住了。
❷使冻僵(或冻伤、冻死)
He was frozen stiff after sitting so long.
他坐了好长时间,人都冻僵了。
❸使呆住;使战栗
She froze her noisy children with a single look.
她一瞪眼,她吵闹的孩子们马上动也不敢动。

freezing 〔ˈfriziŋ ‖ ˈfri:ziŋ〕
a. ❶冻结的;冰冻的;极冷的
❷(态度)非常冷淡的

French 〔frɛntʃ ‖ frentʃ〕
n. 法国人;法语
a. 法国的;法语的

frequent 〔ˈfrikwənt ‖ ˈfri:kwənt〕
a. ❶时常发生的,频繁的;屡次的,经常的
We had frequent snowfall last year.
去年这儿时常下雪。
❷惯常的;习以为常的
a frequent visitor
常客

frequently 〔ˈfrikwəntlɪ ‖ ˈfri:kwəntlɪ〕
ad. 频繁地,屡次地

fresh 〔frɛʃ ‖ freʃ〕
[比]fresher;[最]freshest
a. ❶新鲜的;未经加工或处理过的
They buy fresh meat.
他们买新鲜肉。

❷(水等)淡的
This kind of fish lives in fresh water.
这种鱼生活在淡水中。
❸新的;新到的;刚发生的[(+from)]
She is fresh from university.
她刚大学毕业。
❹(空气)清新的;凉爽的
fresh air
清新的空气

freshman [ˈfrɛʃmən ‖ ˈfreʃmən]
n. [C] ❶(大学等的)一年级生,新生

> 大一学生 freshman,大二学生 sophomore,大三学生 junior,大四学生 senior
>
> **用法工具箱**

❷新人;新手;生手

Friday [ˈfraɪde ‖ ˈfraɪdɪ]
n. 略作 Fri. 星期五
He'll arrive on Friday.
他星期五到。

fridge [frɪdʒ ‖ frɪdʒ]
n. 【英】【口】电冰箱

friend [frɛnd ‖ frend]
n. [C] ❶(可用作称呼)朋友,友人
He is a close friend of mine.
他是我的挚友。
❷赞助者;支持者[(+of/to)]
That rich lady is a friend of arts.
那位富婆是艺术的赞助者。

常用短语

make friends with 交朋友
I made friends with him.
我和他交了朋友。

friendly [ˈfrɛndlɪ ‖ ˈfrendlɪ]
a. ❶友好的,亲切的[(+to/towards)]
He is friendly to me.
他对我很亲切。
❷朋友关系的[(+with)]
He is friendly with me.
他和我很要好。

friendship [ˈfrɛndʃɪp ‖ ˈfrendʃɪp]
n. ❶ 友谊;友好[U]
Their friendship was as close as ever it had been.
他们的友谊跟以往一样亲密。
❷友谊的表现;友好的感情(或行为等)[C]

frighten [ˈfraɪtn̩ ‖ ˈfraɪtən]
[过去式]frightened;[过去分词]frightened
vt. ❶使惊恐,使害怕

The ghost story frightened the child.
这个鬼怪的故事使孩子十分惊恐。
❷吓唬……使其……[(+ away/off/into)]
The alarm frightened the burglar away.
警报铃声吓走了窃贼。

frog 〔frɑg ‖ frɒg〕
n. 蛙，青蛙 [C]

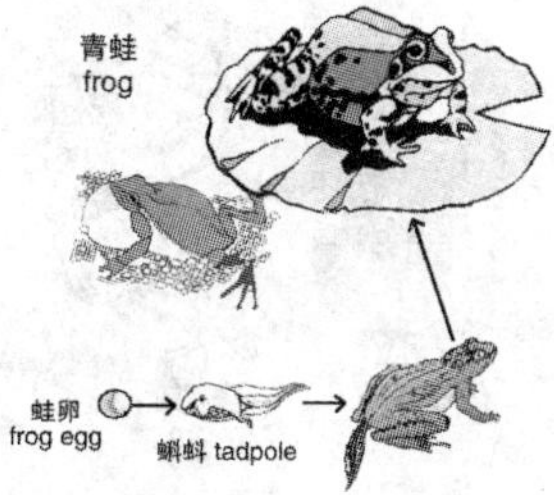

from 〔frɑm ‖ frɒm〕
prep. ❶从……起，始于
She is singing from morning to night.
她从早唱到晚。
❷从；由
He rose from office boy to managing director in 15 years.
他 15 年里从普通职员升到总经理。
❸离(开)
Our school is two miles from the station.
我们学校离车站两英里。
❹从……来；出自
Where are you from?
你从哪儿来？
❺(表示去除，免掉，去掉，阻止，剥夺等)
Bill was absent from school.
比尔没上学。
❻(表示区别，比较)
Can you tell a wolf from a dog?
你能区别狼和狗吗？
❼(表示原料)由[用于看不出原料本质的场合；能看出原材料的用 of]
Cheese is made from milk.
乳酪是由牛奶制成的。
The desk is made of wood.
这桌子是由木头制成的。
❽因为，由于；出于
He died from wound.
他因伤致死。

front 〔frʌnt ‖ frʌnt〕
n. ❶前面；正面[C][(+of)]
The front of the postcard shows a picture of the Summer Palace.
明信片的正面是一幅颐和园的照片。

F

❷临海（或临街）的地方；海滨散步道

The hotel is right on the sea front.

旅馆就在海滨。

❸前线；战线[C]

He has just returned from the front.

他刚从前线回来。

frontier〔frʌn'tɪr || 'frʌntɪə〕

n. 国境，边境；边疆[(＋between/with)][C]

frontier spirit

拓荒精神

the frontier between China and Russia

中国和俄罗斯的边境线

frost〔frɔst || frɒst〕

n. ❶霜[C][U]

The frost killed the young tomato plants.

寒霜冻死了番茄幼苗。

❷冰冻，严寒；冰点以下的温度

There'll be frost tonight.

今晚有严寒。

frown〔fraʊn || fraʊn〕

[过去式]frowned；[过去分词]frowned

vi. 皱眉；表示不满[(＋at/on/upon)]

The father frowned on his son's behavior.

父亲不满他儿子的行为。

frozen〔'frozn̩ || 'frəuzn〕

a. 冰冻的；结冰的；极冷的

a frozen river

结冻的河

fruit〔frut || fru:t〕

n. ❶水果[C][U]

I like fruit and vegetables.

我喜欢水果和蔬菜。

❷果实，果类[U]

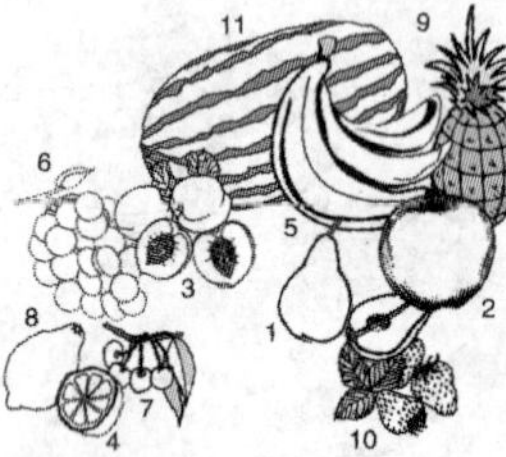

1.pear梨 2.apple苹果 3.peach桃子 4.orange橘子 5.banana香蕉 6.grape葡萄 7.cherry樱桃 8.lemon柠檬 9.pineapple菠萝 10.strawberry草莓 11.watermelon西瓜

❸成果，产物[C]

They enjoy the fruits of their hard labor.

他们享受着自己辛勤劳动的成果。

fry〔fraɪ || fraɪ〕

[过去式]fried；[过去分词]fried

vt. 油煎,油炸,油炒
She fried eggs for breakfast.
她煎蛋当早餐。
vi. 在油里煎(或炸,炒)
The fish is frying.
正在煎鱼。

fuel 〔ˈfjuəl ‖ ˈfjʊəl〕
n. 燃料[C][U]

full 〔ful ‖ fʊl〕
[比]fuller;[最]fullest
a. ❶满的;充满的[(+of)]
The room was full of people.
室内挤满了人。
❷吃饱的
I can't eat any more; I'm full up.
我不能再吃了;我已经饱了。
❸(程度等)完全的;最大的;最高的;正式的
He is a full member of the committee.
他是委员会的正式成员。

常用短语

in full 全部地
Write your name in full.
写上你的全名。
to the full 完全地
He enjoyed himself to the full.
他尽情享受。

fun 〔fʌn ‖ fʌn〕
n. [U] ❶娱乐,乐趣
What fun we had!
我们玩得多开心!
❷玩笑,嬉戏
His uncle is fond of fun.
他的叔父喜欢开玩笑。
❸有趣的人(或事物)
Mr. Smith is great fun.
史密斯先生是一个很有趣的人。

常用短语

make fun of 取笑
They made fun of him.
他们开他的玩笑。

function 〔ˈfʌŋkʃən ‖ ˈfʌŋkʃən〕
[过去式]functioned;[过去分词]functioned
n. [C] ❶机能,功能,作用
The teacher did not explain its grammatical function.
老师没有解释它的文法功能。
❷职务,职责
What is his function on the committee?
他在委员会里担任什么职务?
❸盛大的集会(或聚会,宴会,宗教仪式)
I attended many social functions while working abroad.
我在国外工作期间出席了许多社交会。
vi. ❶(机器等)工作,运行

The refrigerator is not functioning well.
冰箱有点问题。
❷起作用[(+as)]
The sofa functions as a bed at night.
这沙发在夜里可以当床。

fund 〔fʌnd ‖ fʌnd〕
n. 资金,基金,专款[C]
They are raising funds for a new laboratory.
他们在募款筹建一个新的实验室。

F

fundamental 〔ˌfʌndəˈmɛntl̩ ‖ ˌfʌndəˈmentl〕
a. 基础的;根本的,十分重要的[(+to)]
Hard work is fundamental to success.
勤奋工作是成功的基础。

funeral 〔ˈfjunərəl ‖ ˈfjuːnərəl〕
n. 丧葬,葬仪;出殡行列[C]
He attended the funeral.
他参加了葬礼。

funny 〔ˈfʌnɪ ‖ ˈfʌnɪ〕
[比]funnier;[最]funniest
a. ❶有趣的;滑稽可笑的;爱开玩笑的
That's the funniest joke I've ever heard.
那是我所听过的最风趣的笑话了。
❷【口】古怪的,稀奇的
I heard a funny noise.
我听到一个奇怪的声响。
❸【口】稍有不适的;神志不太正常的
He felt funny all day yesterday.
昨儿一整天他都觉得不舒服。

fur 〔fɝ ‖ fɜː〕
n. ❶(兽类的)软毛[U]
That cat has soft white fur.
那只猫的毛又软又白。
❷毛皮;皮子
❸(皮衣等)毛皮制品[P]
Many people wear furs in winter.
冬天许多人穿毛皮衣服。

furnace 〔ˈfɝnɪʃ ‖ ˈfɜːnɪs〕
n. [C] ❶火炉,熔炉
❷(建筑物内的)暖气炉

furniture 〔ˈfɝnɪtʃɚ ‖ ˈfɜːnɪtʃə〕
n. 家具[U]
Some articles of furniture were lost when we moved.
我们搬家的时候有几件家具丢失了。

further 〔ˈfɝðɚ ‖ ˈfɜːðə〕
a. ❶更远的;较远的
the further side of the mountain
山的那一边

❷另外的;进一步的;深一层的
Do you need further help?
你还需要帮忙吗?
ad. ❶更远地
The post office is a mile further.
邮局有一英里远。
❷进一步地;深一层地
We will help you further.
我们会进一步帮助你的。
❸而且;另外;再者
The house is not big enough for us; and further, it is too far from the town.
这房子对我们来说太小了;再者,它离城也太远。

furthermore 〔ˌfɝðɚˈmɔr ‖ ˌfɜːðəˈmɔː〕
ad. 而且,此外,再者
I don't want to go there; furthermore, I have no time to do so.
我不想去那儿,而且我也没时间。

future 〔ˈfjutʃɚ ‖ ˈfjuːtʃə〕
n. ❶未来,将来[the]
He felt confident in the future.
他对未来充满信心。
❷前途[C]
You have a great future.
你前途无量。
a. ❶未来的,将来的
I met my future wife at a dance.
我是在一个舞会上结识了我未来的妻子的。
❷【文】将来(时)的

F

gain 〔gen ‖ geɪn〕

［过去式］gained；［过去分词］gained

vt. ❶ 得到；获得，赢得（战争，诉讼等）

Our army gained the battle.

我们的军队赢得了那场战役。

❷使得到

He had gained himself a reputation for unfairness.

他使自己得到了一个不公正的名声。

❸增加，增添

I gained 5 pounds in a week.

我一个星期体重增加了 5 磅。

vi. ❶获利，赚钱；得益［(＋by/from)］

We all gained from the experience.

我们都从这次经历中获益。

❷（逐渐）取得进展；（逐渐）得到改善；增进健康

The singer is gaining in popularity.

这位歌手越来越受到人们的欢迎。

n. ❶获得；增加；获利［C］［U］

The baby had a gain of half a pound.

那个婴儿的体重增加了半磅。

❷获得物；收益，利润［C］

No gains without pains.

不辛劳，无收获。

gallery 〔'gælərɪ ‖ 'gælərɪ〕

n. 画廊，美术馆[C]
The gallery is having a show of French oil paintings.
这个美术馆正在举办法国油画展。

game 〔gem ‖ geɪm〕
n. ❶游戏；运动；游戏（或运动）器具[C]
Football is a game which interests me a lot.
足球是我很感兴趣的运动。
❷竞赛；运动会[P]
The First East Asian Games were held in Shanghai in 1993.
第一届东亚运动会于 1993 年在上海举行。
❸（比赛等的）一局，一场[C]
He won two games out of three.
他在三局比赛中胜了两局。

gap 〔gæp ‖ gæp〕
n. [C] ❶豁口，裂口，缺口[（＋in）]
The cat went out through a gap in the fence.
猫从篱笆的缺口跑出去了。
❷分歧，隔阂；差距[（＋between）]
There was a great gap between the views of the two.
他们两个人的意见有很大分歧。
the generation gap
代沟

garage 〔gæˈrɑʒ ‖ ˈgærɑːʒ〕
n. [C] ❶车房，车库；飞机库
❷汽车修理厂

garbage 〔ˈgɑrbɪdʒ ‖ ˈgɑːbɪdʒ〕
n.【主美】垃圾；剩菜；废物
Put the garbage in the can.
把剩菜倒在桶内。

garden 〔ˈgɑrdn̩ ‖ ˈgɑːdn〕
n. 花园；菜园；果园；庭院[C]
a rose garden
玫瑰园
a kitchen garden
菜园

gas 〔gæs ‖ gæs〕
n. ❶ 气体[C][U]
There are several kinds of gas in the air.
空气中有几种气体。
❷【矿】瓦斯[U]
❸可燃气；煤气；沼气[U]
Gas is now widely used for cooking and heating.
现在普遍用煤气烧饭、取暖。
❹【美】【口】汽油[U]
Is there any gas station nearby?
附近有加油站吗？

gasoline 〔ˈgæsl̩in ‖ ˈgæsəliːn〕
n. 汽油[U]

gate〔get ‖ geɪt〕

n.［C］❶大门；栅栏门；围墙门

I'll wait for you at the gate.

我在大门口等你。

❷出入口；门道；登机门

Our flight is boarding at gate number 4.

我们的航班在 4 号门登机。

gather〔'gæðɚ ‖ 'gæðə〕

［过去式］gathered；［过去分词］gathered

vt. ❶收集；召集；使聚集

He is gathering materials for a new book.

他正在收集资料，准备写一本新书。

❷积聚；积蓄

This cloth gathers dust.

这种布容易积灰尘。

❸收拾；摘；采集；收割

The girl is gathering flowers.

那个女孩在采花。

vi. 积聚；集合

A crowd gathered at the scene of the accident.

出事地点聚集了一群人。

gay〔ge ‖ geɪ〕

a. ❶【美】【俚】(一般指男子)同性恋的

❷鲜艳的；艳丽的；衣着华丽的

The package was tied with gay ribbons.

包裹用色彩鲜艳的丝带捆扎好。

❸快乐的；爽朗的；轻快的

Tonight she was gay, anxiety-free.

今晚她无忧无虑，很是高兴。

general〔'dʒɛnərəl ‖ 'dʒenərəl〕

［比］more general；［最］most general

a. ❶一般的，普遍的；通常的；非专业性的

This is a general magazine.

这是一本普通杂志。

❷全体的；公众的

That is a matter of general anxiety.

那是一个大家忧虑的问题。

❸大体的，笼统的

We had a general talk about drama.

我们泛泛谈论戏剧。

n. 将军；上将［C］

Washington was a famous general.

华盛顿是一位著名的将领。

generally〔'dʒɛnərəlɪ ‖ 'dʒenərəlɪ〕

ad. ❶通常，一般地

I generally get up at 7.

我通常 7 点起床。

G

❷广泛地，普遍地
It is generally believed that smoking is bad for the health.
人们普遍相信吸烟有害健康。

常用短语

generally speaking 总的来说
Generally speaking, man is stronger than woman.
一般而言，男人比女人强壮。

generation 〔ˌdʒɛnəˈreʃən ‖ ˌdʒenəˈreɪʃən〕
n. [C]❶世代，一代
from generation to generation
世代相传
❷同时代的人，一代人；一代事物；(计算机、音响、武器系统等的)代
the fifth generation computer
第5代计算机
Our generation has seen a lot of changes.
我们这一代人经历了许多变化。

generous 〔ˈdʒɛnərəs ‖ ˈdʒenərəs〕
a. ❶慷慨的，大方的[(+with/in/to)]
She is generous in giving help.
她乐于助人。
❷宽宏大量的，宽厚的[(+to/towards)]
He is generous towards his subordinates.
他待部属很宽厚。
❸大量的；丰富的；丰盛的
She gave me a generous lunch.
她请我吃了一顿丰盛的午餐。

genius 〔ˈdʒinjəs ‖ ˈdʒiːnjəs〕
n. ❶天资，天赋，才华[U]
She has genius.
她有天赋。
❷天才，英才[C]
Einstein was a great scientific genius.
爱因斯坦是一个伟大的科学天才。
❸才能，才干[(+for)]
He has a genius for getting along with children.
他擅长与孩子们打成一片。

gentle 〔ˈdʒɛntḷ ‖ ˈdʒentl〕
[比]gentler；[最]gentlest
a. ❶温和的；和善的，仁慈的
He is a gentle person.
他是个温和的人。
❷轻柔的；和缓的
She gave me a gentle push.
她轻轻推了我一下。
❸驯服的，温驯的
Ours is a gentle horse.
我们的马很温驯。

gentleman 〔ˈdʒɛntḷmən ‖

ˈdʒentlmən〕

n. [C]❶绅士;有教养的男子

He is a perfect gentleman.

他是一个十足的君子。

❷先生,男士

Please bring this gentleman a cup of coffee.

请给这位先生拿一杯咖啡。

〔反义〕lady 女士

geography 〔dʒiˈɑgrəfɪ ‖ dʒɪˈɒgrəfɪ〕

n. ❶地理学[U]

❷地形;地势[the][(+of)]

geometry 〔dʒiˈɑmətrɪ ‖ dʒɪˈɒmətrɪ〕

n. 几何学[U]

G

German 〔ˈdʒɝmən ‖ ˈdʒɜːmən〕

a. ❶德国的;德国人的

❷德语的

n. ❶德国人

❷德语

Germany 〔ˈdʒɝmənɪ ‖ ˈdʒɜːmənɪ〕

n. 德国

get 〔gɛt ‖ get〕

[过去式]got;[过去分词]got, gotten

vt. ❶获得;得到;赢得

He gets first prize in the listening contest.

他获得听力比赛第一名。

❷挣到;买到

I got a new coat in that store last week.

上礼拜我在那家商店买了一件新外套。

❸捉住,捕获

The police got the thief.

警察捉住了贼。

❹(不用被动式)收到,接到

Did you get my letter?

你收到我的信了吗?

❺为……弄到;为……买到

Get me a chair.

替我拿把椅子来。

❻(使役用法)

I got my arm broken.

我的手臂断了。

vi. ❶到达

When did your father get to Hong Kong?

你爸爸什么时候到的香港?

❷变成,成为

It's getting cold.

天气变冷。

❸有可能,有机会[+to-v]

He never gets to go to school.

他从没有机会上学。

❹开始[+v-ing]

They got talking.

他们开始谈话。

❺被……[+v-ed]

They got married.
他们结婚了。

常用短语

get along 生活;进展
How are you getting along?
您好吗?(日子过得怎么样?)
I'm getting along with my roommate very well.
我和我的室友相处得很好。
How are you getting along with your study?
你的学习进展如何?

get at 拿得到
The baby tried to get at the toy.
婴孩设法拿到那个玩具。

get away 逃脱
The criminal got away from the police.
罪犯摆脱了警察逃跑了。

get back 回来
He will soon get back.
他很快就回来。

get in 乘(车),进入
Get in the car.
上车。

get into 陷入(某种状态)
He got into trouble.
他陷入了困境。

get off 从……下来
He got off the train.
他下了火车。

get on 搭乘(车);骑(马)
〈乘(火车,船,巴士,飞机)是 get on,乘计程车是 get in a taxi〉
He got on the train.
他搭乘火车。

get over 克服
We have to get over many difficulties.
我们得克服许多困难。

get through
❶**办完**
He got through the work yesterday.
他昨天完成了工作。
❷**通过**
The train got through the tunnel.
火车穿过隧道。

get up 起床,站起来
I usually get up at 7.
我通常7点起床。
He suddenly got up from the chair.
他突然从椅子上站起来。

ghost 〔gost ‖ gəust〕
n. 鬼,幽灵[C]

giant 〔'dʒaɪənt ‖ 'dʒaɪənt〕
n. [C] ❶巨人
❷(力量、智力超群的)伟人
Shakespeare is a literary giant.

莎士比亚是一位大文豪。
❸巨物;巨大的动物(或植物)
That company is a giant in the electronics industry.
那家公司在电子工业中的实力最强。

gift 〔gɪft ‖ gɪft〕
n. ❶礼品[C]
She has got lots of birthday gifts.
她得到了许多生日礼物。
❷天赋;才能[C][(+for)]
Dee has a gift for making everyone feel at ease.
迪有种能让大家放松的天赋。

girl 〔gɝl ‖ gɜːl〕
n. [C] ❶姑娘,少女
This school is for girls only.
这个学校只招收女生。
❷女儿
My little girl is at school.
我小女儿在上学。

girlhood 〔ˈgɝlhʊd ‖ ˈgɜːlhʊd〕
n. ❶少女时代,少女时期[U]
❷(总称)少女们

give 〔gɪv ‖ gɪv〕
[过去式]gave;[过去分词]given
vt. ❶给;送给
I gave him a book. = I gave a book to him.
我给了他一本书。
❷给予(某人时间,机会等);授予;赐予
I'd like to give him another chance.
我想再给他一次机会。
❸供给,生成;带来
Sorry to have given you trouble.
对不起,打扰了。
❹做(一动作)
give a cry
叫一声
give a kick
踢一下
give a push
推一把
give a reply
回答
give an order
下命令
❺(为……)举办,举行;(为……)上演
give a concert
开音乐会
give a party
开晚会
give a lecture
作演讲
❻交给;托付
I gave the porter my baggage.
我把行李交给脚夫。

常用短语

give in **投降，屈服**
He gave in to her request.
他对她的要求让步。
give off **发散，放出**
The rose gave off a nice smell.
玫瑰散发出香气。
give out **让出**
give up **❶放弃** **❷戒掉**
My father gave up smoking.
我父亲戒烟了。

glad 〔glæd ‖ glæd〕
［比］gladder；［最］gladdest
a. ❶高兴的，快活的［(＋at/about/for/of)］［＋to-v］［＋(that)］
We're glad that he's got a job.
我们为他找到工作而高兴。
❷乐意的［＋to-v］
I'll be glad to do it for you.
我很乐意为你做这件事。
❸令人高兴的
The glad news excited them.
好消息令他们兴奋不已。

glance 〔glæns ‖ glɑːns〕
［过去式］glanced；［过去分词］glanced
vi. ❶(粗略地)看一下，一瞥；扫视［(＋at/round/over/through)］
He glanced round the conference room.
他扫视了一下会议室。
❷闪烁，闪耀
Their bayonets glanced in the sunlight.
他们的刺刀在阳光下闪耀。
vt. ❶用(眼睛)扫视；瞥见
❷擦过；使擦过
The bullet glanced the tree.
子弹穿过那棵树。
n. 一瞥；扫视［(＋at/into/over/through)］［C］
Have you got time for a glance at this report?
你有没有时间浏览一下这份报告？

glass 〔glæs ‖ glɑːs〕
n. ❶玻璃［U］
A mirror is made of glass.
镜子是用玻璃制的。
❷玻璃制品［U］
We have a set of table glass.
我们有一套玻璃餐具。
❸玻璃杯［C］
❹一杯(的容量)［C］
Drink a glass of water.
喝一杯水。
❺眼镜［P］
Our teacher wears a pair of glasses.
我们的老师戴一副眼镜。

G

glimpse 〔glɪmps ‖ glɪmps〕
[过去式]glimpsed；[过去分词] glimpsed
n. 瞥见；一瞥[C]
She drew aside the window-curtain and had a glimpse of the river.
她拉开窗帘，瞥了一眼那条河。
vi. 看一眼，瞥见[(+at)]
He glimpsed at my new watch and said it was a good bargain.
他看了一眼我的新表，说买得很划算。
vt. 瞥见
They glimpsed a village through the trees.
他们透过林隙隐约看见一个村庄。

globe 〔glob ‖ gləʊb〕
n. ❶球；球状物[C]
an electric light globe
电灯泡
❷地球仪[C]

地球仪
terrestrial globe

❸地球[the]
This plant can grow in many parts of the globe.
这种植物能在地球上许多地方生长。

glorious 〔'glɔrɪəs ‖ 'glɔːrɪəs〕
a. ❶光荣的，荣耀的；辉煌的
We gained a glorious victory.
我们赢得了辉煌的胜利。
❷壮观的，壮丽的
a glorious sunset
壮观的日落

glue 〔glu ‖ gluː〕
n. 胶，胶水；黏着剂[C][U]

glove 〔glʌv ‖ glʌv〕
n. [C] ❶手套

手套 glove
长手套 gauntlet
连指手套 mitten

He put on his gloves and began to repair the truck.
他戴上手套，开始修理卡车。
❷拳击手套；棒球手套

GMT
abbr. =Greenwich mean time

【天】格林尼治标准时间

go 〔go ‖ gəʊ〕

［过去式］went；［过去分词］gone

vi. ❶去；离去

When did she go?

她什么时候离开的？

go to school

去上学

〔反义〕come 来

❷行走；旅行；移动

We went by train.

我们搭火车去。

❸做（事）；从事（活动）［＋v-ing］

go swimming

去游泳

go shopping

去购物

❹变为，成为

go mad

疯了

go bad

变坏了

❺（事物）进行

How are things going?

情况怎样？

Everything went well.

一切进展良好。

❻(be) going to do

表示现在有迹象或倾向表明将来的事情或状态（即现在开始的将来）

Oh, dear! I think he is going to jump.

天哪！我想他要跳楼。

〈be going to 可以和任何时态、动词形式连用〉

"She looks happy."

"她看起来很高兴。"

"Yes, I understand that she may be going to have a baby."

"是的，我想她可能要生孩子了。"

常用短语

go about 着手（工作）

Go about your business.

去做你自己的事吧。

（不要多管闲事）

go after 追求

He went after fame.

他追求名誉。

go away 离去，出去

He went away for a change.

他出去散心。

go back 回去

He went back empty-handed.

他空手而回。

go by 过去，逝去

Many hours went by.

好几个小时过去了。

go down 下降，下跌

Prices are expected to go down.

价格可望下跌。

go for 出去(干)

go for a walk 去散步

go for a drive 出去兜风

go in for 爱好

He goes in for tennis.

他爱打网球。

go into 进入;讨论,详细调查

He went into the room.

他进入室内。

Let's not go into that matter now.

咱们现在不要再讨论那件事情了吧。

go off 离去,逃走;(事情)进行

He went off with the money.

他卷款而逃。

The party went off well.

舞会进行得很顺利。

go on 向前行;继续

Let's go on a little farther.

咱们再往前走点吧。

go on with the work 继续工作

go on talking 继续说

go out 出去;熄灭

He went out just now.

他刚出去。

The light went out.

灯熄灭了。

go over 检查;复习

He went over the homework carefully.

他仔细检查作业。

go through 通过;经历

He went through two wars.

他经历了两次战争。

go through with 完成

They will go through with the plan.

他将完成这个计划。

go up 上升,上涨

Prices went up.

物价上涨了。

goal 〔gol ‖ gəul〕

n. [C] ❶(赛跑等的)终点;(旅行的)目的地

He was the first to cross the goal.

他是第一个越过终点的。

❷目的,目标

His goal in life is to be a great scientist.

他人生的目标就是成为一个伟大的科学家。

❸(足球等运动的)球门;得分数

goat 〔got ‖ gəut〕

n. 山羊[C]

kid 小山羊
sheep 绵羊
lamb 小绵羊

用法工具箱

god 〔gɑd ‖ gɒd〕

n. ❶(大写)上帝,造物主

❷男神[C]

〔反义〕goddess 女神

常用短语

God knows 天晓得

God knows where he has gone.

没人知道他去哪儿了。

for God's sake 务请,千万

For God's sake, stop quarreling.

求求你们不要再吵了。

gold 〔gold ‖ gəʊld〕

n. ❶金[U]

People used to pay in gold.

人们过去以黄金支付。

❷金币;财富[U]

❸金色,金黄色[U]

The sun shone on the gold of her hair.

太阳照在她金黄色的头发上。

a. ❶金(制)的;含金的

a gold watch

金表

a gold ring

金戒指

❷金色的

❸金唱片奖的(销售逾百万的)

go gold (指唱片)销售逾百万张

golden 〔'goldn̩ ‖ 'gəʊldən〕

a. ❶金色的,金黄色的;黄金般的

❷金的;金制的

goldfish 〔'goldˌfɪʃ ‖ 'gəʊldˌfɪʃ〕

n. 金鱼[C]

goldsmith 〔'goldˌsmɪθ ‖ 'gəʊldˌsmɪθ〕

n. 金匠[C]

golf 〔gɑlf ‖ gɒlf〕

n. 高尔夫球运动[U]

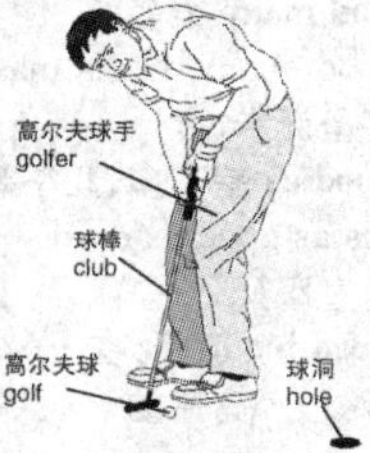

good 〔gʊd ‖ gʊd〕

[比]better;[最]best

a. ❶好的,令人满意的

He is my good friend.

他是我的好朋友。

❷有益的;有效的;适合的[(+for/to)]

Exercise is good for health.

运动有益于健康。

❸愉快的

We all had a good time on the beach.

我们在海滩上玩得很开心。

G

❹擅长的，有本事的[(＋at)]
He is good at swimming.
他擅长游泳。
❺非常的；十足的；充分的
a good deal of oil
很多油
a good long time
很长时间

常用短语

a good many 很多的
a good many Christmas cards
很多圣诞卡
as good as 差不多，几乎等于
He is as good as dead.
他简直跟死了一样。
be good for 适于；在……期间有效；对……有用的
His son is good for nothing.
他儿子一无是处。
The ticket is good for two days.
这张票两日内有效。
n. ❶利益；好处，用处[U]
What good will it do you?
这会给你带来什么好处呢？
❷善；好事；慷慨的行为[U]
There is good in her, in spite of her bad reputation.
尽管她名声不佳，她还是有善的一面。
❸长处，优点[U]
❹(总称)好人[the]
Christians believe the good will go to heaven when they die.
基督教徒相信好人死了进天堂。

常用短语

be no good 毫无用处，毫无价值
This dictionary is no good.
这本字典毫无价值。
do…good＝ do good to 对某人有利
The medicine will do you good.
这药对你有益。

good-bye 〔gʊdˈbaɪ ‖ gʊdˈbaɪ〕
int. 再见！
n. 告辞；告别

good-looking 〔ˌgʊdˈlʊkɪŋ ‖ ˌgʊdˈlʊkɪŋ〕
a. 好看的，漂亮的；美貌的

goods 〔gʊdz ‖ gʊdz〕
n. ❶商品；货物
He buys and sells leather goods.
他买卖皮货。
❷动产
Our neighbors sold their household goods before they moved out.
我们的邻居在搬家前把家用品先卖掉。

G

goose 〔gus ‖ guːs〕
[名复] geese
n. ❶鹅；雌鹅
We saw a flock of geese swimming in the lake.
我们看见一群鹅在湖里游水。

❷鹅肉[U]
I don't care much for goose.
我不太喜欢吃鹅肉。

gossip 〔'gɑsəp ‖ 'gɒsɪp〕
n. 闲话，聊天；流言飞语[C][U]
Her letter were full of gossip about her neighbors' troubles.
她的信净是些东家长西家短的闲话。

government 〔'gʌvə·nmənt ‖ 'gʌvənmənt〕
n. ❶(常大写)政府，内阁[C]
❷政体；体制；政治[U]

grab 〔græb ‖ græb〕
[过去式]grabbed；[过去分词]grabbed
vt. 攫取，抓取，夺取，霸占
The man grabbed my wallet and ran away.
那个人抢了我的钱包跑掉了。
vi. 抓(住)，夺(得)[(+at)]
grab at an opportunity
抓住机会

grace 〔gres ‖ greɪs〕
n. ❶优美；优雅[U]
She moved with grace.
她风姿秀逸。
❷风度，魅力；美德[P]
She is full of graces.
她充满魅力。
❸恩惠，善意[U]
an act of grace
仁慈的行为

graceful 〔'gresfəl ‖ 'greɪsfəl〕
a. ❶优美的，雅致的，典雅的
What a graceful dancer she is!
她的舞姿多优美呀！
❷懂礼貌的，得体的

grade 〔gred ‖ greɪd〕
n. [C] ❶等级；级别；阶段
These are second-grade grapes.
这些是次级葡萄。
❷【美】(中、小学的)年级；(某年级的)全体学生
The twins will enter the fourth grade this fall.
这对双胞胎今年秋季将升到四年级。

G

【英】form 年级
❸【美】成绩，评分
He received a failing grade on the term paper.
他的期末论文不及格。
〔同义〕mark 分数

gradually 〔ˈɡrædʒʊlɪ ‖ ˈɡrædjʊəlɪ〕
ad. 逐步地，渐渐地
His health is gradually improving.
他渐渐恢复了健康。

graduate 〔ˈɡrædʒʊˌɪt ‖ ˈɡrædjʊeɪt〕
［过去式］graduated；［过去分词］graduated
vt.【美】准予……毕业；授予……学位
Our university graduates 1,000 students every year.
我们大学每年有 1,000 名学生毕业。
He was graduated from that college.
他毕业于那所大学。
vi.【英】大学毕业；【美】毕业［(＋from)］
I graduated from a high school.
我高中毕业。
n.【英】大学毕业生；【美】毕业生；学位获得者
a high school graduate
高中毕业生
a graduate in medicine
医科毕业生
a. ❶毕业了的
❷【美】研究生的
a graduate school
(大学的)研究生院

graduation 〔ˌɡrædʒʊˈeʃən ‖ ˌɡrædjʊˈeɪʃən〕
n. ❶毕业［U］
❷毕业典礼［C］

grain 〔ɡren ‖ ɡreɪn〕
n. ❶谷粒［C］
Not a grain of rice was wasted.
一粒米也没有浪费。
❷谷物，谷类［C］［U］
Farmers grow grain and keep cattle.
农民种谷养牛。
❸(沙，盐等的)粒，细粒［C］
There is a grain of sand in his eye.
他眼里有一粒沙子。
❹(常用于否定句)一点儿［C］［(＋of)］
She has no a grain of common sense.
她一点常识也没有。

grammar 〔ˈɡræmɚ ‖ ˈɡræmə〕
n. ❶语法［U］
He had great difficulty in learn-

ing English grammar.
他学习英文语法困难重重。
❷语法书[C]
❸(符合语法规则的)文理,措辞[U]
Her grammar is bad.
她的文理不通。

granddaughter [ˈgrændˌdɔtɚ ‖ ˈgrænˌdɔːtə]
n. 孙女;外孙女[C]

grandfather [grændˌfɑðɚ ‖ grændˌfɑːðə]
n. [C] ❶祖父;外祖父
❷老祖宗

grandmother [ˈgrændˌmʌðɚ ‖ ˈgrændˌmʌðə]
n. 祖母;外祖母[C]

grandparent [ˈgrændˌpɛrənt ‖ ˈgrændˌpeərənt]
n. 祖父;祖母;外祖父;外祖母祖父母;外祖父母[P]

grandson [ˈgrændˌsʌn ‖ ˈgrændsʌn]
n. 孙子;外孙[C]

granny [ˈgrænɪ ‖ ˈgrænɪ]
n.【口】奶奶;外婆;老太太,老奶奶[C]

grape [grep ‖ greɪp]
n. ❶(指果实)葡萄[P]
Wine is made from grapes.
葡萄酒是葡萄酿成的。

葡萄 grape

❷葡萄树[C]
❸葡萄酒[the]

grasp [græsp ‖ grɑːsp]
[过去式]grasped;[过去分词]grasped
vt. ❶抓牢;握紧;抱住
The little girl grasped her mother's arm.
小女孩抓住了她母亲的手臂。
❷领会,理解
I don't grasp your meaning.
我不懂你的意思。
vi. 抓
He will grasp at anything that might help him achieve fame.
他会抢着做任何有助于他成名的事情。
n. ❶抓,紧握;抱
He held my hand in a friendly grasp.
他友好地紧握着我的手。
❷理解,领会
His ideas are beyond my grasp.
他的想法我不能理解。

G

❸能力所及的限度；范围
Victory seemed within the team's grasp.
看来这个队胜利唾手可得。

grass 〔græs ‖ grɑːs〕
n. ❶(青)草；牧草
Cattle eat grass.
牛吃草。
❷草地；草坪；牧地[U]
They are sitting on the grass.
他们坐在草地上。

gravity 〔'grævətɪ ‖ 'grævɪtɪ〕
n. ❶【物】重力；引力；地心吸力
❷严重性；危险性；重大[C]
I don't realize the gravity of the situation.
我没认识到情势的严重。

gray 〔gre ‖ greɪ〕
[比]grayer；[最]grayest
a. ❶灰色的；偏灰的
His hair is gray.
他头发灰白。
❷灰白头发的
He was already gray at 30.
他 30 岁时头发就已经灰白了。
❸(指脸因恐惧，受惊，生病等)苍白的
He was still looking gray and very tired.
他看上去仍然面色苍白，疲惫不堪。
n. ❶灰色[C][U]
❷灰色颜料；灰色衣服[U]
They were dressed in gray.
他们穿着灰色衣服。

great 〔gret ‖ greɪt〕
[比]greater；[最]greatest
a. ❶(数量，规模等)极大的，巨大的
There is a great tree in front of our house.
我们的屋前有棵大树。
❷伟大的，优秀的
Einstein was a great scientist.
爱因斯坦是个优秀的科学家。
❸重大的，重要的
It was a great decision for her.
这对她来讲是一个重大的决定。
❹【口】美妙的，极好的

greatly 〔'gretlɪ ‖ 'greɪtlɪ〕
ad. 极其，非常，大大地

Greece 〔gris ‖ griːs〕
n. 希腊

Greek 〔grik ‖ griːk〕
n. ❶希腊人[C]
❷希腊语[U]
a. 希腊的；希腊人的；希腊语的

green 〔grin ‖ griːn〕
[比]greener；[最]greenest
a. ❶绿的；青葱的
The hills are very green in

spring.
春天山上一片葱绿。
❷(果实等)未熟的;嫩的
Green tomatoes are sour.
未熟的番茄是酸的。
n. ❶绿色,青色[C][U]
The room was decorated in bright green.
这房间以鲜艳的绿色装饰着。
❷草坪,公共草地[C]
They are dancing on the village green.
他们正在村子里的草地上跳舞。
❸蔬菜;植物[P]
I had a dish of greens.
我吃了一盘蔬菜。

greet 〔grit ‖ griːt〕
[过去式]greeted;[过去分词]greeted
vt. ❶问候,迎接,招呼[(+with)]
She greeted her guests at the door.
她在门口迎接客人。
❷(以特定方式)接受;对……作出反应[(+with)]
They greeted her speech with warm applause.
他们对她的演讲报以热烈的掌声。

greeting 〔'gritɪŋ ‖ 'griːtɪŋ〕
n. ❶问候,迎接,招呼[C][U]
She smiled in greeting.
她微笑着打招呼。
❷(生日等场合的)祝愿词;贺词;问候语[P]
He sent his greetings to you in the letter.
他在这封信里向你致以问候。

grocery 〔'grosəɪ ‖ 'grəusərɪ〕
n. ❶【美】食品杂货店[C]
【英】grocer's
I bought sugar at the grocery.
我在食品杂货店买的糖。
❷食品杂货,南北货[P]
She bought a box of groceries.
她买了一箱食品杂货。

gross 〔gros ‖ grəus〕
a. ❶总的;毛的
gross weight
毛重
〔反义〕net 净的
❷粗俗的;下流的
gross manner
粗俗的举止
n. ❶总额,总量[the]
❷箩(计算单位,等于12打或144个)[C]

ground 〔graund ‖ graund〕
n. ❶地面[the]
Snow covers the ground.

雪覆盖着地面。
❷土壤；土地；田产[U]
The ground is fertile.
这片土地很肥沃。
❸(为某种目的的)场所，场地[C]
Our school has a large football ground.
我们学校有一个大足球场。
❹根据，理由[U][P][(+for)][+to-v]
We have good grounds to believe his story.
我们有充分理由相信他的故事。

group 〔grup ‖ gru:p〕
n. ❶群；组；类[C]
There appeared a group of aeroplanes in the sky.
天空中出现了机群。
❷集体；团体[C]
He belonged to the left-wing group.
他属于左翼集团。

grow 〔gro ‖ grəʊ〕
[过去式]grew；[过去分词]grown
vi. ❶成长，生长；发育
She has grown into a beautiful young lady.
她长成一位年轻漂亮的女子。
❷增大，增加；发展
John's reputation is growing fast.
约翰的名声正在迅速扩大。
❸渐渐变得[+to-v]
His cold is growing worse.
他的感冒正在加重。
vt. ❶种植，栽培
We grow flowers and vegetables in our garden.
我们在庭园里种植鲜花和蔬菜。
❷使生长；留(须，发)
David is growing a beard.
大卫在蓄须。

常用短语

grow up 成长
The boy grew up (to be) a great musician.
这个男孩长大后成了一个伟大的音乐家。

grown-up 〔ˌgron'ʌp ‖ ˌgrəʊn'ʌp〕
a. 成熟的；成人的

growth 〔groθ ‖ grəʊθ〕
n. ❶生长，发育；增长，发展[U]
❷种植，栽[U]
❸生长物；产物[C]

guarantee 〔ˌgærən'ti ‖ ˌgærən'ti:〕
[过去式]guaranteed；[过去分词]guaranteed

n. ❶保证；商品保证；保证书
a refrigerator with 3 years' guarantee
保用 3 年的冰箱
❷担保品，抵押品[C]
He offered his house as a guarantee.
他拿出他的房屋做抵押。
vt. 保障，保证……免受损失（或伤害等）[（＋against/from）]
This insurance guarantees you against loss by fire.
这个保险保证你不因火灾受损。

guard 〔gɑrd ‖ gɑːd〕
n. ❶哨兵；卫兵；警备员；看守员[C]
A guard was placed at the door.
门口设了一个警卫。
❷护卫队[the]
A heavy guard remained around the building.
建筑物周围一直有重兵守卫。
❸守卫；警戒；看守[U]
A policeman kept guard over the prisoners.
一名警察看守囚犯。

guess 〔gɛs ‖ ges〕
[过去式]guessed；[过去分词]guessed
vt. ❶猜测；推测
Can you guess the height of the tree?
你能猜出这树的高度吗？
❷猜中，猜对
I guessed his thoughts.
我猜着了他的想法。
❸【美】【口】想，认为[＋(that)]
I guess(that) we'll have to wait a few more minutes.
我想我们得再等几分钟。
vi. ❶猜；推测[（＋at/about）]
We can only guess at the result.
我们只能猜测结果。
❷猜中
❸想，认为
n. 猜测；推测[C]
My guess is that it will rain tomorrow.
我猜明天会下雨。

guest 〔gɛst ‖ gest〕
n. [C]❶客人，宾客
We're expecting guests to dinner.
我们正等候客人进餐。
❷旅客；顾客
The motel manager showed the guests to their room.
汽车旅馆经理把旅客领到他们

房间。

❸特别来宾(或演奏者,演讲者等);客座教授

guide 〔gaɪd ‖ gaɪd〕

[过去式]guided;[过去分词]guided

n. [C] ❶向导,导游;指导者

A guide will show you round the Summer Palace.

一位导游将陪你们参观颐和园。

❷指导;指南

Let conscience be your guide.

让良心指引你吧。

vt. ❶为……领路;带领

Martin guided him to the reception room.

马丁将他领到接待室。

❷引导;指导

He guided the company through the difficulties.

他带领公司渡过了难关。

❸管理;操纵

He guided the ship safely into harbor.

他驾驶轮船安全入港。

guilty 〔ˈgɪltɪ ‖ ˈgɪltɪ〕

a. ❶有罪的,犯……罪的

He was found guilty.

他被判有罪。

❷有过失的[(+of)]

The manager was guilty of an important misjudgment.

经理犯了一个重大的判断错误。

❸自知有过错的,内疚的

I felt guilty after breaking my promise.

我违背诺言后感到内疚。

guitar 〔gɪˈtɑr ‖ gɪˈtɑː〕

n. 吉他[C]

gulf 〔gʌlf ‖ gʌlf〕

n. 海湾[C]

gum[1] 〔gʌm ‖ gʌm〕

n. ❶树胶,树脂[U]

❷橡皮糖,口香糖[U]

gum[2] 〔gʌm ‖ gʌm〕

n. 齿龈,牙床[P]

The gums hurt badly.

牙龈疼得要命。

gun 〔gʌn ‖ gʌn〕

n. 枪;炮[C]

He taught Mary how to shoot a gun.

他教玛丽如何射击。

> 各种枪炮:
> cannon 大炮
> rifle 来复枪
> pistol 手枪
>
> **用法工具箱**

G

guy 〔gaɪ ‖ gaɪ〕

n.【美】【口】家伙；朋友；小伙子［C］

a nice guy

好人

Dave's a nice guy when you get to know him.

戴夫是个好人，你认识他后就知道。

The bad guy is very dark.

那个坏人很阴险。

gymnastics 〔dʒɪmˈnæstɪks ‖ dʒɪmˈnæstɪks〕

n. ❶体操；体育

Gymnastics is a required subject.

体育是必修的学科。

❷技巧；绝技；体操技巧

舵手 helmsman

母鸡 hen

H

汉堡包 hamburger

野兔 hare

ha 〔hɑ ‖ hɑː〕
int.（表示惊讶、欢乐、怀疑等）哈；嘿

habit 〔ˈhæbɪt ‖ ˈhæbɪt〕
n. ❶习惯［C］［U］
Smoking isn't a habit with me.
我没有抽烟的癖好。
❷（动、植物的）习性［C］［U］
Ivy has a climbing habit.
常春藤有攀缘向上的习性。

had 〔hæd ‖ hæd〕
（have 的过去式和过去分词）
had＋过去分词，构成过去完成时
I had met him before that time.
我在那之前曾经遇见过他。
had to
（那时候）不得不
I had to get up early.
我必须早起。

hair 〔hɛr ‖ heə〕
n. ❶毛发；兽毛［C］
The horse has a fine coat of hair.
这匹马长了一身好毛。
❷头发［C］［U］
There are a few hairs in the book.
书里有几根头发。

haircut 〔ˈhɛrˌkʌt ‖ ˈheəkʌt〕
n. 理发

half 〔hæf ‖ hɑːf〕［名复］halves
n. ❶一半，二分之一［C］
A half of 10 is 5.
10 的一半是 5。
❷（足球赛等的）半场；【棒】半局［C］
Our team scored 3 goals in the second half.
我们队在下半场进了 3 个球。
a. ❶一半的，二分之一的
We walk half a mile every day.

我们每天走半英里。
❷不完整的,不完全的
A half truth is often no better than a lie.
半真半假的话常常跟谎言一样糟。
ad. ❶部分地;相当地
I'm half inclined to go.
我有点儿想去。
❷一半地
The theater was half empty.
剧院的座位一半是空着的。
❸几乎
The little boy was half dead from hunger.
那个小男孩饿得半死。

hall 〔hɔl ‖ hɔːl〕
n. [C] ❶会堂,大厅
The mayor's office is in the town hall.
市长的办公室在市政大厅。
❷门厅;走廊
Leave your umbrella in the hall.
把雨伞放在门厅内。
❸【英】(大学中的)餐厅

ham 〔hæm ‖ hæm〕
n. 火腿
ham and egg
火腿蛋

hammer 〔'hæmə ‖ 'hæmə〕
n. 木槌,榔头[C]

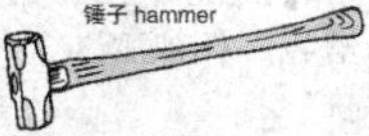

hand 〔hænd ‖ hænd〕
[过去式]handed;[过去分词]handed
n. [C] ❶手
She went to prepare him a meal with her own hands.
她去亲手为他做了一顿饭。
❷(钟表等的)指针
A watch has 3 hands — the second hand, minute hand and hour hand.
手表有 3 根指针——秒针、分针和时针。
❸方面,方向
❹人手,表的指针
left hand/ right hand
左手 / 右手

常用短语

at hand ❶在手边 ❷即将到来
Christmas is at hand.
圣诞节快到了。
at first hand 第一手得来的;直接的
at second hand 间接得来的

H

hand in hand ❶手拉手地 ❷连在一起地

vt. ❶面交，给，传递

He handed me a glass of beer.

他递给我一杯啤酒。

❷搀扶

He handed the old lady out of the cab.

他将这位上了年纪的女士从车上扶下来。

handbag 〔ˈhændˌbæg ‖ ˈhændbæg〕

n. [C] ❶(女用)手提包

❷小旅行袋，旅行包

handful 〔ˈhændˌful ‖ ˈhændful〕

n. ❶一把，一握[C][(+of)]

3 handfuls of beans

3把豆

❷少数，少量[C][(+of)]

a handful of people

少数人

handkerchief 〔ˈhæŋkəˑtʃɪf ‖ ˈhæŋkətʃɪf〕

n. [C] ❶手帕

❷围巾；颈巾

handle 〔ˈhændl̩ ‖ ˈhændl〕

[过去式]handled；[过去分词]handled

n. [C] ❶柄，把手；柄状物

I turned the handle and opened the door.

我转了转拉手，把门打开。

❷可乘之机，把柄，口实

Don't let your conduct give any handle for gossip.

别让你的行为成为人家说三道四的话柄。

vt. ❶触，摸；拿；弄；搬动

Do not handle the exhibits.

请勿触摸展品。

❷操作；操纵；指挥；管理

He knows how to handle the machine.

他会操作这台机器。

❸对待，处理

I didn't know how to handle these people.

我不知道如何对付这些人。

handsome 〔ˈhænsəm ‖ ˈhænsəm〕

a. (男子)英俊的；(女子)健美的，端庄的

He looked handsome and healthy.

他看上去英俊而健康。

handwriting 〔ˈhændˌraɪtɪŋ ‖ ˈhændˌraɪtɪŋ〕

n. [U] ❶书写；手写

❷笔迹；笔法

Is that signature in your handwriting?

那个签名是你的笔迹吗？

H

hang 〔hæŋ ‖ hæŋ〕
[过去式]hung, hanged;[过去分词]hung, hanged
vt. ❶把……挂起
He hung his coat on the hook.
他把衣服挂在钩子上。
❷(hanged;hanged)绞死;吊死
The man was hanged for murder.
那男子因谋杀罪被处绞刑。
vi. ❶悬挂,吊着
The curtains hang well.
窗帘挂得很好。
❷垂下,披下
Her hair hung down on her shoulders.
她的头发披在肩上。
❸(hanged;hanged)被绞死;被吊死
He hanged for murder.
他因谋杀罪被绞死。

happen 〔ˈhæpən ‖ ˈhæpən〕
[过去式]happened;[过去分词]happened
vi. ❶(偶然)发生
A funny thing happened.
发生了一件好笑的事。
❷碰巧[+to-v]
I happened to sit by her in the cinema.
在电影院我碰巧坐在她旁边。

happily 〔ˈhæpɪlɪ ‖ ˈhæpɪlɪ〕
ad. 幸福地,快乐地
They danced happily.
他们快乐地跳着舞。

happiness 〔ˈhæpɪnɪs ‖ ˈhæpɪnɪs〕
n. 幸福,快乐,愉快[U]
The family lived in happiness.
那家过得很幸福。

happy 〔ˈhæpɪ ‖ ˈhæpɪ〕
[比]happier;[最]happiest
a. ❶(感到)高兴的;乐意的[(+at/about)][+to-v][+that]
I am happy to accept your invitation.
我很高兴接受你的邀请。
❷满足的;满意的[(+about/with)]
He won't be happy with the result.
他对结果不会满意。
❸幸运的;幸福的
Happy New Year!
新年快乐!

harbor 〔ˈhɑrbɚ ‖ ˈhɑːbə〕
n. [C]❶港湾,海港
During the gale the ships stayed in the harbor.
刮大风时船只停泊在港内。
❷避难所,躲藏处,避风港

hard 〔hɑrd ‖ hɑːd〕
[比]harder;[最]hardest
a. ❶硬的,坚固的
The ice is as hard as rock.
冰像石头一样硬。
❷困难的,费力的[+to-v]
George is hard to get along with.
乔治很难相处。
❸猛力的;辛苦的
He gave the door a hard kick.
他猛力踢门。
❹刻苦的;努力的
He is a hard worker.
他工作勤奋。
❺艰难的;难受的
We had a hard time.
我们有过困苦的时期。
❻冷酷无情的;严厉的;严格的[(+on)]
You are too hard on your son.
你对你儿子太严厉了。
ad. ❶努力地;艰苦地
She tried hard, but failed.
她努力尝试过,但未能成功。
❷猛烈地;重重地
It's raining hard.
雨下得很大。
❸困难地;困苦地
The old man is breathing hard.
这位老人呼吸困难。

hardly 〔ˈhɑrdlɪ ‖ ˈhɑːdlɪ〕
ad. ❶几乎不,简直不
My legs were so weak that I could hardly stand.
我的腿虚弱得简直无法站立。
❷不十分;尽,刚
He had hardly arrived when it began to snow.
他一到,天就下起雪来了。

常用短语

hardly… when 刚刚……就(同 as soon as)
He had hardly left home when it began to rain.
他刚出门,雨就下起来了。

hardship 〔ˈhɑrdʃɪp ‖ ˈhɑːdʃɪp〕
n. 艰难,困苦[C][U]
He never feared hardship.
他从来不怕艰苦。

hardware 〔ˈhɑrdˌwɛr ‖ ˈhɑːdweə〕
n. [U]❶金属器件,五金器具

> ware 用复合字时作"……器"解
> ironware 铁器
> silverware 银器
> chinaware 瓷器
>
> **用法工具箱**

H

❷【计算机】硬件
〔反义〕software 软件

hare 〔hɛr ‖ heə〕
n. 野兔[C]

harm 〔hɑrm ‖ hɑːm〕
n. 损伤,伤害;危害[U]
Harm set, harm get.
害人反害己。

常用短语

do somebody harm 损害某人
Too much drinking will do you harm.
喝太多酒对你有害。

harmful 〔ˈhɑrmfəl ‖ ˈhɑːmfəl〕
a. 有害的[(+to)]
Smoking can be harmful to your health.
吸烟有害你的健康。

harmless 〔ˈhɑrmlɪs ‖ ˈhɑːmlɪs〕
a. ❶无害的
❷无恶意的;无辜的

harmony 〔ˈhɑrmənɪ ‖ ˈhɑːmənɪ〕
n. 和睦;融洽;一致[U]
They lived in perfect harmony.
他们相处得很融洽。

harvest 〔ˈhɑrvɪst ‖ ˈhɑːvɪst〕
n. ❶收获;收获季节[C][U]
The farmer hired extra workers for the harvest.
农场主为收割增添了雇工。
❷收成,产量[C]
It happened that the harvest was bad in 1988.
碰巧 1988 年的收成很糟。
❸结果;后果;成果
The new medicine is the harvest of 30 years' research.
这种新药是 30 年研究的成果。

has 〔(强)hæz ‖ hæz;(弱)həz ‖ həz〕
(have 的第三人称单数现在式)

haste 〔hest ‖ heɪst〕
n. [U] ❶急忙,迅速
More haste, less speed.
欲速则不达。
❷慌忙,性急
In my haste I forgot to lock the door.
匆忙中我忘了锁门。

hat 〔hæt ‖ hæt〕
n. (有边的)帽子[C]
She was wearing a white hat.
她戴着一顶白帽子。
〈无边的帽子是 cap〉

hatch 〔hætʃ ‖ hætʃ〕
[过去式]hatched;[过去分词]

H

hatched
vt. 孵出
Don't count your chickens before they are hatched.
不要在未孵出小鸡之前先数小鸡。
[别打如意算盘](谚语)

hate 〔het ‖ heɪt〕
[过去式]hated;[过去分词]hated
vt. ❶仇恨,憎恨
You hate her, don't you?
你恨她,不是吗?
❷嫌恶,不喜欢[+to-v][+v-ing]
To tell you the truth, I hate to do it.
老实告诉你,我不愿意做这事。
❸遗憾,抱歉[+to-v][+v-ing]
He hated to have quarrelled with her.
和她吵了一架,他感到很遗憾。
n. ❶仇恨,憎恨;厌恶,反感[U]
She looked at him with hate in her eyes.
她用憎恨的目光看着他。
❷憎恨之物[C]

have 〔(强)hæv ‖ hæv;(弱)həv ‖ həv〕
[过去式]had;[过去分词]had;[第三人称单数]has
v. aux. ❶(加过去分词,构成完成时态)已经;曾经
They haven't finished the job yet.
他们尚未完成该项工作。
❷(用于假设语气,表示与过去事实相反的假设)(假如那时)……的话
She might have come if she hadn't been so busy.
当时若不是那么忙,她可能会来的。
vt. ❶有,拥有
This coat has no pockets.
这件衣服没有口袋。
❷怀有,持有
Many people have doubts about the new project.
许多人对这项新工程有怀疑。
❸体验;经验;患
We had a wonderful time on the beach.
我们在海滩上玩得好极了。
❹要;叫;使
I had my son go instead.
我让我儿子代我去。
❺必须,不得不[+to-v]
I have to leave now.
我得走了。
❻拿到;得到,取得

I had 3 letters yesterday.
我昨天收到 3 封信。
❼吃；喝；吸(烟)
Which do you have，tea or coffee?
你喝什么，茶还是咖啡？

常用短语

have…on 穿，戴
She had a hat on.
她戴着帽子。
have… to do with 与……有关系
He has nothing to do with the affair.
他与此事无关。

hawk 〔hɔk ‖ hɔːk〕
n. 鹰，隼[C]

hay 〔he ‖ heɪ〕
n. (做饲料用的)干草[U]
Make hay while the sun shines.
要把握时机。(谚语)

he 〔hi ‖ hiː〕
pron. (主格) ❶他
He is an engineer.
他是位工程师。
❷任何人
He who laughs last laughs best.
笑到最后的人才笑得最开心。
❸(用来指雄性动物或其他事物)他，它

head 〔hɛd ‖ hed〕
[过去式]headed；[过去分词]headed
n. [C] ❶头
He was hit on the head.
他被击中头部。

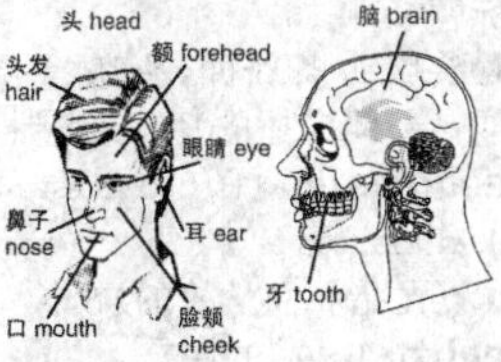

❷(东西的)头；上端；前端；上首[the][(+of)]
The young man walked at the head of the parade.
那个年轻人走在游行队伍最前面。
❸头脑，才智
Steve has a good head for mathematics.
史蒂夫擅长数学。
vt. 作为……的首领；率领；站在……的前头
A car headed the procession.
一辆汽车为游行队伍开路。
vi. (向特定的方向)出发，(船)驶往
Our ship headed south.
我们的船朝南开。

H

headache 〔ˈhɛdˌek || ˈhedeɪk〕

n. 头痛[C]

I have a bad headache.

我头痛得厉害。

headline 〔ˈhɛdˌlaɪn || ˈhedlaɪn〕

n. [C] ❶(报纸等的)标题;大标题

❷头版头条新闻;头版重要新闻,(新闻广播的)内容提要[P]

headmaster 〔ˈhɛdˌmæstɚ || ˌhedˈmɑːstə〕

n. (尤指私立学校的)校长

health 〔hɛlθ || helθ〕

n. ❶健康[U]

Smoking does harm to health.

吸烟有损健康。

❷健康状况[U]

She is in poor health.

她身体不好。

❸祝健康的干杯

We all drank a health to the bride.

我们都为新娘的健康干杯。

healthy 〔ˈhɛlθɪ || ˈhelθɪ〕

a. 健康的;健全的

He is healthy.

他很健康。

hear 〔hɪr || hɪə〕

[过去式] heard; [过去分词] heard

vt. ❶听见;听

I heard him say so.

我听他这么说过。

❷听说,得知[+(that)][(+about/of)]

I heard that he was ill.

我听说他病了。

❸注意听,听取

We'll be glad to hear your opinion of them.

我们将乐于听取你对他们的看法。

vi. 听得见;听

I can't hear very well.

我听不太清楚。

> hear 是“听见”之意;listen 是“注意听”
>
> I listened but I heard nothing.
>
> 我听了半天但什么也没听见。

用法工具箱

常用短语

hear from 收到……的信(或电报等)

I heard from him yesterday.

我昨天收到了他的信。

heart 〔hɑrt || hɑːt〕

n. ❶心脏;胸[C]

The boy's heart gave a jump.
这个男孩的心猛地一跳。
❷内心；心肠[C]
He has a cold heart.
他冷酷无情。
❸感情；爱情；爱好[C]
She gave her heart to him.
她真心爱他。
❹中心；要点[the][(+of)]
the heart of the city
城市的核心
❺勇气；精神[U]
Don't lose your heart.
别失去信心。

常用短语

at heart ❶本质上；实际上 ❷心里；内心是
He is a good-natured man at heart.
他是个本性善良的人。
break one's heart 伤心
by heart 靠记忆
He learned the poem by heart.
他背诵了那首诗。

heartbroken 〔ˈhɑrtˌbrokən ‖ ˈhɑːtˌbrəʊkən〕
a. 悲伤的

heat 〔hit ‖ hiːt〕
[过去式] heated; [过去分词] heated
vt. 把……加热；使暖
The stove heats the room.
暖炉使房间温暖起来。
vi. 变热，发热
The water is heating on the stove.
炉子上的水在变热。
n. ❶热度；温度[U]
The sun gives off heat.
太阳散发出热。
❷暑热；高温[U]
You can't walk about in the heat.
大暑天，你不要到处乱走。
❸热烈；激烈；激怒[U]
In the heat of the argument I lost my self-control.
在激烈的争论中，我失去了自制力。

heaven 〔ˈhɛvən ‖ ˈhevn〕
n. ❶【宗】(常大写)天国；上帝[U]
May her soul rest in Heaven.
但愿她的灵魂在天国安息。
❷天空[P]
Millions of stars were shining in the heavens.
天空中繁星闪烁。

heavy 〔ˈhɛvɪ ‖ ˈhevɪ〕
a. ❶重的，沉的
The box is too heavy for me.
我觉得这盒子太重了。

H

❷沉重有力的；剧烈的；热烈的
I heard his heavy steps on the stairs.
我听到他上楼的沉重脚步声。
❸大的；大量的，多的
There was heavy rain yesterday.
昨天下了场大雨。
❹令人忧郁的；(心情)沉重的
He received a heavy blow.
他受到了沉重打击。
❺(食物等)难消化的
I had a heavy dinner.
我吃了一顿大餐。

词汇拓展

heavily *ad.* 沉重地

H

height 〔haɪt ‖ haɪt〕
n. ❶高，高度，海拔[C][U]
The tree grew to a height of 20 feet.
那树长到 20 英尺高。
❷身高[C][U]
His height makes him stand out in the crowd.
他的高大身材使他在人群中很显眼。

helicopter 〔ˈhɛlɪˌkɑptɚ ‖ ˈhelɪkɒptə〕
n. 直升机[C]

直升机 helicopter

hell 〔hɛl ‖ hel〕
n. ❶(常大写)地狱，冥府
❷悲惨境地，人间地狱[U]
She suffered every hell after her husband died.
她在丈夫死后吃尽苦头。
❸(用于加强语气)究竟，到底[the]
What the hell do you want?
你究竟要什么？
int.【俚】(用于咒骂)混蛋，见鬼，该死
Oh hell! The car broke down again.
噢，该死！车子又抛锚了。

hello 〔həˈlo ‖ həˈləʊ〕
int. ❶(用以打招呼或唤起注意)喂，你好
Hello, Jim! How are you?
喂，吉姆！你好吗？
❷(用作打电话时的招呼语)喂
❸(表示惊讶等)嘿；啊
n. 表示问候(或惊奇，唤起注意时)的叫声[C][U]
She said hello to me when she

saw me.
她见到我时向我打招呼。

help 〔hɛlp ‖ help〕
[过去式]helped;[过去分词]helped
vt. ❶帮助[(+with)]
Could you help me up with this suitcase?
你帮我把这个箱子搬到楼上好吗?
❷援助;助长,促进
Foreign investments help our economic development.
外国投资有助于我们的经济发展。
❸补救;治疗
What have you got that will help a cold?
你有什么药能治感冒?
❹(与 can, could 连用)避免,阻止[+v-ing]
I couldn't help laughing.
我忍不住大笑。
❺(将食物等)分给;取用(食物等)[(+to)]
He helped her some cake.
他给了她一些饼。
Please help yourself to wine.
请随便用酒。
vi. 帮助;有用
Your sympathy helps a lot.
你的同情帮助很大。
n. ❶帮助[U]
She cried for help.
她大声求救。
❷有益的东西;有帮助的人[C]
Thanks. You've been a big help.
谢谢,你帮了个大忙。
❸帮手,助手
She is quite a help to her mother.
她是她妈妈的得力助手。

helpful 〔ˈhɛlpfəl ‖ ˈhelpfəl〕
a. 有利于……的,有帮助的,有益的
You have been very helpful.
你帮了(我们)很大忙。

helpless 〔ˈhɛlplɪs ‖ ˈhelplɪs〕
a. 无力的,无助的,未受到帮助的,无依无靠的
The injured lay helpless.
受伤的人无助地躺着。

hen 〔hɛn ‖ hen〕
n. 母鸡[C]
Hens lay eggs.
母鸡生蛋。

her 〔(强)hɝ ‖ hɜ:;(弱)hɚ ‖ hə〕
pron. ❶(she 的所有格)她的
I saw Mary with her mother.
我看见玛丽同她妈妈在一起。
❷(she 的宾格)她
I met her in the park.

我在公园里遇见了她。

here 〔hɪr ‖ hɪə〕

ad. ❶这里,在这里;向这里

We live here in winter.

我们冬天住在这里。

❷在这点上;这时

Here the speaker paused.

这时演讲人停顿了一下。

❸(用于句首,唤起对方注意某人或某物)瞧;在这里;向这里来

It's 10 o'clock and here is the news.

现在 10 点钟,新闻广播开始了。

❹(用于名词后,引起注意或加强语气)在此,这里

n. 这里

My hometown is 100 miles away from here.

我的家乡离这里有 100 英里路。

〔反义〕there 那里

int. ❶(用以引起注意等)喂!嘿!

Here, don't cry.

得啦,别哭了。

❷(点名时的回答)到!有!

常用短语

here and now 此刻

here, there and everywhere 到处

hero 〔ˈhɪro ‖ ˈhɪərəʊ〕

n. 〔C〕❶英雄;勇士

He was a national hero.

他是个民族英雄。

❷男主角,男主人公

He identifies with the hero of a novel.

他把自己设想成一部小说中的主人公。

heroine 〔ˈhɛro · ɪn ‖ ˈherəʊɪn〕

n. 〔C〕❶女英雄,女杰

❷(小说、电影等的)女主角

hers 〔hɝz ‖ hɜːz〕

pron. (she 的名词性物主代词)她的东西,她的家属(或有关的人)

This is not Jane's pen; hers is over there.

这不是简的笔,她的在那边。

herself 〔hɚˈsɛlf ‖ hɜːˈself〕

pron. ❶(she 的反身代词)她自己

Barbara stared at herself in the mirror.

巴巴拉凝视着镜中的自己。

❷(用以加强语气)她亲自,她本人

She does not believe it herself.

她本人都不相信这件事。

hesitate 〔ˈhɛzə͵tet ‖ ˈhezɪteɪt〕

〔过去式〕hesitated;〔过去分词〕

hesitated

vi. 踌躇;犹豫

Don't hesitate about that. Do it at once.

对于那件事不要再犹豫了,马上去做吧。

vt. 有疑虑,不愿意[+to-v]

He did not hesitate to ask her to sit beside him.

他毫不犹豫地请她坐在他身旁。

hesitation 〔ˌhɛzəˈteʃən ‖ ˌheziˈteiʃən〕

n. 踌躇,犹豫

hey 〔he ‖ hei〕

int. (表示惊讶、疑问、喜悦或用以唤起注意等)嗨;喂

hide 〔haid ‖ haid〕

[过去式]hid;[过去分词]hidden

vt. ❶把……藏起来,隐藏

I keep my diary hidden.

我藏起了我的日记。

❷隐瞒[(+from)]

My husband never hides anything from me.

我丈夫从不对我隐瞒什么。

❸遮掩掉,掩蔽

Lies can not hide facts.

谎言掩盖不了事实。

vi. 躲藏,隐藏

I ran quickly up the stairs and hid behind my bed.

我快速跑上楼,躲在我的床后。

high 〔hai ‖ hai〕

[比]higher;[最]highest

a. ❶高的

He lives in a high building.

他住在一幢高楼里。

❷(用于名词后)有……高度的

This building is 9 stories high.

这幢楼高9层。

❸高音调的

The speaker has a very high voice.

这位演讲人声音很大。

❹(价值、评价等)高的;昂贵的;高速的

The prices are high.

物价很高。

❺(地位、等级、质量等)高级的;重要的

He is a high official.

他是个高级官员。

ad. ❶高,向(或在)高处

The eagle flies high.

鹰飞得很高。

❷强烈地;高声地;奢侈地

The rich men live high.

富人们生活奢侈。

❸(地位等)显赫地

He's risen high in the world.

他已经发迹了。

n. ❶高水平;高峰[C]

The temperature reached a new high this summer.

今年夏天气温达到新的最高纪录。

❷天空,天上[U]

On high the great white clouds slid swiftly.

大片大片的白云在高空飘过。

❸【俚】由麻醉品等引起的快感[C]

Methadone does not produce the "high" brought on by heroin.

美沙酮不产生海洛因引起的那种快感。

highway 〔ˈhaɪˌwe ‖ ˈhaɪweɪ〕

n. 公路;干道[C]

There are many highways to Beijing.

很多条公路通往北京。

hill 〔hɪl ‖ hɪl〕

n. 小山;丘陵

His red house stands on a hill.

他的红房子位于小山上。

him 〔(强)hɪm ‖ hɪm;(弱)hɪm ‖ ɪm〕

pron. ❶(he 的宾格)他

I don't like him.

我不喜欢他。

❷【口】(作主格补语,用来代替 he)(是)他

Is that him?

那就是他吗?

❸【口】(用于 than 或 as 后面,代替 he)他

John is as tall as him.

约翰和他一样高。

himself 〔hɪmˈsɛlf ‖ hɪmˈself〕

pron. ❶(he 的反身代词)他自己

He introduced himself to the people in the room.

他向房间里的人作了自我介绍。

❷(用以加强语气)他亲自,他本人

He does not like it himself.

他自己都不喜欢它。

hire 〔haɪr ‖ ˈhaɪə〕

[过去式] hired; [过去分词] hired

vt. ❶租,租借

They hired a big hall.

他们租了一间大厅。

❷雇,雇用

We hired a driver to take us on a tour of the city.

我们雇用了一个司机带我们游览这个城市。

his 〔(强)hɪz ‖ hɪz;(弱)ɪz ‖ ɪz〕

pron. ❶(he 的所有格)他的
His hat is the brown one.
他的帽子是棕色的那顶。
❷(he 的名词性物主代词)他的东西;他的家属(或有关的人)
The suit is his.
这套衣服是他的。

historian 〔hɪs'tɔrɪən ‖ hɪs'tɒrɪən〕
n. 历史学家[C]

historic 〔his'tɔrɪk ‖ hɪ'stɒrɪk〕
a. 历史上著名的;历史上有重大意义的
a historic event
历史上著名的事件

historical 〔hɪs'tɔrɪkḷ ‖ hɪ'stɒrɪkəl〕
a. 历史的,史学的,基于史实的
a historical play
历史剧

history 〔'hɪstrɪ ‖ 'hɪstərɪ〕
n. ❶历史;史学[U]
History is full of things like that.
历史上充满了那样的事件。
❷来历,沿革,由来[U]
Do you know the history of the company?
你知道这家公司的发展史吗?
❸历史书[C]
They are writing a new history of Africa.
他们正在写一部新的非洲史。
❹履历;病历;经历[C]
I wrote my personal history.
我写了我的履历。

hit 〔hɪt ‖ hɪt〕
[过去式]hit;[过去分词]hit
vt. ❶打,打击;击中
A bullet hit him on the leg.
一颗子弹击中了他的腿。
❷碰撞;使碰撞
The ship hit a rock and wrecked.
船触礁撞毁了。
❸袭击,使遭受
The storm will hit the town.
暴风雨将要袭击这个镇。
vi. ❶打,打击;击中
The boys are hitting at the dog.
男孩们正在打狗。
❷碰撞[(+against)]
The ball hit against the window.
球撞在窗子上。
n. [C] ❶打击;击中
They got five hits and one miss.
他们五次击中,一次未中。
❷碰撞
❸成功而风行一时的事物
The new play is the hit of the

season.
这出新戏是本季最叫座的。

hobby 〔ˈhɑbɪ ‖ ˈhɒbɪ〕
n. 业余爱好，癖好，嗜好[C]
My hobby is collecting stamps.
我的业余爱好是集邮。

hold 〔hold ‖ həʊld〕
[过去式]held；[过去分词]held
vt. ❶握着；抓住；夹住
He held a knife in his hand.
他手里握着一把刀。
❷托住；支撑
The roof was held up by pillars.
屋顶由柱子支撑着。
❸使保持某种姿态等
She held her head up.
她抬起头来。
❹抑制，约束
He held his breath.
他屏住呼吸。
❺拥有，握有，持有
He held shares in the business.
他持有该企业的股份。
❻容纳；包含
The bottle holds two pints.
这个瓶子有两品脱容量。
❼认为；持有(见解等)[＋that]
They held that he was a fool.
他们认为他是个傻瓜。
❽举行
We are going to hold a meeting this afternoon.
今天下午我们要开个会。
vi. 持续，保持
I hope the beautiful weather will hold.
我希望这种好天气将持续下去。

hole 〔hol ‖ həʊl〕
n. [C]❶洞；破洞；孔眼[(＋in)]
There is a hole in the wall.
墙上有一个洞。
❷(动物的)洞穴，窝

holiday 〔ˈhɑləˌde ‖ ˈhɒlədɪ〕
n. [C] ❶节日，假日；休息日，休业日
Friday is a holiday in Muslim countries.
在伊斯兰教国家里星期五是假日。
❷【英】假期[P]

holy 〔ˈholɪ ‖ ˈhəʊlɪ〕
a. ❶神圣的，供神用的
Teaching is one of the holiest tasks.
教书是最神圣的工作之一。
❷献身于宗教的；虔诚的
❸圣洁的；至善的
The poem sings the praise of holy love.

这首诗歌颂圣洁的爱。

home〔hom ‖ həʊm〕

n. ❶家，住家[C][U]

Now he has his home in Manchester.

他现在定居在曼彻斯特。

❷家庭，家庭生活[C][U]

He is planning to establish a home.

他正计划组建家庭。

❸(动植物的)生息地，产地；发源地[the][(＋of)]

the home of democracy

民主的发源地

❹故乡；祖国[U]

He left home for America.

他离开家前往美国。

❺收容所；养育所；疗养所[C]

a home for orphans

孤儿院

ad. 在家；回家；到家；回本国

The delegation will be home next week.

代表团将于下周回国。

a. ❶家庭的

This is my home phone number.

这是我家的电话号码。

❷本国的，国内的；故乡的

These products are for home sale.

这些产品是供国内销售的。

❸总部的

Our home office is in New York.

我们的总部设在纽约。

词汇拓展

home-made *a.* 自制的

a home-made cake 自制蛋糕

homesick 〔ˈhomˌsɪk ‖ ˈhəʊmsɪk〕

a. 怀乡病的，思家的

The girl became homesick after a week's stay at her aunt's.

女孩在姑妈家住了一个星期就想家了。

homework 〔ˈhomˌwɝk ‖ ˈhəʊmwɜːk〕

n. (学生的)家庭作业[U]

I have finished my homework.

我已经完成了家庭作业。

honest〔ˈɑnɪst ‖ ˈɒnɪst〕

a. ❶诚实的；正直的

All my life I have tried to be an honest man.

我一生都想做一个诚实的人。

❷用正当手段获得的

All this is honest money.

这些钱都是正大光明地赚来的。

❸真诚的，坦率的

H

The young man has an honest face.
这个年轻人有一张真诚的脸。

honesty 〔ˈɑnɪstɪ ‖ ˈɒnɪstɪ〕
n. 正直;诚实;坦率[U]
Honesty is the best policy.
诚实为上策。

honey 〔ˈhʌnɪ ‖ ˈhʌnɪ〕
n. ❶蜂蜜[U]
Honey is sweet, but the bee stings.
蜜甜蜂蜇人。
❷(常用于称呼)宝贝儿[C]
I love you, honey.
亲爱的,我爱你。

honeymoon 〔ˈhʌnɪˌmun ‖ ˈhʌnɪmuːn〕
n. 蜜月;蜜月假期;蜜月旅行[C]
They went to Hawaii for their honeymoon.
他们去夏威夷度蜜月。

hono(u)r 〔ˈɑnɚ ‖ ˈɒnə〕
n. ❶荣誉;名誉,面子[U]
We fight for the honor of our country.
我们为祖国的荣誉而战。
❷信誉,信用[U]
The business honor of the company is beyond suspicion.
这个公司的商业信誉毋庸置疑。
❸光荣的事或人[(+to)]
He is an honor to our school.
他是我们学校的光荣。
❹敬意[U]
He was held in honor by everybody.
他受到每个人的尊敬。
❺(大学的)优等成绩[P]
He graduated with honors.
他以优异成绩毕业。
❻(大写)(对法官和某些高级官员的尊称,与 Your, His 或 Her 连用)阁下
Yes, Your Honor.
是的,阁下。

常用短语

in honor of 纪念,庆贺,对……表示敬意
A farewell party was held in honor of him.
为他举行了一个欢送会。

词汇拓展

honorable *a.* 高尚的,光荣的
honorary *a.* 荣誉的,名誉的

hook 〔hʊk ‖ hʊk〕
[过去式]hooked;[过去分词]hooked
n. [C] ❶钩,挂钩;(衣服的)钩扣;吊钩

Will you hang my coat on the hook?
帮我把我的外套挂在钩上行吗?
❷钓鱼钩
vt. ❶用钩钩住(或挂起);扣(衣服)的扣子
Will you hook my coat for me?
你帮我把上衣挂好行吗?
❷钓(鱼)
I have hooked a fish.
我钓到一条鱼。

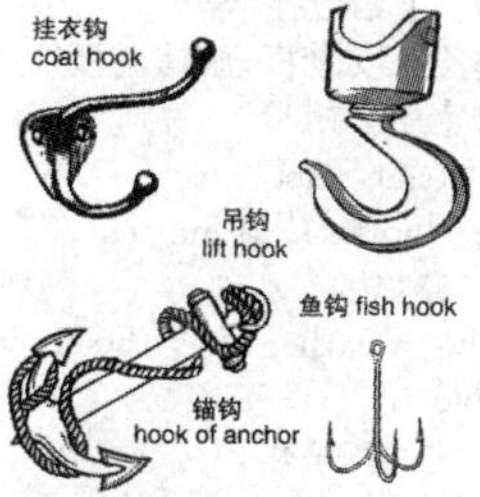

hope 〔hop ‖ həʊp〕
[过去式]hoped;[过去分词]hoped
vt. 希望,盼望[+to-v][+that]
I hope that he will succeed.
我期望他会成功。
vi. 希望,期待
Everyone hopes for snow.
人人盼望下雪。
n. ❶希望,期望[C][U]
You mustn't give up hope.
你一定不要绝望。
❷可能性;期待[C][U][(+of)][+that]
You have no hope of being accepted.
你不可能被接受。
❸被寄托希望的人(或物)[C]
You are my only hope.
你是我唯一的希望。

horizon 〔hə'raɪzn̩ ‖ hə'raɪzn〕
n. ❶地平线[the]
The sun has risen above the horizon.
太阳已从地平线升起。
❷(知识,经验等的)范围;眼界;视野[C]
Good novels broaden your horizons.
好小说开阔人的眼界。

horrible 〔'hɑrəbl̩ ‖ 'hɒrəbl〕
a. ❶可怕的,令人毛骨悚然的
a horrible murder
恐怖的谋杀案
❷【口】极讨厌的,糟透的
The food at the hotel was horrible.
旅馆里的食物糟透了。

horror 〔'hɔrɚ ‖ 'hɒrə〕

n. ❶恐怖，震惊，毛骨悚然[U]
She sat motionlessly with horror.
她惊恐地呆坐着。
❷极端厌恶 [(＋of)]
He expressed his horror of war.
他表示了对战争的憎恶。
❸恐怖性，惨状[U]
❹令人恐怖的事物[C][P]
We should not expose our children to horrors.
我们不应该让孩子看恐怖片。

horse 〔hɔrs ‖ hɔːs〕
n. 马[C]

马 horse

I am learning to ride a horse.
我正在学习骑马。

hospital 〔ˈhɑspɪtl̩ ‖ ˈhɒspɪtl〕
n. 医院[C][U]
His sick father is in the hospital.
他生病的父亲正在住院治疗。

hospitality 〔ˌhɑspɪˈtæləti ‖ ˌhɒspɪˈtælɪtɪ〕
n. 好客；殷勤招待[U]
I received the hospitality of the family.
我受到了这一家人的款待。

host 〔host ‖ həʊst〕
n. [C] ❶主人，东道主
Yesterday we were hosts to a few friends.
昨天我们接待了几位朋友。
❷旅馆老板
❸(广播，电视的)节目主持人

hostess 〔ˈhostɪs ‖ ˈhəʊstɪs〕
n. [C] ❶女主人
❷旅社女老板；旅馆老板娘
❸空中小姐

hot 〔hɑt ‖ hɒt〕
[比]hotter；[最]hottest
a. ❶热的
The weather has been very hot.
天气一直很热。
〔反义〕cold 冷的
❷辣的
This curry is too hot.
这咖喱太辣了。
❸急躁的；激动的；猛烈的
He's got a hot temper.
他脾气急躁。

hot dog 〔ˈhɑtˌdɔg ‖ ˈhɒtdɒg〕
n. 热狗

hotel 〔hoˈtɛl ‖ həʊˈtel〕

n. 旅馆；饭店［C］
We stayed at a resort hotel during the holidays.
假期里我们住在一家观光旅馆。

hour〔aʊr ‖ aʊə〕
n.［C］❶小时
It took us 5 hours to finish the job.
我们花了5个小时完成这项工作。
❷时刻，时间
At what hour did they meet?
他们什么时间见面？
❸一小时的路程；一小时内能做完的工作
We live about an hour from the station.
我们住的地方离车站大约一个钟点的路程。
❹(工作，营业等的)时间［P］
school hours
授课时间
business hours
营业时间
office hours
办公时间
the rush hours
高峰时间

house〔haʊs ‖ haʊs〕
n.［C］❶房子；住宅
They built a house by the roadside.
他们在路边盖了一间房子。
❷家庭，家人
She keeps house.
她管理家务。
❸(大写)议院［the］
the Royal House of England
英国皇室
the House of Commons
【英】下议院
the House of Representatives
【美】众议院

household〔ˈhaʊsˌhold ‖ ˈhaʊshəʊld〕
n. 一家人；家眷；家庭，户［C］
Cecil Burns was the spoilt child of that household.
塞西尔·伯恩斯是那个家庭中被宠坏了的孩子。
a. ❶家的，家庭的；家用的
This is a good household soap.
这是一种质量优良的家用肥皂。
❷普通的；为人所熟知的
He is a household legendary figure.
他是个家喻户晓的传奇性人物。

housekeeper〔ˈhaʊsˌkipə ‖ ˈhaʊsˌkiːpə〕

H

n. [C] ❶女管家;女佣人领班 ❷(旅馆,医院等的)勤杂工女领班

housewife [ˈhausˌwaɪf ‖ ˈhauswaɪf]

n. 家庭主妇[C]

housework [ˈhausˌwɝk ‖ ˈhauswɜːk]

n. 家事[U]

The young couple shared housework.

这对年轻夫妇分担家务事。

how [hau ‖ hau]

ad. ❶(指方式,方法等)怎样,怎么

How did you climb to the top of that building?

你是如何爬上楼顶的?

❷(指健康等情况)怎样

How is Mrs. Smith?

史密斯太太身体好吗?

❸(指数量,程度)多少

How many students are there in your class?

你班里有多少学生?

How much is the book?

这本书多少钱?

How old are you?

你多大年纪了?

How long are you going to stay here?

你打算在这儿待多久?

How often have you been here?

你多久到这儿一次?

❹(表感叹)多么 [how+ 形容词]

How fast he runs!

他跑得多快呀!

conj. (用于间接陈述中,意义和作用与 that 相仿)

This is how we became acquainted.

我们就是这样认识的。

常用短语

How about…? ……如何;怎样

How about a cup of coffee?

喝杯咖啡吧?

How are you?

你好吗?

(用于日常寒暄)

How do you do?

你好,幸会。

(用于初次见面的寒暄)

however [hauˈɛvɚ ‖ hauˈevə]

ad. ❶ 无论如何,不管怎样

However hot it is, he will not take off his coat.

无论多热,他也不会脱掉外衣。

❷不管用什么方法

However he tries, he never seems able to work satisfactorily.

不管他怎么努力,他的工作好

像总不能令人满意。

❸究竟怎样，到底如何

However did you know that?

你到底怎么知道那件事的？

❹可是，然而

He was ill. However, he decided to go.

他病了，可他仍决定要去。

> however 可用于句首，句中或句尾，且要用逗号与句子分开。but 只能用于句首。
>
> **用法工具箱**

huge [ˈhjudʒ ‖ ˈhjuːdʒ]

a. ❶庞大的；巨大的

She spent a huge amount of money on that coat.

她花了大笔的钱买那件衣服。

❷非常的

human [ˈhjumən ‖ ˈhjuːmən]

a. ❶人的；人类的

This meat is not fit for human consumption.

这种肉不适合人食用。

❷凡人皆有的

It's only human nature to want a comfortable life.

人的本性就是要过舒服的生活。

❸有人性的

He is quite human after all.

他毕竟还是挺善良的。

n. 人[C]

Wolves will not usually attack humans.

狼通常不会袭击人。

humanity [hjuˈmænətɪ ‖ hjuːˈmænɪtɪ]

n. [U]❶人性；人道；慈爱；博爱；仁慈

❷(总称)人；人类

humble [ˈhʌmbl̩ ‖ ˈhʌmbl]

[比]humbler；[最]humblest

a. ❶谦逊的；谦恭的

Many famous people are surprisingly humble.

许多知名人士都出奇地谦恭。

❷(身份，地位等)低下的，卑微的，低级的

He is of humble birth.

他出身卑微。

❸(东西)粗糙的，简陋的

The family lived in a humble cottage.

这户人家住在一所简陋的农舍里。

humid [ˈhjumɪd ‖ ˈhjuːmɪd]

a. 潮湿的

humo(u)r [ˈhjumɚ ‖ ˈhjuːmə]

n. ❶幽默感，幽默[U]
Humor is often more than a laughing matter.
幽默常常不只是一笑了之的事。
❷心情，情绪
in a good humor
高兴
in a bad humor
不高兴
out of humor
不悦
❸气质，性情[U]

词汇拓展

humorous *a.* 幽默的，滑稽的

hundred 〔ˈhʌndrəd ‖ ˈhʌndrəd〕

H

n. ❶一百[C]
The child can count from one to a hundred.
这个孩子能从 1 数到 100。
❷数以百计；许多[P][(＋of)]
Hundreds of people took to the streets to protest against police brutalities.
数百名群众上街抗议警察暴行。
a. ❶一百的
It cost me one hundred dollars.
这花去我 100 美元。
❷很多的
I have got a hundred things to do.
我有许许多多事情要做。

hunger 〔ˈhʌŋgɚ ‖ ˈhʌŋgə〕

n. ❶饿，饥饿[U]
Thousands of people are dying from hunger every day.
每天都有成千上万人因饥饿而死。
❷渴望[(＋for/after)]
He has a hunger for/after knowledge.
他有强烈的求知欲。

hunt 〔hʌnt ‖ hʌnt〕

[过去式]hunted；[过去分词]hunted

vt. ❶追猎，猎取
November is a good time to hunt deer.
11 月正是猎鹿的好时节。
❷在……中狩猎；驱使（或指

挥)……行猎
Indians hunted the prairie for buffalo.
印第安人在北美大草原上捕猎野牛。
❸搜索;寻找
I'm hunting a job.
我在找工作。
vi. ❶打猎
We'll go hunting in the afternoon.
我们下午将出去打猎。
❷搜寻[(+for/after)]
John set out that day to hunt for work.
约翰那天外出找工作。

hunter 〔ˈhʌntɚ ‖ ˈhʌntə〕
n. [C] ❶猎人
❷猎犬;猎马
❸追求者;搜寻者[(+after/for)]

hurriedly 〔ˈhɝɪdlɪ ‖ ˈhʌrɪdlɪ〕
ad. 仓促地,匆忙地;草率地

hurry 〔ˈhɝɪ ‖ ˈhʌrɪ〕
[过去式]hurried;[过去分词]hurried
vt. 使赶紧;催促
The salesman hurried the customer to make a choice.
售货员催促顾客作出选择。
vi. 赶紧;匆忙
She hurried home to tell them the news.
她匆匆回家告诉他们这一消息。
n. [U] ❶急忙;仓促;忙乱
In her hurry she forgot to leave her phone number.
匆忙间她忘了留下电话号码。
❷(用于否定句和疑问句)必须赶快[+to-v]
There is no hurry to make a decision.
没有必要匆忙作出决定。
❸渴望,急切
She was in a hurry to see her child.
她急切地想见到她的孩子。

hurt 〔hɝt ‖ hɜːt〕
[过去式]hurt;[过去分词]hurt
vt. ❶使受伤
No one was seriously hurt in the traffic accident.
在这次交通事故中没有人受重伤。
❷使疼痛
The tight shoe hurt my foot.
这只鞋太紧,把我的脚挤疼了。
❸伤……的感情;使(感情)受到伤害
He inadvertently hurt her feelings.

H

他无意中伤了她的感情。

vi. ❶疼痛

My right leg hurts.

我右腿疼。

❷带来痛苦；造成损失

It won't hurt to postpone the meeting for a few more days.

会议再推迟几天也无妨。

n. ❶(精神上的)创伤[C][U][(+to)]

It was a real hurt to her vanity.

这对她的虚荣心真是一个打击。

❷伤；痛[C][U]

The massage made the hurt go away.

按摩使疼痛消失了。

hurt 可指精神上的痛苦；
injure 指受伤，不能活动；
wound 指刀枪的伤

用法工具箱

husband 〔ˈhʌzbənd ‖ ˈhʌzbənd〕

n. 丈夫[C]

Jack will make an ideal husband for her.

杰克将是她理想的丈夫。

〔反义〕wife 妻子

hut 〔hʌt ‖ hʌt〕

n. (简陋的)小屋[C]

We built a hut by the river.

我们在河边建了个小屋。

I

I〔aɪ ‖ aɪ〕

pron. 我(第一人称单数主格,指说者、作者自己,所有格为my,宾格为me)

格＼数	单数	复数
主格	I 我	we 我们
所有格	my 我的	our 我们的
宾格	me 我	us 我们

ice〔aɪs ‖ aɪs〕

n. ❶冰[U]

The pond will soon turn into ice.

这个池塘很快就会结冰。

❷【英】冰淇淋[C]

Don't eat so many ices.

不要吃那么多冰淇淋。

icy〔'aɪsɪ ‖ 'aɪsɪ〕

a. 覆盖着冰的;冰冷的;像冰一样滑的

an icy wind

寒风

an icy road

结满冰的路

idea〔aɪ'dɪə ‖ aɪ'dɪə〕

n. ❶主意;打算;计划[C][(+of)][+to-v][+that]

I like the idea of living at the foot of the hill.

我喜欢在山脚下居住的建议。

❷构想;概念[C][U][(+of)]

Have you any idea of what he is up to?

你知道他想干什么吗?

❸了解,明白[C][(+of)][+wh-]

I have no idea what to do.

我不知道该怎么办。

ideal〔aɪ'dɪəl ‖ aɪ'dɪəl〕

a. ❶理想的,完美的

You're an ideal father.

你真是个完美的父亲。

❷空想的，不切实际的

Nobody would approve your ideal plans for rcforming the system of government.

没有人会赞成你的关于改革政体的不切实际的计划。

identify 〔aɪˈdɛntəˌfaɪ ‖ aɪˈdentɪfaɪ〕

［过去式］identified；［过去分词］identified

vt. ❶确认；识别；鉴定，验明［(＋as)］

She identified him as her attacker.

她认出他就是袭击她的人。

❷视……(与……)为同一事物［(＋with)］

Never identify wealth with happiness.

千万不要把财富和幸福等同起来。

vi. (与……)认同；一致；感同身受［(＋with)］

I identified with the heroine of the novel.

我与小说中的那个女主人公感同身受。

identity 〔aɪˈdɛntətɪ ‖ aɪˈdentɪtɪ〕

n. ❶身份；本身；本体［C］［U］

identity card

身份证

❷同一(性)；相同(处)，一致(处)［C］［U］

the identity of the two crimes

两件犯罪性质相同

idiom 〔ˈɪdɪəm ‖ ˈɪdɪəm〕

n. 惯用语；成语；习惯语［C］

if 〔ɪf ‖ ɪf〕

conj. ❶(表示条件)如果

He will come if you invite him.

如果你请他，他会来的。

❷(表示假设)假如，要是

If I were you, I would never do that.

如果我是你，我决不做那件事。

❸(表示让步)即使

We'll go even if it rains.

即使下雨我们也要去。

❹是否

I don't know if the news is true.

我不知道这个消息是否确切。

❺(表示因果关系)每一次……的时候(总是会)

My mother comes if I need her.

我一需要母亲的时候她就会来。

ignorance 〔ˈɪgnərəns ‖ ˈɪgnərəns〕

n. ［U］❶无知，不学无术；愚昧 ❷不知

ignorant 〔ˈɪgnərənt ‖ ˈɪgnərənt〕
［比］more ignorant；［最］most ignorant
a. ❶无知的，不学无术的；没有受教育的
He was an ignorant man.
他是个无知的人。
❷不知道的［（＋of/about）］［＋that］
I'm quite ignorant of the plan.
我对这个计划一无所知。

ignore 〔ɪgˈnɔr ‖ ɪgˈnɔː〕
vt. 不顾，不理会；忽视
His letters were ignored.
他的信无人理会。

ill 〔ɪl ‖ ɪl〕
［比］worse；［最］worst
a. 生病的，不健康的；要呕吐的［（＋with）］
Mary's son is ill today.
玛丽的儿子今天病了。
ad. ❶坏；冷酷地；不友善地；恶劣地
She was ill treated.
她遭受虐待。
❷困难地；几乎不
I can ill afford the time.
我简直抽不出时间。

illegal 〔ɪˈligḷ ‖ ɪˈliːgəl〕
a. 不合法的，非法的；违反规则的
He committed an illegal act.
他干了不法行为。

illness 〔ˈɪlnɪs ‖ ˈɪlnɪs〕
n. 患病（状态）；身体不适［U］
He didn't come because of illness.
他因病没来。

image 〔ˈɪmɪdʒ ‖ ˈɪmɪdʒ〕
n.［C］❶像，肖像；雕像；偶像

国会山四总统像
images of four presidents in the Mountain Rushmore

金字塔 pyramid
狮身人面像 sphinx

自由女神像
the Statue of Liberty

The coin bore an image of the President.
这枚硬币上有总统的肖像。
❷（心目中的）形象；印象［（＋of）］
I always had an image of her by the window.
在我的脑海中始终有一幅她倚窗而立的画面。
❸映像；影像；图像
❹酷似的人（或物），翻版［the］

[(+of)]
She is the image of her mother.
她是她母亲的翻版。

imagination 〔ɪˌmædʒəˈneʃən ‖ ɪˌmædʒɪˈneɪʃən〕
n. 想象力；创造力[C][U]；想象出来的东西，幻想物[U]
He is a man of imagination.
他是一个富有想象力的人。
Of course nobody was trying to kill him — It was all imagination.
当然没有人试图杀害他——那全是幻觉。

imagine 〔ɪˈmædʒɪn ‖ ɪˈmædʒɪn〕
[过去式]imagined；[过去分词]imagined
vt. ❶想象[+wh-][+(that)][+v-ing]
I can't imagine what has happened.
我想象不出发生了什么事。
❷猜想，料想[+(that)]
I imagine you are tired from the journey.
我想你旅途劳累了。

immediate 〔ɪˈmidɪɪt ‖ ɪˈmiːdɪət〕
a. ❶立即的，即刻的
Mr. Shaw made no immediate answer.
肖先生没有立即回答。
❷现在的，当前的
We must do something to meet the refugees' immediate needs.
我们必须设法满足难民眼下的需求。
❸最接近的，紧接的
Is there a gas station in the immediate area?
附近有加油站吗？

immediately 〔ɪˈmidɪɪtlɪ ‖ ɪˈmiːdɪətlɪ〕
ad. ❶直接地；接近地
He lives immediately next to us.
他住在我们隔壁。
❷立即，即刻，马上
He came home immediately after work.
他一下班就马上回家。
conj.【主英】一……(就……)
Immediately he came home, I told him about it.
他一回家我就告诉了他这件事。

impatient 〔ɪmˈpeʃənt ‖ ɪmˈpeɪʃənt〕
a. ❶无耐心的，不耐烦的；无法忍受的[(+of/at/with)]
He was very impatient with students who could not follow

him.
他对听不懂他讲课的学生很不耐心。
❷切盼的，急欲的[(+for)][+to-v]
Philip was impatient to learn the news.
菲利普急于想知道这个消息。

impolite [ˌɪmpəˈlaɪt ‖ ˌɪmpəˈlaɪt]
a. 无礼的

import [ɪmˈpɔrt ‖ ɪmˈpɔːt]
[过去式]imported；[过去分词]imported
vt. 进口，输入；引进[(+from)]
We import crude oil from Arab.
我们从阿拉伯进口原油。

importance [ɪmˈpɔrtn̩s ‖ ɪmˈpɔːtəns]
n. [U] ❶重要，重大；重要性
Here I would stress the importance of mathematics to the whole of science.
这里我要强调数学对整个科学的重要性。
❷重要的地位(或身份)
Was he related to anyone of importance?
他跟什么重要人物有关系吗？
❸自大，傲慢
with an air of importance
趾高气扬

important [ɪmˈpɔrtn̩t ‖ ɪmˈpɔːtənt]
a. ❶重要的，重大的[(+to/for)]
It is important to see that everything goes well.
重要的是确保一切顺利。
❷地位高的，有权力的
He is an important official in the government.
他是政府的要员。
❸狂妄自大的
He has an important air about him.
他显得盛气凌人。

impossible [ɪmˈpɑsəbl̩ ‖ ɪmˈpɒsəbl]
a. ❶不可能的，办不到的[+to-v][+(that)]
Don't ask me to do impossible things.
别叫我做不可能的事情。
❷不可能发生的；不真实的[+to-v][+(that)]
Living in space is not an impossible dream.
在外层空间居住不是不可能实现的梦想。

❸无法忍受的，很难对付的
He is an impossible fellow.
他这个人实在让人受不了。

impress 〔ɪm'prɛs ‖ ɪm'pres〕
［过去式］impressed；［过去分词］impressed
vt. ❶给……极深的印象；使感动；使铭记
The picture impressed me very much.
这张画使我深受感动。
❷印，压印；盖(印)于［＋on/into］
He impressed a mark on the plate.
他在盘子上盖了印。

impression 〔ɪm'prɛʃən ‖ ɪm'preʃən〕
n. ❶印象［C］［U］［(＋on)］
The new teacher made a good impression on the students.
新老师给学生们留下了一个好印象。
❷模糊的观念；感想［C］［＋that］
I have the impression that I've seen that man before.
我觉得我以前见过那个人。
❸压印；印记；压痕［C］
The robber left an impression of his feet in the mud.

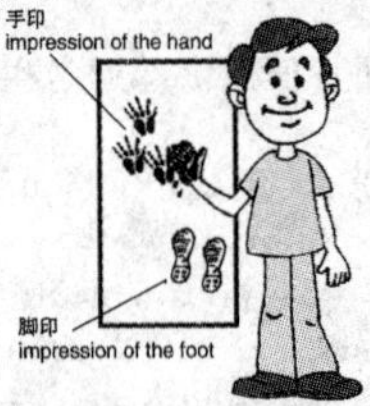

强盗在烂泥里留下了他的脚印。

improper 〔ɪm'prɑpɚ ‖ ɪm'prɒpə〕
a. 不合适的，不适当的；不成体统的
Laughing aloud is improper for a lady.
大笑是不合淑女身份的。

improve 〔ɪm'pruv ‖ ɪm'pruːv〕
［过去式］improved；［过去分词］improved
vt. ❶改进，改善；增进
He put forward a plan for improving the rate of production.
他提出了一个提高生产率的计划。
❷利用(机会等)
She improved her leisure by learning foreign languages.
她利用闲暇时间学习外语。
vi. ❶改善，变得更好
Their working conditions are

improving.
他们的工作条件正在改善。
❷增加，提高
The price of steel improved.
钢材价格提高了。

常用短语

improve in 在……方面有进步
He improved in English.
他英文有了进步。
improve on 改良；使变得更好
It's hard to improve on the plan.
要改良这个计划是很难的。

improvement 〔ɪm'pruvmənt ‖ ɪm'pruːvmənt〕
n. ❶改进，改善；增进[C][U][(+in)]
❷改进处，改善处[C]
❸改善的事物；胜过他人的人[C][(+on/over)]

in 〔ɪn ‖ ɪn〕
prep. ❶在……里，在……上
The two brothers study in the same class.
两兄弟在同一个班里上课。
❷在……之内；在……方面
He is lacking in courage.
他缺乏勇气。
❸从事于；参加着
She is in business.
她做生意。
❹穿着，戴着
She was dressed in black.
她穿着黑衣服。
❺(表示手段，方法，材料)用，以
He wrote the letter in English.
他用英语写的这封信。
❻在……期间；在……以后
The war broke out in 1941.
战争在1941年爆发。
He will be back in a week.
他一个星期内回来。
❼处在……中
My father is in good health.
我父亲身体很健康。
❽(表示数量，程度，比例)按，以；在……中
Fish are caught in great quantities.
捕到大量的鱼。
ad. ❶进；在里头
Please come in.
请进。
❷在屋里；在家
I called on him, but he wasn't in.
我去拜访他，但他不在家。
❸(车，船，季节等)已到达，已来临
Spring is in at last.
春天终于来了。

I

inch 〔ɪntʃ ‖ ɪntʃ〕[名复]inches
n. [C]❶英寸

I am five feet six inches tall.
我身高五尺六寸。
❷少许，一点儿
He escaped death by an inch.
他险些送了命。

常用短语

every inch 完全
He is every inch a gentleman.
他是个十足的绅士。
within an inch of 差点儿
I came within an inch of falling from the cliff.
我差一点儿就从悬崖上跌下来。

incident 〔ˈɪnsədənt ‖ ˈɪnsɪdənt〕
n. 事件；事变［C］
He made up his mind never to tell anyone about the incident.
他决定永远不跟任何人谈这件事。

incline 〔ɪnˈklaɪn ‖ ɪnˈklaɪn〕
［过去式］inclined；［过去分词］inclined
vi. 有……倾向，易于［（＋to/towards）］
We incline to luxury.
我们流于奢侈。
vt. ❶使倾斜；屈（身）；弯（腰）；低（头）
He inclined his body to embrace the boy.
他屈身抱住小男孩。
❷使倾向于，使想要
I am inclined to go there.
我想去那里。
He is inclined to grow fat.
他有发胖的倾向。

include 〔ɪnˈklud ‖ ɪnˈkluːd〕
［过去式］included；［过去分词］included
vt. ❶包括，包含［＋v-ing］
The price includes both house and furniture.
价钱包括房子和家具。
❷算入，包含于……里面
I include him among my friends.
我把他当做朋友。

用法工具箱

include 和 contain
The tour includes a visit to Paris.
（这次旅行包括游览巴黎。）
包括作为整体的一部分或要素。
The basket contains a variety of fruits.
（这篮子里装有各种水果。）
某物容纳在比其更大的容器之中。

income 〔ˈɪnˌkʌm ‖ ˈɪnkʌm〕

n. 收入；收益；所得[C][U]

Tony lives beyond his income.

托尼入不敷出。

inconvenience 〔ˌɪnkənˈvinjəns ‖ ˌɪnkənˈviːnɪəns〕

n. 不便；麻烦，打扰[U]

I cause inconvenience to him.

我给他带来不便。

词汇拓展

inconvenient *a.* 不便的，有困难的

incorrect 〔ˌɪnkəˈrɛkt ‖ ˌɪnkəˈrekt〕

a. 不正确的；错误的

He gave an incorrect answer.

他答错了。

increase 〔ɪnˈkris ‖ ɪnˈkriːs〕

[过去式]increased；[过去分词] increased

vt. 增大；增加；增强

The rich diet increased his weight.

丰富的饮食使他的体重增加了。

vi. 增大；增加；增强

The number of cars is increasing.

汽车的数量越来越多。

词汇拓展

increasingly *ad.* 逐渐地

incredible 〔ɪnˈkrɛdəbl̩ ‖ ɪnˈkredəbl〕

a. 不能相信的，不可信的

an incredible story

难以置信的故事

indeed 〔ɪnˈdid ‖ ɪnˈdiːd〕

ad. ❶（加强语气）真正地，确实，实在

A friend in need is a friend indeed.

患难之交才是真正的朋友。

❷（表示让步）当然，固然

He is indeed young, but he is competent.

他固然年轻，但他很称职。

❸（表示进一层的意思）更确切地；甚至

I am hungry; indeed, I am almost starving.

我饿了；我简直要饿死了。

int. （表示惊讶，讽刺，轻蔑等）真是；哦，不见得吧

"He left without saying a word."

"他一句话没讲就走了。"

"Did he, indeed?"

"一句话没讲，真的？"

I

independence 〔ˌɪndɪˈpɛndəns ‖ ˌɪndɪˈpendəns〕

n. 独立

independent 〔ˌɪndɪˈpɛndənt ‖ ˌɪndɪˈpendənt〕

a. 独立的，自治的，自主的[(＋of)]

India 〔ˈɪndɪə ‖ ˈɪndɪə〕

n. 印度

Indian 〔ˈɪndɪən ‖ ˈɪndɪən〕

n. 印度人；印第安人

a. 印度的；印第安的

indicate 〔ˈɪndəˌket ‖ ˈɪndɪkeɪt〕

[过去式]indicated；[过去分词]indicated

vt. ❶指示；指出

The sign indicates the way to go.

这路标指出路向。

❷表明；象征；暗示

His hesitation indicates unwillingness.

他的犹豫表明不愿意。

indirect 〔ˌɪndəˈrɛkt ‖ ˌɪndɪˈrekt〕

a. ❶间接的；非直接相关的；次要的

an indirect answer

不得要领的答案

❷迂回的，曲折的

an indirect route

曲折的道路

词汇拓展

indirectly *ad.* 间接地

individual 〔ˌɪndəˈvɪdʒʊəl ‖ ˌɪndɪˈvɪdʒʊəl〕

a. ❶个人的，个体的

individual differences

个人差异

❷个别的，单独的

individual word

个别单词

n.[C]个人；个体

Exceptions can not be made for individuals.

对个人不能有例外。

indoors 〔ˈɪnˈdɔrz ‖ ˌɪnˈdɔːz〕

ad. 在室内，在屋里；往室内

He ran indoors.

他跑进室内。

〔反义〕outdoors 在室外

industry 〔ˈɪndəstrɪ ‖ ˈɪndəstrɪ〕

n. ❶工业；企业；行业[C][U]

Our automobile industry is expanding.

我们的汽车工业在发展。

❷勤勉[U]

Industry and thrift favor success.

勤劳和节俭有助于成功。

〔同义〕diligence 勤奋；勤勉

词汇拓展

industrial *a.* 工业的，产业的
industrious *a.* 勤勉的

inexpensive 〔ˌɪnɪk'spɛnsɪv ‖ ˌɪnɪk'spensɪv〕

a. 花费不多的；价钱低廉的

inferior 〔ɪn'fɪrɪɚ ‖ ɪn'fɪərɪə〕

a. ❶（地位等）低等的；下级的；低于……的[（+to）]

inferior classes

下层阶级

❷（质量等）次的；较差的；次于……的[（+to）]

He is inferior to you in all respects.

他各方面都比你差。

用法工具箱

用于比较时，用 inferior to 不用 inferior than

n.（地位等）低于他人者；部下，属下[C]

He is generous to his inferiors.

他对他的部下很宽宏大量。

〔**反义**〕superior 优秀的；上司

infinite 〔'ɪnfənɪt ‖ 'ɪnfɪnɪt〕

a. 无限的；无边的，极大的

infinite time/ space/ distance

无限的时间/空间/距离

infinite wisdom

无穷的智慧

influence 〔'ɪnflʊəns ‖ 'ɪnflʊəns〕

[过去式]influenced；[过去分词]influenced

n. ❶影响，作用[C][U][（+on/upon）]

The teacher has a great influence on his pupils.

这位老师对学生们有很大的影响。

❷影响力；势力，权势[U][（+over/with）]

Mr. Smith is a man of influence in this town.

史密斯先生是这个镇上有权势的人物。

vt. 影响，感化；左右

I don't want to influence you. You must decide for yourself.

我不想影响你，你必须自行决定。

词汇拓展

influential *a.* 有影响的，有势力的

influenza 〔ˌɪnflʊ'ɛnzə ‖ ˌɪnflʊ'enzə〕

n. [U] ❶【医】流行性感冒

❷【兽医】家畜流行性感冒

informal 〔ɪn'fɔrml̩ ‖ ɪn'fɔːməl〕

a. ❶非正式的，非正规的

an informal party

非正式的宴会

❷口语的；会话体的，通俗的

informal English

日常英语

information 〔ˌɪnfɚ'meʃən ‖ ˌɪnfə'meɪʃən〕

n. 报告；消息；报道；情报资料；信息[U][(+about/on)]

The book contains much useful information.

这本书包含了许多有用的资料。

a piece of information

一则信息

inhabit 〔ɪn'hæbɪt ‖ ɪn'hæbɪt〕

[过去式]inhabited;[过去分词]inhabited

vt. 居住于；(动物)栖息于；存在于；占据

These districts are densely inhabited.

这些地区人口稠密。

inhabitant 〔ɪn'hæbətənt ‖ ɪn'hæbɪtənt〕

n. (某地区的)居民，居住者[C]

The small town has about 1,000 inhabitants.

这个小镇大约有1,000居民。

inject 〔ɪn'dʒɛkt ‖ ɪn'dʒekt〕

[过去式]injected;[过去分词]injected

vt. 注射(药液等)[(+into)]；为(某人)注射[(+with)]

injure 〔'ɪndʒɚ ‖ 'ɪndʒə〕

[过去式]injured;[过去分词]injured

vt. 伤害；损害；毁坏

I hope I didn't injure her feelings.

我希望我没有伤害她的感情。

词汇拓展

injury *n.* 伤害，损害

ink 〔ɪŋk ‖ ɪŋk〕

n. 墨水；油墨；墨汁[U]

He wrote a letter in blue ink.

他用蓝墨水写信。

词汇拓展

ink-pad *n.* 打印台

inky 〔'ɪŋkɪ ‖ 'ɪŋkɪ〕

[比]inkier;[最]inkiest

a. 如墨水的，漆黑的

inky darkness

一片漆黑

inn 〔ɪn ‖ ɪn〕

n. 小旅馆，客栈，小饭店[C]

stay at an inn
投宿小旅馆

innocent 〔ˈɪnəsn̩t ‖ ˈɪnəsnt〕
[比]more innocent; [最]most innocent

a. ❶无罪的,清白的[(+of)]
He was pronounced innocent of the charge.
他被宣告无罪。
〔反义〕guilty 有罪的

❷无害的
The butterfly is an innocent insect.
蝴蝶是一种无害的昆虫。

❸天真的,单纯的
Don't be so innocent as to believe everything he says.
不要这么天真,竟相信他所说的一切。

inquire 〔ɪnˈkwaɪr ‖ ɪnˈkwaɪə〕
[过去式]inquired; [过去分词]inquired

vt. 询问;查问;调查
She inquired why he had not thought of that before.
她查问为何他以前没想到那一点。

vi. 询问;调查[(+about/into)]
Why don't you inquire by telephone?
你为何不打电话询问?

常用短语

inquire after 问候
inquire for 求见

inquiry 〔ɪnˈkwaɪrɪ ‖ ɪnˈkwaɪərɪ〕

n. ❶询问,打听;质询[C][U][(+about/into)]
❷调查[C][(+into)]

insect 〔ˈɪnsɛkt ‖ ˈɪnsekt〕

n. [C]昆虫

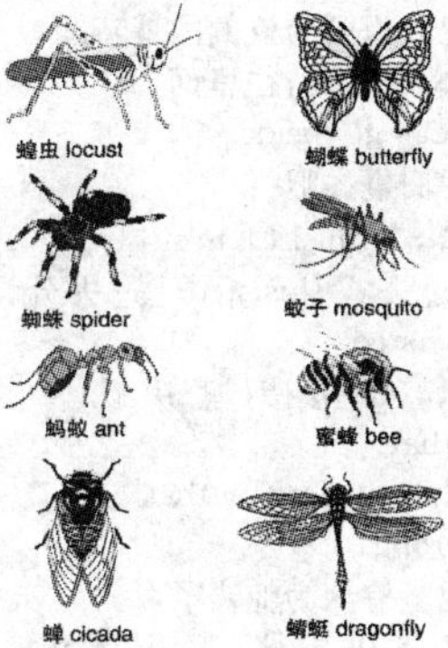

The bee is a diligent insect.
蜜蜂是勤劳的昆虫。

inside 〔ɪnˈsaɪd ‖ ɪnˈsaɪd〕

n. ❶内部,里面[C]
There is a label on the inside of the box.
盒子内侧有个标签。
❷(人行道,道路的)内侧[the]

That car tried to pass me on the inside.
那辆汽车试图从道路的内侧超过我。
a. ❶里面的，内侧的；在屋里的
the inside seat
里面的座位
❷内幕的，秘密的
He's got inside news about the meeting.
他已得到会议的内幕新闻。
ad. 在里面；往里面
Let's go inside.
我们进去吧。

insist 〔ɪn'sɪst ‖ ɪn'sɪst〕
［过去式］insisted；［过去分词］insisted
vt. ❶坚持；坚决认为［＋(that)］
She insisted that he was wrong.
她坚持认为他错了。
❷坚决主张；坚决要求［＋(that)］
He insisted that we (should) accept these gifts.
他一定要我们收下这些礼物。
vi. ❶坚持，坚决认为；强调［(＋on/upon)］
He insists on his innocence.
他坚持说自己是无辜的。
❷坚决主张；一定要［(＋on/upon)］
He insisted on/upon my going with him.
他坚持要我跟他一起去。

inspect 〔ɪn'spɛkt ‖ ɪn'spekt〕
［过去式］inspected；［过去分词］inspected
vt. ❶检查；审查
He inspected every part of the machine.
他检查了机器的每一部分。
❷检阅；视察
The governor inspected the new power station.
总督视察了新的发电站。

词汇拓展
inspection *n.* 检查，视察

instance 〔'ɪnstəns ‖ 'ɪnstəns〕
n. ［C］ ❶例子，实例［(＋of)］
I will give you an instance of it.
我给你举个例子。
❷情况，场合
I won't give in in any instance.
在任何情况下我都不会妥协。
常用短语
for instance 例如

instant 〔'ɪnstənt ‖ 'ɪnstənt〕
a. ❶立即的，即刻的

The telegram was asked for an instant reply.
这封电报要求立即回复。
❷紧迫的，迫切的；迫在眉睫的
The flood victims were in instant need of help.
水灾难民急需救助。
❸(食品)速食的；即溶的
a cup of instant coffee
一杯速溶咖啡
n. 顷刻，一刹那
An instant later, the explosion occurred.
一会儿之后，爆炸就发生了。

instead 〔ɪn'stɛd ‖ ɪn'sted〕
ad. ❶作为替代
He is too busy; let me go instead.
他太忙了，让我去吧。
❷反而，却
Instead of talking to me, she just went out.
她不和我说话，反而出去了。

常用短语

instead of 代替

institute 〔'ɪnstəˌtjut ‖ 'ɪnstɪtjuːt〕
n. [C] ❶学会，学社，协会；会馆
❷(专科性的)学校，学院，大学；研究所

instruction 〔ɪn'strʌkʃən ‖ ɪn'strʌkʃən〕
n. ❶教学，讲授；教育[U][(+in)]
His instruction is given in English.
他用英文教学。
❷教诲；教导[U]
We should follow our teachers' instruction.
我们要听从老师的教诲。
❸命令，指示[P][+to-v][+(that)]
give instructions to these computer
给这些计算机发指令
❹用法说明；操作指南[P]

instructive 〔ɪn'strʌktɪv ‖ ɪn'strʌktɪv〕
a. 有教育意义的；有启发性的
The movie is instructive.
这部电影有教育意义。

instrument 〔'ɪnstrəmənt ‖ 'ɪnstrəmənt〕
n. [C] ❶仪器；器具，器械
The dentist picked up several instruments.
那位牙科医生把几把器械收拾好。
❷乐器
❸手段，工具；促成某事的东西

Language is an instrument for communication.
语言是交际的工具。

insult¹〔ˈɪnsʌlt ‖ ˈɪnsʌlt〕
n. 侮辱，羞辱[C][(+to)]
Your remark is an insult to him.
你的话对他是种侮辱。

insult²〔ɪnˈsʌlt ‖ ɪnˈsʌlt〕
[过去式]insulted；[过去分词]insulted
vt. 侮辱，羞辱
His girlfriend insulted him.
他的女朋友羞辱了他。

insurance 〔ɪnˈʃʊrəns ‖ ɪnˈʃʊərəns〕
n. ❶保险；保险契约[U][(+against)]
take out insurance against fire and theft
办理火险和盗窃保险
❷保险业[U]
She works in insurance.
她从事保险业。
❸保险金额；赔偿金[U][(+on)]
He has ＄100，000 life insurance，which his wife will receive if he dies first.
他有10万美元的人寿保险，如果他先去世，他的妻子将得到这笔钱。

intellectual 〔ˌɪntl̩ˈɛktʃʊəl ‖ ˌɪntɪˈlektʃʊəl〕
a. ❶智力的；理智的
❷智力发达的，聪明的
n. 知识分子；有很高智力的人[C]

intelligence 〔ɪnˈtɛlədʒəns ‖ ɪnˈtelɪdʒəns〕
n. [U] ❶智能；智慧；理解力
He's obviously a man of very high intelligence.
显然他是个非常聪明的人。
❷情报；情报工作；情报机关
Our intelligence shows that the enemy is advancing.
我们的情报显示敌人正在向前行进。

词汇拓展

intelligent *a.* 聪明的

intend〔ɪnˈtɛnd ‖ ɪnˈtend〕
[过去式]intended；[过去分词]intended
vt. ❶想要；打算[+to-v][+v-ing][+(that)]
He intends his son to manage the company.
他打算让他儿子经营该公司。
❷打算使……(成为)；(为……

而)准备[(+for/as)]
That trap is intended for you.
那个圈套是为你而设的。

词汇拓展

intention *n.* 打算,意图

interest [ˈɪntərɪst ‖ ˈɪntrɪst]
n. ❶兴趣;关注;爱好[C][U][(+in)]
I developed an interest in the machine.
我对这台机器产生了兴趣。
❷趣味性[U][(+to)]
Local color added interest to the novel.
地方色彩增加了这部小说的吸引力。
❸感兴趣的事物或人[C]
His two great interests in life are music and painting.
他生活中的两大兴趣是音乐和绘画。
❹利益;利害[P]
He is always seeking his own interests.
他总是追求自己的利益。
❺利息[U]
capital and interest
本金和利息
❻股份,股权[C][(+in)]
He has financial interest in the company.
他在公司有股份。

interesting [ˈɪntərɪstɪŋ ‖ ˈɪntrɪstɪŋ]
[比] more interesting; [最] most interesting
a. 有趣的;引起兴趣的;令人关注的[(+for/to)]
The film was interesting.
这个电影很有趣。

international [ˌɪntəˈnæʃənḷ ‖ ˌɪntəˈnæʃənəl]
a. 国际性的,国际的
international trade
国际贸易

interrupt [ˌɪntəˈrʌpt ‖ ˌɪntəˈrʌpt]
[过去式]interrupted; [过去分词]interrupted
vt. ❶打断(讲话或讲话人)
I don't want to interrupt you. Go on with your story.
我不想打断你。请把你的故事讲下去。
❷中断;遮断;阻碍
The war interrupted the trade between the two countries.
战争使两国的贸易中断了。
vi. 打断
Go on. I don't want to inter-

rupt.
说下去，我不想打断你说话。

interview 〔ˈɪntəˌvju ‖ ˈɪntəvjuː〕
［过去式］interviewed；［过去分词］interviewed
n.［C］❶接见，会见
He asked for an interview with the president.
他要求与校长会面。
❷（记者的）采访，访谈；访谈录
❸面谈，面试
Don't be late for your interview, or you won't get the job.
面试不要迟到，否则你就得不到工作了。
vt. ❶接见，会见；访问，采访
We are now going to interview the Minister of Education.
我们现在就去采访教育部部长。
❷对……进行面谈，面试
She has interviewed most of the applicants for the job.
她已和大部分申请这份工作的人面谈过了。

into 〔ˈɪntu ‖ ˈɪntuː〕
prep. ❶（表示动作的方向）到……里
The man walked into the house in the dark.
那人摸黑走进了屋里。
〔反义〕out of 往外
❷（表示时间的推移）进入到
He worked late into the night.
他工作到深夜。
❸（表示变化）成，为；转入
All the buildings had been turned into hospitals.
所有房子都改成了医院。

introduce 〔ˌɪntrəˈdjus ‖ ˌɪntrəˈdjuːs〕
［过去式］introduced；［过去分词］introduced
vt. ❶介绍，引见［（＋to）］
It was my younger brother who introduced me to jazz.
是我的弟弟介绍我听爵士乐的。
❷引进；传入；采用［（＋to/into）］
Coffee was introduced into England from the Continent.
咖啡是从欧洲大陆传入英国的。
❸提出；制定；推行
The vice chairman of the committee introduced a topic for discussion.
委员会副主席提出议题供大家讨论。

introduction 〔ˌɪntrəˈdʌkʃən ‖

ˌɪntrəˈdʌkʃən〕

n. ❶介绍；正式引见[C][U][P]

He was shaking her hand before I could finish the introduction.

未等我介绍完，他就在握她的手了。

❷引进，传入[U][(＋of/to/into)]

The government saw the introduction of new technology as vital.

政府认为引进新技术至关重要。

❸采用；被采用的东西；引种[C][U]

Television is a later introduction than radio.

电视的使用比无线电要晚。

❹引言，序言；绪论[C][(＋to)]

❺入门(书)[C][(＋to)]

invade〔ɪnˈved ‖ ɪnˈveɪd〕

[过去式]invaded；[过去分词]invaded

vt. ❶侵入，侵略

The enemy invaded our country.

敌人侵犯我国。

❷侵犯，侵扰

You invaded my private rights.

你侵犯了我的个人权利。

词汇拓展

invasion *n.* 侵略，侵犯

invent〔ɪnˈvɛnt ‖ ɪnˈvent〕

[过去式]invented；[过去分词]invented

vt. ❶发明，创造

He invented a new type of stethoscope.

他发明了一种新型听诊器。

❷捏造，虚构

We must invent an excuse for being late.

我们必须找一个迟到的借口。

invention〔ɪnˈvɛnʃən ‖ ɪnˈvenʃən〕

n. ❶发明，创造[U]

Necessity is the mother of invention.

需要是发明之母。

❷发明物，创意[C]

The machine was his own invention.

这台机器是他自己发明的。

inventor〔ɪnˈvɛntɚ ‖ ɪnˈventə〕

n. 发明家，发明者；创作者[C]

investigate〔ɪnˈvɛstəˌget ‖ ɪnˈvestɪgeɪt〕

［过去式］investigated；［过去分词］investigated

vt. 调查，研究

The detective was sent to investigate the crime.

那位侦探被派去调查该犯罪。

vi. 调查，研究［(＋into)］

The principal promised to investigate into that affair.

校长答应去调查那件事情。

invitation 〔ˌɪnvəˈteʃən ‖ ˌɪnvɪˈteɪʃən〕

n. ❶邀请［C］［U］［(＋to)］［＋to-v］

She received an invitation to the party.

她接到参加聚会的邀请。

❷请帖［C］

They sent out 200 invitations to their wedding.

他们发出了200张婚礼请帖。

invite 〔ɪnˈvaɪt ‖ ɪnˈvaɪt〕

［过去式］invited；［过去分词］invited

vt. ❶邀请；招待［(＋to)］

He invited several of his friends to the show.

他邀请了几个朋友去看表演。

❷请求；征求

After his lecture the visiting professor invited questions.

客座教授作完讲座就请大家提问题。

❸引起，招致；吸引；诱惑

Recklessness invites disaster.

莽撞招致灾难。

involve 〔ɪnˈvɑlv ‖ ɪnˈvɒlv〕

［过去式］involved；［过去分词］involved

vt. ❶使卷入，连累；牵涉［(＋in/with)］

That's no concern of mine. I'm not involved.

那与我无关，我未卷入。

❷需要，包含，意味着［(＋in)］［＋v-ing］

His work involves occasional journeys.

他的工作偶尔需要出差。

❸使专注，使忙于［(＋in)］

He was involved in writing his doctoral dissertation.

他在聚精会神地写他的博士论文。

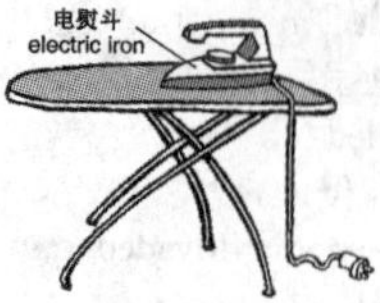

iron 〔ˈaɪɚn ‖ ˈaɪən〕

n. ❶铁；(食物中所含的)铁质

[U]

❷熨斗[C]

irony ['aɪrənɪ ‖ 'aɪərənɪ]

n. 反语；冷嘲；讽刺[U]

He called the foolish boy "Genius" in irony.

他戏称这个蠢男孩为"天才"。

irrigate ['ɪrəˌget ‖ 'ɪrɪgeɪt]

[过去式]irrigated；[过去分词] irrigated

vt. 灌溉

irrigation [ˌɪrə'geʃən ‖ ˌɪrɪ'geɪʃən]

n. 灌溉[U]

is [ɪz ‖ ɪz]

vi. （用于第三人称单数现在式）是

The picture on the wall is beautiful.

墙上的画很美。

v. aux. （与 v-ing 连用构成现在进行时；与 v-ed 连用构成被动语态）

Mr. Ward is known as a great painter.

沃德先生是一位闻名遐迩的大画家。

island ['aɪlənd ‖ 'aɪlənd]

n. 岛[C]

He lived on a small island off the shore.

他住在离海边不远的一个小岛上。

it [ɪt ‖ ɪt]

pron.

格＼数	单数	复数
主格	it 它	they 它们
所有格	its 它的	their 它们的
宾格	it 它	them 它们

❶（指已提及的或心目中的人或事物）这，那，它

This is our new car. I bought it yesterday.

这是我们的新车。我昨天买的。

❷（指无生命物，动植物，性别不详的幼孩等）它

What a beautiful baby — is it a boy?

多漂亮的孩子啊！它是男孩吗？

❸（作无人称动词的主词，表示时间，气候，距离等）

It's about 50 kilometers from here to my ranch.

从这儿到我的牧场约有 50 公里。

It is 10 o'clock.

10 点钟了。

It is cold.

天好冷。

❹(置于句首或句中,引导后面的词组或从句)

It doesn't matter what you say.

你说什么都没关系。

❺(作为形式上的主语或宾语,用于表示强调的句型中)

It was the last dance that I enjoyed the most.

最后一个舞蹈是我最欣赏的。

Italian 〔ɪˈtæljən ‖ ɪˈtælɪən〕

n. 意大利人;意大利语

a. 意大利的; 意大利人(语)的

Italy 〔ˈɪtḷɪ ‖ ˈɪtəlɪ〕

n. 意大利

item 〔ˈaɪtəm ‖ ˈaɪtəm〕

n. [C] ❶项目;品目;条款

She checked the items in the bill.

她检查了账单上的账目。

❷(新闻等的)一则,一条,一项

There was an item of news in yesterday's paper about the return of the hostages.

昨天的报上有一条关于放回人质的新闻。

its 〔ɪts ‖ ɪts〕

pron. (it 的所有格)它的

The dog wagged its tail.

狗摇尾巴。

itself 〔ɪtˈsɛlf ‖ ɪtˈself〕

pron. ❶(it 的反身代词)它自己

The team surprised itself by winning.

该队竟然得胜,连它们自己都感到惊奇。

❷(用以加强语气)它自身,它本身

The work itself is easy.

这个工作本身很容易。

J

jacket 〔ˈdʒækɪt ‖ ˈdʒækɪt〕
n. [C] ❶夹克，上衣
（指西装或女套装的上衣等开前襟的短上衣）
❷（书籍的）护套；（唱片的）封套；公文套
The dictionary is protected by a jacket of clear plastic.
词典带有一个透明塑料的护封。

jade 〔dʒed ‖ dʒeɪd〕
n. 翡翠；玉，绿玉色[U]

jail 〔dʒel ‖ dʒeɪl〕
n. 监狱；拘留所；监禁[C][U]
sent to jail= put in jail 下狱
be in jail
在狱中
break jail
越狱

jam[1] 〔dʒæm ‖ dʒæm〕
[过去式]jammed；[过去分词] jammed
vt. ❶塞进；挤进；把……塞满；使挤满
He jammed the clothes into a bag.
他把衣服塞进袋中。
The train was jammed with passengers.
火车里挤满了旅客。
❷堵住，塞住
The accident jammed the traffic.
这场意外事故使交通阻塞。
n. 拥挤；堵塞；轧住[C]
a traffic jam

J

交通阻塞

jam² 〔dʒæm ‖ dʒæm〕

n. 果酱[U]

apple jam

苹果酱

January 〔ˈdʒænjuˌɛrɪ ‖ ˈdʒænjuərɪ〕

n. 略作 Jan. 一月

I was born on January 1, 1969.

我生于 1969 年 1 月 1 日。

Japan 〔dʒəˈpæn ‖ dʒəˈpæn〕

n. 日本

Japanese 〔ˌdʒæpəˈniz ‖ ˌdʒæpəˈniːz〕

n. ❶日本人

❷日语

a. 日本(人)的

jar 〔dʒɑr ‖ dʒɑː〕

n. [C]❶罐,坛,(宽口的)瓶

❷一罐(或一坛等)的量

We ate a whole jar of jam.

我们吃掉整整一罐果酱。

坛子jar 罐 jug

jaw 〔dʒɔ ‖ dʒɔː〕

n. 颌;颚[C]

the lower (upper) jaw

下(上)颚

jazz 〔dʒæz ‖ dʒæz〕

n. 爵士乐(舞)[U]

jealous 〔ˈdʒɛləs ‖ ˈdʒeləs〕

a. ❶妒忌的[(+of)]

He was jealous of his friend's reputation.

他妒忌朋友的声誉。

❷吃醋的

If other men spoke to her intimately, he was immediately jealous.

一见到别的男人跟她亲热地说话,他便醋意大发。

jealousy 〔ˈdʒɛləsɪ ‖ ˈdʒeləsɪ〕

n. 妒忌;猜忌[C][U]

burning jealousy

强烈的妒忌心

jeep 〔dʒip ‖ dʒiːp〕

n. 吉普车

吉普车
jeep

Jesus 〔ˈdʒizəs ‖ ˈdʒiːzəs〕

n. 耶稣

jet 〔dʒɛt ‖ dʒet〕

n. [C] ❶喷射;喷出物[(+of)]

the jet of water
喷出的水
❷喷气式飞机；喷射引擎
We are going to travel by jet.
我们打算乘喷气式飞机旅行。

喷气式飞机 jet

Jew 〔dʒu ‖ dʒuː〕
n. [C]❶犹太人
❷犹太教徒

词汇拓展

Jewish *a.* 犹太的，犹太人的

jewel 〔ˈdʒuəl ‖ ˈdʒuːəl〕
n. [C] ❶宝石
❷宝石饰物，首饰[P]

job 〔dʒɑb ‖ dʒɒb〕
n. [C] ❶工作；职业
She has a job at a children's hospital.
她在儿童医院工作。
❷零工
He did all kinds of odd jobs.
他做各种零活。
❸费力的事情
The construction of the new building was a big job.
建造新大楼是项大工程。

join 〔dʒɔɪn ‖ dʒɔɪn〕
[过去式]joined；[过去分词]joined
vt. ❶ 连接；使结合[(＋to/together/up)]
He joined the two pieces of wood together with glue.
他用胶水将这两块木料粘在一起。
❷与……会合；与……交接
This path joins the highway ahead.
这条路在前面与公路相接。
❸ 和……一起做同样的事；和……作伴[(＋in/for)]
Will you join us for dinner?
你和我们一起吃晚饭好吗？
vi. ❶汇合；相遇
Where do the two rivers join?
这两条河在什么地方汇合？
❷参加；同……一起[(＋in)]
He never joined in the usual sports of the boys.
他从不参加孩子们的一般体育活动。
❸邻接
The two estates join at the foot of the hill.
这两处庄园在山脚下相毗连。
n. 接合点；接连处[C]

The joins can hardly be seen.
接缝几乎看不出来。

joint 〔dʒɔɪnt ‖ dʒɔɪnt〕
n. [C] ❶接头，接缝；接合点
The pipe was rusted at the joint.
管子的接合处生锈了。
❷关节
finger joint
指关节

joke 〔dʒok ‖ dʒəʊk〕
n. [C] ❶玩笑，戏谑
You have taken my little joke too much to heart.
你把我的小玩笑太当真了。
❷笑柄，笑料
He's the joke of the whole village.
他是全村的笑柄。

常用短语

make a joke 开玩笑
play a joke on somebody 同某人开玩笑

J

journal 〔ˈdʒɝnḷ ‖ ˈdʒɜːnəl〕
n. [C] ❶日报；杂志；期刊
Professor King often contributes to the medical journal.
金教授常为那个医学刊物撰稿。
❷日记；日志
My father keeps a journal of his everyday activities.
我父亲把自己每天的活动记录了下来。
〔同义〕diary 日记

journalism 〔ˈdʒɝnḷˌɪzəm ‖ ˈdʒɜːnəlɪzəm〕
n. 新闻工作；新闻业[U]

journalist 〔ˈdʒɝnḷɪst ‖ ˈdʒɜːnəlɪst〕
n. 新闻工作者，新闻记者；报界人士[C]

joy 〔dʒɔɪ ‖ dʒɔɪ〕
n. ❶欢乐，高兴[U]
Success brought him joy.
成功给他带来喜悦。
❷乐事；乐趣[C]
On a hot day, a cool swim is a joy.
大热天来一次凉快的游泳是件乐事。

joyful 〔ˈdʒɔɪfəl ‖ ˈdʒɔɪfəl〕
a. 高兴的，充满喜悦的；使人高兴的
He had a joyful look on his face.
他脸上充满喜悦。

judge 〔dʒʌdʒ ‖ dʒʌdʒ〕
[过去式]judged；[过去分词]judged
vt. ❶审判；判决
Who will judge the case?

谁将审判这个案子?

❷裁判;评定;裁决,认为

You can't judge a book by its cover.

你不能根据封面来评价一本书。

We must judge whether he is guilty.

我们必须判定他是否有罪。

vi. 判断

Judging from what you say, he must be a reliable man.

由你的话看来,他一定是个可靠的人。

n. [C] ❶法官,审判官

The prisoner was taken before the judge.

囚犯被提审。

❷裁判员

He was one of the judges at the horse race.

他是赛马会上的裁判员之一。

❸鉴定人;鉴赏家

He is no judge in such matters.

他在这些事上是外行。

词汇拓展

judgement *n.* ❶审判,判断 ❷判断力,鉴赏

juice 〔dʒus ‖ dʒuːs〕

n. (水果,蔬菜等的)汁[C][U]

I'd like a glass of tomato juice.

我想要一杯番茄汁。

July 〔dʒuˈlaɪ ‖ dʒʊˈlaɪ〕

n. 略作 Jul. 七月

jump 〔dʒʌmp ‖ dʒʌmp〕

[过去式]jumped;[过去分词]jumped

vi. ❶跳;跳跃

The horse jumped over the ditch.

马跳过了那条沟。

❷(因喜悦,紧张等)跃起;猛跳[(+at/for)]

My heart jumped at the news.

听到这消息我的心猛地跳了一下。

vt. ❶跳过,越过

He jumped the wall easily.

他轻松地跳过墙去。

❷使跳跃;使惊起

He jumped his horse across the stream.

他纵马跳过小溪。

跳 jump

n. [C] ❶跳跃
He got to his feet with a jump.
他霍地站了起来。
❷(需跳跃的)障碍物
The horse cleared all the jumps.
那匹马越过了所有的障碍物。

June 〔dʒun ‖ dʒuːn〕
n. 略作 Jun. 六月

jungle 〔ˈdʒʌŋgl ‖ ˈdʒʌŋgl〕
n. (热带)丛林,密林
There are many animals in jungles.
丛林里有很多动物。

junior 〔ˈdʒunjɚ ‖ ˈdʒuːnɪə〕
a. ❶年纪较轻的[(+to)]
He is junior to me by two years.
他比我小两岁。
❷资历浅的;地位较低的;晚辈的[(+to)]
My cousin is a junior officer.
我表弟是个下级军官。
❸【美】(四年制大学或中学中)三年级(生)的
❹(置于姓名后表示同名父子中的子或同姓两人中的较年幼者,略作 Jr. 或 jr.)小
Mr. Smith Jr. is in charge of this department.
小史密斯先生负责这个部门的工作。
n. ❶较年少者
I am three years her junior.
我比她小三岁。
❷等级较低者;晚辈
Of the two clerks, he is the junior.
这两个职员中他职务较低。
❸(美国四年制大学或中学的)三年级学生

jury 〔ˈdʒurɪ ‖ ˈdʒuərɪ〕
n. [C] ❶【律】陪审团
The jury found the prisoner guilty.
陪审团判定在押犯有罪。
❷(竞赛等的)评审委员会

just 〔(强) dʒʌst ‖ dʒʌst; (弱) dʒəst ‖ dʒəst〕
ad. ❶正好,恰好
That is just what I want to know.
那正是我想知道的。
❷仅仅,只是
He is just a child.
他只是一个孩子。
❸刚才
He is just out of hospital.
他刚刚出院。
a. ❶正义的;正直的;公平的
You are a just man.
你是一个正直的人。

J

❷应得的

He has received a just punishment.

他已受到应得的惩罚。

❸合理的；恰当的

This is a just decision.

这是一个恰当的决定。

justice〔ˈdʒʌstɪs ‖ ˈdʒʌstɪs〕

n. ❶正义；公平；正当的理由；合法[U]

All men should be treated with justice.

人人都应受到公平待遇。

❷司法，审判，法律制裁[U]

Those who break the law are subjected to justice.

违法者要受到法律制裁。

❸法官[C]

juvenile〔ˈdʒuvənl̩ ‖ ˈdʒuːvənaɪl〕

a. 少年的；适合少年的；少年特有的

juvenile books

少年读物

juvenile literature

儿童文学

n. [C] ❶青少年；孩子

❷少儿读物

书报亭
kiosk

风筝
kite

K

袋鼠
kangaroo

骑士
knight

keep 〔kip || ki:p〕
［过去式］kept；［过去分词］kept
vt. ❶（长期或永久）持有，保有
You may keep the book.
你可以留下这本书。
❷（一时）拥有；保管
Please keep the watch for me while I go swimming.
我去游泳，请代我保管这块表。
❸存放，保留，保存
We keep food in a refrigerator.
我们把食物存放在冰箱里。
❹使……保持在（某一状态）
Keep you hands clean.
让你的手保持干净。
❺履行；遵守；保守
Keep your word.
遵守你的诺言。
❻阻止，妨碍；控制住［（＋from）］
Rain kept him from going there.
下雨使他无法去那里。
❼记（日记，账等）
I keep a diary in English.
我用英文记日记。
❽抚养；饲养
I keep two dogs.
我养了两只狗。
❾ 经营，开设（商店等）
She keeps a bookstore.
她经营一家书店。
vi. ❶保持着某一状态
Please keep quiet.
请保持安静。
❷（食物）保持不坏
Will the food keep in hot weather?
这种食品在热天能经久不坏吗？
❸继续不断［＋v-ing］
The child kept asking me ques-

tions.
这孩子老是问我问题。

常用短语

keep away 不接近;使离开
He keeps away from drinking.
他戒了酒。
keep from ❶阻止;避开 ❷克制
You should try to keep from sitting up late at night.
你应避免熬夜。
keep off (使)不接近;挡开
Keep off the grass.
请勿践踏草地。
keep on 继续,(使)不停
He kept on telling the same story over and over.
他不断地反复说同一件事。
keep up with 跟上
We must study to keep up with the times.
我们必须用功,以赶上时代的要求。

keeper 〔ˈkipɚ ‖ ˈkiːpə〕
n. [C] ❶饲养者;保管人
❷看守人;守卫;(足球等的)守门员

key 〔ki ‖ kiː〕
n. [C] ❶钥匙
❷(解决问题的)线索;秘诀;答案;关键
The detective believes the missing gun is the key to the mystery.
那个侦探认为那把丢失的枪是侦破这宗疑案的线索。
❸(钢琴,打字机等的)键
a. 重要的,基本的,关键的
Self-confidence is the key factor to success.
自信是成功的关键因素。

kick 〔kɪk ‖ kɪk〕
[过去式]kicked;[过去分词]kicked
vt. ❶踢
He kicked the football out of the field.
他把足球踢出了场外。
❷踢进(球门);得分
He kicked a goal.
他踢进了一个球。
vi. 踢;踢腿
The baby was kicking and crying.
那婴孩正又踢又叫。
n. 踢
He gave the outer door a good kick just to open it.
为了打开外门,他使劲踢。

kid 〔kɪd ‖ kɪd〕
n. ❶小山羊,小羚羊[C]
❷小山羊皮革[U]
❸(食用的)小山羊肉[U]

❹【口】小孩[C]
Many kids were playing in the park.
很多小孩在公园里玩。

kidnap 〔ˈkɪdnæp ‖ ˈkɪdnæp〕
[过去式]kidnapped, kidnaped; [过去分词]kidnapped, kidnaped
vt. 诱拐，绑架；劫持(小孩等)
A boy was kidnapped.
一个小男孩被绑架了。

kill 〔kɪl ‖ kɪl〕
[过去式]killed; [过去分词]killed
vt. ❶杀死；宰
He was killed in the air crash.
他在空难中死去。
❷扼杀，毁掉
This has killed my hope.
这使我的希望破灭了。
❸中和；抵消；削弱
The noise killed the music.
噪声淹没了音乐声。
❹消磨(时间)
I am just killing time.
我只是在打发时间。

K

killer 〔ˈkɪlɚ ‖ ˈkɪlə〕
n. 杀人者，凶手；嗜杀成性的人(或动物)[C]

kilo 〔ˈkɪlo ‖ ˈkiːləʊ〕
n. 公斤(kilogram)的简称

kind 〔kaɪnd ‖ kaɪnd〕
[比]kinder; [最]kindest
n. 种类[C][(+of)]
There are all kinds of animals in the zoo.
动物园里有各种各样的动物。
She is not the kind of person to tell lies.
她不是那种撒谎的人。
a. ❶亲切的；和蔼的[(+to)]
They are very kind to me.
他们对我很好。
❷富于同情心的，宽容的
A kind girl tries to help people and make them happy.
有同情心的女孩是会设法帮助人并使他们快乐的。
❸【口】体贴的；令人感激的
It's very kind of you to tell me the truth.
你真好，告诉我真相。

kindergarten 〔ˈkɪndɚˌgɑrtn̩ ‖ ˈkɪndəˌgɑːtn〕
n. 幼儿园[C]

kindhearted 〔ˌkaɪndˈhɑrtɪd ‖ ˌkaɪndˈhɑːtɪd〕
a. 好心肠的；仁慈的；同情的

kindly 〔ˈkaɪndlɪ ‖ ˈkaɪndlɪ〕
[比]kindlier; [最]kindliest
a. 亲切的；和蔼的；善良的；体贴的

kindly heart
仁慈的心
ad. 亲切地；和蔼地；好心地
Speak kindly to little kids.
对小孩子说话要和气。

kindness 〔ˈkaɪndnɪs ‖ ˈkaɪndnɪs〕
n. ❶仁慈；和蔼；好意[U][(+to)]
She was known to all for her kindness.
她的仁慈人人皆知。
❷友好的行为；好事[C]
I thanked them for many kindnesses they showed me.
我感谢他们对我的许多帮助。

king 〔kɪŋ ‖ kɪŋ〕
n. [C]❶(常大写)王，国王，君主，首领
They made him King of England.
他们拥戴他为英国国王。
〔**反义**〕Queen 女王
❷(某范围内)最有势力者，最重要者，大王
He is a steel king.
他是钢铁大王。

kingdom 〔ˈkɪŋdəm ‖ ˈkɪŋdəm〕
n. ❶王国[C]
❷领域[C]

kiss 〔kɪs ‖ kɪs〕
[过去式]kissed；[过去分词]kissed
vt. 吻
The children kissed their parents goodnight.
孩子们吻了吻父母以道晚安。
vi. 接吻
They kissed and said goodbye.
他们接吻道别。
n. 吻[C]
She gave her husband a kiss.
她吻了她的丈夫一下。

kitchen 〔ˈkɪtʃɪn ‖ ˈkɪtʃɪn〕
n. 厨房[C]

kite 〔kaɪt ‖ kaɪt〕
n. [C] ❶鸢 ❷风筝
He is flying a kite.
他在放风筝。

风筝
kite

kitten 〔ˈkɪtn̩ ‖ ˈkɪtn〕
n. 小猫[C]

knee 〔ni ‖ niː〕
n. [C] ❶膝，膝盖，膝部
She was on her knees weeding the garden.
她跪着给花园除杂草。

K

❷(裤子,长袜等的)膝部
She mended the holes in the knees of his trousers.
她把他裤子膝部的洞眼缝补好了。

knife 〔naɪf ‖ naɪf〕[名复]knives
n. [C]刀,小刀;菜刀;手术刀
Put your knife and fork down on the plate if you've finished eating.
要是你吃完了就把刀叉放在盘子上。

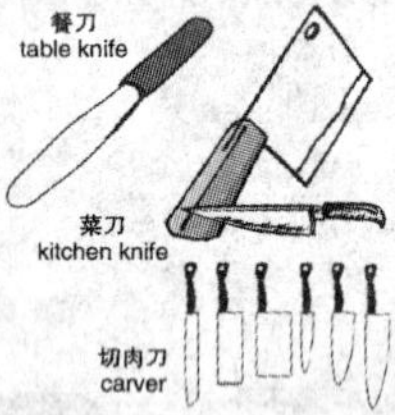

knit 〔nɪt ‖ nɪt〕
[过去式]knitted, knit;[过去分词]knitted, knit
vt. 编织
She's knitting her father a sweater.
她在为父亲织毛衣。
vi. 编织
She is knitting in her room.
她在她的房间里织毛衣。

knock 〔nɑk ‖ nɒk〕
[过去式]knocked;[过去分词]knocked
vi. ❶相撞,碰击[(+against)]
His legs knocked against the chair.
他的两条腿撞到了椅子。
❷敲,击,打[(+on/at)]
He knocked at the door and entered.
他敲了敲门便走进来了。
vt. ❶敲,击,打
The falling bottle knocked him on the head.
跌落的瓶子砸在他的头上。
❷击(撞)成……
The blow knocked her senseless.
那一击把她打昏了。
n. 敲;击,打[C]
I heard a knock on/at the door.
我听见有人敲门。

know 〔no ‖ nəʊ〕
[过去式]knew;[过去分词]known
vt. ❶知道;了解;懂得
I knew she was against us.
我知道她反对我们。
❷认识;熟悉
We have known each other for many years.

K

我们相识多年了。

❸认出；辨别[(＋by/from)]

I know right from wrong.

我能辨别是非。

vi. 知道；了解，懂得[(＋about/of)]

There is one or two things I'd like to know about.

有一两件事我很想知道。

常用短语

be known to 为……所知

He is known to everybody.

他是众人所熟知的人物。

God knows… 天知道(强调没人知道)

God knows where he has gone.

天知道他去了哪里！

as far as I know 据我所知

knowledge 〔'nɑlɪdʒ ‖ 'nɒlɪdʒ〕

n. ❶知识，学识，学问[U][(＋of)]

knowledge of economics

经济学知识

❷知道，了解；消息[U][(＋of)]

My knowledge of Mr. Read is not very great.

我对里德先生的了解不是很多。

❸认识[U]

known 〔non ‖ nəʊn〕

a. 大家知道的；已知的；知名的

He is a known artist.

他是一个知名的艺术家。

Korea 〔kə'rɪə ‖ kə'rɪə〕

n. 朝鲜半岛

词汇拓展

Democratic People's Republic of Korea *n.* 朝鲜

Republic of Korea *n.* 韩国

K

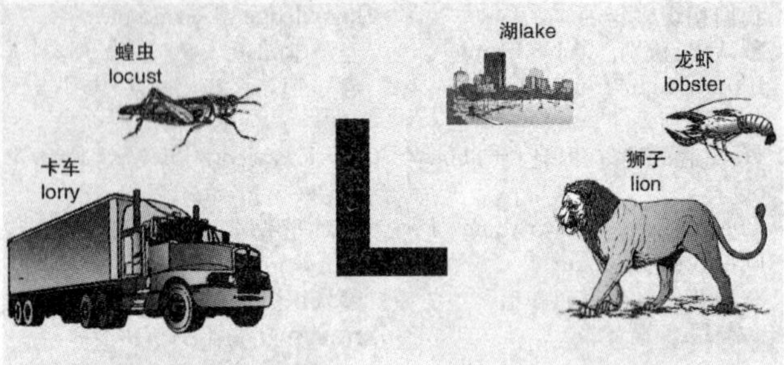

labo(u)r 〔ˈlebɚ ‖ ˈleɪbə〕
[过去式]labored;[过去分词]labored

n. ❶劳动[U]

All wealth comes from human labor.

一切财富都来源于人类的劳动。

❷劳工,劳方[U]

The country is short of skilled labor.

这个国家缺乏熟练工人。

laboratory 〔ˈlæbrəˌtɔrɪ ‖ ləˈbɒrətrɪ〕

n. [C] ❶实验室,研究室

This is our new language laboratory.

这是我们新的语言实验室。

❷化学工厂,药厂

lack 〔læk ‖ læk〕
[过去式]lacked;[过去分词]lacked

vt. (通常不用被动态) 缺少;没有;不足

I don't seem to lack anything.

我好像什么也不缺。

vi. 缺少;不足;没有[(+for)]

They lacked for nothing.

他们什么都不缺。

n. ❶欠缺;不足;没有[U][(+of)]

He can not buy it because of his lack of money.

他因缺钱买不起这个。

❷缺少的东西;需要的东西[C]

Water is a lack of this region.

这个地区缺水。

ladder 〔ˈlædɚ ‖ ˈlædə〕

n. [C] ❶梯子

❷梯状物;阶梯;(发迹等的)途径;梯级

Diligence is often a ladder to

success.
勤勉常常是通往成功的阶梯。

lady 〔ˈledɪ ‖ ˈleɪdɪ〕
n. [C]❶女士，夫人，小姐
"A lady wants to see you, sir."
"先生，一位女士想见您。"
❷淑女，家世好的女子，贵妇人
She is the daughter of an earl, a lady by birth.
她是伯爵的女儿，生来就是一位贵族小姐。
❸(大写)(英国对贵族妻女的尊称)……夫人；……小姐
Lady Elizabeth
伊丽莎白小姐
❹(大写)公共女厕所，女盥洗室[P]

lake 〔lek ‖ leɪk〕
n. 湖[C]
He has a villa by the lake.
他在湖畔有一所别墅。

lamb 〔læm ‖ læm〕
n. ❶小羊[C]
❷羔羊肉；羔羊皮[U]
Which do you prefer, lamb chops or pork chops?
你比较喜欢羊排，还是猪排？

lame 〔lem ‖ leɪm〕
[比]lamer；[最]lamest
a. 跛脚的，瘸的
She's lame in the right leg.
她右脚是瘸的。

lamp 〔læmp ‖ læmp〕
n. [C]灯，油灯，灯火
an electric lamp
电灯
street lamps
街灯

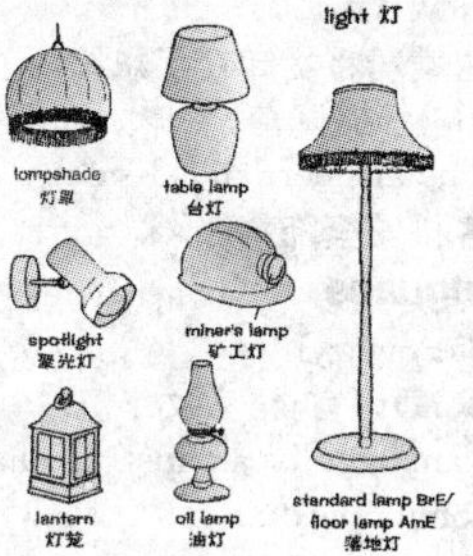

land 〔lænd ‖ lænd〕
[过去式]landed；[过去分词]landed
n. ❶陆地[U]
Most mammals live on land.
大多数哺乳动物生活在陆地上。
❷土地；田地[U]
He owns 300 acres of land.
他拥有 300 英亩土地。
❸国土，国家[C]
He has visited many distant lands.
他访问过许多遥远的国家。

vt. ❶使登陆;使降落;使下车
The pilot landed the helicopter in a rice field.
飞行员将直升机降落在一片稻田里。
❷卸货
The ship landed the goods at New York.
这艘船将货卸在了纽约。
vi. 登陆;降落
The airliner landed safely.
客机安全降落。

language 〔ˈlæŋgwɪdʒ ‖ ˈlæŋgwɪdʒ〕
n. ❶语言;语言文字[U]
Language is an instrument for communication.
语言是交际的工具。
❷(国家,民族等的)语言文字[C]
He can speak several languages.
他会讲好几种语言。

lantern 〔ˈlæntɚn ‖ ˈlæntən〕
n. 灯笼;提灯[C]
the Lantern Festival
元宵节(灯节)

large 〔lɑrdʒ ‖ lɑːdʒ〕
a. ❶大的,宽大的;大规模的
I want a large box; this one is too small.
我要一个大盒子;这个太小了。
❷多的,多量的,多数的
The concert drew a large audience.
音乐会吸引了大量的观众。
❸广博的;广泛的
The President is a man of large experience.
总统是一位经验丰富的人。
ad. ❶大,大大地
Do not write so large.
不要把字写得这么大。
❷夸大地
He tends to talk large.
他经常讲大话。

largely 〔ˈlɑrdʒlɪ ‖ ˈlɑːdʒlɪ〕
ad. ❶大部分;主要地
❷大量地,广泛地

last 〔læst ‖ lɑːst〕
a. ❶最后的
He was the last person to leave.
他是最后离开的人。
❷仅剩的
I've spent my last dollar.
我把我的钱全部花光了。
❸最后过去的;紧接前面的
We had dinner together last Sunday.
我们上个星期日在一起吃饭。
❹最不可能……的

He is the last person to steal.
他决不可能偷东西。
❺最近的，最新的
ad. ❶最后地
He left last.
他最后离开。
❷上次，最近
I saw him last in New York.
我上次见到他是在纽约。
n. ❶最后的人(或东西)[＋to-v]
He was the last of the passengers to leave the ship.
他是最后一个下船的乘客。
❷最后；末尾
They had been friends to the last.
他们始终是好朋友。

常用短语

at last 最后；终于
He succeeded at last.
他终于成功了。

late 〔let ‖ leɪt〕
a. ❶迟的；[(＋for)][(＋in)][＋v-ing]
He was late for school.
他上学迟到了。
❷晚的；晚期的
He came back in the late afternoon.
他在傍晚回来。
❸去世不久的；已故的
She was an admirer of the late President.
她是已故总统的崇拜者。
❹不久前才卸任的；前任的
the late professor
前任教授
❺最近的
the late storm
不久前的暴风雨
ad. ❶迟到，来不及
Tom came to school late and missed the first class.
汤姆迟到且错过了第一堂课。
❷晚；在晚期
He often worked late into the night.
他常常工作到深夜。

lately 〔ˈletlɪ ‖ ˈleɪtlɪ〕
ad. 近来，最近；不久前
I haven't seen him lately.
我近来未曾见到他。

later 〔ˈletɚ ‖ ˈleɪtə〕
a. ❶较晚的，更晚的
❷以后的
We will discuss this in detail in a later chapter.
我们将在以后的一章中对这一点作详细的探讨。
ad. ❶较晚地，更晚地
I went to bed later than usual.

我比往常更晚上床。
❷后来；以后
I'll tell you later.
我以后再告诉你。

常用短语

sooner or later 迟早
She will come sooner or later.
她迟早会来。

latest 〔ˈletɪst ‖ ˈleɪtɪst〕
a. 最新的；最近的
This hat is of the latest fashion.
这顶帽子是最新样式。

latter 〔ˈlætɚ ‖ ˈlætə〕
a. ❶后面的；后半的；末了的
This latter point was of great importance.
后面这点极为重要。
❷(两者中)后者的
Here are Tom and David; the latter is my younger brother.
这是汤姆和大卫；后者是我的弟弟。
〔反义〕former 前者

laugh 〔læf ‖ lɑːf〕
［过去式］laughed；［过去分词］laughed
vi. 笑；嘲笑［(＋at)］
He was laughed at by everybody.
人人都嘲笑他。
n. 笑，笑声［C］
She gave a hearty laugh.
她爽朗地笑了起来。

laughter 〔ˈlæftɚ ‖ ˈlɑːftə〕
n. 笑；笑声［U］
She burst into laughter.
她突然大笑起来。

launch 〔lɔntʃ ‖ lɔːntʃ〕
［过去式］launched；［过去分词］launched
vt. ❶使(船)下水
The ship will be launched next Monday.
这只船将于下星期一下水。
❷发射；投掷；使升空

law 〔lɔ ‖ lɔː〕
n. ❶法，法律［U］［the］
That is against the law.
那是违反法律的。
❷(个别的)法律，法规［C］［(＋against)］
There ought to be a law against cutting down trees.
应该制定一部禁止伐树的法律。

lawn 〔lɔn ‖ lɔːn〕
n. 草坪，草地［C］
The lawn needs mowing.
草坪需要修剪。

lawyer 〔ˈlɔjɚ ‖ ˈlɔːjə〕
n. 律师［C］

L

I suggest he consult a lawyer.
我建议他请教律师。

lay 〔le ‖ leɪ〕
[过去式]laid;[过去分词]laid
vt. ❶放,搁
Please lay the packages on the table.
请把包裹放在桌上。
❷铺设;砌(砖);涂
The workers are laying the tracks.
工人们在铺设铁轨。
❸准备,安排;拟定
They laid down a number of rules.
他们制定了一些规则。
❹下蛋;产卵
vi. 下蛋;产卵
The hens began laying in October.
这些母鸡10月份开始下蛋。

layman 〔ˈlemən ‖ ˈleɪmən〕
n. [C] ❶(未受神职的)一般信徒;俗人
❷外行人,门外汉

lazy 〔ˈlezɪ ‖ ˈleɪzɪ〕
a. ❶懒散的,怠惰的
His teacher thought he was very lazy.
他的老师认为他很懒。
❷使人倦怠的;懒洋洋的
The weather was lazy.
这天气使人无精打采。

lead[1] 〔lid ‖ liːd〕
[过去式]led;[过去分词]led
vt. ❶引导;领(路)
She led me into the drawing-room.
她带我进入客厅。
❷走在(队伍等)的最前头
The military band led the parade.
军乐队走在游行队伍的前面。
❸诱使;致使
What led him to resign his office?
什么事导致他辞职的?
❹领导;指挥;率领
❺过(活);使过(某种生活)
They led a happy life.
他们过着快乐的日子。
vi. ❶领路
You lead and we'll follow.
你领路,我们跟着。
❷通向,导致
That door leads into the garden.
那扇门通向花园。
❸领导
He has a desire to lead.
他有领导欲。
n. [C]❶指导,榜样

All the children followed his lead.
所有的孩子都以他为榜样。
❷领先地位[the]
Our team was in the lead at half time.
我们队在前半场领先。

lead² 〔lɛd ‖ led〕
n. ❶铅[U]
❷黑铅，铅笔芯[C][U]
❸铅制品

leader 〔ˈlidɚ ‖ ˈliːdə〕
n.[C] ❶领袖，领导者，指挥者
He is a decisive leader.
他是一个有决断力的领袖。
❷领先的人(或事物)[(+of/in)]
Our community is a leader in the conservation of wildlife.
我们社区在野生动物保护方面走在前头。

leaf 〔lif ‖ liːf〕[名复]leaves
n. ❶叶子[C]
The trees are thick with leaves.
这些树长着浓密的树叶。
❷(书籍等的)一张，一页[C]
He tore a leaf from his notebook.
他从笔记本上扯下一页。

league 〔lig ‖ liːg〕
n.[C] ❶同盟，联盟
❷盟约
❸联合会，社团；【体】(球队)俱乐部联合会
a football league
足球联合会

lean¹ 〔lin ‖ liːn〕
[过去式]leaned, leant；[过去分词]leaned, leant
vi. ❶倾斜
trees leaning in the storm
暴风雨中倾斜的树木
❷倾身，屈身
She leaned down to hear the child.
她弯下身子听孩子说话。
❸倚，靠[(+on/upon/against)]
She leaned lightly against his shoulder.
她轻轻地靠在他的肩上。
❹依赖，依靠[(+on/upon)]
She leaned on me for help.
她依靠我的帮助。
vt. ❶使倾斜
He leaned his head forward.
他将头向前倾。
❷把……靠在(某种东西上)[(+on/upon/against)]
Lean your head on my shoulder.
把你的头靠在我的肩膀上。

L

lean² 〔lin ‖ liːn〕

［比］leaner；［最］leanest

a. ❶(肉)无脂肪的，精瘦的

Lean meat is healthier for you than fatty meat.

对你来说，瘦肉比肥肉更有利于健康。

❷(人或动物)瘦的

A lean and hungry cat came to my door.

一只饥饿的瘦猫走到我家门口。

❸贫瘠的；贫乏的；收益差的

It's been a lean year for business.

这是生意清淡的一年。

leap 〔lip ‖ liːp〕

［过去式］leaped，leapt；［过去分词］leaped，leapt

vi. 跳，跳跃

He leapt from the horse.

他从马上跳下来。

鱼跳出了水面。
The fish leapt out of the water.

learn 〔lɜ˞n ‖ lɜːn〕

［过去式］learned，learnt；［过去分词］learned，learnt

vt. ❶学习；学会

He has learnt a new skill.

他学会了一项新技能。

❷认识到［＋(that)］

He has learned that dishonesty does not pay.

他已经认识到不诚实是没有好报的。

❸记住

The boy soon learned the poem by heart.

这个男孩不久便能熟背这首诗了。

vi. ❶学，学习［(＋from)］

Why don't you learn from my mistakes?

你为何不从我的错误中吸取教训呢？

❷得知，获悉［(＋of/about)］

We learned of his marriage in the newspapers.

我们从报上获悉他结婚了。

常用短语

learn from 从……中吸取教训

learn of 获悉

least 〔list ‖ liːst〕

a. (little 的最高级)

❶最小的；最少的

He did the work without the

L

least difficulty.
他毫不费力地做了这工作。
❷最不重要的；地位最低的
This is the least useful of the four books.
四本书中这一本用处最小。
ad. (little 的最高级)
❶最小；最少
He works least.
他工作得最少。
❷最不
Math is the least interesting subject.
数学是最没意思的学科。
n. 最小；最少[the]
Giving him food was the least we could do.
给他饭吃是我们能做的最起码的事。

常用短语

at (the) least 至少
A child must sleep at least 8 hours a day.
小孩每天必须睡 8 个小时。
in the least 丝毫
It does not matter in the least.
这毫无关系。

leather 〔ˈlɛðɚ ‖ ˈleðə〕
n. ❶皮革[U]
These gloves are made of leather.
这些手套是用皮革制成。
❷(骑摩托车穿的)皮革防护衣[P]
a. 皮的；皮革制的
Your leather shoes need shining.
你的皮鞋要擦一擦。

leave[1] 〔liv ‖ liːv〕
[过去式]left；[过去分词]left
vt. ❶离开(某处)[(+for)]
Mr. Smith left the room for the office at two o'clock.
史密斯先生两点离开房间，去了办公室。
❷离开(某人)的身边；遗弃，离弃，抛弃
Her husband has left her.
她的丈夫把她遗弃了。
❸辞去(工作等)；脱离(组织等)
Mary left school last year and she is working in a shop now.
玛丽去年退了学，现正在一家商店工作。
❹遗忘；丢下
I left my bag in your room.
我把包落在你的房间里了。
❺听任，使处于某种状态
Please leave me alone.
请不要管我。
❻把……交给；委托[(+with/

to)][+v-ing]
Leave it to me.
把它交给我吧。
❼剩下
There is no time left.
时间所剩不多了。
vi. 离去；动身[(+for)]
We will leave for London next week.
我们下周动身去伦敦。

leave² 〔liv ‖ liːv〕
n. ❶准假；休假；休假期[U]
I got two weeks' leave.
我获得两周的假期。
❷许可，同意[U][+to-v]
Have you got leave to come here this afternoon?
你得到许可今天下午来这里吗？
❸离去，告别[U]
The guests took leave after thanking the host.
客人们对主人表示谢意之后告辞。

left 〔lɛft ‖ left〕
a. ❶左方的；左侧的
Some people write with their left hands.
有些人用左手写字。
❷(常大写)(政治上)左派的；左翼的
ad. 在左边；向左
Walk three blocks and then turn left at the corner.
走过三个街区然后向左转。
n. ❶左，左边[the]
John was seated on her left.
约翰坐在她的左边。
❷(常大写)左派；激进分子们[the]
The left oppose the tax increase.
左翼人士反对增税。

left-hand 〔ˌlɛftˈhænd ‖ ˈlefthænd〕
a. 左手的；左侧的

leg 〔lɛg ‖ leg〕
n. ❶腿，足；小腿[C]
He crossed his legs.
他两腿交叉。
❷(桌，椅等的)脚[C]
the legs of a table
桌子腿

legal 〔ˈligl̩ ‖ ˈliːgəl〕
a. ❶法律上的，有关法律的
He intends to take legal action.
他打算采取法律行动。
❷合法的，正当的
Gambling is not legal here.
赌博在这儿是不合法的。
❸法定的
When you drive, you must not

exceed the legal limit.
开车时的速度不能超过汽车行驶的法定速度。

legend 〔ˈlɛdʒənd ‖ ˈledʒənd〕
n. 传说；传奇故事；传奇文学[C][U]
There are a lot of legends in China.
中国有很多传奇故事。

leisure 〔ˈliʒɚ ‖ ˈleʒə〕
n. 闲暇，空暇时间[U]
I have no leisure to read.
我没有闲暇读书。

常用短语

at leisure
❶有空的
I am at leisure now.
我现在有空。
❷从容地
Do your work at leisure.
慢慢干你的工作吧。

lemon 〔ˈlɛmən ‖ ˈlemən〕
n. ❶柠檬[C][U]
❷柠檬汁[U]
She drank a glass of lemon.
她喝了一杯柠檬汁。
❸柠檬色，淡黄色[U]

L

lend 〔lɛnd ‖ lend〕
[过去式]lent；[过去分词]lent
vt. ❶把……借给
Who lent you the bike?
谁借给你这辆自行车的？
❷贷（款）
He used to lend money at an extremely high rate of interest.
他过去经常放高利贷。

length 〔lɛŋθ ‖ leŋθ〕
n. ❶（距离，尺寸的）长度[C][U]
The fish is two feet in length.
这条鱼有两英尺长。
❷（时间的）长短，期间[C][U]
The length of the movie is two hours.
影片长两小时。

常用短语

at full length 全身伸展地
He lay on the bed at full length.
他舒展地躺在床上。
at length
❶最后，终于
At length the work was finished.
这工作终于完成了。
❷详细地
He explained it at length.
他把事情讲得很详尽。

lengthen 〔ˈlɛŋθən ‖ ˈleŋθən〕
[过去式]lengthened；[过去分词]lengthened

vt. 使加长，使延长
She lengthened the skirt.
她把裙子加长了。
vi. 变长，延长

lens 〔lɛnz ‖ lenz〕
n. [C] ❶透镜；镜片
❷（照相机等的）镜头
❸（眼球的）晶状体

less 〔lɛs ‖ les〕
a. （little 的比较级）较小的，较少的[+than]
Thunderstorms are much less common in Ireland than in England.
爱尔兰的雷雨比英格兰的少。
ad. （little 的比较级）较小地，较少地；不如[+than]
n. 更少的数（量，额）[U]
I could do no less.
这是我起码要做的。

常用短语

no less… than 同……一样
She is no less beautiful than her elder sister.
她和她姐姐一样漂亮。
none the less 仍然
He has fault, but I like him none the less.
他有缺点，但我仍然喜欢他.
no less than （数量）不少于
He has no less than 1,000 dollars.
他的钱不少于 1,000 美元。
（含有感叹意味）
not less than 至少有
（没有 no less than 那种感叹意味）
He has not less than 1,000 dollars.
他至少有 1,000 美元。
not less… than 不比……差
This tool-machine is not less useful than that one.
这台机床使用起来不比那台差。

lesson 〔ˈlɛsn̩ ‖ ˈlesn〕
n. [C] ❶功课；课业
Lessons begin at 8∶00.
8 点钟开始上课。
❷课程[P][(+in/on)]
All new students are given lessons in how to use the library.
所有新生都要上如何利用图书馆的课。
❸一节课；（教科书中的）一课
They usually have 4 lessons in the morning.
上午他们通常有 4 节课。

lest 〔lɛst ‖ lest〕
conj. 【文】❶[lest 后面的从句用动词原形或 should+ 动词原形]唯恐；免得

He walked slowly lest he (should) slip.
他慢慢地走以免滑倒。
❷(用于 be afraid, fear 之后)担心
I was afraid lest he (should) be involved in the scandal.
我怕他受到丑闻的牵连。

let [lɛt ‖ let]
[过去式]let;[过去分词]let
vt. ❶(通常不用被动式)允许
She would not let the child do it.
她不会让孩子做这事的。
❷(用于祈使句,表示建议,请求,命令等)让
Let us go.
我们走吧。
❸出租,租给[(+ to)][(+ out)]
Mrs. White let a room to me.
怀特太太租给我一间房间。
vi. 出租
That apartment lets for $500 a month.
那种公寓房间以每月 500 美元出租。

letter [ˈlɛtɚ ‖ ˈletə]
n.[C] ❶信,函件
He wrote me a letter last month.
他上个月给我写来一封信。
❷字母;文字
There are 26 letters in the English alphabet.
英语字母有 26 个。
[同义] character 字母

level [ˈlɛvl̩ ‖ ˈlevl]
n. ❶水平线;水平面[C]
The village is 1,000 meters above sea level.
这村子海拔 1,000 米。
❷高,高度[C][U]
The flood rose to a level of 50 feet.
洪水涨到 50 英尺高。
❸(文化等的)水平,程度,标准[C][U]
These students have not reached an advanced level yet.
这些学生尚未达到高级班的标准。
a. 水平的,平的
Some streets are not level in the city.
城市中有的街道不平。

liar [ˈlaɪɚ ‖ ˈlaɪə]
n. 说谎的人[C]
He is anything but a liar.
他决不是一个撒谎的人。

liberty [ˈlɪbɚtɪ ‖ ˈlɪbətɪ]
n. ❶自由;自由权[U][+to-v]

Women used to have little liberty.
过去妇女没有多少自由。
❷自由活动于(或使用)某地的权利[U]
You may have the liberty of my study.
你可以使用我的书房。
❸失礼,越轨;未经许可的行为[C]
He allowed himself the liberties of reading her letters.
他未经她许可就看了她的信。

library 〔ˈlaɪˌbrɛrɪ ‖ ˈlaɪbrərɪ〕
n. [C] ❶图书馆,藏书室;图书室,书库
I borrowed this novel from the school library.
我从学校的图书馆借来这本小说。
❷藏书;(指唱片,手稿等)收藏的作品
Professor Hunter has a library of about 5,000 books.
亨特教授约有 5,000 册藏书。
❸丛书;文库
❹(个人的)书房,书库
I found he was working in his library when I called on him.
我去拜访他时看到他在书房里工作。

词汇拓展
librarian *n.* 图书馆管理员

licence 〔ˈlaɪsn̩s ‖ ˈlaɪsəns〕
n. ❶(法律上的)许可,特许[U][+to-v]
He sells cigarettes under license.
他经许可出售香烟。
be given full licence to do something
受权放手做某事
❷许可证;特许证;执照;牌照[C][+to-v]
You need a licence to fish in this river.
你在这条河里钓鱼要有许可证。

lid 〔lɪd ‖ lɪd〕
n. [C] ❶盖子
Put the lid on the box.
把箱子的盖子盖上。
❷眼睑
The lid is swollen.
眼皮肿了。

lie¹ 〔laɪ ‖ laɪ〕
[过去式]lay;[过去分词]lain
vi. ❶(人,动物)躺,卧;(东西)被平放
His hat and gloves were lying

L

on the table.
他的帽子和手套都放在桌上。
❷呈……状态，置于
The whole city lay in ruins after the earthquake.
地震之后整个城市成了一片废墟。
❸(事情)在于；(错误等)发现
The remedy lies in education.
补救的办法在于教育。
❹位于
The mountain lies in the west of the town.
这座山在镇子的西面。

lie² 〔laɪ ‖ laɪ〕
[过去式]lied；[过去分词]lied
vi. ❶撒谎
He lied about his age.
他在年龄上撒了谎。
❷造成错觉，欺骗
That clock must be lying; it isn't noon yet.
那钟肯定走得不准，现在还不到中午。
n. 谎话[C]
The newspapers were full of lies.
报纸上一片谎言。

life 〔laɪf ‖ laɪf〕[名复] lives
n. ❶生命；生存[U]
How did life begin?
生命是如何起源的？
❷生物，活的东西[U]
There is no life on the moon.
月球上没有生物。
❸(个人的)性命[C]
He risked his life to save the child.
他冒着生命危险救那个孩子。
❹人生；世上[U]
enjoy life
享受人生
❺生活(状态)；生计[C][U]
He leads a happy life.
他过着快乐的生活。

常用短语

all one's life 一生
bring to life 使苏醒
come to life 苏醒过来
for life 终身

lifeboat 〔ˈlaɪfˌbot ‖ ˈlaɪfbəʊt〕
n. 救生艇，救生船[C]

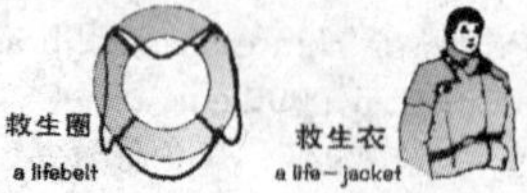

lifetime 〔ˈlaɪfˌtaɪm ‖ ˈlaɪftaɪm〕
n. (有时与代词的所有格连用)一生，终身；(事物的)使用期，寿命
a. 一生的，终身的

lift 〔lɪft ‖ lɪft〕

［过去式］lifted；［过去分词］lifted

vt. ❶举起；抬起［（＋up）］

This box is too heavy for me to lift.

这个箱子太重了，我提不起来。

Lift your foot up, please.

请把你的脚抬一抬。

❷振作（精神）；提高（声音等）［（＋up）］

The good news lifted up our spirits.

这个好消息使我们精神振奋。

❸空运

Food is being lifted in by helicopter.

食品正用直升机空运进来。

vi. ❶被提（或举）起；升起

The window won't lift.

窗子提不起来。

❷（云，雾等）消散

The rain stopped and the overcast lifted.

雨过天晴。

❸耸立

The Monument to the People's Heroes lifts above Tian An Men Square.

人民英雄纪念碑耸立在天安门广场。

n. ［C］❶提，吊，升，举

With a graceful lift of her hand, she dismissed him.

她轻盈地一抬手就把他打发走了。

❷【英】电梯

He took the lift to the top floor.

他搭电梯来到顶楼。

❸顺便搭载

He gave me a lift to the station.

他让我搭便车去车站。

light[1] 〔laɪt ‖ laɪt〕

［比］lighter；［最］lightest；［过去式］lighted，lit；［过去分词］lighted，lit

n. ❶光；光线；光亮［U］

She was reading by the light of a candle.

她在蜡烛光下读书。

❷光源；灯；灯火［C］

Turn off the lights when you leave.

离开时把灯关掉。

❸日光；日间［U］

They set off at first light.

他们天一亮就出发了。

vt. ❶点（火）；点燃［（＋up）］

He lit up a match.

他划着了一根火柴。

❷照亮[(＋up)]
The room is brilliantly lighted up and full of guests.
房间里灯火辉煌，宾客济济。
❸使容光焕发[(＋up)]
A smile of triumph lit up her face.
她的脸上绽放出胜利的微笑。
vi. ❶点着
The match lights easily.
这根火柴容易划着。
❷变亮
Her face lighted up at the good news.
她听到这个好消息面露喜色。
a. ❶明亮的
The room is very light.
这个房间很亮。
❷浅色的
The dress is light blue.
这裙子是浅蓝色的。

light² 〔laɪt ‖ laɪt〕
[比]lighter；[最]lightest
a. ❶(重量)轻的
The suitcase is very light.
这个箱子很轻。
❷(数量，程度)少量的；轻微的
There was a light rain falling outside.
外面下着小雨。
❸(负担)轻的；轻松愉快的
Let's see a light film for a change.
咱们看部轻松的影片调剂一下。
❹清淡的；易消化的；(酒)淡的
a light supper
清淡的晚餐
ad. 轻地；轻装地
I like to travel light.
我喜欢轻装旅行。

lighter 〔'laɪtə ‖ 'laɪtə〕
n. ❶点火者
❷打火机；点火器

lighting 〔'laɪtɪŋ ‖ 'laɪtɪŋ〕
n. [U]❶照明；点火
❷(总称)舞台灯光

lightning 〔'laɪtnɪŋ ‖ 'laɪtnɪŋ〕
n. 闪电，电光[U]
The little girl is afraid of thunder and lightning.
这小女孩害怕雷声和闪电。

like¹ 〔laɪk ‖ laɪk〕
[过去式]liked；[过去分词]liked

vt. ❶喜欢[＋v-ing][＋to-v]
She likes playing the piano.
她喜欢弹钢琴。
❷(用于否定句中)愿意[＋v-ing][＋to-v]
I don't like deceiving him.
我不愿意欺骗他。
❸(与 should, would 连用)希望,想,想要[＋to-v]
He would like you to make that trip.
他希望你走一趟。
vi. 喜欢;愿意;希望
You can do exactly as you like.
你爱怎么做就怎么做。

like[2] 〔laɪk ‖ laɪk〕
prep. ❶像,如
They are like brothers and sisters.
他们就像兄弟姐妹一样。
❷(做法,程度等)和……一样
Dick acts like a gentleman.
迪克的举止如同绅士。
❸与相称的
It's not like her to be so careless.
她通常是不会这么粗心的。
a. ❶相像的
The brothers are very like.
这几个兄弟很相像。
❷有相同性质的;类似的
His uncle promised him ＄100 if he could earn a like sum.
他的伯伯答应给他 100 美元,如果他能自己挣到同样数目的钱的话。
conj.【口】如同,好像
It was just like you said.
情况正如你所说的那样。

likely 〔ˈlaɪklɪ ‖ ˈlaɪklɪ〕
a. ❶很可能的[＋to-v][＋that]
John is likely to be in London this autumn.
今年秋天约翰可能在伦敦。
❷适当的,正合要求的[(＋for)]
The park is a likely place for the picnic.
这个公园倒是个适合野餐的地方。

limb 〔lɪm ‖ lɪm〕
n. [C] ❶肢;臂;脚;翼
He stood up and stretched his limbs.
他站起来,伸了伸胳膊和腿。
❷大树枝,主枝
He sat on a limb of the tree and looked down.
他坐在一根大树枝上往下看。

limit 〔ˈlɪmɪt ‖ ˈlɪmɪt〕
[过去式]limited;[过去分词]

limited

n. [C] ❶界线;界限

That wall is the limit of the schoolyard.

那堵围墙是校园的界限。

❷限度;限制;极限

He knows his own limits.

他自知能力有限。

❸范围,境界[P]

Drive slowly within the city limits.

在市区内车子要开得慢点。

vt. 限制;限定[(+to)]

The teacher limited his students' compositions to 500 words.

老师把学生的作文限制在500字以内。

limitation [ˌlɪməˈteʃən ‖ ˌlɪmɪˈteɪʃən]

n. ❶限制,限制因素;局限[C][U]

❷极限,限度[P]

line [laɪn ‖ laɪn]

[过去式]lined;[过去分词]lined

n. [C] ❶ 绳,线,索

She hung the wash on the line.

她将洗好的衣服晾在绳子上。

❷线条

Draw a line from A to B.

从A点画一条线到B点。

❸列,排;(等待顺序的)行列

There is a long line at the ticket office.

售票处排着长队。

❹交通线;航线;铁路线

vt. ❶用线标示;划线于

He lined the paper with a blue pencil.

他用蓝铅笔在纸上划了线。

❷使有线条,使起皱纹

His face was lined with worry.

忧虑使他脸上布满了皱纹。

❸沿……排列

The streets were lined on both sides with people.

街道两旁都站着人。

vi. 排队,排齐[(+up)]

The troops lined up and marched away.

部队列队走开了。

linger [ˈlɪŋgɚ ‖ ˈlɪŋgə]

[过去式]lingered;[过去分词]lingered

vi. ❶继续逗留,徘徊

Davis lingered for a moment in the bar.

戴维斯在酒吧逗留了一会儿。

❷持续,缓慢消失

The sound lingered in the air.

那声音在空中持续了好久。

❸磨蹭，拖延[(＋over)]
They lingered over coffee and missed the train.
他们慢吞吞地喝咖啡，结果误了火车。
vt. 消磨，缓慢度过[(＋away/out)]
They lingered away the whole evening at the tea-house.
他们在茶馆消磨了整整一个晚上。

link 〔lɪŋk ‖ lɪŋk〕
[过去式]linked；[过去分词]linked
n. [C] ❶(链状物的)环，节
❷环节；纽带；联系，关系
vt. vi. 连接，结合；联系
The road links the two villages.
这条路连接两个村子。

lion 〔ˈlaɪən ‖ ˈlaɪən〕
n. [C] ❶狮子
The soldier was as brave as a lion.
那个士兵如狮子般勇猛。
❷勇猛的人

lip 〔lɪp ‖ lɪp〕
n. 嘴唇[C]
She compressed her lips and kept silent.
她紧闭嘴唇，一声不吭。

liquid 〔ˈlɪkwɪd ‖ ˈlɪkwɪd〕
n. 液体[C][U]
Oil, milk and water are all liquids.
油、牛奶和水都是液体。
a. ❶液体的；液态的，流动的
He took liquid diet today.
他今天吃的是流食。
❷清澈的，透明的
The child has large liquid eyes.
这个孩子有一双水汪汪的大眼睛。

list 〔lɪst ‖ lɪst〕
[过去式]listed；[过去分词]listed
n. 表；名册；目录[C]
His name was dropped from the list.
他的名字从名单上除去了。
vt. ❶把……编列成表，把……编入目录
These names are to be listed in the catalog.
这些名字将被列入目录。
❷列举
The reasons are listed below.
理由列举如下。

listen 〔ˈlɪsn̩ ‖ ˈlɪsn〕
[过去式]listened；[过去分词]listened
vi. ❶听，留神听[(＋to)]

She's listening to the radio.
她正在听广播。
❷听从，听信[(+to)]
Children should listen to their parents.
孩子应该听父母的话。

literature 〔ˈlɪtərəˌtʃʊr ‖ ˈlɪtərətʃə〕
n. ❶文学；文学作品[C][U]
He majors in Russian literature.
他主修俄罗斯文学。
❷文献，图书资料[C][U]
She went through the literature on the subject.
她仔细查阅了有关这个问题的资料。

little 〔ˈlɪtḷ ‖ ˈlɪtl〕
[比]less；[最]least
a. ❶小的；小巧可爱的
The little dog followed the boy everywhere.
那条小狗到哪儿都跟着那个男孩。
❷短暂的
Let's rest a little while.
让我们稍微休息一会儿。
❸幼小的
He is too little to drive a car.
他太小了，不能开车。
❹少的，不多的（否定意味）
I have little money.
我没多少钱。
❺（加 a）少许，一点儿（肯定意味）
There is a little milk left in the bottle.
瓶子里有少许牛奶。
ad. ❶很少
You rest too little.
你休息得太少了。
❷（用在 know，suspect 等动词之前）毫不
We little believed that he would harm us.
我们一点也不相信他会伤害我们。

live[1] 〔lɪv ‖ lɪv〕
[过去式]lived；[过去分词]lived
vi. ❶活，活着
Are your parents living?
你父母健在吗？
❷继续活
He lived to the age of 70.
他活到 70 岁。
❸住，居住
She lives about 10 miles from my house.
她住在离我们的屋子大约 10 英里远处。
❹生活，过生活
vt. ❶过（生活）；度过
That young man lived a life of

L

luxury.
那个年轻人过着奢侈的生活。
❷实践;经历
None of the others have lived my experiences.
其他人没有一个经历过我的这些遭遇。

live² 〔laɪv ‖ laɪv〕
a. ❶活的,有生命的
We sell live fish.
我们出售活鱼。
❷燃烧着的
We cooked the steak over live coals.
我们在燃烧着的炭上煎牛排。
❸通着电流的
Stay away. That wire is live.
别碰它。那根电线是带电的。
❹实况播送的
ad. 在(或从)表演现场;以实况(转播)
The football game was televised live.
足球比赛由电视现场直播。

lively 〔'laɪvlɪ ‖ 'laɪvlɪ〕
[比]more lively;[最]most lively
a. 精力充沛的;活泼的,轻快的,愉快的
a lively girl
活泼的女孩
a lively dance
轻盈的舞蹈

living 〔'lɪvɪŋ ‖ 'lɪvɪŋ〕
a. ❶活的;活着的
All the living Presidents attended Nixon's funeral.
所有的总统都参加了尼克松的葬礼。
❷在活动中的;在使用着的
a living language
一种仍在使用的语言
❸充满生气的;活跃的;生动的
The wilderness is a living museum of natural history.
这片荒野是一座活生生的自然历史博物馆。
❹生活的;维持生活的
n. ❶生计
He earns his living as a salesman.
他靠当推销员为生。
❷生活(方式)[U]
We advocate plain living.
我们提倡俭朴的生活。
❸活;生存[U]
He seemed tired of living.
他似乎对生活感到厌倦。

load 〔lod ‖ ləʊd〕
[过去式]loaded;[过去分词]loaded
n. [C] ❶负载;担子
The load on that beam is more than it bears.

那根梁上的载重超过了它所能承受的量。

❷(精神方面的)负担;重任

The good news has taken a load off my mind.

听到这个好消息我就放心了。

❸(车,船等的)装载量;一车(或一船等)货物

The truck was carrying a load of sand.

卡车装运一车沙子。

vt. ❶装,装载[(+with)]

The dockers are loading the ship with coal.

码头工人正把煤装上船。

❷把弹药装入(枪,炮);把胶卷装入(照相机)

Don't forget to load your camera.

别忘了给你的相机装胶卷。

❸使摆满;使充满;使长满

The air was loaded with soot.

空气中充满了煤烟。

loaf 〔lof ‖ ləʊf〕[名复]loaves

n. (一条或一块)面包[C]

two loaves of bread

两条面包

local 〔ˈlokl̩ ‖ ˈləʊkəl〕

a. 地方性的;当地的,本地的

He works at the local post office.

他在本地的邮局工作。

locate 〔ˈloket ‖ ˈləʊkeɪt〕

[过去式]located;[过去分词]located

vt. ❶把……设置在

The company located its branch office in the suburbs.

该公司把它的分公司设在郊区。

❷使……坐落于

The museum is located on Main Street.

博物馆位于梅因街。

❸探出,找出

The police are trying to locate the missing man.

警方正设法查明那个失踪者的下落。

location 〔loˈkeʃən ‖ ləʊˈkeɪʃən〕

n. 位置;场所,所在地[C]

lock 〔lɑk ‖ lɒk〕

[过去式]locked;[过去分词]locked

n. 锁[C]

I left the key in the lock.

我把钥匙留在锁上。

锁 lock

vt. 锁，锁上[(＋up)]
See that the door is locked up before you go to bed.
睡觉前切记把门锁上。
vi. 锁住；锁得上
The door won't lock.
这扇门锁不上。

locust [ˈlokəst ‖ ˈləʊkəst]
n. [C] ❶【昆】蝗虫
❷【昆】蝉

log [lɔg ‖ lɒg]
n. 圆木；原木；木料[C]
The cabin was built of logs.
这间小屋是用原木建造的。

logic [ˈlɑdʒɪk ‖ ˈlɒdʒɪk]
n. [U] ❶逻辑；逻辑学
❷推理(法)

London [ˈlʌndən ‖ ˈlʌndən]
n. 伦敦(英国首都)

lonely [ˈlonlɪ ‖ ˈləʊnlɪ]
a. 孤独的，寂寞的，孤寂的
I was alone, but not lonely.
我独自一人但并不孤单。

词汇拓展

loneliness *n.* 孤独，寂寞

long [lɔŋ ‖ lɒŋ]
[比]longer；[最]longest
a. ❶长的；远的
The railway is 1, 000 miles long.
这条铁路长 1,000 英里。
❷长久的
She was abroad for a long time.
她在国外待了很久。
❸冗长的；过久的
He gave a long, tiring report.
他的报告冗长，令人厌倦。
ad. ❶长久地
You can keep my book as long as you like.
我的书你要借多久随你的便。
❷始终
She worked all day long.
她工作了一整天。
〔反义〕short 短的；近的

常用短语

before long 不久以后
He will be back before long.
他不久就会回来。
as long as 只要；有……之久
I'll work as long as I live.
只要我活着，我就会工作。
He has been ill as long as 5 years.
他已经病了 5 年。
no longer ＝**not… any longer** 不再；已不
You are no longer a child. ＝ You are not a child any longer.
你不再是小孩子了。
so long as 只要……的话
We'll go so long as the weather

is good.
只要天气好我们就去。

look 〔luk‖luk〕
［过去式］looked；［过去分词］looked

vi. ❶看［(＋at)］
These flowers are good to look at.
这些花很好看。

see 看见(有内容)，探望
I can see you.
我能看见你。
I will see you soon.
我很快去看望你。
see a film
看电影
look 看(强调动作)
I looked but I saw nothing.
我注意看了，但什么也没看见。
watch 观看，守望
watch TV
看电视
watch play
看戏
watch football match
看球赛

用法工具箱

❷注意，留神
If you look deeper, you'll see the difference between them.
如果你更留心一点，你就会看出它们之间的差别了。
❸好像；看起来
She looks happy.
她看上去很幸福。

vt. ❶(常用于祈使句)留心，注意，留神
Please look what time the plane takes off.
请留心飞机起飞时间。
❷看起来相称
She doesn't look her age.
她看起来和她的年龄不相符。

常用短语

look about 四下环顾
look after 照顾
The nurse looked after the babies.
护士照料着婴儿。
look at 看
Look at the blackboard.
请看黑板。
look down on 轻视
Don't look down on him.
不要看不起他。
look for 寻找
What are you looking for?

你在找什么？

look forward to 盼望

I'm looking forward to seeing you.

我盼望能见到你。

look as if 看起来像

He looks as if he has been ill.

他看起来好像生病了。

look up 查询；仰视

Look up the word in the dictionary.

在字典里查一查这个字。

n.［C］❶看；瞥［(＋at)］

Jane took another look at herself in the glass.

简又对着镜子照了照自己。

❷脸色；眼神；表情

The boss had a happy look on his face.

老板脸上带着高兴的神色。

❸外表，样子［the］

He has the look of a winner.

他有一副胜利者的样子。

❹面容；美貌［P］

loose〔lus ‖ luːs〕

［比］looser；［最］loosest；［过去式］loosed；［过去分词］loosed

a. ❶松的，宽的；松散的

She wore loose garments in the summer.

她在夏天穿宽松的衣服。

❷未予束缚的；未控制的

The dog ran loose on the street.

这只狗在街上到处乱跑。

❸松开的，松掉了的

I have got a loose tooth.

我有一颗牙齿松动了。

vt. 解开(结等)

She helped the child loose the laces of his shoes.

她帮孩子解开鞋带儿。

lose〔luz ‖ luːz〕

［过去式］lost；［过去分词］lost

vt. ❶失，丢失，丧失

Carl's father lost his job last month.

卡尔的父亲上个月失业了。

❷使失去

A bad cold had lost me some time.

一场重感冒使我失去了一些时间。

❸输去；未赢得

He has lost his case.

他的官司打输了。

❹迷失；使迷路

He lost his way.

他迷了路。

❺浪费，白费

There is no time to lose.
珍惜光阴。
❻(钟表)慢
My watch loses two minutes a day.
我的表每天慢两分钟。
vi. ❶输掉,失败[(＋by/to)]
Cambridge lost to Oxford.
剑桥队输给了牛津队。
❷受损失;赔钱[(＋on)]
We lost on that transaction.
我们在那笔交易上赔了钱。
❸(钟,表)走慢
Your watch is losing.
你的表走慢了。

loss 〔lɔs ‖ lɒs〕
n. ❶丧失;遗失[C][U]
He suffered a temporary loss of memory.
他暂时丧失了记忆。
❷损失;亏损(额)[C][U]
It is a great loss to her.
这对她来说是一个巨大的损失。
❸输,失败[C]
The loss of the first game did not discourage them.
第一场比赛的失败并没有令他们沮丧。

lost 〔lɔst ‖ lɒst〕
a. ❶弄丢的,遗失的
The lost ring was never found.
遗失的戒指再也没有找到。
❷迷途的
He took the lost child to the policeman.
他把迷路的小孩儿领到警察那里。
❸逝去的;丧失的
She felt great grief over her lost youth.
她对逝去的青春感到极大的悲伤。

lot 〔lɔt ‖ lɒt〕
n. ❶【口】很多,多数,多量[P][(＋of)]
There are a lot of people in the railroad station.
火车站里有许许多人。
❷(作特定用处的)一块地[C]
a parking lot
停车场
❸签[C]
draw lots
抽签
❹命运,运气
Her lot was not a happy one.
她的命运不佳。

loud 〔laʊd ‖ laʊd〕
[比]louder;[最]loudest

a. ❶大声的,响亮的
He has a loud voice.
他的嗓门很大。
❷喧噪的;(举止等)招摇的,炫耀的
Joe is a loud, vulgar person.
乔是一个爱招摇的,庸俗的人。
❸(衣服颜色等)鲜艳的,花哨的,俗艳的
She wore a loud dress.
她穿着一件艳丽的连衣裙。
ad. 大声地,响亮地
He should not speak so loud.
他不该如此大声说话。

loudly [ˈlaudlɪ ‖ ˈlaudlɪ]
ad. ❶高声地;吵闹地
❷花哨地;华丽地

loudspeaker [ˈlaudˈspikɚ ‖ ˌlaudˈspiːkə]
n. 扬声器,扩音器,喇叭[C]

love [lʌv ‖ lʌv]
[过去式]loved;[过去分词]loved
n. ❶爱;热爱;爱戴[U][(+for/of/to/towards)]
My mother's love for me was very great.
我母亲对我的爱是很深的。
❷恋爱,爱情[U]
John and Mary are in love.
约翰和玛丽在恋爱。
❸酷爱,爱好[U][(+of/for)]
He was sincere in his love for literature.
他对文学的爱好是很真诚的。
vt. ❶爱,热爱;爱戴;疼爱
You should love your students.
你应该爱你的学生。
❷爱好,喜欢[+v-ing][+to-v]
Bill loves playing football.
比尔喜欢踢足球。
❸(与 would, should 连用)想要,想做[+to-v]
She said she'd love to come sometime.
她说她很想某个时候来。

lovely [ˈlʌvlɪ ‖ ˈlʌvlɪ]
[比]lovelier;[最]loveliest
a. ❶秀美动人的,可爱的
She looks lovely in white.
她穿白色衣服看上去很漂亮。
❷【口】令人愉快的;美好的
We had a lovely holiday.
我们假期过得很愉快。

lover [ˈlʌvɚ ‖ ˈlʌvə]
n.[C] ❶恋人,情人(尤指男性);(一对)情侣[P]
❷爱好者,热爱者[(+of)]

loving [ˈlʌvɪŋ ‖ ˈlʌvɪŋ]
a. 钟爱的;深情的;表示爱的

Your loving daughter, Mary.
爱你的女儿,玛丽。
(信的结尾用语)

low 〔lo ‖ ləʊ〕
[过去式] lower; [过去分词] lowest
a. ❶低的,矮的;浅的
The office is in a low building.
办公室设在一幢低矮的房子里。
❷(在量,度,价值等方面)少的,小的,低的
The temperature is very low today.
今天气温很低。
❸没有精神的,情绪低落的
He is in low spirit.
他情绪低落。
❹地位低的,卑微的
a man of low birth
出身低微的人
ad. ❶低,向下地
Her head was bent low.
她的头低着。
❷低声地;以低音调
She spoke lowly and hurriedly.
她低声地很快地说着话。
❸低价地;程度低地
He bought low and sold high.
他贱买贵卖。
❹卑微地;下贱地

loyal 〔lɔɪəl ‖ lɔɪəl〕
a. 忠诚的,忠心的[(+to)]
She was loyal to her faith.
她忠于自己的信念。

luck 〔lʌk ‖ lʌk〕
n. [U] ❶运气,命运
It's a matter of luck whether we are successful.
我们能否成功是碰运气的事。
❷好运;幸运;侥幸
She had no luck finding a job.
她很不幸,找不到工作。
❸带来好运的东西;吉祥物

lucky 〔'lʌkɪ ‖ 'lʌkɪ〕
a. 幸运的,好运的[+to-v][+(that)]
He was lucky enough to marry a beautiful girl.
他有幸娶到一位漂亮姑娘。
〔**反义**〕unlucky 不幸的

luggage 〔'lʌgɪdʒ ‖ 'lʌgɪdʒ〕
n. 【主英】行李[U]
They had left the luggage at the station.
他们将行李留在车站了。

lunch 〔lʌntʃ ‖ lʌntʃ〕
n. 午餐;【美】便餐;便当[C][U]
Lunch is from 11 : 00 to

1：00.
午饭从 11 点供应到 1 点。

lung 〔lʌŋ ‖ lʌŋ〕
n. 肺[C]

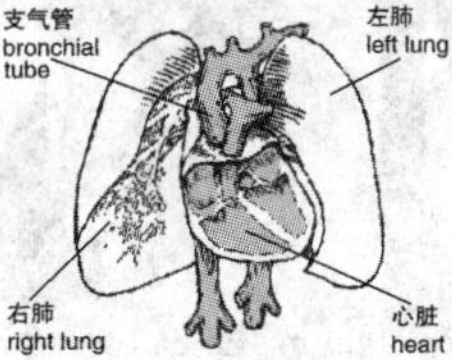

luxury 〔ˈlʌkʃərɪ ‖ ˈlʌkʃərɪ〕
n. ❶奢侈，奢华[U]
They live in luxury.
他们生活奢华。
❷奢侈品[C]
A fridge was then a luxury.
那时候冰箱是一种奢侈品。
❸享受；乐趣
She enjoyed the luxury of doing good.
她以行善为乐事。

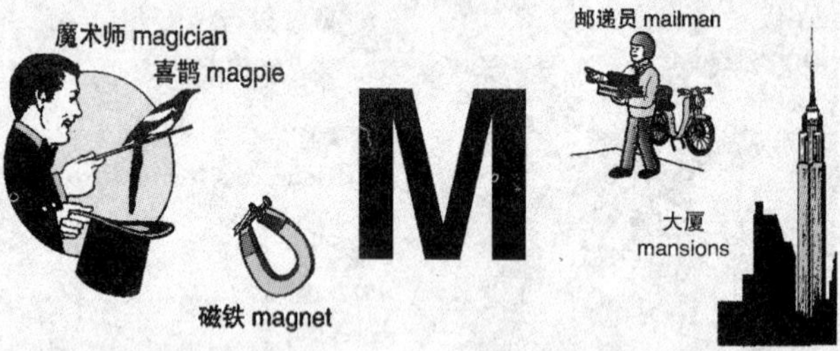

machine 〔mə'ʃin ‖ mə'ʃiːn〕

n. 机器;机械[C]

The washing machine has gone wrong.

洗衣机坏了。

machinery 〔mə'ʃinərɪ ‖ mə'ʃiːnərɪ〕

n. 机器;机械[U]

Many products are made by machinery rather than by hand.

许多产品是机器造的而不是手工做的。

mad 〔mæd ‖ mæd〕

[比]madder;[最]maddest

a. ❶发疯的,发狂的

She went mad after the death of her son.

儿子死后她就疯了。

❷愚蠢的;鲁莽的

It was a mad idea to climb the mountain in the bad weather.

在这种坏天气去爬山真是愚蠢。

❸【口】狂热的,着迷的[(+about/on/for)]

Both brothers are mad about tennis.

兄弟俩对网球都很入迷。

❹【口】恼火的[(+at/with)]

Don't be mad with/ at her.

不要跟她发脾气。

madam 〔'mædəm ‖ 'mædəm〕

n. ❶(对妇女的恭敬称呼)夫人,太太,小姐

Can I help you, madam?

夫人,我能为您效劳吗?

❷(大写)(正式书信中对妇女的尊称)女士

❸(大写)(用于职称或姓名前面的称呼)女士,夫人

magazine 〔ˌmægəˈzin ‖ ˌmægəˈziːn〕

n. 杂志,期刊[C]

He writes short stories for a monthly magazine.

他为一家月刊杂志撰写短篇小说。

magic 〔ˈmædʒɪk ‖ ˈmædʒɪk〕

n. [U] ❶魔法,巫术

The fairy's magic changed the two brothers into swans.

仙子使用魔法将两兄弟变成了天鹅。

❷魔术,戏法

He is going to perform magic at the party.

他将在晚会上表演魔术。

❸神奇的力量,魔力,魅力

The magic of her voice charmed the audience.

她那歌声的魅力令观众陶醉。

a. ❶巫术的;魔术的

The Caliph of Baghdad flew on his magic carpet to Arabia.

巴格达的哈里发驾着魔毯飞到了阿拉伯半岛。

❷有魔力的;不可思议的

That was a truly magic moment.

那真是不可思议的一刻。

magnet 〔ˈmægnɪt ‖ ˈmægnɪt〕

n. 磁铁,磁石[C]

mail 〔mel ‖ meɪl〕

[过去式]mailed;[过去分词]mailed

n. ❶【美】邮递;邮政[U][the]

Air mail is quicker than sea mail.

航空邮寄比海路邮寄快。

❷邮件[U]

Is there any mail this morning?

今天上午有邮件吗?

vt.【美】邮寄[(+to)]

I have mailed the letter.

我已邮了那封信。

〔同义〕post 邮寄

mailbox 〔ˈmelˌbɑks ‖ ˈmeɪlbɒks〕

n.【美】❶邮筒;邮箱[C]

❷电子邮箱[C]

main 〔men ‖ meɪn〕

a. 主要的,最重要的

She noted down the main points of the speech.

她把演说的要点记了下来。

M

mainland 〔ˈmenˌlænd ‖ ˈmeɪnlənd〕
n. 大陆，本土[the]
a. 大陆的，本土的
I came from mainland Greece.
我来自希腊大陆。

mainly 〔ˈmenlɪ ‖ ˈmeɪnlɪ〕
ad. 主要地；大致地

maintain 〔menˈten ‖ meɪnˈteɪn〕
[过去式]maintained；[过去分词]maintained
vt. ❶维持；保持；使继续
China maintains friendly relations with the United States.
中国和美国保持着友好关系。
❷维修；保养
He maintains his house very well.
他把房子养护得很好。
❸坚持；主张；断言[＋(that)]
He maintained that he was innocent.
他坚持说自己是无辜的。
❹供养，扶养；负担，支持
He maintained a large family.
他养着一大家子人。

major 〔ˈmedʒɚ ‖ ˈmeɪdʒə〕
[过去式]majored；[过去分词]majored
a. ❶较大的；较多的
The house needs major repairs.
这幢房子需要大修。
❷主要的；重要的
He is a major writer.
他是位大作家。
❸主修的
Her major subject is chemistry.
她的主修科目是化学。
〔反义〕minor 较小的；次要的
n.[C] ❶成年人；已到法定年龄者
❷(常大写)陆军(或空军、海军陆战队)少校
❸(大学中的)主修科目
Physics was his major.
物理是他的主修科目。
❹(大学专业的)主修学生
He is a mathematics major.
他是主修数学的学生。
vi. 主修[(＋in)]
Alice majors in economics.
艾丽斯主修经济学。

majority 〔məˈdʒɔrətɪ ‖ məˈdʒɔːrɪtɪ〕
n. ❶多数，过半数，大多数[the][(＋of)]
The majority were on Ben's side.
大多数人都站在本的一边。
❷多数党；多数派[the]
The Democrats become the majority in the election.

M

民主党在这次选举中变成了多数党。
❸多得的票数[C]
He won by a majority of two: the vote was 7 to 5.
他以两票的多数获胜:票数是7比5。
〔反义〕minority 少数

make〔mek ‖ meɪk〕
[过去式] made; [过去分词] made
vt. ❶做;制造;建造[(+ of/from/out of/for)]
Mary made a paper boat.
玛丽做了一只纸船。
❷作出(某种举动)
I didn't make any promise.
我没有作出任何承诺。
❸使得;使……做……
The news made John irritable.
这消息使约翰烦躁不安。
❹到达;赶上
He will never make the summit.
他永远到不了山顶。
❺获得,挣得;赢得
He made a fortune by industry.
他因努力而发财。
❻认为;估计,推算
I make its height about 50 feet.
据我估计,其高度有50英尺。
❼总计;等于
Two and two makes four.
2加2等于4。
❽准备;整理;布置
Shall I make tea?
要我泡茶吗?
❾引起;生成
Don't make a noise.
不要发出噪音。
❿成为,变成;成为……的成员
She will make a good teacher.
她会成为一个好老师。

maker〔ˈmekɚ ‖ ˈmeɪkə〕
n. 制作者;制造业者;制造厂[C]

make-up〔ˈmekˌʌp ‖ ˈmeɪkʌp〕
n. ❶构成;构造[C][U]
❷化妆;装扮;化妆品[C][U]

male〔mel ‖ meɪl〕
a. ❶男性的,男子的
A male nurse took my temperature.
一位男护士给我量了体温。
❷雄的,公的
n. [C] 男子;雄性动物
Males are generally taller than females.
雄性动物通常长得比雌性动物高。

mammy〔ˈmæmɪ ‖ ˈmæmɪ〕
n. [C] ❶【英】【方】(儿语)妈咪

❷【美】(照看白人孩子的)黑人保姆

man 〔mæn ‖ mæn〕

n. ❶成年男子;男人[C]

He is a nice young man.

他是一个很好的青年。

❷人[C]

All men are born equal.

人生而平等。

❸人类[U]

This happens time and again in the course of the history of man.

在人类历史的进程中,这种事一次又一次地发生。

manage 〔ˈmænɪdʒ ‖ ˈmænɪdʒ〕

[过去式]managed;[过去分词]managed

vt. ❶管理;经营;处理

He manages a hotel for his father.

他替他父亲经营一家旅馆。

❷控制;照管;驾驭

She doesn't know how to manage her naughty children.

她不知道怎样管好自己那顽皮的孩子。

❸使用;操纵

Can the child manage chopsticks now?

孩子会用筷子了吗?

❹设法做到;勉力完成[+to-v]

He managed to keep out of debt.

他设法不借贷。

vi. ❶管理;经营生意;处理事务;安排

Who will manage while the boss is away?

老板不在时谁来管理?

❷设法应付过去

He had such a great deal of work to do, but somehow he managed.

他手头的工作实在太多,但他还是顶下来了。

manager 〔ˈmænɪdʒɚ ‖ ˈmænɪdʒə〕

n. [C](商店,公司等的)负责人;主任;经理

He is a store manager.

他是一位商店经理。

mankind 〔mænˈkaɪnd ‖ mænˈkaɪnd〕

n. 人类[U]

manner 〔ˈmænɚ ‖ ˈmænə〕

n. ❶ 方式,方法;态度,举止

We walked in a leisurely manner, looking in all the shop windows.

我们慢悠悠地走着,看遍了所有的橱窗。

❷礼貌，规矩；（民族、时代的）风俗，习惯[P]

It is bad manners to interrupt.

打断别人的话是不礼貌的。

manufactory 〔ˌmænjəˈfæktərɪ ‖ ˌmænjʊˈfæktərɪ〕

n. 制造厂，工厂

manufacture 〔ˌmænjəˈfæktʃɚ ‖ ˌmænjʊˈfæktʃə〕

[过去式]manufactured；[过去分词]manufactured

vt. ❶（大量）制造，加工

The company manufactures cars.

这家公司制造汽车。

❷捏造，虚构（证据，借口等）

Who manufactured the rumor?

是谁编造这种谣言的？

n. ❶（大量）制造[U]

The bikes are of home manufacture.

这些自行车是本国制造的。

❷制造业[U]

❸制品，产品[P]

This country imports many foreign manufactures.

这个国家进口许多外国产品。

many 〔ˈmɛnɪ ‖ ˈmenɪ〕

a. 许多的，多的

How many brothers do you have?

你有几个兄弟？

pron. 许多人；许多

I don't need so many.

我不需要这么多。

many 用来修饰可数名词；much 用来修饰不可数名词

用法工具箱

常用短语

a good/great many 很多

A good many people supported him.

许多人支持他。

as many as 和……一样多

Take as many as you want.

你需要多少就拿多少。

many a 许多的

Many a man believes the story.

许多人相信这个故事。

map 〔mæp ‖ mæp〕

n. 地图[C]

a world map

世界地图

march 〔mɑrtʃ ‖ mɑːtʃ〕

[过去式]marched；[过去分词]marched

n. ❶（大写）略作 Mar. 三月

❷行进；行军；行程[C][U]

vi. (齐步)前进;行军
The soldiers marched by the reviewing stand.
士兵们从检阅台前齐步走过。

margin ['mɑrdʒɪn ‖ 'mɑːdʒɪn]
n. [C] ❶边,边沿,边缘
I stood at the margin of the lake for about an hour.
我在湖边站了差不多一个小时。
❷页边空白;栏外
the margin of the page
页边空白处

mark[1] [mɑrk ‖ mɑːk]
[过去式]marked;[过去分词]marked
n. ❶痕迹;污点;瘢疤[C]
The scandal left a mark on his reputation.
那件丑事玷污了他的名声。
❷记号;符号;标记[C]
You can see in him the marks of an educated man.
从他身上你可以看到受过教育的人的特点。
❸【英】分数;成绩[C]
I got full marks in English.
我英语得了满分。
❹靶子;目标[C]
He fired a shot, and hit the mark.
他开了一枪且正中目标。
vt. ❶做记号于;留痕迹于;标明;标示
The box of eggs was marked "With Care".
这个鸡蛋盒标上了"小心"字样。
❷标志;表示……的特征
Long ears mark a rabbit.
长耳朵是兔子的特征。
❸给(试卷等)打分数
The teacher marked the examination papers.
教师给试卷打了分数。
❹注意,留心[+wh-]
Mark carefully what I say.
认真注意听我说。

mark[2] [mɑrk ‖ mɑːk]
n. (2002 年前德国的货币单位)马克[C]

market ['mɑrkɪt ‖ 'mɑːkɪt]
n. ❶市场;股票市场;市集[C]
They put a new product on the market.
他们向市场推出一种新产品。
❷销路,需求[U]
There's no market for these goods.
这些货物没有销路。
❸行情,市况[C]
the stock market

股市行情

marriage 〔ˈmærɪdʒ ‖ ˈmærɪdʒ〕

n. ❶结婚，婚姻[C][U]

Their marriage was a happy one.

他们的婚姻是美满幸福的。

❷结婚典礼[C]

The marriage will take place in May.

婚礼将于五月举行。

married 〔ˈmærɪd ‖ ˈmærɪd〕

a. 已婚的，有配偶的

a married couple

已婚夫妇

marry 〔ˈmærɪ ‖ ˈmærɪ〕

[过去式]married；[过去分词] married

vt. ❶娶；嫁，和……结婚

He's going to marry Jane.

他将与简结婚。

❷(牧师等)为……证婚

The old priest married the young man and the young girl.

老牧师为这对青年男女主持婚礼。

❸把(女儿等)嫁出[(＋off/to)]

He married his daughter to the actor.

他把女儿嫁给了那个演员。

vi. 结婚

He didn't marry until he was 50.

他直到50岁才结婚。

mask 〔mæsk ‖ mɑːsk〕

n. 假面具；伪装；遮蔽物[C]

面具 mask

I bought him a mask.

我给他买了个面具。

a surgical mask

医用口罩

a gas mask

防毒面具

master 〔ˈmæstɚ ‖ ˈmɑːstə〕

[过去式]mastered；[过去分词] mastered

n. [C] ❶主人；雇主；户主

The dog ran to its master.

那条狗向它的主人跑去。

❷男教师

❸能手，名家，大师；师傅

The young writer learned a great deal from the works by masters in literature.

这位青年作家从文学大师的作品中学到了许多东西。

M

❹(常大写)硕士;硕士学位

❺(大写)(用在人名前作称呼)少爷

a. 精通的,熟练的

I'm sure he'll make a master boxer.

我相信他会成为一名身手不凡的拳师。

vt. ❶控制;制服;统治

She learned to master her anger.

她学会了控制自己不发火。

❷精通,掌握

I found it difficult to master Russian.

我发现掌握俄语很难。

match[1] 〔mætʃ ‖ mætʃ〕

[过去式]matched;[过去分词]matched

n.[C] ❶比赛,竞赛

Our side beat the other in the match.

我方在竞赛中击败了对方。

❷对手,敌手;相配者[(+for)]

The blue shirt and gray tie are a good match.

蓝衬衫和灰领带很相配。

vt. ❶使较量,使比赛[(+against/with)]

Read will be matched against Stone in the semifinal.

里德将在半决赛中与斯通较量。

❷敌得过,比得上[(+for/in)]

His latest film doesn't match his previous ones.

他最新的一部影片比不上他以前的一些影片。

❸和……相配,和……相称

The color of the shirt does not match that of the tie.

衬衫的颜色与领带不相配。

match[2] 〔mætʃ ‖ mætʃ〕

n. 火柴[C]

He struck a match and lit his cigarette.

他擦了根火柴点燃香烟。

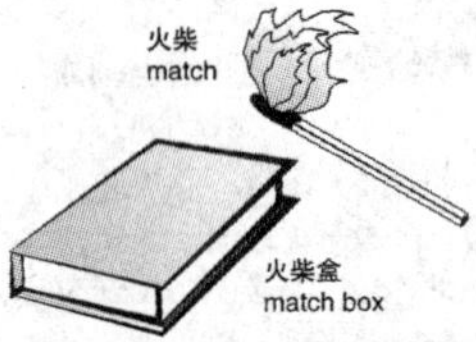

material 〔məˈtɪrɪəl ‖ məˈtɪərɪəl〕

a. 物质的,有形的

A warm house and good food are material comforts.

温暖的家和美味佳肴都是物质享受。

n. ❶材料,原料[C][U]

Wood and stone are the only

M

raw materials on the island.
木材和石头是这个岛上仅有的原材料。
❷素材;资料[U][(+for)]
He collected material for the history of China.
他搜集中国历史的资料。
❸工具,用具[P]
Your writing materials are in the top drawer of your desk.
你的书写文具在你书桌的最上面的抽屉里。

mathematics 〔ˌmæθəˈmætɪks ‖ ˌmæθɪˈmætɪks〕
n. [U] ❶数学
Mathematics is her favorite subject.
数学是她最喜欢的科目。
❷数学运算;数学应用
His mathematics are weak.
他的计算能力很差。

matter 〔ˈmætɚ ‖ ˈmætə〕
[过去式]mattered;[过去分词]mattered
n. ❶事情;问题;事件[C]
It was a matter of life and death for them.
这对他们来说是生死攸关的事情。
❷麻烦事,毛病[the][(+with)]
There' s the matter with this car.
这辆汽车有点儿毛病。
❸物质[U]
Matter exists in three states: solid, liquid and gas.
物质以三种形态存在,即固态、液态和气态。
vi. 有关系,要紧
It doesn't matter who wins.
谁赢了并不重要。

maximum 〔ˈmæksəməm ‖ ˈmæksɪməm〕
n. 最大量,最大数,最大限度[C][(+of)]
You can borrow a maximum of 10 books from the liberary.
你最多可向图书馆借10本书。

may 〔me ‖ meɪ〕
[过去式]might
v. aux. ❶(表示可能性)可能,也许
She may be a nurse.
她可能是个护士。
❷(表示许可或请求许可)可以
"May I come in?"
"我可以进来吗?"
"Yes, please."
"请。"
❸(表示希望、祝愿等)祝,愿
May you succeed!
祝你成功!

M

❹(表示让步)无论;尽管
I will come, no matter what may happen.
无论发生什么事,我一定会来。

常用短语

may as well do 最好……
We may as well go home.
我们该回家了。

May 〔me ‖ meɪ〕
n. 五月

maybe 〔ˈmebɪ ‖ ˈmeɪbɪ〕
ad. 大概,或许,可能
Maybe you'll have better luck next time.
也许下次你的运气会好一点。
〔同义〕perhaps 或许

mayor 〔ˈmeɚ ‖ meə〕
n. 市长,镇长[C]
He is the mayor of the city.
他是这个城市的市长。

me 〔(强)mi ‖ miː;(弱)mɪ ‖ mɪ〕
pron. ❶(I的宾格)我
He doesn't know me.
他不认识我。
❷【口】(作主语补语,代替I)(是)我
"Who's there?"
"谁在那儿?"
"It's me."
"是我。"
❸【口】(用于as或than的后面,代替I)我
He is taller than me.
他比我高。

meal 〔mil ‖ miːl〕
n. [C] ❶膳食;一餐
I have four meals a day.
我一天吃四餐。
❷进餐;进餐时间
Please don't eat between meals.
在两顿饭之间请不要进食。

mean¹ 〔min ‖ miːn〕
a. ❶吝啬的,小气的[(+about/over/with)]
Her husband is very mean about money.
她的丈夫在金钱上很吝啬。
❷卑鄙的,心地不好的[(+to)]
You're so mean to your stepmother.
你对你继母太过分了。
❸卑贱的;鄙陋的
The young couple made their home in a mean dwelling.
这对年轻夫妇在一个简陋的住处安了家。

mean² 〔min ‖ miːn〕
[过去式]meant;[过去分词]meant
vt. ❶(言辞等)表示……的意思,作……解释

M

What does the phrase mean?
这词组是什么意思?
❷意指,意谓
I realized what he meant.
我明白他的意思了。
❸意欲,意图,打算[+to-v]
I mean her no harm.
我无意伤害她。
❹意味着;有……的意义[+(that)][+v-ing][(+to)]
The company means a great deal to me.
这公司对我很重要。

meaning〔'minɪŋ‖'mi:nɪŋ〕
n.[C][U] ❶意思;含义
Do you know the meaning of the word?
你知道这个单词的意思吗?
❷意义,目的
What is the meaning of life?
生活的意义何在?

means〔minz‖mi:nz〕
n. ❶手段,方法;工具[C]
There are no means of getting there.
没有办法到那儿。
❷财产;资力;收入[P]
He is a man of means.
他是个有钱人。

常用短语

by all means 无论如何,必须
Read the book by all means.
必须读这本书。
by means of 用……的方式
We express our feelings by means of words.
我们借助言辞表达我们的感情。
by no means 决不
Translation is by no means easy.
翻译绝不是件容易的事。

meanwhile〔'minˌhwaɪl‖'mi:nwaɪl〕
n. 其时,其间[the]
In the meanwhile I'll visit an old friend of mine.
在这期间我将去拜访我的一位老朋友。
ad. 其间;同时
Mother went shopping; meanwhile, I cleaned the house.
母亲去买东西;我打扫屋子。

measure〔'mɛʒɚ‖'meʒə〕
[过去式]measured;[过去分词]measured
vt. ❶测量;计量
We measured the distance.
我们测量了距离。
❷打量;估量
She measured the stranger with her eyes.

她用双眼打量着那个陌生人。

vi. 有……长(或宽,高等)

The lake measures 130 by 80 kilometers.

这条湖长 130 千米宽 80 千米。

n. ❶尺寸;分量[U]

❷度量单位[C]

An hour is a measure of time.

小时是计时单位。

卷尺 band tape

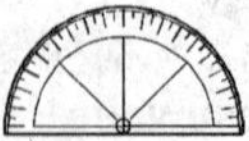

量角器 protractor

直尺 ruler

量具 measure

❸措施;手段;方法[P]

The government was urged to take measures to combat the spread of AIDS.

人们敦促政府采取措施防止艾滋病的传播。

meat [mit ‖ miːt]

n. [U] ❶(食用的)肉

a slice of meat

一片肉

❷(蛋,贝类,果子等的)食用部分,肉

the meat of a nut

胡桃肉

mechanical [məˈkænɪkḷ ‖ mɪˈkænɪkəl]

a. ❶机械的,用机械的

They were using a mechanical shovel to clear up the streets.

他们用机械铲土机清理街道。

❷机械似的,呆板的,无表情(或感情)的,无意识的

Blink is a mechanical action of the eyelids.

眨眼是眼睑的无意识动作。

medal [ˈmɛdḷ ‖ ˈmedl]

n. 奖章,纪念章,勋章[C]

金牌 gold medal

奖章 medal

She won an Olympic gold medal in swimming.

她获得一枚奥林匹克游泳金牌。

medicine [ˈmɛdəsṇ ‖ ˈmedɪsn]

n. ❶药;内服药[C][U]

Why did the patient refuse to take the medicine?

那个病人为什么不肯服药?

❷医学;医术;内科学[U]

Anesthesia was a great innova-

M

tion in medicine.
麻醉是医学上的重大创新。

medium〔'midɪəm ‖ 'miːdɪəm〕
[名复] media, mediums
n. [C] ❶中间;中庸;适中
His opinion is the medium between the extremes.
他的意见是介于两个极端之间的中庸之道。
❷媒介物,媒体;传导体[(+for)]
Air is medium for sound.
空气是传导声音的媒介物。
❸手段,工具;宣传工具;新闻媒介[(+of)]
TV is the modern media of communication.
电视是现代传媒。
a. ❶中间的,中等的,适中的
a shirt of medium size
中号的衬衣
❷(肉类)烧得适中的,中等熟度的

meet〔mit ‖ miːt〕
[过去式]met;[过去分词]met
vt. ❶遇见;碰上
I met her at the gymnasium.
我在体育馆遇见了她。
❷认识;会见
❸迎接
Shall we go to the station to meet your mother?
我们去车站接你的母亲好吗?
❹对抗;和……交手
❺遭遇,经历
A policeman could meet danger any minute of his working day.
警察在值勤时随时都可能碰到危险。
❻满足;符合
I wish I could meet your wishes.
我希望我能让你满意。
vi. ❶ 相遇;相会;相识
The two trains met at a small station.
这两列火车在一个小站相遇(即错车)。
❷集合;聚会;开会
❸接触;接合;会合
The two rivers meet near the capital.
这两条河在首都附近汇合。
n.【美】集会;竞赛大会[C]
He broke two national records in a track meet.
他在一次田径比赛中打破了两项全国纪录。

meeting〔'mitɪŋ ‖ 'miːtɪŋ〕
n. 会议;集会;会[C]
Mr. White isn't here, and he's at a meeting.

M

怀特先生不在这儿，他在开会。

melody 〔ˈmɛlədɪ ‖ ˈmelədɪ〕

n.【音】旋律；主调[C][U]

These songs have beautiful melodies.

这些歌很好听。

melon 〔ˈmɛlən ‖ ˈmelən〕

n. ❶瓜；甜瓜[C]

❷圆鼓鼓像瓜似的东西；大肚子[C]

melt 〔mɛlt ‖ melt〕

[过去式]melted；[过去分词]melted

vi. ❶融化；熔化

The snow has melted.

雪已经融化了。

❷溶化；熔解

The sugar melted in the tea.

糖在茶水中溶解了。

vt. ❶使融化；使熔化；使溶解

Great heat melts iron.

高温使铁熔化。

❷使软化；使柔软

Her tears melted his heart.

她的眼泪使他心软了。

❸使消散；使消失

The sun melted the fog.

日出雾散。

M

member 〔ˈmɛmbɚ ‖ ˈmembə〕

n.[C] ❶(团体等的)成员；会员；一分子

Several members of the family got involved in the crime.

这一家族中有好几个人参与作案。

❷(身体的)一部分

His lower members were numb with cold.

他的下肢冻僵了。

memorial 〔məˈmorɪəl ‖ mɪˈmɔːrɪəl〕

n. 纪念物；纪念碑；纪念馆；纪念活动[C]

We visited the Lincoln Memorial last week.

我们上周参观了林肯纪念馆。

memorize 〔ˈmɛməˌraɪz ‖ ˈmeməraɪz〕

[过去式]memorized；[过去分词]memorized

vt. 记住；背熟

Memorize these sentence patterns.

记住这些句型。

memory 〔ˈmɛmərɪ ‖ ˈmemərɪ〕

n. ❶记忆；记忆力[U][(+for)]

His phone number has slipped my memory.

他的电话号码我记不起来了。

❷留在记忆中的人(或事物)；回忆[C]

The photograph brings back many pleasant memories.
这张照片使人回想起许多愉快的往事。
❸纪念[U]
They dedicated the library to their grandfather's memory.
他们用这座图书馆来纪念他们的祖父。

mend 〔mɛnd ‖ mend〕
[过去式]mended;[过去分词]mended
vt. ❶修理,修补;缝补
He asked her to mend his socks.
他叫她替他补袜子。
❷改善,改良;纠正,改正
He promised that he would mend his ways.
他保证他将改过自新。
vi. ❶渐愈;好转
The child is mending nicely.
这孩子的病情在很快好转。
❷改过;改善
The economy is mending.
经济情况正在好转。
n. ❶修缮部位[C]
The mend in your dress scarcely shows.
你衣服上补过的地方几乎看不出来。
❷好转;痊愈[the]
His health is on the mend.
他的健康正在好转中。

mental 〔ˈmɛntl̩ ‖ ˈmentl〕
a. ❶精神的,心理的
Her problem is mental, not physical.
她的毛病是精神方面的,而不是身体方面的。
❷智力的,脑力的
All humans do have some kind of innate mental ability.
凡是人确有某种天生的智力。
❸内心的;在脑中进行的
Her mental anguish was beyond words.
她内心的痛苦难以用言语形容。
❹精神病的

mention 〔ˈmɛnʃən ‖ ˈmenʃən〕
[过去式]mentioned;[过去分词]mentioned
vt. ❶提到,说起[+v-ing][+(that)][+wh-]
They have three dogs to look after, not to mention the cat and the bird.
他们有三只狗要照顾,更别提那只猫和鸟了。
❷提名表扬
Mr. Stevenson was mentioned

in the annual report for his co-operation.
史蒂文森先生因乐于合作因此在年度报告中被提名表扬。
n. 提及，说起[C][U]
The actor's wedding got a mention in the newspapers.
报上提到了这位演员的婚礼。

常用短语

Don't mention it. **别客气。**
make mention of **提及**
not to mention **更不必说**

menu ['mɛnju ‖ 'menjuː]
n. [C] ❶菜单
Let us see what is on the menu today.
让我们看看今天菜单上有些什么菜。
❷饭菜，菜肴
We all enjoyed the fine menu.
我们都津津有味地吃了这餐佳肴。
❸【计算机】项目单，(功能)选择单

mercy ['mɝsɪ ‖ 'mɜːsɪ]
n. ❶慈悲，怜悯；仁慈，宽容[U][(+on)]
The commander showed mercy to the prisoners of war.
司令官对战俘十分怜悯。
❷仁慈行为，善行[C][(+for)]
❸【口】幸运，侥幸
It was a mercy that the whole family survived in the earthquake.
这次地震中一家人都幸免于难，真是不幸中之大幸。
❹救济，救难
Distributing food among the homeless was an act of mercy.
发配食物给无家可归的人是救苦救难的行为。

mere [mɪr ‖ mɪə]
a. 仅仅的，只不过的
The mere thought of the ruffian made her shudder.
她一想到那个恶棍就不寒而栗。

merely ['mɪrlɪ ‖ 'mɪəlɪ]
ad. 只是，仅仅，不过
Instead of answering, she merely smiled.
她没有回答，只是笑了笑。

merry ['mɛrɪ ‖ 'merɪ]
[比]merrier；[最]merriest
a. 欢乐的，愉快的，兴高采烈的
He is in a very merry mood today.
他今天心情极为愉快。
Merry Christmas!
圣诞快乐！

message ['mɛsɪdʒ ‖ 'mesɪdʒ]

n.［C］❶口信，信息；消息，音信，电文，通讯［＋to-v］［＋that］［（＋for）］
We've just received a congratulatory message from them.
我们刚刚收到他们的贺电。
❷咨文
The President's message to Congress has to do with taxes.
总统向国会提出的咨文与税有关。

metal〔ˈmɛtl̩ ‖ ˈmetl〕
n. 金属；合金［C］［U］
Heat expands metal.
热使金属膨胀。

method〔ˈmɛθəd ‖ ˈmeθəd〕
n. ❶方法，办法［C］［（＋of/for）］
It's a new method of solving the problem.
这是解决这个问题的一个新方法。
❷条理；秩序［U］
His book is totally without method.
他写的那本书毫无条理。

metre, meter〔ˈmitɚ ‖ ˈmiːtə〕
n.【英】米

mice〔maɪs ‖ maɪs〕
n. 老鼠（mouse 的复数）

microphone〔ˈmaɪkrəˌfon ‖ ˈmaɪkrəfəʊn〕
n. 扩音器；麦克风［C］

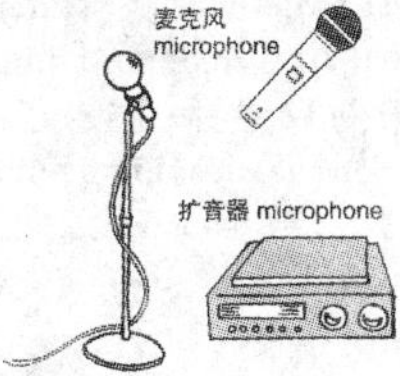

microscope〔ˈmaɪkrəˌskop ‖ ˈmaɪkrəskəʊp〕
n. 显微镜［C］

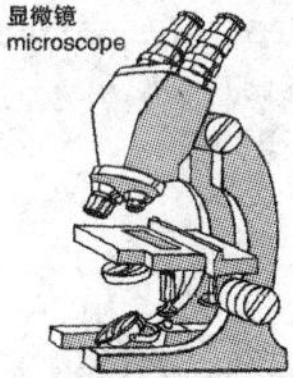

midday〔ˈmɪdˌde ‖ ˌmɪdˈdeɪ〕
n. 正午；中午；日中［U］
a. 正午的；中午的；日中的

middle〔ˈmɪdl̩ ‖ ˈmɪdl〕
a. ❶中部的，中间的
They sat in the middle row.
他们坐在中间一排。
❷中等的，中级的
He was a man of middle height.
他是中等个子。
n. 中部，中途；中央［C］［the］

M

I was in the middle of my work when he called.
他打电话来的时候,我正在忙。

midnight 〔ˈmɪdˌnaɪt ‖ ˈmɪdnaɪt〕
n. 半夜12点钟;午夜;子夜[C]
A train was leaving at midnight for New Orleans.
有一班火车将于夜间12点开往新奥尔良。

midsummer 〔ˈmɪdˈsʌmɚ ‖ ˈmɪdˌsʌmə〕
n. [U] ❶仲夏
❷盛夏

midwinter 〔ˈmɪdˈwɪntɚ ‖ ˈmɪdˌwɪntə〕
n. [U] ❶仲冬
❷冬至

might[1] 〔maɪt ‖ maɪt〕
n. 力量,威力;势力[U]
To be frank, this mission is beyond my might.
说实话,这一使命非我能力所及。

might[2] 〔maɪt ‖ maɪt〕
v. aux. ❶(may的过去式)(表示可能、不确定、期望、许可等,相当于may,但更带迟疑、婉转等色彩)可能;可以
It might rain.
可能下雨。
❷(用于表示与事实相反情况的假设语气中)会,能
If you were older you might understand.
假如你年龄再大一点,你就会理解了。
❸(表示请求或婉转的责备)请;应该
You might at least apologize.
你至少应该表示一下歉意。

mild 〔maɪld ‖ maɪld〕
[比]milder;[最]mildest
a. ❶温和的,温柔的
He is the mildest man alive.
他是世上最和善的人了。
❷温暖的,暖和的
It's been a mild winter this year.
今年的冬天一直很暖和。
❸味淡的,不浓烈的
Please make my drink a mild one.
请把我的酒调得淡一点。

mile 〔maɪl ‖ maɪl〕
n. 英里[C]
At first we covered about 100 miles a day.
起初我们每天差不多行100英里。

military 〔ˈmɪləˌtɛrɪ ‖ ˈmɪlɪtərɪ〕
a. ❶军事的;军用的
There used to be a military base in the region.

M

这个地区过去是个军事基地。

❷军人的;军队的

He did a year's military service.

他服过一年兵役。

❸陆军的

milk〔mɪlk ‖ mɪlk〕

n.[U] ❶乳;牛奶

He drank a glass of milk.

他喝了一杯奶。

❷(植物、果实的)乳汁,乳液

million〔ˈmɪljən ‖ ˈmɪljən〕

n.[C] ❶百万;百万元(镑、美元、欧元等)

❷无数[P]

He has millions of books.

他有许多许多书。

millionaire〔ˌmɪljənˈɛr ‖ ˌmɪljəˈneə〕

n.百万富翁,巨富[C]

mind〔maɪnd ‖ maɪnd〕

[过去式]minded;[过去分词]minded

n. ❶头脑,智力[C][U]

He has a brilliant mind.

他智力超群。

❷记忆力[U]

It completely slipped my mind.

对此,我一点儿也记不起来了。

❸意向[C][U]

He has a good mind to quit that job.

他很想辞去那份工作。

vt. ❶注意,留意,记住要

Mind the wet paint.

当心油漆未干。

❷(用于否定句和疑问句中)介意,反对

Do you mind my smoking here?

我在这儿抽烟你不介意吧?

vi. 介意

If you don't mind, I'll open the window.

如果你不介意,我就开窗。

Do you mind if I put my bag here?

我把袋子放在这儿你不介意吧?

mine¹〔maɪn ‖ maɪn〕

pron. ❶(I的名词性物主代词)我的东西

Is this book mine?

这本书是我的吗?

❷(I的名词性物主代词)我的

He is a friend of mine.

他是我的朋友。

mine²〔maɪn ‖ maɪn〕

n.[C]❶矿;矿山,矿井

❷宝库,源泉[(+of)]

My neighbor is a mine of information about history.

我的一位邻居历史知识十分渊博。

M

mineral 〔ˈmɪnərəl ‖ ˈmɪnərəl〕

n. 矿物[C]

Tin is a mineral.

锡是一种矿物。

minimum 〔ˈmɪnəməm ‖ ˈmɪnɪməm〕

n. 最小量，最小数；最低限度[C][(+of)]

with a minimum of effort

没费什么劲

minority 〔məˈnɔrətɪ ‖ maɪˈnɒrɪtɪ〕

n. ❶少数[the]

This kind of people are in the minority.

这种人是少数的。

❷少数派；少数群体；少数民族[C]

minus 〔ˈmaɪnəs ‖ ˈmaɪnəs〕

prep. 减(去)

10 minus 6 is 4.

10 减 6 等于 4。

a. 负的，减去的

a minus number

负数

n.【数】负号，减号；负数，负量[C]

minute 〔ˈmɪnɪt ‖ ˈmɪnɪt〕

n. [C] ❶分(钟)(时间单位)

It is 5 minutes after/ past 10.

现在是 10 点 5 分。

❷一会儿，片刻

I'll be back in a minute.

我马上就回来。

常用短语

the minute that … 一……就……

I'll tell her the minute she gets here.

她一来我就告诉她。

miracle 〔ˈmɪrəkl̩ ‖ ˈmɪrəkəl〕

n. 奇迹；奇迹般的人(或物)，惊人的事例[C]

It was a miracle that he survived.

他能生还是个奇迹。

mirror 〔ˈmɪrɚ ‖ ˈmɪrə〕

n. [C] ❶镜子

The motorist saw in his rear-view mirror that a police car was following him.

那位汽车驾驶员从他的后视镜里看到一辆警车正跟着他。

❷反映，真实的写照[(+of)]

His novel is a mirror of the times.

他的小说是当代的真实写照。

❸榜样，典型

She is the very mirror of virtue.

她是贞洁的典范。

misery 〔ˈmɪzərɪ ‖ ˈmɪzərɪ〕

n. 痛苦；不幸；悲惨；穷困；苦难

▲Subjects 学科

数学 mathematics

化学 chemistry

物理学 physics

地理学 geography

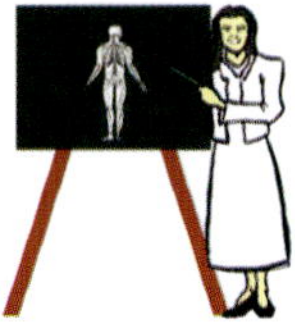

医学 medicine

历史学 history

生物学 biology

考古学 archaeology

天文学 astronomy

音乐学 musicology

美术学 art

经济学 economics

▲Sports 运动

football足球

basketball 篮球

volleyball 排球

tennis 网球

table tennis 乒乓球

race 赛跑

discus throw 铁饼

boxing 拳击

hurdle race 跨栏赛跑

shooting 射击

high jumping 跳高

weightlifting 举重

side horse 鞍马

ice show 冰上表演

fencing 击剑

▲Military Weapons 军事兵器

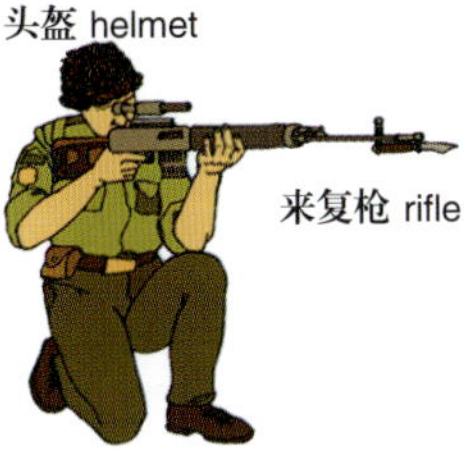

士兵 soldier

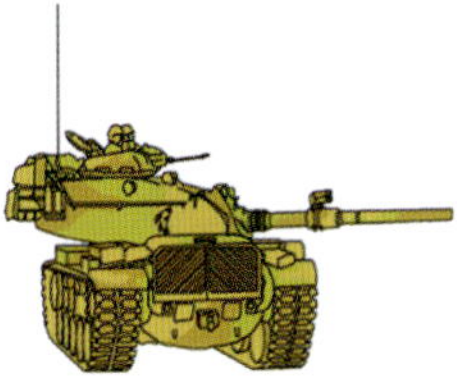

坦克 tank

导弹
guided missile

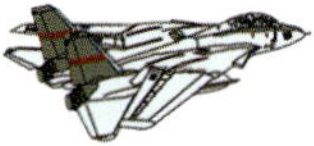

战斗机
fighter plane

军舰 naval vessel

武装直升机
armed helicopter

预警飞机
early warning plane

航空母舰
aircraft carrier

潜水艇 submarine

火炮 cannon

大炮 gun

手枪 handgun

▲Vehicles 交通工具

马车 carriage

轿车 car

直升机 helicopter

出租车 taxi

客机
passenger plane

热气球
hot-air balloon

货车 lorry

有轨电车 tramcar

吉普车
jeep

公共汽车
bus

火车 train

救护车 ambulance

汽艇 motorboat

客轮 liner

自行车
bike

帆船 sailing ship

摩托车 motorcycle

▲Animals 动物

熊猫 panda

斑马 zebra

袋鼠 kangaroo

猩猩 orangutan

骆驼 camel

虎 tiger

鹿 deer

长颈鹿 giraffe

狗熊 bears

狼 wolf

树袋熊 koala

大象 elephants

狮 lion

豹 leopard

鸵鸟 ostrich

企鹅 penguins

犀牛
rhinoceros

羚羊 antelope

老鹰 eagle

天鹅
swan

▲Clothes 服装

墨镜 sunglasses
长裙 dress
毛衣 sweater
夹克衫 jacket
T恤衫 T-shirt
手提包 bag
衬衣 shirts
裤子 trousers
手套 gloves
领带 tie
坎肩 waistcoat
围巾 scarf
套服 suit
短裤 shorts
袜子 socks
帽子 cap
凉鞋 sandals
高筒皮鞋 leather boots
运动鞋 sports shoes
风衣 parka
外衣 coat
裙子 skirt
皮鞋 leather shoes

▲Fruits and Vegetables 水果蔬菜

苹果 apples

猕猴桃 kiwi fruits

桃 peaches

橘子 tangerine

草莓 strawberries

西瓜 watermelons

梨 pears

香蕉 bananas

橙子 oranges

黄瓜 cucumbers

菠萝 pine apples

葡萄 grapes

西红柿 tomatoes

豆角 beans

蘑菇 mushrooms

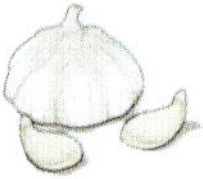
大蒜 garlic

南瓜 pumpkins

胡萝卜 carrots

土豆 potatoes

辣椒 hot peppers

大葱 scallions

茄子 eggplants

白菜 Chinese cabbage

▲Antonyms 反义词

软 soft
硬 hard

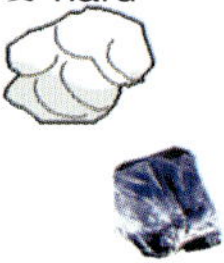

买 buy
卖 sell

少 young
老 old

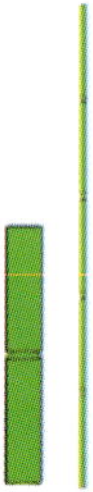

大 big
小 small

笑 laugh
哭 cry

新 new
旧 old

单 single
双 double

长 long
短 short

胖 fat
瘦 thin

弱 weak
强 strong

勇敢 brave
胆小 timid

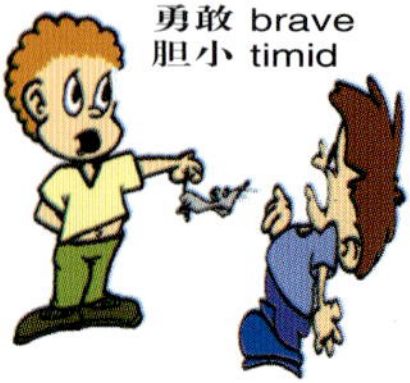

上 up
下 down

多 more
少 less

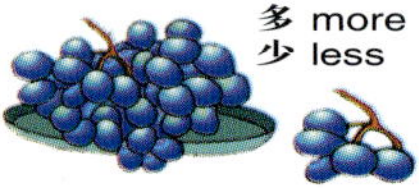

[C][U]
She felt most severely the miseries of mankind.
她极为强烈地感受到了人类的种种苦难。

词汇拓展

miserable *a.* 可怜的,不幸的

miss[1] 〔mɪs ‖ mɪs〕
[过去式]missed;[过去分词]missed
vt. ❶未击中;未得到;未达到;未看到;未听到;未领会
He missed my meaning.
他没有领会我的意思。
❷未履行;未出席;未赶上,错过[+v-ing]
She missed going to the party on Saturday.
星期六她没能出席聚会。
❸想念,惦记
I know how you miss your mother.
我了解你多么想念你的母亲。
vi. 未击中;打偏
Aim carefully or you'll miss.
仔细瞄准,否则会击不中的。
n. [C] ❶未中;得不到;达不到
He hit the target three times without a miss.
他三发三中。
❷失败
❸逃脱;幸免

miss[2] 〔mɪs ‖ mɪs〕
n. ❶(通常大写)(用于姓名或姓之前,尤指对未婚女子的称呼)小姐[C]
Miss Brown is a popular teacher.
布朗小姐是位很受欢迎的教师。
❷(可单独使用的称呼语)小姐
❸少女,姑娘[C]
❹(通常大写)(用于选美会等,加于国名等之前)……小姐,……皇后
Her daughter was chosen as Miss Hong Kong 6 years ago.
她女儿6年前当选为香港小姐。

missile 〔'mɪsl̩ ‖ 'mɪsaɪl〕
n. ❶飞弹,导弹
❷投射物;投射武器

mission 〔'mɪʃən ‖ 'mɪʃən〕
n. ❶外交使团,使节团[C][(+to)]
a financial mission
财政使节团
❷使命,任务[C][U]
He accomplished the mission.
他完成了使命。

M

❸布道；传教[C][U]

mist 〔mɪst ‖ mɪst〕

n. 薄雾，霭[C][U]

The mist has cleared off.

雾已经散了。

mistake 〔mə'stek ‖ mɪ'steɪk〕

[过去式]mistook；[过去分词]mistaken

vt. ❶弄错，误解

You mistook my meaning entirely.

你完全误会了我的意思。

❷把……误认为[(＋for)]

He was mistaken for the minister.

人们错把他当做牧师了。

❸挑选错；估计错

It was wise of you not to mistake your own strength.

你没有错误估计自己的力量是明智的。

vi. 弄错，搞错

You mistake, my dear.

亲爱的，你错了。

n. 错误，过失；误会[C][U]

Tom didn't make a single spelling mistake in his composition.

汤姆在这篇作文里一个字也没拼错。

M

常用短语

make a mistake 犯错，弄错

misunderstand 〔ˌmɪsʌndɚ'stænd ‖ ˌmɪsʌndə'stænd〕

[过去式]misunderstood；[过去分词]misunderstood

vt. 误会；曲解

You misunderstood me.

你误会我了。

mix 〔mɪks ‖ mɪks〕

[过去式]mixed；[过去分词]mixed

vt. ❶使混合，掺和

The workmen mixed sand, gravel, and cement to make concrete.

工人们把沙、石子和水泥混合成混凝土。

❷使结合；使结交[(＋with)]

We can sometimes mix business with pleasure.

我们有时能把工作和娱乐结合起来。

❸(给……)配制；调制[(＋for)]

The doctor mixed a bottle of medicine for him.

医生为他配了一瓶药。

❹混淆，搞混[(＋with)]

vi. ❶相混合，相溶[(＋with)]

Oil doesn't mix with water.

油和水不能相溶。

❷交往，交游[(＋with)]

He's mixing with the wrong people.
他交友不慎。
❸发生牵连；参与[(+in)]
Did he mix in the quarrel?
他有没有参与那场争吵？

常用短语

mixed up in 参与
mix up 拌和
n. ❶混合，搅和；结合[C][U]
❷混合物；混杂的一群人[(+of)]
A mix of people attended the meeting.
各色人等参加了那个会议。

mixture ['mɪkstʃɚ || 'mɪkstʃə]
n. 混合，混和[U]
a mixture of eggs, flour and milk
鸡蛋、面粉还有牛奶的混合物

model ['mɑdl̩ || 'mɒdl]
n.[C] ❶模型，雏形；原型[(+of/for)]
He made a clay model of the Eiffel Tower.
他做了一个埃菲尔铁塔的黏土模型。
❷模范，典型[(+of/for)]
His mother is a model of industry.
他母亲是勤劳的典范。
❸模特儿；时装模特儿
Lily is a fashion model.
莉莉是个时装模特儿。
❹(汽车等的)型号，样式
a. ❶用作模型的
❷模范的，榜样的
They are a model couple.
他们是一对模范夫妻。

moderate ['mɑdərɪt || 'mɒdərɪt]
a. 中等的，适度的；有节制的，不过分的
He is moderate in everything.
他每件事都适可而止。
n. 温和主义者，稳健派

modern ['mɑdɚn || 'mɒdn]
a. ❶现代的；近代的
In the afternoon they went to an exhibition of modern art.
他们下午去参观了现代艺术展。
❷现代化的；时髦的；最新的
His office is tastefully furnished with modern furniture.
他的办公室用新式家具装饰得十分雅致。
❸(常大写)(指语言)现代的；近代的

modest ['mɑdɪst || 'mɒdɪst]
[比] more modest; [最] most modest

M

a. ❶谦虚的，审慎的[(＋about)]
He's got a drawer full of medals, but he's too modest to wear them.
他有满满一抽屉的奖章，但是他很谦虚，从不戴它们。
❷(女性及其衣饰)端庄的；稳重的
She wore a modest bathing suit.
她穿一件不太暴露的游泳衣。
❸不太大(或多)的；适度的，有节制的
Prices tended to rise year by year, but at a modest rate.
物价年年上涨，但幅度不大。

moist 〔mɔɪst ‖ mɔɪst〕
[比]moister；[最]moistest
a. ❶潮湿的，微湿的；多雨的[(＋with)]
The path was moist with dew.
小路有露水，湿湿潮潮的。
❷含泪的，泪汪汪的[(＋with)]
Her eyes were moist with tears.
她的眼里噙着泪水。

词汇拓展

moisture *n.* 湿度，水分

moment 〔'momənt ‖ 'məumənt〕
n. ❶瞬间；片刻[C]
Just a moment; she's coming.
请稍等，她马上来。
❷指定时刻[C]
Both of them arrived at the same moment.
他们俩同时到达。
❸契机；时机；重要时刻，关头[＋to-v]
I'll have to pick my moment to tell my wife.
我得选个合适的时机将这件事告诉我妻子。

常用短语

at any moment 随时
A fire may happen at any moment.
火灾随时都有可能发生。
the moment that 当时，那时
He hid himself the moment he saw me.
他一看见我就藏了起来。

Monday 〔'mʌndɪ ‖ 'mʌndɪ〕
n. 略作 Mon. 星期一

money 〔'mʌnɪ ‖ 'mʌnɪ〕
n. ❶钱；货币[U]
Do they accept French money?
他们接受法国货币吗？
❷财产，财富[U]

monkey 〔'mʌŋkɪ ‖ 'mʌŋkɪ〕

M

n. 猴子；顽童[C]

month 〔mʌnθ ‖ mʌnθ〕

n. 月，一个月的时间[C]

She flew to Japan last month.

上个月她乘飞机去了日本。

monthly 〔ˈmʌnθlɪ ‖ ˈmʌnθlɪ〕

a. 每月的；每月一次的；一个月有效的

It is a monthly magazine.

这是月刊。

ad. 每月；每月一次

I pay my rent monthly.

我每月付一次房租。

mood 〔mud ‖ muːd〕

n. ❶心情，心境，情绪[C][+to-v]

I am not in the mood to argue.

我没有心情争辩。

❷心情不好，生气[C]

She was in a bit of a mood this morning.

今天早晨她情绪欠佳。

❸喜怒无常[P]

He is a man of moods.

他是一个喜怒无常的人。

moon 〔mun ‖ muːn〕

n. ❶月球[the]

The moon rises.

月亮升起来。

❷月亮

a full moon 满月

a half moon 半月

a new moon 新月

moonlight 〔ˈmunˌlaɪt ‖ ˈmuːnlaɪt〕

n. 月光[U]

We were walking in the moonlight.

我们在月光下散步。

moral 〔ˈmɔrəl ‖ ˈmɒrəl〕

a. ❶道德(上)的

He refused the request on moral grounds.

基于道德上的考虑，他拒绝了这个请求。

❷讲道德的，品行端正的

My grandmother was a very moral woman, and she'd never allow cursing.

我祖母是很讲究道德的人，她从不允许诅咒。

M

❸教训的

❹精神上的，心理上的；道义(德)上的

We will give them moral support.

我们会给他们精神支持。

n.［C］❶道德上的教训；寓意

What is the moral of this story?

这个故事的寓意是什么？

❷道德；品行；风纪[P]

Some people have no business morals.

有些人毫无商业道德。

more〔mor ‖ mɔː〕

a. ❶（many，much 的比较级）更多的；更高程度的[＋(than)]

He has more chance than ever.

他从来没有这样的大好机会。

❷另外的，附加的

If you still feel hungry，there is more food in the kitchen.

如果你还饿，厨房里还有东西。

pron. ❶更多的数量；更多的人(或事物)[(＋of/than)]

Instead of fewer accidents，there were more.

意外事故非但没有减少，反而增多了。

❷额外的数目；另外的一些

ad. ❶(用以构成形容词或副词的比较级)更[(＋than)]

His illness was more serious than the doctor first thought.

他的病情比医生原先预料的更严重。

❷(much 的比较级)更多；更大程度地

You should sleep more than you do.

你应该有更多的睡眠。

❸另外；再

They stayed there two days more.

他们在那里又待了两天。

❹而且

常用短语

(and) what is more 而且

more and more 越来越

He became more and more excited.

他越来越激动。

more or less 多少有些；大约

I was more or less tired after the trip.

旅行之后我多少有点儿累。

no more ❶不再

I saw her no more.

我再也没见过她。

❷也不

I have no more money.

我也没钱。

not any more 不再

no more than 不过，只

He wrote no more than three novels.

他只写了三部小说。

not more than

至多，不比……多

He wrote not more than three novels.

他最多写了三部小说。

the more… the more 越……越……

The more you have, the more you want.

你拥有越多，想得到的就越多。

morning 〔ˈmɔrnɪŋ‖ˈmɔːnɪŋ〕

n. 早晨；上午[C][U]

Mother goes shopping on Tuesday and Friday mornings.

我母亲总是在星期二和星期五上午上街购物。

most 〔most‖məʊst〕

a. ❶(many, much 的最高级)最多的；最高程度的

Which of you has made the most mistakes?

你们当中谁错得最多？

❷多数的；大部分的

Most birds can fly.

多数的鸟会飞。

pron. ❶最大量，最多数，最高额[the]

I did the most I could.

我已尽最大的努力去做了。

❷大部分，大多数[(+of)]

Of course most of them don't agree with his opinion.

当然，他们中大多数人都不同意他的意见。

ad. ❶(用以构成形容词或副词的最高级)最

Of the three questions, this is the most difficult.

三个问题中这是最难的。

❷(much 的最高级)最多，最大限度地

She gave money most generously.

她付钱最大方。

❸非常，很

It is really most unfortunate.

这真是太不幸了。

mostly 〔ˈmostlɪ‖ˈməʊstlɪ〕

ad. 大多数地，大部分地；主要地；多半

It is mostly made of iron.

它主要是由铁组成的。

mother 〔ˈmʌðɚ‖ˈmʌðə〕

n. [C] ❶母亲；妈妈

She is a mother of five children.
她是五个孩子的母亲。
❷起源，根由［the］［(＋of)］
Necessity is the mother of invention.
需要乃发明之母。

motion〔ˈmoʃən ‖ ˈməʊʃən〕
n. ❶(物体的)运动，移动；(天体的)运行［U］
The train was in motion.
火车开动了。
❷动作，姿态；手势，眼色［C］
All her motions were graceful.
她的一举一动都很优美。
❸动机，意向［U］
He did that of his own motion.
他出于自愿做了那事。

常用短语

motion picture（美）电影

motive〔ˈmotɪv ‖ ˈməʊtɪv〕
n.［C］❶动机；主旨；目的［(＋of/for)］
His sole motive was to make her happy.
他唯一的目的就是使她幸福。
❷(文艺作品的)主题

motor〔ˈmotɚ ‖ ˈməʊtə〕
n.［C］❶原动力
❷马达，发动机；内燃机；电动机
This sewing machine is driven by an electric motor.
这台缝纫机是靠电动机驱动的。

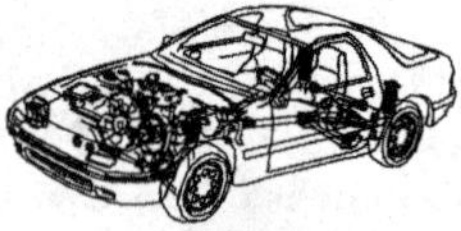

马达
motor

motorcar〔ˈmotɚˌkɑr ‖ ˈməʊtəkɑː〕
n.［C］❶【英】汽车
❷(铁道上的)电动车

motorcycle〔ˈmotɚˌsaɪkl̩ ‖ ˈməʊtəˌsaɪkl〕
n. 摩托车［C］

mountain〔ˈmaʊntn̩ ‖ ˈmaʊntɪn〕
n. ❶山［C］
❷山脉［P］

mouse〔maʊs ‖ maʊs〕［名复］mice
n.［C］❶鼠
❷胆小怕羞的人
Are you a man or a mouse?
你是一个男子汉还是一个胆小

鬼?

❸【计算机】鼠标

mouth 〔mauθ ‖ mauθ〕

n.［C］❶(人,动物的)嘴

Open your mouth wider, please.

请把嘴张大些。

❷口状物;进出口;河口;(瓶子等的)口

A big rock blocked the mouth of the cave.

一块大石头堵住了洞口。

move 〔muv ‖ muːv〕

［过去式］moved;［过去分词］moved

vt. ❶使移动,搬动;开动

That chair is in the way; move it please.

那把椅子挡着路,请把它移开。

❷使感动［(+to)］

They were much moved by her story.

他们被她所说的深深打动。

❸(在会上)提议,动议［+that］

He moved that the meeting be continued after dinner.

他提议晚饭后继续开会。

vi. ❶移动;离开;前进

The train was already moving when we arrived at the railroad station.

当我们到达火车站时,火车已经开动了。

❷(事情等)进展

❸迁移;搬家［(+in/into/out/away)］

When are you moving to the suburbs?

你们什么时候搬到郊区去?

movement 〔ˈmuvmənt ‖ ˈmuːvmənt〕

n. ❶运动,活动［C］［U］

He lay there without movement.

他躺在那里,一动也不动。

❷动作,姿态［C］

❸倾向;动向;变迁［C］［U］

There is a movement towards simple designs in clothing.

时下服装设计趋于朴素。

❹(政治,社会,思想)运动［C］

We're starting a movement against smoking.

我们正掀起一场反对吸烟的运动。

movie 〔ˈmuvɪ ‖ ˈmuːvɪ〕

n.［C］❶电影,影片

This movie is worth seeing.

这部影片值得一看。

❷电影的放映,一场电影［the

M

P]
Let's go to the movies.
咱们去看电影吧。

Mr. [ˈmɪstɚ || ˈmɪstə]
n. (mister的简称,用于男士的姓、姓名或职务之前)先生[C]
Mr. Lee is a well-known scholar in ancient Chinese history.
李先生是中国古代史著名学者。

Mrs. [ˈmɪsɪz || ˈmɪsɪz]
n. (mistress的简称,用于已婚女性的夫姓或夫的姓名之前)夫人,太太[C]
Mrs. Smith lives in Paris.
史密斯太太住在巴黎。

much [mʌtʃ || mʌtʃ]
[比]more;[最]most
a. 许多;大量的;很大程度的
How much rent do you pay?
你付多少租金?
pron. 许多,大量
Much of the time was wasted.
许多时间都浪费掉了。
ad. ❶非常;很
I don't much care for television.
我不太喜欢看电视。
❷(加强比较级或最高级)远为,……得多
She is much the most active member in our group.
她绝对是我们组最活跃的成员。
❸常常;好久
Do you dine out much?
你常在外面用餐吗?

常用短语

as much 同样地
I thought as much.
正如我所预料的。
as much as 尽;尽……那样多
Eat as much as you like.
尽量多吃。
as much…as 同样多
He drinks as much milk as I do.
他喝的牛奶和我喝的一样多。
how much 多少
How much is this tie?
这领带多少钱?

mud [mʌd || mʌd]
n. 泥;泥浆[U]
The car got stuck in the mud.
那辆车陷入泥里了。

muddy [ˈmʌdɪ || ˈmʌdɪ]
a. ❶多烂泥的;泥泞的
The boy's pants were muddy.
那男孩的裤子沾了很多泥。
❷浑浊的;模糊的
muddy water

M

污浊的水

murder 〔ˈmɝdə ‖ ˈmɜːdə〕

〔过去式〕murdered；〔过去分词〕murdered

n. 谋杀，凶杀；谋杀罪〔C〕〔U〕

There has been a decrease in the number of murders in the city.

城里凶杀案件的数量有所减少。

vt. 谋杀，凶杀

She'll murder you when she finds out what you've done.

等她发现你干了什么事的时候，她会气得把你给杀了。（口语：气极了）

muscle 〔ˈmʌsḷ ‖ ˈmʌsl〕

n. ❶【解】肌；肌肉〔C〕〔U〕

He developed the muscles in the legs by running.

他通过跑步使腿部的肌肉发达了。

❷体力，膂力〔U〕

It'll take a lot of muscle to remove the rock.

搬走那块石头要费很大的气力。

museum 〔mjuˈzɪəm ‖ mjuːˈzɪəm〕

n. 〔C〕 ❶博物馆

His works were hung in many museums.

他的作品被许多博物馆收藏。

❷【美】展览馆，陈列馆

music 〔ˈmjuzɪk ‖ ˈmjuːzɪk〕

n. 〔U〕 ❶音乐；乐曲；音乐作品

A bit of music will cheer you up.

听会儿音乐会使你的心情愉快起来。

❷乐谱

read music

看乐谱

musical 〔ˈmjuzɪkḷ ‖ ˈmjuːzɪkəl〕

a. ❶音乐的，关于音乐的

❷音乐般的，美妙的，悦耳的

乐器 musical instruments

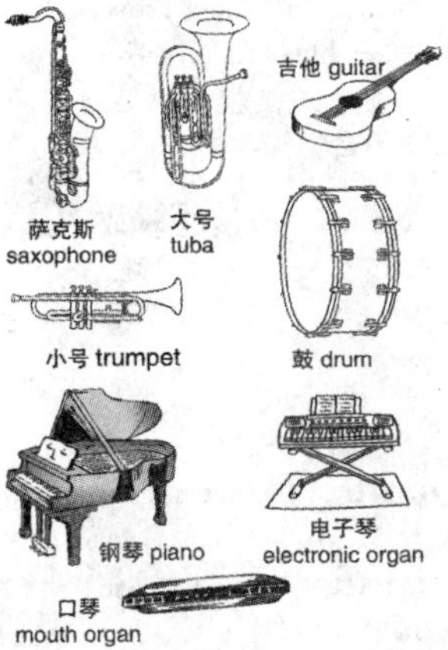

musician 〔mjuˈzɪʃən ‖ mjuːˈzɪʃən〕

n. 音乐家；乐师；作曲家[C]

must 〔mʌst ‖ mʌst〕

v. aux. ❶(表示必要、命令或强制)必须，得

You mustn't talk like that.

你可不能这样说话。

❷(表示肯定的推测)一定是，谅必，八成

This must be your room.

这一定是你的房间了。

> must 这一意思的否定式是 cannot
>
> She can't be happy with her husband in prison.
>
> 她丈夫在监狱里她肯定不会幸福。
>
> **用法工具箱**

❸(表示不可避免性)必然要，必定会

All men must die.

人总有一死。

mustache 〔ˈmʌstæʃ ‖ məˈstɑːʃ〕

n. 髭，小胡子[C]

mutton 〔ˈmʌtn̩ ‖ ˈmʌtn〕

n. 羊肉[U]

my 〔maɪ ‖ maɪ〕

pron. ❶(I 的所有格)我的

I'm looking for my glasses.

我在找我的眼镜。

❷(用于若干词组，表示惊奇等)哎呀！哇！

My goodness!

天哪！

int. (表示惊奇等)哎呀！喔唷！

myself 〔maɪˈsɛlf ‖ maɪˈself〕

pron. ❶(I 的反身代词)我自己

I am teaching myself French.

我在自修法语。

❷(用以加强语气)我亲自，我本人

I myself wrote the report.

我自己写的报告。

❸我的正常情绪；我的正常健康状况

I am feeling myself again.

我觉得健康如昔。

mysterious 〔mɪsˈtɪrɪəs ‖ mɪˈstɪərɪəs〕

a. 神秘的；不可思议的

I saw a mysterious object in the sky.

我看见天空中有个神秘物体。

mystery 〔ˈmɪstrɪ ‖ ˈmɪstərɪ〕

n. ❶神秘的事物；难以理解的

事物；谜[C]
His death has remained a mystery.
他的死仍是个谜。
❷神秘，秘密[U]
That case is wrapped in mystery.
那件案子笼罩在神秘的气氛之中。
❸神秘小说，推理小说[C]
I like reading mysteries.
我喜欢读推理小说。

myth 〔mɪθ ‖ mɪθ〕
n. ❶神话[C][U]
❷虚构的人(或事物)[C]
He is interested in the Greek myths.
他对希腊神话感兴趣。

M

nail 〔nel ‖ neɪl〕

n. [C] ❶钉子

The nail has been pulled out.

那只钉子被拔出来了。

❷(手、脚的)指甲;(鸟、兽的)爪

❸(鸟禽)喙上的硬甲壳

name 〔nem ‖ neɪm〕

n. ❶名字,姓名;名称[C]

What's your name?

你叫什么名字?

❷名声,声誉

His actions have given him a bad name.

他的行为给他带来了不好的名声。

nap 〔næp〕

[过去式]napped;[过去分词]napped

n. 打盹儿,午睡[C]

He takes a nap every afternoon.

他每天都午睡。

vi. 打盹,小睡

He is napping in the sofa.

他正在沙发上小睡。

narrow 〔ˈnæro ‖ ˈnærəʊ〕

[比]narrower;[最]narrowest

a. ❶狭的,狭窄的

The street is too narrow for a truck to pass.

这条街太窄,卡车无法行驶。

❷范围狭小的

He has only a narrow circle of friends.

他交友不广。

❸心胸狭窄的
She has a narrow mind.
她心胸狭隘。

nation〔neʃən ‖ neɪʃən〕
n.[C] ❶国民
He is loved by the whole nation.
他受到全国人民的爱戴。
❷国家
Each nation has a flag of its own.
每个国家都有自己的国旗。
❸民族

national〔ˈnæʃənḷ ‖ ˈnæʃənl〕
a. ❶全国性的,国有的,国立的
a national newspaper
全国性的报纸
a national hospital
国立医院
❷民族的,国家的,国民的
a national hero
民族英雄

nationality〔ˌnæʃənˈælətɪ ‖ ˌnæʃəˈnælɪtɪ〕
n. ❶国籍[C][U]
What's your nationality?
你是哪国人?
❷民族[C]

native〔ˈnetɪv ‖ ˈneɪtɪv〕
a. ❶天生的
He has native ability as an actor.
他有当演员的天赋。
❷出生地的,祖国的,家乡的
They are native speakers of English.
他们的母语是英文。
❸本土的,本国的,土生的[(+to)]
The giant panda is native to China.
大熊猫是中国特有的动物。
❹土著人的,土著的
Native American
美洲土著居民;印第安人
n.[C] ❶本地人,本国人
Are you a native here, or just a visitor?
你是本地人? 还是过客?
❷土著[P]

natural〔nætʃərəl ‖ nætʃərəl〕
[比] more natural; [最] most natural
a. ❶自然的;有关自然界的
We visited a museum of natural history.
我们参观了一个自然博物馆。
❷天然的
Coal and oil are natural products.

N

煤和石油是天然物产。

❸不做作的

Try to look natural for your photograph.

拍照要尽量显得自然一些。

naturally〔ˈnætʃərəlɪ ‖ ˈnætʃərəlɪ〕

ad. ❶天生地，天然地

He is naturally shy.

他天生害羞。

❷自然地

Speak more naturally.

说得再自然点儿。

❸当然

Naturally they got angry.

他们当然生气。

nature〔ˈnetʃɚ ‖ ˈneɪtʃə〕

n. ❶（常大写）自然；自然界[U]

Nature does not provide everything we want.

自然界并不提供我们所需要的一切东西。

❷性质，本质[C][U]

The nature of iron differs greatly from that of wood.

铁与木头的性质有很大区别。

naught〔nɔt ‖ nɔːt〕

n.【数】零[U]

naughty〔ˈnɔtɪ ‖ ˈnɔːtɪ〕

a. 顽皮的，淘气的；撒野的

It's naughty of you to pull the dog's tail.

你拽狗尾巴，真是顽皮。

navy〔ˈnevɪ ‖ ˈneɪvɪ〕

n. [C] ❶（常大写）海军

He is an officer in the Navy.

他是一个海军军官。

❷海军舰队

near〔nɪr ‖ nɪə〕

[比]nearer；[最]nearest

a. ❶近的

The post office is quite near.

邮局很近。

❷（关系、程度上）接近的；近似的；几乎是的

Her aunt is her nearest relative.

她姨妈是她最近的亲戚。

❸（两者中）较近的

the near bank of the river

较近的那一边河岸

ad. ❶近，接近

He lives quite near.

他住得很近。

❷几乎，差不多

It is near impossible.

那是几乎不可能的。

prep. 在……附近

He sat in a chair near the door.

他坐在靠门的一把椅子上。

nearby 〔ˈnɪrˈbaɪ ‖ ˈnɪəbaɪ〕

a. 附近的

I went fishing in the nearby river.

我去附近的河钓鱼。

ad. 在附近

He lives nearby.

他住在附近。

nearly 〔ˈnɪrlɪ ‖ ˈnɪəlɪ〕

ad. ❶几乎，差不多

She is nearly 50 now.

她将近 50 岁了。

❷密切地，亲密地

They are nearly related.

他们是至亲。

nearsighted 〔ˈnɪrˈsaɪtɪd ‖ ˌnɪəˈsaɪtɪd〕

a. ❶近视的；近视眼的

❷目光短浅的，短视的

neat 〔nit ‖ niːt〕

[比]neater；[最]neatest

a. ❶整洁的；整齐的

He keeps his desk neat.

他的课桌总是那么整洁。

❷工整的；匀称的，样子好的

She had small, neat writing.

她的字写得小而工整。

❸熟练的；灵巧的

She is a neat worker.

她做事干净利落。

necessarily 〔ˈnɛsəˌsɛrəlɪ ‖ ˈnesɪserɪlɪ〕

ad. 必定；必然地，必要地

War necessarily causes unhappiness.

战争必然导致不幸。

necessary 〔ˈnɛsəˌsɛrɪ ‖ ˈnesɪsərɪ〕

[比]more necessary；[最]most necessary

a. ❶必要的，必需的[(＋for/to)]

Oxygen is necessary for life.

氧气是生命所必需的。

❷必然的，无法避免的

I will go there again, if necessary.

有必要的话，我再去那儿一趟。

necessity 〔nəˈsɛsətɪ ‖ nɪˈsesətɪ〕

n. ❶需要，必要性[U][(＋of/for)]

She felt the necessity of accepting the invitation.

她认为必须接受这一邀请。

❷必需品[C]

Television is considered a necessity by a lot of people.

许多人认为电视是一件生活必需品。

neck 〔nɛk ‖ nek〕

N

n. ❶颈，脖子[C]
❷衣领，领子[C]
The neck of a shirt gets dirty easily.
衬衫的领口很容易弄脏。

necklace 〔ˈnɛklɪs ‖ ˈneklɪs〕
n. 项链[C]

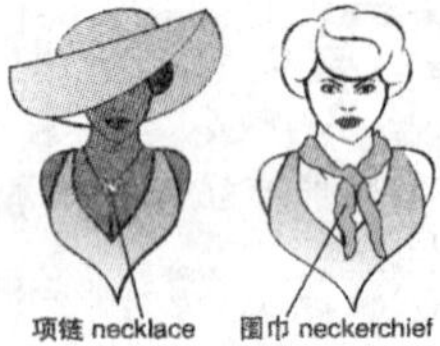

need 〔nid ‖ niːd〕
[过去式]needed；[过去分词]needed
n. 需要；必要；需求；要求[(＋of/for)][＋to-v]
We have no need to be afraid of them.
我们不必怕他们。
vt. 需要，有……必要[＋to-v][＋v-ing]
The garden needs watering.(＝The garden needs to be watered.)
花园该浇水了。
v.aux. (多用于疑问句和否定句)需要；必须
Need you go so soon?
你需要走这么早吗？

needle 〔ˈnidl̩ ‖ ˈniːdl〕
n. 针；编织针；唱针；注射针[C]
The needle of the compass shows that we're facing south.
指南针上的磁针显示我们正面朝南方。

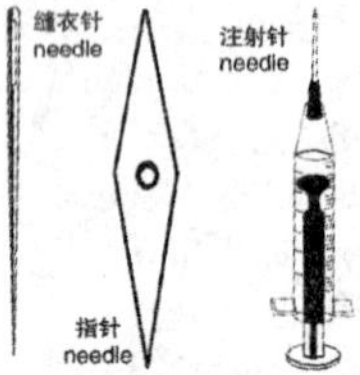

negative 〔ˈnɛgətɪv ‖ ˈnegətɪv〕
a. ❶否定的；否认的
He gave me a negative answer.
他给了我一个否定的答案。
❷反面的；消极的
Their criticism was not negative.
他们的批评并不是负面的。

neglect 〔nɪˈglɛkt ‖ nɪˈglekt〕
[过去式]neglected；[过去分词]neglected
vt. ❶忽视，忽略
He was so busy that he neglected his health.
他忙得连身体健康都无暇顾

及。

❷疏忽，玩忽

He was dismissed for neglecting his duties.

他因玩忽职守而被解雇。

❸漏做，忘了做[＋to-v]

She neglected to pay the fine.

她忘了缴罚金。

negotiate 〔nɪˈgoʃɪˈet ‖ nɪˈɡəʊʃɪˌeɪt〕

[过去式]negotiated；[过去分词]negotiated

vi. 谈判，协商，洽谈[(＋with/for)]

vt. 通过谈判达成，谈成[(＋with)]

Negro 〔ˈnigro ‖ ˈniːɡrəʊ〕

n. 黑人[C]

> Negro(现在用已过时)一般被认为有冒犯性，相当于 black，作“黑人”解。在美国，现在多用 African American。
>
> **用法工具箱**

neighbo(u)r 〔ˈnebɚ ‖ ˈneɪbə〕

n. [C] ❶邻居；邻近的人(或物)

❷邻国

Canada and the United States are neighbors.

加拿大和美国是邻邦。

neighborhood 〔ˈnebɚˌhʊd ‖ ˈneɪbəhʊd〕

n. ❶邻近地区[C]

They live in the neighborhood of the TV station.

他们住在电视台附近。

❷近邻，整个街坊[the]

The whole neighborhood talks about it.

整个街坊都在议论这件事。

neither 〔ˈniðɚ ‖ ˈniːðə〕

a. 两者都不

Neither shoe fits comfortably.

两只鞋都不合脚。

pron. (两者之中)无一个

Neither of my friends has come yet.

我的两个朋友都还没来。

ad. ❶(与 no，not，never 等连用)也不

“John can't swim.”

“约翰不会游泳。”

“Neither can I.”

“我也不会。”

❷(与 nor 连用)既不……也不……；也不

We had neither money nor food.
我们既没有钱，也没有食物。

nephew 〔ˈnɛfju ‖ ˈnefjuː〕
n. 侄儿；外甥[C]

nervous 〔ˈnɝvəs ‖ ˈnɜːvəs〕
[比] more nervous; [最] most nervous
a. ❶神经质的；紧张不安的
I was nervous on the stage.
我在舞台上很紧张。
❷神经的
a nervous breakdown
精神崩溃

nest 〔nɛst ‖ nest〕
n. 巢；窝；穴；(鸟等的)一窝，一群[C]
A bird lays eggs in the nest it has built.
鸟将蛋下在自己所筑的巢里。

net 〔nɛt ‖ net〕
n. ❶网；网状物；网状制品[C][U]
They caught fish with their nets.
他们用网捕鱼。
❷罗网，陷阱[C]
The criminal was finally caught in the net of justice.
罪犯终于落入法网。
❸网状系统；通信网；广播网；间谍网[C]
❹(网球等的)落网球[C]

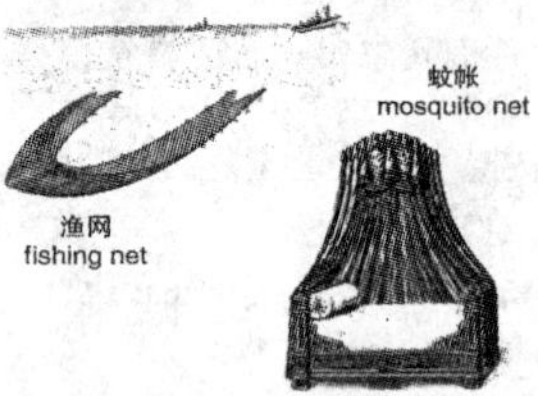

Netherlands 〔ˈnɛðɚləndz ‖ ˈneðələndz〕
n. 荷兰

neutral 〔ˈnjutrəl ‖ ˈnjuːtrəl〕
a. 中立的；中立国的；中立地带的
Switzerland remained neutral during the Second World War.
瑞士在第二次世界大战期间保持中立。

never 〔ˈnɛvɚ ‖ ˈnevə〕
ad. ❶从未；永不；决不
He will never go there again.
他再也不会去那里了。
❷不；没有；不要；不可能
Never mind.
没关系。

nevertheless 〔ˌnɛvɚðəˈlɛs ‖ ˌnevəðəˈles〕

N

ad. 仍然，不过，然而

She was angry; nevertheless, she listened to me.

她很生气，但还是听了我的话。

new 〔nju ‖ nju:〕

［比］newer；［最］newest

a. ❶新的；新鲜的；新型的

He bought a new dictionary.

他买了一本新字典。

New Year

新年

New Year's Day

元旦

New Year's Eve

除夕

❷没有经验的；陌生的［(＋to)］

Her name is new to me.

她的名字对我来说是完全陌生的。

news 〔njuz ‖ nju:z〕

n. ❶新闻；消息；报道［U］［(＋of/about)］

A few days later he told me an exciting piece of news.

几天之后他告诉我一个令人振奋的消息。

❷新闻节目［the］

The news is at 8：00.

新闻节目在8点播出。

newspaper 〔ˈnjuzˌpepɚ ‖ ˈnjusˌpeɪpə〕

n. ❶报纸，报［C］

❷报社［C］

❸新闻用纸，白报纸［U］

newsreel 〔ˈnjuzˌril ‖ ˈnju:zri:l〕

n. 新闻(短)片

newsstand 〔ˈnjuzˌstænd ‖ ˈnju:zstænd〕

n. 报刊出售摊

New York 〔njuˈjɔrk ‖ nju:ˈjɔ:k〕

n. 纽约

next 〔ˈnɛkst ‖ ˈnekst〕

a. ❶紧邻的，贴近的

He rose to fetch a chair from the next room.

他立起身来去隔壁房间搬一张椅子。

❷紧接在后的；接下去的；下一班的

Is he coming this weekend or next weekend?

他这个周末来还是下个周末来？

❸居后的，次于的

ad. ❶接下去，然后

What happened next?
然后发生了什么事情?
❷下次
❸次于,第二
I like this best and that next.
我最喜欢这个,其次是那个。
prep. 靠近,贴近,次于
She sat next her mother.
她坐在她母亲身边。

nice 〔naɪs ‖ naɪs〕
[比]nicer;[最]nicest
a. ❶好的;美好的,宜人的;可爱的
It's a nice day.
天气真好。
❷好心的,友好的
It's very nice of you to invite us to the party.
你真太好了! 邀请我们参加晚会。
❸细微的,精细的
a nice difference of meaning
意义上的细微差别
❹有教养的,体面的,正派的
A nice girl would never go there.
好女孩决不会去那里。

niece 〔nis ‖ niːs〕
n. [C] ❶侄女
❷外甥女

night 〔naɪt ‖ naɪt〕
n. 夜;晚上[C][U]
We arrived at the village before night fell.
我们在夜幕降临前到达那个村庄。

常用短语

at night 在晚上
We arrived there late at night.
我们深夜才到那里。
last night 昨晚

nine 〔naɪn ‖ naɪn〕
a. 九的;九个的
n. 九;九个

nineteen 〔ˌnaɪnˈtin ‖ ˌnaɪnˈtiːn〕
a. 十九(个、人、岁)的
n. 十九(个、人、点、分、岁)

nineteenth 〔ˈnaɪnˈtinθ ‖ ˌnaɪnˈtiːnθ〕
a. ❶(与 the 连用)第十九的,第十九个的
❷十九分之一的
n. [C] ❶(与 the 连用)第十九(个);月的第十九日
❷十九分之一

ninetieth 〔ˈnaɪntɪɪθ ‖ ˈnaɪntɪɪθ〕
a. 第九十的;九十分之一的
n. 第九十;九十分之一

ninety 〔ˈnaɪntɪ ‖ ˈnaɪntɪ〕

a. 九十(个、人、岁)的
n. ❶ 九十(个、人、岁)
❷九十年代;九十到九十九岁[the]
He is in his early nineties.
他是九十出头的人。

ninth 〔naɪnθ ‖ naɪnθ〕
a. ❶(与 the 连用)第九的,第九个的
❷九分之一的
n.[C] ❶(与 the 连用)第九(个);月的第九日
❷九分之一

no 〔no ‖ nəʊ〕
a. ❶没有
He has no friends in this city.
在这个城市里他没有朋友。
❷不许;不要;没有
No smoking!
严禁吸烟!
ad. ❶(用以表示否定的回答)不,不是,没有
"Is the baby a boy?"
"婴儿是男孩吗?"
"No, it's a girl."
"不,是女孩。"
❷(用在比较级之前)一点也不
He is no older than you.
他并不比你年长。
❸(用于形容词前)并非,并无
It is no different.
这没有什么不同。

Nobel Prize 〔ˈnoˌbɛlˈpraɪz ‖ ˈnəʊbelˌpraɪz〕
n. 诺贝尔奖

noble 〔ˈnobl̩ ‖ ˈnəʊbl〕
a. ❶高贵的,高尚的,崇高的
His friend is a man of noble mind.
他的朋友是个思想高尚的人。
❷贵族的;显贵的
It was said that he was from a noble family.
据说他出身于贵族家庭。

nobody 〔ˈnoˌbɑdɪ ‖ ˈnəʊbɒdɪ〕
pron. 无人,没有人
There was nobody in the room.
房间里没有人。
n. 无足轻重的人,小人物[C]
I am a nobody.
我无足轻重。

nod 〔nɑd ‖ nɒd〕
[过去式]nodded;[过去分词]nodded
vi. ❶点头
She nodded to me friendly.
她友好地向我点了点头。
❷打盹,打瞌睡
She sat nodding by the fire.
她坐在火旁打盹。

N

vt. ❶点(头)

He nodded his head and smiled.

他点头微笑。

❷点头表示;向……点头表示

He nodded his agreement.

他点头表示同意。

n. 点头;打盹,打瞌睡

He greeted us with a nod.

他点头向我们打招呼。

noise 〔nɔɪz ‖ nɔɪz〕

n. 声响;喧闹声[C][U]

What's up? There's such a loud noise in the corridor.

出什么事啦? 走廊里喧闹声那么大。

常用短语

make a noise 发出噪音

Baby is asleep. Don't make a noise.

孩子正在睡觉,不要弄出声音来。

noisy 〔'nɔɪzɪ ‖ 'nɔɪzɪ〕

[比]noisier;[最]noisiest

a. 喧闹的,嘈杂的

Don't be noisy!

别吵闹!

none 〔nʌn ‖ nʌn〕

pron. 没有任何人(或物)[(+of)]

None of the telephones are/is working.

所有的电话都坏了。

None would take the risk.

谁也不愿冒此风险。

ad. 毫不,决不

He spent two weeks in hospital but he's none the better for it.

他在医院住了两星期,但未见好转。

nonsense 〔'nɑnsɛns ‖ 'nɒnsəns〕

n. 胡说;胡闹,愚蠢的举动[U]

He is always talking nonsense.

他老是胡扯。

int. 胡说! 废话!

Nonsense! I don't believe it.

胡扯! 我才不信呢。

noon 〔nun ‖ nuːn〕

n. 正午,中午[U]

The accident happened a little before noon.

事故是在中午前一会儿发生的。

no one 〔'nowʌn ‖ 'nəʊˌwʌn〕

n. 没有人

No one is at home.

没人在家。

nor 〔nɔr ‖ nɔː〕

conj. ❶(用在 neither 之后)也不

I have neither time nor money.

我既没时间也没钱。

❷(用在 not, no, never 等之后)也不

The story is not interesting nor instructive.

这个故事没有趣味，也没有教育意义。

❸(用在句首，句子必须倒装)也不

You do not like him, nor do I.

你不喜欢他，我也不喜欢。

normal 〔ˈnɔrml̩ ‖ ˈnɔːməl〕

a. ❶正常的，正规的，标准的

The doctor said the child's temperature was normal.

医生说孩子体温正常。

❷(人的精神、身体等)正常发育的

He did not seem normal to her.

她觉得他似乎精神不正常。

north 〔nɔrθ ‖ nɔːθ〕

n. 北，北方[the]

I live in a small room facing the north.

我住在一个朝北的小房间里。

〔反义〕 south 南，南方

常用短语

in the north of 在……的北部

Beijing is in the north of China.

北京在中国的北部。

(to the) north of 在……以北

Taipei is to the north of Taichung.

台北在台中以北。

on the north of 邻接……的北方

Russia is on the north of China.

俄罗斯与中国北面接壤。

a. 北的，北方的，北部的

Mexico is in the south of North America.

墨西哥在北美洲南部。

A north wind was blowing hard last night.

昨晚北风刮得很紧。

ad. 向北方；在北方；自北方

He walked north.

他往北走去。

northern 〔ˈnɔrðɚn ‖ ˈnɔːðən〕

a. (在)北方的；向北方的；来自北方的

Our office is on the northern side of the building.

我们的办公室在大楼的北侧。

Norway 〔ˈnɔrwe ‖ ˈnɔːweɪ〕

n. 挪威

nose 〔noz ‖ nəʊz〕

n. 鼻子[C]

He often blows his nose.

他经常擤鼻子。

not 〔nɑt ‖ nɒt〕

ad. ❶不[放在助词或动词后，构成否定]

He is not a member of the Union.

他不是工会会员。

I do not know his name.

我不知道他的名字。

❷(用来代替并否定一个词组或句子)不，不会

Drop that gun! If not, you'll be sorry.

把枪扔下！否则你会后悔的。

❸(与否定词一起构成双重否定表肯定)并非，不怎么

They refused her request not without good reason.

他们不无道理地拒绝了她的请求。

❹(与 all，both，every 连用表示部分否定)不都是，不全是

I don't know all the boys.

我并不认识所有的男孩。

常用短语

not… at all 毫不，一点也不

I do not like it at all.

我一点也不喜欢它。

not…but… 不是……而是……

She is not a student but a teacher.

她不是学生而是老师。

not only … but also … 不但……而且……

He is not only brave but also wise.

他不仅勇敢而且聪明。

note 〔not ‖ nəʊt〕

n. ❶笔记；记录[C]

He never took notes in class.

他上课从不记笔记。

❷注，注释[C]

❸便条；(外交上的)照会[C]

Tom opened the note from his father.

汤姆打开了父亲写给他的便条。

❹纸币；票据[C]

He sent me 4 50-yuan notes.

他寄给我 4 张 50 元面额的钞票。

常用短语

take notes 记笔记

notebook 〔ˈnotˌbʊk ‖ ˈnəʊtbʊk〕

n. ❶笔记本；手册；期票簿[C]

❷笔记本计算机

nothing 〔ˈnʌθɪŋ ‖ ˈnʌθɪŋ〕

pron. 无事；无物；没什么

There is nothing on the table.

桌上什么都没有。

n. 微不足道的事(或人)

His latest play is nothing.
他的新戏一文不值。
ad. 一点也不,并不
Your approach to teaching differs nothing from hers.
你的教学方法同她的教学方法并无不同之处。

常用短语

nothing but 除了,只不过
She is nothing but a child.
她只不过是个孩子。

notice 〔ˈnotɪs ‖ ˈnəʊtɪs〕
[过去式]noticed;[过去分词]noticed
n. ❶公告,通知,贴示[C]
Don't put a notice on the wall.
不要在墙上贴公告。
❷警告;预先通知[U]
They have received notice of the approaching typhoon.
他们已收到台风即将来临的预报。
❸注意;察觉[U]
His special talents attracted my notice.
他特殊的才干引起了我的注意。
vt. ❶注意,注意到
She didn't notice that I had entered the room.
她没有看到我已经走进屋里。
❷通知
The plane was noticed to take off at 6 o'clock.
飞机接到通知 6 点起飞。

noticeable 〔ˈnotɪsəbl̩ ‖ ˈnəʊtɪsəbl〕
a. 显而易见的,显著的,值得注意的
The class made noticeable improvement.
这个班取得了显著的进步。

noun 〔naʊn ‖ naʊn〕
n. 【文】名词[C]

novel 〔ˈnɑvl̩ ‖ ˈnɒvəl〕
n. (长篇)小说[C]
He has written several novels.
他写过好几部小说。

novelist 〔ˈnɑvl̩ɪst ‖ ˈnɒvəlɪst〕
n. 小说家[C]

November 〔noˈvɛmbɚ ‖ nəʊˈvembə〕
n. 略作:Nov. 十一月

now 〔naʊ ‖ naʊ〕
ad. ❶现在,当前,此刻
What time is it now?
现在几点了?
❷立刻,马上
Go now or you'll be late.
你得马上走,不然就要迟到了。

N

❸(用来引出后面的话或加强语气)嗨;那么;喂;却说;好
Now, let's play football.
让我们踢足球吧。

常用短语

just now 刚才
He started for Shanghai just now.
他刚刚动身去了上海。
right now 立刻
Do your homework right now.
马上写作业。
conj. 既然;由于
Now (that) you have come, you may as well stay.
你既然来了,不妨就住下。
n. 现在,当前,此刻[U]
Now is the best time to visit Paris.
当前是造访巴黎的最佳时节。

nowadays 〔ˈnauəˌdez ‖ ˈnauədeɪz〕
ad. 现今,时下
Nowadays young men wear their hair long.
现在年轻人都把头发留长。

nowhere 〔ˈnoˌwɛr ‖ ˈnəuhweə〕
ad. 任何地方都不
He goes nowhere on a rainy day.
下雨天他哪儿都不去。

nuclear 〔ˈnjuklɪə ‖ ˈnjuːklɪə〕
a. 核的;原子核的;原子能的;原子弹的
nuclear weapons
核武器

numb 〔nʌm ‖ nʌm〕
a. 失去感觉的,麻木的[(+with)]
My hands are numb with cold.
我的手冻僵了。

number 〔ˈnʌmbə ‖ ˈnʌmbə〕
n. ❶数,数字[C]
The number of students absent is 5.
有5名学生缺席。
9 is an odd number and 10 is an even number.
9是奇数,10是偶数。
❷号码;第……号[C]
Sam lives at number 20 Park Street.
萨姆住在派克街20号。

常用短语

a large number of 多数的,很多的,许多的
He has a large number of books.
他有很多书。
a number of 很多,一些

N

A number of books are missing.

丢了很多书。

nun 〔nʌn ‖ nʌn〕

n. 修女；尼姑［C］

nurse 〔nɝs ‖ nɜːs〕

n.［C］❶护士

She is a nurse for ward duty.

她是一位病房护士。

❷保姆，奶妈

She left the baby with the nurse.

她把孩子留给保姆。

nursery 〔ˈnɝsərɪ ‖ ˈnɜːsərɪ〕

n. 幼儿室，育儿室，托儿所［C］

Many children are brought up in a nursery.

许多孩子在托儿所长大。

nut 〔nʌt ‖ nʌt〕

n.［C］❶坚果；坚果仁

❷螺母，螺帽

❸难事；难题，难对付的人

Painting the ceiling was a tough nut to crack.

油漆天花板是件难事。

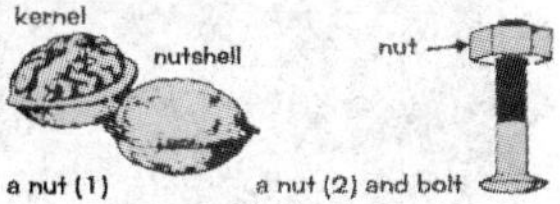

nutrition 〔njuˈtrɪʃən ‖ njuːˈtrɪʃən〕

n. 营养，滋养，食物［U］

Proper nutrition is important for good health.

适当的营养对健康很重要。

nylon 〔ˈnaɪlɑn ‖ ˈnaɪlɒn〕

n. ❶尼龙［U］

The poncho is made of nylon.

这雨披是用尼龙制造的。

❷尼龙长袜［P］

She bought a pair of nylons.

她买了一双尼龙长袜。

N

O

oak 〔ok ‖ əʊk〕
n. 橡树，橡木[C][U]

obedient 〔əˈbidɪənt ‖ əˈbiːdɪənt〕
a. 服从的，顺从的；恭顺的[(＋to)]
He is obedient to his parents.
他很听父母的话。
〔反义〕disobedient 不服从的

obey 〔oˈbe ‖ əʊˈbeɪ〕
[过去式]obeyed；[过去分词]obeyed
vt. 服从；听从；执行；遵守
You didn't obey the manager's instructions.
你没有执行经理的指示。
vi. 服从；听话
The child obeyed and went to bed.
孩子听话，睡觉去了。

object[1] 〔ˈɑbdʒɪkt ‖ ˈɒbdʒɪkt〕
n. ❶物体[C]
I saw a strange object in the sky.
我看见天空中有个不明物体。
❷对象；目标[C][(＋of)]
The object of the game is to score 100 points.
这个游戏的目标是得到100分。
He has no definite object in life.
他没有确定的人生目标。
❸【文】宾语[C]

object[2] 〔əbˈdʒɛkt ‖ əbˈdʒekt〕
[过去式]objected；[过去分词]objected
vi. 反对[(＋to)]
We all objected to the plan.
我们全都反对这个计划。
vt. 提出……作为反对的理由[＋(that)]
He objected that the plan was risky.

他表示反对，说这个计划太冒险。

objection 〔əb'dʒɛkʃən ‖ əb'dʒekʃən〕

n. 反对；异议；不喜欢，反对的理由[C][(+to/against)]

We have no objection to your plan.

我们对你的计划没有异议。

obligation 〔ˌɑblə'geʃən ‖ ˌɒblɪ'geɪʃən〕

n. ❶(道义上或法律上的)义务；责任[C][U]

I have an obligation to help him.

我有义务帮助他。

❷恩惠[C][(+to/toward)]

I feel an obligation to him for his help.

我对于他的帮忙很感激。

oblige 〔ə'blaɪdʒ ‖ ə'blaɪdʒ〕

[过去式]obliged；[过去分词]obliged

vt. ❶ 使不得不，迫使

I was obliged to abandon that idea.

我不得不放弃那个想法。

❷施恩于；答应……的请求

Please oblige me by turning down the radio.

劳您驾，请帮我把收音机音量调低一些。

❸使感激

We're much obliged to you for your information.

我们很感谢你提供的消息。

observation 〔ˌɑbzɚ'veʃən ‖ ˌɒbzə'veɪʃən〕

n. 观察；观测；观察力[C][U]

The experiment requires careful observation.

这个实验需要仔细观察。

observe 〔əb'zɝv ‖ əb'zɜːv〕

[过去式]observed；[过去分词]observed

vt. ❶看到，注意到

He observed a stranger hanging around the store.

他看到一个陌生人在商店附近闲逛。

❷观察，观测；监视

They carefully observed the behavior of deer.

他们仔细观察了鹿的生活习性。

❸遵守，奉行

This law must be strictly observed.

这项法律必须严格遵守。

obstacle 〔'ɑbstəkl̩ ‖ 'ɒbstəkl〕

n. 障碍(物)；妨碍[C][(+to)]

obtain 〔əb'ten ‖ əb'teɪn〕

[过去式]obtained；[过去分词]

O

obtained

vt. 得到，获得

He failed to obtain a scholarship.

他没有获得奖学金。

vi. 得到公认；通用；流行；存在

Those conditions no longer obtain.

那些情形已不存在。

obvious 〔ˈɑbvɪəs ‖ ˈɒbvɪəs〕

a. 明显的；显著的

It was quite obvious that she was not going home.

很显然她不准备回家。

obviously 〔ˈɑbvɪəslɪ ‖ ˈɒbvɪəslɪ〕

ad. 明显地；显然地

occasion 〔əˈkeʒən ‖ əˈkeɪʒən〕

n. ❶场合，时刻；重大活动，盛典[C]

I met her on several occasions.

我在好几种场合遇到过她。

The anniversary was quite an occasion.

周年纪念是件大事。

❷时机，机会[C][(＋for)]

He seized the occasion to invite her home for dinner.

他抓住机会邀请她到家里吃饭。

occasional 〔əˈkeʒənl̩ ‖ əˈkeɪʒənəl〕

a. ❶偶尔的，非经常的

She likes an occasional glass of wine.

她喜欢偶尔喝杯酒。

❷特殊场合的，应景的

Occasional music was played at the graduation.

毕业典礼上演奏了庆典的音乐。

occupation 〔ˌɑkjəˈpeʃən ‖ ˌɒkjʊˈpeɪʃən〕

n. ❶工作，职业[C]

He is a bus driver by occupation.

他的职业是公共汽车司机。

❷占领，占据；占领时期[U]

The Japanese occupation of Taiwan lasted 51 years.

日本占领台湾达51年之久。

职业的各种问法：
What do you do?
你是做什么工作的？
Where do you work?
你在哪里工作？
What is your occupation?
你的职业是什么？
What line are you in?
你是从事哪一行的？

用法工具箱

occupy 〔ˈɑkjəˌpaɪ ‖ ˈɒkjʊˌpaɪ〕

[过去式]occupied;[过去分词]occupied

vt. ❶占领,占据

The enemy soon occupied the town.

敌人很快占领了这个城镇。

❷占(时间、空间),占用,居(某种地位)

Reading occupies most of my free time.

阅读占去了我大部分的空闲时间。

❸(常与 oneself 连用或作被动式)使忙碌,使从事[(+ in/with)]

This game will keep the children occupied.

这个游戏让孩子有得忙了。

She occupied herself with routine office tasks.

她忙于办公室的日常工作。

occur 〔əˈkɚ ‖ əˈkɜː〕

[过去式]occurred;[过去分词]occurred

vi. ❶发生

Earthquakes occur frequently in this area.

这个地区经常发生地震。

❷被想起,被想到,浮现[(+ to)]

It occurred to me to visit my teacher.

我想到要去看看我的老师。

ocean 〔ˈoʃən ‖ ˈəuʃən〕

n. 海洋;海[the]

Humans may be able to live in the depths of the ocean some day.

有朝一日人类也许能在海洋深处生活。

o'clock 〔əˈklɑk ‖ əˈklɒk〕

ad. ……点钟

He left at 5 o'clock.

他 5 点出发。

October 〔ɑkˈtobɚ ‖ ɒkˈtəubə〕

n. 略作 Oct. 十月

odd 〔ɑd ‖ ɒd〕

a. ❶奇特的,古怪的

He's an odd old man.

他是个古怪的老头儿。

❷单只的,不成对的;零散的

It's no use keeping this odd stocking.

单只的袜子留着没什么用。

❸奇数的,单数的

5 and 9 are odd numbers.

5 和 9 是奇数。

❹临时的,不固定的;非经常的

I did many odd jobs.

我干过很多临时工作。

odo(u)r 〔ˈodɚ ‖ ˈəudə〕

n. 气味;香气;臭气[C]

The odor filled the room.
那气味充满了房间。
〔同义〕smell 气味

of〔(强)ɑv ‖ ɒv;(弱)əv ‖ əv〕
prep. ❶……的,属于
One of the legs of the table is broken.
桌子的一条腿坏了。
❷用……做成的;由……制成
The house is made of stone.
这房子是石头建的。
❸……的,……的量
I'd like to have a cup of coffee.
我想喝杯咖啡。
❹……之中的;……的成员
Of all the students in this class, Tom is the best.
在这个班级中,汤姆是最优秀的。
❺(表示同位)
the city of Beijing
北京市
❻(表示宾格关系)
his knowledge of English (= that he knows English)
他的英语知识
❼(表示主格关系)
the play of Shakespeare (= Shakespeare's play)
莎士比亚的著作
❽来自……的;出自
the people of China
中国人民
❾因为
He died of cancer.
他死于癌症。

off〔ɔf ‖ ɔːf〕
ad. ❶(离)开,(走)开,(隔)开
They went off together and left me sitting there.
他们一同离开了,留下我独自坐在那里。
❷(时间、空间上)离,距
The town is 5 miles off.
那个城镇离这儿5英里远。
❸切断,关掉,停止;取消;不在工作,休息
He turned off the light before going out.
他出门前把灯关了。
❹完,光,直到最后
He drank it off.
他把这全喝光了。

常用短语

be well off 富有
prep. ❶离开……,隔着……,从……脱落,从……掉下
He lifted a cup off the table.
他从桌上拿起一只杯子。
❷偏离……;失去……
You're going off the subject.
你们离题了。

offend 〔əˈfɛnd ‖ əˈfend〕
[过去式]offended;[过去分词] offended
vt. ❶冒犯;触怒;伤害……的感情
We were offended by his rude words.
我们被他无礼的话所激怒。
❷使不舒服
The smell offends me.
这气味令我作呕。

offer 〔ˈɔfɚ ‖ ˈɔːfə〕
[过去式]offered;[过去分词] offered
vt. ❶给予,提供;拿出,出示 [(+to)]
He offered a glass of wine to me.
他端给我一杯酒。
❷愿意;试图(做某事);提议 [+to-v]
They offered to help me.
他们表示愿意帮助我。
❸出(价);开(价)
We offered him the calculator for $50.
这台计算机我们向他开价 50 美元。
n. 提供,提议[C][(+of)][+to-v]
Thank you for your kind offer of help.
感谢你想给予帮助的好意。

office 〔ˈɔfɪs ‖ ˈɔːfɪs〕
n. ❶办公室,营业处,政府机关,公署[C]
His office is on the third floor.
他的办公室在三楼。
❷官职,职务[C][U]
He was elected to the office of mayor.
他被选上担任市长一职。

officer 〔ˈɔfəsɚ ‖ ˈɔːfɪsə〕
n. [C] ❶军官
The officers live here, and the enlisted men live over there.
军官住在这里,士兵住在那里。
❷(政府)公务员,官员;干事,高级职员
Bank officers are well-paid.
银行高级职员薪金高。
❸警官,警察
A police officer came to our help when our car broke down on the way.
我们的汽车在路上出了毛病,一位警官帮了我们忙。

official 〔əˈfɪʃəl ‖ əˈfɪʃəl〕
a. ❶官员的;公务上的
The President's official duties include being Commander in Chief.

O

总统的职责包括担任总司令。
❷官方的，法定的；正式的
Is the news official?
这个消息是官方发布的吗？
❸摆官架子的；讲究形式的
His official airs offended her.
他那副官架子令她十分不快。

often 〔'ɔfən ‖ 'ɔ:fn〕
［比］oftener，more often；［最］oftenest，most often
ad. ❶常常，时常
We often go hunting.
我们常常去打猎。
❷往往，通常
Man is often taller than woman.
一般说来男子比女子高。

常用短语

how often 多久一次
How often have you been there?
你多久去那里一次？

oh 〔o ‖ əʊ〕
int. ❶（表示惊讶，恐惧等）哦，啊，哎呀
Oh, what a nightmare!
啊，真是一场噩梦！
❷（用于招呼）喂，噢
Oh, George, have you seen this?
嗨，乔治，你看见过这个吗？

oil 〔ɔɪl ‖ ɔɪl〕
n. ❶油，石油，汽油［U］
Mexico is self-sufficient in oil.
墨西哥在石油方面可自给自足。
❷油画颜料［P］
He is good at painting in oils.
他擅长画油画。

O. K. 〔o'ke ‖ əʊ'keɪ〕
a.【口】❶可以的；不错的
The new schedule is O. K. with me.
新日程表对我是合适的。
❷很好的
Everything is O. K.
一切都好。
ad.【口】❶尚可；挺好
She is doing O. K. at school.
她在学校挺好。
❷对吧
"What do you know about life here?"
"对这里的生活情况你了解多少？"
"O. K. , so I wasn't born here, but I've spent a lot of time here."
"对，我不是在这儿出生的，可我已在这里生活了很久。"
int.【口】好，行
"Shall we go now?"
"我们现在就去好吗？"

O

"O. K."
"好的。"

old 〔old ‖ əʊld〕
[比]older;[最]oldest
a. ❶老的,上了年纪的,古老的
Oxford is an old university.
牛津大学是一所古老的大学。
❷旧的;破旧的
❸……岁(的)
My father is 50 years old.
我的父亲50岁了。
❹以前的,原来的
He got his old job back.
他恢复了原来的工作。

old-fashioned 〔ˌold'fæʃənd ‖ ˌəʊld'fæʃənd〕
a. 旧式的,过时的
He had a very old-fashioned watch.
他有一只旧式手表.

olive 〔'ɑlɪv ‖ 'ɒlɪv〕
n. ❶橄榄[C]
❷橄榄树[C]

橄榄树
olive

❸橄榄色[U]

Olympics 〔ə'lɪmpɪks ‖ ə'lɪmpɪks〕
n. 奥林匹克运动会(=Olympic Games)
The Olympics are held every 4 years.
奥运会每4年举办一次。

omit 〔o'mɪt ‖ əʊ'mɪt〕
[过去式]omitted;[过去分词]omitted
vt. ❶遗漏;省略;删去[(+from)]
You may omit the second paragraph from the article.
这篇文章的第二段你可以略去。
❷忽略不做;忘记[+to-v][+v-ing]
He omitted reading the second page.
他忘了读第二页。

on 〔ɑn ‖ ɒn〕
prep. ❶在……上(位置)
He laid a hand on my shoulder.
他把一只手放在我肩上。
❷以……支持,挂在……上;以……为轴
There is a picture on the wall.
墙上有一幅画。
He jumped on one leg.
他单腿跳。

O

once

❸朝，向，靠近，在……旁，沿着
She stood on my left.
她站在我左边。
❹在……的时候（特定的时间）
We have no school on Sunday.
我们星期天不上学。

用法工具箱

on ＋日
It happened on Monday.
这事发生在星期一。
in ＋ 年或月
I was born in June.
我在六月出生。
at ＋ 时间
I got up at 6 o'clock.
我 6 点钟起床。

❺关于，有关
This is a book on history.
这是本有关历史的书。
❻以……方式，通过
I watched the game on television.
我从电视上看了这场比赛。
❼凭……，靠……；使用……，吃……
The Chinese live on rice.
中国人主要吃米饭。
❽处于……状态，进行中
The building is on fire.
那栋建筑物着火了。
ad. ❶继续
They talked on until midnight.
他们一直谈到深夜。
❷穿上，盖上；连接上
It's cold today. Why don't you put your overcoat on?
今天很冷。为什么不把大衣穿上？
❸（机器）处于工作状态；开着；通着
He left the engine on while waiting for Joe.
他在等候乔时让汽车引擎开着。
〔反义〕off 关着

常用短语

on and on 继续不断地
He talked on and on.
他不停地说话。
on doing 一……就……
On arriving at the station, I telephoned her.
一到车站，我就给她打了电话。

once 〔wʌns ‖ wʌns〕
ad. ❶一次，一回
I see them once every two months.
我每两个月与他们见一次面。
❷昔日，曾经

one

He once knew her, but they are no longer friends.
他以前认识她,但他们已经不是朋友了。

常用短语

once and again 一再地
She was late once and again.
她一再迟到。
once in a while 有时,偶尔
I heard from her once in a while.
我偶尔收到她的来信。
once again＝ once more 再次
Write it once more.
重写一遍。
once upon a time 从前(讲故事的开头语)
Once upon a time there was an old man.
从前有个老人。
n. 一次,一回
Once is enough.
一次就够了。

常用短语

all at once 突然
All at once we heard a loud noise.
突然间我听到一声巨响。
at once 立刻,马上
Do it at once!
马上干!
conj. 一旦,一经……便……
Once you get into a bad habit, you'll find it hard to get out of it.
一旦染上坏习惯,想改掉就难了。

one 〔wʌn ‖ wʌn〕
n. ❶ 一;一个
One plus two equals three.
一加二等于三。
❷一个人;一件事物
Is this the one I gave you?
这是我给你的那一个吗?
a. ❶一个的
One swallow does not make a summer.
一燕不成夏(单凭一事不足以下判断)。
❷某一个的
One Thursday afternoon he got seriously injured in an accident.
一个星期四下午,他在事故中受了重伤。

常用短语

for one thing 一则
I cannot go. For one thing I have no money.
我不去,理由之一是我没钱。
pron. ❶一个人;任何人
One can not learn a language

O

well unless one works hard.
学好一种语言非下苦功不可。
❷(表示与别的对照)这一个人(或物)
Here are two pens; one is for you and the other is for your younger sister.
这儿有两支钢笔;这支给你,另一支给你妹妹。
❸(代替上下文中的名词或名词词组)
I need a pen. Can you lend me one?
我需要笔。你能借我一支吗?

one 指不特定的东西;it 指特定的东西
I don't have a knife. Lend me one.
我没有刀,借我一把。
I want your knife. Lend it to me.
我要你的刀,把它借给我。

用法工具箱

O

常用短语

one after another 一个接一个
They came in the classroom one after another.
他们陆续走进教室。
one another 彼此,互相
They helped one another.
他们互相帮助。

oneself 〔wʌn'sɛlf ‖ wʌn'self〕
pron. ❶(反身代词)自己,自身
At the age of 6 one ought to dress oneself.
到6岁,就应该自己穿衣服了。
❷亲自,本人
To do something oneself is often easier than getting someone else to do it.
自己去办理一件事常常比请人去做来得容易。

onion 〔'ʌnjən ‖ 'ʌnjən〕
n.【植】洋葱[C]

洋葱头
onion

We grow onions in the backyard.
我们在后院里种上洋葱。

only 〔'onlɪ ‖ 'əʊnlɪ〕
a. ❶唯一的,仅有的
He is an only son.

他是独生子。

❷最好的，最合适的，无可匹敌的，独一无二的

She is the only person for the job.

她是担任这个工作最合适的人选。

ad. ❶只，仅仅，才

At present we can only wait and see.

当前我们只好等等再说。

❷不料；反而，结果却

I walked all the way from home to the library, only to find it closed.

我从家里一路走到图书馆，不料已经关门了。

常用短语

not only…but also… 不仅……而且……

I can speak not only English but also French.

我不仅会说英语还会说法语。

onto 〔'ɑntʊ || 'ɒntʊ〕

prep. 到……之上；向……之上

The cat jumped onto the chair.

猫跳到椅子上了。

onward 〔'ɑnwəd || 'ɒnwəd〕

ad. 向前；在前面

The world is moving onward.

世界正向前发展。

a. 向前的，前进的

The plane's onward movement was slowed by adverse winds.

飞机前进的速度因逆风而减慢。

open 〔'opən || 'əupən〕

［过去式］opened；［过去分词］opened

vt. ❶开，打开；铺开，展开

I opened the window after I got up.

我起床后便把窗子打开。

❷开始

The Conference was opened on October 15.

大会于 10 月 15 日开始。

❸使开张（营业）

He opened a grocery last month.

上个月他开了一个杂货铺。

❹开通，开辟

They opened a way through the forest.

他们开了一条穿过森林的路。

vi. ❶开；张开；展开

The buds are starting to open.

花蕾开始绽放。

❷开始；开业

The fair opened on March 17.

交易会于 3 月 17 日开幕。

❸展现

A great future opens before them.
远大的前程展现在他们面前。
a. ❶打开的
My door is always open to visitors.
我的门永远向来访者敞开。
❷开阔的，空旷的
In front of us we saw a stretch of open fields.
我们看到在我们的眼前是一片开阔的田野。
❸敞开的，开着的；无顶的
an open car
敞篷车
an open drain
排水明沟
❹悬而未决的，未定的
This is still an open question.
这仍然是一个尚未解决的问题。
❺营业的，办公的；开放的，可以自由参加的[(＋to)]
The swimming pool is open to the pubic.
这个游泳池对公众开放。
The store is open from 10 a. m. to 6 p. m.
这家店从上午10点到下午6点营业。
❻愿意接受的；易招致……的[(＋to)]
Children are open to various influences.
孩子容易受到各种影响。

open-air 〔ˌopən'ɛr ‖ ˌəʊpən'eə〕
a. 露天的；户外的；野外的

opener 〔'opənɚ ‖ 'əʊpənə〕
n. 开启的工具[C]
a can opener
开罐器

opera 〔'ɑpərə ‖ 'ɒpərə〕
n. 歌剧[C]
Carmen is a well-known opera.
《卡门》是一部有名的歌剧。

operate 〔'ɑpəˌret ‖ 'ɒpəreɪt〕
[过去式]operated；[过去分词]operated
vi. ❶工作；运作；运转
The machine is not operating properly.
机器运转得不正常。
❷营业，运营
His company operates in several countries.
他的公司在几个国家有业务活动。
❸起作用，影响，生成效果
The medicine operated quickly.
这药很快起作用。
❹动手术，开刀[(＋on/for)]
The doctor operated on my fa-

ther.
这个医生给我父亲做手术。
vt. 操作;开动(机器)等
Who operates that machine?
那台机器由谁操作?

operation 〔ɑpəˈreʃən ‖ ˌɒpəˈreɪʃən〕
n. ❶操作;运转[U]
The operation of this machine is simple.
这个机器的操作很简单。
❷经营;营运[U]
The operation of a railroad needs many men.
铁路的营运需要很多人。
❸作用;效力[U]
The operation of natural law is constant.
自然法则的作用是永恒的。
❹【医】手术[C][(+on/for)]

operator 〔ˈɑpəˌretɚ ‖ ˈɒpəˌreɪtə〕
n. [C] ❶操作者,技工
❷接线员

opinion 〔əˈpɪnjən ‖ əˈpɪnjən〕
n. ❶意见,见解;主张[C][(+of/on/about)]
Opinions differ on this matter.
对这件事各人看法不一。
❷(群体的)观点,信仰[U]
Public opinion is in favor of the plan.
舆论支持这个计划。

opium 〔ˈopɪəm ‖ ˈəupɪəm〕
n. [U] 鸦片

opponent 〔əˈponənt ‖ əˈpəunənt〕
n. 对手;敌手,反对者[C]
She defeated her opponent in the match.
她在比赛中击败了对手。

opportunity 〔ˌɑpɚˈtjunətɪ ‖ ˌɒpəˈtjuːnɪtɪ〕
n. 机会;良机[C][U][(+of/for)][+to-v]
There may be an opportunity for you to see the chairman of the board tomorrow.
明天你也许有机会见到董事长。

oppose 〔əˈpoz ‖ əˈpəuz〕
[过去式]opposed;[过去分词]opposed
vt. ❶反对;反抗;妨碍[+v-ing]
He would oppose changing the law.
他将反对改变这个法规。
❷使相对;使对抗[(+to)]
They were bitterly opposed to the scheme.
他们强烈反对这个计划。

opposite 〔ˈɑpəzɪt ‖ ˈɒpəzɪt〕
a. ❶相反的,对立的[(+to)]

O

They have opposite views on the question.
在这个问题上他们持相反的观点。
Idealism is opposite to materialism.
唯心论和唯物论是对立的。
❷对面的，相对的[(＋to)]
His store is opposite to mine.
他的店在我的店的对面。
prep. 在……对面
The post office is opposite the bank.
邮局在银行对面。
ad. 在对面
They sat opposite on the lawn.
他们面对面坐在草坪上。

opposition 〔ˌɑpəˈzɪʃən ‖ ˌɒpəˈzɪʃən〕
n. 反对；反抗；对抗[(＋to)][U]
Mother was in opposition to my plan.
母亲反对我的计划。

oppress 〔əˈprɛs ‖ əˈpres〕
[过去式]oppressed；[过去分词]oppressed
vt. ❶压迫；压制
High prices are oppressing our daily life.
高物价压迫着我们的生活。
❷使(心情)沉重；使烦恼，折磨
Many troubles oppressed me.
许多麻烦困扰着我。

oppression 〔əˈprɛʃən ‖ əˈpreʃən〕
n. ❶压迫，压制[C][U]
❷压抑；沉闷[U]

optimism 〔ˈɑptəˌmɪzəm ‖ ˈɒptɪmɪzəm〕
n. 乐观；乐观主义[U]

or 〔(强)ɔr ‖ ɔː；(弱)ɚ ‖ ə〕
conj. ❶或者；还是
Either you or I am to go.
你我之间总有一个人要去。
❷否则，要不然
Hurry up, or you'll be late.
快点，否则你会迟到的。
❸也就是说，换言之
It is zoology, or the study of animals.
这是动物学，也就是动物的研究。

常用短语

or so 大约
We cannot master a foreign language in a year or so.
我们无法在一年左右掌握一门外语。

oral 〔ˈɔrəl ‖ ˈɔːrəl〕
a. 口头的，口述的
an oral examination

口试

orange〔'ɔrɪndʒ ‖ 'ɔːrɪndʒ〕

n. ❶橙,柑橘[C]

He bought a crate of oranges for his children.

他给孩子们买了一箱柑橘。

❷橙色,橘黄色[U]

orbit〔'ɔrbɪt ‖ 'ɔːbɪt〕

n. (天体等的)运行轨道[C][U]

The satellite was launched into the orbit around the moon.

卫星被发射进入绕月球运行的轨道。

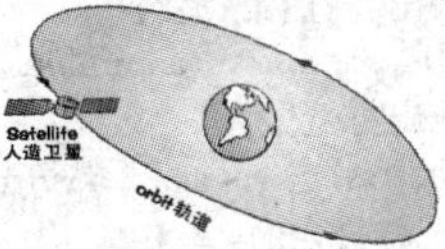

orchestra〔'ɔrkɪstrə ‖ 'ɔːkɪstrə〕

n. 管弦乐队[C]

The orchestra played a Mozart symphony.

乐队演奏了一首莫扎特的交响曲。

order〔'ɔrdɚ ‖ 'ɔːdə〕

[过去式]ordered;[过去分词]ordered

vt. ❶命令;指挥[+(that)]

The mayor ordered that free food be distributed.

市长命令发放免费食品。

❷订购;叫(菜或饮料)[(+for)]

Please order a copy for me.

请给我订购一本。

n. ❶顺序,次序[U]

The names are in alphabetical order.

名字按字母顺序排列。

❷状况;良好的状况[U]

Things were in terrible order.

情况一团糟。

❸秩序,治安;规律[U]

The young teacher can't keep order in her classes.

那位年轻教师无法维持课堂秩序。

❹命令,指示[C]

You must obey my orders.

你必须服从我的命令。

❺订购;订货[C]

He placed an order with the company for the books.

他向那家公司订购了这些书。

O

常用短语

in order 整齐的

Put the books in order.

把书放整齐。

in order that/ in order to… 为了……

He worked hard in order that

he could succeed. (= He worked hard in order to succeed.)
他努力工作是为了成功。

ordinary [ˈɔrdn̩ˌɛrɪ ‖ ˈɔːdɪnərɪ]
a. ❶通常的,平常的
She had in an ordinary dress.
她穿着平常的衣服。
❷普通的,平凡的
The novel describes the way of life of the ordinary people there.
这部小说描写了那里普通人的生活方式。

organ [ˈɔrgən ‖ ˈɔːgən]
n. [C] ❶器官
The heart is one of the body's important organs.
心脏是人体的重要器官之一。
❷机构,机关
A court is an organ of government.
法庭是一个政府机构。

O

organization [ˌɔrgənəˈzeʃən ‖ ˌɔːgənaɪˈzeɪʃən]
n. ❶组织,机构,团体[C]
It is a non-profit organization.
这是一个非营利性的组织。
❷组织工作;体制,编制[U]
He is engaged in the organization of a new club.
他正参与组建一个新的俱乐部。
❸条理,系统[U]
Efficiency depends on good organization.
高效率依赖于良好的组织。

Orient [ˈɔrɪˌənt ‖ ˈɔːrɪənt]
n. (大写)亚洲;东方(国家)[the]

origin [ˈɔrədʒɪn ‖ ˈɔːrɪdʒɪn]
n. [C][U]❶起源;由来;起因
What was the origin of the quarrel?
这场争吵的起因是什么?
❷出身;门第;血统
His origins were humble.
他出身低微。

original [əˈrɪdʒənl̩ ‖ əˈrɪdʒənl]
a. ❶最初的,本来的;原始的
The original price of the car was a bit too high.
这辆汽车原来的价格有点高。
❷有独创性的;新颖的;奇特的
He is an original dramatist.
他是个有独创性的剧作家。
❸原作的;原本的
This is an original painting by Picasso.
这是一幅毕加索的原作。
n. [C]❶原物,原著,原画,原版,原文

The original of this picture was nowhere to be found.
这幅画的原作已无处寻觅。
❷原著的语言［the］
He can read Shakespeare in the original.
他能读原版本的莎士比亚作品。

orphan〔ˈɔrfən ‖ ˈɔːfən〕
n. 孤儿［C］

other〔ˈʌðɚ ‖ ˈʌðə〕
a. ❶（两者中）另一个的；其余的
Her firstborn is a doctor. Her other children are all in the army.
她的长子是医生，其余几个孩子都在部队服役。
❷别的，其他的；更多的，额外的，不同的
There are other ways to do this exercise.
做这个练习还可用别的方法。

常用短语

the other day 几天前
I saw him the other day.
我几天前见过他。

pron. ❶（两个中的）另一个人（或物）；另一方［the］
It is hard to tell the twin brothers one from the other.
这对孪生兄弟很难分辨。
❷其余的人（或物）
Some boys are reading; others are listening to the radio.
有些孩子在阅读，有些则在听收音机。

常用短语

each other 相互
They love each other.
他们互相爱慕。

one after the other 交互地
He lifted his feet one after the other.
他交互抬脚。

otherwise〔ˈʌðɚˌwaɪz ‖ ˈʌðəwaɪz〕
ad. ❶用别的方法；不同样地
We'll get there somehow, by boat or otherwise.
我们总要设法去那里的，乘船也好，用其他办法也好。
❷在其他方面；除此以外
The rent is a bit high, but otherwise the house is satisfactory.
这所房子租金贵了点，但在其他方面倒是令人满意的。
❸否则，不然
I'm not feeling very well today, otherwise I would do it myself.
今天我身体不太舒服，否则这

事我就亲自去做了。

ought 〔ɔt ‖ ɔːt〕

v. aux. ❶(表示义务,责任等)应当,应该

Students ought to study hard.

学生应该努力学习。

❷(表示愿望)应该,该

You ought to read his novels.

你应该读读他的小说。

❸(表示可能性,期望)该

It ought to be a fine day tomorrow.

明天该是个好天气。

ounce 〔aʊns ‖ aʊns〕

n. ❶盎司,英两[C]

There are 16 ounces in 1 pound.

1 磅有 16 盎司。

❷(常用于否定句)一点点,少量[(+of)]

The dancers didn't have an ounce of energy left.

舞蹈演员们用尽了体力。

O

our 〔'aʊr ‖ 'aʊə〕

pron. (we 的所有格)我们的

Our country is rich in resources.

我国资源丰富。

ours 〔'aʊrz ‖ 'aʊəz〕

pron. (we 的名词性物主代词)我们的东西;我们的家属

Ours is an industrial city.

我们的城市是个工业城市。

ourselves 〔ˌaʊr'sɛlvz ‖ ˌaʊə'selvz〕

pron. ❶(we 的反身代词)我们自己

We have bought ourselves a new house.

我们给自己买了一栋新房子。

❷(用以加强语气)我们亲自,我们本人

We have a bathroom to ourselves.

我们自己有一间浴室,不必和人共用。

out 〔aʊt ‖ aʊt〕

ad. ❶出外;在外;向外

Let's go out for a walk.

我们出去散散步吧。

❷在外;不在家(或办公室);在室外

All yesterday he was out.

昨天他整天在外。

〔反义〕in 在内

❸消失,用完

The oil has run out.

油已经用完了。

❹出现;问世;显露

His secret got out.

他的秘密泄露了。

❺从……向外

He came out of the room.
他从房间里出来。
❻完全；彻底
I was tired out.
我累死了。
❼脱离……状态
The patient is out of danger.
病人已脱离险境。
❽(用)完；熄灭；(机器)停转
The wind blew the candle out.
风把烛火吹熄了。

outbreak 〔ˈaʊtˌbrek ‖ ˈaʊtˌbreɪk〕
n. 爆发[C][(＋of)]
He was born just before the outbreak of the war.
他是在战争爆发前出生的。

outburst 〔ˈaʊtˌbɝst ‖ ˈaʊtbɜːst〕
n. (情感、力量等的)爆发，迸发[C][(＋of)]
an outburst of temper
发脾气

outdoors 〔ˌaʊtˈdɔrz ‖ ˈaʊtˈdɔːz〕
ad. 在户外，在野外，在露天；往户外
〔反义〕indoors 在室内

outline 〔ˈaʊtˌlaɪn ‖ ˈaʊtlaɪn〕
n. ❶[C]外形；轮廓[(＋of)]
the outline of a footprint in the snow
雪中脚印的轮廓
❷提纲，概要；要点；草案[(＋of)]
He gave me an outline of the plan.
他向我说明那个计划的概要。

outlook 〔ˈaʊtˌlʊk ‖ ˈaʊtlʊk〕
n. [C]❶观点，看法[(＋on)]
a correct outlook on life
正确的人生观
❷展望，前景[(＋for)]
The business outlook for next year is not good.
明年的商业前景并不乐观。
❸景色，景致
The outlook around the house is fine.
这所房子的周围景色优美。

out-of-date 〔ˌaʊtəvˈdet ‖ ˌaʊtəvˈdeɪt〕
a. 旧式的；不流行的

output 〔ˈaʊtˌpʊt ‖ ˈaʊtpʊt〕
n. [C][U]❶产量
the annual output
年产量
❷【计算机】输出；输出信息
〔反义〕input 输入

outside1 〔ˈaʊtˈsaɪd ‖ ˌaʊtˈsaɪd〕
n. ❶外面，外部[the]
The outside of the house is painted white.
房子外部漆成白色。

〔反义〕inside 里面

❷外表，外观

He has a rough outside but a good heart.

他外表粗鲁，但心地善良。

a. 外边的，外部的，外面的

The outside walls are brick.

外墙是砖砌的。

ad. 在外面，向外面

A car is waiting outside.

外面有辆车在等着。

〔反义〕inside 在里面

outside²〔aut'said ‖ aut'said〕

prep. 在……外；向……外

Outside the window it is a wonderful spring morning.

窗外是一片美妙的春天晨景。

outstanding〔aut'stændiŋ ‖ aut'stændiŋ〕

a. 显著的；杰出的；重要的

an outstanding person

杰出的人物

outward〔'autwəd ‖ 'autwəd〕

O

a. ❶向外的；往外去的

The outward flow of gold is very rapid.

黄金的外流非常快。

❷外表的；表面的

That's only outward cheerfulness.

那只是表面的欢乐。

ad. 向外；出海，出港

The door opens outward.

这扇门向外开。

〔反义〕inward 向内

oven〔'ʌvən ‖ 'ʌvən〕

n.［C］❶炉，灶

❷烤箱

She took the pie out of the oven and turned the gas off.

她将派从烤箱中拿出来并关掉了瓦斯。

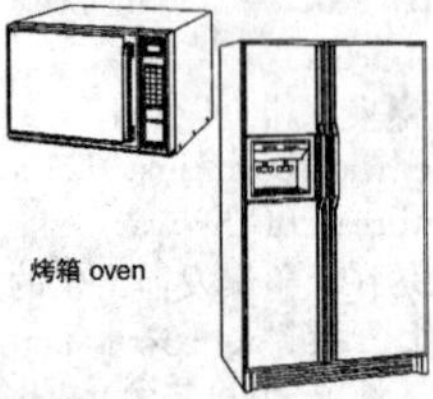

烤箱 oven

over〔'ovə ‖ 'əuvə〕

prep. ❶在……之上，在正上方

We live over a small bookstore.

我们住在一家小书店的楼上。

❷(覆盖)在……上面

We spread a carpet over the floor.

我们给地板铺上了地毯。

❸越过……

A plane flew over the house.

一架飞机飞过了房子。

❹遍及，到处

He traveled all over the world.
他游遍了世界。
❹职位等高于;支配;监督
He ruled over the country.
他统治着那个国家。
❻超过,多余
Over 40 boys and girls came to see me.
有40多个男孩女孩来看过我。
❼在……期间
I stayed at home over the holidays.
假期我一直待在家里。
❽一面……一面……
We had a chat over a cup of coffee.
我们一边喝咖啡一边聊天。
ad. ❶在上方;在上空
I heard a plane flying over.
我听见飞机从上空飞过。
❷倒下,翻倒
He fell over on the ice.
他跌倒在冰上。
❸从一边至另一边;越过
She stepped over to the other side to avoid meeting him.
她走到大街另一边,避免与他相遇。
❹越出边缘;溢出
The soup spilled over.
汤溢出来了。
❺剩余;更多,较大
Is there any cement over?
有多出来的水泥吗?

常用短语

over and over (again) 再三
She read the letter over and over again.
她把那封信读了好几遍。
over there 在那边
You will see a tall building over there.
在那边你会看到一个高大的建筑物。
a. ❶结束的,完了的
Summer is over. It is autumn now.
夏天过去了。秋天到了。
❷上面的;上方的
❸(蛋)双面煎的

overcoat 〔ˈovɚˌkot ‖ ˈəuvəkəut〕
n. 外套,大衣[C]

大衣 overcoat

overcome 〔ˌovɚˈkʌm ‖ ˌəuvəˈkʌm〕

[过去式]overcame;[过去分词]overcome
vt. ❶战胜;克服
The learner of a second language has many obstacles to overcome.
第二语言学习者有许多障碍要克服。
❷(被动语态)使软弱,受不了[(+by/with)]
He was overcame by the heat.
他热得受不了。

overhear 〔ˌovəˈhɪr ‖ ˌəuvəˈhɪə〕
[过去式]overheard;[过去分词]overheard
vt. 偶然听到,无意中听到;偷听到
Do not talk so loud, you may be overheard.
别这么大声说话,别人会听见的。

overlook 〔ˌovəˈluk ‖ ˌəuvəˈluk〕
[过去式]overlooked;[过去分词]overlooked
vt. ❶眺望;俯瞰
The house on the hill overlooks the valley.
从小山上的房子能俯瞰山谷。
❷看漏;忽略
My calculation was wrong because I overlooked one tiny point.
由于忽略了一个细微之处,我的计算错了。
❸宽恕,宽容
He has been kind enough to overlook my fault.
他很宽容,原谅了我的错。

overnight[1] 〔ˈovəˈnaɪt ‖ ˌəuvəˈnaɪt〕
ad. 通宵;整夜;在夜里
The weather changed overnight.
天气在夜里变了。

overnight[2] 〔ˈovəˈnaɪt ‖ ˈəuvənaɪt〕
a. 一整夜的
an overnight trip
一宿的旅行

overseas 〔ˈovəˈsiz ‖ ˌəuvəˈsiːz〕
ad. 在(或向)海外;在(或向)国外
〔同义〕abroad 在国外
a. (在)海外的;(在)国外的

oversleep 〔ˈovəˈslip ‖ ˈəuvəˈsliːp〕
[过去式]overslept;[过去分词]overslept
vi. 睡过头
He overslept and was late for school.
他睡过了头,因而上学迟到了。

O

overwhelm 〔ˌovɚˈhwɛlm ‖ ˌəʊvəˈwelm〕

［过去式］overwhelmed；［过去分词］overwhelmed

vt. 战胜；征服；压倒，使受不了；使不知所措［(＋by/with)］

She was overwhelmed by grief.

她不胜悲伤。

We overwhelmed them by numbers.

我们的人数压倒了他们。

overwork 〔ˌovɚˈwɝk ‖ ˌəʊvəˈwɜːk〕

［过去式］overworked；［过去分词］overworked

vt. vi. (使)过分劳累；(使)工作过度

He has been overworking.

他已经劳累过度了。

owe 〔o ‖ əʊ〕

［过去式］owed；［过去分词］owed

vt. ❶欠(债等)［(＋to/for)］

I owe the landlord 100 dollars. (＝ I owe 100 dollars to the landlord.)

我欠房东 100 美元。

❷(应)感激［(＋to)］

We owe a great deal to our parents.

我们深受父母之恩。

❸应该把……归功于［(＋to)］

We owe the principle of gravitation to Newton.

我们全靠牛顿才知道引力的原理。

vi. 欠钱

I still owe for my car.

我还欠着买汽车的钱。

owl 〔aʊl ‖ aʊl〕

n. ［C］ ❶【动】猫头鹰

❷常熬夜的人，惯于夜间活动的人

猫头鹰
owl

own 〔on ‖ əʊn〕

［过去式］owned；［过去分词］owned

vt. 有，拥有

He owns 3 cars.

他有 3 辆汽车。

a. ❶自己的

I saw the whole accident with my own eyes.

我亲眼看到这次事故发生的全过程。

❷特有的

He left the company to start a business of his own.
他离开公司去创办自己的企业。
He had a room of his own.
他有自己的房间。

owner 〔ˈonɚ ‖ ˈəʊnə〕
n. 物主；所有人[C]
Who is the owner of that motorcycle?
谁是那辆摩托车的主人？
I met the owner of the local hotel.
我碰见了当地那家旅馆的主人。

ox 〔ɑks ‖ ɒks〕[名复]oxen
n. [C] ❶牛
❷去势公牛，阉牛(未阉割的是bull)

oxygen 〔ˈɑksədʒən ‖ ˈɒksɪdʒən〕
n. 【化】氧；氧气[U]

O

钢琴
piano

P

电话phone

花生peanut

装甲
plate armour

pace 〔pes ‖ peɪs〕

n. ❶一步；一步跨出去的长度(约 2.5 尺)［C］

Walk 10 paces forward.

向前走 10 步。

❷步速；速度；进度

The work progressed at a slow pace.

这项工作进展缓慢。

Pacific 〔pəˈsɪfɪk ‖ pəˈsɪfɪk〕

n. 太平洋［the］

pack 〔pæk ‖ pæk〕

［过去式］packed；［过去分词］packed

vt. ❶装(箱)；给(某人)将(某物)装入行李

Please don't forget to pack me a razor.

请别忘了给我放一把剃须刀进去。

❷将……挤(塞，装)入；挤(塞，装)满

Visitors packed the gallery.

参观者挤满了画廊。

❸捆扎；包装

We packed the books before we moved.

我们在搬迁前把书本捆好了。

n. ［C］ ❶包；捆；包裹；背包

The tourist carried a pack on his back.

那个观光旅行者背了个包。

❷【美】一包(盒，箱，袋)［(＋of)］

He used to smoke a pack of cigarettes a day.

他过去经常一天抽一包香烟。

package 〔ˈpækɪdʒ ‖ ˈpækɪdʒ〕

n. ［C］❶包裹；包

He undid the package.

他解开了那个包裹。

❷(香烟等的)一包

P

page 〔pedʒ ‖ peɪdʒ〕
n. (书等的)页[C]
Do the exercises on page 10.
做第 10 页上的练习。

pain 〔pen ‖ peɪn〕
n. ❶痛,疼痛;痛苦[U]
The death of her son gave her infinite pain.
她儿子的去世使她悲痛欲绝。
❷(身体特定部位的)疼痛[C]
She has a pain in her stomach.
她胃痛。
❸辛苦,努力[P]
No pains, no gains.
不劳则无获。

painful 〔ˈpenfəl ‖ ˈpeɪnfʊl〕
a. ❶疼痛的;引起痛苦的
The wound was painful.
伤处很痛。
❷费力的;困难的;麻烦的
a painful task
困难的任务

paint 〔pent ‖ peɪnt〕
[过去式]painted;[过去分词]painted
vt. ❶油漆;涂以颜色
The door was painted blue.
门被漆成蓝色。
❷画,绘画
The boy is painting a tiger.
那个男孩在画一只老虎。
n. ❶油漆,涂料[U]
❷绘画颜料;一套颜料[P]
He bought me a box of paints.
他给我买了一盒颜料。

painter 〔ˈpentɚ ‖ ˈpeɪntə〕
n. [C] ❶(油)漆工
❷画家

painting 〔ˈpentɪŋ ‖ ˈpeɪntɪŋ〕
n. ❶绘画;绘画艺术,画法[U]
He took up painting as a hobby.
他将绘画当做一种业余爱好。
❷画,油画,水彩画[C]
There is a painting on the wall.
墙上有幅画。
〈 painting 是油画;drawing 是铅笔画〉

pair 〔pɛr ‖ peə〕
n. ❶一对,一双,(两部分形成的)一件[C][(+of)]
a pair of shoes
一双鞋
a pair of socks
一双袜子
a pair of glasses
一副眼镜
a pair of scissors
一把剪刀
a pair of trousers
一条裤子
❷一对(夫妻,情侣,舞伴等)

P

[C]
That pair are always quarreling.
那对夫妻老是争吵。

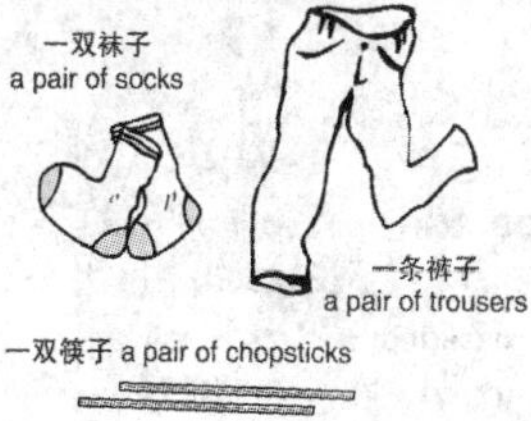

palace [ˈpælɪs ‖ ˈpælɪs]
n. 皇宫,宫殿[C]
The Queen of England lives in Buckingham Palace.
英国女王住在白金汉宫。

pale [pel ‖ peɪl]
a. ❶苍白的,灰白的
She was pale with fear.
她吓得脸色发白。
❷(颜色)淡的
Her beauty seemed pale beside Mary's.
她的美貌与玛丽的相比似乎显得黯然失色。
❸(光)微弱的,暗淡的

palm [pɑm ‖ pɑːm]
n. 手掌,手心[C]
She placed the money in his palm.
她把钱放在他的手心里。

pamphlet [ˈpæmflɪt ‖ ˈpæmflɪt]
n. 小册子[C]

pan [pæn ‖ pæn]
n. [C]平底锅
a frying pan
煎锅

panic [ˈpænɪk ‖ ˈpænɪk]
n. 恐慌,惊慌,(经济)大恐慌[C][U]
The explosion caused a panic among the people.
爆炸引起了人们的恐慌。

pants [pænts ‖ pænts]
n. [P]❶裤子,宽松的长裤
This jacket will match those pants nicely.
这件夹克和那条裤子会十分相

配。

❷【英】短裤；妇女用紧身短内裤(＝underpants)

papa ['pɑpə ‖ pə'pɑː]

n.【口】爸爸[C]

paper ['pepɚ ‖ 'peɪpə]

n. ❶纸[U]

a sheet of paper

一张纸

a bit of paper

一张纸片

a strip of paper

一张纸条

❷报纸[C]

What news is there in the papers this morning?

今天早上报纸上有点儿什么新闻？

❸试题，试卷，答案(纸)[C]

Hand in your papers now.

现在交卷。

❹论文，报告[C]

He is writing a paper on the subject.

他正在就这个题目写论文。

❺文件[P]

I had my important papers stolen.

我的重要文件被偷了。

parachute ['pærəˌʃut ‖ 'pærəʃuːt]

n. 降落伞[C]

降落伞
parachute

parade [pə'red ‖ pə'reɪd]

[过去式]paraded；[过去分词]paraded

vt. vi. 在……游行，在……列队行进

They paraded the street.

他们沿街游行。

n. 列，游行[C][U]；夸耀[C]

I saw a big parade on the street.

我在街上看到庞大的游行队伍。

paradise ['pærəˌdaɪs ‖ 'pærədaɪs]

n. ❶(通常大写)天堂[U]

❷【宗】(通常大写)伊甸园[U]

❸乐园，像天堂一样的地方[C]

Hong Kong is a shopper's paradise.

香港是购物者的天堂。

paragraph ['pærəˌgræf ‖ 'pærəgrɑːf]

n. [C] ❶(文章的)段，节

Translate the following paragraphs into Chinese.

将下列各个段落译成中文。

❷(报刊的)短评，短讯

Did you see the paragraph about the stock market?

你有没有看到有关股票市场的那则短讯？

parallel 〔'pærəˌlɛl ‖ 'pærəlel〕

a. 平行的，同方向的；相同的；类似的[(＋to)]

The road runs parallel to the railroad.

这条路和铁路平行。

n. 平行线；平行面；类似的人(或事物)，可相比拟的人(或事物)[C][(＋to/with)]

The town has a close parallel to that.

这个镇和那个镇很相似。

parcel 〔'pɑrsl̩ ‖ 'pɑːsl〕

n. [C]❶小包，包裹

I sent a parcel to my mother at home.

我寄了个包裹给家乡的母亲。

❷(土地的)一块，一片

pardon 〔'pɑrdn̩ ‖ 'pɑːdn〕

[过去式]pardoned；[过去分词]pardoned

n. 原谅，饶恕，宽恕[C][U]

I beg your pardon. I suppose I should have knocked.

请原谅。我想我应该先敲一下门的。

I beg your pardon. 有三种含义：I beg your pardon.[读降调]

请原谅，对不起。

I beg your pardon.[读升调]

请再说一遍。

I beg your pardon …用于开始与人说话或在谈话中插入自己的意见

用法工具箱

vt. 原谅，饶恕[(＋for)]

Pardon me for not writing to you sooner.

请原谅我未能及早给你写信。

parent 〔'pɛrənt ‖ 'peərənt〕

n. [C] ❶父亲；母亲

❷双亲[P]

She still lives with her parents.

她仍然与父母住在一起。

Paris 〔'pærɪs ‖ 'pærɪs〕

n. 巴黎

Paris is the capital of France.

巴黎是法国的首都。

park 〔pɑrk ‖ pɑːk〕

[过去式]parked；[过去分词]parked

vt. 停放(车辆等)
Don't park the car on this street.
别把汽车停放在这条街上。
vi. 停放车辆
He parked behind his house.
他把车子停放在房子后面。
n.[C] ❶公园;游乐场
This city has many beautiful parks.
这座城市有许多美丽的公园。
❷停车场
There's a car park over there.
那儿有个停车场。

parliament 〔ˈpɑrləmənt ‖ ˈpɑːləmənt〕
n. ❶[C]议会,国会
He was the first farmworker to get into parliament.
他是第一个进入议会的农场工人。
❷(大写)(英国,加拿大等的)国会

parrot 〔ˈpærət ‖ ˈpærət〕
n. 鹦鹉[C]

鹦鹉
parrot

part 〔pɑrt ‖ pɑːt〕
n. ❶一部分,部分[C][U][(+of)]
Parts of the book are interesting.
这本书有几部分很有意思。
❷部,篇;分册,分辑;节,段;集[C]
That's a radio serial in 10 parts.
那是一部10集广播连续剧。
❸部件,零件[C]
Our workshop turns out parts for generators.
我们车间生产发动机零件。
❹本分,职责,作用,角色
Who plays the part of Ophelia?
谁扮演奥菲莉亚?

常用短语

play a part in 在……中起作用;参与
take part in 参加

partial 〔ˈpɑrʃəl ‖ ˈpɑːʃəl〕
a. ❶部分的,局部的;不完全的
The film was only a partial success.
这部电影仅仅是部分成功。
❷【贬】不公平的,偏袒的[(+to/towards)]
She is partial to her youngest boy.

她偏爱她的小儿子。

participate 〔pɑr'tɪsəˌpet ‖ pɑː'tɪs'ɪpeɪt〕

[过去式]participated;[过去分词]participated

vi. 参加,参与[(+in)]

No professionals participated in the contest.

没有职业选手参加这个比赛。

participle 〔'pɑrtəˌsɪpl̩ ‖ 'pɑːtɪsɪpl〕

n. 【文】分词[C]

particle 〔'pɑrtɪkl̩ ‖ 'pɑːtɪkl〕

n. 微粒,颗粒,极小量[C][(+of)]

There is not a particle of truth in his story.

他的故事没一点儿真实性。

particular 〔pə'tɪkjələ ‖ pə'tɪkjʊlə〕

a. ❶特殊的;特定的;特别的

The teacher showed particular concern for the disabled child.

老师特别关心那个残疾儿童。

❷特有的,独特的;异常的

Her particular way of smiling left a good impression on me.

她特有的微笑给我留下了美好的印象。

❸(过于)讲究的;苛求的,挑剔的[(+about/over)][(+wh-)]

She is particular about what she eats.

她过分讲究吃。

词汇拓展

particularly *ad.* 特别地

partly 〔'pɑrtlɪ ‖ 'pɑːtlɪ〕

ad. 部分地;不完全地;在一定程度上

I study English partly because I like it and partly because it is useful.

我学习英文一方面是由于喜好,一方面是由于它有用。

partner 〔'pɑrtnə ‖ 'pɑːtnə〕

n. [C] ❶(一起行动的)伙伴,拍档

They were partners in crime.

他俩是同谋犯。

❷合伙人,共同出资人

The shop is owned by two partners.

这家商店为两个合伙人所拥有。

❸(舞蹈,游戏等的)搭档

The partners all joined hands and danced in a big circle.

舞伴们全都手拉手绕成一个大圈子跳舞。

part-time 〔'pɑrtˌtaɪm ‖ ˌpɑːt'taɪm〕

P

a. 部分时间的，非全日的，兼任的，兼职的
I 'm looking for a part-time job.
我正在找一份兼职的工作。

party 〔ˈpɑrtɪ ‖ ˈpɑːtɪ〕
n. [C] ❶聚会，集会，派对
I met a childhood friend at the party.
在宴会上我遇见一个儿时的朋友。
❷（共同工作或活动的）一团人，一伙人，一行人[（＋of）]
The bus was rented by a party of tourists.
一群游客租用了那辆公共汽车。
❸政党，党派
Which party does John belong to?
约翰属于哪个党派？
❹（契约等的）当事人，一方
Both the parties agreed about that.
双方都对此表示同意。

P

pass 〔pæs ‖ pɑːs〕
[过去式]passed；[过去分词]passed
vi. ❶前进；通过；经过；超过
You cannot pass. Stop where you are.
你不能过去。原处停下。
❷终止，消失；离开，死亡
The pain passed.
疼痛消失了。
❸（时间）推移，流逝；变化，转化；转移
The 10 days passed quickly.
这10天很快就过去了。
❹（考试等）及格；通过；被批准
vt. ❶经过，穿过，越过，超过
We passed several stores before we came to the barber's.
我们走过几家商店才到了理发店。
❷传递；传达；传（球）
Please pass me the salt.
请把盐递给我。
❸通过（考试；检查等）；使及格；批准（议案等）
The bill was passed in 1908.
这项议案是1908年通过的。

常用短语

pass away ❶消失 ❷过世
pass by ❶经过；过去 ❷（时间）过去，错过
n. [C]❶穿过，经过
❷通行证；护照；入场证
No pass, no passage.
没有通行证不得通过。
❸及格；及格分数
He got a pass in English.
他英语考试得了个及格分数。

passage [ˈpæsɪdʒ ‖ ˈpæsɪdʒ]

n. ❶通行；通过[U]

The road is too narrow to allow the passage of truck.

这条街太窄卡车不能通过。

❷通路；水路；出入口[C]

Magellan was trying to find a passage to the Indian Ocean.

麦哲伦试图找到一条通向印度洋的通道。

❸走廊，过道[C]

His office is at the end of the passage.

他的办公室在走廊的尽头。

❹(时间的)推移[U]

passenger [ˈpæsn̩dʒɚ ‖ ˈpæsəndʒə]

n. 乘客，旅客[C]

This bus can carry 50 passengers.

这辆公共汽车可载 50 名乘客。

passer-by [ˈpæsɚˈbaɪ ‖ ˌpɑːsəˈbaɪ]

n. 过路人[C]

He begged from passers-by.

他向过路人乞讨。

passion [ˈpæʃən ‖ ˈpæʃən]

n. ❶热情，激情[C][U]

They sang with great passion.

他们满怀激情地歌唱。

❷恋情；情欲[(＋for)]

You may have a passion for her, but it isn't love.

你也许对她怀有强烈的情欲，但这不是爱情。

❸盛怒，愤怒

At those words of mine he broke into a violent passion.

他听了我说的那些话便勃然大怒。

passionate [ˈpæʃənɪt ‖ ˈpæʃənət]

a. ❶ 热情的；热烈的，激昂的

He made a passionate speech.

他做了一次热情洋溢的演讲。

❷易怒的，性情暴躁的

a man of passionate nature

性格暴躁的人

passive [ˈpæsɪv ‖ ˈpæsɪv]

a. ❶被动的；消极的

❷【语】被动的；被动语态的

passport [ˈpæsˌpɔrt ‖ ˈpɑːsˌpɔːt]

n. 护照[C]

past [pæst ‖ pɑːst]

a. ❶过去的；刚过去的

His past life was a happy one.

他过去的生活很幸福。

❷过去了的；完了的

The danger is past.

危险已过。

❸以前的；前任的

John Smith is a past president of our club.

约翰·史密斯是我们俱乐部的前任主席。

❹【文】过去式的

prep.（指时间，数量等）过；通过，经过

It's half past 10.

现在是 10 点半。

n. 过去，昔日［the］

In the past he had to read by candlelight.

过去他只得在烛光下攻读。

pastime〔ˈpæsˌtaɪm ‖ ˈpɑːsˌtaɪm〕

n. 消遣；娱乐［C］

I often travel as a pastime.

我以旅行为消遣。

pat〔pæt ‖ pæt〕

［过去式］patted；［过去分词］patted

n. 轻拍，轻打［C］

I gave the cute child a pat.

我轻轻拍了拍那个惹人喜爱的小孩。

vt. 轻拍，抚拍

The headmaster patted the pupil on the shoulder.

校长轻轻拍了拍那个学生的肩膀。

vi. 轻拍

Snowflakes were patting against the windowpane.

雪花轻轻拍打着玻璃窗。

path〔pæθ ‖ pɑːθ〕

n.［C］❶小径，小路

They walked along the path through the woods.

他们沿着林间小路走去。

❷ 通路，道路，途径［(＋through)］

His path through life was hard.

他的人生历程十分坎坷。

❸路线，轨道［(＋of)］

The path of an arrow is a curve.

箭的轨道是一条曲线。

patience〔ˈpeʃəns ‖ ˈpeɪʃəns〕

n. 耐心；忍耐；耐性；毅力［U］

She has reached the limit of her patience.

她已到了忍无可忍的地步。

patient〔ˈpeʃənt ‖ ˈpeɪʃənt〕

a. ❶有耐心的，能忍受的，能容忍的

He's a very patient man.

他是个很有耐心的人。

❷（人）勤奋的；（工作等）需要耐性的

n. 病人［C］

The doctor is very patient with his patients.

那位医生对病人十分耐心。

patrol〔pəˈtrol ‖ pəˈtrəʊl〕

P

[过去式]patrolled;[过去分词]patrolled

n. ❶巡逻,侦察[C][U]

A policeman on patrol found the fire.

一名警察在巡逻中发现了火灾。

❷巡逻队[C]

vt. 巡逻;侦察

Watchmen patrolled the school grounds.

警卫在学校操场巡查。

pattern [ˈpætɚn ‖ ˈpætən]

n. [C] ❶花样,图案

I don't like the pattern on the fabric.

我不喜欢那块布料上的图案。

❷形态,样式;格局

They like new patterns of family life.

他们喜欢新的家庭生活方式。

❸(服装裁剪的)纸样,(浇铸用的)模具

Mary used a paper pattern to make her new dress.

玛丽按照纸样缝制她的新衣服。

❹模范,榜样,典型

pause [pɔz ‖ pɔːz]

[过去式]paused;[过去分词]paused

n. 暂停,中断,间歇[C]

After a brief pause the speaker continued.

稍稍停顿一下后演讲者继续讲下去。

vi. ❶中断,暂停;停顿

He paused when he heard steps behind him.

他听到后面有脚步声便停了下来。

❷犹豫,考虑

She paused before consenting to marry him.

她在同意嫁给他前曾犹豫不定。

pavement [ˈpevmənt ‖ ˈpeɪvmənt]

n.【英】人行道[C]

paw [pɔ ‖ pɔː]

n. 脚爪;爪子[C]

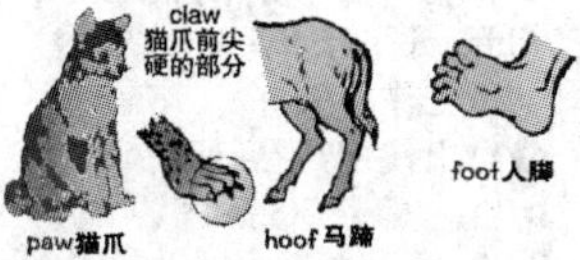

Get your paws off those cakes.

别用你的手碰那些蛋糕。

pay [pe ‖ peɪ]

[过去式]paid;[过去分词]paid

vt. ❶付,支付;付款给[(+

for/to)]
She paid the money to me.
她将钱付给了我。
❷偿还;补偿;向……报复[(＋out)]
I've paid him out for the trick he played on me.
他捉弄我,我已对他进行了报复。
❸给予(注意);致以(问候);进行(访问)[(＋to)]
We'll pay a visit to Japan this winter.
今年冬天我们要去访问日本。
vi. ❶付款;偿还债务
I'll pay by check.
我将用支票付款。
❷有利,划算
It will pay to be kind to others.
好心会有好报。
❸有利;(工作等)有报酬
This job pays well.
这份工作报酬好。
❹付出代价;受到惩罚
n. [U] ❶薪俸;报酬
The miners went on strike for higher pay.
矿工举行罢工,要求增加工资。
❷报偿;惩罚

payment ['pemənt ‖ 'peɪmənt]
n. ❶支付,付款[U]
Full payment must be made before we get the new car.
我们在得到新汽车之前必须付清全部款项。
❷支付的款项(或实物)[C]
We made our last house payment today.
我们今天付了我们购房的最后一期款子。
❸报偿;惩罚[U]

peace [pis ‖ piːs]
n. [U]❶和平;和约;和睦
We live in peace with our neighbors.
我们与邻居和睦相处。
❷(社会)治安,秩序[the]
break /keep the peace
扰乱/维持社会治安
❸(心的)平静,安详;宁静
I told him to go away and leave me in peace.
我叫他走开,别来打扰我。

peaceful ['pisfəl ‖ 'piːsful]
[比] more peaceful; [最] most peaceful
a. 平静的,安宁的,和平的
The village looked very peaceful.
这个村子看起来很安静。

peach [pitʃ ‖ piːtʃ]
n. ❶桃子,桃树[C]

P

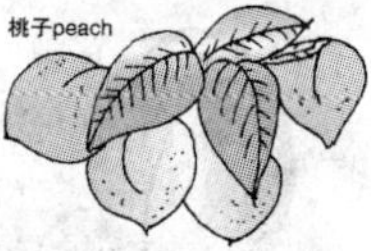

❷桃色[U]
❸【俚】特别惹人喜爱的人;漂亮的女孩;极好的事物
The new office girl is a real peach. All the guys want to date her.
办公室里新来的女孩是个漂亮小妞儿,所有的男士都想跟她约会。

pear 〔pɛr ‖ peə〕
n. [C] ❶梨
❷梨树

pearl 〔pɝl ‖ pəːl〕
n. 珍珠[C]
The necklace is made of natural pearls.
这条项链是用天然珍珠做成的。

peasant 〔ˈpɛzn̩t ‖ ˈpeznt〕
n. [C] ❶农夫,小耕农
Just before sunset the peasants quit laboring in the fields.
农民们直到日落才结束在田间的劳动。
❷【口】乡下人;粗野的人
He is a real peasant.
他是一个十足的乡巴佬儿。

peculiar 〔pɪˈkjuljɚ ‖ pɪˈkjuːlɪə〕
[比] more peculiar; [最] most peculiar
a. ❶奇怪的;乖僻的;罕见的
He looked at me with a very peculiar expression.
他用一种奇特的眼神看着我。
❷(个人或团体)特有的,独具的;独特的[(+to)]
This style is peculiar to him.
这一风格是他独有的。
❸特别的,特殊的
It is a matter of peculiar interest.
这是一件有特殊意义的事。

pedestrian 〔pəˈdɛstrɪən ‖ pɪˈdestrɪən〕
a. 徒步的,步行的,行人的
a pedestrian crossing
行人穿越道
n. 步行者,行人[C]

peel 〔pil ‖ piːl〕
[过去式] peeled; [过去分词] peeled
vt. 削去……的皮,剥去……的壳;替……削(或剥)……
peel a banana
剥去香蕉皮
n. (水果,蔬菜等的)皮;(对虾等的)壳[U]

pen 〔pen ‖ pen〕

n. [C]❶笔，钢笔

The contract must be signed with a pen, not a pencil.

这份合同一定要用钢笔而不用铅笔签字。

❷文笔；笔调；笔法

He has a lively pen.

他的笔法生动逼真。

penalty 〔ˈpenl̩tɪ ‖ ˈpenltɪ〕

n. ❶处罚；刑罚[C][(+for)]

There are now stiffer penalties for drunken drivers.

现在对酗酒开车的处罚更严厉了。

❷罚款[C][(+for)]

The penalty for spitting is $10.

随地吐痰罚款 10 美金。

❸【体】犯规的处罚；罚球[C]

The referee gave a penalty.

裁判处以罚球。

pencil 〔ˈpensl̩ ‖ ˈpensl〕

n. 铅笔[C]

The last item on the list was added in pencil.

单子上的最后一项是用铅笔加上去的。

penguin 〔ˈpeŋgwɪn ‖ ˈpengwɪn〕

n. 企鹅[C]

penny 〔ˈpenɪ ‖ ˈpenɪ〕

n. ❶【英】便士；一便士硬币[C]

Please give me 10 pennies for this tenpence piece.

请替我把这 10 便士换成 10 个 1 便士硬币。

❷【美】一分；一分硬币[C]

❸一小笔钱；(用于否定句)一文钱

The excursion won't cost you a penny if you go with us.

如果你与我们一起去，这趟旅行就不会花你一文钱。

pension 〔ˈpenʃən ‖ ˈpenʃən〕

n. 退休金；养老金；抚恤金[C]

people 〔ˈpipl̩ ‖ ˈpiːpl〕

n. ❶人们[P]

Who are these people?

这些人是谁?

❷国民；民族；种族[C]

The Chinese are a hard-working people.

中华民族是个勤劳的民族。

P

❸家族;家人;亲属(尤指父母)[P]
All her people are in Australia.
她的家人都在澳大利亚。

pepper ['pɛpɚ ‖ 'pepə]
n. 胡椒粉;辣椒粉;香辣调味品[U]
I'd like to add some pepper to the bean curd.
我想在豆腐里加一点辣椒粉。

per [pɚ ‖ pə]
prep. 经,由,每
a pint of milk per child
每个孩子一品脱奶

perceive [pɚ'siv ‖ pə'siːv]
[过去式]perceived;[过去分词]perceived
vt. ❶察觉;感知
I perceived a man enter the house.
我看到一个人走进这间房子。
❷意识到;理解[＋that][＋wh-]
He gradually perceived that his parents had been right.
他渐渐地意识到他的父母是对的。

percent [pɚ'sɛnt ‖ pə'sent]
n. ❶百分之一[C]
Thirty percent of the farmland has been planted oil crops.
30%的农田已种上油料作物。
❷百分比,百分率;部分
He spends a large percent of his income on food and drink.
他把收入的大部分花在食物和饮料方面。
a. 百分之……的,每一百中有……的
They went on strike on Monday in demand of a 30 percent wage increase.
他们于星期一举行罢工,要求增加30%的工资。

perception [pɚ'sɛpʃən ‖ pə'sepʃən]
n. ❶感知,感觉[U]
❷认识,观念[C]
❸感知能力;洞察力[U]
the perception of a strange sound
听到奇怪的声音
a man of keen perception
感觉敏锐的人

perfect ['pɚfɪkt ‖ 'pəːfɪkt]
a. ❶完美的;理想的
Her acting is really perfect.
她的演技达到了炉火纯青的境界。
❷精通的;娴熟的
Practice makes perfect.
熟能生巧。

❸对……最适当的[(+for)]

The weather is perfect for a garden party.

这是举行露天招待会的理想天气。

❹完全的，十足的

He is a perfect stranger to me.

对我来说他完全是个陌生人。

perfectly 〔ˈpɚfɪktlɪ ‖ ˈpəfɪktlɪ〕

ad. 完美地；完全地

His guess was perfectly right.

他的猜想完全正确。

perform 〔pɚˈfɔrm ‖ pəˈfɔːm〕

[过去式]performed；[过去分词]performed

vt. ❶履行；运行；完成；做

The young doctor performed the heart operation.

这位年轻医生为病人做了心脏手术。

❷演出，表演，演奏

The students will perform an opera next Friday.

这些学生下星期五将演出一出歌剧。

vi. ❶演出，表演，演奏[(+in/at)]

The singer had never performed in London before.

那位歌手过去从未在伦敦演出过。

❷(机器)运转；(人)行动，表现

Our team performed well in the match yesterday.

我队在昨天的比赛中表现得很出色。

performance 〔pɚˈfɔrməns ‖ pəˈfɔːməns〕

n. ❶演出；演奏；表演[C]

The evening performance begins at 8 o'clock.

晚上的演出 8 点开始。

❷履行；执行；完成[U][(+of)]

He failed completely in the performance of his duty.

他完全没有履行他的职责。

perfume 〔ˈpɚfjum ‖ ˈpəːfjuːm〕

n. [C][U]❶香味，芳香

It has the perfume of roses.

它有蔷薇的香味。

❷香水；香料

She sprayed perfume over her chest.

她在胸前洒上香水。

perhaps 〔pɚˈhæps ‖ pəˈhæps〕

ad. 大概，或许，可能

"Will he come?"

"他会来吗?"

"Perhaps not."

"大概不会。"

period 〔ˈpɪrɪəd ‖ ˈpɪərɪəd〕

n. [C] ❶时期，期间
This was the most difficult period of his life.
这是他一生中最艰难的时期。
❷时代
the period of the Civil War
美国南北战争年代
❸(一堂)课，课时
We have 4 periods of English a week.
我们每星期上 4 节英语课。
❹周期；月经

permanent 〔ˈpɝmənənt ‖ ˈpɜːmənənt〕
a. ❶永久的，永恒的；永远的
Nature is permanent.
自然是永恒的。
❷固定性的；常在的
This is my permanent address.
这是我的固定地址。

permission 〔pɚˈmɪʃən ‖ pəˈmɪʃən〕
n. 允许，许可，同意[U][＋to-v][(＋from)]
We have obtained permission from the directors to use some of our funds.
我们已得到董事的许可，可以动用部分资金。

permit 〔pɚˈmɪt ‖ pəˈmɪt〕
[过去式]permitted；[过去分词]permitted
vt. 允许，许可，准许
Smoking is permitted in this room.
这间房间可以吸烟。
vi. 允许，容许[(＋of)]
His late arrival permits of no excuse.
为自己的迟到他没有辩解的余地。

常用短语

weather permitting 如果天气允许的话
Weather permitting, I will go.
天气允许的话我会去。
n. 许可证，执照[C]
a permit to hunt
狩猎许可证

perpetual 〔pɚˈpɛtʃuəl ‖ pəˈpetʃuəl〕
a. ❶永久的；长期的
Do you believe in perpetual life?
你相信永生吗？
❷【口】无休止的；连续不断的
I am bored with his perpetual talking.
我厌倦了他说个不停。

persist 〔pɚˈsɪst ‖ pəˈsɪst〕
[过去式]persisted；[过去分词]persisted

P

vi. ❶坚持;固执[(+in/with)]
He persisted in his opinion.
他固执己见。
❷持续;存留
The snow persists in the valley.
山谷中的雪仍未消融。

person [ˈpɜ˞sn̩ ‖ ˈpɜːsn]
n. ❶人;家伙[C]
A strange person is asking to see you.
有个陌生人想见你。
❷【书】(人的)身体,人身;外表,容貌[C]
The young man has a fine person.
那个小伙子相貌堂堂。
❸【文】人称

personal [ˈpɜ˞sn̩l ‖ ˈpɜːsnl]
a. ❶个人的,私人的
It's all a matter of personal taste.
这纯粹是个人的兴趣问题。
❷本人的,亲自的
The plan was drawn up under the chief engineer's personal guidance.
这一方案是在总工程师的亲自指导下制定的。
❸涉及私事的;攻击个人的
Frank is always making personal remarks about his cousins.
弗兰克老是对他表兄弟进行人身攻击。
❹身体的;容貌的
She is proud of her personal beauty.
她对自己漂亮的容貌很自豪。

personality [ˌpɜ˞sn̩ˈælətɪ ‖ ˌpɜːsənˈælətɪ]
n. ❶人格,品格[C][U]
His personality left a deep impression on us.
他的人品给我们留下了深刻的印象。
❷个性,性格[C][U]
He has a strong personality.
他性格坚强。

personnel [ˌpɜ˞sn̩ˈɛl ‖ ˌpɜːsəˈnel]
n. ❶(总称)人员,员工[P]
All the personnel of this factory have gathered in the hall.
这个工厂的全体员工都在会场集合。
❷人事部门;人事科(或室等)[U]

persuade [pə˞ˈswed ‖ pəˈsweɪd]
[过去式]persuaded;[过去分词]persuaded
vt. ❶说服,劝服[(+into/out of)]

P

She persuaded me into buying it.
她说服我买下了它。
❷使某人相信[(＋of)][＋that]
How can I persuade you of my sincerity?
我怎样才能使你相信我的诚意呢?

pet〔pɛt‖pet〕
n. 供玩赏的动物,宠物[C]
The little girl keeps a lamb as a pet.
那个小女孩养了一只羔羊作为宠物。
This store sells pet food.
这家商店出售宠物食品。

petrol〔ˈpɛtrəl‖ˈpetrəl〕
n. [U]【英】汽油;【美】gasoline

petroleum〔pəˈtrolɪəm‖pɪˈtrəʊlɪəm〕
n. 石油[U]

phenomenon〔fəˈnɑməˌnɑn‖fəˈnɒmɪnən〕[名复] phenomena
n. 现象[C]
Rainbow is one of the most beautiful phenomena of nature.
彩虹是美丽的自然现象之一。

philosopher〔fəˈlɑsəfɚ‖fəˈlɒsəfə〕
n. [C] ❶哲学家,思想家,学者,贤哲
❷达观的人,(逆境中)泰然自若的人

philosophy〔fəˈlɑsəfɪ‖fəˈlɒsəfɪ〕
n. ❶哲学[U]
He majors in philosophy.
他主修哲学。
❷人生观;主义[C][U]
His philosophy is not sound.
他的人生观不健全。

phoenix〔ˈfinɪks‖ˈfiːnɪks〕
n. 长生鸟;凤凰[C]

phone〔fon‖fəʊn〕
[过去式]phoned;[过去分词]phoned
n. ❶电话[U]
She spoke to me by phone last night.
她昨晚与我通了电话。
❷电话机[C]
The phone is ringing.
电话在响。

电话机
phone

❸听筒,耳机[C]
vt. 打电话给……[(＋up)]

I must phone her up tonight.
我必须今夜给她打电话。

photo 〔ˈfoto ‖ ˈfəutəu〕
n. 【口】照片[C]
He took a photo of me.
他给我照了张相。

photograph 〔ˈfotəˌgræf ‖ ˈfəutəgrɑːf〕
[过去式]photographed; [过去分词]photographed
n. 照片[C](=photo)
I took a photograph of my girlfriend.
我给女朋友拍了张照片。
vt. 为……拍照
She photographed the ancient tower.
她把古塔拍了下来。

phrase 〔frez ‖ freɪz〕
n. [C] ❶词组
Try to learn by heart these English words and phrases.
努力把这些英语单词和词组记住。
❷成语，惯用语
❸措辞，说法
The speaker certainly has a way with a phrase.
这位演讲者无疑善于辞令。

physical 〔ˈfɪzɪkl̩ ‖ ˈfɪzɪkl〕
a. ❶身体的，肉体的
Playing basketball is one form of physical exercise.
打篮球是体育活动的一种形式。
❷物质的
I have no idea how large the physical universe is.
我不知道物质世界有多大。
❸自然科学的，按自然法则的
There may be a physical explanation for these strange happenings.
这些奇怪现象也许有符合自然法则的解释。
❹物理的；物理学的

physician 〔fəˈzɪʃən ‖ fɪˈzɪʃən〕
n. [C] ❶医师
The physician prescribed him some medicine.
医生给他开了一些药。
❷内科医生

physicist 〔ˈfɪzəsɪst ‖ ˈfɪzɪsɪst〕
n. 物理学家[C]

physics 〔ˈfɪzɪks ‖ ˈfɪzɪks〕
n. 物理学[U]
According to our present ideas of physics, nothing can travel faster than light.
根据我们现在物理学的概念，

没有什么东西的速度能超过光速。

pianist 〔pɪ'ænɪst ‖ pɪ'ænɪst〕

n. 钢琴家；钢琴演奏者[C]

piano 〔pɪ'æno ‖ pɪ'ænəʊ〕

n. 钢琴[C]

大钢琴
grand piano

Maggie plays the piano very well.

玛吉钢琴弹得很好。

pick 〔pɪk ‖ pɪk〕

[过去式]picked；[过去分词]picked

vt. ❶挑选，选择

Please pick a good book for me.

请为我挑一本好书。

❷采，摘

He picked her a rose.

他给她采了一朵玫瑰花。

❸(用手指或尖形工具)挖；剔；扒；啄[(＋from/out of)]

She picked the meat from the bones.

她将骨头上的肉剔去。

❹撬(锁)；扒窃

I had my pocket picked in the train.

我的钱包在火车上被偷了。

pickpocket 〔'pɪkˌpɑkɪt ‖ 'pɪkˌpɒkɪt〕

n. 扒手[C]

picnic 〔'pɪknɪk ‖ 'pɪknɪk〕

n. (自带食物的)郊游，野餐；(个人自带食品的)聚餐[C]

We went on a picnic to the hill.

我们到山上去野餐。

picture 〔'pɪktʃɚ ‖ 'pɪktʃə〕

[过去式]pictured；[过去分词]pictured

n. [C] ❶画；画像；图片；照片

I had some pictures taken this morning.

今天上午我拍了几张照片。

❷【美】电影

I have seen the picture before.

我以前看过这部电影。

❸(心中的)形象，想象；(生动的)描写；写照[(＋of)]

This book gives a good picture of life in China today.

这本书生动地描述了当代中国的生活情况。

vt. ❶想象

P

Can you picture Bill dressed as a fairy?
你能想象得出比尔扮作仙女的模样吗?
❷画,用图表示,拍摄;(生动地)描绘,描述
The painter pictured the general sitting on a horse.
画家给骑着马的将军画像。

pie 〔paɪ ‖ paɪ〕
n. [C][U] ❶派(酥壳有馅的饼);馅饼
an apple pie
苹果馅饼
❷【口】极简单的事;不堪一击的对手
That job was as easy as pie.
那项工作容易极了。

piece 〔pis ‖ piːs〕
n. ❶一个,一张,一片;一块[C][(+of)]
Could you give me a piece of paper?
你能给我一张纸吗?
❷(艺术)作品;曲,篇[C]
The pianist played a piece by Chopin.
钢琴家演奏了一曲肖邦的作品。
❸一则消息,报道
Here is a good piece of news for you.
有个好消息要告诉你。

pig 〔pɪg ‖ pɪg〕
n. 猪[C]
He keeps pigs as a career.
他以养猪为业。

pigeon 〔ˈpɪdʒən ‖ ˈpɪdʒɪn〕
n. 鸽子[C]
A pigeon was cooing up in one of the elms.
一只鸽子在榆树上咕咕地叫。

pile 〔paɪl ‖ paɪl〕
[过去式] piled; [过去分词] piled
n. [C] ❶堆;一堆[(+of)]
A pile of dirty clothes lay by the washing machine.
一堆脏衣服放在洗衣机旁边。
❷【口】大量;大数目[P][(+of)]
He's got piles of work to do this morning.
今天上午他有大量工作要做。
vt. 堆积,叠;累积
He piled the books on top of each other.
他把书一本本地叠起来。
vi. ❶堆积;累积
Her work is piling up.

她的工作越积越多。

❷拥，挤[(+in/into/out/off)]

They piled into my car.

他们挤进我的车。

pill 〔pɪl ‖ pɪl〕

n. 药丸，药片[C]

sleeping pills

安眠药

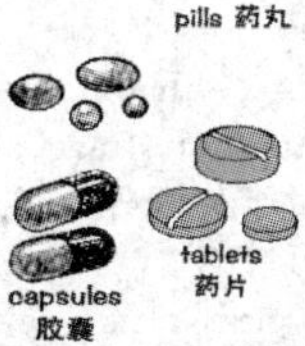

pillow 〔ˈpɪlo ‖ ˈpɪləʊ〕

n. 枕头[C]

In bed, I rest my head on a soft pillow filled with feathers.

在床上，我把头搁在用羽毛作为枕心的软枕头上。

pilot 〔ˈpaɪlət ‖ ˈpaɪlət〕

n. [C] ❶(船舶的)引航员，领航员；舵手

Mark Twain was once a river pilot on the Mississippi.

马克·吐温曾当过密西西比河上的领航员。

❷(飞机等的)驾驶员，飞行员

an airline pilot

航空公司的飞行员

pin 〔pɪn ‖ pɪn〕

n. 大头针；别针[C]

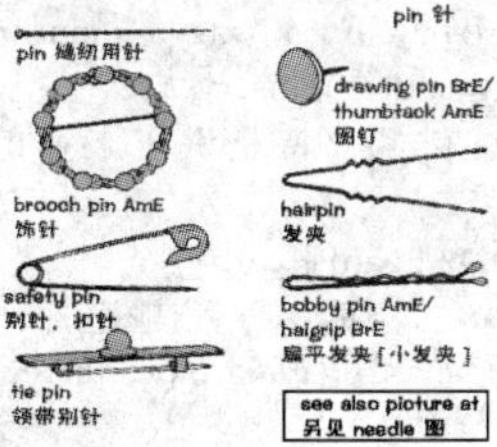

ping-pong 〔ˈpɪŋˌpaŋ ‖ ˈpɪŋpɒŋ〕

n. 乒乓球，桌球[U]

pine 〔paɪn ‖ paɪn〕

n. ❶松树[C]

❷松木[U]

pink 〔pɪŋk ‖ pɪŋk〕

n. 粉红色，桃红色[C][U]

She was dressed in pink.

她穿着粉红色的衣服。

a. ❶粉红色的；桃红色的

The tree was covered with beautiful pink blossom.

这棵树开满了美丽的粉红色的花。

❷面红耳赤的；激动的；愤怒的

She went pink with shame.

她羞得满脸通红。

pioneer 〔ˌpaɪəˈnɪr ‖ ˌpaɪəˈnɪə〕

n. [C]❶拓荒者，开拓者

P

They were the pioneers of the American West.
他们是美国西部的开拓者。
❷先驱者[(+in/of)]、
Henry Ford was a pioneer in the auto industry.
亨利·福特是汽车工业的先驱。

pipe 〔paɪp ‖ paɪp〕
n. [C]❶管,导管,输送管
They are laying pipes under the road.
他们正在铺设路下面的管子。
❷烟斗
His father is a pipe-smoker.
他父亲抽烟斗。
❸管乐器;笛
He is playing a tune on his pipe.
他在用笛子吹奏一支曲子。

pirate 〔'paɪrət ‖ 'paɪərət〕
n. [C] ❶海盗;劫掠者
❷海盗船

pistol 〔'pɪstḷ ‖ 'pɪstl〕
n. [C] ❶手枪
❷信号枪;发令枪

pitiful 〔'pɪtɪfəl ‖ 'pɪtɪfəl〕
a. 可怜的,令人同情的
The thin girl was a pitiful sight.
那个瘦骨伶仃的女孩看起来真可怜。

pity 〔'pɪtɪ ‖ 'pɪtɪ〕
n. ❶怜悯;同情[U]
The villagers took pity on the hungry travellers and gave them hot food.
村民们很同情饥饿的旅行者,端出热的食物给他们吃。
❷可惜的事,憾事[C][+(that)]
It's a pity that he missed the opportunity to travel abroad.
他错过了去国外旅游的机会,真是可惜。

place 〔ples ‖ pleɪs〕
[过去式]placed;[过去分词]placed
n. [C]❶地方,地点;地区;位置;居民点
Keep it in a cool place.
把它放在阴凉的地方。
❷住所,寓所
We ate lunch at her place.
我们在她家吃了中饭。
❸席位,座位
The people took their places.
大家都就座了。
❹名次,(第……)名
Mary won the first place in the singing contest.
玛丽在歌咏比赛中得了第一

名。

❺社会地位，身份

That playwright has a high place in the history of American literature.

那位剧作家在美国文学史上占有重要地位。

❻工作，职务，职责

He got a place in the bank.

他在银行得到了一个职位。

vt. ❶放置，安置，安排；将……寄托于

He placed cups and saucers on the table.

他把杯子和茶碟放到桌上。

❷投(资)；存(款)；开出(订单)

I placed an order with them for 500 pairs of shoes.

我向他们订购了500双鞋子。

plain 〔plen ‖ pleɪn〕

[比]plainer；[最]plainest

a. ❶简朴的；朴素的；不掺杂的

He advocates plain living.

他提倡过简朴的生活。

❷清楚的；明白的；平易的

The meaning of the sentence is very plain.

这个句子的意思十分清楚。

❸坦白的，直率的

I must be plain with you.

我必须坦白地对你说。

❹【婉】(相貌)平常的；丑的

n. 平原；旷野[C]

the Great Plains

(美国密西西比河流域以西的)大平原

词汇拓展

plainly *ad.* 朴素地，率直地

plan 〔plæn ‖ plæn〕

[过去式]planned；[过去分词]planned

n. [C] ❶计划；方案；打算[(＋for/of)][＋to-v]

What's your plan for the weekend?

你打算如何过周末？

❷图纸；平面图

the plan of the house

房子的设计图

vt. ❶计划；打算

She asked about the journey he had planned.

她问起他所筹划的旅行。

❷设计；绘制……的平面图

vi. 计划；打算[(＋for/on)]

They plan on coming at Christmas.

他们计划圣诞节来。

plane 〔plen ‖ pleɪn〕

n.【口】飞机[C]

P

I have never traveled by plane.
我从没坐飞机旅行过。

planet 〔'plænɪt ‖ 'plænɪt〕
n. 行星[C]
The planets move around the sun.
行星绕着太阳转。

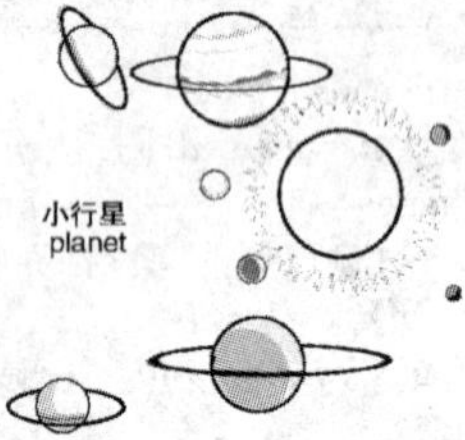

plant 〔plænt ‖ plɑːnt〕
[过去式]planted;[过去分词] planted
n. [C]❶植物,农作物

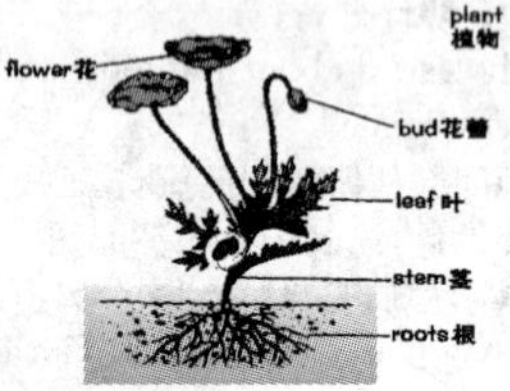

❷工厂;车间
He works at a power plant.
他在发电厂工作。
vt. 栽种;播种
We planted a lot of flowers in our garden.
我们在庭院里种了很多花。

plastic 〔'plæstɪk ‖ 'plæstɪk〕
a. ❶可塑的,塑性的
The shop assistant helped Mary put fruit into a plastic shopping bag.
售货员帮玛丽把水果装入一个塑胶购物袋里。
❷造型的,塑造的,塑像的
Sculpture is a plastic art.
雕塑是一种造型艺术。
❸柔顺的,易受影响的
The mind of a child is plastic.
儿童的思想是很容易受外界影响的。
n. ❶塑胶;塑胶制品[P]
Plastics don't rust like metal.
塑胶不像金属那样会生锈。
❷信用卡

plate 〔plet ‖ pleɪt〕
n. ❶盘子,盆,碟[C]
The child soon finished the food on his plate.
那个孩子很快把自己盘子里的食物吃完了。
❷一盘食物[C]
He had a plate of beef for lunch.
他午餐吃了一盘牛肉。

P

plateau 〔plæ'to ‖ 'plætəʊ〕

n. 高原[C]

platform 〔'plæt,fɔrm ‖ 'plætfɔːm〕

n. [C] ❶平台,台

a helicopter landing platform

直升机升降平台

❷讲台;戏台

The speaker mounted the platform.

演讲者登上了讲台。

❸(铁路等的)月台

He was coming by train, so I waited on the platform.

他坐火车来,所以我在月台上等。

play 〔ple ‖ pleɪ〕

[过去式]played;[过去分词]played

vi. ❶玩耍;游戏;戏弄;玩弄

Children like to play.

孩子们喜欢玩。

❷演奏;弹奏;吹奏;放音

The organ is playing.

管风琴在演奏。

❸参加竞赛

He played in the game.

他参加了比赛。

❹表演;上演

What's playing at the theatre?

剧场里在演什么戏?

vt. ❶演奏;放(唱片等)

Play us your favorite record.

请把你最喜欢的唱片放给我们听听。

❷同……比赛;玩(游戏等);打(球);踢(球);打(牌);下(棋)

He plays golf nearly every weekend.

他差不多每个周末都打高尔夫球。

❸开(玩笑);玩弄[(+on)]

Don't play a joke on him.

别拿他开玩笑。

❹扮演(角色);上演(戏剧)

I am to play Juliet.

我将扮演朱丽叶。

n. ❶游戏;玩耍[U]

All work and no play is no fun.

只工作,不娱乐,不会使人开心。

❷戏剧;剧本[C]

How did you enjoy the TV play?

你喜欢那个电视剧吗?

player 〔'pleɚ ‖ 'pleɪə〕

n. [C] ❶游戏的人;打牌的人;下棋的人

❷(球类)运动员

❸演员;演奏者;(电)唱机;(不能录音的)随身听,单放机

playground 〔'ple,graʊnd ‖

P

ˈpleɪɡraʊnd〕

n. [C]（学校的）操场，运动场；（儿童）游乐场

The students gathered on the playground.

学生们在操场上集合。

playmate〔ˈpleˌmet ‖ ˈpleɪmeɪt〕

n. 游伴，玩伴[C]

pleasant〔ˈplɛzn̩t ‖ ˈpleznt〕

a. ❶令人愉快的；舒适的

The walk was very pleasant.

那次散步很愉快。

❷讨人喜欢的；和蔼可亲的

The new manager is a pleasant Chinese American.

新任经理是个和气的美籍华人。

please〔pliz ‖ pliːz〕

[过去式]pleased；[过去分词]pleased

vt. 使高兴，使喜欢，使满意

It is very difficult to please him.

要取悦他很难。

vi. ❶使人满意，令人高兴，讨人喜欢；讨好

She is always anxious to please.

她老是极力想讨好人。

❷愿意；喜欢

Go where you please.

你想去哪儿就去哪儿。

❸（用于请求或命令）请

“May I come in?”

“我可以进来吗？”

“Come in, please.”

“请进。”

常用短语

if you please 请；对不起

be pleased with 中意，满足

He is pleased with the gift.

他对礼物很满意。

pleased〔plizd ‖ pliːzd〕

a. 高兴的，喜欢的；满意的[（+at/about/by/with）][+to-v][+that]

I am pleased to lend you the book.

很高兴把书借给你。

She had a pleased smile in he face.

她露出满意的微笑。

pleasure〔ˈplɛʒɚ ‖ ˈpleʒə〕

n. ❶愉快，高兴；满足[U]

He finds great pleasure in reading books.

他从读书中得到很大乐趣。

❷乐事；乐趣[C]

It is a pleasure to work with you.

和你一起工作真是件愉快的事。

常用短语

with pleasure 愉快地，乐意

He showed her around the city with pleasure.

他欣然陪同她游览了这座城市。

"Will you come with me?"

"你也一起来吧。"

"With pleasure."

"我很乐意"

plentiful 〔'plɛntɪfəl ‖ 'plentɪfʊl〕

a. 丰富的，充足的；多的

a plentiful supply of rice

充足的大米供应

plenty 〔'plɛntɪ ‖ 'plentɪ〕

n. 丰富；充足；大量[U][(+of)]

He has plenty of humorous stories to tell.

他有许多幽默故事可讲。

plot 〔plɑt ‖ plɒt〕

n. [C] ❶阴谋；秘密计划[(+against)][+to-v]

A plot to assassinate the President was uncovered by government agents.

刺杀总统的阴谋被政府特工人员发觉了。

❷(小说，戏剧等的)情节

The play has a very complicated plot.

这出戏的情节相当复杂。

plow, plough 〔plaʊ ‖ plaʊ〕

n. 犁[C]

Plows are still pulled by oxen in some countries.

在一些国家犁头仍由牛拖拉。

plug 〔plʌg ‖ plʌg〕

n. [C] ❶塞子，栓；堵塞物

She pulled out the plug of the bathtub.

她拔出浴缸的塞子。

❷(电器的)插头；(墙上的)插座；接头

plus 〔plʌs ‖ plʌs〕

prep. 加，加上

2 plus 5 is 7.

2 加 5 等于 7。

P. M., p. m.

abbr. = post meridiem 下午；午后

I took the 7 : 00 p. m. train to Beijing.

我搭下午 7 点的火车去北京。

pocket 〔'pɑkɪt ‖ 'pɒkɪt〕

n. 口袋[C]

He was standing with his hands in his pockets.

他站在那儿，两手插着口袋。

poem 〔'po・ɪm ‖ 'pəʊɪm〕

n. (一首)诗[C]

poet 〔'po・ɪt ‖ 'pəʊɪt〕

n. 诗人[C]

poetic 〔po'ɛtɪk ‖ pəʊ'etɪk〕

a. 诗的；诗人的；充满诗意的

His speech was very poetic.

他的演说很富有诗意。

poetry 〔'po·ɪtrɪ ‖ 'pəʊɪtrɪ〕

n. （总称）诗，诗歌[U]

Shakespeare and Milton were masters of English poetry.

莎士比亚和弥尔顿是英国诗歌的艺术大师。

point 〔pɔɪnt ‖ pɔɪnt〕

[过去式]pointed；[过去分词]pointed

n. ❶尖，尖端，尖头[C]

Do you have a pencil with a sharper point?

你有尖一点儿的铅笔吗？

❷特点，特征[C]

Dancing is not her strong point.

她不擅长跳舞。

❸分数；（比赛等的）得分[C]

In the game we got 10 points while the Medical School got only 3.

比赛中我们得了 10 分，而医学院只得了 3 分。

❹点；中心思想[the]

What's the point of your argument?

你主张的论点是什么？

❺意义；目的；用途[U][(+in/of)]

I see no point in talking to him.

我看不出和他谈还有什么意义。

❻【数】点；小数点；标点[C]

vt. ❶把……指向，把……对准；瞄准[(+at/towards)]

It's rude to point your fingers at people.

用手指指人是很不礼貌的。

❷指出[(+out)]

He pointed out that they were mistaken.

他指出他们错了。

pointed 〔'pɔɪntɪd ‖ 'pɔɪntɪd〕

a. ❶有尖头的，尖的

a pointed stone

尖利的石头

❷尖锐的；深刻的；中肯的

She made a pointed remark on the plan.

她对这个计划提出了尖锐的意见。

poison 〔'pɔɪzn̩ ‖ 'pɔɪzn〕

[过去式]poisoned；[过去分词]poisoned

n. 毒；毒药；毒物[C][U]

Gas is a poison.

煤气是有毒气体。

P

vt. 使中毒;毒死;污染
Industrial wastes have poisoned the river.
工业废弃物污染了这条河。

poisonous 〔ˈpɔɪzn̩əs ‖ ˈpɔɪzənəs〕
a. ❶有毒的;有害的
a poisonous snake
毒蛇
❷恶毒的,有恶意的
poisonous rumor
恶毒的流言

polar 〔ˈpolɚ ‖ ˈpəʊlə〕
a. ❶北极的,南极的;极地的
❷(有)极的;极性的;磁极的;电极的

pole[1] 〔pol ‖ pəʊl〕
n. 杆;柱;竿[C]
We used a branch as a fishing pole.
我们用树枝做钓竿。

pole[2] 〔pol ‖ pəʊl〕
n. [C] ❶(地球的)极;极地区域,极地
A big white bear lives near the North Pole.
一种大白熊栖居于北极附近。
❷【物】电极;磁极
The opposite poles of magnets attract each other.
磁体的南北两极相互吸引。

police 〔pəˈlis ‖ pəˈliːs〕
n. 警察,警方[P][the]
We must inform the police.
我们必须通知警方。

policeman 〔pəˈlismən ‖ pəˈliːsmən〕
n. 警察,警员[C]
A policeman asked me several questions.
有个警官问了我好几个问题。

policy 〔ˈpɑləsɪ ‖ ˈpɒləsɪ〕
n. [C][U] ❶政策,方针
One of the new government's policies is to cut taxes.
新政府的政策之一是减税。
❷策略,手段
Honesty is the best policy.
诚实是上策。

polish 〔ˈpɑlɪʃ ‖ ˈpɒlɪʃ〕
[过去式]polished;[过去分词]polished
vt. ❶磨光,擦亮
He polished his spectacles with a handkerchief before answering the questions.
回答问题之前,他用手帕擦拭了一下眼镜。
❷使优美,使精炼;润饰
The speaker spent several days polishing her lecture.
演讲者花了几天时间润饰她的

演讲稿。

n. ❶磨光，擦亮

Give your shoes a polish.

把你的鞋子擦一擦。

❷光滑，光泽

A hot plate will spoil the polish on this table.

热盘子会毁坏桌面的光泽。

polite 〔pə'laɪt ‖ pə'laɪt〕

a. 有礼貌的，客气的；殷勤的

He's always so polite to people.

他对人总是非常有礼貌。

political 〔pə'lɪtɪkḷ ‖ pə'lɪtɪkəl〕

a. 政治的；政治上的

a political party

政党

politician 〔ˌpɑlə'tɪʃən ‖ ˌpɒlɪ'tɪʃən〕

n. 政治家，政客[C]

He is a dishonest politician.

他是个狡诈的政客。

politics 〔'pɑləˌtɪks ‖ 'pɒlɪtɪks〕

n. 政治，政治学[U]

Politics was one of his university subjects.

政治学是他大学的课程之一。

pollution 〔pə'luʃən ‖ pə'lu:ʃən〕

n. [U] ❶污染

environmental pollution

环境污染

air pollution

空气污染

❷污染物；污染地区

She was horrified by all the pollution on the beach.

她对海滩上的污染感到震惊。

pond 〔pɑnd ‖ pɒnd〕

n. 池塘[C]

Some cattle were drinking at the pond.

几头牛正在池塘边饮水。

pony 〔'ponɪ ‖ 'pəʊnɪ〕

n. [C] ❶矮种马；小马

The children rode their ponies all over the farm.

孩子们骑着小马在农场上到处跑。

❷小型的东西

She drank a pony of brandy.

她喝了一小杯白兰地。

pool 〔pul ‖ pu:l〕

n. [C]❶水塘，水池，小水坑

After the heavy rain there were pools on the road.

大雨过后路上有一些小水坑。

❷(液体等的)一摊，一片[(+of)]

Fatally shot, he lay in a pool of blood.

他遭致命枪击，躺在血泊之中。

❸游泳池

I swam in the swimming pool.

我在游泳池里游泳。

poor 〔pur ‖ puə〕

[比]poorer;[最]poorest

a. ❶贫穷的,贫困的

My family used to be poor.

我家过去很穷。

❷粗劣的,蹩脚的

My English is very poor.

我的英语很糟。

❸贫乏的,缺少的,不充足的

That country is poor in natural resources.

那个国家自然资源贫乏。

❹体弱的

He's still in poor health after his illness.

他病后身体仍很虚弱。

❺可怜的,不幸的

The poor little girl began to cry.

这个可怜的小姑娘哭了起来。

popcorn 〔'pɑpˌkɔrn ‖ 'pɒpkɔːn〕

n. 爆玉米花[U]

popular 〔'pɑpjələ˞ ‖ 'pɒpjʊlə〕

a. ❶民众的;大众的

popular representatives

人民代表

❷得人心的,受欢迎的[(+with/among)]

She is now a popular film star.

她现在是有名的影星。

He is popular with girls.

他很受女孩子欢迎。

❸普通的,广为流传的,流行的,通俗的,大众化的

Many young people love popular songs.

许多年轻人喜爱流行歌曲。

popular novels

通俗小说

population 〔ˌpɑpjə'leʃən ‖ ˌpɒpjʊ'leɪʃən〕

n. ❶人口[U]

The population of this country rose by 10 percent.

这个国家的人口增长了百分之十。

❷(某地域的)全部居民[the]

Only ten percent of the population here is illiterate.

这里只有百分之十的居民是文盲。

P

populous 〔'pɑpjələs ‖ 'pɒpjʊləs〕

a. 人口众多的,人口稠密的

a populous city

人口众多的城市

pork 〔pɔrk ‖ pɔːk〕

n. 猪肉[U]

porridge 〔'pɔrɪdʒ ‖ 'pɒrɪdʒ〕

n. 粥,糊,麦片粥[U]

port 〔pɔrt ‖ pɔːt〕

n. ❶港[C][U]
We must reach port by evening.
我们必须在傍晚前抵港。
❷港市，口岸[C]
The former fishing village has now become an important port.
过去的渔村现已成为重要港口。
❸机场，航空站[C]

portable ['pɔrtəbl̩ || 'pɔːtəbl]
a. 便于携带的，手提式的(计算机)；轻便的
a portable radio
便携式收音机

porter ['pɔrtɚ || 'pɔːtə]
n. (车站，机场等的)搬运工人，脚夫[C]
The porter carried our baggage.
那个脚夫帮我们提行李。

portion ['pɔrʃən || 'pɔːʃən]
n. ❶(一)部分[C][(+of)]
He left the major portion of his money to the foundation.
他将大部分钱留给了这个基金会。
❷(食物等的)一份，一客[C]
He was very hungry and ordered two portions of roast duck.
他很饿，因而叫了两份烤鸭。

portrait ['pɔrtrɪt || 'pɔːtrɪt]
n. 肖像，画像；相片[C]
This portrait looks real.
这幅肖像看起来栩栩如生。

portray [pɔr'tre || pɔː'treɪ]
[过去式]portrayed；[过去分词]portrayed
vt. 画(人物，风景等)；(用语言)描写
The picture portrays a beautiful sunset.
那幅画描绘了落日的美景。

Portugal ['pɔrtʃəgl̩ || 'pɔːtjugəl]
n. 葡萄牙

Portuguese ['pɔrtʃəˌgiz || ˌpɔːtjʊ'giːz]
n. 葡萄牙人；葡萄牙语
a. 葡萄牙的；葡萄牙人的；葡萄牙语的

position [pə'zɪʃən || pə'zɪʃən]
n. ❶位置，地点，方位[C]
The bed used to be in this position.
床原来是放在这儿的。
❷姿势，姿态[C]
The girl is drawn in a standing position.
那个少女站立的姿势被画了下来。
❸地位，身份；位次[C][(+

in)]
He has a high position in society.
他社会地位很高。
❹形势,境况[C]
He made a study of the position of the middle class in Britain.
他研究过英国中产阶级的状况。
❺立场,态度[C]
I am in no position to help you.
以我的境遇,我无法帮助你。
❻职位,职务;工作[C][(+with/in)]
She got a position in that company.
她在那家公司谋了个职位。

positive 〔ˈpɑzətɪv‖ˈpɒzətɪv〕
a. ❶确定的;确实的
There is positive proof that he did it.
有确凿的证据证明他做了这件事。
❷确信的;有自信的[(+of/about)][+(that)]
Are you positive that you saw him?
你肯定你看到他了吗?
❸积极的,建设性的
He has a positive attitude towards life.
他对生活持积极的态度。

possess 〔pəˈzɛs‖pəˈzes〕
[过去式]possessed;[过去分词]possessed
vt. 拥有,持有;具有;占有
The country possesses rich mineral deposits.
这个国家拥有丰富的矿藏。

possession 〔pəˈzɛʃən‖pəˈzeʃən〕
n. ❶拥有;占有[U]
The possession of a degree does not guarantee you a job.
拥有一个学位不能保证你找到工作。
❷所有物;财产[P]
Her possessions could fit in one suitcase.
她的全部财物可以装在一个手提箱内。

possibility 〔pɑsəˈbɪlətɪ‖ˌpɒsəˈbɪlɪtɪ〕
n. ❶可能性[(+of)][+that]
There is a good possibility of rain tonight.
今晚很可能要下雨。
❷可能的事,可能发生的事[C]
Life on other planets is a possibility.
其他行星上有生物是可能的。
❸发展前途,潜在价值[P]
He is a man of possibilities.

P

他是一个有发展前途的人。

possible〔ˈpɑsəbl̩ ‖ ˈpɒsəbl〕

a. ❶可能的

I'll do everything possible to help you.

我将尽一切可能帮助你。

❷有可能的[+that]

It's possible that he will not accept the invitation.

他有可能不接受邀请。

❸合适的，尚可的

He is the only possible man for this position.

他是唯一适合担任此职的人。

常用短语

as … as possible 尽可能

Do it as quickly as possible.

要尽快做。

if possible 如有可能

Do so if possible.

如果可能的话就这样做吧。

P

possibly〔ˈpɑsəblɪ ‖ ˈpɒsəblɪ〕

ad. ❶也许，可能

Possibly you are right.

也许你是对的。

❷无论如何，究竟（用于否定句、疑问句）

I cannot possibly go to the party.

我怎么也不会去参加晚会。

post¹〔post ‖ pəust〕

[过去式] posted; [过去分词] posted

n. ❶【主英】邮政(制度)；邮寄[U]

If you could get the book, please send it to me by post.

如果你能弄到那本书，请邮寄给我。

❷邮件；邮件的一次发送(或收进)[U]

The last post had arrived and there was no letter for her.

最后一批邮件已到，但没有她的信。

vt. 邮寄，投寄

Do you mind posting a letter for me?

你能帮我寄封信吗?

post²〔post ‖ pəust〕

n. 柱；桩；杆[C]

The notice was nailed to a post.

布告钉在一根柱子上。

postage〔ˈpostɪdʒ ‖ ˈpəustɪdʒ〕

n. 邮资，邮费[U]

How much is the postage on this package?

这个包裹需要多少邮费?

postcard〔ˈpostˌkɑrd ‖ ˈpəustˌkɑːd〕

n. 邮政明信片[C]

postman 〔 ˈpostmən ‖ ˈpəustmən〕

n. 【英】邮差，邮递员［C］

postpone 〔posˈpon ‖ pəusˈpəun〕

［过去式］postponed；［过去分词］postponed

vt. 使延期，延迟，延缓［(＋to/until)］［＋v-ing］

The party was postponed to the next week.

集会延期至下周举行。

postwar 〔ˈpostˈwər ‖ ˈpəustˈwɔː〕

a. 战后的

a postwar problem

战后的问题

〔反义〕prewar 战前的

pot 〔pɑt ‖ pɒt〕

n. ❶罐；壶；锅［C］

壶 pot

❷一罐（壶，锅）之量［C］［(＋of)］

She made a pot of tea for her guests.

她给客人沏了一壶茶。

potato 〔pəˈteto ‖ pəˈteɪtəu〕

n. 马铃薯［C］［U］

Potato is grown in many parts of the world.

马铃薯在世界许多地区都有种植。

potential 〔pəˈtɛnʃəl ‖ pəˈtenʃəl〕

a. 潜在的，可能的

Education develops potential abilities.

教育能开发潜能。

pound 〔paʊnd ‖ paʊnd〕

n. ❶（重量单位）磅［C］

These potatoes weigh 4 pounds.

这些马铃薯有 4 磅重。

❷英镑［C］

She paid 20 pounds for the suit.

她花了 20 英镑买了那件套装。

pour 〔pər ‖ pɔː〕

［过去式］poured；［过去分词］poured

vt. ❶倒，灌，注

She poured herself another cup of tea.

她为自己又倒了一杯茶。

❷倾注；大量投入；大量生产

They have poured money into the tourist industry.
他们已经把大笔钱投入了旅游业。
vi. ❶倾泻，涌流
The crowd poured out of the concert hall.
人群从音乐厅涌了出来。
❷斟茶
Shall I pour?
我来斟茶好吗？
❸(雨)倾盆而下[(+down)]
The rain poured steadily down.
大雨不停地倾盆而下。

poverty 〔'pɑvətɪ ‖ 'pɒvətɪ〕
n. [U] ❶贫穷，贫困
His family lives below the poverty line.
他的一家生活极端艰苦。
❷贫乏，缺少[(+of/in)]
The article shows a poverty of imagination.
这篇文章显得缺乏想象力。

powder 〔'paudɚ ‖ 'paudə〕
n. ❶粉，粉末[C][U]
He crushed a piece of chalk to powder.
他将一支粉笔压成粉末。
❷扑粉，化妆用粉[U]
There's too much powder on your nose.
你鼻子上的粉擦得太多了。
❸火药，炸药[U]

power 〔'pauɚ ‖ 'pauə〕
n. ❶权力；势力，能力，本领[U]
She lost her power of speech.
她失去了说话的能力。
❷力，力量；动力，电力；功率[U]
The shortage of power dimmed the streets.
由于电力不足，街道昏暗。

powerful 〔'pauɚfəl ‖ 'pauəfəl〕
[比]more powerful；[最]most powerful
a. 强有力的，强大的
a powerful army
强大的军队

practical 〔'præktɪkḷ ‖ 'præktɪkəl〕
[比]more practical；[最]most practical
a. ❶实践的，实际的
Practical experience is often very important.
实践经验往往是很重要的。
❷实用的，有实用价值的
Your invention is very practical.
你的发明很实用。
❸注重实效的，讲究实际的，有

实际经验的
She was a simple, practical, hardworking woman.
她简朴,实际,勤奋。
❹可实施的

practically 〔ˈpræktɪklɪ ‖ ˈprækətɪklɪ〕
ad. ❶【口】几乎,差不多
The work is practically finished.
那项工作几乎完成了。
❷实际上;事实上
He is practically the boss of the group.
他是那个集团真正的老板。
❸从实际出发
Practically speaking, the plan is not good.
实际上说,那个计划并不好。

practice 〔ˈpræktɪs ‖ ˈpræktɪs〕
[过去式]practiced;[过去分词]practiced
n. ❶实行,实施,实践[U]
I am afraid the idea would never work in practice.
恐怕这个想法实际上行不通。
❷(反复的)练习,学习[C][U]
Learning a language needs a lot of practice.
学习语言需要勤练不辍。
❸(医生、律师等的)业务,工作,营业[C]
Dr. Pat is no longer in practice here.
帕特医生不在这儿行医了。
❹习惯,常规,惯例[C][U]
vt. ❶实践,实行
What I preach, I am resolved to practice.
我所讲的道理,我必定身体力行。
❷练习,实习;训练
The young girl practices the violin every day.
这个小女孩每天练习拉小提琴。
vi. ❶实践,实行
❷练习,实习
I don't think you practice enough.
我认为你练习得不够。
❸(医生,律师等)开业[(+as)]
He practices as a lawyer in Hong Kong.
他在香港当律师。

praise 〔prez ‖ preɪz〕
[过去式]praised;[过去分词]praised
n. 赞扬,称赞[U]
I'm sure I don't deserve so much praise.
我肯定自己不值得这么多赞

扬。

vt. 赞美，表扬；歌颂

The publishers praised his novel pretty highly.

出版商们对他的小说评价甚高。

pray 〔pre ‖ preɪ〕

［过去式］prayed；［过去分词］prayed

vt. 祈祷，祈求

They prayed that they would defeat their enemies soon.

他们祈祷尽快打败敌人。

vi. 祈祷，祈求；请求，恳求［(＋to/for)］

The athletic meet is on Saturday, so we're praying for a fine day.

学校的运动会是星期六，所以我们虔心祈求好天气。

P

precede 〔prɪ'sid ‖ prɪ'siːd〕

［过去式］preceded；［过去分词］preceded

vt. （顺序，位置或时间上等）处在……之前

He preceded me into the classroom.

他比我先进入教室。

precious 〔'prɛʃəs ‖ 'preʃəs〕

［比］more precious；［最］most precious

a. ❶贵重的，宝贵的，珍贵的

He has sent me most precious gifts.

他送给我极为珍贵的礼物。

❷珍爱的，宝贝的

His children are very precious to him.

他极疼爱自己的孩子。

precise 〔prɪ'saɪs ‖ prɪ'sais〕

［比］more precise；［最］most precise

a. 精确的；准确的；明确的；清晰的

The precise sum was 63 cents.

准确的数目是 63 美分。

词汇拓展

precisely *ad.* 准确地，精确地

precision 〔prɪ'sɪʒən ‖ prɪ'sɪʒən〕

n. 精确（性）；精密（度）；准确（性）；确切（性）［U］

We guarantee the precision of the watch.

我们可以保证这块表的准确性。

predict 〔prɪ'dɪkt ‖ prɪ'dɪkt〕

［过去式］predicted；［过去分词］predicted

vt. 预言；预料；预报［＋that］［＋wh-］

Some scientists predict that there will be a great earthquake.
有些科学家预言将会有一场大地震。

prediction 〔prɪˈdɪkʃən ‖ prɪˈdɪkʃən〕
n. 预言；预报[C][U]

preface 〔ˈprɛfɪs ‖ ˈprefɪs〕
n. [C] ❶序言，绪言；引语
The book has a preface written by the author.
该书有作者写的序言。
❷【口】开端，序幕；前奏[(+ to)]
The accident was the preface to a great scientific discovery.
这一偶然事件成了一项重大科学发现的前奏。

prefer 〔prɪˈfɝ ‖ prɪˈfɜː〕
[过去式]preferred；[过去分词]preferred
vt. 宁可，宁愿(选择)；更喜欢
I prefer the quiet countryside to the noisy cities.
我喜欢安静的乡村胜过喧闹的城市。
I prefer walking.
我比较喜欢散步。
He preferred to die rather than (to) steal/instead of stealing.
他宁可死也不愿偷。
〈后接不定式时，与 rather than 或 instead of 连用〉

preference 〔ˈprɛfərəns ‖ ˈprefərəns〕
n. 喜爱，偏爱的事物(或人)
My preference is for beef rather than pork.
比起猪肉我比较喜欢吃牛肉。

prejudice 〔ˈprɛdʒədɪs ‖ ˈpredʒʊdɪs〕
n. 偏见，歧视[C][U][(+ against)]
He had a prejudice against foreigners.
他对外国人有偏见。

preparation 〔ˌprɛpəˈreʃən ‖ ˌprepəˈreɪʃən〕
n. ❶准备，预备[U][(+ of/for)]
He sharpened his knife in preparation for carving the meat.
他磨快了刀准备切肉。
❷(具体的)准备工作，准备措施[P][(+for)]
We made preparations for the trip.
我们为旅行做准备。
❸【英】【书】预习；备课[U]

prepare 〔prɪˈpɛr ‖ prɪˈpeə〕
[过去式]prepared；[过去分词]

prepared

vt. ❶准备;使……准备好[(+for)]

They prepared themselves for the worst.

他们作了最坏的打算。

❷筹备,筹划[(+for)]

❸做(饭菜);制作;调制

When we arrived home, mother had already prepared dinner for us.

当我们到家时,母亲已为我们准备好了晚餐。

vi. 做准备,预备[(+for)][+to-v]

I was preparing for bed when I heard a knock at the door.

我正准备睡觉时听到有人敲门。

presence 〔'prɛzṇs ‖ 'prezns〕

n.[U] ❶出席,在场;存在

I was aware of his presence at the party.

我注意到他在晚会上出现了。

❷面前,眼前

He felt shy in the presence of the ladies.

他在女士面前很腼腆。

present[1] 〔'prɛzṇt ‖ 'preznt〕

a. ❶出席的,在场的

All the students were present.

所有的学生都出席了。

〔**反义**〕absent 缺席的

❷现在的,当前的

The present King is loved by the people.

现在的国王很受人民的爱戴。

present[2] 〔'prɛzṇt ‖ 'preznt〕

n. 礼物,赠品[C]

I have a present for you.

我有礼物给你。

preserve 〔prɪ'zɝv ‖ prɪ'zɜːv〕

[过去式]preserved;[过去分词]preserved

vt. ❶保存,保藏;防腐[(+from)]

Oil preserves metal from rust.

油能防止金属生锈。

❷保护;维护;维持

We have taken effective measures to preserve our natural resources.

我们已采取有效措施保护自然资源。

❸腌(肉等);把……做成蜜饯(或果酱);把……制成罐头食品[(+in)]

We preserve fish in salt.

我们用盐腌鱼。

n. ❶蜜饯;果酱[C][U]

Mother used to make peach preserves.

妈妈过去常常自制桃子果酱。

❷(动植物)保护区;禁猎区[C]

president 〔ˈprɛzədənt ‖ ˈprezɪdənt〕

n. [C] ❶(大写)总统[(+of)]

The President of France visited our country last week.

上星期法国总统访问了我国。

❷会长;校长;大臣;长官;(会议)主席

❸总裁;董事长

press 〔prɛs ‖ pres〕

[过去式]pressed;[过去分词]pressed

vt. ❶按,压,挤

Press this button to start the engine.

按此钮发动引擎。

❷紧抱,紧握(手)

She pressed the frightened child to her heart.

她把受了惊吓的孩子搂在怀里。

❸催促,敦促;催逼;强迫;(极力)劝说

He pressed the man to pay his debts.

他逼那个人还债。

vi. ❶挤向前,奋力前进

Many people pressed forward to shake hands with him.

许多人挤向前和他握手。

❷紧迫

Time presses and we must get back to work.

时间紧迫,我们得回去上班了。

n. ❶报刊;新闻界;记者们;通讯社[the]

The power of the press is very great.

新闻报刊的力量是极大的。

❷新闻舆论;报刊评论

The government's new policy received a good press.

政府的新政策受到新闻舆论的好评。

pressure 〔ˈprɛʃɚ ‖ ˈpreʃə〕

n. ❶压力;压迫;紧迫;催促[C][U]

He works well under pressure.

他在有压力的情况下工作很出色。

❷【物】压力;压强[C][U]

presume 〔prɪˈzum ‖ prɪˈzjuːm〕

[过去式]presumed;[过去分词]presumed

vt. ❶擅自(做);冒昧(做)[+to-v]

May I presume to ask where you work?

对不起,您在哪儿工作?

❷假定,假设;推测,认为[+

(that)]
Don't presume that he is guilty.
不要假定他有罪。
❸推定，意味着[＋(that)]
I presumed (that) you were tired.
我想你累了。

pretend 〔prɪˈtɛnd ‖ prɪˈtend〕
[过去式]pretended；[过去分词]pretended
vt. ❶佯装；假装[＋to-v][＋(that)]
He pretended that he was innocent.
他假装无辜。
❷自命，自称[＋to-v][＋(that)]
He does not pretend to be a scholar.
他并不自命为学者。
❸(尤指孩子)(在游戏中)假扮；装作[＋to-v][＋(that)]
Let's pretend that we're on an island.
让我们装作在一孤岛上。
vi. ❶假装
She wasn't really crying; she was only pretending.
她并非真的在哭；她只是假装而已。
❷自封，自称；妄求[(＋to)]
She pretends to great knowledge.
她自称具有广博的知识。

pretty 〔ˈprɪtɪ ‖ ˈprɪtɪ〕
[比]prettier；[最]prettiest
a. ❶(用于女性，小孩及小物件)漂亮的；秀丽的；可爱的
What a pretty house it is!
多漂亮的一栋房子！
❷优美的；悦耳的；令人愉快的
She's got a pretty voice.
她的声音很悦耳。
ad. 相当，颇，很，非常
Her sister is still pretty sick.
她的妹妹仍病得很重。

prevent 〔prɪˈvɛnt ‖ prɪˈvent〕
[过去式]prevented；[过去分词]prevented
vt. ❶防止，预防
Vitamin C is supposed to prevent colds.
维生素C被认为能预防感冒。
❷阻止；制止；妨碍[(＋from)]
Who prevents their plans from being carried out?
谁阻止他们的计划，不让实施？

previous 〔ˈpriviəs ‖ ˈpriːviəs〕
a. 先的，前的，以前的
I remember you mentioned the same thing on a previous occasion.

我记得你在以前某个场合提及过同一件事情。

prewar〔priˈwɔr ‖ ˈpriːwɔː〕

a. 战前的

〔反义〕postwar 战后的

price〔praɪs ‖ praɪs〕

n. ❶价格，价钱[C]

Prices keep going up.

物价持续上涨。

❷代价[(＋of/for)]

The country paid a heavy price for her independence.

该国为独立付出了沉重的代价。

常用短语

at any price 不惜任何代价；无论如何

I'll do it at any price.

我会不惜任何代价去做。

pride〔praɪd ‖ praɪd〕

n. ❶自豪，得意[U][(＋in)]

He looked at his painting with pride.

他得意地看着他的画儿。

He took pride in his work.

他为自己的工作感到自豪。

❷引以自豪的人(或物)[C][(＋of)]

He is the pride of the family.

他的家人以他为荣。

❸骄傲，傲慢，自大[U]

He has far too much pride.

他太骄傲了。

priest〔prist ‖ priːst〕

n. [C] ❶(基督教)牧师；(天主教)神父

The priest conducts the church service.

牧师主持教堂的礼拜仪式。

❷神职人员；教士；僧人；祭司

primary〔ˈpraɪˌmɛrɪ ‖ ˈpraɪmərɪ〕

a. ❶首要的，主要的

A primary cause of Tom's failure is his laziness.

懒惰是汤姆失败的主要原因之一。

❷初级的，初等的；基层的

I started primary school when I was 5 years old.

我5岁时开始读小学。

primitive〔ˈprɪmətɪv ‖ ˈprɪmɪtɪv〕

a. ❶原始的；远古的；早期的

Primitive people lived in caves.

原始人住在山洞里。

❷粗糙的；简单的；未开化的

a primitive straw hut

简陋的茅屋

prince〔prɪns ‖ prɪns〕

n. 王子，亲王[C]

princess〔ˈprɪnsɪs ‖ ˌprɪnˈses〕

n. 公主；王妃[C]

principal 〔ˈprɪnsəpḷ ‖ ˈprɪnsəpəl〕

a. 主要的，首要的，最重要的

Drinking is a principal cause of traffic accidents.

酗酒是发生交通事故的主要原因。

n. 校长；社长；首长[C]

The school principal read the honor roll list.

校长宣读优秀生名单。

principle 〔ˈprɪnsəpḷ ‖ ˈprɪnsəpl〕

n. ❶原则；原理[C]

I take this seriously. It's a matter of principle.

我对此很认真。这是原则问题。

❷主义；信条[C]

❸道义，节操[U]

He is a man of high principle.

他是一个有高度道德原则的人。

print 〔prɪnt ‖ prɪnt〕

[过去式]printed；[过去分词]printed

vt. ❶印，印刷

The book was printed on rough yellow paper.

这本书用粗糙的黄纸印刷。

❷出版，发行

Their dictionary was printed last month.

他们的字典已于上个月出版发行。

❸用印刷体写

Please print your name and address.

请用印刷体书写你的姓名和地址。

n. ❶印出的字；印刷字体[U]

This book has clear print.

这本书的字体很清晰。

❷印痕，印记[C]

His feet left prints in the soft soil.

松软的泥土上留下了他的脚印。

printing 〔ˈprɪntɪŋ ‖ ˈprɪntɪŋ〕

n. 印刷；印刷术；印刷业[U]

When was printing invented?

印刷术是什么时候发明的？

prior 〔ˈpraɪɚ ‖ ˈpraɪə〕

a. 在先的，在前的；居先的

I have a prior engagement.

我已与人有约在先。

常用短语

prior to… 在……之前

She traveled in America prior to her marriage.

她结婚之前去美国旅行了一趟。

priority 〔praɪˈɔrətɪ ‖ praɪˈɒrətɪ〕

n. ❶优先权[U]

Old people have priority over young people in taking seats.

老年人比年轻人优先入坐。

❷优先考虑的事[C]

prison 〔ˈprɪzn̩ ‖ ˈprɪzn〕

n. ❶监狱[C][U]

He was sent to prison for damaging public property.

他因破坏公共财产被处监禁。

❷监禁[U]

Are there alternatives to prison?

除了监禁还有其他办法吗?

prisoner 〔ˈprɪzn̩ɚ ‖ ˈprɪzənə〕

n. 犯人,囚犯,俘虏[C]

Two prisoners have escaped.

有两个犯人逃跑了。

private 〔ˈpraɪvɪt ‖ ˈpraɪvɪt〕

a. ❶个人的,私人的

That's my private view.

那是我个人的观点。

❷私下的,非公开的,秘密的

I wish to have a private talk with you.

我希望私下和你谈谈。

❸私营的,私立的,私有的

If you go to a private hospital, you must pay.

如果你去一家私立医院就诊,你得付费。

privilege 〔ˈprɪvl̩ɪdʒ ‖ ˈprɪvɪlɪdʒ〕

n. ❶特权;优惠[C][U]

He enjoys diplomatic privileges.

他享有外交特权。

❷(个人的)恩典,殊荣

It is a great privilege to know you.

认识你真是莫大的荣幸。

prize 〔praɪz ‖ praɪz〕

n. [C] ❶奖赏;奖品;奖金

His poem won the first prize in the contest.

他的诗作在比赛中获得第一名。

❷(值得)竞争的目标,极有价值的东西

To some men wealth is the greatest prize in life.

对一些人来说,财富是人生最有价值的东西。

P

probability 〔ˌprɑbəˈbɪlətɪ ‖ ˌprɒbəˈbɪlɪtɪ〕

n. ❶可能性,或然性[U][(+of)][+that]

The probability of making a mistake increases when you are tired.

你累的时候犯错误的可能性就会增加。

❷或有的事；可能的结果[C]
A surprise test is a strong probability.
突然考试很有可能。
❸【数】概率，或然率，几率[U]

probable 〔ˈprɑbəbḷ ‖ ˈprɒbəbl〕
a. 很可能发生的；很可能成为事实的；很有希望的
He's a probable candidate.
他是很有希望的候选人。

probably 〔ˈprɑbəblɪ ‖ ˈprɒbəblɪ〕
ad. 大概，或许，很可能
He will probably refuse the offer.
他很可能会拒绝这一提议。

problem 〔ˈprɑbləm ‖ ˈprɒbləm〕
n. 问题，疑难问题[C]
Measures have been taken to solve traffic problems in big cities.
业已采取措施以解决大城市的交通问题。

procedure 〔prəˈsidʒɚ ‖ prəˈsiːdʒə〕
n. [C]❶过程；手续；步骤
The chairman was quite familiar with the procedure for conducting a meeting.
主席对开会的过程很熟悉。
❷常规；常规的做法
The first step in the procedure for making a kite is to build the frame.
制作风筝的第一步是做骨架。

proceed 〔prəˈsid ‖ prəˈsiːd〕
[过去式]proceeded；[过去分词]proceeded
vi. ❶继续进行；继续做(或讲)下去[(＋to/with)]
The old man took a drink from his cup and proceeded with his story.
老人拿起杯子喝了一口，继续讲他的故事。
❷开始，着手，出发[＋to-v]
After everyone was seated, the chairman proceeded to announce his plan.
大家就座后，主席开始宣布他的计划。
❸进行，开展
The project is proceeding as planned.
工程正在按计划进行。

process 〔ˈprɑsɛs ‖ ˈprɒses〕
[过去式]processed；[过去分词]processed
n. [C]❶过程，进程
I will tell you all the complicated process sooner or later.
我早晚要将整个复杂过程告诉

你。
❷步骤;过程;工序;制作法
They are using a new process to make glass.
他们正在用一种新方法制造玻璃。
vt. ❶加工
Supermarkets sell many vegetables that have been processed.
超级市场出售许多已经加工过的蔬菜。
❷处理,办理;用计算机处理
The information is being processed.
信息正在处理中。

procession 〔prəˈsɛʃən ‖ prəˈseʃən〕
n. ❶(人或车辆等的)行列,队伍[C]
Thousands of workers joined the funeral procession.
数千名工人加入了送葬行列。
❷(行列的)行进[U]
The demonstrators marched in procession to the minister's office.
示威者列队向部长的办公室走去。

produce 〔prəˈdus ‖ prəˈdjuːs〕
[过去式]produced;[过去分词]produced
vt. ❶生产,出产;制造;创作
The factory produces tires.
这家工厂生产轮胎。
❷生育;产(仔)
❸拿出;出示;提出
She produced a comb out of her handbag.
她从手提包里拿出一把梳子。
❹引起,生成;招致
Hard work produces success.
努力工作可获得成功。

product 〔ˈprɑdʌkt ‖ ˈprɒdʌkt〕
n. [C] ❶产品,产物;产量;出产【喻】产物
They came here in search of new markets for their products.
他们来这儿为他们的产品寻找新市场。
❷结果,成果
The plan was the product of many days of careful thought.
这个计划是许多天仔细考虑的成果。
❸作品,创作

production 〔prəˈdʌkʃən ‖ prəˈdʌkʃən〕
n. ❶生产[U]
Thousands of men were employed in the production of cars.

P

成千上万的人被雇用来生产汽车。
❷制作;(电影)摄制;(戏剧)演出[U]
The production of the film cost 20 million US dollars.
这部影片的摄制耗资2,000万美元。
❸产量[U]
Production was up last month.
上个月产量上升了。
❹(艺术)作品;(研究)成果,产物[C]

productive 〔prəˈdʌktɪv ‖ prəˈdʌktɪv〕
a. ❶生产的,生产性的
Farming is productive labor.
农业是生产性劳动。
❷出产……的;生成……的[(+of)]
Rude words are productive of quarrels.
粗鲁的言辞会导致争吵。

profession 〔prəˈfɛʃən ‖ prəˈfeʃən〕
n. (尤指受过良好教育或专门训练者,如律师,医生,教师的)职业[C]
What made you choose law as a profession?
是什么使你选择法律工作作为职业的?

professional 〔prəˈfɛʃənl̩ ‖ prəˈfeʃənəl〕
a. ❶(具有专门知识的)职业的
Doctors and lawyers are professional people.
医生和律师是专业人员。
❷职业性的,非业余性的
He is a professional wrestler.
他是职业摔跤手。
〔反义〕amateur 业余的

professor 〔prəˈfɛsɚ ‖ prəˈfesə〕
n. 教授[C]
She was a professor of chemistry at Chicago University.
她曾是芝加哥大学的化学教授。

profit 〔ˈprɑfɪt ‖ ˈprɒfɪt〕
n. ❶利润,赢利;收益,红利[C][U]
He made a profit of 50 thousand dollars on his house.
他卖掉房子获利5万美元。
❷利益,益处;得益[U]
We gained a lot of profit from your advice.
我们从你的建议中获益匪浅。

profound 〔prəˈfaʊnd ‖ prəˈfaʊnd〕
a. ❶深深的;深刻的;深切的;深度的

He gave a profound sigh.
他深深叹了口气。
❷渊博的,造诣深的;深奥的
a profound scholar
渊博的学者

program(me)〔ˈprəʊgræm ‖ ˈprəʊgræm〕
n.[C] ❶节目单;过程表
The last item on the program was a grand display of fireworks.
最后一项节目是大型烟火表演。
❷节目,表演,演出
What is your favorite television program?
你最喜爱的电视节目是什么?
❸计划;方案;过程
What is the program for tomorrow?
明天计划做什么?
❹(政党的)纲领
❺(教学)大纲;课程
❻【计算机】程序;过程设计

progress〔ˈprɑgrɛs ‖ ˈprəʊgres〕
[过去式]progressed;[过去分词]progressed
n.[U] ❶前进,行进
They made slow progress towards the mountaintop.
他们向山顶缓慢地前进。
❷进步,上进;发展
The boy has made great progress this year.
这个男孩今年进步很多。
❸进行,进展
A grand reception is in progress.
大型招待会正在进行。
vi. ❶前进;进行
The building of the railroad is progressing.
铁路正在建造中。
❷上进,提高,进步
The boy has progressed in his studies.
这个男孩学习方面有进步。

progressive〔prəˈgrɛsɪv ‖ prəˈgresɪv〕
a. 进步的;先进的;渐次的,逐渐的;累进的
a progressive party
革新派

prohibit〔proˈhɪbɪt ‖ prəˈhɪbɪt〕
[过去式]prohibited;[过去分词]prohibited
vt. (以法令,规定等)禁止
Alcohol is prohibited here.
这里是禁酒的。
〔同义〕forbid 禁止

prohibition〔ˌproəˈbɪʃən ‖ prəʊhɪˈbɪʃən〕

n. ❶禁止[U][(+of)]
the prohibition of smoking
禁止吸烟
❷(常大写)禁酒[U]
❸禁令;禁律[C][(+against/on)]
a prohibition against selling alcohol to people under the age of 18
禁止向18岁以下青少年售酒的法令

project ['prɑdʒɛkt ‖ 'prɒdʒekt]
n. [C]❶方案,计划,企划
They formed a project to build a new school building.
他们拟订了盖一幢新校舍的计划。
❷工程
❸科研项目

promise ['prɑmɪs ‖ 'prɒmɪs]
[过去式]promised;[过去分词]promised
n. ❶承诺,诺言[C][(+of)][+(that)][+to-v]
Give me your promise that you will never be late again.
答应我你决不再迟到了。
❷希望,前途[U]
The young man shows promise as a poet.
这位青年有成为诗人的希望。
vt. ❶允诺,答应
He promised me the book.
他答应给我这本书。
❷给人以……的指望;有……的可能[+to-v]
It promises to be fine tomorrow.
明天有可能是个好天气。
❸【口】向……保证,向……断言
vi. ❶允诺,作出保证
❷有指望,有前途
That project promises well.
那个工程很有希望成功。

promote [prə'mot ‖ prə'məʊt]
[过去式]promoted;[过去分词]promoted
vt. ❶晋升[(+to)]
He was promoted to be section chief.
他被提升为科长。
❷促进;发扬;引起
We should promote world peace.
我们应当促进世界和平。

pronoun ['pronaʊn ‖ 'prəʊnaʊn]
n. 【文】代词[C]

pronounce [prə'naʊns ‖ prə'naʊns]
[过去式]pronounced;[过去分词]pronounced

vt. ❶发……的音；注……的音
She knows a lot of French words but pronounces them incorrectly.
她认识很多法文，但发音不准确。
❷宣称；断言；表示[＋that]
The doctor pronounced that he was recovering nicely.
医生宣称他正在顺利康复。
❸宣判[(＋on/upon)]
The judge pronounced a sentence of death on the murderer.
法官宣判凶手死刑。
vi. ❶发音
He pronounces distinctly.
他发音清晰。
❷(尤指在法庭上)发表意见；作出判断[(＋on/upon/for/against)]
The judge pronounced against him.
法官做了对他不利的判决。

proof 〔pruf ‖ pru:f〕
n. ❶证据；物证[C][U][(＋of)][＋that]
I can give you more than one proof that it is true.
我能给你好几个证据证明它的真实性。
❷证明；论证[U]
In proof of this theory, I shall make certain studies.
为了证明这一理论，我将进行某些研究。
a. 不能穿透的，能抵挡[(＋against)]
This cloth is proof against water.
这种布是防水的。

propaganda 〔ˌprɑpəˈgændə ‖ ˌprɒpəˈgændə〕
n. 宣传，宣传活动(或计划、方法)[U]

proper 〔ˈprɑpɚ ‖ ˈprɒpə〕
a. ❶适合的，适当的，恰当的[＋to-v][＋that]
He wondered whether it would be proper to knock at her door.
他不知道敲她的门是否恰当。
〔同义〕fit 合适的
❷合乎体统的，循规蹈矩的；正派的，高尚的
Many young people think old people are too proper.
许多年轻人认为老人太循规蹈矩。

property 〔ˈprɑpɚtɪ ‖ ˈprɒpətɪ〕
n. ❶财产，资产；所有物[U]
This small house is my only property.
这所小房子是我唯一的财产。

P

❷房产，地产[C][U]

He has several properties in this street.

他在这条街上有几处房产。

❸特性，性能，属性[C]

He is studying the medicinal properties of wild plants.

他正在研究野生植物的药物特性。

proportion 〔prəˈpɔrʃən ‖ prəˈpɔːʃən〕

n. ❶比例；比率[C][U][(+of/to)]

the proportion of boys to girls

男孩儿跟女孩儿的比率

❷调和；均衡，相称[U][P]

The painting lacks proportion.

这幅画儿比例失调。

❸部分，份儿[C][(+of)]

A large proportion of the country is desert.

这个国家的大部分地区是沙漠。

proposal 〔prəˈpozl̩ ‖ prəˈpəuzəl〕

n. ❶(建议等的)提出，计划；提案[C][U]

Proposal is easier than performance.

建议容易实行难。

The proposal was turned down.

这个建议被否决了。

❷求婚[C]

She has had a proposal.

已经有人向她求婚了。

propose 〔prəˈpoz ‖ prəˈpəuz〕

[过去式]proposed；[过去分词] proposed

vt. ❶提议，建议，提出[+v-ing][+(that)]

It was proposed (that) we go to the station to meet our guests.

有人建议我们去车站接客人。

❷提(名)，推荐

I proposed Mr. Hunter for the job.

我提议亨特先生来干这项工作。

❸计划，打算[+to-v]

They propose to begin tonight.

他们打算今晚开始。

❹求(婚)

He proposed to the girl.

他向这个女孩儿求婚了。

prosperity 〔prɑsˈpɛrətɪ ‖ prɒsˈperɪtɪ〕

n. 兴旺，繁荣，昌盛，成功[U]

The business finally restored prosperity.

商业终于恢复了繁荣。

prosperous 〔ˈprɑspərəs ‖ ˈprɒspərəs〕

a. 兴旺的，繁荣的，昌盛的

P

He was prosperous in his time.
他有过一段辉煌的时期。

protect 〔prə'tɛkt ‖ prə'tekt〕
[过去式]protected;[过去分词]protected
vt. 保护，防护[(＋against/from)]
May God protect you from harm.
愿上帝保佑你免受伤害。

protection 〔prə'tɛkʃən ‖ prə'tekʃən〕
n. ❶保护，防护；警戒[U][(＋against/from)]
The construction workers wore metal helmets for protection.
建筑工人为了防护而戴金属头盔。
❷防护物[(＋against/from)]
A thin jacket is a poor protection against cold.
一件单薄的夹克衫不足以御寒。

protest 〔'protɛst ‖ 'prəutest〕
n. 抗议，异议，反对[C][U]
They made a protest against the high price.
他们抗议物价高涨。

proud 〔praud ‖ praud〕
[比]prouder;[最]proudest
a. ❶傲慢的，自负的
He's too proud to speak to poor people like us.
他太骄傲了，从不与我们这样的穷人说话。
❷自豪的，得意的[(＋of)][＋to-v][＋(that)]
We are proud of you.
我们为你感到自豪。

prove 〔pruv ‖ pru:v〕
[过去式]proved;[过去分词]proved, proven
vt. ❶证明，证实[＋(that)]
I'll prove to the world that he was right.
我将向世人证明他是对的。
❷表现，显示
She has proved herself unreliable.
她的表现说明她靠不住。
vi. 证明是；原来是
The rumor proved true.
这个谣传结果是真的。

proverb 〔'prɑvɝb ‖ 'prɒvɜ:b〕
n. 谚语，俗语，常言[C]

provide 〔prə'vaɪd ‖ prə'vaɪd〕
[过去式]provided;[过去分词]provided
vt. ❶提供
On Sundays his landlady provided dinner as well as breakfast.

星期天，他的女房东不但供给早餐，还供给晚餐。
❷装备，供给[(+with)]
Somehow she managed to provide her children with food and clothing.
她总是设法使她的孩子有饭吃，有衣穿。
vi. ❶抚养，赡养[(+for)]
He tried to earn more money to provide for a large family.
他设法多挣钱以供养一个子女众多的家。
❷做准备；预防[(+for/against)]
Provide for your old age.
为自己老年做个打算吧。

provided 〔prəˈvaɪdɪd ‖ prəˈvaɪdɪd〕
conj. 以……为条件；假如
I will go, provided (that) you go.
假如你去，我就去。

providing 〔prəˈvaɪdɪŋ ‖ prəˈvaɪdɪŋ〕
conj. 以……为条件；假如
I will go, providing you go.
假如你要去，我就去。

province 〔ˈprɑvɪns ‖ ˈprɒvɪns〕
n. 省，州[C]
British Columbia is a province of Canada.
不列颠哥伦比亚是加拿大的一个省。

psychology 〔saɪˈkɑlədʒɪ ‖ saɪˈkɒlədʒɪ〕
n. ❶心理学[U]
She is studying child psychology.
她正研究儿童心理学。
❷心理，心理特点[C][U]
female psychology
女性心理

public 〔ˈpʌblɪk ‖ ˈpʌblɪk〕
a. ❶公众的，公共的，公用的
public welfare
公共福利
You mustn't do that in a public place.
你不许在公共场所做那件事。
❷政府的，公务的
a public official
官吏
❸公然的；众所周知的
They made the secret public.
他们公开了这个秘密。
n. ❶公众，民众[the]
The public were provoked to anger.
公众被激怒了。
❷(某方面的)大众，群众；……界，众人

P

the buying public
消费大众
the novel-reading public
小说的读者

常用短语

in public 公然地,公开地
He hates to be seen in public.
他讨厌在公开场合露面。

publication 〔ˌpʌblɪˈkeʃən ‖ ˌpʌblɪˈkeɪʃən〕
n. ❶出版;发行[U]
The magazine has ceased publication.
该杂志已经停止出版。
❷出版物;刊物[C]
A newspaper is a publication.
报纸是一种出版物。
❸发表,宣布,公布[U]
The widespread publication of traffic laws helps prevent accidents.
广泛公布交通法规有助于防止事故的发生。

publish 〔ˈpʌblɪʃ ‖ ˈpʌblɪʃ〕
[过去式]published;[过去分词]published
vt. ❶出版;发行
The publishing house has published 5 dictionaries.
这家出版社已出版了 5 部词典。
❷刊载,刊登
The magazine published a short story written by a high school student.
这家杂志刊登了一篇一个中学生所写的短篇小说。
❸发表
When are you going to publish this work of yours?
你什么时候出版你这部作品?
vi. ❶出版,发行
The newspaper publishes in Taipei.
这份报纸在台北出版。
❷(著作人)发表作品

publisher 〔ˈpʌblɪʃɚ ‖ ˈpʌblɪʃə〕
n. [C] ❶出版(或发行)者;出版(或发行)公司;出版商
❷发表者,公布者

pudding 〔ˈpʊdɪŋ ‖ ˈpʊdɪŋ〕
n. 布丁[C][U]
Rice pudding is nourishing.
大米布丁富于营养。

pull 〔pʊl ‖ pʊl〕
[过去式]pulled;[过去分词]pulled
vt. ❶拉,拖,牵,拽;搬走
She pulled his sleeve to get his attention.
她拉他的袖子以引起他的注意。
❷拔;采,摘;揪下;拉开;扯破[(+out/up)]

He had a bad tooth pulled out.
他拔掉了一颗坏牙。
vi. ❶拉，拖，牵；拔，摘
The child pulled at my sleeve.
那个小孩儿拉了拉我的衣袖。
❷(能)被拉(或拖，拔)动
The door pulled open.
门拉开了。
n. ❶拉，拖[C]
He gave a strong pull at the rope.
他用力拉了拉绳子。
❷拉力；引力
The moon's pull affects the tide on earth.
月球的引力影响地球上的潮汐。

pulse 〔pʌls ‖ pʌls〕
n. 脉搏；脉的一次跳动[C]
feel the patient's pulse
给病人把脉

P

pump 〔pʌmp ‖ pʌmp〕
[过去式]pumped；[过去分词]pumped
n. 泵，唧筒[C]
We have a pump for drawing water from the well.
我们用一个水泵从井里抽水。
vt. ❶用唧筒抽(水等)；用唧筒抽吸……中的水等
The fire brigade pumped water out of the flooded house.
消防队将水从被淹的房子里抽出去。

❷打(气)；为……打气
This tire was flat; you didn't pump enough air in.
这个轮胎没气了，你并没打足气。

punch 〔pʌntʃ ‖ pʌntʃ〕
n. 用拳打[C][(+in/on)]
He gave me a punch on the jaw.
他一拳打在我下巴上。

punctual 〔ˈpʌŋktʃuəl ‖ ˈpʌŋktʃuəl〕
a. 严守时刻的；准时的[(+for/in)]
She's always very punctual for appointments.
她总是准时赴约。

punctuation 〔ˌpʌŋktʃuˈeʃən ‖ ˌpʌŋktʃuˈeɪʃən〕
n. 标点法；标点[U]

A piece of writing without any punctuation is difficult to understand.
一篇没有任何标点符号的文章是很难懂的。

punish 〔ˈpʌnɪʃ ‖ ˈpʌnɪʃ〕
[过去式]punished;[过去分词]punished
vt. 罚;惩罚,处罚[(+for)]
Motorists should be severely punished for speeding.
超速驾车的人应受严厉惩罚。

punishment 〔ˈpʌnɪʃmənt ‖ ˈpʌnɪʃmənt〕
n. 处罚,惩罚;刑罚[C][U]
punishment for murderer
对谋杀犯的刑罚

pupil 〔ˈpjupḷ ‖ ˈpjuːpl〕
n.[C] ❶学生,小学生;弟子
The school has 1,500 pupils.
这所学校有1,500名小学生。
❷瞳孔

purchase 〔ˈpɝtʃəs ‖ ˈpɜːtʃəs〕
[过去式]purchased;[过去分词]purchased
vt. ❶买,购买
He purchased this stamp at an auction.
他在拍卖会中购得这枚邮票。
❷赢得,获得,努力取得
We treasure this dearly purchased victory.
我们珍惜这次以惨重的代价换来的胜利。
n. ❶买,购买[C][U]
He worked all the summer to save money for the purchase of a piano.
他工作了一整个夏天,为的是存钱买架钢琴。
❷所购之物[C]
He filled the car with his purchases.
他把买的东西装满车子。

pure 〔pjʊr ‖ pjʊə〕
[比]purer;[最]purest
a. ❶纯粹的,不掺杂的;地道的
Is the cup made of pure gold?
这只杯子是纯金做的吗?
❷纯净的;洁净的;清澈的
The air by the sea is pure and healthy.
海边的空气清新又有益健康。
❸完全的,十足的
It was pure luck that he was at home when we called.
非常幸运,我们打电话时他在家里。

purely 〔ˈpjʊrlɪ ‖ ˈpjʊəlɪ〕
ad. 纯粹地,完全,仅仅,只不过
It was purely accidental.
那完全是意外。

purple 〔ˈpɝpḷ ‖ ˈpɜːpl〕

a. 紫的，紫红的

His face turned purple with rage.

他气得脸色发紫。

purpose 〔ˈpɝpəs ‖ ˈpɜːpəs〕

n. ❶目的，意图[C]

What is the purpose of his visit?

他来访的目的是什么？

❷用途；效用，效果[C]

The purpose of a trap is to catch and hold animals.

陷阱是用来捕捉野兽的。

❸意志，决心[U]

He is weak of purpose.

他的意志薄弱。

常用短语

on purpose 故意地

He said so on purpose.

他是故意这么说的。

purse 〔pɝs ‖ pɜːs〕

n. [C]❶钱包；(女用)手提包

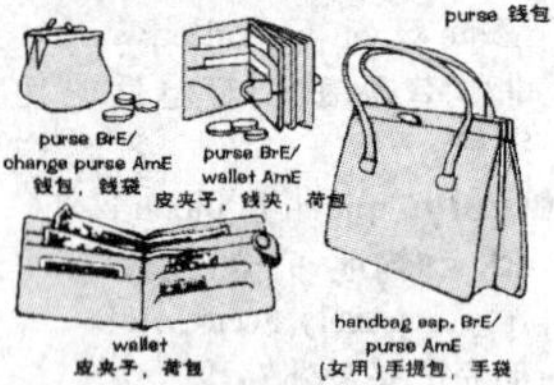

The lady put her wallet in her purse.

那位女士将皮夹子放在手提包里。

❷(钱包形的)小袋，小包

pursue 〔pɚˈsu ‖ pəˈsjuː〕

vt. ❶追赶；追踪；追捕

Police pursued the car at high speed.

警察高速追赶那辆汽车。

❷(疾病等)纠缠；跟随

He has been pursued by misfortune.

他厄运连连。

❸追求；向……求爱

She pursued the goal of perfection in her art.

她的目标是追求艺术上的完美境界。

pursuit 〔pɚˈsut ‖ pəˈsjuːt〕

n. ❶追踪，追击[U]

He was captured without much pursuit.

没有经过多少追捕就把他捉住了。

❷追求，寻求[U][(+of)]

He wasted his life in vain in pursuit of pleasure.

他为了追求享乐而白白虚度了一生。

❸事务；职业；消遣[P]

He is engaged in scientific pursuits.
他从事科学研究。
Fishing is my favorite pursuits.
钓鱼是我最大的消遣。

push 〔puʃ ‖ puʃ〕
［过去式］pushed;［过去分词］pushed
vt. ❶推;推动,推进
He pushed the library door open.
他推开了图书馆的门。
❷逼迫;催促,促使［(＋to)］
She pushed her son to pursue an academic career.
她督促儿子从事学术。
vi. ❶推;推开
❷推进;向前挤
Our troops pushed northward.
我军向北推进。
n. ❶推;推进［C］
He opened the door with one push.
他一推门就开了。
❷奋发,努力,奋进［C］
We must make a push to get the job done.
我们必须加把劲儿把这事干完。

put 〔put ‖ put〕
［过去式］put;［过去分词］put
vt. ❶放,摆,装
Where did you put the book?
你把书放哪儿啦?
❷使处于(某种状态)
They have just put through a business deal.
他们刚刚谈成一笔生意。
❸施加,强加［(＋on)］
They tried to put the blame on him.
他们力图将责任推在他身上。
❹提出［(＋to/before)］
She put a question to him about it.
她就这件事向他提出了问题。
❺写上,标上,表达,表述,翻译
Put your name here.
把你的名字写在这儿。
Put the sentence into English.
把这句话翻译成英语。
I can't put it in words.
我无法用言语来表达。

常用短语

put down ❶放下 ❷写下
Put down your name and address.
写下你的姓名和地址。
The bus put down some passengers.
一些乘客下了公共汽车。
put off 推迟;拖延

P

Don't put off writing to him.
别拖了，给他写信吧。
put on 穿上
I put on my coat in a hurry.
我匆忙穿上外套。

puzzle 〔'pʌzḷ ‖ 'pʌzl〕
［过去式］puzzled；［过去分词］puzzled
vt. ❶使迷惑；使为难，使窘困
What puzzles me is why they didn't show up.
令我百思不解的是他们为什么没有出现。
❷苦思而得出［(＋out)］
I could not puzzle out her intentions.
我猜不出她的意图。
vi. ❶感到迷惑
❷苦思，冥思苦想［(＋about/over/as to)］
I have been puzzling about this question for weeks now.
我对这个问题已冥思苦想了好几个星期。
n. ［C］❶(游戏的)猜谜，智力竞赛
❷难题，谜，难以理解之事
Her decision was a puzzle to him.
她的决定对他来说是个谜。
❸困惑，迷惑
I'm in a puzzle as to how to cope with the new situation.
我不知道该如何应付这个新局面。

pyramid 〔'pɪrəmɪd ‖ 'pɪrəmɪd〕
n. (古埃及建造的)金字塔［C］

P

quake 〔kwek ‖ kweɪk〕
[过去式]quaked;[过去分词] quaked
vi. ❶颤抖,哆嗦[(+at/with/for)]
He quaked with fright.
他吓得发抖。
❷震动;摇晃
The house quaked.
房子震动了。

qualification 〔ˌkwɑləfəˈkeʃən ‖ ˌkwɒlɪfɪˈkeɪʃən〕
n. 资格,能力[P][(+for)][+to-v]
He has no qualification for the job.
他没有资格担任这项工作。

quality 〔ˈkwɑlətɪ ‖ ˈkwɒlɪtɪ〕
n. ❶质,质量[U]
Quality often matters more than quantity.
质量往往比数量更重要。
❷特性[C]
merchandise of quality
优质商品
One quality of wood is that it can burn.
木料的一个特点是能燃烧。

quantity 〔ˈkwɑntətɪ ‖ ˈkwɒntɪtɪ〕
n. ❶量[U]
Mathematics is the science of pure quantity.
数学是研究纯量的科学。
❷数量;分量[C][(+of)]
There is a small quantity of water left in the bottle.
瓶子里还剩下少量的水。
❸大量,大宗[C][P][(+of)]
She has quantities of good clothes.
她有许多好衣服。

Q

quarrel 〔ˈkwɔrəl ‖ ˈkwɒrəl〕
［过去式］quarreled；［过去分词］quarreled
n.［C］❶争吵；不和；吵闹［(＋with/between/about)］
He is good-natured and has never had a quarrel with anyone.
他脾气很好，从不和任何人争吵。
❷争吵的原因；怨言；责备［(＋with/against)］
I have no quarrel with what you say.
我对你的话没有反对意见。
vi. ❶争吵，不和［(＋with/about/over)］
She often quarreled with her husband over trivial matters.
她常因小事情与丈夫争吵。
❷埋怨；责备；挑剔［(＋with)］
He quarreled with my suggestion that television caused violence.
他反对我关于电视会引起暴力事件的看法。

quarter 〔ˈkwɔrtɚ ‖ ˈkwɔːtə〕
n. ❶四分之一；四等分之一［C］；季度
She cut the cake into quarters.
她把蛋糕切成4份。
❷一刻钟［C］
a quarter to 7 o'clock
差一刻钟到7点
❸付款的季度［C］
We pay our rent at the end of each quarter.
我们于每个季度末付房租。
❹(美国，加拿大的)25分硬币［C］
❺地方，地域［P］
He traveled in all quarters of the earth when he was young.
他年轻时曾周游世界。

queen 〔kwin ‖ kwiːn〕
n. ［C］❶(大写)女王，王后［(＋of)］
❷(权力，地位或相貌等)出众的女人，皇后，名媛［(＋of)］
She was the queen of society then.
那时她是社交界女王。

question 〔ˈkwɛstʃən ‖ ˈkwestʃən〕
n. ❶问题；询问［C］
She asked me many questions about my adventures in the Arctic.
她问了我许多有关我在北极探险的问题。
❷怀疑；疑问［C］［U］［(＋about)］

Q

There's no question about his honesty.
他无疑是诚实的。

quick 〔kwɪk ‖ kwɪk〕
[比]quicker;[最]quickest
a. ❶快的,迅速的
Some children are very quick.
有些孩子很敏捷。
❷敏捷的;伶俐的[+to-v][(+of/in/at)]
She is quick at learning a foreign language.
她学外语学得快。
ad. 快,迅速地
He runs as quick as a deer.
他跑得跟鹿一样快。

quickly 〔ˈkwɪklɪ ‖ ˈkwɪklɪ〕
ad. ❶快,迅速地
❷立即,马上

quiet 〔ˈkwaɪət ‖ ˈkwaɪət〕
a. ❶安静的;轻声的;沉默的
Be quiet!
安静!
❷宁静的,安定的;平静的
The sea was quiet before the storm struck.
暴风雨来袭前海面很平静。
❸文静的,温和的
He was a quiet man who didn't let small things upset him.
他是个性格平和的人,从不为小事生气。
n. [U] ❶安静;寂静
I'd like a few hours for quiet after the day's work.
一天工作下来我想有几小时的安静。
❷安稳;和平

quite 〔kwaɪt ‖ kwaɪt〕
ad. ❶完全,彻底
She wore a hat quite out of fashion.
她戴着一顶完全过时的帽子。
❷相当,颇
I quite like watching volleyball games.
我相当喜欢看排球比赛。
❸【美】很
Ann is quite pretty.
安长得很漂亮。
❹【英】(用作回答)的确如此

quiz 〔kwɪz ‖ kwɪz〕
n. ❶考查,测验;提问[C]
We had a quiz in English today.
我们今天有个英语小考。
❷(电视等节目中的)智力竞赛

quotation 〔kwoˈteʃən ‖ kwəʊˈteɪʃən〕
n. ❶引用,引证[U]
❷引文;语录[C]
❸【商】(股票等的)行情;报价单,估价单[C]

Q

quote〔kwot ‖ kwəʊt〕
［过去式］quoted；［过去分词］quoted
vt. ❶引用；引述
The judge quoted various cases in support of his opinion.
法官引证了各种案例来支持他的判决理由。
To quote an old saying, every dog has its day.
用句老话来说，人人都有得意时。
❷把……放在引号内
The dialogue in old books is not quoted.
旧书里的对话不加引号。
vi. 引用；引证［(＋from)］
The minister quoted from the Bible.
牧师引用《圣经》里的语句。
She quoted from a newspaper article.
她引用了报纸上一篇文章的内容。

rabbit 〔'ræbɪt ‖ 'ræbɪt〕

n. 兔；野兔[C]

A rabbit can make long jumps.

兔子可以跳得很远。

race[1] 〔res ‖ reɪs〕

[过去式] raced；[过去分词] raced

n. 赛跑；比赛，竞赛[C][(+against/between/with)]

He ran a race with me.

他同我赛跑。

vi. ❶比速度；参加竞赛；参加赛马

She's a very good swimmer and often races.

她是一位优秀的游泳选手，经常参加比赛。

❷疾走；全速行进

She raced to the phone.

她飞快地跑向电话。

vt. ❶和……竞赛

❷使急走，使全速行进；使(发动机)猛转

The taxi-driver raced me to the airport.

出租车司机驾车将我飞速送到机场。

race[2] 〔res ‖ reɪs〕

n. ❶人种；种族；民族[C][U]

The British are a sea-going race.

英国是个航海的民族。

❷血统，宗族，门第[U]

He was a man of noble race.

他是个出身高贵的男士。

radar 〔'redɑr ‖ 'reɪdɑː〕

n. 雷达[C][U]

radio 〔'redɪˌo ‖ 'reɪdɪəʊ〕

n. ❶无线电；无线电话(或电报)[C][U]

Ships sent messages to each other by radio.

船只使用无线电互通信息。
❷无线电传送，无线电广播，收音机[the]
She listened to the pop music on the radio.
她听电台的流行音乐。
Father bought her a stereo radio.
父亲给他买了台立体声收音机。

rag 〔ræg ‖ ræg〕
n. ❶破布，碎布；抹布；造纸的破布料[C][U]
He cleaned the car with an oily rag.
他用一块沾满油污的破布擦汽车。
❷破衣烂衫[P]
The beggar was dressed in rags.
这个乞丐穿着破衣烂衫。

rail 〔rel ‖ reɪl〕
n. ❶栏杆，扶手；围栏[C]
He kept his hands on the rail as he climbed the steps.
他上台阶时，手不离扶栏。
❷(门等的)横木[C]
❸铁轨[C]
Hundreds of people were injured when the train run off the rails.
火车出轨时，数百人受伤。
❹铁路[U]
He came back by rail.
他是乘火车回来的。

railroad 〔ˈrelˌrod ‖ ˈreɪlrəʊd〕
n. [C] ❶【美】铁路
A new railroad is under construction.
一条新的铁路正在修建中。
❷铁路公司

railway 〔ˈrelˌwe ‖ ˈreɪlweɪ〕
n. [C]❶【英】铁路；铁道
❷【英】铁路系统；铁路公司

rain 〔ren ‖ reɪn〕
n. 雨，雨水[U]
Do you get much rain?
你们那儿雨水多吗？

rainbow 〔ˈrenˌbo ‖ ˈreɪnbəʊ〕
n. 虹，彩虹[C]

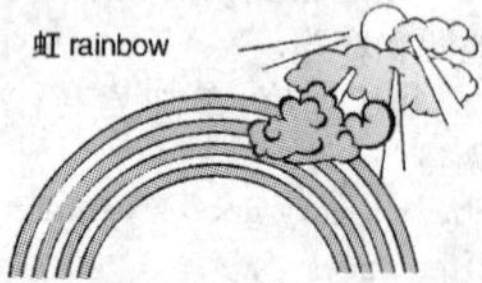

raincoat 〔ˈrenˌkot ‖ ˈreɪnkəʊt〕
n. 雨衣[C]

raindrop 〔ˈrenˌdrɑp ‖ ˈreɪndrɒp〕
n. 雨点，雨滴[C]

rainy 〔ˈrenɪ ‖ ˈreɪnɪ〕

R

a. 下雨的;多雨的
It's a rainy day.
今天下雨。

raise 〔rez ‖ reɪz〕
[过去式]raised;[过去分词]raised
vt. ❶举起,抬起
He raised his glass and said: "Your health, Carl."
他举起杯子说道:"祝你健康,卡尔。"
❷增加;提高;提升[(+to)]
The landlord raised my rent.
房东增加了我的租金。
❸筹(款);招(兵);集结
They are going to raise funds for the school buildings.
他们将为盖校舍筹集资金。
❹养育;种植;饲养
raise wheat
种小麦
raise cattle
养牛
raise a family
养家
n. ❶【美】加薪;加薪额[C]
I am going to ask the boss for a raise.
我要找老板要求加薪。
❷提高,举,升

range 〔rendʒ ‖ reɪndʒ〕
n. ❶排,行;一系列[C]
The library has ranges of books in perfect order.
这个图书馆的书一排一排放得井井有条。
❷山脉[C]
❸(变化等的)幅度;(知识等的)范围;区域[C]
The houses are sold out within this price range.
在这个价位范围之内的房子已售完。
❹【军】射程;距离;(加足燃料后车辆等的)最大行程[C][U]
What is the range of this telescope?
这架望远镜的有效距离是多大?

rank 〔ræŋk ‖ ræŋk〕
[过去式]ranked;[过去分词]ranked
n. ❶等级;地位,身份[C][U]
people of all ranks
社会各阶层人士
an artist of the first rank
第一流的艺术家
❷排,横列;【军】行列[C]
soldiers in the front rank
前排的士兵
vt. ❶排列,把……排成行
The commander ranked his sol-

diers in a column of fours.
指挥官将士兵们排成 4 列纵队。
❷把……分等;把……评级
She ranked her students according to their grades.
她按成绩排列学生的名次。
vi. 列为
They ranked high in their class.
他们是班上的优等生。

rapid 〔'ræpɪd ‖ 'ræpɪd〕
[比]rapider;[最]rapidest
a. 快的,迅速的;动作快的
He had a rapid recovery from his illness.
他复原得很快。

R

rapidly 〔'ræpɪdlɪ ‖ 'ræpɪdlɪ〕
ad. 很快地,立即,迅速地

rare 〔rɛr ‖ reə〕
[比]rarer;[最]rarest
a. ❶稀有的,罕见的
These flowers are very rare in this country.
这些花在这个国家很少见。
❷杰出的,珍贵的
Gold is a rare metal.
金子是贵重金属。
❸稀薄的,稀疏的
The higher you climb up the mountain, the rarer the air is.
越往山上爬,空气越稀薄。
❹【口】非常好的,极度的

rarely 〔'rɛrlɪ ‖ 'reəlɪ〕
ad. 很少,难得
He rarely comes here.
他很少来这儿。

rat 〔ræt ‖ ræt〕
n. 鼠[C]
Rats carry very nasty diseases.
老鼠传播讨厌的疾病。

rate 〔ret ‖ reɪt〕
n. ❶比例,率;比率[C]
The unemployment rate is rising in that country.
那个国家的失业率正在上升。
❷速度,速率[the][C]
The car was going at the rate of 60 miles an hour.
汽车以每小时 60 英里的速度行驶。
❸费用,价格;行市[C]
The room rates at this motel range from $30 to $50 per day.

这个汽车旅馆的房价每天从 30 美元到 50 美元不等。

❹等级[U]

rather 〔'ræðɚ ‖ 'rɑːðə〕

ad. ❶相当，颇，有点儿

I'm feeling rather sleepy.

我有点困倦。

❷(常与 would 或 had 连用)宁可，宁愿；(与其……)倒不如；而不是

He would rather walk than take the bus.

他宁愿步行，也不愿坐公共汽车。

❸(常与 or 连用)更确切地说

He left late last night, or rather early this morning.

他昨夜很晚，或者应该说是今天一大早才走。

❹【英】(用于回答问题)确是如此；当然

rational 〔'ræʃənḷ ‖ 'ræʃənl〕

[比] more rational; [最] most rational

a. ❶理性的，有理性的；明白事理的

Man is a rational animal.

人是有理性的动物。

❷基于理性的，合理的

He thought in a rational way.

他以理性的方式思考。

raw 〔rɔ ‖ rɔː〕

[比]rawer; [最]rawest

a. ❶生的，未煮过的

Most fruits are eaten raw.

大部分的水果是生吃的。

❷未加工的；处于自然状态的

All the raw materials are imported.

所有原料全部是进口。

❸未经训练的，无经验的

The new teacher is very capable, but he's still a bit raw.

这位新教师很能干，但是还缺少点经验。

ray 〔re ‖ reɪ〕

n. 光线[C]；射线，辐射线[P]

The gun can fire invisible rays.

这枪能发出看不见的射线。

the sun's rays

太阳光

razor 〔'rezɚ ‖ 'reɪzə〕

n. 剃刀[C]

reach 〔ritʃ ‖ riːtʃ〕

[过去式]reached; [过去分词] reached

vt. ❶抵达，到达；达到

When will they reach Los Angeles?

他们什么时候抵达洛杉矶？

❷伸出(手)；伸手及到，够到

He reached his hand out for the

R

book I offered him.
他伸出手来接我给他的书。
❸与……取得联系
We tried to reach them by cable.
我们试着用电报跟他们联络。
vi. ❶伸出手(或脚)
She reached up and picked a pear off a branch.
她抬起手从一根枝上摘下一个梨。
❷达到,及到;延伸
The speaker's voice couldn't reach to the back of the auditorium.
演讲人的声音礼堂后排听不见。
n. ❶(手、能力、智力、影响等)可及之范围[U][(+of)]
It was put out of the child's reach.
把它放在孩子拿不到的地方。
❷(江、河的)一段流域;地带;大片地区[C]
the upper reaches of the river
河的上游地区

react 〔rɪ'ækt ‖ rɪ'ækt〕
[过去式]reacted;[过去分词]reacted
vi. 作出反应,反应[(+to)]
The eyes react to light.
眼睛对光有反应。

reaction 〔rɪ'ækʃən ‖ rɪ'ækʃən〕
n. [C][U]❶反应,感应[(+to)]
What was his reaction to the plan?
他对这个计划有什么反应?
❷【化】【物】反应,反作用
Putting an acid and a metal together causes a reaction.
将酸和金属放在一起会引起反应。

read 〔rid ‖ ri:d〕
[过去式]read;[过去分词]read
vt. ❶读,阅读;朗读
I read a good article in today's paper.
我在今天的报纸上读到了一篇好文章。
❷读懂;觉察
She read his thoughts.
她看出了他的心思。
❸读到;获悉[+(that)]
I read in a magazine that drinking a lot of tea could be a preventive against cancer.
我从一本杂志上读到,大量喝茶有可能是预防癌症的一种措施。
vi. ❶阅读,朗读
He seldom reads in his free

R

hours.
他空余时间很少看书。
❷读起来
Your compositions read well.
你的作文读起来很不错。

reader 〔'ridɚ ‖ 'riːdə〕
n. [C] ❶读者;爱好阅读者
❷读物,读本

reading 〔'ridɪŋ ‖ 'riːdɪŋ〕
n. ❶阅读;朗读 [U]
❷读物,阅读材料[U]

ready 〔'rɛdɪ ‖ 'redɪ〕
[比]readier;[最]readiest
a. ❶(用作表语)准备好的[(+for)][+to-v]
He is ready for the trip.
他已准备好去旅行。
❷愿意的,乐意的[(+with)][+to-v]
I am always ready to work for you.
我随时愿意为你效劳。
❸敏捷的,机灵的
She has a ready tongue.
她口齿伶俐。

real 〔'riəl ‖ 'riːəl〕
a. ❶真的,真正的;衷心的;真诚的
His affection for the girl was real.
他对那个女孩的爱是真心的。
❷现实的,实际的,实在的
The TV play was based on real life.
那出电视剧是根据现实生活写成的。
❸完全的,十足的
a real idiot
十足的傻瓜

reality 〔rɪ'ælətɪ ‖ rɪ'ælɪtɪ〕
n. ❶现实;真实[U]
He is out of touch with reality.
他脱离现实。
❷事实,实际存在的事物[C]
His dream has become a reality.
他的梦想已成为现实。

realize 〔'riəˌlaɪz ‖ 'rɪəlaɪz〕
[过去式]realized;[过去分词]realized
vt. ❶领悟,了解,认识到[+(that)][+wh-]
I realized what he meant.
我明白了他的意思。
❷实现;使成为事实
Her wish to become a movie star was finally realized.
她当电影明星的愿望终于实现了。

really 〔'rɪəlɪ ‖ 'rɪəlɪ〕
ad. ❶真正地,确实,实际上
She isn't really young.

她实际上并不年轻。

❷很，十分，全然

realm 〔rɛlm ‖ relm〕

n. 【书】王国；国土，领土界，领域；范围[C]

the realm of science

科学领域

reap 〔rip ‖ riːp〕

[过去式]reaped；[过去分词]reaped

vt. 收割(庄稼)；收获

rear 〔rɪr ‖ rɪə〕

n. 后部，后面；背后，背面[the]

At the rear of the house is a piece of woodland.

在房子后面是一块林地。

R

reason 〔ˈrizn̩ ‖ ˈriːzn〕

n. ❶ 理由，原因，动机[C][U]

The reason (that) she did it is still a mystery.

她为什么做那件事仍是一个谜。

❷理性，理智；判断力，推理[U]

Beasts do not have reason.

野兽不具理性。

❸道理，情理；明智[U]

Why won't you listen to reason?

你为什么不听劝告？

❹正常心智，正常神志[U]

reasonable 〔ˈrizn̩əbl̩ ‖ ˈriːznəbl〕

a. ❶通情达理的，讲道理的

Why aren't you more reasonable?

你为什么不能通情达理些呢？

❷合理的，正当的；适当的

Your answer is not reasonable.

你的回答不合理。

rebel[1] 〔rɪˈbɛl ‖ rɪˈbel〕

[过去式]rebelled；[过去分词]rebelled

vi. 造反；反叛；反抗[(＋against)]

The people rebelled against the tyrant.

人民起来反抗暴君。

rebel[2] 〔ˈrɛbl̩ ‖ ˈrebəl〕

n. 造反者；反抗者；反叛者[C]

The rebels armed themselves against the government.

反叛分子武装自己对抗政府。

rebellion 〔rɪˈbɛljən ‖ rɪˈbeljən〕

n. 反叛，造反；叛乱[C][U][(＋against)]

They raised a rebellion against the king.

他们作乱反叛国王。

recall 〔rɪˈkɔl ‖ rɪˈkɔːl〕

[过去式]recalled；[过去分词]recalled

vt. ❶回想，回忆；使想起

I recalled my last evening with

her.
我回忆和她在一起的最后一个晚上。
❷叫回，召回[(+from/to)]
The Prime Minister recalled the ambassador to Japan.
首相召大使回日本。

receipt 〔rɪ'sit ‖ rɪ'siːt〕
n. ❶收到，接到[U]
On receipt of the article, I will send you money.
东西一收到我就寄钱给你。
❷收据，收条[C]

receive 〔rɪ'siv ‖ rɪ'siːv〕
[过去式]received；[过去分词]received
vt. ❶收到，接到
I've just received a telegram.
我刚收到一份电报。
❷得到，受到，遭受
They received the support of the workers.
他们得到工人们的支持。
❸接待，欢迎；接受，接纳；承认
His speech was well received.
他的演讲很受欢迎。

receiver 〔rɪ'sivɚ ‖ rɪ'siːvə〕
n.[C] ❶受领人；收件人，收款人；收受者
❷接待人
❸电话听筒，受话器

recent 〔'risn̩t ‖ 'riːsnt〕
a. 新近的，最近的；近来的；近代的
recent history
近代历史

recently 〔'risn̩tlɪ ‖ 'riːsntlɪ〕
ad. 最近，新近，近来
I have not heard from her recently.
我最近没收到她的信。

reception 〔rɪ'sɛpʃən ‖ rɪ'sepʃən〕
n. ❶接待，接见；欢迎
Jim had an enthusiastic reception when he returned home.
吉姆回到家时受到了热情的接待。
❷接待会；欢迎会；宴会[C]
Our school gave a reception to our new principal.
我们学校为新校长举行了欢迎会。

recite 〔rɪ'saɪt ‖ rɪ'saɪt〕
[过去式]recited；[过去分词]recited
vt. 背诵；朗诵，当众吟诵
He recited the long poem.
他背诵了这首长诗。

reckless 〔'rɛklɪs ‖ 'reklɪs〕
a. 不注意的，不在乎的；鲁莽的，不顾后果的

Some of these young motorcyclists are very reckless.
有些年轻的摩托车骑士很鲁莽。

recognition 〔ˌrɛkəgˈnɪʃən ‖ ˌrekəgˈnɪʃən〕
n. ❶认出，识别；认识[U]
He has changed beyond recognition.
他已经变得认不出来了。
❷承认；确认；认可[U]

recognize 〔ˈrɛkəgˌnaɪz ‖ ˈrekəgnaɪz〕
[过去式]recognized；[过去分词]recognized
vt. ❶认出，识别；认识[(＋as)]
The policeman recognized her as a pickpocket.
警察认出她是个小偷。
❷正式承认；认可，认定
Many countries recognized the new government.
许多国家承认了新政府。
❸承认(事实)；认清[(＋as)][＋(that)]
I recognized that I had made a mistake.
我认识到自己犯了一个错误。

recommend 〔ˌrɛkəˈmɛnd ‖ ˌrekəˈmend〕
[过去式]recommended；[过去分词]recommended
vt. ❶推荐，介绍
Can you recommend me some new books on this subject?
你能推荐一些有关这个学科的新书给我吗？
❷建议，劝告
I recommend you to comply with safety regulations.
我劝你遵守安全规则。

record[1] 〔ˈrɛkɚd ‖ ˈrekɔːd〕
n. ❶记录，记载[C][U][(＋of)]
the record of their lives
他们的生活记录
❷履历，经历；成绩；前科记录[C]
He had a good school record.
他的学习成绩优良。
❸最高纪录，最佳成绩[C][(＋for)]
He holds the record for the high jump.
他保持跳高的纪录。
❹唱片[C][(＋of)]
Will you play the record?
你能替我放唱片吗？

record[2] 〔rɪˈkɔrd ‖ rɪˈkɔːd〕
[过去式]recorded；[过去分词]recorded
vt. 记载，记录，将(声音，影像

等)录下
I'll record his speech.
我要将他的演说录下来。

recorder〔rɪˈkɔrdɚ ‖ rɪˈkɔːdə〕
n. [C] ❶记录者,书记员;录音师
❷记录器;录音机;印码电报机
❸竖笛

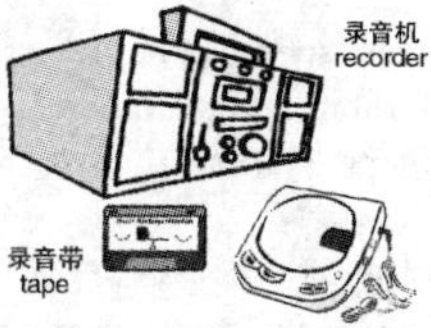

recover〔rɪˈkʌvɚ ‖ rɪˈkʌvə〕
[过去式]recovered;[过去分词]recovered
vt. ❶重新获得;重新找到
Jane recovered her lost wallet.
简寻回了丢失的钱包。
❷恢复;使恢复原状
Joan made a great effort to recover herself.
琼努力使自己镇定下来。
❸挽回,弥补
It's hard to recover lost time.
弥补失去的时间并不容易。
vi. 恢复健康;恢复原状;恢复[(+from)]
It took a long time for him to recover from a bad cold.
他患重感冒,很长时间才康复。

recovery〔rɪˈkʌvərɪ ‖ rɪˈkʌvərɪ〕
n. ❶重获;复得[U]
An anonymous call led to the recovery of the stolen jewels.
一个匿名电话使被盗珠宝失而复得。
❷恢复,复苏;复原,痊愈[(+from)]
She made a quick recovery from her illness.
她很快病愈。

recreation〔ˌrɛkrɪˈeʃən ‖ ˌrekrɪˈeɪʃən〕
n. [C][U] ❶消遣;娱乐,游戏
❷(身心的)休养

red〔rɛd ‖ red〕
[比]redder;[最]reddest
a. 红的,红色的
The little girl's eyes were red with weeping.
那个小女孩哭得两眼通红。
n. ❶红,红色[C][U]
❷红衣服[U]
The girl in red is his younger sister.
那个穿红衣服的女孩是他妹妹。
❸赤字,负债,亏损[the]

R

reduce 〔rɪˈdus ‖ rɪˈdjuːs〕
［过去式］reduced；［过去分词］reduced
vt. ❶减少；缩小；降低
He is trying to reduce expenses.
他正试图减少开支。
❷使处于(某种状态)；使化为，使变为［(＋to)］
The fire reduced the paintings to ashes.
大火将这些画作烧成了灰烬。

reduction 〔rɪˈdʌkʃən ‖ rɪˈdʌkʃən〕
n. 减少；削减［C］［U］
They sell everything at a reduction of 10 percent at the store.
这家店所有货品都减一成出售。

R

refer 〔rɪˈfɝ ‖ rɪˈfɜː〕
［过去式］referred；［过去分词］referred
vt. ❶认为……起源(于)，把……归因(于)［(＋to)］
He referred all his troubles to bad luck.
他将他的一切麻烦都归因于运气不好。
❷把……归类(于)，把……归属(于)［(＋to)］
Botanists refer this flower to the rose family.
植物学家将这花归入蔷薇科。
❸将……提交，交付［(＋to)］
We referred the proposal to the board of directors.
我们把这一建议提交董事会处理。
vi. ❶论及，谈到，提及［(＋to)］
In his speech, he referred to the Bible several times.
他在演说中好几次提到《圣经》。
❷查阅，参考；查询，打听
Please refer to the last page of the book for answers.
寻找答案，请查阅书的最后一页。
❸涉及，有关［(＋to)］
The rule refers only to special cases.
这条规则只涉及一些特殊的情况。

referee 〔ˌrɛfəˈri ‖ ˌrefəˈriː〕
n. (篮球、足球、拳击等的)裁判员［C］

reference 〔ˈrɛfərəns ‖ ˈrefərəns〕
n. ❶提及；涉及［C］［U］［(＋to)］
The boss didn't make any reference to his former employer.

老板没有提及他以前的雇主。
❷参考，参照；参考文献；出处[C][U]
References are given in full at the end of this article.
正文末尾处有全部的参考书目。
❸证明；推荐；证明人，推荐人；推荐函[C]
My professor gave me a good reference.
我的教授给我写了很好的推荐信。

reflect 〔rɪˈflɛkt ‖ rɪˈflekt〕
[过去式]reflected；[过去分词]reflected
vt. ❶反射；照出，映出
The still water reflected the full moon.
平静的水面映出了满月。
❷反映，表现[＋wh-]
That choice reflects your good taste.
那个选择反映了你的高雅品味。
vi. ❶反射；映现
❷深思；反省[(＋on/upon)]
He reflected on his past mistakes.
他反省过去的错误。

reflection 〔rɪˈflɛkʃən ‖ rɪˈflekʃən〕
n. ❶反射；回响；反射光，回声[U]
❷映像，倒影[C]
❸深思，熟虑；反省[U][(＋on/upon)]

reform 〔rɪˈfɔrm ‖ rɪˈfɔːm〕
[过去式]reformed；[过去分词]reformed
vt. ❶改革，革新，改良
He raised some proposals to reform the Labor Party.
他提出了一些改革工党的建议。
❷革除(弊端等)
There is a strong demand to reform social abuses.
人们强烈要求革除社会弊端。
❸改造，使悔改
We should try to reform criminals rather than punish them.
我们应该尽力改造罪犯，而不是惩罚他们。
vi. 改正，改邪归正
Harry has completely reformed.
哈里已弃恶从善了。
n. 改革，改良；改过，自新[C][U]
The new government made many necessary reforms.

新政府进行了许多必要的改革。

refrigerator 〔rɪˈfrɪdʒəˌretɚ ‖ rɪˈfrɪdʒəreɪtə〕

n. 冰箱，雪柜；冷藏室；冷冻库[C]

refuge 〔ˈrɛfjudʒ ‖ ˈrefjuːdʒ〕

n. ❶躲避；避难；庇护[U][(+from)]

She took refuge in a friend's house.

她在朋友家躲避。

❷避难所；藏身处；(受虐妇女的)庇护所；收容所[C][(+from)]

refusal 〔rɪˈfjuzl̩ ‖ rɪˈfjuːzl〕

n. 拒绝[C][U]

She gave me a flat refusal.

她断然拒绝了我。

refuse 〔rɪˈfjuz ‖ rɪˈfjuːz〕

[过去式]refused；[过去分词]refused

vt. ❶拒绝；拒受；拒给；不准

He refused my offer of help.

他拒绝了我的帮助。

❷拒不；不肯，不愿[+to-v]

The engine refused to start.

引擎怎么也发动不起来。

vi. 拒绝

It never occurred to me that you would refuse.

我从未想到你会拒绝。

regain 〔rɪˈgen ‖ rɪˈgeɪn〕

[过去式]regained；[过去分词]regained

vt. 取回，收回；收复，恢复

He regained his health.

他恢复了健康。

regard 〔rɪˈgɑrd ‖ rɪˈgɑːd〕

[过去式]regarded；[过去分词]regarded

n. ❶注重，注意；考虑；关心[U][(+to/for)]

No one showed the least regard for his feelings.

没有人关心他的感受。

❷尊敬；尊重；器重[U][(+for)]

I have a very high regard for your abilities.

我非常器重你的能力。

❸问候，致意[P]

vt. ❶把……看做，把……认为[(+as)]

He is regarded as the best doctor in town.

他被公认为是城里最好的医生。

❷(常用于否定句)注重，注意，考虑

You seldom regard my advice.

你很少考虑我的劝告。

❸尊敬，尊重
She regards her teacher highly.
她很尊重她的老师。

常用短语

regard as 把……视为
as regards 至于
in/with regard to 关于

regarding〔rɪˈgɑrdɪŋ‖rɪˈgɑːdɪŋ〕
prep. 关于；就……而论
I know nothing regarding the future.
对于未来我一无所知。

regardless〔rɪˈgɑrdlɪs‖rɪˈgɑːdlɪs〕
a. 不注意的，不留心的；不关心的
I'll take the job regardless of the pay.
不管报酬多少我都要做这份工作。

常用短语

regardless of 不顾
She went out, regardless of his objection.
她不顾他的反对还是出去了。

region〔ˈridʒən‖ˈriːdʒən〕
n.［C］❶地区，地带；行政区域
I prefer to live in a cold region.
我宁愿住在寒冷的地区。
❷(艺术，科学等的)领域，范围
He is an authority in the region of chemistry.
他是化学界的权威。

register〔ˈrɛdʒɪstɚ‖ˈredʒɪstə〕
［过去式］registered；［过去分词］registered
n. ❶登记，注册［C］
No register of his death was found.
没有查到他的死亡记录。
❷登记簿，花名册［C］
vt. ❶登记，注册，申报
Waldo went to the city hall to register the birth of his son.
沃尔多去市政厅为他儿子做出生登记。
❷(仪器等)标示，指示；记录
The thermometer registered 70 degrees.
温度计显示读数为 70 度。
vi. 登记，注册
I registered at a hotel near the train station.
我在靠近火车站的一家旅馆登记住宿。

regret〔rɪˈgrɛt‖rɪˈgret〕
［过去式］regretted；［过去分词］regretted
vt. ❶懊悔；因……而遗憾［＋v-ing］［＋that］
I regret that you see it like

R

that.
你那样看待这件事，我很遗憾。
❷痛惜；哀悼；思念
I regret his death.
我对他的逝世痛惜不已。
❸为……抱歉，遗憾[+to-v][+that]
I regret to say that I am unable to help you.
很抱歉，我爱莫能助。

regular ['rɛgjələ˞ || 'regjʊlə]
a. ❶规则的，有规律的；固定的；正常的
He's got no regular job.
他没有固定的工作。
❷定期的，定时的
He made a regular visit to his parents.
他定期看望父母亲。
❸经常的，习惯性的
Laura was one of his regular customers.
劳拉是他的老顾客之一。

reject [rɪ'dʒɛkt || rɪ'dʒekt]
[过去式]rejected；[过去分词]rejected
vt. 拒绝，抵制
He rejected our proposal.
他拒绝了我们的提议。

relate [rɪ'let || rɪ'leɪt]
[过去式]related；[过去分词]related
vt. ❶讲，叙述[(+to)]
To him we related our troubles, asking his advice.
我们向他讲述了我们的困难，请他指导。
❷使有联系[(+to/with)]
Can you relate what happened in your childhood to your present state of mind?
你能把你童年时的遭遇同当前的心境联系起来吗？
vi. ❶有关，涉及[(+to)]
I don't know to what this relates.
我不知道这与什么有关。
❷符合[(+with)]
Your statement does not relate well with the facts.
你的说法与事实不太符合。
❸相处[(+to)]
She doesn't relate well to her peers.
她和同辈处不来。

relation [rɪ'leʃən || rɪ'leɪʃən]
n. ❶ 关系，关联[C][U]
Their relations seemed quite close.
他们的关系似乎十分密切。
❷亲戚，亲属[C]
He had no other near relations.

他没有其他近亲。

relative 〔ˈrɛlətɪv ‖ ˈrelətɪv〕

a. ❶相对的，比较的

Relative to its size, the city is sparsely populated.

与它的面积相比，这座城市人口极为稀少。

❷与……有关系的，相关的[(＋to)]

He asked me some questions relative to the subject.

他问了我一些有关这个题目的问题。

n. 亲戚，亲属[C]

My aunt is my only immediate relative.

我姑母是我唯一的至亲。

relax 〔rɪˈlæks ‖ rɪˈlæks〕

[过去式]relaxed；[过去分词]relaxed

vt. vi. 使松弛，使松懈，放松

Relax your muscles.

放松你的肌肉。

release 〔rɪˈlis ‖ rɪˈliːs〕

[过去式]released；[过去分词]released

vt. ❶释放，解放

Release the dog. It has been chained up for hours.

放开这条狗。它已被拴了好几个小时了。

❷放松，松开；发射，投掷

He quickly released her hand.

他很快地放开了她的手。

❸豁免；赦免；免除[(＋from)]

This releases them from personal responsibility.

这免除了他们的个人责任。

❹发行；发表

n. ❶释放，解放；豁免；赦免[U][(＋from)]

After my examination I had a feeling of release.

考试之后，我感到如释重负。

❷发行，发表；发行的书(或电影等)，(发布的)通讯稿，新闻稿[C][U]

The film is scheduled for release next month.

该片定于下月发行。

reliable 〔rɪˈlaɪəbḷ ‖ rɪˈlaɪəbl〕

[比]more reliable；[最]most reliable

a. 可信赖的；可靠的；确实的

a reliable man

一个可靠的人

relieve 〔rɪˈliv ‖ rɪˈliːv〕

[过去式]relieved；[过去分词]relieved

vt. ❶缓和，减轻；解除

The medicine will relieve your pain.

R

这药会减轻你的痛苦。
❷换……的班，接替
The guard will be relieved at midnight.
守卫将在半夜换班。
❸调剂，使不单调乏味
The brown hills were relieved by patches of green.
褐色的群山缀有片片绿坡，因而显得不单调。
❹救济；救援；解围

religion〔rɪˈlɪdʒən ‖ rɪˈlɪdʒən〕
n. ❶ 宗教[U]
Buddhism is the religion founded by Buddha in the North of India.
佛教是佛陀始创于印度北部的宗教。
❷宗教信仰；宗教生活，修道生活[U]
He is a man without religion.
他是个没有宗教信仰的人。

reluctant〔rɪˈlʌktənt ‖ rɪˈlʌktənt〕
[比]more reluctant；[最]most reluctant
a. 不情愿的；勉强的[＋to-v]
She was reluctant to marry.
她不愿结婚。

rely〔rɪˈlaɪ ‖ rɪˈlaɪ〕
[过去式]relied；[过去分词]relied
vi. ❶依靠，依赖；依仗[(＋on/upon)]
We relied on him for help.
我们依靠他帮忙。
❷信赖，相信；指望[(＋on/upon)]
He cannot be relied upon.
不能指望他。

remain〔rɪˈmen ‖ rɪˈmeɪn〕
[过去式]remained；[过去分词]remained
vi. ❶剩下，余留
Not so much remains to be done.
没剩多少事要做。
❷(人)留下；逗留
They went, but I remained.
他们走了，但我留下了。
❸保持，仍是
He remained a bachelor all his life.
他终身未娶。

remark〔rɪˈmɑrk ‖ rɪˈmɑːk〕
[过去式]remarked；[过去分词]remarked
vt. 谈到；评论；说[＋(that)]
A local newspaper remarked that crime was on the decrease.
一家地方报纸评论说犯罪案件在减少。

vi. 谈论，议论；评论[(＋on/upon)]
Prof. Smith remarked on the differences between the two dictionaries.
史密斯教授谈到了这两本词典的不同之处。
n. 言辞；谈论，评论[C]
He had a habit of making humorous remarks.
他惯于幽默的谈吐。

remarkable 〔rɪˈmɑrkəbl̩ ‖ rɪˈmɑːkəbl〕
a. 值得注意的；非凡的；卓越的
He is a remarkable linguist.
他是一位杰出的语言学家。

remedy 〔ˈrɛmədɪ ‖ ˈremədɪ〕
n. [C][U] ❶治疗；治疗法；药物[(＋for/against)]
I know a remedy for headaches.
我知道一种治头疼的药。
❷补救(法)；纠正(法)[(＋for)]
I don't suppose there'll ever be a remedy for that.
我想那件事不会有任何补救办法。

remember 〔rɪˈmɛmbɚ ‖ rɪˈmembə〕
[过去式]remembered；[过去分词]remembered
vt. ❶记得，想起，回忆起[＋(that)][＋v-ing]
I remember telling you about it once.
我记得这事和你谈过一次。
❷记住，牢记，不忘[＋to-v]
Remember to write us when you get there.
到了那儿别忘了给我们写信。
❸代……致意，代……问好[(＋to)]
Remember me to your parents.
请代我向你父母问好。
vi. 记得，记起，记住
If I remember correctly, your brother went to Canada 10 years ago.
如果我记得没错的话，你弟弟10年前就到加拿大去了。

remind 〔rɪˈmaɪnd ‖ rɪˈmaɪnd〕
[过去式]reminded；[过去分词]reminded
vt. 提醒；使想起，使记起[(＋of)][＋that][(＋about)]
I reminded Gerald of his promise.
我提醒杰拉尔德他曾许下的诺言。

remote 〔rɪˈmot ‖ rɪˈməʊt〕
[比]remoter；[最]remotest
a. 相隔很远的，遥远的；偏僻的

R

the remote future
遥远的未来
a remote village
偏僻的乡村

remove〔rɪˈmuv ‖ rɪˈmuːv〕
[过去式]removed;[过去分词] removed
vt. ❶移动,搬开;调动[(+from/to)]
Students removed several desks to another classroom.
学生们把几张书桌搬到另外一间教室。
❷脱掉;去掉,消除
She saw he had removed his glasses.
她看到他摘下了他的眼镜。
❸使离去;把……免职;撤去[(+from)]
He was removed from the post.
他被解雇了。
vi. 迁移,搬家[(+from/to)]
The manager's office has removed to another building.
经理的办公室已搬到另外一幢大楼里了。

renew〔rɪˈnju ‖ rɪˈnjuː〕
[过去式]renewed;[过去分词] renewed
vt. ❶(使)更新,更换;使复原;使恢复
renew a carpet
更新一块地毯
renew one's health
恢复健康
❷重新开始;继续
renew an attack
开始了再一次攻击
❸准予(契约等)延期;续借;续订;换(执照等)
renew a contract
续签合同

rent〔rɛnt ‖ rent〕
[过去式]rented;[过去分词] rented
n. ❶租金,租费[C][U]
I've got to pay my rent this morning.
今天上午我必须付房租。
❷出租的财产(指房,地产等)
vt. ❶租用,租入
They rented a cabin for their vacation.
他们为度假租了一间小屋。
❷租出[(+to/out)]
I have rented out the house to a very nice family.
我把房子出租给了一户很好的人家。
vi. 出租[(+at/for)]
This house rents for $800 a month.

这间屋子月租 800 美元。

repair 〔rɪˈpɛr ‖ rɪˈpeə〕

［过去式］repaired；［过去分词］repaired

vt. ❶修理；修补

The roof should be repaired soon.

这屋顶应及早修整。

❷补救；纠正

Tom tried to repair his mistake.

汤姆努力纠正自己的错误。

❸恢复

It took a long time for him to repair his health.

他过了好长时间才恢复健康。

n. ❶修理；修补［U］

The road is badly in need of repair.

这条路急需修理。

❷修理工作；修补工作［P］

Repairs must be done to the house before we move in.

在我们搬进去之前，房屋必须修整。

repeat 〔rɪˈpit ‖ rɪˈpiːt〕

［过去式］repeated；［过去分词］repeated

vt. ❶重复；重做；重说［＋wh-］

The teacher asked him to repeat what he had said.

老师要他重复他所讲的话。

❷复述，背诵

Mary could repeat many poems from memory.

玛丽能背诵许多诗歌。

❸照着说；照着写

Please repeat the following sentence after me.

请跟我朗读下面这个句子。

vi. ❶重复；重做；重说

Experiences repeat.

经历是会重复的。

❷(食物)留有余味

Garlic repeats on him.

他嘴里有大蒜味。

repetition 〔ˌrɛpɪˈtɪʃən ‖ ˌrepɪˈtɪʃən〕

n. 重复；反复；重说；重做［C］［U］

Repetition helps learning.

重复有助于学习。

replace 〔rɪˈples ‖ rɪˈpleɪs〕

［过去式］replaced；［过去分词］replaced

vt. ❶把……放回(原处)

Replace the book where it was.

把书放回原处。

❷取代；以……代替［(＋with/by)］

He was injured and replaced by another player.

R

他受伤了,别的选手接替了他。
replace a wore tire with a new one
换掉旧轮胎改用新的

reply 〔rɪ'plaɪ‖rɪ'plaɪ〕
[过去式]replied;[过去分词]replied
vi. 回答,答复[(+to)]
They did not reply to our new proposal.
他们对我们的新建议没有作出答复。
vt. 答复[+(that)]
She replied that she was happy to accept our invitation.
她回复说她很高兴接受我们的邀请。
n. 回答,答复[C][(+to)]
What did you say in reply to her request?
在答复她的请求时你是怎么说的?

report 〔rɪ'port‖rɪ'pɔːt〕
[过去式]reported;[过去分词]reported
vt. ❶报告
He reported that he had seen her.
他报告说他见到她了。
❷报道;记述,描述[+that]
It is reported that 20 men were killed in the clash.
据报道,在这次冲突中有20人被打死。
❸告发,揭发[(+for/to)]
He was reported to the police for speeding.
他因超速被人检举。
vi. ❶报告;报道[(+on/from)]
He reported on the whole event to the vice-premier.
他把整个事件向副总理作了汇报。
❷报到[(+for/to)]
She failed to report for duty on the date indicated.
她没有在指定日期报到上班。
n. ❶报告;报告书[C]
an investigation report
调查报告
❷通讯[C]
a newspaper report
新闻报道
❸传闻[C][U]
I never believe idle reports.
我从来不信捕风捉影的传闻。
❹【英】成绩单[C]
My son got an excellent report last semester.
我儿子上学期成绩出色。

reporter 〔rɪ'portɚ‖rɪ'pɔːtə〕
n. [C] ❶报告人,申报人

❷记者;通讯员

represent 〔ˌrɛprɪˈzɛnt ‖ ˌreprɪˈzent〕

［过去式］represented;［过去分词］represented

vt. ❶描绘,(抽象地)表现

This picture represents a scene at King Arthur's court.

这幅画描绘了亚瑟王法庭的一个场面。

❷象征;表示

The dove represents peace.

鸽子象征和平。

❸作为……的代表

They said that they represented the committee.

他们说他们代表该委员会。

representation 〔ˌrɛprɪzɛnˈteʃən ‖ ˌreprɪzenˈteɪʃən〕

n. ❶代表,代理;代表权[U]

❷表示,表现;表述[C][U]

representative 〔ˌrɛprɪˈzɛntətɪv ‖ ˌreprɪˈzentətɪv〕

a. [(＋of)] ❶表现的;代表性的,典型的

This case is representative of the attitudes of the police.

这个事例典型地反映了警方的态度。

❷代表的,代理的;议会制的

representative government

代议政体

n. 代表,代理人[C]

She is the club's representative at the convention.

她是该俱乐部派来参加会议的代表。

republic 〔rɪˈpʌblɪk ‖ rɪˈpʌblɪk〕

n. 共和国;共和政体[C]

the People's Republic of China

中华人民共和国

reputation 〔ˌrɛpjəˈteʃən ‖ ˌrepjʊˈteɪʃən〕

n. 名誉,名声,好名声,声望;信誉[C][U][(＋for)]

The store has an excellent reputation for fair in buying and selling.

该店买卖公平,声誉极佳。

This restaurant has a fine reputation.

这家餐厅信誉很好。

request 〔rɪˈkwɛst ‖ rɪˈkwest〕

［过去式］requested;［过去分词］requested

n. ❶要求,请求[C][U]

Mr. Paine made a request that I should help him.

潘恩先生要求我帮助他。

❷请求的事;(电台等的)点播曲[C]

All my requests were granted.

R

我所请求的事情全都被答应了。

vt. 要求，请求；请求给予

I requested him to come before 10∶00.

我要求他10点以前来。

require 〔rɪ'kwaɪr ‖ rɪ'kwaɪə〕

［过去式］required；［过去分词］required

vt. ❶需要［＋v-ing］［＋that］

The roof requires repairing.

屋顶需要修理了。

❷【书】要求，命令［（＋of）］［＋that］

The director required that we should work all night.

主任要求我们通宵工作。

requirement 〔rɪ'kwaɪrmənt ‖ rɪ'kwaɪəmənt〕

n. 需要；必需品，要求；必要条件［C］

I cannot meet your requirement.

我不能满足你的要求。

rescue 〔'rɛskju ‖ 'reskjuː〕

［过去式］rescued；［过去分词］rescued

vt.（从危险中）援救；营救；挽救［（＋from）］

He rescued 3 children from the burning building.

他从失火的建筑物内救出了3个孩子。

n. 援救；营救［C］［U］

Rescue was at hand.

救援近在咫尺。

research 〔rɪ'sɝtʃ ‖ rɪ'sɜːtʃ〕

［过去式］researched；［过去分词］researched

n. 研究；调查，探究［P］［（＋in/into/on）］

a research into the causes of cancer

癌症病因的研究

vi. 作学术研究；调查，探究［（＋in/into/on）］

He is researching into the causes of cancer.

他正在研究癌症的起因。

vt. 研究，探究

The historical background to the play has been very carefully researched.

这部剧本的历史背景已有人做过仔细的研究。

resemble 〔rɪ'zɛmbl̩ ‖ rɪ'zembl〕

［过去式］resembled；［过去分词］resembled

vt.（外表，性格）像，类似

She was not beautiful; she did not resemble her mother.

她不漂亮，也不像她的母亲。

resent 〔rɪˈzɛnt ‖ rɪˈzent〕
［过去式］resented;［过去分词］resented
vt. 愤慨;怨恨
He did not appear to resent it.
他好像对此并不生气。

词汇拓展
resentment *n.* 怨恨,愤慨

reserve 〔rɪˈzɝv ‖ rɪˈzɜːv〕
［过去式］reserved;［过去分词］reserved
vt. ❶储备,保存;保留［(+for)］
These seats are reserved for special guests.
这些座位是为特别的来宾保留的。
❷预约,预订
They have reserved rooms at a hotel.
他们已预订了旅馆房间。
n. ❶储备(物);储备金;保留(物);储藏量［C］［U］［(+of)］
The old man kept a large reserve of firewood for cold weather.
这位老人贮存了大量的柴薪以备天冷时用。
❷保留地;保护区;禁猎区［C］
❸克制;沉默寡言;含蓄;冷淡［U］
He spoke with reserve.
他说话谨慎。
❹预备军,后备队;预备役军人［P］
The reserves were quickly mobilized during the war.
战争期间后备队很快动员起来。

reservoir 〔ˈrɛzɚˌvɔr ‖ ˈrezəvwɑː〕
n. ［C］❶蓄水库;贮水池(或槽);贮存器
❷储藏所,仓库

residence 〔ˈrɛzədəns ‖ ˈrezɪdəns〕
n. ❶居住;合法居住资格［U］
❷住所;住宅;官邸［C］
the mayor's official residence
市长的官邸

resident 〔ˈrɛzədənt ‖ ˈrezɪdənt〕
n. ［C］❶居民,定居者
❷【美】高级专科住院实习医生

resign 〔rɪˈzaɪn ‖ rɪˈzaɪn〕
［过去式］resigned;［过去分词］resigned
vt. ❶放弃,辞去
The general resigned his commission.
将军辞去了他的职务。

R

❷把……托交给，委托[(+to/into)]
She resigned her children to the care of her younger sister.
她把孩子交给她妹妹照管。
❸使听从，使顺从[(+to)]
He is resigned to his fate. =He resigned himself to his fate.
他听天由命。
vi. 辞职
The simplest thing for him is to resign at once.
最简单的做法就是他立即辞职。

resist 〔rɪ'zɪst ‖ rɪ'zɪst〕
[过去式]resisted；[过去分词]resisted
vt. ❶抵抗，反抗；抗拒
The nation was unable to resist the invasion.
该国无力抵抗侵略。
❷抗(酸)，耐(热等)
This special coating is designed to resist rust.
这种特别的涂层具有抗锈性。
❸(常用于否定句)忍耐，忍住[+v-ing]
I couldn't resist the temptation to tease Ollie.
我忍不住要逗奥利玩。
vi. ❶抵抗，反抗，抗拒
If the enemy continue to resist, wipe them out.
如果敌人继续抵抗，就把他们消灭掉。
❷(常用于否定句)忍耐，忍住

resolution 〔ˌrɛzə'luʃən ‖ ˌrezə'luːʃən〕
n. ❶决心；决定[C][+to-v]
He made a resolution to keep a diary.
他决心要记日记。
❷(会议等的)正式决定，决议[C]
The committee passed the resolution.
委员会通过了这个决议。
❸解决；解答；解除[U][(+of)]
❹坚定，刚毅，决断力[U]
He lacks resolution.
他缺乏决断力。

resolve 〔rɪ'zɑlv ‖ rɪ'zɒlv〕
[过去式]resolved；[过去分词]resolved
vt. ❶解决，解答；消除(疑惑等)
The letter resolved all our doubts.
这封信消除了我们的一切疑虑。
❷决心，决定[+to-v][+

(that)]
She resolved (that) she would never speak to him again.
她决心不再和他说话。
❸议决,投票表决[+to-v][+(that)]
The Senate resolved to accept the President's budget proposals.
参议院通过决议接受总统的预算建议。
❹使分解;解析;分辨[(+into)]
vi. ❶决心,决定[(+on)]
He resolved on going abroad to study.
他决定到海外留学。
❷决议,作出正式决定[(+on/against)]
The Government resolved on a bold policy.
政府决定采取大胆的政策。
❸分解,解体;消退
This chemical resolves when distilled at a high temperature.
这种化学品在高温下蒸馏就会分解。
n. ❶决心,决意[C][+to-v]
He made a firm resolve to give up gambling.
他下决心不再赌博。
❷坚决,刚毅,果断[U]
George Washington was a man of great resolve.
乔治·华盛顿是一个非常刚毅的人。

resource 〔rɪ'sors ‖ rɪ'sɔːs〕
n. ❶资源;物力,财力[P]
China is rich in natural resources.
中国自然资源丰富。
❷办法,对策[C]
They appealed to the last resource.
他们诉诸于最后的手段。

respect 〔rɪ'spɛkt ‖ rɪ'spekt〕
[过去式]respected;[过去分词]respected
n. ❶敬重,尊敬[U]
They treated me with respect.
他们对我很敬重。
❷敬意,问候[P][(+to)]
Give my respects to your parents.
代我向你的父母亲问候。
❸尊重,注重,重视[U][(+for/to)]
Some people have no respect for the speed limit and consequently are punished.
有些人全然不顾限速规定,结果受到处罚。

R

❹关系;方面,着眼点[C][U]

vt. ❶尊敬,敬重[(+for/as)]

He is highly respected by everyone for his integrity.

他因清廉而深受大家的尊敬。

❷尊重,重视

I respected their moral standards.

我尊重他们的道德标准。

❸遵守;顾及

We must respect the laws of a country we are in.

我们必须遵守所在国家的法律。

❹关于,涉及

常用短语

R

in one respect 在某一点上

in respect of 关于

He is my senior in respect of this.

从这一点说他是我的长辈。

with respect to 有关

respectable 〔rɪ'spɛktəbl ‖ rɪ'spektəbl〕

a. ❶值得尊敬的,名声好的;体面的

a respectable man

名声好的人

a respectable profession

体面的工作

❷(质、量等)不错的,相当的,可观的

respectable income

可观的收入

respectful 〔rɪ'spɛktfəl ‖ rɪ'spektfəl〕

a. 恭敬的;尊敬人的,尊重人的

He is respectful to his elder.

他对长辈很恭敬。

respective 〔rɪ'spɛktɪv ‖ rɪ'spektɪv〕

a. 分别的;各自的

They sat on their respective chairs.

他们坐在各自的椅子上。

respond 〔rɪ'spɑnd ‖ rɪ'spɒnd〕

[过去式]responded;[过去分词]responded

vi. ❶作答,回答[(+to)]

He responded to my question.

他回答了我的问题。

❷作出反应;响应[(+to/by/with)]

He responded to her kindness.

他感谢她的好意。

response 〔rɪ'spɑns ‖ rɪ'spɒns〕

n. ❶回答;答复[C][(+to)]

He made no response to my question.

他没有回答我的问题。

❷反应,响应[C][U][(+to)]

a stimulus and a response

刺激和反应

responsibility 〔rɪˌspɑnsəˈbɪlətɪ ‖ rɪˌspɒnsəˈbɪlɪtɪ〕

n. ❶责任，责任感[U][(+for)]

A little child does not feel much responsibility.

小孩子没有感到有什么责任。

He is completely lacking in responsibility.

他完全没有责任感。

❷职责，任务；义务，负担[C]

Keeping house is my responsibility.

管理家务是我的事。

responsible 〔rɪˈspɑnsəbḷ ‖ rɪˈspɒnsəbl〕

a. ❶需负责任的，承担责任的[(+for/to)]

Politicians are responsible to the voters.

政治家应对选民负责。

❷作为原因的[(+for)]

Heavy rains were responsible for the shortage of vegetables.

大雨是蔬菜短缺的原因。

❸认真负责的；可信赖的

We should give the job to a responsible person.

我们应将该工作委托给一个可信赖的人。

❹有责任感的

rest[1] 〔rɛst ‖ rest〕

[过去式] rested; [过去分词] rested

n. 休息；休养；休息时间[C][U]

Let's take a rest.

我们休息一下吧。

vi. ❶休息；睡；安息，长眠

Mrs. Whitman rests with her husband.

惠特曼太太与先生长眠一处。

❷支撑在，搁在；依赖，依据[(+on/upon)]

The whole theory rests on a wrong assumption.

整个理论都是建立在错误的假定上。

❸(常用在否定句)安定下来，放心，安心

She will not rest until she gets to the bottom of the matter.

不查明事实真相她不会安心。

vt. ❶使休息；使安息；使轻松

The doctor tried to rest his patient's mind at ease.

医生设法让病人安下心来。

❷使支撑在，使搁在；使(视线等)停留在

He rested his eyes on the newcomer for an instant.

他瞧了一下那个新来的人。

rest²〔rɛst ‖ rest〕

n. 剩余部分；其余的人；其余［the］

The rest of the eggs have gone bad.

其余的鸡蛋都变质了。

restaurant 〔ˈrɛstərənt ‖ ˈrestərɒnt〕

n. 餐馆，饭店［C］

He invited her to dinner at a French restaurant.

他邀请她去一家法国餐馆吃饭。

restless〔ˈrɛstlɪs ‖ ˈrestlɪs〕

a. 不得休息的，没有睡眠的；焦躁不安的，烦躁的

She passed a restless night.

她一夜未眠。

restore〔rɪˈstɔr ‖ rɪˈstɔː〕

［过去式］restored；［过去分词］restored

vt. ❶使恢复健康，使复原［(＋to)］

The town restored order.

这个城市恢复了秩序。

❷修复，整修；修补(受损文物等)

They restored the old church.

他们修复了这个古老的教堂。

❸归还，交还［(＋to)］

❹使复位，使复职［(＋to)］

We restored him to his old post.

我们让他恢复了原职。

restrict〔rɪˈstrɪkt ‖ rɪˈstrɪkt〕

［过去式］restricted；［过去分词］restricted

vt. 限制；限定；约束［(＋to/within)］

The doctor restricted me to a light diet.

医生让我只吃清淡的食物。

result〔rɪˈzʌlt ‖ rɪˈzʌlt〕

［过去式］resulted；［过去分词］resulted

vi. ❶发生，生成［(＋from)］

His failure resulted largely from his laziness.

他的失败主要是懒惰所致。

❷结果；导致［(＋in)］

The accident resulted in 10 deaths.

这次事故造成10人死亡。

n. ❶结果；成果；效果［C］［U］

They worked without result.

他们徒劳无功。

❷战绩；比赛结果［C］［(＋of)］

The result of the match was 2∶1 to Chicago.

比赛结果是芝加哥队以2∶1获胜。

常用短语

as a result of 由于

Many people were injured as a result of the accident.

由于这场事故很多人受了伤。

result from 起因于

result in 导致

resume[1]〔rɪˈzum ‖ rɪˈzjuːm〕

［过去式］resumed；［过去分词］resumed

vt. ❶重新开始，继续

They proposed that he should resume his job as farmhand.

他们建议他应重新做农夫的工作。

❷恢复；重返；重新占用

Those standing may now resume your seats.

诸位站着的现在可以重新坐下了。

❸收回，取回

They won the battle and resumed lost territory.

他们打胜了这一仗并收复了失地。

vi. 重新开始，继续

He paused, drank a glass of wine, reflected for a moment, and resumed.

他停下来，喝了一杯酒，想了一会儿，又继续说了下去。

resume[2]〔ˌrɛzuˈme ‖ ˈrezjuːmeɪ〕

n.［C］❶摘要，梗概

The professor asked Peter to write a resume about this book.

教授要求彼得写这本书的梗概。

❷【美】(个人)简历

You're required to submit a resume.

你必须交一份个人简历。

retail〔ˈritel ‖ ˈriːteɪl〕

a. 零售的

a retail price

零售价

a retail dealer

零售商

retire〔rɪˈtaɪr ‖ rɪˈtaɪə〕

［过去式］retired；［过去分词］retired

vi. ❶退休；退役

Mr. Weller retired last month and now lives at his ease.

韦勒先生上个月退休了，现在过着悠闲的生活。

❷退出；退隐［(＋from/to)］

She retired to the country.

她退隐到乡下去了。

❸后退，撤退

Our armies have retired to regroup for a fresh attack.

我们的军队已经撤下来重新整编，以便发起新的进攻。

❹就寝

retired 〔rɪ'taɪrd ‖ rɪ'taɪəd〕

a. ❶退休的，辞职的，退役的

❷引退的，退隐的；幽静的，僻静的

return 〔rɪ'tɝn ‖ rɪ'tɜ:n〕

[过去式]returned；[过去分词] returned

vi. ❶回，返回，归[(＋to/from)]

She did not return home till 11 o'clock.

她11点钟才回家。

❷重新发生；回复，恢复[(＋to)]

The situation has returned to normal in the capital.

首都的局势已恢复正常。

❸归还，退回[(＋to)]

vt. ❶还，归还；送回[(＋to)]

Have you returned the novel to the library?

那本小说你还给图书馆了吗？

❷回答，回报；报答

We decided to return blow for blow.

我们决定以牙还牙。

n. ❶回，归，返回[C][U]

On his return he reported his findings to the committee.

他一回来就向委员会报告调查结果。

❷还，归还[U]

❸回答；报答[C][U]

He expected no return when he decided to give us full support.

他决定全力支持我们时并无图报之意。

❹回复；复发；恢复；再现[C][U]

She had a return of the heart attack.

她心脏病又发作了。

常用短语

in return 回答，回报

Give him something in return.

给他些东西作为回报。

reveal 〔rɪ'vil ‖ rɪ'vi:l〕

[过去式]revealed；[过去分词] revealed

vt. ❶展现，显露出

Little by little he revealed his ambition.

渐渐地，他暴露出他的野心。

❷揭示，揭露；暴露；泄露

He revealed the secret by accident.

他不小心泄露了这个秘密。

revenge 〔rɪ'vɛndʒ ‖ rɪ'vendʒ〕

[过去式]revenged；[过去分词]

revenged

vt. ❶替……报仇[(+on)]

I revenged myself on him.

我报复了他。

❷报复,洗雪

I will revenge that insult.

我要洗雪那个耻辱。

n. 报仇;报复[U][(+for/on)]

People of the village took revenge on the thieves by beating them with sticks.

村子里的人们用棍棒打窃贼报仇。

reverse 〔rɪˈvɜ˞s ‖ rɪˈvɜːs〕

[过去式]reversed;[过去分词]reversed

vt. ❶颠倒,翻转

reverse a glass

倒置玻璃杯

reverse the order

颠倒顺序

❷使倒退,使倒转;使反向

Please reverse the car.

请倒车。

n. ❶相反[the][(+of)]

He did the reverse of what I told him.

他做的与我说的正相反。

❷背面,反面[the]

the reverse of a coin

硬币的反面

review 〔rɪˈvju ‖ rɪˈvjuː〕

[过去式]reviewed;[过去分词]reviewed

vt. ❶批评,评论

He promised to review the film in one of the evening papers.

他答应在一家晚报上评论这部电影。

❷回顾,回忆

Before falling asleep, she reviewed the day's happenings.

入睡以前,她回顾了一天所发生的事情。

❸复习,温习

Review your lessons every day.

要每天复习功课。

n. ❶批评,评论[C][U]

His new book got mixed reviews.

对他的新书的评论毁誉参半。

❷评论杂志(文章)[C]

He writes reviews for The New Yorker.

他为《纽约人》撰写评论文章。

❸阅兵[C]

❹复习,温习[C][U]

revise 〔rɪˈvaɪz ‖ rɪˈvaɪz〕

[过去式]revised;[过去分词]revised

vt. ❶修订;校订

The dictionary was revised in

1997.
这本字典是 1997 年修订的。
❷修改,修正
He revised his opinion.
他改变了意见。

revolution 〔ˌrɛvəˈluʃən ‖ ˌrevəˈluːʃən〕
n. ❶革命,革命运动[C][U]
The American Revolution gave independence to the Colonies.
美国独立战争使 13 个州得到了独立。
❷革命性剧变,大变革[C][(+in)]
The automobile caused a revolution in our way of traveling.
汽车使旅行的方式发生了根本性的变化。
❸(天体的)运行,公转[C][U][(+round)]
One revolution of the earth around the sun takes a year.
地球绕太阳运行一周需一年时间。

revolutionary 〔ˌrɛvəˈluʃənˌɛrɪ ‖ ˌrevəˈluːʃənərɪ〕
a. ❶革命的
❷大变革的;完全创新的

reward 〔rɪˈwɔrd ‖ rɪˈwɔːd〕
[过去式]rewarded;[过去分词]rewarded
n. ❶报答;报偿;奖赏;报应[C][U]
It is unfair that he gets very little in reward for his hard work.
他工作很辛苦,报酬却很少,这不公平。
❷酬金;赏金;奖品[C][(+for)]
A large reward is offered for the capture of the criminals.
巨额悬赏捉拿这些罪犯。
vt. 报答,报偿;酬谢;奖励
Winners will be rewarded a trip to England.
优胜者将获得去英国旅游的奖赏。

rewrite 〔riˈraɪt ‖ ˌriːˈraɪt〕
[过去式]rewrote;[过去分词]rewritten
vt. 重写;改写;修改
Rewrite the following into a simple sentence.
把下列句子改写成简单句。

rhyme 〔raɪm ‖ raɪm〕
n. ❶韵,韵脚,押韵[U]
❷同韵词,押韵词[C][(+for/to)]

rhythm 〔ˈrɪðəm ‖ ˈrɪðəm〕
n. ❶节奏;韵律[C][U]
❷节拍[C]

ribbon 〔ˈrɪbən ‖ ˈrɪbən〕

R

n. 缎带；丝带；饰带[C][U]
The young girl's hair was tied up with a red ribbon.
这个小女孩的头发用一条红缎带扎了起来。

rice 〔raɪs ‖ raɪs〕
n. [U] ❶稻，谷
Rice is an important crop.
稻是重要的粮食作物。
Most of Asians live on rice.
大多数亚洲人以大米为主食。
❷米饭

rich 〔rɪtʃ ‖ rɪtʃ〕
[比]richer；[最]richest
a. ❶有钱的，富有的
He grew rich from selling used cars.
他靠卖旧车致富。
❷富于……的，有很多……的[(+in)]
The country is rich in resources.
这个国家资源丰富。
❸贵重的；富丽的；奢华的
She put on rich jewels.
她戴上了昂贵的珠宝。
❹(食物)营养价值高的；油腻的；味浓的
I don't like rich food.
我不喜欢油腻的食品。
❺肥沃的，富饶的
The soil here is rich.
这儿的土地很肥沃。

rid 〔rɪd ‖ rɪd〕
[过去式]rid，ridded；[过去分词]rid，ridded
vt. 使免除；使摆脱；从……清除[(+of)]
We'll have to get rid of him.
我们必须摆脱他。

常用短语

get rid of 摆脱

riddle 〔ˈrɪdl̩ ‖ ˈrɪdl〕
n. 谜，谜语[C]

ride 〔raɪd ‖ raɪd〕
[过去式]rode；[过去分词]ridden
vi. ❶骑马，乘车；骑马(或乘车)旅行
She rode home on her bicycle.
她骑自行车回家。
❷(马，车等)适于乘(或骑)；(道路等)骑起马来……
The car rides smoothly.

这辆车乘坐平稳。

vt. ❶骑(马等);乘(车等)

He learned to ride a horse at the age of 9.

他 9 岁时学会了骑马。

❷骑马通过;乘车行经

We have ridden 600 miles.

我们已经行驶 600 英里了。

n.[C] ❶骑;乘坐;搭乘

He gave me a ride to the plaza.

他让我搭车去市场。

❷骑马(或乘车)旅行,兜风

We went for a ride in the car.

我们开车兜风。

ridiculous 〔rɪˈdɪkjələs ‖ rɪˈdɪkjʊləs〕

a. 可笑的,荒谬的;滑稽的

It's the most ridiculous thing I ever heard in my life.

这是我一生中所听过的最可笑的事情。

rifle 〔ˈraɪfl̩ ‖ ˈraɪfl〕

n. 步枪,来复枪[C]

He pulled the trigger of his rifle.

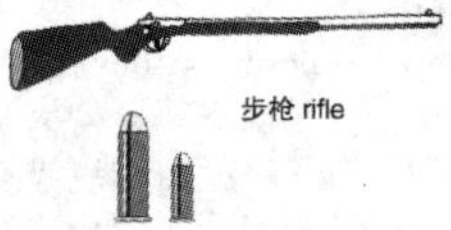

步枪 rifle

他扣响了步枪的扳机。

right 〔raɪt ‖ raɪt〕

a. ❶右的,右边的,右侧的

the right bank of the river

河的右岸

❷(常大写)(政治上)右翼的

❸正当的,对的,正义的[+to-v]

The editors were right to refuse this article.

编辑们不接受这篇文章是有道理的。

❹正确的,准确的[(+in)]

She was right in her answer.

她答对了。

常用短语

all right 适宜的,健康的;(感叹)好吧,行

Everything is all right.

一切都很好。

He will be all right again.

他会好起来的。

All right, let's do it again.

好吧,再来一次。

ad. ❶向右,向右方,向右侧

Turn right.

向右转。

❷正确地,无误地;恰当地

He guessed right.

他猜得不错。

❸不偏不倚地,正好;恰好,就

Your glasses are right on the

table.
你的眼镜就在这个桌子上。
❹直接地；径直地
Go right to the end of this street and then turn left.
一直走到这条街的尽头，然后左转。
❺【口】立即，马上

常用短语

right away 立刻，马上
He hurried to the station right away.
他立刻赶往车站。
n. ❶右，右边，右面
The man standing on her right is her younger brother.
站在她右边的那个人是她弟弟。
❷正确，对，是［U］
We must teach our children how to tell right from wrong.
我们应该教会孩子如何明辨是非。
❸正当；公正；正义；合法［U］
❹权利［C］［U］［＋to-v］
You must stand up for your rights.
你一定要维护自己的权利。

rim 〔rɪm‖rɪm〕
n. ［C］❶（尤指圆形物的）边，缘；边缘
the rim of a cup
杯口
❷（镶在器物周围的）框边

ring¹ 〔rɪŋ‖rɪŋ〕
n. ［C］❶圈；环；环形物
Fatigue brought on dark rings round her eyes.
劳累使她眼睛周围出现了黑圈。

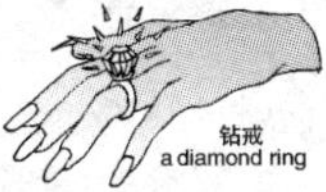

钻戒
a diamond ring

❷戒指；耳环

ring² 〔rɪŋ‖rɪŋ〕
［过去式］rang；［过去分词］rung
vi. （钟，铃等）鸣，响
I was making the bed when the telephone bell rang.
电话铃响时我正在铺床。
vt. ❶按（铃）；摇（铃）；敲（钟）
She felt bad and rang the bedside bell for a nurse.
她觉得身体不适，按了床边的铃叫护士来。
❷【主英】打电话给［（＋up）］
Your wife has rung you twice since lunch time.
午饭后你太太已给你来过两次电话了。
n. 铃声，钟声；按铃，敲钟［C］

[(+of)]
There was a ring of laughter in the corridor.
走廊里传来银铃般的笑声。

常用短语

give somebody a ring 打电话给某人

ripe 〔raɪp ‖ raɪp〕
a. ❶(水果或庄稼)成熟的;适宜食用的,醇美的
ripe apples
成熟的苹果
❷成年的,圆滑的,老成的[(+in)]
He is ripe in judgement.
他具有成熟的判断力。
❸准备妥当的,时机成熟的[(+for)]
The time is ripe for a new foreign policy.
采用新外交政策的时机已成熟。

rise 〔raɪz ‖ raɪz〕
[过去式]rose;[过去分词]risen
vi. ❶上升;升起;上涨;升高;增加
The sun has not yet risen.
太阳还没升起。
❷高耸;高出
An immense building rose before their eyes.
他们眼前耸立起一座巨大的建筑物。
❸起立
He rose and left the room.
他站起身走出屋去。
❹【书】起床
n. ❶(数量,程度等)增加,上涨[C][(+in)]
There will be a rise in unemployment next year.
明年失业人数将会增加。
❷上升,兴起,发展,提升,加薪[C][U]
His rise to power surprised me.
他上台掌权令我感到意外。

risk 〔rɪsk ‖ rɪsk〕
[过去式]risked;[过去分词]risked
n. ❶危险,风险[C][U][(+of)]
He saved my life at the risk of losing his own.
他冒着生命危险救了我的性命。
❷(保险业承担的)险;危险率;保险金额;保险对象[C]
vt. ❶使遭受危险,以……作为赌注
The brave man risked his life in trying to save the child.
那位勇敢的人冒着生命危险试

图救那孩子。

❷冒……的风险[+v-ing]

They risked losing their jobs.

他们冒着失去工作的风险。

❸冒险于[+v-ing]

I don't think they will risk holding an election.

我想他们是不会冒风险举行选举的。

常用短语

at risk 处于危险中

at the risk of 冒……危险；以……为赌注

He rescued the drowning child at the risk of his life.

他冒着生命危险救那个溺水的小孩。

take risks/a risk 冒险

river 〔ˈrɪvɚ ‖ ˈrɪvə〕

n. [C] ❶江，河

❷巨流；大量[(+of)]

He drinks rivers of tea every day.

他每天喝大量茶水。

road 〔rod ‖ rəʊd〕

n. 路，道路，公路，街道，马路[C]

roar 〔rɔr ‖ rɔː〕

[过去式]roared；[过去分词]roared

vi. ❶(狮，虎等)吼叫；(风等)呼啸；(雷，炮等)轰鸣

Day and night heavy trucks roared past their houses.

重型卡车日夜不停地从他们家门口呼啸而过。

❷大声叫喊；狂笑；大声歌唱[(+at/with)]

He roared with anger.

他气得大吼。

n. 吼，啸；怒号；轰鸣声；喧闹声[C]

The little girl was frightened by the tiger's roars.

小女孩被老虎的吼叫声吓坏了。

roast 〔rost ‖ rəʊst〕

[过去式]roasted；[过去分词]roasted

vt. ❶烤，炙，烘

He roasted a chicken for dinner.

他烤了一只鸡作为晚餐。

❷烤得使变热(或烫)，烘暖

The sun was roasting us.

太阳炙烤着我们。

rob 〔rɑb ‖ rɒb〕

[过去式]robbed；[过去分词]robbed

vt. ❶抢劫，劫掠，盗取[(+of)]

He robbed me of my wallet.

R

他抢了我的钱包。

❷非法剥夺，使丧失[(＋of)]

They robbed the people of their liberty.

他们夺走了人民的自由。

vi. 抢劫

He said he would not rob again.

他说他再也不抢劫了。

robber 〔'rɑbɚ ‖ 'rɒbə〕

n. 抢劫者，强盗[C]

rock 〔rɑk ‖ rɒk〕

n. ❶岩，岩石，磐石[C][U]

His purpose remains as firm as a rock.

他的意志仍坚如磐石。

❷【美】【口】石块，石子儿[C]

❸【俚】钻石，宝石[P]

rocket 〔'rɒkɪt ‖ 'rɒkɪt〕

n. 飞弹，火箭；火箭发动机[C]

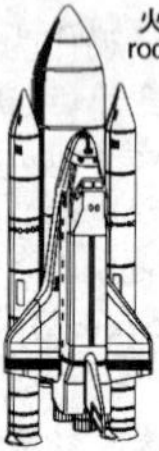

The rocket was launched to the moon.

火箭被发往月球。

role 〔rol ‖ rəʊl〕

n. [C] ❶角色

She played the leading role in the school play.

她在学校的戏里扮演主角。

❷作用，任务

He denied any role in the robbery.

他否认曾参与这起抢劫案。

roll 〔rol ‖ rəʊl〕

[过去式] rolled; [过去分词] rolled

vi. ❶滚动；打滚

The coin rolled under the bed.

硬币滚到床底下去了。

❷(眼睛等)转动

❸(船等)左右摇晃

The boat rolled badly.

船摇晃得很厉害。

❹发出隆隆声；蛙鸣

The drums rolled.

鼓声隆隆。

vt. ❶使滚动；使打滚

He rolled a snowball.

他滚了一个雪球。

❷卷，绕[(＋up)]

She rolled up her sleeves and began to prepare for supper.

她卷起袖子开始准备晚餐。

❸转动；旋转；用车载运

He rolled his eyes on her.
他的眼珠对着她骨碌碌地转。
n. ❶滚动；打滚[C]
❷(一)卷；卷状物[C][(+of)]
Please buy a roll of film for me.
请给我买一卷胶片。
❸擂鼓声；隆隆声[the][(+of)]
The roll of thunder was thunderous.
隆隆的雷声震耳欲聋。
❹名单，名册[C]

Roman 〔ˌroˈmən ‖ ˈrəumən〕
a. ❶罗马的；罗马人的
❷古罗马语的
n. ❶罗马人
❷古罗马语，拉丁语

romance 〔roˈmæns ‖ rəuˈmæns〕
n. ❶中世纪骑士故事[C]
❷传奇小说，爱情小说，冒险故事[C]
She liked to read romances.
她喜欢读传奇故事。
❸罗曼蒂克气氛，浪漫情调[U]
There was an air of romance about the old inn.
这家老客栈颇有些浪漫气氛。
❹爱情关系，风流韵事[C]
They didn't want anyone to know about their romances.
他们不想让任何人知道他们的恋情。

Rome 〔rom ‖ rəum〕
n. 罗马(意大利首都)

roof 〔ruf ‖ ru:f〕
n. [C] ❶屋顶；车顶
The rain's coming in. We have to fix the roof.
雨水滴进来了。我们得把屋顶修理一下。
❷住屋，家
All sorts of people found shelter under his roof.
各种各样的人在他家找到了栖息之所。
❸顶部；最高处；天花板[the]

room 〔rum ‖ ru:m〕
n. ❶房间，室[C]
❷空间，场所；位置[U][(+for)][+to-v]
There isn't enough room for all the furniture.
没有足够的地方放置全部家具。
❸余地；机会[U][(+for)][+to-v]
There is still room for improvement.
还有改进的余地。

root 〔rut ‖ ru:t〕
n. [C] ❶(植物的)根；地下茎[P]

R

These plants have very deep roots.
这些植物的根长得很深。
❷(牙齿，头发等的)根，根部
❸根；根基；本质
This is the root cause of poverty.
这是贫穷的根本原因。
❹根源，来源；根由
Money is the root of all evil.
金钱是万恶之源。
❺祖先
❻词根

rope 〔rop ‖ rəʊp〕
n. 绳，索[C][U]
This ladder is made of rope.
这架梯子是用绳索做的。

rose 〔roz ‖ rəʊz〕
n. ❶ 蔷薇花，玫瑰花[C]
There is no rose without a thorn.
没有无刺的玫瑰。
❷玫瑰色，玫瑰红[U]
❸红润的面色[P]
The girl has roses on her cheeks.
这姑娘的双颊红润。

rosy 〔'rozɪ ‖ 'rəʊzɪ〕
a. 玫瑰色的，玫瑰红的；红润的；(因害羞等)涨红脸的
rosy cheeks
红润的双颊

rough 〔rʌf ‖ rʌf〕
[比]rougher；[最]roughest
a. ❶粗糙的；表面不平的
Her hands were rough with work.
她的双手因工作而变得粗糙。
❷未加工的；粗加工的，粗制的
They built a rough model out of sticks and wire.
他们用木条和金属丝做了个粗制的模型。
❸粗略的，初步的
I had a rough idea where the sunk ship lay.
我大略知道沉船的位置。
❹粗暴的；粗野的，粗俗的
He is rough in speech.
他言语粗俗。
❺暴风雨的；狂暴的；剧烈的
a rough sea
波涛汹涌的海

round 〔raʊnd ‖ raʊnd〕
a. ❶圆的，圆形的；球形的
The earth is round.
地球是圆的。
❷丰满的，圆胖的
She looks round in this dress.
她穿上这身衣服显得很丰满。
prep. ❶围绕，环绕
They sat round the table.
他们围桌而坐。

❷去……的四处；在……的各处；在……周围
I'll show you round the town.
我带你们到城里各处看看。
❸在……拐弯处
❹大约
We set out round 7 o'clock.
我们是 7 点左右出发的。

route 〔rut ‖ ruːt〕
n. 路；路线；路程；航线[C]
This is the shortest route from Boston to New York.
这是从波士顿到纽约的最短路线。

routine 〔ru'tin ‖ ruː'tiːn〕
n. 例行公事；日常工作；惯例；惯常的过程[C][U]
I am tired of my daily routine.
我对每天例行的公事感到厌烦。

row 〔ro ‖ rəʊ〕
n. (一)列，(一)排；(一排)座位[C]
The teacher told the children to stand in a row.
老师叫孩子们站成一排。

royal 〔'rɔɪəl ‖ 'rɔɪəl〕
a. ❶王的，女王的；王室的
The royal family consists of the king and queen and their relations.
王室由国王、王后以及他们的亲属组成。
❷(大写)(英国)皇家的；英国的

royalty 〔'rɔɪəltɪ ‖ 'rɔɪəltɪ〕
n. ❶(总称)皇族或王族(成员)[U]
❷王位；王权；王威[U]

rubber 〔'rʌbɚ ‖ 'rʌbə〕
n. ❶橡胶[U]
There are a lot of rubber plantations in this region.
这个地区有许多橡胶园。
❷橡皮，橡皮擦子[C]

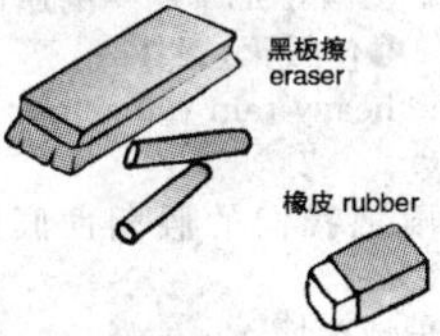

rubbish 〔'rʌbɪʃ ‖ 'rʌbɪʃ〕
n. 垃圾；废物[U]
a pile of rubbish
一堆垃圾

rude 〔rud ‖ ruːd〕
a. ❶粗野的，粗鲁的，无礼的
I did not intend to be rude.
我并不想粗鲁无礼。
❷粗糙的，简陋的
People of the Stone Age used

rude tools.
石器时代的人使用粗糙简陋的工具。
❸未加工的，天然的
They are buying rude cotton.
他们正在收购原棉。

ruin 〔'ruɪn ‖ 'ruːɪn〕
n. ❶毁灭；崩溃；毁坏[U]
476B. C. saw the ruin of Roman Empire.
公元前476年罗马帝国灭亡。
❷废墟；遗迹[P]
We visited the ruins of the temple.
我们参观了那个庙宇的遗迹。
vt. ❶使毁灭；毁坏
The heavy rain ruined our holiday.
大雨把我们的假期彻底搞糟了。
❷使成废墟
The hurricane ruined all the houses here.
飓风使这里所有的房屋成为废墟。

R

rule 〔rul ‖ ruːl〕
[过去式]ruled；[过去分词]ruled
n. ❶规则，规定，章程，条例[C]
It's against the rules of the school to smoke.
吸烟是违反校规的。
❷习惯，通例，常规[C]
He's made it a rule to rise early last year.
他去年养成早起的习惯。
❸支配，统治；统治期间[U]
vt. 统治，管辖；控制，支配
The queen ruled her country for 20 years.
这位女王统治了她的国家20年。
vi. 统治，管辖；控制，支配[(+over)]
He ruled over the country for 10 years.
他统治这个国家10年。

ruler 〔'rulɚ ‖ 'ruːlə〕
n. 统治者；管理者；支配者[C]

rumor 〔'rumɚ ‖ 'ruːmə〕
n. 谣言，谣传；传闻，传说[C][U]

run 〔rʌn ‖ rʌn〕
[过去式]ran；[过去分词]run
vi. ❶跑，奔
He had to run to catch the bus.
他不得不跑过去赶搭那辆公共汽车。
❷逃跑
The enemy cut and ran.
敌人匆忙逃窜。

❸竞赛；竞选［（＋for）］
Will he run for Governor?
他会竞选州长吗？
❹赶紧；赶去
❺（车，船）行驶
Buses run every 10 minutes.
巴士每 10 分钟开一班。
❻（机器等）运转；进行
The machine runs smoothly.
这台机器运转正常。
❼流，淌；滴；（墨水等）渗开
The river runs into the sea.
河流入了大海。
❽变（成），变得
The oil is running short.
油快用光了。
❾蔓延；传播
vt. ❶使跑，使奔
He ran his horse up and down.
他让他的马跑来跑去。
❷参加（赛跑，竞赛）；同……比赛；使（马等）比赛
run a race
参加赛跑
❸驾驶，开（车）
She ran the car off the road.
她把车开离了道路。
❹开动（机器）
He has learned to run farm machines.
他学会了开农场的机器。
❺办；经营，管理
They have the right to run their own affairs.
他们有权管理自己的事务。
❻冒（危险）
He ran the risk of losing his life.
他冒着失去生命的危险。
n. 跑［C］
The bank is a 10 minutes' run from the hotel.
从旅馆到银行跑步需 10 分钟。

runaway 〔ˈrʌnəˌwe ‖ ˈrʌnəweɪ〕
a. 脱离控制的；失控的；逃跑的；私奔的
n. 逃跑的人（或动物）［C］

runner 〔ˈrʌnɚ ‖ ˈrʌnə〕
n. 跑步者；赛跑者［C］
He is a fast runner.
他跑得很快。

rural 〔ˈrʊrəl ‖ ˈrʊərəl〕
a. 农村的；田园的；村民的；有乡村风味的
rural life
田园生活

rush 〔rʌʃ ‖ rʌʃ〕
［过去式］rushed；［过去分词］rushed
vi. ❶冲，奔，闯
He sprang up and rushed to the door.

他跳起身向门口跑去。
❷赶紧；仓促行动；冒失地做[(+to/into)]
Don't rush to a conclusion.
不要急于下结论。
❸(河水等)奔腾；涌
Torrents of water came rushing down from the mountains.
洪水从山里倾泻下来。
vt. ❶使急速行动；急送；急派
The injured passengers were rushed to the hospital.
受伤的乘客被急忙送到医院。
❷匆忙地做(或吃等)
We rushed the work.
我们赶做工作。

R

n. ❶冲，奔，急速行动[C]
❷匆忙，紧急[U]
It was a bit of a rush to get the job done in two hours.
两小时内完成这项工作是有点匆忙。
❸忙碌(时刻)，(交通等的)繁忙[U]
rush hour
上下班高峰期

Russia 〔ˈrʌʃə ‖ ˈrʌʃə〕
n. 俄罗斯，俄国

Russian 〔ˈrʌʃən ‖ ˈrʌʃən〕
a. 俄国的；俄语的
n. 俄国人；俄语

sacrifice 〔ˈsækrəˌfaɪs ‖ ˈsækrɪfaɪs〕

[过去式]sacrificed;[过去分词]sacrificed

n. ❶(供奉神的)牲礼,祭品;献祭[C][U]

❷牺牲;牺牲的行为[C][U]

Parents often make sacrifices for their children.

父母常常为子女作出牺牲。

❸亏本出售,大贱卖;亏本促销品[C]

He will sell his house at a sacrifice because he needs money.

因为缺钱,他将亏本出售他的房子。

vt. ❶牺牲;献出[(+for)]

He sacrificed himself for his country.

他为了国家而牺牲了自己。

❷亏本出售

He sacrificed his car when he went abroad to work.

他到海外去工作的时候亏本出售了他的汽车。

❸献祭

The ancient Greeks sacrificed lambs or calves before engaging in battle.

古希腊人参战前都要献祭羔羊或牛犊。

sad 〔sæd ‖ sæd〕

[比]sadder;[最]saddest

a. 悲哀的;令人悲痛的,可悲的

She is still very sad over the death of her aunt.

她对姑妈的死至今仍悲伤不已。

safe 〔sef ‖ seɪf〕

[比]safer;[最]safest

a. ❶安全的,无危险的,保险的[(+from)]

The house is not safe from theft.
这房子不安全，容易遭窃。
❷平安的，无损的
We were glad she was safe.
她平安无事，我们很高兴。
❸无害的，不能为害的[+to-v]
Water from this well is safe to drink.
这口井里的水可安全饮用。
❹稳健的，可靠的
We need a safe driver.
我们需要一个谨慎的驾驶员。

常用短语

safe and sound 安然无恙
He returned home safe and sound.
他平安地回来了。

safety ['seftɪ ‖ 'seɪftɪ]
n. ❶安全，平安[U]
You can't take action alone for safety's sake.
为了安全起见，你不能单独采取行动。
❷安全设施[C]

常用短语

in safety 安全的
He came home in safety.
他平安地回家了。

sail [sel ‖ seɪl]
[过去式] sailed; [过去分词] sailed
n. ❶帆，篷[C][U]
❷乘船航行，乘船游览
They took a sail to Shanghai.
他们乘船去上海。
vi. ❶航行，(坐船)游览
A yacht is sailing on the lake.
一艘游艇正在湖上航行。
❷起航，开船
Our ship sails tomorrow for Hong Kong.
我们的船明天起航前往香港。
vt. ❶在……上航行；飘过；飞过……
Clouds are sailing the skies.
云在天空飘移。
❷驾驶(船)
Can you sail a boat?
你会驾驶船吗？

sailboat ['selˌbot ‖ 'seɪlbəʊt]
n. 【美】帆船[C]

sailing ['selɪŋ ‖ 'seɪlɪŋ]
n. ❶航海，航行，起航[C]
The sailing is at 8：00 a. m.
上午8点起航。
❷游艇比赛[U]

常用短语

plain sailing 一帆风顺

sailor ['selɚ ‖ 'seɪlə]
n. 船员；水手；水兵[C]

He had been a sailor in the U. S. Navy.
他曾在美国海军当水兵。

saint [sent || seɪnt]
n. [C]❶(教会正式承认的)圣徒,圣者
❷似圣徒般的人;道德高尚的人;虔诚的人
You would need to be a saint to put up with her children.
只有圣人才能容忍她的那几个孩子。
❸(大写)圣……(缩写为 St.;加在专有名词之前)
St. George
圣·乔治

sake [sek || seɪk]
n. 目的,理由;缘故(用于下列短语)[C][the]
for the sake of= for one's sake
为……
John did it for his own sake.
约翰为了自身的利益做了这件事情。
for God's[goodness', heaven's, mercy's] sake
看在上帝的分上;务请
Save me for God's sake.
看在上帝的分上救救我吧。

salad ['sæləd || 'sæləd]
n. 色拉,凉拌菜[C][U]
I am not fond of salad.
我不喜欢吃色拉。

salary ['sælərɪ || 'sælərɪ]
n. 薪金,薪水[C][U]
He finally got a job in a company paying good salaries.
他终于在一家公司里找到一份薪水高的工作。

sale [sel || seɪl]
n. ❶卖,出售[C][U]
These goods are entirely unfit for sale.
这些货物完全不宜销售。
❷销售额[C][P]
Sales are down this month.
这个月的销售额减少了。
❸销路[C][U]
There was no sale for black and white TV sets.
黑白电视机没有销路。
❹(尤指季节性或存货的)廉价出售[C]
The store is having a sale this week.
这家店本周大减价。

常用短语

for sale 待售
on sale ❶上市,出售❷廉价销售;特价

salesman ['selzmən || 'seɪlzmən]
n. [C] ❶(男)推销员

S

Four salesmen were showing people suits and sweaters.
四个推销员在给人们展示套装和毛衣。
❷男店员，男售货员

salt 〔sɔlt ‖ sɔːlt〕
n. 盐[U]
Pass me the salt, please.
请把盐递给我。

salty 〔ˈsɔltɪ ‖ ˈsɔːltɪ〕
a. 有盐分的；咸味浓的

salute 〔səˈlut ‖ səˈluːt〕
[过去式]saluted；[过去分词]saluted
vt. 向……行礼，向……致敬；打招呼
The students saluted each other warmly.
学生们互相热情地打招呼。
n. ❶敬礼[C]；敬礼姿势[the]
❷致敬；致意[C][U]

salvation 〔sælˈveʃən ‖ sælˈveɪʃən〕
n. ❶救助，拯救[U]
❷【宗】对灵魂的拯救，救度[U]

same 〔sem ‖ seɪm〕
a. ❶（通常与 the 连用）同一的，同样的
This is the same skirt that she was wearing a year ago.
这就是她一年前穿的那条裙子。
Those shirts are all the same size.
那几件衬衫大小都一样。
❷（与指示代词连用）上述的
The accident happened on that same afternoon.
事故就是在那天下午发生的。
❸（通常与 the 连用）无变化的；千篇一律的，单调的
ad. （通常与 the 连用）同样地
"Right" and "write" are pronounced the same.
"right"和"write"发音相同。
pron. （通常与 the 或指示代词连用）同样的人；同样的事物
His birthday and hers are the same.
他和她的生日是同一天。

常用短语

the same as 跟……一样

sample 〔ˈsæmpl̩ ‖ ˈsæmpl〕
n. 样品，样本；试用品[C]
Show me a sample of cloth.
把布的样品给我看看。

sand 〔sænd ‖ sænd〕
n. ❶沙[U]
Sand is insoluble in water.
沙在水中是不溶解的。
❷沙地；沙滩；沙洲[P]
Several children were playing

on the sands.
有几个小孩在沙滩上玩。

sandwich 〔ˈsænwɪtʃ ‖ ˈsændwɪtʃ〕
n. 三明治[C]
He ate sandwiches in the office for lunch.
他在办公室吃三明治当午餐。

Santa Claus 〔ˈsæntəˌklɔz ‖ ˈsæntəˌklɔːz〕
n. 圣诞老人

圣诞老人
Santa Claus

Santa Claus is believed to come through a chimney.
人们认为圣诞老人从烟囱进来。

Satan 〔ˈsetn̩ ‖ ˈseɪtən〕
n. 撒旦;魔鬼

satellite 〔ˈsætl̩ˌaɪt ‖ ˈsætəlaɪt〕
n. [C] ❶【天】卫星
❷人造卫星

satire 〔ˈsætaɪr ‖ ˈsætaɪə〕
n. 讽刺作品,讽刺[C][U]

satisfaction 〔ˌsætɪsˈfækʃən ‖ ˌsætɪsˈfækʃən〕
n. ❶满意,满足;称心[U]
He smiled in satisfaction when he won the race.
他赢得赛跑后满意地笑了。
❷快事,乐事;愉快[C]
Playing tennis is one of his greatest satisfactions.
打网球是他最大的乐趣之一。

satisfactory 〔ˌsætɪsˈfæktərɪ ‖ ˌsætɪsˈfæktərɪ〕
a. 令人满意的;符合要求的;良好的
The work was satisfactory.
这份工作令人很满意。

satisfy 〔ˈsætɪsˌfaɪ ‖ ˈsætɪsfaɪ〕
[过去式]satisfied;[过去分词]satisfied
vt. ❶使满意,使高兴;使满足
That answer won't satisfy her.
那个回答不能令她满意。
❷满足(需要,欲望等)
Our company will do everything to satisfy the needs of our customers.
我们公司将尽一切努力令顾客满意。
❸符合,达到(要求,标准等)
You can't apply for the job until

you have satisfied certain conditions.
只有符合这些条件，你才能申请这个工作。

Saturday 〔'sætɚde ‖ 'sætədɪ〕
n. 略作 Sat. 星期六

sauce 〔sɔs ‖ sɔːs〕
n. ❶调味汁，酱汁[C][U]
❷【美】果酱[U]

sausage 〔'sɔsɪdʒ ‖ 'sɔːsɪdʒ〕
n. 香肠，腊肠[C][U]

savage 〔'sævɪdʒ ‖ 'sævɪdʒ〕
a. ❶野性的；凶猛的；残酷的；猛烈的
The poor man received a savage beating.
那可怜的人被毒打了一顿。
❷未开化的，野蛮的，原始的
The inhabitants were still in the savage state.
这些居民仍处于未开化的状态。
❸粗鲁的，无理的
She was irritated by his savage behavior.
他的不文明行为激怒了她。
❹未开发的，荒凉的
n.[C] ❶野蛮人，未开化的人
These civilizations flourished while Europeans were still savages living in caves.
当欧洲人还未开化，住在山洞里的时候，这些文明已经处在发达的时期。
❷残暴成性的人

save 〔sev ‖ seɪv〕
[过去式] saved; [过去分词] saved
vt. ❶救，挽救[(+from)]
He saved me from drowning.
他救了我，使我免遭溺死。
❷节省，省去；避免
The computer will save us a lot of time.
计算机将使我们省下许多时间。
❸储蓄；储存[(+for)]
❹保留[(+for)]
He promised to save a room for me.
他答应给我留个房间。
vi. ❶储蓄；积蓄[(+up/for)]
We've been saving for 5 years to buy a house.
为了买房子，我们已经储蓄了 5 年。
❷节省，节约
I save on fares by walking to work.
我步行上班可以节省车费。

saving 〔'sevɪŋ ‖ 'seɪvɪŋ〕
n. ❶节俭，节约[C][U]

The discount gave me a saving of $25.
这个折扣使我节约了25美元。
❷储蓄金，存款，储蓄额[P]
She lived on her savings.
她靠存款过日子。

saw 〔sɔ ‖ sɔː〕
n. 锯子；锯条[C]

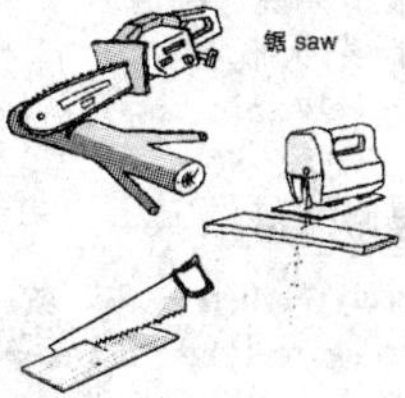

say 〔se ‖ seɪ〕
[过去式]said；[过去分词]said
vt. ❶说，讲[+(that)]
The doctor said she would be all right in a few days.
医生说她过几天就会好的。
❷假定，假设[+(that)]
Let's say you miss the train, what do you plan to do?
假定你赶不上火车，你准备怎么办？
❸(常用作插入语)比如说，例如；估计；约莫
You may learn to play the violin, say, three years.
你可以，比如说，在三年内学会拉小提琴。
vi. 说，讲；发表意见
It's not for me to say.
这不应由我发表意见。

常用短语

that is to say 那就是说
His whole family, that is to say, four persons were staying there.
他的全家，也就是说，有四个人住在那里。

saying 〔'seɪŋ ‖ 'seɪɪŋ〕
n. 格言，警句，谚语[C]

scale¹ 〔skel ‖ skeɪl〕
n. [C]❶ 刻度；尺度；刻度尺
This ruler has one scale in centimeters and another in inches.
这把尺有厘米和英寸两种刻度。
❷比率；缩尺
This map is drawn to a scale of 1 inch to 50 miles.
这幅地图是以1英寸代表50英里的比例绘制的。
❸等级；级别
Are teachers high on the social scale?
教师的社会等级高吗？

scale² 〔skel ‖ skeɪl〕
n. [C] ❶天平，秤[P]

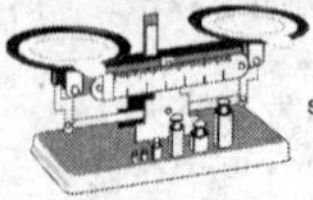

天平
scale

台秤
platform scale

My kitchen scales are not accurate.
我的厨房秤不精确。
❷天平盘,秤盘

scandal 〔ˈskændḷ ‖ ˈskændl〕
n. 丑闻,丑事[C][U]
His career is marked by a lot of scandals.
他的经历中有很多丑闻。

S

scar 〔skɑr ‖ skɑː〕
n. [C]❶疤;伤痕;(物品等的)损伤痕
He had a scar on his chin.
他下巴上有一块疤。
❷(心灵上的)创伤

scarce 〔skɛrs ‖ skeəs〕
a. ❶缺乏的;不足的
In the past, food and fuel were scarce in this region.
在过去,这地区食物和燃料都很缺乏。
❷稀有的,珍贵的
Old stamps are scarce.
年代久的邮票是珍贵的。

scarcely 〔ˈskɛrslɪ ‖ ˈskeəslɪ〕
ad. ❶几乎不,几乎没有
I can scarcely hear you.
我几乎听不见你讲话。
〔同义〕hardly 几乎不
❷决不
He can scarcely have said that.
他决不会说这种话。
❸不很;大概不
I scarcely think so.
我可不这么想。

常用短语

scarcely…when 一……就……
I had scarcely got home when it began to rain.
我一到家就下起雨来。

scare 〔skɛr ‖ skeə〕
[过去式]scared;[过去分词]scared
vt. ❶惊吓,使恐惧
They are scared that the ship might be wrecked.
他们怕船失事。
❷把……吓跑[(+away/off)]
The watchdog scared away the thief by barking.
看门狗大声叫吓走了窃贼。
❸把……吓出来[(+out/up)]
She was scared out of her wits.
她被吓得不知所措。

vi. 受惊
My horse scares easily.
我的这匹马容易受惊。
n. 惊恐;惊吓
You did give me a real scare.
你可真把我吓了一跳。

scarf 〔skɑrf ‖ skɑːf〕
[名复]scarfs, scarves
n. 围巾;披巾;头巾[C]
The wind made the girl pull her woollen scarf tightly around her neck.
由于刮风,那个女孩子将她的羊毛围巾紧紧地围在脖子上。

scene 〔sin ‖ siːn〕
n. ❶(戏剧的)一场;(电影,电视的)一个镜头[C]
❷场面;事件[C]
❸景色,景象;(舞台)布景[C]
What a fantastic mountain scene!
多么迷人的山景!
❹(事件发生的)地点,现场;(戏剧等的)背景[the][(+of)]
The criminal fled the scene.
罪犯逃离了现场。

scenery 〔ˈsinərɪ ‖ ˈsiːnərɪ〕
n. [U]❶风景,景色
The scenery is beautiful.
这风景很美。
❷【戏】舞台布景

scent 〔sɛnt ‖ sent〕
n. 气味,香味[C]
The scent of the narcissi was in the air.
空气中散发着水仙花的香味。

schedule 〔ˈskɛdʒul ‖ ˈskedʒʊl〕
n. [C]❶表;清单;目录
❷【美】时间表;课程表;(火车等的)时刻表
The train is behind the schedule.
火车晚点了。
❸计划表;日程安排表
I have a full schedule for tomorrow.
我明天的工作时间表排得很满。

常用短语

ahead of schedule 提前
behind schedule 落后于预计计划/时间
on schedule 按照预订时间

scheme 〔skim ‖ skiːm〕
n. [C] ❶计划;方案
Jack's scheme for raising money is practicable.
杰克筹款的计划是可行的。
❷诡计,阴谋[+to-v]
He revealed a scheme to kill the king.
他揭露了谋杀国王的计划。

S

scholar 〔'skɑlɚ ‖ 'skɒlə〕

n. [C]学者(尤指人文学科的学者)

scholarly 〔'skɑlɚlɪ ‖ 'skɒləlɪ〕

a. ❶学者的;学者风度的

❷博学的;学问精深的;学术水平高的

scholarship 〔'skɑlɚʃɪp ‖ 'skɒləʃɪp〕

n. ❶学问,学识;学术成就[U]

The book is a fine piece of scholarship.

这部书是一个优秀的学术成果。

❷奖学金[C][(+to)]

He won a scholarship to Harvard.

他获得奖学金去哈佛读书。

school 〔skul ‖ sku:l〕

n. ❶学校[C]

Which school does your child go to?

你的孩子在哪所学校念书?

❷上学,学业;功课[U]

School begins at 8 o'clock.

8点钟开始上课。

❸全校学生;全校师生

The whole school likes/like the headmaster.

全校师生都喜欢这位校长。

science 〔'saɪəns ‖ 'saɪəns〕

n. ❶科学;自然科学[U]

The computer is a marvel of modern science.

计算机是现代科学的一个奇迹。

❷(一门)科学,学科[C][U]

Some people think that chess is a science, not just a game.

一些人认为国际象棋是一门科学,而不仅是一种游戏。

scientist 〔'saɪəntɪst ‖ 'saɪəntɪst〕

n. 科学家;科研人员[C]

剪刀 scissors

scissors 〔'sɪzɚz ‖ 'sɪzəz〕

n. 剪刀

She took a pair of scissors and cut the string.

她拿了一把剪刀把绳子剪断了。

scold 〔skold ‖ skəuld〕

[过去式]scolded;[过去分词]scolded

vt. 骂,责骂;唠唠叨叨地责备

She scolded her son for returning home late.

她责骂她的儿子回家晚了。

score 〔skɔr ‖ skɔː〕

n. [C] ❶(比赛中的)得分,比数;(测验的)成绩,分数

His total score was 5.

他的总积分是 5 分。

❷二十,二十人,二十个

A man's life is but three score and ten years.

一个人一辈子不过七十年。

❸大量,许多[P][(＋of)]

scores of books

许多书

Scotland 〔ˈskɑtlənd ‖ ˈskɒtlənd〕

n. 苏格兰(英国的一部分,在大不列颠岛北部)

scrap 〔skræp ‖ skræp〕

n. ❶碎片,小块[C]

He wrote it on a scrap of paper.

他把它写在纸片上。

❷少量,一点儿[(＋of)]

There is not a scrap of truth in his remarks.

他的话没一点儿是真的。

scream 〔skrim ‖ skriːm〕

[过去式]screamed;[过去分词]screamed

vi. ❶尖叫;放声大哭;放声大笑[(＋for/with)]

Someone is screaming for help.

有人在大喊救命。

❷(机器,汽笛等)发出尖锐刺耳的声音;(动物等)尖鸣;(风)呼啸

They were about to leave when they heard a siren screaming behind them.

他们正要离开时,突然听到警报器在背后尖叫起来。

❸吵嚷着抗议;强烈要求[(＋for)]

The whole gang was screaming for the immediate release of their leader.

那帮人吵嚷着要求立即释放他们的头儿。

vt. ❶尖叫着说;尖叫着发出

A newsboy is screaming an extra.

一个报童正在尖声叫卖号外。

❷尖叫得使……

She screamed herself hoarse.

她尖叫得把嗓子喊哑了。

n. 尖叫;尖锐刺耳的声音;呼啸声[C]

I was awakened by the sound of screams.

我被阵阵尖叫声惊醒。

screen 〔skrin ‖ skriːn〕

n. [C] ❶屏;幕;帘;帐;隔板

He hid behind the screen and

S

listened in on their conversation.
他躲在帘子后面偷听他们的谈话。
❷纱窗,纱门
We have screens on our windows to keep out the flies.
我们窗户上有纱窗挡苍蝇。
❸掩蔽物,遮挡物
A screen of trees hides the villas from the beach.
这些别墅有树木遮掩从海滩上是看不见的。

S

screw 〔skru ‖ skruː〕
[过去式]screwed;[过去分词]screwed
n. [C] ❶螺钉,螺丝钉;螺栓,螺杆
Turn the screw to the right to tighten it.
将螺钉向右旋紧。

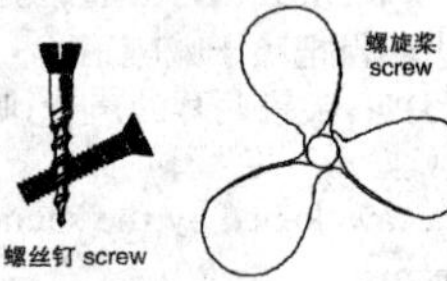

❷(螺丝钉的)一转,一拧
He gave it another screw and the lid was tightly on.
他又拧了一下,盖子就紧紧旋上了。
❸螺旋形,螺旋体
vt. 旋,拧
Could you screw the lid off the jar?
你能把这瓶的盖子给旋开吗?

scribble 〔ˈskrɪbl̩ ‖ ˈskrɪbl〕
[过去式]scribbled;[过去分词]scribbled
vt. 潦草地书写;在……上面乱涂(或乱画)
He scribbled his name on the card.
他在卡片上潦草地写上他的名字。

sculpture 〔ˈskʌlptʃɚ ‖ ˈskʌlptʃə〕
n. ❶雕刻品,雕塑品;雕像[C][U]
❷雕刻术,雕塑术[U]
He is skilled in sculpture.
他善于雕刻。

sea 〔si ‖ siː〕
n. ❶海,海洋[U][the]
We saw many boats sailing on the sea.
我们看到许多条船在大海上航行。
❷海浪,波涛[C]
There's a rough sea today.
今天海面上波涛汹涌。

seal[1] 〔sil ‖ si:l〕

［过去式］sealed；［过去分词］sealed

n. ［C］❶印章，图章，印记

There was no official seal on the document.

这公文上没有公章。

❷封（印）；封印纸

The envelope's seal was torn open.

信封封缄被撕开了。

❸密封物

The seal on the jar was broken.

瓶的封口被打开了。

vt. ❶封，密封

She forgot to seal her letter before mailing it.

她忘记在寄信前将信封上。

❷盖章，盖印于

The treaty was signed and sealed by both governments.

两国政府已经在条约上签字盖章。

seal[2] 〔sil ‖ si:l〕

n. 【动】海豹［C］

search 〔sɝtʃ ‖ sə:tʃ〕

［过去式］searched；［过去分词］searched

vt. 搜查；在……中搜寻［（＋for）］

The police are searching the buildings for survivors.

警察正在建筑物中搜寻幸存者。

vi. 搜查；搜寻［（＋for/through）］

a bird searching for food

正在觅食的小鸟

n. 搜查，搜寻［C］［U］［（＋for）］

They made a long search for the lost child.

他们花了很长时间寻找失踪的孩子。

常用短语

in search of 寻找

He is now in search of a house.

他现在正在找房子。

seashore 〔ˈsiˌʃɔr ‖ ˈsi:ʃɔ:〕

n. 海岸，海滨［C］［the］

The girls were playing on the seashore.

女孩子们正在海滨玩耍。

seasick 〔ˈsiˌsɪk ‖ ˈsi:sɪk〕

a. 晕船的

seaside ['siˌsaɪd ‖ 'siːsaɪd]

n. 海边,海滨[the][U]

We were planning to playing on the seaside for the summer.

我们打算去海滨避暑。

season ['sizn̩ ‖ 'siːzn]

n. [C]❶季,季节

There are four seasons in a year.

一年之内有四季。

❷节期,时令;旺季;活跃季节

the rainy season 雨季

the harvest season 收获季节

S

seat [sit ‖ siːt]

n. [C]❶座,座位

Excuse me. Is this seat taken?

对不起,请问这座位有人吗?

❷席位,职位

His party has one third of the seats in Parliament.

他所在的党在议会中占三分之一席位。

常用短语

take one's seat 就座

second[1] ['sɛkənd ‖ 'sekənd]

a. ❶第二的;第二次的

She lives on the second floor.

她住在二楼。

❷另一的,附加的

It is not likely that you will be given a second opportunity.

人家不大可能再给你一次机会。

ad. ❶居第二位

The American swimmer came second.

美国游泳选手得第二。

❷第二,其次

He is the second tallest boy in the class.

他是班上第二高的男孩儿。

n. ❶第二名,第二位,二等奖[the]

I got a second in the speech contest.

我在演讲比赛中得了第二名。

❷二日,初二[the]

the second of May

五月二号

second[2] ['sɛkənd ‖ 'sekənd]

n. ❶(时间,角度的)秒[C]

There are 40 seconds left.

还剩 40 秒。

❷瞬间,片刻

She'll be back in a second.

她一会儿就回来。

secondhand [ˌsɛkənd'hænd ‖ 'sekəndˌhænd]

a. ❶(资料等)第二手的,非原始的,间接的

❷用过的;旧的

a secondhand book
旧书
secondhand clothes
旧衣服

secret 〔ˈsikrət ‖ ˈsiːkrɪt〕
a. 秘密的，机密的
He kept his illness secret from his parents.
他没有告诉他父母他生病的事。
n. [C] ❶秘密，机密；内情
I'll tell you a secret that I've never told anybody.
我要告诉你一个我从未告诉过任何人的秘密。
❷秘诀，诀窍；秘方[the][(+of)]
One of the secrets of good health is regular exercise.
身体健康的诀窍之一是定时运动。

常用短语

in secret 秘密地
keep a secret 保守秘密

secretary 〔ˈsɛkrəˌtɛrɪ ‖ ˈsekrətrɪ〕
n. [C] ❶ 秘书[(+to)]
Mary is private secretary to the company chairman.
玛丽是公司董事长的私人秘书。
❷(政府机关等的)秘书官，书记官
❸(大写)(政府各部的)部长[the]
He was the then Secretary of Defense.
他是当时的国防部长。

section 〔ˈsɛkʃən ‖ ˈsekʃən〕
n. [C]❶切下的部分，片，块
Mother cut the cake into 6 equal sections.
母亲把蛋糕切成相等的6块。
❷(事物的)部分
He occupied the other section of Martin's house.
他占用了马丁房子的另一部分。
❸(文章等的)节；(条文等的)款，项
This chapter has four sections.
这一章有四节。
❹部门；处；科；股；组
the account section 会计科

secure 〔səˈkjur ‖ sɪˈkjʊə〕
a. ❶安全的，无危险的[(+from/against)]
Now my house is secure against burglary.
现在我的房子无被盗窃的危险。
❷安心的，无忧虑的

You have made me feel secure.
你使我觉得放心。

security 〔sə'kjʊrətɪ ‖ sɪ'kjuːrɪtɪ〕

n. ❶ 安全,安全感[U]

I want to live in security.
我希望生活在安全之中。

❷防备,保安;防护,防御(措施)[C][U]

They tightened security during the President's visit.
他们在总统访问期间加强了安全防卫。

❸保证;保障;担保(品)[C][U]

A life-insurance policy may serve as security for a loan.
人寿保险单可作贷款的抵押。

S

see 〔si ‖ siː〕

[过去式]saw;[过去分词]seen

vt. ❶看见,看到

He was seen to come out.
有人看见他走出来。

❷遭受;经历

They have seen hard times.
他们经历过艰难时世。

❸理解,领会;发现

I see what you mean.
我理解你的意思。

❹会见,访问

He came to see me yesterday.
他昨天来看我了。

❺陪,送

I will see you home.
我送你回家。

❻参观,观看(戏,电影等)

I want to see a film tonight.
我今晚想去看电影。

vi. ❶看,看见;观看

Can you see without your glasses?
你不戴眼镜能看得见吗?

❷看出,理解;知道

I don't see at all.
我一点也不明白。

❸想,考虑;查看,调查

Let me see.
让我想一想。

seed 〔sid ‖ siːd〕

n. ❶种子,籽[C][U]

❷原因,根源[C]

He was cursed for sowing seeds of discord among his friends.
他因在朋友中挑拨离间而被人咒骂。

seeing 〔'siɪŋ ‖ 'siːɪŋ〕

conj. 鉴于,由于;因为

Seeing (that) he says so, it must be true.
既然他这么说,那一定是真的。

seek 〔sik ‖ siːk〕

[过去式]sought;[过去分词]sought

vt. ❶寻找;探索;追求

They were seeking employment.
他们在找工作。
❷在……中搜索，搜查遍（某处）[（＋through）]
Something suspicious was found after the room was sought through.
房间被彻底搜查后，发现了一点可疑的东西。
❸企图，试图[＋to-v]
He sought to speak to her.
他寻找机会与她说话。
vi. 寻找；探索[（＋after/for）]
He sought vainly for the answer.
他寻求答案，但无结果。

seem 〔sim ‖ siːm〕
[过去式]seemed；[过去分词]seemed
vi. ❶看来好像，似乎
She seems very happy with the new job.
她对新工作好像很满意。
❷似乎存在；好像发生
There seems to be something wrong with him.
他似乎有点儿不对劲。
❸感到好像，觉得似乎
I seem to hear someone knocking at the door.
我好像听到有人在敲门。

seize 〔siz ‖ siːz〕
[过去式]seized；[过去分词]seized
vt. ❶抓住；捉住
The police seized an escaping convict.
警察抓住了一个在逃犯。
❷夺取；攻占
The enemy seized the town after a violent attack.
敌人猛攻后占领了这个城镇。
vi. 抓住，捉住；夺取[（＋on/upon）]
We seized on his remark and regarded it as a promise.
我们抓住他的话，把它当做是一种承诺。

seldom 〔ˈsɛldəm ‖ ˈseldəm〕
ad. 不常，很少；难得
She seldom showed her feelings.
她很少表露感情。

select 〔səˈlɛkt ‖ sɪˈlekt〕
[过去式]selected；[过去分词]selected
vt. 选择，挑选，选拔[（＋for/from）]
Mr. Reed has been selected to represent us on the committee.
里德先生代表我们已被选入委

员会。

selection 〔sə'lɛkʃən ‖ sɪ'lekʃən〕

n. 选择;选拔[U]

I want to make my own selection.

我要作出自己的选择。

self 〔sɛlf ‖ self〕

n. ❶自身,自己;自我[C][U]

Much importance should be attached to the development of the individual self.

应该十分重视个人自身的发展。

❷本性,本质[C]

She hates her former self.

她痛恨过去的自己。

❸私利,私心[U]

He never has any thought of self.

他从不考虑个人得失。

selfish 〔'sɛlˌfɪʃ ‖ 'selfɪʃ〕

a. 自私的,利己主义的;只顾自己的

She is rather selfish.

她非常自私。

词汇拓展

selfishness *n.* 自私

sell 〔sɛl ‖ sel〕

[过去式]sold;[过去分词]sold

vt. ❶卖,销售

He sold me his camera.

他把照相机卖给了我。

❷推销;促进……的销售

Television sells many products.

电视促进许多商品的销售。

❸达到……销售额

The novel has sold about 200 thousand copies.

这部小说已销售约 20 万册。

vi. ❶卖,出售

Eggs sell by the dozen.

蛋按打出售。

❷(商品)(以……价格)售出[(+at/for)]

This oil painting sells for 500 dollars.

这幅油画售价 500 美元。

❸有销路

Is that item selling?

那种商品销路好吗?

seller 〔'sɛlɚ ‖ 'selə〕

n. 销售者,卖方;行销货[C]

the best-seller book

畅销书

semester 〔sə'mɛstɚ ‖ sɪ'mestə〕

n. 半学年;一学期[C]

The first semester begins in September.

第一学期从九月份开始。

senate 〔'sɛnət ‖ 'senɪt〕

n. (大写)(美国等的)参议院

[C]
The Senate opens this week.
参议院本周开始会议。

senator〔ˈsɛnətɚ ‖ ˈsenətə〕
n. 参议员[C]

send〔sɛnd ‖ send〕
[过去式]sent;[过去分词]sent
vt. ❶发送,寄[(+to)]
She sent me a Christmas card.
她给我寄来一张圣诞贺卡。
❷派遣,打发;使进(学校等)
He sent his son to return the books to the library.
他派他儿子把书还给图书馆。
vi. 差使;派人;送信[+to-v]
She sent to warn me.
她捎信儿来让我注意。

senior〔ˈsinɪɚ ‖ ˈsiːnjə〕
a. ❶年长的,年纪较大的[(+to)]
My brother is senior to me by two years.
我哥哥比我大两岁。
〔**反义**〕junior 年幼的
❷地位较高的;年资较深的
He is a senior member of the club.
他是这个俱乐部的资深会员。
❸【美】四年级生的;【英】高年级生的
❹(置姓名后表示年长者,常大写)老……;大……
Alfred Kennedy, Sr.
老阿尔弗雷德·肯尼迪
n. [C]❶较年长者
He was your senior by five years.
他比你大五岁。
❷前辈;上司;学长;资深人士
He was my senior at college.
他是我大学的学长。
❸【美】(大学或中学)四年级生;【英】(大学)高年级生
senior high school
高中

sensation〔sɛnˈseʃən ‖ senˈseɪʃən〕
n. [C]❶感觉,知觉[+that]
I felt a sensation of happiness.
我有一种幸福的感觉。
❷轰动的事件(或人物)
The show was a sensation for weeks.
这演出轰动了好几个星期。

sense〔sɛns ‖ sens〕
[过去式]sensed;[过去分词]sensed
n. ❶感官;官能[C]
The dog has a keen sense of smell.
狗有灵敏的嗅觉。
❷感觉;意识;观念[(+of)][+

S

(that)]
She has no sense of time.
她没有时间观念。
❸见识,智慧[U][(+of)]
He had the good sense to withdraw from the election contest.
他很明智,退出了竞选。
❹意义;意思[C]
The word here is used in its figurative sense.
此词在这儿取的是它的比喻意义。
vt. 感觉到,意识到[+(that)][+wh-]
I sensed that I had made a serious mistake.
我意识到自己犯了个严重的错误。

S

常用短语

in a sense 就某种意义来说
He is right in a sense.
从某种意义上说他是对的。
make sense 有意义
What you said does not make sense.
你所说的话毫无意义。

sensible ['sensəbḷ ‖ 'sensəbl]
a. ❶明智的;合情理的
He is a sensible man.
他是个通达的人。
❷意识到的,察觉到的
There was a sensible fall in temperature.
气温显著下降了。

sensitive ['sɛnsətɪv ‖ 'sensɪtɪv]
a. ❶敏感的;易受伤害的[(+to)]
The eyes of a cat are sensitive to light.
猫的眼睛对光敏感。
❷神经过敏的;易怒的[(+to/about)]
She is very sensitive about her figure.
她对自己的身材很在意。

sentence ['sɛntəns ‖ 'sentəns]
[过去式]sentenced;[过去分词]sentenced
n. ❶【文】句子[C]
A sentence usually contains a subject and a predicate.
句子通常包括主语和谓语。
❷【律】判决,宣判;课刑[C][U]
The sentence was 10 years in prison.
判决是10年徒刑。
vt. 宣判;判决[(+to)]
He was sentenced to death.
他被判死刑。

sentiment ['sɛntəmənt ‖ 'sentɪmənt]
n. ❶ 感情,心情;情操[C][U]

The song aroused patriotic sentiment.
这首歌唤起了爱国情操。
❷情绪[C][U][(＋for/towards)]
They have hostile sentiments towards us.
他们对我们怀有敌意。
❸感伤，多愁善感[C][U]
She is a woman of sentiment.
她是一个多愁善感的女人。

separate〔ˈsɛprət ‖ ˈsepəreɪt〕
[过去式]separated;[过去分词]separated
vt. 分隔;分割;使分离;使分散
They separate the big eggs from the small ones.
他们把大鸡蛋和小鸡蛋分开。
vi. 分开;脱离;分手;分散
The family separated everywhere.
这家人分散各处。
a. ❶分开的，分离的
He lives separate from his family.
他和家人分开住。
❷分别的，单独的
The word has two separate meanings.
这个词有两个不同的意思。

separately〔ˈsɛpərətlɪ ‖ ˈsepəreɪtlɪ〕
ad. 分离地;个别地;分别地
We want to pay for the two coffees separately.
这两杯咖啡我们各自付账。

September〔sɛpˈtɛmbɚ ‖ sepˈtembə〕
n. 略作 Sept. 九月

sequence〔ˈsikwəns ‖ ˈsiːkwəns〕
n. ❶连续;接续;一连串[C][(＋of)]
They suffered a sequence of defeats.
他们经受了一连串的失败。
❷次序;顺序;先后[C][U]
in alphabetical sequence
依照字母顺序

sergeant〔ˈsɑrdʒənt ‖ ˈsɑːdʒənt〕
n. 中士;警官[C]

series〔ˈsɪriz ‖ ˈsɪəriːz〕
n. [C] ❶连续;系列[(＋of)]
Since then, it began a series of wet days that spoiled our vacation.
之后就是一连串的下雨天，把我们的假期弄得一团糟。
❷(邮票)套;丛书;辑;组
This publishing firm is planning a new series of school textbooks.
这家出版公司正打算出一系列

新的教材。

serious〔'sɪrɪəs ‖ 'sɪərɪəs〕

a. ❶严重的;危急的,危险的;令人担心的

His error is serious.

他的错误很严重。

❷严肃的,庄严的

He was kind and affectionate, but very serious.

他仁慈、亲切,但非常严肃。

❸认真的;不是开玩笑的;当真的[(+about/in)]

I was pretty serious about what I said at dinner.

我晚餐时说的话是当真的。

seriously〔'sɪrɪəslɪ ‖ 'sɪərɪəslɪ〕

ad. ❶严肃地,认真地;当真地

He takes things too seriously.

他太较真儿了。

❷严重地

He was seriously injured in the traffic accident.

他在车祸中受了重伤。

serpent〔'sɝpənt ‖ 'sɜːpənt〕

n. ❶蛇(尤指大蛇、毒蛇)[C]

❷狡猾的人;阴险毒辣的人[C]

❸(常大写)魔鬼,撒旦[the]

servant〔'sɝvənt ‖ 'sɜːvənt〕

n.[C] ❶仆人,佣人,雇工

The millionaire kept 39 servants.

这百万富翁雇用了 39 个佣人。

❷公务员,公仆

He is a civil servant.

他是一位文职官员。

serve〔sɝv ‖ sɜːv〕

[过去式]served;[过去分词]served

vt. ❶为……服务;为……服役

Children must be educated to serve their country when they grow up.

必须教育孩子长大后为国家服务。

❷供应[(+with)]

The company serves the city with gas.

这家公司提供城里的煤气。

❸侍候(顾客等);供应(饭菜);端上[(+to/with)]

She served me a cup of coffee.

她给我端上一杯咖啡。

❹任(职);服(刑);当(学徒)[(+as/for/in)]

He served 8 years in prison.

他坐过 8 年牢。

❺适合(特定用途或目的);对……有用;供……使用

The sofa serves us as a bed.

这个沙发我们可当床用。

vi. ❶服务;服役;供职;帮佣[+(in/on/under)]

S

My father served in the navy during the Second World War.
我父亲在第二次世界大战期间在海军服役。
❷招待,侍候;上酒,端菜
Pearl is serving at table.
珀尔在侍候进餐。
❸适用;有用;足够[(+for/as)][+to-v]
A simple example will serve to illustrate the point.
一个简单的例子可以说明这一点。

service 〔'sɜ˞vɪs ‖ 'sɜːvɪs〕
n. ❶ 服务;效劳;帮助[P]
He died in the service of his country.
他为国捐躯。
❷招待,服侍;服务态度[U]
That hotel is noted for its fine service.
那家旅馆以服务优良著称。
❸公共设施;公用事业,服务业[C][U]
There is a good bus service into the city.
往市内的公共汽车十分方便。
postal service
邮政业
❹军种;服役;勤务[C][U]
My uncle is in the service.
我叔叔在部队服役。
❺宗教仪式;礼拜式[C]
We attended morning service.
我们参加早礼拜。

session 〔'sɛʃən ‖ 'seʃən〕
n. ❶(议会等的)开会;(法庭的)开庭[C]
❷会议,集会,会[C]
❸会期;开庭期间[C]

set 〔sɛt ‖ set〕
[过去式]set;[过去分词]set
vt. ❶放,置;竖立;使接触;使处于(特定位置);使坐落;安装
He set down the bag and rested for a while.
他放下袋子,休息了一会儿。
❷为(小说,舞台等)设置背景
The play is set in 15th-century Italy.
这出戏以15世纪的意大利为背景。
❸使处于(特定状态)
She set the caged bird free.
她放走了关在笼中的那只鸟。
❹分派(工作);指定(作业)
They set her to do the work.
他们派她做这工作。
❺放(火),点燃(火)
He set fire to his own house.
他放火烧了自己的房子。
vi. ❶ (日,月等)落,下沉;衰落

S

When we reached the hotel, the sun had set.
我们到达旅馆时，太阳已经下山了。
❷凝结，凝固；固定，定型
The cement will set in a few hours.
水泥几小时后就会凝固。
❸(折骨)接合
❹着手于，开始[(+to)]
They set to work as soon as they arrived.
他们一抵达就开始工作。
a. ❶固定的，不变的；老一套的
He is a man of set opinions.
他是个固执已见的人。
❷规定的；(书等)指定的
She got to the park before the set time.
她在约定的时间之前到了公园。
n. ❶一套，一部，一副[C][(+of)]
She bought a dinner set of Chinese make.
她买了一套中国制造的餐具。
a tea set
一套茶具
❷收音机，电视机[C]
I bought a new television set.
我买了台新电视机。
❸一伙人；(特殊)阶层[the]
I warned her to keep away from that bad set.
我警告过她不要接近那帮坏蛋。

常用短语

set about 着手
He set about washing his car.
他着手开始洗车。
set aside 保留，存储
She set aside part of the money in the bank.
她把一部分钱存在了银行。
set off 出发
set out 开始，着手
They set out to examine the ship.
他们着手检查那艘船。
set to 开始认真干起来
They set to work at once.
他们马上展开工作。
set up 成立
They set up a tent near the stream.
他们在溪流附近搭起一个帐篷。

setting [ˈsɛtɪŋ ‖ ˈsetɪŋ]
n. ❶环境；背景[C]
We designed a sea setting for the play.
我们为这出戏设计了个海景。

❷(日、月的)沉落[U]
He would never forget the setting of the sun that day.
他永远也忘不了那天落日的情景。

settle ['sɛtḷ || 'setl]
[过去式]settled;[过去分词] settled
vt. ❶安放;安顿;安排;料理
He settled himself in the armchair.
他安坐在安乐椅上。
❷使(自己)安下心来;使(心情)平静下来,使安宁
After the excitement I tried to settle myself.
激动过后,我设法平静下来。
❸确定,决定[+(that)][+wh-]
I've settled that I'll drop medicine and take up physics.
我已决定放弃学医,开始学物理。
❹解决(问题等);结束(争端,纠纷等)
He settled the controversy.
他解决了纠纷。
❺使定居;殖民于
They are settled in their new house.
他们迁入了新居。
vi. ❶坐下;安顿下来
You'd better marry and settle down.
你最好结婚并安定下来。
❷停息;下沉;沉淀
The powder will settle in the bottle after a few days.
粉末过几天就会沉淀在瓶子里。
❸稳定下来;平静下来;镇定下来[(+down/to)]
She cannot settle to work.
她安不下心来工作。
❹和解;结束争端[(+with)]
❺安家,定居;殖民
The family has settled in New Zealand.
这家人已定居新西兰。

settlement ['sɛtḷmənt || 'setlmənt]
n. ❶解决[U]
Our dispute has reached a settlement.
我们的纷争已经和解。
❷殖民;定居,殖民地
Australia used to be a settlement of England.
澳大利亚过去是英国的殖民地。

settler ['sɛtlɚ || 'setlə]
n.【美】移居者;殖民者;开拓者

S

[C]
They were the first settlers here.
他们是这里的第一批定居者。

seven 〔'sɛvən ‖ 'sevn〕
a. 七的；七个的
n. 七；七个

seventeen 〔ˌsɛvən'tin ‖ ˌsevn'tiːn〕
a. 十七的；十七个的；十七人的
n. 十七(个，人，岁，点)
sweet seventeen
妙龄十七岁

S

seventeenth 〔ˌsɛvən'tinθ ‖ ˌsevn'tiːnθ〕
a. ❶(与 the 连用)第十七的，第十七个的
❷十七分之一的
n. [C] ❶(与 the 连用)第十七(个)；月的第十七日
❷十七分之一

seventh 〔'sɛvənθ ‖ 'sevnθ〕
a. ❶(与 the 连用)第七的，第七个的
❷七分之一的
n. [C] ❶(与 the 连用)第七(个)；月的第七日
❷七分之一

seventieth 〔'sɛvəntɪəθ ‖ 'sevntɪɪθ〕
a. ❶第七十的
❷七十分之一的
n. ❶第七十
❷七十分之一

seventy 〔'sɛvəntɪ ‖ 'sevntɪ〕
a. ❶七十的；七十个的；七十人的
❷七十岁的
n. ❶七十(个，人，岁)[C]
❷七十年代；七十到七十九岁[the P]
in the seventies
七十年代
He is in his seventies.
他七十多岁了。

several 〔'sɛvrəl ‖ 'sevərəl〕
a. 几个的，数个的
He was seriously injured in the accident and died several days later.
他在那次事故中受了重伤，几天后就死了。

severe 〔sə'vɪr ‖ sɪ'vɪə〕
[比]severer；[最]severest
a. ❶严重的；剧烈的；凛冽的
a severe winter
严冬
a severe illness
重病
❷严厉的；苛刻的[(+with/on/upon)]
My uncle became severe when I

was late.
当我迟到时，我的叔父变得严厉起来。

sew〔so‖səʊ〕
［过去式］sewed；［过去分词］sewn，sewed
vt. ❶缝合；缝上；缝入［(＋on/in)］
She sewed a button on my coat.
她在我外衣上面缝了个扣子。
❷缝制；缝补
Mother used to sew me shoes.
母亲过去总为我缝制鞋子。
vi. 缝，做针线活
The old lady did not stop sewing until midnight.
老太太直到半夜才放下针线活。

sex〔sɛks‖seks〕
n. ❶性别［U］
What sex is the baby?
这婴儿是什么性别?
❷男性；女性［C］
the male sex 男性
the female sex 女性
❸性，色情［U］
There's too much sex in the film.
这电影里色情场面太多。

sexual〔ˈsɛkʃʊəl‖ˈsekʃʊəl〕
a. 性的，性别的

shade〔ʃed‖ʃeɪd〕
［过去式］shaded；［过去分词］shaded
n. ❶荫；阴凉处；阴暗［the］
I saw him sitting in the shade of a tree.
我看见他坐在树荫下。
❷遮光物，遮太阳的东西［C］
❸(图画，照片等的)阴影部分［U］
❹(色彩的)浓淡，色度［C］
vt. 遮蔽，蔽荫［(＋from)］
She shaded her eyes from the sun.
她遮着眼睛，以避开阳光。

shadow〔ˈʃædo‖ˈʃædəʊ〕
n. ❶荫；阴暗处［U］［the］
Sometimes she sits alone in the shadow.
有时候她独自一人坐在幽暗处。
❷影子［C］
Lunar eclipse occurs when the earth's shadow falls on the moon.
地球的影子落在月球上时，就发生月食。
❸征兆，阴影［C］
The scandal cast a shadow on his career.
这件丑闻给他的事业蒙上了一

S

层阴影。

shake 〔ʃek ‖ ʃeɪk〕

[过去式] shook; [过去分词] shaken

vt. ❶摇，摇动；震动；抖动

His heavy steps shook the room.

他沉重的脚步使房间都为之震动。

❷握(手)

He came forward and shook me by the hand.

他走上前来和我握手。

❸动摇，减弱

This shook Arthur's religious faith.

这动摇了阿瑟的宗教信仰。

vi. 摇动；震动；发抖

He was shaking with anger.

他气得浑身发抖。

n. ❶摇动；震动；握手

It is customary to welcome a visitor with a shake.

习惯上大家都握手迎接客人。

❷【口】一刹那[C]

He finished the bottle of wine in a shake.

他片刻功夫就把一瓶酒喝完了。

Shakespeare 〔ˈʃekˌspɪr ‖ ˈʃeɪkspɪə〕

n. 莎士比亚(1564-1616，英国诗人、剧作家)

shall 〔ʃæl ‖ ʃæl〕

v. aux. ❶(用于第一人称，表示将来)将，会

I shall be 30 next year.

明年我就30岁了。

❷(用在问句中表示征求对方意见，主要用于第一、第三人称)……好吗？要不要……？

Shall we begin now?

我们现在开始好吗？

❸(用于陈述句中的第二，第三人称，表示说话人的意图、允诺、警告、命令、决心等)必须，应，可

You shall have it back next week.

下星期一定还给你。

❹(用在条约，规章，法令等文件中表示义务或规定，一般用于第三人称)应，必须

The student shall wear uniforms.

学生应该穿校服。

shallow 〔ˈʃælo ‖ ˈʃæləʊ〕

[比]shallower；[最]shallowest

a. ❶浅的

The lake is quite shallow.

这个湖泊很浅。

❷浅薄的，肤浅的

All his books are shallow.
他的书都很肤浅。

shame 〔ʃem ‖ ʃeɪm〕
［过去式］shamed；［过去分词］shamed

n. ❶羞耻（心），羞愧（感）［U］［（＋at）］
She felt great shame at having failed in the exam.
她考试不及格，感到极其羞愧。
❷羞辱，耻辱［U］［（＋on）］
Your bad behavior brings shame on the whole school.
你的恶劣行径给整个学校带来耻辱。
❸带来耻辱的人（或事）［（＋to）］
He is a shame to us.
他是我们引以为耻的人。
❹憾事；倒霉的事；令人憎恶的事；不应该的事
It's a shame I haven't heard from you for years.
真遗憾，我多年没有收到你的信了。

vt. ❶使感到羞耻
She was shamed and frightened.
她既羞愧又惊慌。
❷使感羞愧而……［（＋into/out of）］
He was shamed into admitting his guilt.
他羞愧地承认犯了罪。
❸胜过，使相形见绌
Her academic achievements shamed her brothers.
她的学术成就使她的兄弟们相形见绌。

shameful 〔ˈʃemfəl ‖ ˈʃeɪmfəl〕
［比］more shameful；［最］most shameful

a. 可耻的，丢脸的
He is not ashamed of his shameful act.
他不为自己可耻的行为感到羞耻。

shape 〔ʃep ‖ ʃeɪp〕
［过去式］shaped；［过去分词］shaped

n. ❶形状；样子，外形［C］［U］

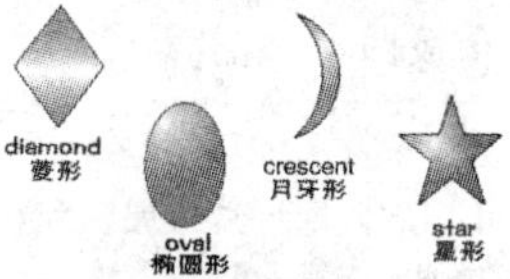

The sculptor worked the clay into the shape of a woman.
雕刻家将泥土捏成一个妇女的形状。
❷（表现）形式；体现，具体化［C］［U］

The writer's dreams find a shape in his novel.
作者的理想在他的小说中得到体现。
vt. ❶使成形；塑造，制作[(+into/from/out of)]
The potter shaped the clay into a vase.
陶工将泥土塑成花瓶。
❷形成
Childhood experiences often play a big part in shaping one's character.
童年经历在形成一个人的性格方面往往起重要作用。
❸使合身[(+to)]
The dress was shaped to her figure.
这件连衣裙做得很适合她的身材。
vi. 成长，发展
Our vacation plans are shaping well.
我们的假期计划进展顺利。

share [ʃɛr ‖ ʃeə]
[过去式]shared；[过去分词]shared
n. ❶一份，份儿；(分担的)一部分[C][(+in/of)]
I have done my share of the work.
我已经做了我分内的工作。
These young engineers had a large share in modernizing the factory.
这些年轻工程师在工厂现代化的过程中尽了很大的力。
❷股份；股票[C][(+in)]
vt. ❶均分；分摊；分配[(among/between)]
The money was shared between them.
这笔钱由他们两人分。
❷分享；分担；共有；共同使用[(+with/among/between)]
Sam share a house with two other classmates.
萨姆和其他的两位同学合住一所房子。
vi. 分享；分担[(+in)]
My wife shared with me in distress.
妻子与我共患难。

shark [ʃark ‖ ʃɑːk]
n.【鱼】鲨鱼[C]

鲨鱼 shark

sharp 〔ʃɑrp ‖ ʃɑːp〕
［比］sharper；［最］sharpest
a. ❶锋利的；尖的
You must be very careful with this sharp knife.
你用这把锋利的刀子时必须很小心。
❷陡的；急转的
The driver found the sharp turn to the left very difficult.
司机发现车子左急转弯时很难开。
❸急剧的；激烈的
In the past few days I had a sharp pain in the back.
前几天我的背痛得厉害。
❹敏锐的，机警的［（＋at）］
She studied the young man with her sharp bright eyes.
她以其明亮锐利的眼睛端详这位年轻男士。
ad. ❶整（指时刻）
The lecture started at 3 o'clock sharp.
讲座于 3 点整开始。
❷锐利地；机警地；急剧地；突然地
❸【音】偏高地
He is singing sharp.
他唱得偏高。

she 〔ʃi ‖ ʃiː〕
pron. ❶（主格）她
How can you talk to her like that? She's your mother.
你怎么能这样对她说话？她可是你的母亲啊。
❷（用来指雌性动物或国家，船舶，地球，月亮等）她，它
That's my new car. She's beautiful, isn't she?
那是我的新车。很漂亮，对不对？

shed[1] 〔ʃɛd ‖ ʃed〕
［过去式］shed；［过去分词］shed
vt. ❶流出；流下
She shed tears over her loss.
她因遭受损失而流泪。
❷散发；放射
The sun sheds light and warmth.
太阳发出光和热。
❸脱；使（籽，毛发等）脱落；蜕（壳等）
Most trees shed their leaves in autumn.
大多数树在秋天落叶。

shed[2] 〔ʃɛd ‖ ʃed〕
n. ［C］ ❶棚，小屋
He left his bicycle in the shed.
他将自行车放在车棚内。
❷堆房；库房；车库

sheep 〔ʃip ‖ ʃiːp〕

n. ❶羊，绵羊[C]
He keeps a flock of sheep.
他养了一群羊。
❷羊皮[U]
❸害羞而忸怩的人；胆小鬼；蠢人；驯服的人[C]
Are you a man or a sheep?
你是个男子汉，还是个懦夫？

sheet [ʃit ‖ ʃiːt]
n. [C] ❶床单
My mother changes the sheets every week.
我妈妈每周换床单。
❷(纸等的)一张，薄板，薄片[(+of)]
She wrote her name and address on a sheet of paper.
她把名字和地址写在一张纸上。

shelf [ʃɛlf ‖ ʃelf]
n. [C] ❶(壁橱、书橱等的)架子；搁板
He put the old books on the bottom shelf.
他将旧书放在底层书架上。
❷架子(或搁板)上的东西；搁板的容量
He read the whole shelf in a week.
他一个星期之内把这整个架子上的书都看了。

shell [ʃɛl ‖ ʃel]
n. [C][U]❶壳，果壳
Peanuts have shells.
花生有壳。
❷贝壳，甲
The seashore was scattered with shells.
海滩上到处是贝壳。

shelter [ˈʃɛltɚ ‖ ˈʃeltə]
[过去式]sheltered；[过去分词]sheltered
n. ❶遮盖物；躲避处；避难所[C][(+from)]
The umbrella is a poor shelter from heavy rain.
雨伞不能遮挡住大雨。
❷掩蔽，遮蔽；庇护，保护；避难[U][(+from)]
We took shelter from the rain in a cave.
我们在一个山洞里避雨。
vt. (使)掩蔽，遮蔽；庇护；保护[(+from)]
The wall sheltered us from the wind.
墙壁遮挡着，使我们免遭风吹。
vi. 躲避；避难[(+from)]
They sheltered from the sun under a tree.
他们在树底下乘凉。

shepherd [ˈʃɛpɚd ‖ ˈʃepəd]

S

n. 牧羊人,羊倌[C]
The shepherd guided his sheep down the hill.
牧羊人赶着羊下山了。

shift 〔ʃɪft ‖ ʃɪft〕
[过去式]shifted;[过去分词]shifted
vt. ❶转移;移动,搬移
We shifted our furniture.
我们移动了家具。
❷替换,更换;变动,改变
The wind shifted to the west.
风转向西吹。
❸推卸,转嫁[(+onto/on)]
He always tries to shift the blame onto someone else.
他总是试图将过错推卸给别人。
vi. ❶转移;移动
The boy shifted uncomfortably in his chair.
这男孩不舒服地在椅子里动来动去。
❷变换,改变
He shifted hastily to a new subject.
他匆忙转换一个新的话题。
❸设法应付;自己谋生
The man went abroad, leaving his wife and children to shift for themselves.
那个男人去了海外,留下妻子儿女自谋生计。
n. [C] ❶转换;转移;转变[(+in)]
A sudden shift in weight caused the boat to turn over.
重量突然转移把船弄翻了。
❷手段,办法;权宜之计[P]
The lazy man tried every shift to avoid doing his work.
这懒汉采取各种手段回避工作。
❸轮班;轮班工作时间
She works the night shift.
她上夜班。

shilling 〔'ʃɪlɪŋ ‖ 'ʃɪlɪŋ〕
n. 先令(原英国货币单位,=1/20英镑)[C]

shine 〔ʃaɪn ‖ ʃaɪn〕
[过去式]shone, shined;[过去分词]shone, shined
vi. ❶发光;照耀
The sun shone bright and warm.
阳光灿烂和煦。
❷显露;发亮
The joy shone clear on his face.
他喜形于色。
❸出众,杰出[(+at/in)]
He shines at golf.
他高尔夫球打得很出色。

S

vt. ❶把……的光投向，把……照向
He shone the flashlight on the water.
他用手电筒照了照水面。
❷(shined; shined) 擦亮
Have you shined your boots?
你的皮靴擦过没有？
n. 光，光亮；光泽；光彩
The waxed floor had a good shine.
打蜡地板闪闪发光。

ship 〔ʃɪp ‖ ʃɪp〕
n. 船，舰[C]
They crossed the Pacific by ship.
他们乘船横渡太平洋。

shipwreck 〔ˈʃɪpˌrɛk ‖ ˈʃɪprek〕
n. 船舶失事，海难，失事船的残骸[C]
Few people were saved from the shipwreck.
在这次船只失事中很少人获救。

shirt 〔ʃɝt ‖ ʃɜːt〕
n. [C] ❶衬衫；男式衬衫
❷内衣；汗衫
❸女用(仿男式)衬衫

shiver 〔ˈʃɪvɚ ‖ ˈʃɪvə〕
[过去式]shivered；[过去分词]shivered
vi. 发抖，打颤[(＋with)]
She was shivering with cold.
她冷得发抖。
〔同义〕tremble 发抖
n. 颤抖[C]
A shiver ran through her.
她全身发抖。

shock 〔ʃɑk ‖ ʃɒk〕
[过去式]shocked；[过去分词]shocked
n. ❶冲击，冲撞；震动[C][U]
Earthquake shocks are often felt in Japan.
在日本常常感觉到地震引起的震动。
❷震惊；引起震惊的事件(或东西)；打击[C][U]
The news of his death was a shock to us.
他去世的消息令我们震惊。
❸【医】休克；中风
The traffic accident sent him into a state of shock.
那次交通事故使他处于休克状态。
vt. ❶使震惊(或愤慨，厌恶等)
They were shocked by her rudeness.
他们对她的无礼感到震惊。
❷使电击；使休克
She got shocked when she tou-

ched the live wire.
她在触到通电的电线时受到电击。
❸震惊得使……[(＋into/out of)]
His deeds shocked her out of making friends with him.
他的行径使她大为震惊，不想与他交朋友了。

shoe 〔ʃu ‖ ʃuː〕
n. 鞋[C]
Mother bought her a pair of tennis shoes.
母亲给她买了一双网球鞋。

shoelace 〔ˈʃuˌles ‖ ˈʃuːleɪs〕
n. 鞋带[C]

shoot 〔ʃut ‖ ʃuːt〕
[过去式]shot；[过去分词]shot
vt. ❶发射，放射
He shot the arrow from the bow.
他拉弓把箭射了出去。
❷开(枪)，放(炮)；射出(光线等)
The searchlight shot a long ray across the sky.
探照灯射出一道长长的光柱划过天空。
❸射中；射伤；射死
He shot a wild duck.
他射中一只野鸭。
vi. ❶射出；放出；抛出
Hearing the sad news, he felt the tears shooting from his eyes.
一听到这令人伤心的消息，他就感到泪水从眼中涌了出来。
❷(箭一般)飞驰；飞快地移动
A meteor suddenly shot across the sky.
一颗流星急速掠过天空。
❸射击；射猎
I used to shoot in the winter.
过去我经常在冬天打猎。
n. 幼芽，幼枝[C]
A giraffe were eating the shoots on the trees.
一只长颈鹿正在吃树上的嫩枝。

shop 〔ʃɑp ‖ ʃɒp〕
[过去式]shopped；[过去分词]shopped
n. [C]【主英】❶商店，零售店
She keeps a flower shop.
她经营一家花店。
❷工作坊，工厂；修理厂
My father works in a carpenter's shop.
我父亲在木工场工作。
vi. 购物，逛商店
My mother has gone shopping in town.

S

母亲到城里买东西去了。

shopkeeper 〔ˈʃɑpˌkipɚ ‖ ˌʃɒpˈkiːpə〕

n. 店主，商店经理[C]

shopping 〔ˈʃɑpɪŋ ‖ ˈʃɒpɪŋ〕

n. [U] ❶买东西，购物

Mother does her shopping on Wednesdays and Saturdays.

母亲在星期三和星期六去买东西。

❷所购买的物品

She put her shopping away in the kitchen.

她把购买来的东西在厨房里放好。

❸商业设施

New York has good shopping.

纽约商业设施齐全。

shore 〔ʃɔr ‖ ʃɔː〕

n. ❶岸，滨[C][U]

The sailor was held up while he was on shore.

那个水手在岸上遭到抢劫。

❷陆地[U]

short 〔ʃɔrt ‖ ʃɔːt〕

[比]shorter；[最]shortest

a. ❶短的；矮的

The railway station is only a short distance from here.

火车站离这里很近。

Tom is shorter than Jack by a head.

汤姆比杰克矮一头。

❷缩写的[(+for)]

UN is short for the United Nations.

UN 是 the United Nations（联合国）的缩写。

❸短暂的；短促的

❹短缺的；不足的[(+of)]

We are short of skilled labor.

我们缺少技术工人。

n. 短裤；裤衩[P]

He bought a new pair of shorts.

他买了一条新的短裤。

shortage 〔ˈʃɔrtɪdʒ ‖ ˈʃɔːtɪdʒ〕

n. 缺少，不足，匮乏[C][U]

a water shortage

水缺乏

a shortage of 10 dollars

缺 10 美元

shortcoming 〔ˈʃɔrtˌkʌmɪŋ ‖ ˈʃɔːtˌkʌmɪŋ〕

n. 缺点，短处[P]

We all have shortcomings.

我们都有些缺点。

shorten 〔ˈʃɔrtn̩ ‖ ˈʃɔːtn〕

vt. 使变短；缩短；减少

She had her skirt shortened an inch.

她请人把裙子改短了一英寸。

vi. 变短,缩短;变小
The days shorten in the autumn.
秋天白昼变短。

shortly ['ʃɔrtlı || 'ʃɔːtlı]
ad. ❶立刻,马上,不久
She will arrive shortly.
她很快就来了。
❷简短地,扼要地
Speak shortly to the point.
简单扼要地说。

shot [ʃɑt || ʃɒt]
n. [C]❶射击,开枪;枪(炮)声
The policeman fired a warning shot.
警察鸣枪示警。
❷【体】射门;投篮;一击
❸【体】铅球
❹快照
I took a shot of the twin sisters.
我给那对孪生姊妹拍了一张照片。

should [ʃʊd || ʃʊd]
v. aux. ❶(shall 的过去时,表示过去将来)将
We hoped that we should be able to do that.
我们希望我们能这样做。
❷(表示语气较强的假设)万一,竟然
If the car should break down on the way, you would have to walk back.
万一汽车中途抛锚,你就得走回来。
❸(表示可能性,推测,推论或期待)可能,该
She should be here at any minute.
她该马上就到。
❹(表示义务,责任)应该,应当
You should phone your mother every week.
你应该每周给你母亲打一次电话。
❺(表示建议,命令,决定等)应该,必须
You should brush your teeth before you go to bed.
上床前要刷牙。
❻(用 should have +过去分词)本应该……(但实际没那样做)
You should have posted those letters. Why didn't you?
那些信你该寄出去了,为什么没寄呢?
❼表假设
Should there be a problem, I hope you will call me immediately.

如果有问题的话，我希望你立刻打电话给我。

shoulder 〔ˈʃoldɚ‖ˈʃəʊldə〕

n. 肩，肩膀[C]

Too much work has been placed on his shoulders.

压在他身上的工作太多了。

shouldn't 〔ˈʃʊdn̩t‖ˈʃʊdnt〕

＝should not

You shouldn't tell a lie.

你不应该撒谎。

shout 〔ʃaʊt‖ʃaʊt〕

[过去式]shouted；[过去分词]shouted

vi. ❶呼喊，喊叫

The sick child shouted with pain.

那个得病的孩子痛得叫了起来。

❷叫嚷；大声说；大声笑

vt. ❶高呼；大声说出；嚷着说出[(＋out)]

The commanding officer shouted his orders.

指挥官高声发出命令。

❷叫喊得使……

He shouted himself hoarse.

他喊叫得嗓子都嘶哑了。

n. 呼喊；喊叫声[C]

Children's shouts of joy shook the classroom.

孩子们的欢呼声使教室都震动了。

show 〔ʃo‖ʃəʊ〕

[过去式]showed；[过去分词]shown

vt. ❶显示，露出

She shows great interest in American drama.

她对美国戏剧很感兴趣。

❷陈列，展出

The paintings were shown at the Art Gallery.

这些画曾在美术馆展出。

❸演出；放映

❹证明，表明[＋(that)][＋wh-]

His remarks showed that he misunderstood my position on the question.

他的话说明他误解了我在这一问题上的立场。

❺出示，给……看

Please show me your passport.

请出示您的护照。

❻带领，引导

I will show you around the campus.

我会领你在校园里转转。

vi. ❶显现；露面

Her worry showed in her eyes.

她的眼神显露出忧愁。

❷上演；放映

Where is the film showing?

这部影片在哪儿上映？

常用短语

show around 带领……参观

show off 炫耀

She showed off her ring.

她炫耀她的戒指。

show up 出现

He showed up late.

他姗姗来迟。

n. ❶展览，展览会；陈列品[C]

We visited an art show this morning.

今天上午我们参观了一个画展。

❷表演；演出节目[C]

He is in show business.

他从事演艺事业。

❸表现，显示[(+of)]

Some delegates walked out in a show of protest.

有几位代表退出会场以示抗议。

❹炫耀，卖弄[U]

He is fond of show.

他喜欢卖弄。

shower [ˈʃauə || ˈʃauə]

n. [C] ❶阵雨；冰雹（或风雪等）的一阵

He was caught in a shower.

他被阵雨淋湿了。

❷（倾泻般出现的）一大批，大量[(+of)]

I have received a shower of letters recently.

最近我收到了一大批信件。

❸淋浴；淋浴器；淋浴间

I take a cold shower every day.

我每天用冷水淋浴。

shrimp [ʃrɪmp || ʃrɪmp]

n. (小)虾[C]

shrink [ʃrɪŋk || ʃrɪŋk]

[过去式]shrank, shrunk; [过去分词]shrunk, shrunken

vi. ❶收缩，缩短，皱缩

This kind of cloth shrinks in the wash.

这种布缩水。

❷退缩，畏怯

Brave men never shrink from danger.

勇敢的人决不会因危险而退缩。

shrug [ʃrʌg || ʃrʌg]

[过去式]shrugged; [过去分词]shrugged

vt. vi. (表示疑惑，蔑视，无奈等)耸(肩)

He shrugged (his shoulder), and said that he had nothing to do with it.

S

他耸耸肩说此事与他无关。

shut 〔ʃʌt ‖ ʃʌt〕

［过去式］shut；［过去分词］shut

vt. ❶关上，闭上，关闭

Shut the window, please.

请关窗户。

❷把……关住；禁闭

She shut herself in her bedroom sobbing her heart out.

她把自己关在卧室里，哭得死去活来。

❸使停止营业；停止开放

Business is not good. He'll have to shut the shop.

生意不好，他只得打算停业。

vi. ❶关上，合上

The doors shut, and the train moved off.

门都关了，火车已开走了。

❷停止营业；打烊

The stores shut at 9：30 p. m.

这些商店晚上九点半打烊。

shy 〔ʃaɪ ‖ ʃaɪ〕

［比］shyer；［最］shyest

a. ❶怕羞的，羞怯的，腼腆的

He is shy by nature.

他天生怕羞。

❷易受惊的，胆小的，迟疑的，提防的；回避的［(＋of)］

The deer is a shy animal.

鹿是胆小的动物。

sick 〔sɪk ‖ sɪk〕

［比］sicker；［最］sickest

a. ❶病的，有病的；病人的

The sick tree is several hundred years old.

这棵病树已生长了好几百年了。

❷患……病的［(＋with)］

He is sick with influenza.

他患了流行性感冒。

❸想呕吐的，恶心的

She feels sick at the sight of the dead rat.

她一见死老鼠就感到恶心。

sickness 〔'sɪknəs ‖ 'sɪknɪs〕

n. ［U］❶患病

He is absent because of sickness.

他因病缺席。

❷恶心，呕吐

side 〔saɪd ‖ saɪd〕

n. ［C］❶边；面；侧；端

An old man was sitting on the side of the road.

一个老人坐在路边。

❷旁边；身边

The big guy standing at his side may be his bodyguard.

站在他身旁的那个大个子可能是他的保镖。

❸(问题等的)方面；(争论比赛

等的)一方,一派
Whose side are you on?
你支持哪一方?

sidewalk 〔ˈsaɪdˌwɔk ‖ ˈsaɪdwɔːk〕
n.【美】人行道[C]

sideways 〔ˈsaɪdˌwez ‖ ˈsaɪdweɪz〕
ad. (斜)向一边;向旁边
He looked sideways at me.
他斜眼看着我。

sigh 〔saɪ ‖ saɪ〕
[过去式]sighed;[过去分词]sighed
vi. 叹气,叹息
She sighed with relief.
她欣慰地叹了口气。
n. 叹气,叹息[C]
The old man gave a sigh.
老人叹了口气。

sight 〔saɪt ‖ saɪt〕
n. ❶视觉,视力[U]
I'll have my sight tested tomorrow.
我明天去检查视力。
❷视界,视域[U]
Victory is in sight.
胜利在望。
❸看见,目睹[U][(+of)]
The girl dreaded the sight of snakes.
那女孩害怕看到蛇。
❹景色,景象[C]
It was a glorious sight.
那是壮丽的景色。

常用短语

at first sight 初见;初看之下
They fell in love at first sight.
他们一见钟情。
at (the) sight of 一看见
She fainted at the sight of blood.
她一看见血就昏过去了。
catch sight of 看到
We caught sight of a boat over there.
我们看见那边有条小船。
in sight 看得见
The land was still in sight.
陆地仍看得见。
lose sight of 不再看见
We lost sight of the man at last.
我们终于看不见那个人了。
out of sight 在看不见的地方
The plane flew out of sight.
飞机飞得看不见了。

sightseeing 〔ˈsaɪtˌsiŋ ‖ ˈsaɪtsiːɪŋ〕
n. 观光,游览[U]
We went sightseeing to the Great Wall.

S

我们游览了长城。

sign 〔saɪn ‖ saɪn〕
［过去式］signed;［过去分词］signed
n.［C］❶记号，符号
❷标志；招牌；标牌
The sign says "Parking Forbidden".
告示牌上写着"禁止停车"。
❸手势；暗号；表示
I talked with him by signs.
我和他用手势会话。
❹征象；前兆［(+ of)］［+ (that)］
World trade is showing signs of revival.
世界贸易正显示出重新活跃的征兆。
vt. ❶签(名)；写下
He signed his name on the cheque.
他在支票上签了名。
❷以手势(或其他动作)表示
She signed the children to be quiet.
她示意孩子们安静下来。

signal 〔ˈsɪgn̩l ‖ ˈsɪgnəl〕
n.［C］❶信号；暗号
A red lamp is used as a danger signal.
红灯用作危险信号。
❷信号器；交通指示灯；【铁】信号灯
The train must stop when the signal is red.
信号灯是红色时，火车必须停驶。

signature 〔ˈsɪgnətʃɚ ‖ ˈsɪgnɪtʃə〕
n. 签名，署名；画押［C］
He put his signature there.
他在那里签了名。

significance 〔ˈsɪgnɪfɪkəns ‖ sɪgˈnɪfɪkəns〕
n.［U］❶重要性，重要
This is a matter of great significance.
这是件非常重要的事情。
❷意义，含义；意思
What was the significance of his remark?
他的话有什么含义呢？

silence 〔ˈsaɪləns ‖ ˈsaɪləns〕
n.［U］❶无声，寂静
The silence was broken by a loud cry.

宁静被一声喊叫所打破。
❷沉默，默不作声
I can't understand his silence on such an important matter.
我真不懂他对如此重要的事情竟闭口不谈。

silent 〔'saɪlənt ‖ 'saɪlənt〕
［比］more silent；［最］most silent
a. ❶沉默的；寡言的；不做声的
She made a silent protest.
她作无言的抗议。
❷寂静无声的
The park was silent.
公园里静悄悄的。

silk 〔sɪlk ‖ sɪlk〕
n. ❶蚕丝，丝；丝织物(品)，绸布［U］
The princess is wearing a dress of the finest silk.
公主身穿最高级的丝绸衣服。
❷丝绸制品，绸衣［P］
She was dressed in silks.
她穿着绸衣。

silly 〔'sɪlɪ ‖ 'sɪlɪ〕
［比］sillier；［最］silliest
a. ❶愚蠢的；糊涂的
It was silly of me to say such a thing.
我竟然说了这种话，真傻。
❷无聊的
He told a silly story.
他讲了一个无聊的故事。
❸【口】眼花的；失去知觉的
I was knocked silly by the news.
我被这消息惊呆了。
n. 呆子，傻瓜［C］
Well, silly, why not stay!
喂，傻瓜，为什么不留下呢！

silver 〔'sɪlvə ‖ 'sɪlvə〕
n. ［U］❶银
❷银器；银餐具
The silver will need to be polished for the dinner party.
为了宴会，这些银器需要擦得光亮。
❸银币；硬币
Could you tell me where to change paper money into silver?
请问在哪儿可以把纸币兑换成硬币？
a. ❶银的；镀银的；含银的
❷银色的，有银色光泽的
There is not a silver hair on her head.
她头上没有一根银发。
❸(声音)清脆悦耳的
He heard a silver laughter from the next room.
他听到隔壁房间里传来一阵银铃般的笑声。

S

similar ['sɪmələ˞ ‖ 'sɪmɪlə]
[比] more similar; [最] most similar
a. 相像的,相仿的,类似的[(+to)]
His problem is similar to yours.
他的问题和你的相似。

simple ['sɪmpḷ ‖ 'sɪmpl]
[比]simpler;[最]simplest
a. ❶简单的,简易的;简明的
Such a toy is simple to make.
这种玩具做起来很简单。
❷单纯的,朴实的;天真的
My aunt has a simple heart.
我姑妈有一颗单纯的心。
❸坦率的;善良的
❹完全的,纯粹的
His statement was simple racism.
他的陈述纯粹是种族歧视。

S

simply ['sɪmplɪ ‖ 'sɪmplɪ]
ad. ❶简单地,简易地;简明地
He explained it simply.
他简单地做了说明。
❷简朴地,朴素地
She was simply dressed.
她穿着简朴。
❸仅仅,只不过
It's simply a question of money.
这只不过是钱的问题。

simultaneous [ˌsaɪmḷ'tenɪəs ‖ ˌsaɪməl'teɪnjəs]
a. 同时发生的,同时存在的;同步的,一齐的[(+with)]
simultaneous interpretation
同声传译

sin [sɪn ‖ sɪn]
n. ❶(宗教或道德上的)罪,罪孽,罪恶[C][U]
It's a sin to waste food.
浪费食物是一种罪孽。
❷(违反礼节,习俗的)过错,过失;不合常情的事[C][(+against)]
It's a sin to stay indoors on such a fine day.
这样的好天气留在屋里实在不该。

since [sɪns ‖ sɪns]
ad. (常用于现在完成时或过去完成时)
❶此后;从那时到现在
She left school three years ago and has worked as a nurse ever since.
她三年前毕业,从那时起便一直当护士。
❷之前,以前
He killed himself 10 years since.

他10年前自杀了。

prep.（常用于现在完成时或过去完成时）自……以来，从……至今

I haven't heard from him since last year.

我自去年以来未曾收到过他的信。

conj. ❶（常用于现在完成时或过去完成时）自……以来，从……至今

It's been 10 years since they married.

他们结婚到现在已经10年了。

❷既然；因为，由于

He must have taken the book since it isn't here.

他一定是把书拿走了，因为书已不在这里了。

sincere〔sɪn'sɪr ‖ sɪn'sɪə〕

[比]sincerer；[最]sincerest

a. ❶衷心的，真诚的，笃实的；真心实意的

❷忠实的，诚实的，正直的

sincerely〔sɪn'sɪrlɪ ‖ sɪn'sɪəlɪ〕

ad. 真诚地；诚恳地；由衷地

I sincerely hope you'll come with us.

我真诚希望你和我们一起去。

sing〔sɪŋ ‖ sɪŋ〕

[过去式]sang，[过去分词]sung

vi. ❶唱，唱歌

She sang to the guitar.

她和着吉他歌唱。

❷（鸟，虫等）鸣，鸣叫

vt. ❶唱；吟唱

❷给……唱

Our hostess promised to sing us a song after dinner.

女主人答应饭后给我们唱支歌。

❸用诗赞颂（或叙述）

They sang the deeds of heroes.

他们歌颂英雄们的事迹。

singer〔'sɪŋɚ ‖ 'sɪŋə〕

n. 歌唱家，歌手[C]

She is a good singer.

她是一位出色的歌手。

single〔'sɪŋgl̩ ‖ 'sɪŋgl〕

a. ❶单一的，单个的；个别的

❷（用于否定句）连一个也（没有的）

There was not a single person in the house.

屋子里一个人都没有。

❸孤单的；单身的；【植】单瓣的

single parent family

单亲家庭

❹单人用的；【英】单程的

I want a single ticket.

我要一张单程票。

singular〔'sɪŋgjəlɚ ‖ 'sɪŋgjʊlə〕

a. ❶【文】单数的
❷单一的；独个的
❸非凡的，卓越的

sink 〔sɪŋk ‖ sɪŋk〕
［过去式］sank，［过去分词］sunk，sunken
vi. ❶（船等）下沉，沉没；（日，月）落，没
The sun was sinking in the west.
夕阳西下。
❷（面颊等）下陷［（＋in）］
❸（水面）低落，（地面）陷落
His feet sank in the mud.
他的脚陷进烂泥中。
❹（疲倦地）坐下，倒下；（头，肩等）筋疲力尽地垂下［（＋to/into/on）］
She was stunned and sank down on the ground.
她被击昏倒在地上。
vt. ❶使下沉；使陷入；把……插入
The submarine sank two ships.
潜艇击沉了两艘船。
❷使下垂
❸挖掘；刻，雕
The oil workers are sinking a well.
石油工人正在打油井。
❹降低（声音，名誉等）
❺投资于……［（＋in/into）］
He's sunk a large sum of money into buying a new house.
他把一大笔钱投在买一幢新房子上面。

sip 〔sɪp ‖ sɪp〕
［过去式］sipped；［过去分词］sipped
vi. vt 呷，啜
He was sipping brandy.
他在品尝白兰地。
n. 啜饮［U］
He drank coffee in sips.
他细品咖啡。

sir 〔sɝ ‖ sɜː〕
n. ❶先生，阁下；老师；长官
This way, sir.
先生，这边请。
❷（大写）爵士
Sir Walter Scott was a famous British writer.
沃尔特·司各特爵士是英国著名作家。

siren 〔ˈsaɪrən ‖ ˈsaɪərən〕
n. 汽笛；警报器［C］

sister 〔ˈsɪstɚ ‖ ˈsɪstə〕
n.［C］❶姐妹；姐姐，妹妹
She is elder sister of Susan.
她是苏珊的姐姐。
❷（情同姐妹的）挚友；（女性）好友；【喻】姐妹（情同手足的女

子)；女同事
Cathy was like a sister to me.
凯茜待我像亲姐妹一样。
❸女会友；【宗】修女，女教友
a. ❶姐妹关系的
❷如同姐妹的
Ours and theirs are sister schools.
我们学校和他们学校是姐妹学校。

sit 〔sɪt ‖ sɪt〕
[过去式]sat；[过去分词]sat
vi. ❶坐，坐着；就座
Sit down, please.
请坐。
❷(在议会等)占有席位；当委员[(＋on)]
He sits on the committee.
他担任委员会的委员。

site 〔saɪt ‖ saɪt〕
n. 地点，场所，旧址，遗迹[C]
a history site
历史遗迹
a site for a hospital
医院的建筑用地

sitting room 〔ˈsɪtɪŋ rum ‖ ˈsɪtɪŋruːm〕
n. 起居厅(室)；客厅

situation 〔ˌsɪtʃuˈeʃən ‖ ˌsɪtjuˈeɪʃən〕
n. ❶处境，境遇[C]
He is in a difficult situation.
他处境困难。
❷形势；情况；局面[C]
The economic situation is now different.
现在经济形势不同了。
❸地位；(尤指仆役等的)职位，工作[C]
❹(建筑物等的)位置；地点[C]
The house has a beautiful situation on a hill.
房子坐落在小山上，环境优美。
❺(戏剧，小说等的)紧张情节或场面[U]

six 〔sɪks ‖ sɪks〕
a. 六的；六个的
n. ❶六
❷六个，六个人(或物)

sixteen 〔ˌsɪksˈtin ‖ ˌsɪksˈtiːn〕
a. 十六(个，人，岁)的
n. 十六(个，人，岁)[C]

sixteenth 〔ˌsɪksˈtinθ ‖ ˌsɪksˈtiːnθ〕
a. ❶(与 the 连用)第十六的，第十六个的
❷十六分之一的
n. [C]❶(与 the 连用)第十六(个)；月的第十六日
❷十六分之一

sixth 〔sɪksθ ‖ sɪksθ〕
a. ❶(与 the 连用)第六的，第

S

六个的
❷六分之一的
n.［C］❶（与 the 连用）第六（个）；月的第六日
❷六分之一

sixtieth〔ˈsɪkstɪəθ ‖ ˈsɪkstɪɪθ〕
a. ❶第六十的
❷六十分之一的
n. ❶第六十
❷六十分之一

sixty〔ˈsɪkstɪ ‖ ˈsɪkstɪ〕
a. 六十（个，人，岁）的；
n. ❶六十（个，人，岁）［C］
❷六十年代；六十到六十九岁［the P］
in the sixties
六十年代
He is in his sixties.
他六十多岁了。

size〔saɪz ‖ saɪz〕
n. ❶尺寸，大小［C］［U］
What's the size of the park?
这个公园有多大？
❷尺码，号，型［C］
What size shoes do you take?
你穿多大尺码的鞋？

skate〔sket ‖ skeɪt〕
［过去式］skated；［过去分词］skated
vi. ❶滑冰，溜冰
In winter, many people skate on the lake.
冬天时，许多人在湖上溜冰。
❷一带而过，略微触及［（＋over/around/round）］
They prefer to skate around the issue of sex discrimination.
他们不愿多触及性别歧视的问题。

冰鞋 skates

skating〔ˈsketɪŋ ‖ ˈskeɪtɪŋ〕
n. 溜冰，滑冰［U］
She is good at skating.
她擅长溜冰。

skeleton〔ˈskɛlətn̩ ‖ ˈskelɪtn〕
n.［C］❶骨骼；骸骨
❷（房屋等的）骨架；残骸
❸概略，大纲

sketch〔skɛtʃ ‖ sketʃ〕
［过去式］sketched；［过去分词］sketched
n.［C］❶速写，素描
He did a sketch of the ballet dancers.
他为这些芭蕾舞者画了一张素描。

❷略图，草图；粗样；草稿
❸概略，梗概
At the meeting he gave a sketch of recent happenings.
会上他简述了最近发生的事件。
vt. ❶写生；速写；为……绘草图
He sketched the coal miner in a few minutes.
他几分钟就画了一幅那位煤矿工人的素描。
❷草拟；概略地叙述[(＋in/out)]
His rise to power is briefly sketched in the first two chapters.
他得势掌权的经过在头两章里作了简单的描述。
vi. ❶画素描，画速写
He went out sketching on Sunday.
他星期天出去画速写。
❷画草图；打草稿

ski 〔ski ‖ skiː〕
[过去式]skied；[过去分词]skied
n. 滑雪板[C]

vi. 滑雪

skiing 〔ˈskiɪŋ ‖ ˈskiːɪŋ〕
n. [U] ❶滑雪(运动)
Let's go skiing, shall we?
我们去滑雪，好吗？
❷滑雪技术

skilful 〔ˈskɪlfəl ‖ ˈskɪlfəl〕
[比] more skilful；[最] most skilful
a. 有技术的，熟练的
He is skillful at/in teaching.
他教书教得很好。

skill 〔skɪl ‖ ˈskɪl〕
n. ❶(专门)技术；技能，技艺[C]
Reading and writing are different skills.
阅读和写作是不同的技能。
❷熟练[U]

skim 〔skɪm ‖ skɪm〕
[过去式]skimmed；[过去分词]skimmed
vt. ❶撇去……表面的浮物
The cook skimmed the fat from/ off the soup.
厨师把汤上的浮油撇去。
❷使掠过；掠过
Gulls skimmed the water.
海鸥掠过水面。
❸浏览，略读
skim a paper

浏览报纸

skin 〔skɪn ‖ skɪn〕

n. [C][U]❶皮肤，皮

I was caught in a shower of rain and soaked to the skin.

我正赶上一场阵雨，浑身湿透了。

❷(动物的)皮，毛皮；(果实等的)外皮，壳

She peeled off the skin of a banana for the child.

她替孩子剥掉香蕉皮。

skirt 〔skɝt ‖ skɜːt〕

[过去式] skirted；[过去分词] skirted

n. ❶裙子；衬裙[C]

The little girl was dressed in a very short skirt.

小女孩穿了一条很短的裙子。

❷边缘；外围；郊外[P]

Mr. Smith lives on the skirts of the town.

史密斯先生住在城郊。

sky 〔skaɪ ‖ skaɪ〕

n. ❶天，天空；太空[C][U]

There were no clouds in the sky.

天空中万里无云。

❷天气，气候[P]

The radio station forecasts clear skies tomorrow.

无线电台预报明天是晴天。

skyscraper 〔ˈskaɪˌskrepɚ ‖ ˈskaɪskreɪpə〕

n. 摩天大楼，超高层大楼[C]

There are many famous skyscrapers in New York.

在纽约有很多著名的摩天大楼。

slave 〔slev ‖ sleɪv〕

n. [C] ❶奴隶

There were more slaves than citizens in ancient Athens.

在古代的雅典，奴隶比城镇自由民多。

❷奴隶般受控制的人；摆脱不了某种习惯(或影响)的人[(+to/of)]

They are all slaves to fashion.

他们都是拼命赶时髦的人。

slavery 〔ˈslevərɪ ‖ ˈsleɪvərɪ〕

n. ❶奴隶身份；奴役[U]

She was sold into slavery.

她被卖身为奴。

❷奴隶制度

sleep 〔slip ‖ sliːp〕

[过去式] slept；[过去分词] slept

vi. ❶睡，睡觉

He was still sleeping when I went in.

我走进去时他还在睡觉。

❷【婉】长眠，安息
❸静止下来，保持寂静
The whole village was sleeping at night.
夜晚整个村庄一片寂静。
vt. 睡(觉)
I slept a sound sleep.
我睡得很沉。
n. [U]❶睡眠
It seems that you haven't got enough sleep.
看来你睡眠不足。
❷【婉】死亡
He went to his final sleep.
他长眠了。

常用短语

go to sleep 上床睡觉
I went to sleep earlier last night.
我昨晚睡得很早。
sleeping car(火车的)卧铺车厢

sleepy 〔'slipɪ ‖ 'sliːpɪ〕
[比]sleepier;[最]sleepiest
a. ❶想睡的;瞌睡的;困乏的
I felt sleepy.
我瞌睡了。
❷寂静的;不活跃的;呆滞的
a sleepy town
冷清的小镇

sleeve 〔sliv ‖ sliːv〕
n. [C] ❶袖子;袖套
He rolled up his sleeves and got down to work.
他卷起袖子开始工作。
❷【主英】唱片套子
The photograph of the conductor was printed on the record sleeve.
指挥的照片印在唱片套上。

slice 〔slaɪs ‖ slaɪs〕
n. [C] ❶薄片，切片，片[(+of)]
For breakfast, she had only a slice of bread and butter.
她早餐只吃了一片黄油面包。
❷部分，份[(+of)]
Each partner receives his slice of profits.
每一个合伙人得到他的一份利润。

slide 〔slaɪd ‖ slaɪd〕
[过去式]slid;[过去分词]slid
vi. ❶ 滑，滑动
The boys amused themselves by sliding down the banister.
男孩们从楼梯扶手滑下以取乐。
❷滑落;下落
The car slid into the ditch.
汽车滑进了沟里。
❸不知不觉地陷入[(+into)]
He had slid into bad habits.

S

他不知不觉地染上了坏习惯。
vt. ❶使滑动，使滑行
He carefully slid the top off the box.
他小心地将箱盖挪开。
❷悄悄地迅速放入[(＋in/into)]
He slid a pistol into his pocket.
他将一支手枪悄悄地放入口袋。
n. [C] ❶滑，滑行，滑动
The car went into a slide on the iced road.
汽车在结冰的路上打滑了。
❷下落，下降
to stop the slide in living standard
遏止生活水平的下降
❸滑道；滑坡；滑梯
The frozen brook makes a good slide.
冰封的小溪成为滑冰的好地方。
❹雪崩；山崩；土崩
❺幻灯片

slight 〔slaɪt ‖ slaɪt〕
[比]slighter；[最]slightest
a. ❶轻微的；微小的；少量的
She has a slight fever.
她有点儿发烧。
❷极不重要的，不足道的
The boss decided to pass over his slight mistakes.
老板决定原谅他的小错误。
❸细长的；瘦小的
Ann is a slight girl.
安是个瘦弱的女孩。
❹脆弱的；不结实的；不牢靠的

slightly 〔ˈslaɪtlɪ ‖ ˈslaɪtlɪ〕
ad. ❶轻微地；稍微地；微小地
I felt slightly ill.
我觉得有点不适。
❷纤细地；娇弱地；瘦小地
a slightly-built framework
不结实的构架

slim 〔slɪm ‖ slɪm〕
[比]slimmer；[最]slimmest
a. 苗条的；纤细的
Fat girls envy slim girls.
胖女孩儿羡慕苗条的女孩儿。

slip[1] 〔slɪp ‖ slɪp〕
[过去式]slipped；[过去分词]slipped
vi. ❶滑动，滑行
The ship slipped through the water.
船在水面滑行。
❷滑倒，失足
She slipped on the ice.
她在冰上滑倒了。
❸滑落，滑掉；松脱
He woke to find that his quilt

S

had slipped off the bed.
他醒来发现被子从床上滑下来了。
❹溜;悄悄走;(时间)不知不觉地过去
He slipped out of the room.
他悄悄溜出房间。
As the years slipped by, I thought less about her.
随着岁月的流逝,我已把她淡忘了。
vt. ❶使滑动;使滑行
The old lady slipped a hand over the heart.
老太太伸手抚摩胸口。
❷错过;被……忽略;被遗忘
Your telephone number has slipped my mind.
我忘了你的电话号码。
❸摆脱,挣脱
❹匆忙地穿(或脱)[(+on/off)]
He slipped off his clothes and went into the bathroom.
他迅速脱掉衣服,走进浴室。
❺塞入;暗中塞(钱等);把……塞给
He slipped the waiter $1 to get a good table.
为得到好桌位,他悄悄塞给侍者一美元。

n. ❶滑动;滑跤;失足[C]
He took a slip in the bathroom.
他在浴室里滑了一跤。
❷下降
There has been a slip in the quality of your work.
你的工作质量有所下降。

slip²〔slɪp ‖ slɪp〕
n. 片条,板条;纸条[C]
My friend wrote down his address and telephone number on a slip of paper.
我的朋友把他的地址和电话号码写在一张纸条上。

slipper〔ˈslɪpɚ ‖ ˈslɪpə〕
n. (尤指室内穿的)浅口便鞋,拖鞋[P]

slogan〔ˈslogən ‖ ˈsləʊgən〕
n. [C] ❶口号,标语
❷简短醒目的广告语

slope〔slop ‖ sləʊp〕
n. ❶倾斜;坡度[C][U]
The floor of the theater has a slope of four feet from the back seats to the front seats.
这戏院的地板从后排座位到前排座位有四英尺的倾斜。
❷坡;斜面[C]
It is dangerous to climb up a steep slope.
攀登陡坡是危险的。

S

slot machine 〔ˈslɑtməˌʃin ‖ ˈslɒtməˌʃiːn〕
❶自动售货机
❷老虎机
❸公共电话

slow 〔slo ‖ sləʊ〕
［比］slower；［最］slowest；［过去式］slowed；［过去分词］slowed
a. ❶慢的，缓缓的；迟缓的
He's a slow walker.
他走起路来慢吞吞的。
〔**反义**〕fast 快的
❷（表等）慢
My watch is two minutes slow.
我的表慢两分钟。
〔**反义**〕fast 快了的
❸迟钝的；笨的；理解慢的
He is slow in understanding.
他理解慢。
〔**反义**〕quick 敏锐的
ad. ❶慢慢地；迟迟地
Drive slow.
开车要慢行。
❷慢了地
The clock runs slow.
这钟走着走着就慢了。
vt. 使慢，放慢［（＋down/up）］
The car slowed down.
小汽车放慢了速度.
vi. 变慢［（＋down/up）］
The machine slowed down and stopped.
机器转速逐渐减慢，并终于停住了。

slowly 〔ˈslolɪ ‖ ˈsləʊlɪ〕
ad. 缓慢地；悠悠地
Please speak more slowly.
请说慢点。

small 〔smɔl ‖ smɔːl〕
［比］smaller；［最］smallest
a. ❶小的；小型的
My bedroom is smaller than yours.
我的卧室比你的小。
❷少的，少量的；几乎没有的
He has small hope of getting the job.
他获得那份工作的希望渺茫。
❸细小的，瘦小的；幼小的
David is a small man.
戴维长得瘦小。
❹低微的；不重要的
It is just a small problem.
这只是个小问题。
ad. ❶小声地
She spoke as small as possible.
她尽量放低声音说话。
❷小小地，细小地
She writes a bit too small.
她的字写得太小了一点。
❸轻蔑地
They thought small of him at

first.
他们起初都小看他。

smart 〔smɑrt ‖ smɑːt〕
[比]smarter;[最]smartest
a. ❶漂亮的;时髦的;潇洒的
You look smart in the new suit.
你穿这套新衣服很帅气。
❷整齐的,整洁的
The boys in their smart school uniforms marched at the head of the parade.
身着整齐校服的男学生走在游行队伍的前列。
❸伶俐的;机警的;精明的
He is smart and can take care of himself.
他很精明可以照顾他自己。

smell 〔smɛl ‖ smel〕
[过去式]smelled, smelt;[过去分词]smelled, smelt
vt. ❶嗅,闻
Smell the perfume.
闻闻这香水。
❷闻出,嗅到
I bent down to smell the flowers.
我弯下腰闻花香.
❸察觉出
He smelled trouble.
他察觉到会有麻烦。
❹发出……的气味
You both smell brandy.
你俩身上都有股白兰地酒的气味。
vi. ❶嗅,闻[(+at)]
She smelled at the flower.
她闻闻那朵花。
❷有气味;有臭气
This fish smells.
这鱼发臭了。
❸闻起来有某种气味(或迹象)[(+of)]
The meat smells of garlic.
这肉中带有大蒜的味道。
n. ❶气味;香味;臭味[C][U]
The smell of garlic filled the kitchen.
厨房里弥漫着大蒜味道。
❷嗅觉[U]
❸一嗅,一闻
She took a smell at the flower.
她闻了闻那朵花。
❹少许
I need a smell of pepper.
我要一点点胡椒粉。

smile 〔smaɪl ‖ smaɪl〕
[过去式]smiled;[过去分词]smiled
vi. ❶微笑;笑[(+at)][+to-v]
The teacher smiled at my answer.

老师被我的答案逗笑了。
❷(命运,天气等)有利,惠及[(+on/upon)]
You'll get on well as long as the boss smiles on you.
只要老板偏爱你,你会很顺利的。
vt. ❶以微笑表示;以微笑清除
The boss smiled appreciation of my remarks.
老板笑了笑,表示赞赏我的话。
❷露出(笑容)
n. 微笑,笑容[C]
Tom had a big smile on his face when he heard the news.
听到这消息,汤姆满面笑容。

S

smith 〔smɪθ ‖ smɪθ〕
n. 铁匠;锻工[C]

smog 〔smɑg ‖ smɒg〕
n. 烟雾(=smoke and fog)[U]

smoke 〔smok ‖ sməuk〕
[过去式]smoked;[过去分词]smoked
n. ❶烟[U]
She cannot stand the smell of cigarette smoke.
她受不了香烟的气味。
❷一口烟;纸烟;雪茄烟[C]
She offered him a smoke.
她敬了他一支烟。
vi. ❶冒烟,喷烟
A chimney could be seen smoking in the distance.
看得见远处的烟囱在冒烟。
❷冒雾气;冒水汽
❸抽烟;【俚】抽大麻烟
My father has given up smoking.
我父亲已戒烟了。
vt. ❶抽(烟,烟斗)
My grandfather used to smoke a pipe.
我祖父过去抽烟斗。
❷熏制;熏赶;熏染
The boys decided to smoke the snakes out from the hole.
男孩们决定用烟把蛇熏出洞。

smooth 〔smuð ‖ smu:ð〕
[比]smoother;[最]smoothest;[过去式]smoothed;[过去分词]smoothed
a. ❶平滑的,光滑的;平坦的
That road is smooth.
那是一条平坦的路。
❷平静的;平稳的
The sea looks calm and smooth.
海洋看上去风平浪静。
❸(运转)滑顺的;(事情)进行顺利的
Everything is smooth just now.
此时此刻,诸事顺利。

vt. ❶使光滑，使平滑；把……弄平；烫平
She smoothed her dress with an electric iron.
她用电熨斗烫平衣服。
❷轻轻地(或均匀地)涂抹
In winter many people smooth cream over their faces.
冬天，许多人在脸上抹润肤霜。
❸消除(障碍，困难，分歧等)[(+out/over/down/away)]
This kind of beauty cream is said to be able to smooth away wrinkles.
据说这种美容霜能消除皱纹。

smuggle 〔ˈsmʌgḷ ‖ ˈsmʌgl〕
[过去式]smuggled；[过去分词]smuggled
vt. [(+into/out of)]走私；非法私运
He smuggled heroin into the country.
他把海洛因偷运到那个国家。

snack 〔snæk ‖ snæk〕
n. 快餐；小吃，点心[C]
We had a snack there.
我们在那里吃小吃。
snack bar
小吃店

snake 〔snek ‖ sneɪk〕
n. 蛇[C]
The child was frightened by the snake.
这个小孩被蛇吓了一跳。

蛇 snake

sneeze 〔sniz ‖ sniːz〕
[过去式]sneezed；[过去分词]sneezed
vi. 打喷嚏
Cover your mouth when you sneeze.
打喷嚏的时候把嘴巴捂住。

sniff 〔snɪf ‖ snɪf〕
[过去式]sniffed；[过去分词]sniffed
vi. 嗅，闻[(+at)]
The dog sniffed at the stranger.
狗闻了闻那个陌生人。

snow 〔sno ‖ snəʊ〕
[过去式]snowed；[过去分词]snowed
n. ❶雪[U]
A beggar was lying dead in the snow.
一个死了的乞丐躺在雪地里。
❷下雪季节；积雪[P]

S

We often go hunting during the snows.
在下雪季节我们常出去打猎。
vi. ❶下雪
It has snowed for three days.
已经连续下了三天雪了。
❷雪片似地落下；纷至沓来
Presents snowed in on her birthday.
她生日时，礼物雪片似地飞来。

snowball 〔'snoˌbɔl ‖ 'snəubɔːl〕
n. [C] ❶雪球
❷【植】山白刺美洲茶

S

snowman 〔'snoˌmæn ‖ 'snəumæn〕
n. 雪人[C]

snowstorm 〔'snoˌstɔrm ‖ 'snəustɔːm〕
n. 暴风雪[C]

snowy 〔'snoɪ ‖ 'snəuɪ〕
a. 雪的；下雪的；多雪的
It's a snowy day.
下雪了。

so 〔so ‖ səu〕
ad. ❶这么，那么；如此地；【口】多么，非常
I'm so pleased to see you.
看到你我真高兴。
❷就那样，像这样；如此
Hold the fork so.
要这样拿叉子。
❸(so后用倒装结构)也如此，也一样
I was tired, and so were the others.
我累了，其他人也一样。
❹(用于 so… that 结构)如此……以至于
The teacher speaks so clearly that everyone can understand her.
老师讲得那么清楚，每个学生都听懂了。
conj. ❶因此，所以
The manager was ill, so I went in her place.
经理病了，所以我代她去。
❷因而，从而
Mum told him to go to bed early so he could get up early the next morning.
妈妈叫他早点上床睡觉，第二天早上好早点起床。
int. ❶(表示惊讶等)啊，哦
So! You've kept me in the dark

all the time.
哦！原来你一直把我蒙在鼓里。
❷(表示同意等)好，行

常用短语

so as to 以便
or so 大约

soap 〔sop ‖ səʊp〕
n. 肥皂[U]
I bought a piece of soap yesterday.
昨天我买了一块肥皂。

soar 〔sɔr ‖ sɔː〕
[过去式]soared；[过去分词]soared
vi. ❶高飞，翱翔
A plane soared above us.
飞机在我们头上翱翔。
❷猛增；暴涨
Prices have soared.
物价涨了。

sob 〔sɑb ‖ sɒb〕
[过去式]sobbed；[过去分词]sobbed
vi. ❶呜咽；啜泣
She broke down and sobbed aloud.
她禁不住大声哭了起来。
❷(风等)发呜咽声
The wind sobbed in the trees.
风在树林中凄鸣。
n. 呜咽(声)，啜泣(声)[C]
She nodded with a sob.
他啜泣着点了点头。

so-called 〔ˌsoˈkɔld ‖ ˈsəʊˈkɔːld〕
a. 所谓的，号称的(轻蔑，挖苦)
He is the so-called progressive politician.
他就是所谓的进步政治家。

soccer 〔ˈsɑkɚ ‖ ˈsɒkə〕
n. 足球[U]

social 〔ˈsoʃəl ‖ ˈsəʊʃəl〕
a. ❶社会的；社会上的
Opinions on various social questions differ from person to person.
有关各种社会问题的意见因人而异。
❷社交的；交际的；联谊的
George stayed out of the social life of the school.
乔治置身于该校社交生活之外。
❸【动】群居的
Bees and ants are social insects.
蜜蜂和蚂蚁是群居昆虫。

socialism 〔ˈsɒʃəˌlɪzəm ‖ ˈsəʊʃəlɪzəm〕
n. 社会主义[U]

socialist 〔ˈsoʃəlɪst ‖ ˈsəʊʃəlɪst〕
n. 社会主义者[C]

society 〔ˈsəsaɪətɪ ‖ səˈsaɪətɪ〕

S

n. ❶社会[C][U]
It will be a danger to society.
它会对社会构成威胁。
❷社团;协会;公会;俱乐部[C]
She has joined the film society.
她加入了电影协会。
❸社交界;上流社会[U]
❹交际;交往;友谊[U]
Paul spends much time in the society of his friends.
保罗花很多时间与他的朋友交往。

sock 〔sɑk ‖ sɒk〕
n. 短袜[C][P]

sofa 〔'sofə ‖ 'səʊfə〕
n. 沙发,长椅[C]
Please sit on the sofa.
请坐在沙发上。

soft 〔sɔft ‖ sɒft〕
[比]softer;[最]softest
a. ❶柔软的
Silk feels soft and smooth.
丝织品摸起来柔软光滑。
❷(声音)低的;轻柔的
The soft music sounds very pleasing to the ear.
那轻柔的音乐听起来十分悦耳。
❸(光线等)柔和的
❹(天气等)温暖的;和煦的
He is used to the soft climate of the south.
他习惯于南方温暖的气候。
❺温柔的;宽厚的;和蔼的
ad. ❶柔软地;轻柔地
Play softer, please.
请轻点儿弹奏。
❷安静地;轻松地

soften 〔'sɔfən ‖ 'sɒfən〕
[过去式]softened;[过去分词]softened
vt. 使变柔软,缓和
Her words softened my anger.
她的话平息了我的怒气。

soil 〔sɔɪl ‖ sɔɪl〕
n. ❶土,泥土,土壤[C][U]
Some soils are not suitable for farming.
有的土壤不适于耕作。
❷土地,国家,领土[C][U]
He died on British soil.
他死在英国。
❸务农,农业生活[the]
❹温床,滋生地[U]
Parts of this town are soil for crime.
这个城市某几个区是犯罪的温床。

solar 〔'solɚ ‖ 'səʊlə〕
a. 太阳的;日光的;源自太阳的
solar energy
太阳能

solar calendar
阳历

soldier 〔ˈsoldʒɚ ‖ ˈsəʊldʒə〕
n. [C]❶(陆军)兵,士兵
How long has your brother been a soldier?
你兄弟当了多长时间的兵了?
❷(为事业或主义而奋斗的)战士,斗士
Henry is a soldier in the civil rights movement.
亨利是民权运动的斗士。

solid 〔ˈsɑlɪd ‖ ˈsɒlɪd〕
[比]solider;[最]solidest
a. ❶固体的
When water freezes, it becomes solid.
水结冰时变成固体。
❷纯的,纯粹的
This spoon is solid silver.
这把汤匙是纯银的。
❸结实的;坚固的;坚牢的
He is a man of solid build.
他是个体格强健的人。
n. [C]❶固体
Iron and stone are solids.
铁和石头是固体。
❷固体食物,非流质食物[P]
Now he is well enough to take solids.
现在他病好了,可以吃非流质食物了。

solution 〔səˈluʃən ‖ səˈluːʃən〕
n. ❶解答;解决(办法);解释[C][(+to/of/for)]
It may take a long time to find a solution to the problem.
也许要花很长时间才能找到解决这个问题的办法。
❷【数】解法;解式[C]
❸溶解,溶化;溶解状态[U]
Salt can be held in solution in water.
盐能溶于水。
❹溶液,溶剂[C][U]
strong solution
浓溶液

solve 〔sɑlv ‖ sɒlv〕
[过去式]solved;[过去分词]solved
vt. ❶解决;解释;阐明
With the help of his friends, he finally solved the problem.
在朋友们的帮助下,他终于解决了问题。
❷解,解答(数学题)
She tried to solve a crossword puzzle.
她试着解答一道纵横字谜。

some 〔sʌm ‖ sʌm〕
a. ❶(修饰名词的单数形式)某一,某个

S

She is playing chess with some boy.
她正在和一个男孩下棋。
❷(修饰名词的复数形式或不可数名词)某些;若干;一部分的;一些
I have some work to do this evening.
今晚我有些事要做。
❸好些,好几个;不少
He lived in London for some years.
他在伦敦住了好几年。
pron. ❶一些;若干
Some of the students are from the North.
有些学生是北方人。
❷有些人;有些事物
Some smoke and some don't.
有些人吸烟,有些人不吸烟。
ad. ❶【口】稍稍,有几分
His mastery of the language has improved some.
他对该语言的掌握有所提高。
❷【口】很,非常
I felt worried some.
我愁得要命。
❸(与数字连用)约,约莫
Some 20 passengers were killed in the road accident.
这次交通事故中约有 20 名旅客死亡。

somebody [ˈsʌmbədɪ ‖ ˈsʌmbədɪ]
pron. 某人;有人
n. 重要人物,有名气的人[C]
He is somebody in business circles.
他在商界是个有头有脸的人。

somehow [ˈsʌmhaʊ ‖ ˈsʌmhaʊ]
ad. ❶由于某种未知的原因;不知怎么的
Somehow I don't like the singer on TV.
不知怎么地我就是不喜欢电视里那个歌星。
❷以某种方式;用某种方法;设法
We must finish the task somehow.
我们一定设法完成这项工作。

someone [ˈsʌmˌwʌn ‖ ˈsʌmwʌn]
pron. 某人;有人
Someone wants to see you.
有人要见你。

something [ˈsʌmθɪŋ ‖ ˈsʌmθɪŋ]
pron. 某人;某事;若干;什么
He knows something about it.
对于那件事,他知道一些。

常用短语

something like 有点像

An airship is shaped something like a cigar.
飞船的形状有点像雪茄。
something of a 多少有点儿
He is something of a carpenter.
他略懂木工。
or something 诸如此类的什么
She is a teacher or something.
她是个老师什么的。
sometime 〔ˈsʌmˌtaɪm ‖ ˈsʌmtaɪm〕
ad. ❶在(将来或过去)的某一时候
I'll finish it sometime.
我随时会把它完成。
❷日后,改天
I'll come to see you sometime.
我改天来看你。
sometimes 〔ˈsʌmˌtaɪmz ‖ ˈsʌmtaɪmz〕
ad. 有时;间或
I sometimes go to work on foot.
我有时步行去上班。
somewhat 〔ˈsʌmˌhwɑt ‖ ˈsʌm*h*wɒt〕
ad. 有点,稍微
My jacket is somewhat like yours.
我的夹克与你的那件有点像。
somewhere 〔ˈsʌmˌhwer ‖ ˈsʌm*h*weə〕
ad. 在某处;到某处
I must have left my wallet somewhere.
我一定把钱包落在什么地方了。
son 〔sʌn ‖ sʌn〕
n. [C] ❶儿子;养子;继子
Mike was the third of five sons.
在五个儿子中迈克排行第三。
❷女婿
❸男性后裔;子孙[P]
The sons of Confucius are scattered in many parts of China.
孔子的后裔散居在中国的许多地方。
song 〔sɔŋ ‖ sɒŋ〕
n. ❶歌,歌曲[C]
❷诗歌;歌谣[C]
❸唱;歌唱[U]
We raised our voices in song.
我们放声歌唱。
❹(鸟,虫等的)鸣声[C][U]
He was waked by the song of birds in the trees.
他被林中的鸟鸣声闹醒。
son-in-law 〔ˈsʌnɪnˌlɔ ‖ ˈsʌnɪnˌlɔː〕
n. 女婿[C]
soon 〔sun ‖ suːn〕

［比］sooner；［最］soonest

ad. ❶不久，很快地

It will soon be Christmas.

圣诞节很快就要到了。

❷快；早

She didn't finish her homework as soon as she had expected.

她的作业没有她预料的那样快完成。

❸宁可，宁愿，宁肯

I would as soon you didn't tell me about that.

我宁可你不告诉我那件事。

S

常用短语

as soon as … 一……就……

no sooner…than 刚……就……

He had no sooner left home than it began to rain.

他刚离开家就下雨了。

sore 〔sor ‖ sɔː〕

［比］sorer；［最］sorest

a. ❶痛的；疼痛发炎的；一碰就痛的［(＋from)］

I have a sore throat.

我喉咙痛。

❷惹人生气的；使人难过或痛苦的

His origins were a sore point with him.

他的出身是个使他难堪的话题。

sorrow 〔ˈsɑro ‖ ˈsɒrəʊ〕

n. ❶悲痛，悲哀，悲伤，忧伤［U］［(＋at/for/over)］

She felt sorrow at the death of her aunt.

她对姑母的去世感到悲痛。

❷伤心事，不幸的事；悲伤的原因［C］［P］［(＋to)］

Many sorrows turned her hair white.

这许许多多不幸的事使她的头发变白了。

sorry 〔ˈsɔrɪ ‖ ˈsɒrɪ〕

a. ❶感到难过的；感到可怜的［(＋about/for)］［＋(that)］［＋to-v］

I am sorry to hear that your younger brother passed away.

听到你弟弟去世的消息，我很难过。

❷感到抱歉的；感到遗憾的［(＋about/for)］［＋(that)］［＋to-v］

I'm sorry that I can't join you in the discussion.

很遗憾，我不能参加你们的讨论了。

❸可悲的；可怜的；寒酸的

He was in a sorry plight that he became ill and had no money.

他贫病交加，处境困窘。

int. ❶抱歉，对不起
Sorry, I kept you waiting.
对不起，让你久等了。
❷【主英】(未听清对方的话)请再说一下

sort 〔sɔrt ‖ sɔːt〕
n. [C] ❶种类，品种，类型
All sorts of lamps are available in that shop.
在那家商店可买到各式各样的灯具。
❷(常与定语连用)某种人，某类人
She's a happy-go-lucky sort.
她是个乐天派。

soul 〔sol ‖ səul〕
n. ❶灵魂，心灵[C]
Christians believe that the soul is not mortal.
基督徒相信灵魂永生。
❷精神；精力[U]
She puts her whole soul into work.
她把全部精力投入工作。
❸气魄；热情[U]
It's quite an attractive building, but somehow it hasn't got much soul.
那是一幢相当漂亮的建筑，但不知怎么地它没有多少生气。
❹鬼魂[C]
❺人[C]
Not a soul was to be seen.
一个人都看不到。

sound¹ 〔saʊnd ‖ saʊnd〕
[过去式]sounded；[过去分词]sounded
n. 声音，响声；【物】声[C][U]
We heard sounds of laughter from the next room.
我们听到隔壁房间传来的阵阵笑声。
vi. ❶发声；响起；发音
At this moment his footsteps sounded on the stairs.
这时候传来了他走在楼梯上的脚步声。
❷听起来；听上去
The music sounds very pleasing to the ear.
这音乐听起来十分悦耳。

sound² 〔saʊnd ‖ saʊnd〕
a. ❶健康的；健全的
She is sound in body and mind.
她身心健康。
❷完好的；坚固的
I bought this sound house for a song.
我以低价买了这所完好无损的房子。
❸合理的，明智的
I acted on her sound advice.

S

我按她的忠告去做了。
ad. 充分地；酣畅地
He was still sound asleep when I went in.
我走进去时他还在酣睡。

soup 〔sup ‖ suːp〕
n. 汤[C][U]
A bowl of hot chicken soup is good for you.
喝一碗热鸡汤对你有好处。

sour 〔saʊr ‖ ˈsaʊə〕
a. ❶酸的，酸味的
These oranges taste sour.
这些橘子吃起来很酸。
❷酸腐的，酸臭的
The soup has gone sour.
这汤发酸了。
❸发酵的
❹脾气坏的；乖戾的；刻薄的
It is said that the boss is sour toward his employees.
据说这个老板对他的雇员很刻薄。

source 〔sors ‖ sɔːs〕
n. [C] ❶(河的)源头；水源
Do you know the source of Amazon River?
你知道亚马逊河的源头吗？
❷根源；来源[(+of)]
They are required to publish the sources of their campaign funds.
他们必须公布自己竞选经费的来源。
❸提供消息(或证据)者；消息(或证据)来源[P]
The news comes from a reliable source.
这消息来自一位可靠人士。
❹出处；原始资料[P]

south 〔saʊθ ‖ saʊθ〕
n. 南；南方[the]
The house faces to the south.
这房子朝南。
a. 南的；南方的；向南的；(风)来自南方的
A south wind is blowing.
在刮南风。
ad. 在南方；向南方；来自南方
My room faces south.
我的房间向南。

southeast 〔ˌsaʊθˈist ‖ ˌsaʊθˈiːst〕
n. 东南；东南方[the]
a. (在)东南的；向东南的；东南部的
ad. 在东南；向东南；来自东南

southern 〔ˈsʌðɚn ‖ ˈsʌðən〕
a. (在)南方的；向南方的
southern countries
南方诸国

southwest 〔ˌsaʊθˈwest ‖ ˌsaʊθˈwest〕

n. 西南;西南方[the]
a. (在)西南的;向西南的;西南部的
ad. 在西南;向西南;来自西南

souvenir 〔ˌsuvəˈnɪr ‖ ˌsuːvəˈnɪə〕
n. 纪念品,纪念物[C]
He brought some souvenirs from his trip.
他旅行回来带了一些纪念品。

space 〔spes ‖ speɪs〕
n. ❶空间[U]
The table takes up a lot of space.
这张桌子占去很多地方。
❷宇宙,太空,外层空间[U]
We witnessed a missile being launched into outer space.
我们目睹一枚飞弹向外太空发射。
❸场所,空地;【建】生活空间;房间[C][U]
a parking space
停车的空地
❹空白,余地;篇幅[C][U]

spade[1] 〔sped ‖ speɪd〕
n. 铲;锹[C]
He was digging potatoes with a spade.
他正在用铁锹挖马铃薯。

spade[2] 〔sped ‖ speɪd〕
n. (扑克牌中的)黑桃[C]

Spain 〔spen ‖ speɪn〕
n. 西班牙(国名)

Spanish 〔ˈspænɪʃ ‖ ˈspænɪʃ〕
n. 西班牙语;西班牙人
a. 西班牙的;西班牙人的;西班牙语的
He is Spanish.
他是西班牙人。

spare 〔spɛr ‖ speə〕
[过去式]spared;[过去分词]spared
vt. 分出;腾出(时间,人手);分让(多余的东西)[(+for)]
Can you spare me a few minutes?
你能为我抽出几分钟时间吗?
a. ❶多余的,剩下的;空闲的
He has nothing to do in his spare time.
他在闲暇的时候无事可做。
❷备用的
Every car should carry a spare tire.
每辆车子应带一个备用轮胎。
❸节约的;少量的;贫乏的[(+of)]
He is spare of speech.
他很少说话。

spark 〔spɑrk ‖ spɑːk〕
[过去式]sparked;[过去分词]sparked

S

n. [C] ❶火花，火星
A cigarette spark started the fire.
香烟的火星引起了这场火灾。
❷(宝石等的)闪耀
❸【电】火花；火星
Close the circuit and you'll see a blue spark.
接通电路你就会看到蓝色的电火花。
vi. ❶发出火花；飞出火星
The wood burns steadily with no sparking.
这木柴燃烧正常，不爆火花。
❷闪耀；闪光
Her eyes sparked.
她双眼闪闪发光。

S

sparkle [ˈspɑrkl̩ ‖ ˈspɑːkl]
[过去式]sparkled；[过去分词] sparkled
vi. ❶发火花；闪耀
Her eyes sparkled with happiness.
她的双眼闪耀着幸福的光芒。
❷(才智等)焕发；活跃
His wit sparkles.
他才气横溢。
❸(香槟酒等)发泡
n. 火花；闪耀；闪光[C][U]
People always mention the sparkle of her eyes.
人们总是说她的眼睛炯炯有神。

speak [spik ‖ spiːk]
[过去式]spoke；[过去分词] spoken
vi. ❶说话，讲话
He wanted to speak to me.
他想和我说话。
❷谈话，谈论
I have not spoken to him on this subject yet.
我还没有和他谈这件事。
❸发表演说；陈述意见
It was the first time that I spoke in public.
这是我第一次在公共场合发言。
vt. ❶说(某种语言)
Miss Li speaks good English.
李小姐英语说得很好。
❷陈述；表达

speaker [ˈspikɚ ‖ ˈspiːkə]
n. [C] ❶说话者；演讲者；演说家
The chairman introduced the speaker to the audience.
主席将演讲人介绍给听众。
❷讲(某种)语言的人
He is a speaker of French.
他说法文。
❸扬声器，扩音机

spear 〔spɪr ‖ spɪə〕
n. 矛;鱼叉[C]
Spears are their tools for hunting.
矛是他们狩猎的工具。

special 〔ˈspɛʃəl ‖ ˈspeʃəl〕
a. ❶特别的,特殊的
He never drinks except on special occasions.
只有在特别场合,他才喝酒。
❷专门的,专用的
She works as a nurse in a special hospital.
她在一家专门医院做护士。

specialist 〔ˈspɛʃəlɪst ‖ ˈspeʃəlɪst〕
n. [C]❶专家[(+in)]
❷专科医生[(+in)]

specialize 〔ˈspɛʃəˌlaɪz ‖ ˈspeʃəlaɪz〕
[过去式]specialized;[过去分词]specialized
vi. 专攻;专门从事[(+in)]
He specializes in physics.
他专攻物理。

species 〔ˈspiʃiz ‖ ˈspiːʃiːz〕
n. 种类,物种[(+of)]
There are several species of tiger.
老虎有好几种。

specific 〔spɪˈsɪfɪk ‖ spɪˈsɪfɪk〕
a. ❶特殊的,特定的
I bought it for a specific purpose.
我为了特殊的目的买下它。
❷明确的;具体的
I had no specific reason to do it.
我做这件事没有明确的理由。

speech 〔spitʃ ‖ spiːtʃ〕
n. ❶说话能力[U]
Animals lack the faculty of speech.
动物不会说话。
❷说话;言词;言论[U]
We express our thoughts by speech.
我们用言语表达思想。
❸演说,演讲;致词[C]
The chairman made an opening speech.
主席致开幕词。

speed 〔spid ‖ spiːd〕
n. ❶速率,速度[C][U]
The train is traveling at a speed of 60 miles per hour.
火车正以每小时 60 英里的速度行驶。
❷快速,迅速[U]
More haste, less speed.
欲速则不达。

spell 〔spɛl ‖ spel〕

S

[过去式]spelled, spelt;[过去分词]spelled, spelt
vt. 用字母拼;拼写
I don't know how to spell your name.
我不会拼写你的名字。
vi. 拼字
The child cannot spell well.
这孩子不太会拼字。

spend 〔spɛnd ‖ spend〕
[过去式]spent;[过去分词]spent
vt. ❶花(钱),花费[(+on/for)]
I spent $100 on the bike.
我花了100美元买下那辆自行车。
❷花(时间,精力)[(+on)]
They spent three months (in) traveling Europe.
他们花了三个月时间周游欧洲。

spirit 〔ˈspɪrɪt ‖ ˈspɪrɪt〕
n. ❶精神,心灵[C][U]
Nothing could dampen his spirits.
什么事情都不能使他意志消沉。
❷灵魂,精灵;幽灵;妖精[C]
They believe that his spirit still lives after his death.
他们相信他死后灵魂还活着。
❸(时代等的)潮流;精神;风气[U]
He embodied the American spirit of optimistic materialism.
他体现了美国人乐观的实利主义精神。
❹情绪,心情;兴致[P]
He is in good spirits.
他很愉快。

spiritual 〔ˈspɪrɪtʃuəl ‖ ˈspɪrɪtʃuəl〕
a. 精神(上)的,心灵的
She was my adviser in spiritual matters.
她是我在心理问题上的顾问。

spit 〔spɪt ‖ spɪt〕
[过去式]spit, spat;[过去分词]spit, spat
vt. ❶吐(唾液等)[(+out)]
Spit your gum out before you come into the classroom.
进教室之前把口香糖吐掉。
❷口出(恶言,粗话等)[(+out)]
He spat curses at me.
他厉声咒骂我。
vi. ❶吐口水;吐痰
You'll be fined if you spit on the street.
你如果在街上吐痰,是要遭罚

款的。

❷(为表示轻蔑等)吐口水；表示唾弃；表示轻蔑[(+at/on)]

He spat on my suggestion.

他对我的建议表示轻蔑。

spite 〔spaɪt ‖ spaɪt〕

n. 恶意；心术不良；怨恨[(+against/out of/from)] [U]

She broke the vase out of spite.

她故意将花瓶打碎。

常用短语

in spite of 不管

〔同义〕despite 不管

He went fishing in spite of rain.

尽管下雨，他还是出去钓鱼了。

splendid 〔'splɛndɪd ‖ 'splendɪd〕

a. ❶有光彩的；灿烂的

The King was wearing a splendid golden crown.

国王戴着光彩夺目的金王冠。

❷壮丽的；辉煌的

They won another splendid victory.

他们又赢得了辉煌的胜利。

❸显著的；杰出的

❹【口】极好的；令人极其满意的

My kid sister has a splendid memory.

我小妹记忆力极好。

spoil 〔spɔɪl ‖ spɔɪl〕

[过去式]spoiled, spoilt；[过去分词]spoiled, spoilt

vt. ❶损坏；糟蹋；搞糟

The rain spoiled our picnic.

这场雨弄得我们的野餐一团糟。

❷宠坏；溺爱

They spoiled their child.

他们宠坏了孩子。

vi. (食物等)变坏，腐败

The apples spoiled.

苹果烂了。

spoken 〔'spokən ‖ 'spəukən〕

a. 口头讲的，口头的；口语的

spoken English

口头英语

sponge 〔spʌndʒ ‖ spʌndʒ〕

n. 海绵[C]

Sponge absorbs water.

海绵吸水。

sponsor 〔'spɑnsɚ ‖ 'spɒnsə〕

n. [C] ❶发起者；主办者；倡议者

❷(广播、电视节目的)赞助者；资助者

spoon 〔spun ‖ spu:n〕

n. 匙，汤匙[C]

She ate soup with a silver spoon.

她用银匙喝汤。

spoonful 〔'spunˌful ‖ 'spuːnful〕

n. 满满一匙；一匙的量[C]

two spoonfuls of sugar

两匙糖

sport 〔'sport ‖ spɔːt〕

n. ❶游戏，娱乐，消遣[C][U]

He spends all his time in sport and play.

他把全部时间花在消遣和游玩上。

❷运动，体育竞技活动[C][U]

I think football is an exciting sport.

我认为足球是一种刺激的运动。

❸【英】运动会[P]

The school sports will be held next month.

校运会将于下月举行。

sportsman 〔'sportsmən ‖ 'spɔːtsmən〕

n. 喜好运动的人；喜好打猎等户外运动的人；运动员，运动家[C]

He is a keen sportsman.

他是个热衷于户外运动的人。

sportsmanship 〔'sportsmənˌʃɪp ‖ 'spɔːtsmənʃɪp〕

n. 运动员风格，运动道德；体育精神[U]

To show good sportsmanship is very important.

表现良好的体育道德是很重要的。

spot 〔spɑt ‖ spɒt〕

[过去式]spotted；[过去分词]spotted

n. [C] ❶污点；污渍

The boy's white shirt was marked with spots of ink.

那男孩的白衬衫上有墨水渍。

❷疤；痣；丘疹；疮

❸场所，地点

This is the spot where the two trucks collided.

这儿就是两辆卡车相撞的地点。

〔同义〕place 地点，场所

❹职位，职务

She found a spot as a secretary.

她找到一个秘书的职位。

vt. ❶使沾上污点；弄脏[(+with)]

His boots were spotted with mud.

他的靴子上沾有泥渍。

❷玷污；侮辱

The scandal spotted his character.

那件丑闻玷污了他的人格。

❸【口】认出；发现

My father spotted several spell-

ing mistakes in my composition.
我父亲在我作文里发现了好几个拼写错误。

spray 〔spre ‖ spreɪ〕
［过去式］sprayed；［过去分词］sprayed
n. ❶浪花；水花；飞沫［U］
We were wet with the spray.
我们被浪花溅湿。
❷喷雾；喷雾状物［C］
The beer came out of the bottle in a spray.
啤酒从瓶中喷出。
❸喷洒液，喷液［C］［U］
Did you bring along some insect spray?
你有没有带些杀虫喷液来？
vt. 喷洒，喷涂［（＋on/over/with）］
He sprayed water on the flowers in the morning.
他早晨给花浇水。
vi. 喷；（如浪花般）溅散
There was a hole in the hose, and water sprayed out all over me.
软管上有一个洞，水喷出来溅了我一身。

spread 〔sprɛd ‖ spred〕
［过去式］spread；［过去分词］spread
vt. ❶使伸展；使延伸
I spread my arms as far as I could.
我尽可能地将双臂伸展开。
❷张开；展开；摊开
Mom spread a new table-cloth on the table.
妈妈在桌上铺了一块新桌布。
❸涂；敷
❹撒；散布，传播；普及
She was told not to spread this secret around.
她被告知不要把这个秘密传出去。
vi. ❶伸展，延伸；延长［（＋out）］
A wide stretch of land spreads in front of us.
我们面前是一片广阔的土地。
❷传开；蔓延
The fire spread from the factory to the warehouse nearby.
火从工厂蔓延到了附近的仓库。

spring 〔sprɪŋ ‖ sprɪŋ〕
［过去式］sprang，sprung；［过去分词］sprung
n. ❶春季；春天［C］［U］
❷旺盛时期；青春年少时期［U］
❸跳跃［C］

S

He rose with a spring and dashed out the door.
他一跃而起，奔出门去。
❹弹簧；发条[C]
❺弹力；活力[U]
There's little spring in this sofa.
这张沙发几乎没什么弹性。
❻泉[C]

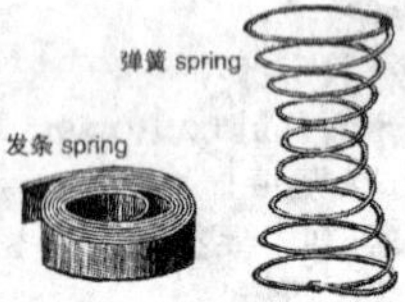

spy 〔spaɪ ‖ spaɪ〕
n. 间谍；密探[C]
She liked the adventures of a spy.
她喜欢间谍的冒险。

square 〔skwɛr ‖ skweə〕
n. [C] ❶正方形；方形物；方块
❷(方形)广场
There is a fair in the town square.
市中心广场有个商品交易会。
❸【数】平方，二次幂[(+of)]
64 is the square of 8.
64是8的平方。
a. ❶正方形的
a square table 方桌
❷成直角的
square angles 直角
❸结实的，魁梧的
The mayor is a man of square frame.
市长是个体格魁梧的人。
❹正直的；公正的
The market calls for a square deal.
市场需要公平交易。
❺直截了当的，断然的
They offered to buy his farm but met a square refusal.
他们出价要买他的农场，却遭到断然拒绝。

squirrel 〔ˈskwɝəl ‖ ˈskwɪrəl〕
n. ❶松鼠[C]
Squirrels feed on nuts.
松鼠以坚果为食。
❷松鼠毛皮[U]

stability 〔stəˈbɪlətɪ ‖ stəˈbɪlɪtɪ〕
n. 稳定，稳定性；安定[U]
She lacks emotional stability.
她情绪不稳定。

stable 〔'stebl̩ ‖ 'steɪbl〕

a. ❶稳定的,牢固的;平稳的

A stable government is essential to economic growth.

稳定的政府对于经济增长是重要的。

❷可靠的,可信赖的,稳重的;坚定的

He is a man of stable character.

他是一个稳重可靠的人。

stadium 〔'stedɪəm ‖ 'steɪdɪəm〕

n. 体育场,运动场;球场;竞技场[C]

staff 〔stæf ‖ stɑːf〕

n. [C]❶(全体)职员;(全体)工作人员

My elder brother is on the editorial staff.

我哥哥是编辑部的职员。

❷幕僚;参谋人员;参谋机构

I have a staff of 15.

我有 15 名幕僚。

❸拐杖;棍;棒

The old man walked with a wooden staff.

那位老汉拄着木拐杖走路。

❹旗杆;标杆;标尺

stage 〔stedʒ ‖ steɪdʒ〕

n. [C] ❶舞台

Some girls are dancing on the stage.

一些女孩儿在舞台上跳舞。

❷戏剧;戏剧艺术;演戏;戏剧界[the]

Novels are often adapted for the stage.

小说常常改编为戏剧。

❸(进展的)阶段;时期

A caterpillar must pass through the cocoon stage to become a butterfly.

毛毛虫必须经过茧的阶段才能变成蝴蝶。

stain 〔sten ‖ steɪn〕

[过去式]stained;[过去分词]stained

vt. 染污;玷污[(+with)]

Blood stained the blanket.

血玷污了毯子。

His crimes stained the family honor.

他的罪行玷污了家庭的名誉。

n. [C]❶污点;污迹;瑕疵

He's got an ink stain on his shirt.

他衬衫上有块墨渍。

〔同义〕spot 污点

❷色斑

stair 〔stɛr ‖ steə〕

n. ❶梯级[C]

the top stair

楼梯最高的一级
❷楼梯[P]
We hurried down the stairs.
我们匆匆下了楼。

stamp 〔stæmp ‖ stæmp〕
[过去式]stamped;[过去分词] stamped
n. [C]❶邮票

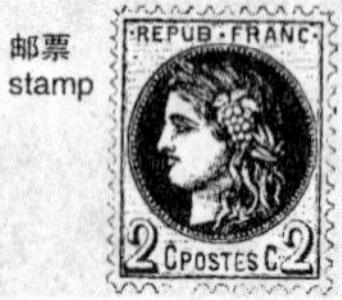

My son is a stamp collector.
我儿子是集邮爱好者。
❷图章;印章;戳子;(印下的)戳记,标记
He is looking for his rubber stamp.
他正在找他的橡皮印章。
vt. ❶贴邮票于;贴印花于
I forgot to stamp the letter.
这封信我忘了贴邮票。
❷盖章于;压印于;打上(标记等)[(+on/with)]
He stamped his name on all his books.
他在他所有的书上都用章盖上自己的名字。
vi. 跺脚;踩[(+on)]
The horse stamped on a cockroach.
这匹马踩死了一只蟑螂。

stand 〔stænd ‖ stænd〕
[过去式]stood;[过去分词] stood
vi. ❶站立,站着
Her legs were so weak that she could hardly stand.
她的腿软得几乎站不住了。
❷站起[(+up)]
Stand up! 起立!
❸(身高、温度、得分等)是……[(+at)]
The thermometer stood at 70 Fahrenheit.
温度计的读数是华氏 70 度。
❹处于某种状态
Mr. Black stands high in the public estimation.
布莱克先生在公众中声望很高。
vt. ❶使站立;使站起
He stood the ladder against the wall.
他把梯子靠墙放着。
❷(常用于否定句或疑问句)忍受,容忍[+v-ing][+to-v]
I can't just stand the cold.
我受不了这么冷。
n. [C] ❶架子,座;讲台

a music stand
乐谱架
an umbrella stand
伞架
❷看台;看台观众[P]
The ball went into the stands.
球飞进了看台。
❸摊子,小贩卖部
a newspaper stand
报摊

standard [ˈstændəd‖ˈstændəd]
n. ❶标准;水平;规格;规范[C][U]
Your recent work has been below standard.
你最近的工作一直达不到标准。
❷度量衡标准;(货币)本位[C]
The kilogram is the international standard of weight.
千克是国际通用的重量标准。
a. ❶标准的
He wrote in standard English.
他用标准英文写作。
❷公认为优秀的;权威的;一流的
This is a standard atlas.
这是一本权威的地图册。
❸合规格的;一般性的

star [stɑr‖stɑː]
n. ❶星,恒星;(日,月等)天体[C]
We can see the stars at night.
在晚上我们可以看到星星。
❷(电影,体育等的)明星;杰出人物
His wish to become a football star has come true.
他想当足球明星的愿望实现了。

stare [stɛr‖steə]
[过去式]stared;[过去分词]stared
vi. 盯;凝视[(+at/into)]
Don't stare at me like that.
别那样盯着我。
vt. 盯;凝视;注视
The old man stared the uninvited guest up and down.
老人把不速之客上下打量了一番。
n. 凝视;注视;瞪眼[C]
He gave her a rude stare.
他粗鲁地瞪了她一眼。

start [stɑrt‖stɑːt]
[过去式]started;[过去分词]started
vi. ❶出发,起程
We'll start at 6：00 on Friday morning.
我们将于星期五早上6点出发。
❷开始,着手

Summer vacation normally starts in early July.
暑假一般在7月初开始。
❸突然跳起;吃惊
She started at the sound of a gun.
她听到枪声,吓了一跳。
vt. ❶使开始;开始[+to-v][+v-ing]
When did you start to learn English?
你何时开始学英语的?
❷引起;发起;创办
He is thinking of starting a newspaper.
他打算创办一份报纸。
❸使开始运转,启动
Do you know how to start the motor?
你会启动马达吗?
n. [C] ❶出发;出发点;起跑点;出发时间
We'll make an early start for the beach.
我们一早出发去海滩。
❷起始;最初;开端
He opposed the scheme from the start.
他一开始就反对这个计划。
❸开动,启动
❹惊跳,惊吓
She woke up with a start.
她惊醒过来。

starvation 〔starˈveʃən ‖ stɑːˈveɪʃən〕
n. 饥饿;挨饿;饿死[U]

starve 〔starv ‖ stɑːv〕
[过去式]starved;[过去分词]starved
vi. ❶饿死
The explorers starved to death in the desert.
探险者们在沙漠中饿死了。
❷挨饿;【口】饿得慌
Let's get something to eat; I'm starving.
我们吃点东西吧,我饿坏了。
❸渴望;极需要[+for][+of]
The plants are starving for water.
这些植物极需要水。
vt. ❶使饿死;使挨饿
He was starved to death.
他被饿死了。
❷以饥饿迫使[(+into)]
They starved the enemy into submission.
他们切断敌军粮援以迫其投降。

state 〔stet ‖ steɪt〕
[过去式]stated;[过去分词]stated

n. ❶状况，状态[C]
The vice president is in a state of poor health.
副总统健康状况不佳。
❷情况；形势[C]
❸形态；心态；兴奋状态[C]
Ice is water in a solid state.
冰是水的固体状态。
❹国家，政府，国土[C][U]
All the land belongs to the state in this country.
在这个国家土地全属国有。
vt. 陈述；声明；说明
The witness stated that she had never seen Mr. Smith.
证人宣称她以前从未见过史密斯先生。

statesman 〔ˈstetsmən ‖ ˈsteɪtsmən〕
n. 政治家[C]
Abraham Lincoln was a great statesman.
亚伯拉罕·林肯是一位非常伟大的政治家。

station 〔ˈsteʃən ‖ ˈsteɪʃən〕
n. [C]❶车站
She got off at Victoria Station.
她在维多利亚车站下了车。
❷(各种机构的)站；所；局；署
The pickpocket was brought to the nearby police station.
小偷被带到附近的警察所。
❸广播电台，电视台；电视频道
I don't like the program. Would you please turn the radio to a music station?
我不喜欢这个节目。您能把收音机调到音乐台吗？

stationery 〔ˈsteʃənˌɛrɪ ‖ ˈsteɪʃənərɪ〕
n. 文具；信纸[U]
Pens, pencils, ink and so on are stationery.
钢笔、铅笔、墨水等都是文具。

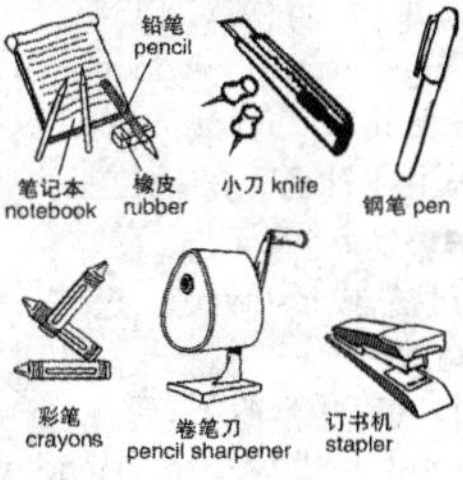

文具 stationery

statistics 〔stəˈtɪstɪks ‖ stəˈtɪstɪks〕
n. 统计，统计学
Statistics show that the population of China is increasing.
统计资料显示中国的人口正日益增长。

statue 〔ˈstætʃʊ ‖ ˈstætʃuː〕

n. 雕像，塑像［C］
The Statue of Liberty stands in New York Bay.
自由女神像耸立在纽约港。

status 〔ˈstetəs ‖ ˈsteɪtəs〕
n. 地位，身份［C］［U］
The status of a doctor is very high in the community.
医生在社会上的地位很高。

stay 〔ste ‖ steɪ〕
［过去式］stayed；［过去分词］stayed
vi. ❶停留；留下；暂住
He stayed with a friend while he was in Paris.
他在巴黎时住在一位朋友家里。
❷继续，保持
I hope the weather will stay fine.
我希望天气能持续放晴。
❸站住；停下；止住
Stay right here.
就在这里停下。

常用短语

stay up 不去睡觉；熬夜
stay with 同……住在一起

n. 停留，逗留
He made few friends during his stay in the village.
他在这个村子逗留期间，没有交上几个朋友。

steady 〔ˈstɛdɪ ‖ ˈstedɪ〕
［比］steadier；［最］steadiest
a. ❶稳固的，平稳的
Is the table steady?
桌子平稳吗？
❷稳定的，不变的
The price of fruits remains steady.
水果的价格保持稳定。
❸坚定的；扎实的，可靠的
We appreciate steady workers.
我们赞赏踏实的工人。

steak 〔stek ‖ steɪk〕
n. 牛排；肉排；鱼排［C］［U］
We had beef steak for dinner.
我们晚餐吃牛排。

steal 〔stil ‖ stiːl〕
［过去式］stole；［过去分词］stolen
vt. 偷，窃取
I think someone has stolen my jacket.

我认为有人偷了我的夹克。

vi. ❶偷东西；行窃

It is wrong to steal.

偷东西是不对的。

❷偷偷地行动；溜

He stole into the house.

他偷偷溜进屋内。

steam 〔stim ‖ stiːm〕

［过去式］steamed；［过去分词］steamed

n.［U］❶蒸汽，水蒸气；水汽；蒸汽压力

Who invented the steam engine?

谁发明了蒸汽机？

❷轮船；乘船旅行

He used to travel by steam.

他过去常乘轮船旅行。

vi. 蒸发；冒热气

The pot was steaming.

这锅正冒着热气。

vt. 蒸；煮

My mother is steaming fish.

我妈妈正在蒸鱼。

steel 〔stil ‖ stiːl〕

n. ［U］❶钢，钢铁

Tools of this kind are made from steel.

这类工具是钢制的。

❷（钢铁般的）坚强；坚固；冷酷

He has a heart of steel.

他是个铁石心肠的人。

step 〔stɛp ‖ step〕

［过去式］stepped；［过去分词］stepped

n. ❶ 脚步［C］

She took a few steps towards the window.

她向窗口走了几步。

❷脚步声［C］

I heard his steps approaching.

我听到他的脚步声临近了。

❸一步的距离；短距离［C］

The museum is only a short step away from our school.

博物馆离我们学校不远。

❹步伐，步调［C］［U］

He went home with heavy steps.

他拖着沉重的脚步回到家。

❺足迹［C］

I found several steps on the mud.

我发现泥里有几个脚印。

❻台阶［C］

He went up the door steps.

他上了台阶。

❼步骤；手段；措施［C］

Steps have been taken to ensure safety.

已采取了安全措施。

❽踏板；梯级；（接近目标的）一

S

步;一阶段[C]
the top step of a ladder
梯子的最上一级
vi. ❶跨步;走;步行
Please step this way.
请这边走。
❷踏(进);跨(入)
She stepped into the room and sat down in a sofa.
她走进屋子在沙发上坐下。
❸踩,踩住[(+on)]
Sorry! Did I step on your toes?
对不起! 我是不是踩到你的脚了?

S

stepfather 〔ˈstɛpˌfɑðɚ ‖ ˈstepfɑːðə〕
n. 继父,后父[C]

stick 〔stɪk ‖ stɪk〕
[过去式]stuck;[过去分词]stuck
n. ❶枝条;柴枝[C]
❷棍,棒,杖;手杖[C]
Grandpa still walks without a stick.
爷爷走路仍不拄拐杖。
❸棒状物[C][(+of)]
I bought the child some sticks of candy.
我给孩子买了几根棒棒糖。
vt. ❶刺;戳;刺死
She stuck her finger with a needle.
她用针刺了手指。
❷粘贴;张贴
They stuck the notice on the wall.
他们把通知贴在墙上。
❸伸,伸出
Don't stick your head out of the train window.
不要把头伸到火车窗外面。
vi. 粘住;钉住
This stamp won't stick.
这张邮票贴不上去。

still 〔stɪl ‖ stɪl〕
[比]stiller;[最]stillest
ad. ❶还,仍旧
Her grandmother is still living.
她祖母仍然健在。
❷尽管如此,然而;(虽然……)还是
He is good-natured. Still, I don't like him.
他脾气很好,可是我还是不喜欢他。
❸(强调比较级)还要,更
It's hot today, but it'll be still hotter tomorrow.
今天很热,但明天会更热。
❹还有
a. ❶静止的,不动的
The little girl kept still in her

chair watching TV.
小女孩一动不动地坐在椅子上看电视。
❷寂静的；静默的；平静的
The lake is still today.
今天湖水十分平静。

stimulate 〔ˈstɪmjəˌlet ‖ ˈstɪmjʊleɪt〕
［过去式］stimulated；［过去分词］stimulated
vt. 刺激；激励；使兴奋；促使
The medicine stimulates the brain.
这种药刺激大脑。

sting 〔stɪŋ ‖ stɪŋ〕
［过去式］stung；［过去分词］stung
vt. ❶刺，蜇，叮
A bee stung him on the back.
一只蜜蜂蜇了他的背。
❷刺痛，使疼痛
The smoke stung my eyes.
烟熏得我眼睛痛。
❸（心灵，感情上的）刺痛；伤害
Their ridicule stung him into making a sharp reply.
他们的嘲弄刺激他作出了尖刻的回答。
vi. ❶刺，叮
Bees do not normally sting without being provoked.
如果没有人惹它，蜜蜂通常是不蜇人的。
❷被刺痛，感到灼痛
My eyes are stinging from the smoke.
我的眼睛被烟熏痛。
n. ❶螫针；（植物的）刺毛［C］
Be careful. The insect has stings.
当心，这昆虫有刺。
❷刺伤（处）；刺痛［C］
The football team felt the sting of defeat.
足球队尝到了失败的痛楚。

stock 〔stɑk ‖ stɒk〕
n. ［C］［U］❶贮存；（知识等的）蓄积
The sailor has a rich stock of tales of adventure.
那个水手满肚子都是探险故事。
❷进货；库存品，存货
There is not much stock in the shop right now.
当前店里存货不多。
❸（公司的）股票，股份
Stocks of the company are falling.
该公司的股票正在下跌。

stomach 〔ˈstʌmək ‖ ˈstʌmək〕
n. ❶胃［C］

S

❷【口】肚子，腹部[C]
He kicked Bill in the stomach.
他一脚踢在比尔的肚子上。
❸(常用于否定句)食欲，胃口；欲望，志趣[U][(+for)]
I have no stomach for any food now.
现在我什么东西都不想吃。

stomachache 〔ˈstʌməkˌek ‖ ˈstʌməkeɪk〕
n. 胃痛；腹痛[C][U]
I have a stomachache.
我肚子痛。

S

stone 〔ston ‖ stəʊn〕
n. 石子，石头，石块[C]
The boy threw some stones into the pond.
那个男孩把几块石头丢进了池里。

stool 〔stul ‖ stuːl〕
n. ❶凳子；搁脚凳[C]

凳子 stools

❷厕所；马桶

stop 〔stɑp ‖ stɒp〕
[过去式]stopped；[过去分词] stopped
vt. ❶停止；中止，止住[+v-ing]
It has stopped raining.
雨停了。
❷阻止，阻挡
The policemen stopped the fight.
警察制止了这场斗殴。
❸塞住；堵塞；填塞
We stopped the leak in the gas pipe by means of lead.
我们用铅堵塞了煤气管上的漏洞。
vi. ❶停止；中止
Stop for a while and take a rest.
停一会儿休息休息。
❷停下来(做别的事)[+to-v]
He stopped to listen to her talking.
他停下来听她说话。
❸【口】逗留；歇宿；(偶然)过访
On my way home I stopped at my aunt's.
回家途中我顺便到姑妈那儿去了一会儿。
n. [C]❶停止；中止；终止；停车
The train came to a stop.
火车停了下来。
❷停车站

I'll get off at the next stop.
我下一站下车。
❸【英】标点(特指句号)
❹逗留;歇宿
We made a stop in Tokyo.
我们在东京停留了一下。

store 〔stor ‖ stɔː〕
[过去式]stored;[过去分词]stored
vt. ❶贮存
Water is stored against the dry season.
蓄水以备旱季使用。
❷保管,收存
The cabbages were stored in the basement.
卷心菜储藏在地下室里。
❸容纳;蓄有
The barn will store 5 tons of grain.
这个谷仓能放5吨粮食。
n.[C] ❶贮存,贮藏
The grain here is for store.
此处的粮食供储备用。
❷仓库,货栈
❸【美】店铺,店;【英】大商店
Another auto store was opened in town yesterday.
昨天镇上又开了一家汽车商行。
❹【英】百货店[P]
She bought the sofa at the stores.
她在百货店买下的这个沙发。
❺贮存品,备用品[P]
They deal in household stores.
他们经营家庭用品。

storey 〔ˈstorɪ ‖ ˈstɔːrɪ〕
n.【英】楼层[C]

storm 〔stɔrm ‖ stɔːm〕
n. 暴风雨[C]
The ship had no sooner dropped anchor than a storm broke.
船刚下锚暴风雨就来了。

story 〔ˈstorɪ ‖ ˈstɔːrɪ〕
n. ❶故事;传闻;叙述[C][(+about)]
I am interested in true stories about great scientists.
我对一些伟大科学家的真实故事很感兴趣。
❷(短篇)小说[C]
❸内情,真相;情况[the]
He is one of the few who know the story.
他是少数知道真相的人。

stove 〔stov ‖ stəʊv〕
n. 火炉;暖炉[C]

straight 〔stret ‖ streɪt〕
[比]straighter;[最]straightest
a. ❶笔直的;挺直的
His friend is a tall, slim girl

with a straight nose.
他的朋友是位鼻子挺直，身材高而苗条的姑娘。
❷正直的，坦率的，有品德的[(＋with)]
The boss is not completely straight with us.
上司对我们并不完全坦诚。
ad. ❶直，挺直地
The soldiers stood straight.
士兵们站得笔直。
❷直接地；一直地
Go straight down the road and then turn left.
沿着这条路一直走，然后左转。
❸正直地；坦率地
Tell me straight what you think of the plan.
请把你对这个计划的看法坦白地告诉我。
❹立刻，马上
He went to bed straight after supper.
他吃完晚饭就去睡了。

strange 〔strendʒ ‖ ˈstreɪndʒ〕
[比]stranger；[最]strangest
a. ❶奇怪的，奇妙的，不可思议的
She was startled by a strange voice.
一个奇怪的声音吓了她一跳。
❷陌生的；生疏的，不熟悉的[(＋to)]
The place is strange to me.
这地方我不熟悉。
❸生手的，外行的；不习惯的[(＋to)]
My uncle is strange to city life.
我叔父不习惯都市生活。

stranger 〔ˈstrendʒɚ ‖ ˈstreɪndʒə〕
n. [C] ❶ 陌生人[(＋to)]
I feel strange in the presence of strangers.
在陌生人面前，我感到不自在。
❷外地人；新来者
Sorry, I don't know. I'm a stranger here myself.
对不起，我不清楚。我对这里也不熟。
❸外行，生手；不习惯于……的人[(＋to)]
He is no stranger to sorrow.
他饱经忧患。

straw 〔strɔ ‖ strɔː〕
n. ❶稻草，麦秆[U]
The local people made fancy straw hats for sale.
当地居民制作花式草帽出售。
❷(一根)稻草；麦秆[C]
Straws are hollow.
麦秆是空心的。
❸吸管[C]

The boy was drinking milk through a straw.
那个男孩在用吸管喝牛奶。

strawberry 〔ˈstrɔˌbɛrɪ ‖ ˈstrɔːbərɪ〕
n.【植】草莓[C]

stream 〔strim ‖ striːm〕
[过去式]streamed;[过去分词] streamed
n. [C] ❶小河;溪流
❷流;流动
People kept coming in streams.
人们川流不息地到来。
❸光线;(光的)束,道
a stream of light
一束光线
❹潮流;趋势
He always goes with the stream.
他总是顺应潮流。
vi. ❶流,流动;淌
The pipe broke and water streamed onto the floor.
水管破了,水流到了地板上。
❷涌入,涌进;川流不息
Blood streamed from the wound.
血从伤口流出。
vt. 流出;涌出
Her nose streamed blood.
她的鼻子流血了。

street 〔strit ‖ striːt〕
n. [C] ❶街,街道
I live on the same street as Peter.
我和彼得住在同一条街上。
❷全街区的居民[the]
The whole street protested such police brutality.
全街区的人都抗议警方这种野蛮行为。

strength 〔strɛŋθ ‖ streŋθ〕
n. ❶力,力量,力气;实力;效力[U]
The medicine has lost its strength.
这药已经失效。
❷长处[C]
1,500-meter race is his strength.
1,500 米赛跑是他的强项。

strengthen 〔ˈstrɛŋθən ‖ ˈstreŋθən〕
[过去式]strengthened;[过去分词]strengthened
vt. vi. 加强;增强;巩固
We want to strengthen our ties with them.
我们要加强与他们的联系。

stress 〔strɛs ‖ stres〕
[过去式]stressed;[过去分词] stressed

S

n. ❶压力;紧张;压迫[C][U]
He did so under (the) stress of necessity.
他受形势所迫才那样做的。
❷着重;重要性[U][(＋on)]
The government lays stress on welfare work.
政府着重于福利事业。
❸【语】重音;重读[C][U][(＋on)]
vt. 强调,着重
He stressed the need for understanding between nations.
他强调国家间相互谅解的必要。

S

strict 〔strɪkt ‖ strɪkt〕
[比]stricter;[最]strictest
a. ❶严格的;严厉的[(＋with)]
He is very strict with his students.
他对学生非常严格。
❷严谨的;精确的
He told the strict truth.
他讲的情况完全属实。
❸完全的,绝对的
She was pledged to keep it a strict secret.
她发誓对此事绝对保密。

strike 〔straɪk ‖ straɪk〕
[过去式]struck;[过去分词]struck, stricken
vt. ❶打,击,攻击
He was struck by lightning.
他被闪电击中。
❷(用爪)抓伤;(用毒牙)咬伤;(疾病)侵袭
The snake struck the man's hand.
蛇咬伤了那个男人的手。
❸(钟)敲响(报时)
The clock struck 12 o'clock.
钟敲过12点。
❹打(火);划(火柴);盖(章)
He struck a match to smoke.
他划火柴点烟。
❺使突然想起
A good idea struck the scientist.
那个科学家想起了一个好主意。
vi. ❶打,击;袭击;进攻
His knee struck against the chair.
他的膝盖撞到了椅子上。
❷突然想到;突然发现[(＋on/upon)]
He struck on a solution to the problem.
他突然想到一个解决问题的办法。
n.[C] ❶打击;攻击;空袭
The commander decided to

make an air strike on the enemy's supply line.
指挥官决定空袭敌人的补给线。
❷罢工；罢课；罢市
The steel workers called a strike.
钢铁工人发动了罢工。
❸(石油、煤等矿藏的)发现，意外成功；走运
He made a lucky strike and in 3 months realized a considerable fortune.
他交了好运，3 个月就发了相当大的一笔财。

strong 〔strɔŋ ‖ strɒŋ〕
[比]stronger；[最]strongest
a. ❶强壮的，强健的
He is strong enough to lift that rock.
他力气很大，能举起那块石头。
❷强大的；(风，水流等)强劲的
A strong wind is blowing.
刮着大风。
❸(性格)坚强的；(态度等)坚决的；强硬的
Our leader has a strong will.
我们的领袖有坚强的意志。
❹坚固的，牢固的
❺(味道，气味)浓的，强烈的；(酒)烈性的
I like drinking strong tea.
我喜欢喝浓茶。

structure 〔ˈstrʌktʃɚ ‖ ˈstrʌktʃə〕
[过去式]structured；[过去分词]structured
n. ❶结构；构造；组织[C][U]
We know a lot about the structure of genes now.
如今我们对基因的结构有了较多的了解。
❷构造体；建筑物[C]
We visited the museum, a steel and glass structure.
我们参观了博物馆，它是一座钢和玻璃的建筑物。
vt. 构造；组织；建造
They structure their communication to meet the needs of the client.
他们创建通讯系统以满足客户的需要。

struggle 〔ˈstrʌgl̩ ‖ ˈstrʌgl〕
[过去式]struggled；[过去分词]struggled
vi. ❶奋斗；斗争[(+ for/against/with)][+to-v]
They struggled for peace.
他们为和平而战。
❷努力；使劲；挣扎[(+ for)][+to-v]

S

She struggled to keep back the tears.
她努力忍住泪水。
❸艰难地行进
The wounded soldier struggled in the forest.
受伤的士兵在森林中艰难地行进。
n. [C] ❶奋斗；斗争[(＋for/against/with)]
The struggle between the two teams was hard.
这两个队之间的斗争很艰苦。
❷努力；使劲；挣扎
The cat made a struggle to get free.
猫努力要挣脱。

stubborn [ˈstʌbɚn ‖ ˈstʌbən]
a. ❶倔强的，顽固的；不听话的
He is as stubborn as a mule.
他倔得像头骡子。
❷顽强的，不屈不挠的
He made a stubborn resistance.
他做了顽强抵抗。

student [ˈstjudn̩t ‖ ˈstjuːdənt]
n. [C] ❶(大中学校的)学生
❷学者；研究者[(＋of)]
He is a student of international politics.
他是研究国际政治的学者。

study [ˈstʌdɪ ‖ ˈstʌdɪ]
[过去式]studied；[过去分词]studied
n. ❶学习；研究；调查[U][P]
The plan is under study.
那个计划正在研究中。
❷研究论文，专题论文[C]
She wrote a study of Shakespeare.
她写了一篇有关莎士比亚的论文。
❸学科[P]
the Department of English studies
英语系
❹书房[C]
vt. ❶学习；研究
For a year he studied Chinese with me.
他跟我学了一年中文。
❷细看，细察
I studied him closely.
我仔细地看了看他。
❸仔细考虑
We need time to study a suitable answer.
我们需要时间去考虑一个适当的答复。
vi. 学习，用功
My daughter often studies late into the night.
我女儿常常学习到深夜。

stuff 〔stʌf ‖ stʌf〕
[过去式]stuffed;[过去分词]stuffed
n. [U] ❶材料,原料;木料
Some parts nowadays are made of plastic or similar stuff.
现在有些零件是由塑料或类似的材料制造的。
❷物品;东西
He picked the stuff up off the floor and put it on the table.
他把那东西从地上捡起来,放在桌子上。
❸素质;本质;要素
The young man has good stuff in him.
那个年轻人素质很好。
vt. ❶装;填;塞[(+up)]
He has a bad cold and his nose is stuffed up.
他患重感冒,鼻子塞住了。
❷把……装满;把……塞进[(+into/with/up)]
He stuffed the suitcase with his clothes.
他把衣服塞进手提箱。

stupid 〔ˈstjupɪd ‖ ˈstjuːpɪd〕
[比]stupider;[最]stupidest
a. ❶愚蠢的,笨的
It is stupid to do such a thing.
做这种事真蠢。
❷麻木的,无知觉的;迟钝的
The sailor was stupid with liquor.
那水手醉得不省人事。
❸无聊的,乏味的,讨厌的
It was a stupid book.
那是一本无聊的书。

style 〔staɪl ‖ staɪl〕
n. ❶风格,作风[C][U]
❷文体;文风;语调[C][U]
The letter is written in a formal style.
这封信以正式文体写成。
❸风度;体面,时髦[U]
That gentleman has great style.
那位先生很有风度。
❹(衣服等的)流行款式[C][U]
Her hat is out of style.
她的帽子过时了。

subject 〔ˈsʌbdʒɪkt ‖ ˈsʌbdʒɪkt〕
n. [C] ❶主题;题目;题材,话题;(议论的)对象
Let's change the subject.
咱们换个话题吧。
❷科目,学科
❸【文】主语

subjective 〔səbˈdʒɛktɪv ‖ səbˈdʒektɪv〕
a. ❶主观的,主观上的

❷个人的

substance 〔ˈsʌbstəns ‖ ˈsʌbstəns〕

n. ❶物质[C]

Ice and snow are different forms of the same substance, water.

冰和雪都是水这一种物质不同的形式。

❷实质；本质；实体；本体[U]

❸要旨；要义；梗概[U]

The substance of his speech was that he was better than the other candidates.

他演说的主要内容就是：他比其他候选人更好。

❹财产，财物[U]

Later he became a man of substance.

后来，他成为拥有大量资产的人。

subtract 〔səbˈtrækt ‖ səbˈtrækt〕

[过去式]subtracted；[过去分词]subtracted

vt. 减，减去；去掉[(＋from)]

Subtract 13 from 17 and you have 4.

17 减 13 得 4。

vi. 作减法

suburb 〔ˈsʌbɝb ‖ ˈsʌbɜːb〕

n. [C] ❶(城市周围的)近郊住宅区(或村，镇)

❷郊区[the P]

subway 〔ˈsʌbˌwe ‖ ˈsʌbweɪ〕

n. [C] ❶【美】地下铁；地下铁火车

❷【英】地下过道，地道

succeed 〔səkˈsid ‖ səkˈsiːd〕

[过去式]succeeded；[过去分词]succeeded

vi. ❶成功，办妥；获得成效[(＋in)]

He succeeded in getting the job.

他谋得了那份工作。

❷继任；继承[(＋to)]

The millionaire's eldest son will succeed to his estate.

这位百万富翁的长子将继承他的产业。

vt. ❶继……之后；接续

The storm was succeeded by calm.

暴风雨后一片宁静。

❷接替；继承

The younger man will succeed Mr. White as director.

那位较年轻的男士将接替怀特先生当主任。

success 〔səkˈsɛs ‖ səkˈses〕

n. ❶成功；成就；胜利[U]

They have achieved remarkable success in their work.
他们在工作方面成绩显著。
❷成功的事；取得成就的人[C]
She was a success as an actress.
她是位成功的女演员。

successful 〔səkˈsɛsfəl ‖ səkˈsesfəl〕
[比]more successful；[最]most successful
a. ❶成功的；结果圆满；胜利的
It was a successful experiment.
那是一次成功的试验。
❷(人)一帆风顺的；有成就的；发迹的
She was a successful novelist.
她是一个有成就的小说家。

such 〔sʌtʃ ‖ sʌtʃ〕
a. ❶这样的，此类的
She has bought paper, pens, and other such stationery.
她买了纸、笔以及诸如此类的文具。
Susan is such a nice girl.
苏珊是如此漂亮的一个女孩。
❷(与 that 连用)如此的……(以致)
He is such a good teacher that all his pupils like him.
他是位极好的老师，所有的学生都喜欢他。
❸(表示惊叹或加强语气)这样的，这等的
It was such an exciting game.
那场比赛真是精彩刺激。

sudden 〔ˈsʌdn̩ ‖ ˈsʌdn〕
a. 突然的；意外的
His rise to power was very sudden.
他的掌权很令人意外。

suddenly 〔ˈsʌdn̩lɪ ‖ ˈsʌdnlɪ〕
ad. 意外地；忽然；冷不防
Suddenly it began to rain.
突然下起雨来。

suffer 〔ˈsʌfɚ ‖ ˈsʌfə〕
[过去式]suffered；[过去分词]suffered
vt. ❶遭受；经历
He suffered many humiliations before he became a football star.
他在成为足球名将前受过许多屈辱。
❷(常用于否定句)忍受
I cannot suffer such rudeness.
我不能容忍这种粗鲁的举止。
vi. ❶受苦；患病[(+from)]
He suffered from poverty all his life.
他一生饱受贫穷之苦。
❷受损害，受损失；变糟

S

This scientific instrument suffered severely.
这部科学仪器受到严重损坏。
❸受惩罚;被处决[(+for)]
He suffered for his offence.
他因自己的过错而受到惩罚。

sufficient 〔sə'fɪʃənt ‖ sə'fɪʃənt〕
a. 足够的,充分的[(+for)][+to-v]
Her income is not sufficient to support her family.
她的收入不够养活家人。

sugar 〔'ʃʊgɚ ‖ 'ʃʊgə〕
n. ❶(食用)糖[U]
❷方糖[C]

S

suggest 〔sə'dʒɛst ‖ sə'dʒest〕
[过去式]suggested;[过去分词]suggested
vt. ❶建议,提议[+v-ing][+(that)][+wh-]
I suggest our going to the park on Sunday.
我建议咱们星期天去公园。
❷暗示;启发[+(that)]
I'm not suggesting that it was his fault.
我并不是说那是他的错。
❸使人想起,使人联想到[(+to)]
That cloud suggests a boat to me.
那朵云使我联想到船。

suggestion 〔sə'dʒɛstʃən ‖ sə'dʒestʃən〕
n. ❶建议,提议[C][U]
I ordered a steak at his suggestion.
我根据他的建议点了一份牛排。
❷暗示,示意,启发;联想[U]
Poetry achieves its finest effects by suggestion.
诗歌借助暗示联想达到最佳意境。
❸微量,细微的迹象[(+of)]
I detected a suggestion of malice in his remarks.
我察觉他的话中带有一点恶意。

suicide 〔'suəˌsaɪd ‖ 'suːɪsaɪd〕
n. 自杀,自杀行为
He committed suicide.
他自杀了。

suit 〔sut ‖ suːt〕
[过去式]suited;[过去分词]suited
n. [C]❶(一套)衣服
I picked out a black suit.
我挑了一套黑色西装。
❷诉讼
He will bring a suit against his boss.

他要对老板提出控告。

vt. ❶适合,中……的意

Would Friday morning suit you?

星期五早上对你合适吗?

❷(不用被动式)与……相配,与……相称

This dress suits you beautifully.

这件衣服你穿非常合适。

❸使合适;使适应[(+to)]

Her speech was well suited to the occasion.

她的讲话在这个场合十分得体。

vi. ❶合适,适当

Will this time suit?

这个时间合适吗?

❷相称;彼此协调[(+ to/with)]

The position suits with his abilities.

这个职位与他的能力相称。

suitable ['sutəbl̩ ‖ 'suːtəbl]

[比]more suitable;[最]most suitable

a. 适当的;合适的;适宜的[(+to/for)]

He was just not suitable for the job.

他就是不适合干这份工作。

suitcase ['sutˌkes ‖ 'suːtkeɪs]

n. 小型旅行箱;手提箱[C]

She packed all her belongings into a suitcase.

她将全部东西都装进了一只手提箱。

sum [sʌm ‖ sʌm]

[过去式]summed;[过去分词]summed

n. [C] ❶总数,总和,总计[the][(+of)]

She paid the sum of $200 for dresses.

她买衣服总共花了200美元。

❷金额;一笔[(+of)]

He earned a large sum of money.

他赚了一大笔钱。

vt. ❶计算……的总和[(+up)]

The accountant summed up the figures.

会计合计了一下数字。

❷总结;概括;概述[(+up)]

The story may be summed up in one sentence.

该故事可以用一句话来概括。

summary ['sʌmərɪ ‖ 'sʌmərɪ]

a. 概括的,扼要的

He presented a summary account.

他做了扼要说明。

S

n. 总结，摘要，一览[C][(+of)]
Give a summary of this chapter.
把这一章做个摘要。

summer ['sʌmɚ || 'sʌmə]
n. 夏天
the summer holiday
暑假

sun [sʌn || sʌn]
n. ❶太阳[the]
The sun rises in the east and sets in the west.
太阳从东方升起，由西方落下。
❷阳光[U]
There is not much sun today.
今天阳光不多。

Sunday ['sʌndɪ || 'sʌndɪ]
n. 略作 Sun. 星期日

sunlight ['sʌnˌlaɪt || 'sʌnlaɪt]
n. 日光[U]

sunny ['sʌnɪ || 'sʌnɪ]
a. ❶阳光充足的；和煦的，暖和的
It's a sunny day.
今天是晴天。
❷快活的；乐观的；性情开朗的；向上的
a sunny smile
愉快的微笑

sunrise ['sʌnraɪz || 'sʌnraɪz]
n. 日出；黎明，日出时间[U]
I get up at sunrise.
我黎明就起床了。

sunset ['sʌnsɛt || 'sʌnset]
n. 日落，日落时间[U]
The sunset here is very splendid.
这里的落日十分壮观。

sunshine ['sʌnˌʃaɪn || 'sʌnʃaɪn]
n. [U]❶阳光
Cats like lying in the sunshine.
猫喜欢躺在阳光下。
❷晴天
After rain comes sunshine.
雨过天晴。

superior [sə'pɪrɪɚ || suː'pɪərɪə]
a. ❶(在职位，地位等方面)较高的，上级的[(+to/in)]
A major is superior to a captain.
少校(职位)高于上尉。
❷(在质量等方面)较好的，优秀的，上等的
This handbag is made of superior leather.
这只手提包是由上等皮革制成的。
❸有优越感的；高傲的；傲慢的
Don't take a superior attitude toward the younger students.
不要对比自己年轻的同学采取傲慢的态度。

n.[C] ❶上司;长官;长辈[P]
She is my superior.
她是我的上司。
❷占优势者,优胜者[(+in)]
He has no superior in this respect.
在这方面没有人能胜过他。

superman 〔ˈsupɚˌmæn ‖ ˈsjuːpəmæn〕
n. 超人;能力非凡的人[C]

supermarket 〔supɚˌmɑrkɪt ‖ ˈsjuːpəˌmɑːkɪt〕
n. 超级市场[C]

supper 〔ˈsʌpɚ ‖ ˈsʌpə〕
n. 晚餐,晚饭[C][U]
What do we have for supper today?
今天晚餐我们吃什么?

supply 〔səˈplaɪ ‖ səˈplaɪ〕
[过去式]supplied;[过去分词]supplied
vt. ❶供给,供应,提供[(+to/for/with)]
Our farm supplies the market with fruits and vegetables.
我们的农场为市场提供水果和蔬菜。
❷补充;满足
It is hard to supply the demand for more meat.
要满足更多的肉类需求是很难的。
n. ❶供给,供应[U]
They are engaged in the supply of small parts for replacement.
他们从事提供备用小零件的工作。
❷供应量;供应品;库存(货)[C]
We have new supplies of fur coats.
我们有新进的皮大衣货。
❸生活用品;补给品;军粮[P]
Our medical supplies are running short.
我们的医疗用品快用完了。

support 〔səˈport ‖ səˈpɔːt〕
[过去式]supported;[过去分词]supported
vt. ❶支撑,支托,扶持
The old man entered the room supported by his grandson.
老人由孙子扶着进了房间。
❷支持,拥护,赞成;资助
They supported the Democratic Party.
他们支持民主党。
❸扶养,赡养
He has a large family to support.
他要扶养一大家人。
n. [U]❶维持生计,扶养;生活

S

费;供养
Hunter is the chief support of the family.
亨特是他一家的主要赡养者。
❷支持,拥护,赞成;鼓舞
We need your support.
我们需要你们的支持。

suppose 〔sə'poz ‖ sə'pəuz〕
[过去式]supposed;[过去分词]supposed
vt. ❶猜想,以为[+(that)]
I suppose (that) he is still in town.
我想他还在城里。
❷期望;认为必须,认为应该
You're not supposed to take the books out of the room.
这些书不能拿出屋去。
❸必须以……为前提
Every effect supposes a cause.
任何事的生成都必然有其原因。
❹(用于祈使语气)让……[+(that)]
Suppose we telephone her first.
我们先打电话给她如何?
❺假定[+(that)]
Suppose you were given 1 million yen, what would you do with it?
要是人家给你100万日元,你要怎么用它?

sure 〔ʃur ‖ ʃʊə〕
[比]surer;[最]surest
a. ❶确信的,有把握的[+(that)][+wh-][(+about/of)]
I'm not sure whether our team will win.
我不能肯定我队是否能赢。
❷一定的,必定的[+to-v]
She is sure to write to you.
她一定会给你写信的。
❸确实的;可靠的
That is a sure proof.
那是个确凿的证据。

surface 〔'sɝfɪs ‖ 'sɜːfɪs〕
n. ❶面,表面[C]
It has a rough surface.
它表面粗糙。
❷水面[C]
The breeze rippled the surface of the lake.
微风吹皱了湖面。
❸外观,外表[the]
Beneath his rough surface he is really a very kind person.
他外表粗俗,但实际上是一个很善良的人。
a. ❶表面的,外观的
It was a surface wound and soon healed.

S

那是一个表面伤，不久便长好了。

❷地面上的；水面上的

The Americans are strengthening their surface fleet.

美国人正在加强他们的水上舰队。

❸表面上的，外表上的

There have been improvements in surface conditions but not in fundamental weaknesses.

表面情况已有改善但根本的弱点依然如故。

surgeon〔ˈsɝdʒən ‖ ˈsɜːdʒən〕

n. 外科医生[C]

A surgeon removed the boy's brain tumor.

一位外科医生为这个男孩切除了脑肿瘤。

surname〔ˈsɝˌnem ‖ ˈsɜːneɪm〕

n. 姓[C]

My surname is Hill.

我姓希尔。

surprise〔səˈpraɪz ‖ səˈpraɪz〕

[过去式]surprised；[过去分词]surprised

n. ❶惊奇，诧异[U]

To my surprise, he refused to cooperate with us.

令我吃惊的是，他不肯与我们合作。

❷使人惊讶的事，意外的事[C]

The incident came as quite a surprise to them.

这一事件完全出乎他们的意料。

vt. ❶使吃惊，使感到意外

I was surprised to learn that he was taking drugs.

听说他在吸毒，我很吃惊。

❷突然袭击；当场捉住

Our troops surprised the enemy while they were still sleeping.

趁敌人还在睡觉，我们的部队出其不意地袭击他们。

surprised〔səˈpraɪzd ‖ səˈpraɪzd〕

a. 感到惊讶的；出人意料的

I was surprised to hear the news.

听到这个消息我很吃惊。

surround〔səˈraund ‖ səˈraund〕

[过去式]surrounded；[过去分词]surrounded

vt. ❶围，围绕；圈住[(＋with/by)]

Our house is surrounded by trees.

我们房子的四周都是树。

❷包围，围困

The police surrounded the house.

警察包围了这幢房子。

surrounding 〔sə'raʊndɪŋ ‖ sə'raʊndɪŋ〕

n. 环境;周围的事物[P]

He didn't pay much attention to his surroundings.

他没有多注意他周围的环境。

a. 周围的;附近的

Foxes started coming in from the surrounding countryside.

狐狸开始从附近的乡下跑进来。

survive 〔sɚ'vaɪv ‖ sə'vaɪv〕

[过去式]survived;[过去分词]survived

vt. ❶在……之后仍然生存,从……中逃生

She survived the accident.

她在事故当中幸存下来。

❷比……活得长;丧失(配偶,亲人等)

She survived her husband by one year.

她比她丈夫多活了一年。

suspect[1] 〔sə'spɛkt ‖ sə'spekt〕

[过去式]suspected;[过去分词]suspected

vt. ❶疑有,察觉

He suspected danger and didn't go near it.

他感到有危险所以没有靠近它。

❷怀疑,不信任[+of][+(that)]

He suspected me of lying.

他怀疑我撒谎。

❸猜想;料想[+(that)]

I suspect that she has known the truth.

我怀疑她知道了真相。

suspect[2] 〔'sʌspɛkt ‖ 'sʌspekt〕

n. 嫌疑犯;可疑分子[C]

The police arrested the suspect of the case.

警察逮捕了该案件的嫌疑犯。

suspicion 〔sə'spɪʃən ‖ sə'spɪʃən〕

n. ❶怀疑,疑心,猜疑[C][U][+(that)]

I had a strong suspicion that Tom had seen me coming.

我很怀疑汤姆看到我进来。

❷嫌疑[U]

She's been arrested on suspicion of spying.

她因涉嫌间谍活动而被捕。

suspicious 〔sə'spɪʃəs ‖ sə'spɪʃəs〕

a. ❶猜疑的,疑心的;多疑的[(+of)]

I'm suspicious of the government's intentions.

我怀疑政府的意图。
❷可疑的，有蹊跷的
There were suspicious circumstances about his death.
关于他的死，有一些值得怀疑的情况。

swan 〔swɑn ‖ swɒn〕
n. 天鹅[C]

swear 〔swɛr ‖ sweə〕
[过去式]swore；[过去分词]sworn
vi. ❶发誓；宣誓
He swore to God.
他对天发誓。
❷诅咒；骂脏话[(＋at)]
He often swears at his wife when he is angry.
他经常在生气的时候咒骂他妻子。
vt. ❶发(誓)；宣(誓)
We swore eternal friendship.
我们誓守永恒的友谊。
❷【口】断言；保证说[＋(that)]
He swore that she was insane.
他断言她有精神病。

sweat 〔swɛt ‖ swet〕
[过去式]sweat, sweated；[过去分词]sweat, sweated
n. 汗，汗水[U]
There was sweat on his forehead.
他额头冒着汗。
vi. 出汗
They saw his face being white and sweating.
他们看到他脸色苍白，并且出着汗。

sweet 〔swit ‖ swiːt〕
a. ❶甜的
The apples taste sweet.
这些苹果很甜。
❷悦耳的；漂亮的；芳香的；美味的
She gave us a sweet song.
她给我们唱了一支好听的歌曲。
❸漂亮的，可爱的
She is a sweet girl.
她是个可爱的姑娘。
❹和蔼的，亲切的；温柔的
She is sweet to her pupils.
她对学生和蔼可亲。
n. ❶【英】糖果[P]
Children love sweets.
小孩子喜欢糖果。
❷【英】(餐后的)甜点[C][U]
Would you like some more sweet?
你想再吃点儿甜点吗？

sweetheart 〔ˈswitˌhɑrt ‖ ˈswiːthɑːt〕
n. 心上人，恋人，情人[C]

swim 〔swɪm ‖ swɪm〕

［过去式］swam;［过去分词］swum

vi. ❶游,游泳

A horse can swim.

马会游泳。

❷旋转,摇晃;眼花,眩晕

I was tired out, and my head was swimming.

我累坏了,头发晕。

vt. 游过;与……比赛游泳

She tried to swim the English Channel.

她试图横渡英吉利海峡。

n. 游泳

Shall we go for a swim?

我们去游泳好吗?

词汇拓展

swimmer *n.* 游泳者

swimming pool *n.* 游泳池

S

switch 〔swɪtʃ ‖ swɪtʃ〕

［过去式］switched;［过去分词］switched

n. 开关,电闸,电键［C］

I couldn't find the switch in the dark.

我在黑暗中找不到开关。

vt. 打开(或关掉)……的开关［(＋on/off)］

He switched on/ off the light.

他打开/关掉灯。

Switzerland 〔ˈswɪtsə·lənd ‖ ˈswɪtsələnd〕

n. 瑞士

sword 〔sword ‖ sɔːd〕

n.［C］❶剑,刀

❷武力;兵权;君权;战争［the］

Do you believe that the pen is mightier than the sword?

你相信笔杆的威力大于武力吗?

symbol 〔ˈsɪmbl̩ ‖ ˈsɪmbəl〕

n.［C］❶象征,标志［(＋of)］

The white bird is a symbol of freedom.

这白色的鸟是自由的象征。

❷记号,符号［(＋for)］

We use x as the symbol for an unknown quantity.

我们用 x 表示一个未知数。

sympathetic 〔ˌsɪmpəˈθɛtɪk ‖ ˌsɪmpəˈθetɪk〕

a. ❶同情的;有同情心的

She is a sympathetic person.

她是个有同情心的人。

❷赞同的,支持的［(＋to/towards)］

He was sympathetic to my opinion.

他赞成我的意见。

sympathy 〔ˈsɪmpəθɪ ‖

ˈsɪmpəθɪ〕

n. ❶同情,同情心[U][P][(+for/with)]

I have no sympathy for beggars.

我不同情乞丐。

❷支持;赞同[U][(+with)]

Many people are in sympathy with your views.

许多人赞同你的看法。

symphony 〔ˈsɪmfənɪ ‖ ˈsɪmfənɪ〕

n. [C] ❶交响乐,交响曲

❷【美】交响乐团,交响乐队

He conducts a symphony.

他指挥一个交响乐团。

system 〔ˈsɪstəm ‖ ˈsɪstəm〕

n. ❶体系;系统[C]

They are devising a road system.

他们在设计道路系统。

❷制度,体制[C]

The present system of education needs to be improved.

当前的教育制度需要改进。

❸秩序,规律[U]

His secretaries work with system.

他的几位秘书工作有条不紊。

S

table 〔'tebḷ ‖ 'teɪbl〕
n. ❶桌子；餐桌；台［C］
We reserved a table for 4 at the restaurant.
我们在餐馆预订了 4 人一桌的位子。
❷食物，菜肴
The nearby restaurant keeps an excellent table.
附近那家餐馆菜肴质量上乘。
❸表；目录［C］
time table
时间表

tablet 〔'tæblɪt ‖ 'tæblɪt〕
n.［C］❶小片，小块
❷药片

tail 〔tel ‖ teɪl〕
n.［C］❶尾巴；尾部；尾状物；发辫
We were at the tail of the bus queue.
我们站在公共汽车候车队伍的末尾。
❷燕尾服［P］
❸盯梢的人，侦探，跟踪者
She couldn't figure out who put a tail on her.
她猜不透谁派人盯她的梢。

tailor 〔'telɚ ‖ 'teɪlə〕
n.（尤指男装）裁缝师；（尤指男装）服装商［C］
He had his dress made by a Paris tailor.
他请巴黎的裁缝师做衣服。

take 〔tek ‖ teɪk〕
［过去式］took；［过去分词］taken
vt. ❶拿，取；握，抱
She took his outstretched hand.
她握住他伸出的手。
❷拿走，取走；夺取，占领；抓，

捕;吸引
The airport had been taken by daybreak.
天亮前机场就被攻占了。
❸带去;带领
Dad took us to the museum last Friday.
上星期五爸爸带我们去了博物馆。
❹就(座),就(职)
He took his seat.
他就了座。
❺取得,获得
His younger brother took the first prize.
他弟弟拿了头奖。
❻接受;采取;修(学科),上(课)
He takes no gifts from anyone.
他不接受任何人的礼物。
❼承担;容纳
❽吃(饭),喝(水),服(药);吸入;吸收
Take this medicine after each meal.
每餐后服用此药。
❾需要;花费;占用
The game took 5 hours.
那场比赛用了5个小时。
❿(表示做一次动作)运行,做
⓫生(根);生成(兴趣等)
⓬乘(车),搭(船)
He took plane for Shanghai.
他乘飞机去上海。
⓭记录;量取;拍摄
I took a picture of the baby.
我给那个婴儿拍了张照片。
⓮以为;把……看做
He took her words as an insult.
他把她的话当作侮辱。

常用短语

take after 像
He takes after his father in appearance.
他外表很像他父亲。
take apart 拆开;拆散
take away 拿走;夺去
Take away those books.
把那些书拿走。
take back 拿回;收回
I took my words back.
我收回我的话。
take off ❶脱下;移去
He took off his shoes.
他脱下鞋。
❷起飞
The plane took off at 3 o'clock.
飞机3点起飞。
❸休假
take on ❶具有;呈现
The city takes on a new look.
这座城市呈现新面貌。

T

❷承担
I don't want to take on any additional work.
我不想承担任何额外工作。
take to ❶沉迷于
He has taken to drink.
他沉迷于杯中物。
❷喜欢
I have taken to my new English teacher.
我开始喜欢我的新英语老师了。

T

take up ❶开始从事
Let's take up the problem.
让我们从这个问题开始。
❷占用；花去
The bookshelf took up too much room.
这个书架占了太多的空间。

tale 〔tel ‖ teɪl〕
n. [C] ❶故事，传说；叙述
Grandpa told the children the tales of his childhood.
爷爷给孩子们讲他童年的故事。
❷谎话，捏造的话
One shouldn't tell tales.
人不应该搬弄是非。

talent 〔ˈtælənt ‖ ˈtælənt〕
n. ❶天才，天资[C][U][(+for)]
He has a talent for music.
他有音乐天赋。
❷天才；有才能的人们；人才[C][U]
She is a new diving talent.
她是一个新的跳水天才。

talk 〔tɔk ‖ tɔːk〕
[过去式]talked；[过去分词]talked
vi. 讲话；谈话；演讲[(+to/with/about)]
I want to talk to your manager about an urgent matter.
我想和你们经理谈一件紧急的事。
vt. ❶讲，说
Don't talk nonsense.
别胡说八道。
❷讨论，商谈
The young people were talking philosophy in Clay's study.
那几个年轻人在克莱的书房里谈论哲学。
n. ❶谈话；会话[C][(+with/about)]
I had a talk with Mr. Jones.
我和琼斯先生谈过话。
❷(非正式)演讲[C]
Professor Kern gave a talk on American drama.
克恩教授作了一次有关美国戏

剧的演讲。

❸话题[the][(+of)]

The divorced woman is the talk of the street.

那个离了婚的女子成了街头巷尾的话题。

常用短语

small talk 闲谈;聊家常

talk about/of 谈论;谈到

What are you talking about?

你们正谈什么呢?

talking of 谈到;至于

Talking of Beijing, have you ever been there in winter?

谈到北京,你冬天去过那里吗?

talk over 商讨;讨论

We talked over the matter with her.

我们和她详细讨论了那件事。

talk with 与……会话

I want to talk with you.

我要和你谈谈。

tall 〔tɔl ‖ tɔːl〕

a. ❶身材高的;高大的

Joe is as tall as Lanny.

乔与兰尼一样高。

❷身高……

She is 5 feet tall.

她身高5英尺。

tame 〔tem ‖ teɪm〕

[比]tamer;[最]tamest;[过去式]tamed;[过去分词]tamed

a. ❶(动物)经驯养的,驯服的

Cows are tame animals.

奶牛是家畜。

❷温驯的,驯良的,听使唤的

Don't be afraid. These horses are tame.

不要怕。这些马很温驯。

vt. ❶驯化,驯养

She is an expert in taming animals.

她是一个驯兽专家。

❷制服,使顺从

Harsh punishment in childhood had tamed him and broken his will.

童年时代所受的严厉惩罚使他变得唯唯诺诺,缺乏意志。

tank 〔tæŋk ‖ tæŋk〕

n. [C] ❶(贮水,油,气等的)柜,罐,箱,槽

Every apartment house has a water tank on its roof.

T

每栋公寓房子的房顶都有一个水塔。

❷坦克，战车

Our infantry is supported by tanks.

我们的步兵有坦克支持。

tape 〔tep ‖ teɪp〕

n. ❶带子，线带；窄布条[C][U]

I used tape to tie up the parcel.

我用带子捆紧包裹。

❷(录音或录像)磁带[C]

I recorded music on tape.

我把音乐录在录音带上。

target 〔ˈtɑrɡɪt ‖ ˈtɑːɡɪt〕

n. 靶子；攻击的目标[C]

The arrow hit the centre of the target.

箭射中了靶心。

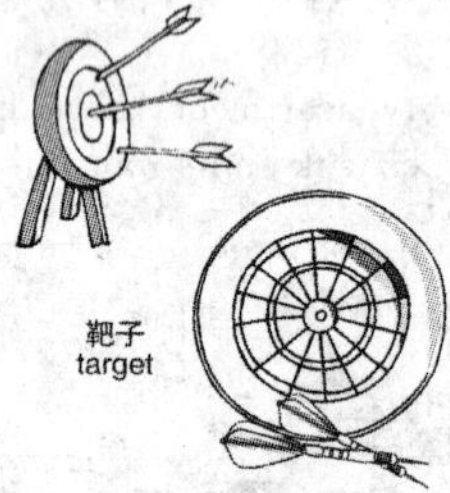

靶子
target

task 〔tæsk ‖ tɑːsk〕

n. [C] ❶任务；工作；作业

The task has been fulfilled.

任务已完成了。

❷困难的工作；苦差事

She had the difficult task of pulling out all the weeds.

她的苦差事是铲除所有的杂草。

taste 〔test ‖ teɪst〕

[过去式] tasted; [过去分词] tasted

n. ❶味觉[U]

❷味道，滋味；感受，体验

The liquid has a bitter taste.

这种药水有苦味。

❸爱好，兴趣[C][U][(＋for/in)]

She has a taste for music.

她爱好音乐。

vt. ❶尝，辨(味)

He tasted both cakes and decided neither was good.

他两块蛋糕都尝了尝，觉得都不好吃。

❷尝到，感到；体验

He has never tasted defeat.

他从未尝过失败的滋味。

vi. ❶吃起来；尝起来

The medicine tastes bitter.

这药有苦味。

❷察觉，有味觉，辨味

I can't taste because of my bad

cold.
因为重感冒，我辨不出味来。

tax 〔tæks ‖ tæks〕
n. 税；税金［C］［U］［(＋on)］
Every citizen must pay taxes.
每个公民都必须纳税。
a tax on cigarettes
香烟税

taxi 〔ˈtæksɪ ‖ ˈtæksɪ〕
n. 出租车［C］
He called a taxi for me.
他为我叫了出租车。

出租车
taxi

tea 〔ti ‖ tiː〕
n. ❶茶；茶叶［U］
I prefer tea to coffee.
我喜欢茶胜于咖啡。
❷(一杯)茶［C］
Three teas and a coffee, please.
请来三杯茶，一杯咖啡。
❸【英】下午茶，午后茶点［C］［U］
We have tea at 4 o'clock.
我们4点钟吃茶点。

teach 〔titʃ ‖ tiːtʃ〕
［过去式］taught；［过去分词］taught
vt. ❶教，讲授；训练［(＋to)］
She taught us how to pronounce those difficult words.
她教我们如何发这些难字的音。
❷教导；使领悟
It has taught us that unity means strength.
这件事使我们认识到团结就是力量。
❸【口】教训，告诫……不要
That accident taught them a lesson.
那次事故给了他们一个教训。
I'll teach you to call his name!
我要告诫你不要叫他的名字！
vi. 教，讲授；当老师
He teaches in Berlin.
他在柏林教书。

teacher 〔ˈtitʃɚ ‖ ˈtiːtʃə〕
n. 老师，教师［C］

teaching 〔ˈtitʃɪŋ ‖ ˈtiːtʃɪŋ〕
n. ❶教学，讲授，执教［U］
She is planning to go into teaching.
她打算从事教学工作。
❷教诲；教导；学说［U］［P］
His teachings still exert a

T

strong influence.
他的教导仍在生成巨大影响。

team 〔tim ‖ tiːm〕
n. 队；组；班[C]
John is a member of the school volleyball team.
约翰是学校排球队队员。

tear[1] 〔tɛr ‖ teə〕
[过去式]tore；[过去分词]torn
vt. ❶撕开，撕裂；扯破，划破
He has torn a hole in his shirt.
他把衬衫扯破了一个洞。
❷拉掉；拔掉；撕掉
I tore a page from my notebook.
我从笔记本上撕下一页纸来。
vi. 被撕裂；被扯破
This material tears easily.
这种料子很容易撕破。

tear[2] 〔tɪr ‖ tɪə〕
n. 眼泪；泪珠[C]
The hot tears welled up in her eyes.
热泪涌出她的眼眶。

technical 〔ˈtɛknɪkl̩ ‖ ˈteknɪkəl〕
a. ❶工艺的；技术的；科技的
He attends a technical school.
他在工艺学校上学。
❷专门的，技术性的
technical terms
术语

technique 〔tɛkˈnik ‖ tekˈniːk〕
n. 技巧；技术；技法[C][U]
The violinist's technique was excellent.
那位小提琴家的技术高超。

technology 〔tekˈnɑlədʒɪ ‖ tekˈnɒlədʒɪ〕
n. 科技；工艺学；工艺，技术[C][U]

teens 〔tinz ‖ tiːnz〕
n. 十几岁（指13至19岁）
He is still in his teens.
他还只有十几岁。

telegram 〔ˈtɛləˌgræm ‖ ˈtelɪgræm〕
n. 电报[C]
She had dispatched telegrams to her father.
她已经给父亲发了许多电报。

telegraph 〔ˈtɛləˌgræf ‖ ˈtelɪgrɑːf〕
n. ❶电报，电信[U]
❷（一份）电报；电报机[C]

telephone 〔ˈtɛləˌfon ‖ ˈtelɪfəun〕
[过去式]telephoned；[过去分词]telephoned
n. 电话机；电话[C][U]
The telephone is ringing.
电话铃响了。
There is a telephone for you.
你的电话。

vt. 打电话给，打电话告知[＋that]
He telephoned me that he couldn't come.
他打电话告诉我他不能来了。

television [ˈtɛləˌvɪʒən ‖ ˈtelɪˌvɪʒən]
n. ❶电视，电视广播[U]
Television advertising boosted their sales.
电视广告促进了他们的销售。
❷电视机[C]
She set the television to the Midnight News.
她将电视机调到午夜新闻档。

tell [tɛl ‖ tel]
[过去式]told；[过去分词]told
vt. ❶告诉；讲述，说
He told us how the accident happened.
他告诉我们那次事故是怎么发生的。
❷吩咐，命令
Tell him not to come tomorrow.
叫他明天别来。
❸识别；辨别[(＋from/apart)]
It's difficult to tell them apart.
很难把他们区分开来。
vi. ❶讲述[(＋of/about)]
The book tells of his younger sister's life in Japan.
这本书谈及他妹妹在日本的生活情况。
❷识别；判定
It's too early to tell.
现在要作出判断为时过早。
❸生成效果；发生影响[(＋on)]
Strain began to tell on his health.
过度劳累开始影响他的健康。
❹【口】告发

temper [ˈtɛmpɚ ‖ ˈtempə]
n. ❶情绪；性情，脾气[C]
She has a sweet temper.
她脾气温和。
❷暴躁；怒气[C][U]
His father is in a temper today.
他父亲今天在发脾气。

temperature [ˈtɛmprətʃɚ ‖ ˈtempərɪtʃə]
n. [C][U]❶温度，气温
The temperature dropped abruptly.
气温骤然下降。
❷体温
A nurse took his temperature.
护士为他量体温。

temple¹ [ˈtɛmpl̩ ‖ ˈtempl]
n. [C]❶(古代希腊，罗马，埃及等的)神殿，圣堂

T

❷(佛教的)寺院,寺庙
There is a Buddhist temple in this town.
在这个镇上有一座佛教寺庙。

temple² 〔ˈtɛmpl̩ ‖ ˈtempl〕
n. 太阳穴,鬓角[C][P]
A stone hit him on the temple.
一块石头击中了他的太阳穴。

temporary 〔ˈtɛmpəˌrɛrɪ ‖ ˈtemprərɪ〕
a. 临时的;暂时的,一时的
This is my temporary residence.
这是我的临时住处。

T

tempt 〔tɛmpt ‖ tempt〕
[过去式]tempted;[过去分词]tempted
vt. ❶引诱,诱惑,勾引
My friends tempted me to drink heavily.
朋友们怂恿我酗酒。
❷吸引,打动;引起
The cake tempts my appetite.
这块蛋糕引起了我的食欲。

temptation 〔tɛmpˈteʃən ‖ tempˈteɪʃən〕
n. 引诱,诱惑,诱惑物[C][U][(+to-v)]
Some advertisements are only temptations to make people spend money.
一些广告只是诱惑人们花钱的招数。

ten 〔tɛn ‖ ten〕
a. 十(个,人,岁,点)的
n. 十,十个

tenant 〔ˈtɛnənt ‖ ˈtenənt〕
n. 房客;佃户;承租人;住户,居住者[C]

tend¹ 〔tɛnd ‖ tend〕
[过去式]tended;[过去分词]tended
vi. ❶走向;趋向[(+to/towards)]
His views tend towards the extreme.
他的观点趋于偏激。
❷易于[+to-v]
Old people tend to get fat.
老年人容易发胖。

tend² 〔tɛnd ‖ tend〕
[过去式]tended;[过去分词]tended
vt. 照管,照料;护理;管理
A shepherd tended the sheep.
牧羊人照顾羊群。

tendency 〔ˈtɛndənsɪ ‖ ˈtendənsɪ〕
n.[C] ❶(发展、思想、行为等的)倾向[(+to/towards)][+to-v]
He has a tendency towards pes-

simism.
他有悲观的倾向。
❷趋势，潮流[(+to/towards)][+to-v]
There is a tendency towards regional cooperation.
目前有一种地区性合作的趋势。

tender [ˈtɛndɚ ‖ ˈtendə]
[比]tenderer;[最]tenderest
a. ❶嫩的；柔软的
There are lots of tender blossoms in the garden.
花园里净是娇嫩的花朵。
❷敏感的，一触就痛的
Her bruised knee is still tender.
她受了淤伤的膝盖仍然一碰就痛。
❸温柔的；体贴的[(+towards)]
The nurse was very tender towards the sick children.
护士对生病的孩子们很温柔。

tennis [ˈtɛnɪs ‖ ˈtenɪs]
n. 网球(运动)[U]

I like playing tennis.
我喜欢打网球。

tense [tɛns ‖ tens]
[比]tenser;[最]tensest
a. 拉紧的，绷紧的；(心理或神经)紧张的；引起紧张的
tense rope
拉紧的绳子
tense nerves
紧张的神经

tension [ˈtɛnʃən ‖ ˈtenʃən]
n. ❶拉紧，绷紧；(精神上的)紧张[U]
❷紧张局势，紧张状况[P][U]

tent [tɛnt ‖ tent]
n. 帐篷[C]
Tents are used by campers and by soldiers in the field.
露营的人和战地的士兵用帐篷。

tenth [tɛnθ ‖ tenθ]
a. ❶(与 the 连用)第十的，第十个的
❷十分之一的
n. [C](与 the 连用)第十(个)；月的第十日

term [tɝm ‖ tɜːm]
n. [C] ❶期，期限
They were sentenced to long terms in prison.
他们被判长期入狱。

❷学期
Are there any examinations at the end of term?
学期结束时有考试吗？
❸任期
The President's term of office is 4 years.
总统任期为 4 年。
❹(契约，谈判等的)条件；条款[P]
the terms of payment
支付条件
❺专有名词，术语；(一般的)词，名称
legal terms
法律术语
medical terms
医学术语

常用短语

in terms of **就……而论；在……方面**
He thinks of everything in terms of money.
他一切都从钱的角度来考虑问题。
in the long term **从长远来看**
in the short term **从眼前来看；从短期来看**

terminal 〔ˈtɝmənl̩ ‖ ˈtɜːmɪnl〕
a. ❶末端的；终点的；极限的
They reached the terminal station.
他们到达了终点站。
❷每期的；定期的；学期的
Our terminal examinations were over.
我们的期末考试结束了。
n. [C] ❶末端；终点；极限
❷(火车，巴士，飞机等的)总站，终点站
❸航空站
❹【电】端子
❺【计算机】终端(设备)

terrible 〔ˈtɛrəbl̩ ‖ ˈterəbl〕
[比] more terrible；[最] most terrible
a. ❶可怕的，吓人的，恐怖的
It was a terrible blow to him.
这对他是一个可怕的打击。
❷极度的，严重的
I'm afraid we have made a terrible mess in your room.
恐怕我们把你的房间搞得一团糟了。
❸令人敬畏的
❹【口】令人讨厌(或不快)的
I smelt a terrible odor.
我闻到一股难闻的气味。
❺【口】极糟糕的，极差的

terribly 〔ˈtɛrəblɪ ‖ ˈterəblɪ〕
ad. ❶可怕地
❷【口】很，非常

I'm terribly sorry.
我很抱歉。

territory 〔ˈtɛrəˌtɔrɪ ‖ ˈterɪtərɪ〕
n. [C][U]❶领土，版图；领地
They recaptured the lost territory.
他们收复了失地。
❷地区；（按某种目的划定的）区域（尤指商业推销区）
❸（行动，知识等的）领域，范围
Physics is outside his territory.
物理学不是他的专长。

test 〔tɛst ‖ test〕
[过去式]tested；[过去分词]tested
n. [C] ❶试验
A simple test will show if this is real gold.
简单的试验就能证明这是否是真金。
❷化验；化验法；化验剂
He had a blood test.
他验过血了。
❸检验；检验标准
❹测验；考察；小考
We are to have a history test next week.
下周我们有历史测验。
vt. 试验；检验；测验
The doctor has his ears tested.
医生检查他的耳朵。

text 〔tɛkst ‖ tekst〕
n. ❶正文，本文[U]
The book contains 200 pages of text.
这本书的正文有200页。
❷课文；课本 [C]

textbook 〔ˈtɛkstˌbʊk ‖ ˈtekstbʊk〕
n. 教科书，课本[C]

Thames 〔tɛmz ‖ temz〕
n. （伦敦）泰晤士河

than 〔（强）ðæn ‖ ðæn；（弱）ðən ‖ ðən〕
conj. ❶比，比较
She looks younger than she is.
她看起来比她实际岁数显得要年轻。
❷（用于 rather，sooner 之后）与其……（宁愿……）
I would rather do some reading at home than go shopping with them.
与其和他们去购物，倒不如我留在家里读点书。
❸（用于 else，other 等之后）除了……（之外）
She has never been to a big city other than Chicago.
除芝加哥外她没有去过别的大城市。
prep. （后接计量数目）超过

My aunt stayed here for more than a week.
我姑妈在这儿待了一个多星期。

thank 〔θæŋk ‖ θæŋk〕
［过去式］thanked；［过去分词］thanked
vt. ❶感谢［（＋for）］
Thank you for your help.
感谢您的帮助。
❷要……负责，责怪
She can thank herself for this accident.
这个事故要怪她自己。
❸（用于 will 之后，表示客气的请求）感谢，请
I will thank you to turn on the lights.
请你把电灯打开。
n. 感谢；谢意；谢辞［P］
I must offer my heartfelt thanks to you.
我要向你表示衷心的感谢。

常用短语

Thanksgiving Day 感恩节

that 〔ðæt ‖ ðæt〕
pron. ❶那；那个；那人；那事；那东西［与指明近处的人或物 this 相对］
That's my English teacher.
那是我的英文老师。
❷（已被提到的）那个；那人；那事；那东西
Who told her that?
是谁告诉她那件事的？
❸（用作关系代词的先行词）那；那个
What is that which you have just stuffed into the plastic cup?
你刚才塞在塑料杯里的是什么东西？
❹（代替句中名词，避免重复）
The population of Japan is greater than that of England.
日本的人口比英国的人口多。
❺（用作关系代词，引导关系从句）
This is the book that I bought yesterday.
这是我昨天买的书。
a. 那，那个
That book isn't mine.
那本书不是我的。
ad.【口】那样，那么
Is the problem that easy?
问题有那么简单吗？
conj. ❶（引导名词从句）
He expressed the hope that we would keep in touch with his firm.
他表示希望我们与他的公司保

持联系。

❷(引导状语从句,表示原因或理由)因为,由于

We are glad that we have accomplished another arduous task.

我们都感到高兴,因为又完成了一项艰巨的任务。

❸(引导状语从句,表示目的或结果)为了,以至于

He is working hard that he can catch up with the class.

他努力学习,以便赶上班上的同学。

the〔ðə ‖ ðə〕,在元音前读作〔(强)ði ‖ ðiː;(弱)ðɪ ‖ ðɪ〕

art. ❶这(个),那(个)

Do you know the man talking to the boss?

你认识那个在跟老板说话的男人吗?

❷这些,那些

Have you got the letters I sent you?

我寄给你的那几封信收到了吗?

ad. ❶(用于形容词,副词比较级前)越……越……

The sooner, the better.

越快越好。

❷(用于比较级前)更加

If you put in a good word for him, he's all the more likely to get the job.

要是你替他说句好话,他就更有可能得到这份工作了。

theater, theatre〔ˈθɪətɚ ‖ ˈθɪətə〕

n. ❶剧场;电影院[C]

Let's go to the theater.

我们看戏去吧。

❷剧,戏剧;剧本,剧作[U]

He's interested in the theater.

他对戏剧感兴趣。

❸戏剧界[the]

❹(剧场等)全场观众[the]

The theater warmly applauded every item.

全场观众对每个节目都报以热烈的掌声。

theft〔θɛft ‖ θeft〕

n. 偷窃,盗窃[U]

He was put in prison for theft.

他因犯了盗窃罪而入狱。

their〔(强)ðɛr ‖ ðeə;(弱)ðɚ ‖ ðə〕

pron. (they 的所有格)他们的;她们的;它们的

That's their business.

那是他们的事。

theirs〔ðɛrz ‖ ðeəz〕

pron. (they 的名词性物主代

词)他(或她,它)们的东西;他(或她)们的家属(或有关的人)
Our house is older than theirs.
我们的房子比他们的古老。

them 〔(强)ðɛm ‖ ðem;(弱)ðəm ‖ ðəm〕
pron. (they 的宾格)他们;她们;它们
I can't find my keys. I forget where I put them.
我找不到钥匙了。我忘了把它们搁在哪儿了。

T

theme 〔θim ‖ θiːm〕
n. [C] ❶题目,主题,主题思想 ❷(音乐的)主题,主旋律

themselves 〔ðəmˈsɛlvz ‖ ðəmˈselvz〕
pron. ❶(they 的反身代词)他们自己;她们自己;它们自己
Heaven helps those who help themselves.
天助自助者。
❷(加强语气)他们(或她们)亲自;他们(或她们)本身
They built the hut themselves.
他们自己建造的这个小屋。

then 〔ðɛn ‖ ðen〕
ad. ❶那时,当时
He worked in that factory then.
他那时在那个工厂工作。
❷然后,接着
They chatted for a while and then went to work.
他们聊了一会儿,然后上班去了。
❸那么,既然这样
When will the manager be available, then?
那么经理什么时候可以接见我呢?
❹于是,所以
❺此外,还有
It was a nice bicycle, and then cheap.
这是部好脚踏车而且又便宜。
n. 那时,当时[U]
We waited for him till then.
我们等他等到那个时候。

常用短语

by then 到那时
from then on 从那时起
since then 从那时以后

theory 〔ˈθiərɪ ‖ ˈθɪərɪ〕
n. ❶学说;论说;……论[C][(+of)][+that]
Darwin spent more than 20 years working on his theory of evolution.
达尔文花了 20 余年时间研究他的进化论。
❷理论;学理,原理[U]

It seems good in theory, but it doesn't work in practice.
理论上它似乎很不错,但实际上却行不通。
❸意见;推测,揣度[C][+that]
My theory is that we'll have a cold winter this year.
依我看今年冬天会很冷。

there 〔ðɛr ‖ ðeə〕
ad. ❶在那里;到那里;向那里
She lives there.
她住在那里。
❷在那时;在那点上;在那方面
You've got a point there.
你这话有道理。
❸(用以引起注意,加强语气等)瞧,你看
There she is. 瞧,她来了。
❹(与动词 be 连用)有
There is a picture on the wall.
墙上有幅画儿。
❺(与动词 seem, appear 连用)好像……;看来……
There seems no doubt about it.
对于那件事似乎没什么疑问。
int. (表示满意,得意,鼓励,安慰,挑衅等)你瞧;好啦;喂
There, there, stop crying.
好啦,好啦,别哭了。
n. 那个地方,那里
They have moved somewhere near there.
他们搬到了那个地方附近。

therefore 〔'ðɛrˌfɔr ‖ 'ðeəfɔː〕
ad. 因此;因而;所以
He was down with the flu, and therefore couldn't come to the party.
他患了流行性感冒,因此未能前来参加宴会。

thermometer 〔θə'mɑmətɚ ‖ θə'mɒmɪtə〕
n. 温度计,寒暑表[C]

these 〔ðiz ‖ ðiːz〕
pron. 这些
These are hers.
这些是她的。
a. 这些的;这
These books are a bit difficult for pupils.
这些书对小学生来说有点儿难。

they 〔ðe ‖ ðeɪ〕
pron. ❶(主格)他们;她们;它们
The children are at school. They will be home around 4:00.
孩子们在学校里上课。他们 4 点左右回家。
❷人们
They say another school will be built here.

据说这里要再建一所学校。

thick 〔θɪk ‖ θɪk〕

[比]thicker;[最]thickest

a. ❶厚的;粗的

How thick is the board?

这块木板有多厚?

The wall is one meter thick.

这堵墙有一米厚。

❷浓的,浓厚的;黏稠的

It is dangerous to drive in a thick fog.

在浓雾天驾车很危险。

❸充满……的;长满……的[(+with)]

The air was thick with smoke.

空气中烟雾弥漫。

ad. ❶厚厚地;密集地

Don't spread jam that thick.

别把果酱涂得那么厚。

❷浓浓地;强烈地

My heart beat thick in the course of the interview.

在面试过程中我的心跳得厉害。

thief 〔θif ‖ θiːf〕

n. 贼,小偷[C]

The thief was caught in the act.

小偷当场被捕。

thigh 〔θaɪ ‖ θaɪ〕

n. 股,大腿[C]

thin 〔θɪn ‖ θɪn〕

[比]thinner;[最]thinnest

a. ❶薄的;细的;瘦的

She looks thinner than before.

她看上去比过去瘦了。

❷稀少的;稀疏的

He has thin hair.

他头发稀疏。

❸稀薄的;淡的

The air became even thinner when I climbed to the top of the mountain.

我爬到山顶时,空气变得更加稀薄了。

ad. 薄;细;稀;疏;微

Don't cut the bread too thin.

别把面包切得太薄。

thing 〔θɪŋ ‖ θɪŋ〕

n. [C] ❶物,东西

I can't see a thing in the dark room.

屋子里黑漆漆的,我什么也看不见。

❷事,事情;事件

We asked our group leader what was the next thing we had to do.

我们问了组长下一步要做什么。

❸【口】人;动物;家伙;东西

❹(尤指穿在外面的)衣服[P]

He flung his things on and rushed out the door.
他匆匆穿上衣服，奔出门去。
❺局面；情况；形势[P]
How are things?
情况如何？

think 〔θɪŋk ‖ θɪŋk〕
[过去式]thought；[过去分词]thought
vt. ❶想；思索
Think how much you can earn if you open a restaurant in such a good location.
想一想，要是你在这样的黄金地段开一家餐馆，你会赚多少钱啊。
❷认为，以为[+(that)]
We think that it is our duty to take care of the orphans.
我们认为照顾这些孤儿是我们的职责。
❸(常与 cannot, could not 连用)想象；理解[+wh-]
I can't think what you mean.
我不懂你是什么意思。
vi. ❶想；思索
Think before you leap.
先思而后行。
❷认为
Do as you think best.
你认为怎样最好就怎样去做。

常用短语

think about 想到
I'm thinking about my friends in the country.
我想起了在乡下的朋友。
think of 考虑到，想念，打算
She often thinks of home.
她常想家。

thinker 〔'θɪŋkɚ ‖ 'θɪŋkə〕
n. 思想家；思考者[C]

third 〔θɝd ‖ θɜːd〕
a. ❶第三的
❷三分之一的
n. ❶第三
He was the third in the speech contest.
他在演讲比赛中获得第三名。
❷三分之一

thirdly 〔'θɝdlɪ ‖ 'θɜːdlɪ〕
ad. 第三

thirsty 〔'θɝstɪ ‖ 'θɜːstɪ〕
a. ❶口干的，渴的
I am thirsty.
我很口渴。
❷干旱的，缺水的；吸水性强的
They watered the thirsty fields.
他们浇灌干旱的田地。
❸渴望的，渴求的[(+for)]
We are thirsty for adventure.

我们渴望冒险。

thirteen 〔θɝˈtin ‖ ˈθɜːtiːn〕

a. 十三(个,人,岁,点)的

n. 十三;十三个

thirteenth 〔ˌθɝˈtinθ ‖ ˌθɜːˈtiːnθ〕

a. ❶(与 the 连用)第十三的,第十三个的

❷十三分之一的

n. [C] ❶(与 the 连用)第十三(个);月的第十三日

❷十三分之一

thirtieth 〔ˈθɝtɪɪθ ‖ ˈθɜːtɪɪθ〕

a. ❶(与 the 连用)第三十的;第三十个的

❷三十分之一的

n. [C] ❶(与 the 连用)第三十(个);月的第三十日

❷三十分之一

thirty 〔ˈθɝtɪ ‖ ˈθɜːtɪ〕

a. 三十(个,人,岁,点)的

n. ❶三十;三十个

❷三十年代[the]

He lived in Canada in the thirties.

三十年代他住在加拿大。

this 〔ðɪs ‖ ðɪs〕

pron. ❶ 这;这个;这人;这事;这东西

Look at this.

瞧瞧这个。

❷以下(或以上)所述

This is how we got to know each other.

以上就是我们认识的经过。

a. ❶这;这个

This pen is mine.

这支笔是我的。

❷今,本

He will treat us to dinner this Friday.

这个星期五他要请我们吃饭。

ad. 【口】这么,这样地

The fish I caught was this big.

我捕到的那条鱼有这么大。

those 〔ðoz ‖ ðəuz〕

pron. 那些

Those who are going camping please gather at the gate.

要去野营的人请在大门口集合。

a. 那些的;那

Those apples are rotten.

那些苹果烂了。

thorough 〔ˈθɝo ‖ ˈθʌrə〕

a. ❶彻底的;完全的

The film was a thorough success.

这部电影获得了极大的成功。

❷周密的;完善的

The doctor was very thorough in his examination of the sick child.

医生对生病的孩子进行了仔细的检查。

❸十足的,彻头彻尾的

He is a thorough scoundrel.

他是一个十足的无赖。

though 〔ðo ‖ ðəʊ〕

conj. 虽然;尽管

Though he is rich, his life is not happy.

他虽然很有钱,但生活并不幸福。

ad. (一般放在句尾)然而,还是

It was a hard job; he took it though.

这是份儿苦差事,可他还是接受了。

thought 〔θɔt ‖ θɔːt〕

n. ❶思维;思考,考虑[U]

After serious thought, he decided to accept their terms.

经过认真考虑,他决定接受他们的条件。

❷想法;见解[C][(+of/about/on)]

Please write and let me have your thoughts on the matter.

请写信让我知道你对此事的看法。

❸(常用在疑问句、否定句中)意图,打算[U][(+of)]

He had no thought of hurting her.

他没想要伤害她。

❹思想,思潮[U]

thoughtful 〔ˈθɔtfəl ‖ ˈθɔːtfəl〕

a. ❶深思的,沉思的

That put us all in a thoughtful mood.

这使我们大家陷入了沉思。

❷细心的,注意的[(+of)]

You should be more thoughtful of your behavior.

你应该更加注意你的举止。

❸体贴的,考虑周到的[(+about/of)]

She is always thoughtful of her mother.

她总是很体贴她的母亲。

thoughtless 〔ˈθɔtlɪs ‖ ˈθɔːtlɪs〕

[比] more thoughtless; [最] most thoughtless

a. ❶欠考虑的,粗心的,轻率的

❷不顾及他人的,不为他人着想的

thousand 〔ˈθaʊzn̩d ‖ ˈθaʊzənd〕

a. ❶一千的;一千个的

❷成千的;许许多多的,无数的

I've warned him a thousand times.

我警告过他无数次了。

n. ❶一千;一千个

The town has a population of

10,000.
这个镇有 10,000 人。
❷数千；许许多多，无数[P][(+of)]
The flood took away thousands of lives.
洪水夺走了成千上万人的生命。

thread 〔θrɛd ‖ θred〕
n. ❶线[C][U]
Please give me a piece of thread.
请给我一段线。
❷线状物；一线，一丝[C]
a thread of hope
一线希望
❸头绪，思路；贯穿着的东西[C]
I must have skipped a page, because I lost the thread of the story.
我一定跳过了一页，因为我弄不清故事的脉络了。

threat 〔θrɛt ‖ θret〕
n. ❶威胁，恐吓[C][U][+to-v][+of]
❷构成威胁的人(或事物)[(+to)]
Some people think that machinery is a threat to their jobs.
一些人认为机器是对他们工作的一种威胁。
❸凶兆；征兆[(+of)]
The clouds brought a threat of rain.
阴云带来下雨的征兆。

threaten 〔'θrɛtn̩ ‖ 'θretn〕
[过去式]threatened；[过去分词]threatened
vt. ❶威胁，恐吓；扬言要[+to-v][+that]
He threatened to call the police.
他威胁着要叫警察。
❷预示，是……的征兆；有……的危险
Dark skies threatened rain.
天空发暗预示要下雨。
vi. 威胁，恐吓
I don't mean to threaten.
我没有威胁的意思。

three 〔θri ‖ θri:〕
a. 三(个，人，点，岁)的
n. 三，三个

throat 〔θrot ‖ θrəʊt〕
n. [C] ❶咽喉，喉咙
I have a sore throat.
我喉咙痛。
❷咽喉状部分；入口；窄路
the throat of a mine
矿井的巷道口
❸嗓音，嗓门

She sang at the top of her throat.
她放开嗓门大声歌唱。

through 〔θru ‖ θru:〕
prep. ❶穿过;通过
The river runs through our village.
这条河穿过我们的村子。
❷以,用,凭借
She got the position through her older brother.
她通过她哥哥获得那个职位。
❸由于,因为
They became unemployed through no fault of their own.
他们的失业不是由于自身的过失造成的。
❹从……开始至终;在……整个期间
I'll stay here from Monday through Friday.
我从星期一到星期五都会待在这儿。
❺完成;(做)完,(耗)尽
We are through school at 3:00.
我们3点放学。
ad. ❶直达[(+to)]
This train goes through to Shanghai.
这列火车直达上海。
❷从头至尾,直至完成
They played cards the whole night through.
他们通宵打牌。
❸(电话)接通[(+to)]
Can you put me through to Mrs. Lodge?
请给我接洛奇太太好吗?
❹透,彻底
We get through in the shower.
我们在雨中淋了个透。
a. ❶直达的,直通的
I'll take a through train.
我想搭直达列车。
❷完成的,结束的[(+with)]
Are you through with your letter?
你信写完了吗?

throughout 〔θru'aʊt ‖ θru:'aʊt〕
prep. ❶遍及,遍布
throughout the world
全世界
❷自始至终,在整个期间
He stayed at home throughout the winter.
整个冬天他都待在家里。
ad. ❶(通常用在句尾) 始终
He remained silent throughout.
他从始到终都保持沉默。
❷彻头彻尾地
The ring is gold throughout.

T

这戒指是纯金的。

throw 〔θro ‖ θrəʊ〕

［过去式］threw；［过去分词］thrown

vt. ❶投，掷，抛，扔［(＋at/to)］

She threw a towel to me.

她丢给我一条毛巾。

❷使突然陷入；把……投进［(＋into)］

The news threw the family into a panic.

这个消息使那一家人顿时惊恐不安。

❸匆匆穿上(或脱下)

She threw a shawl over her shoulders.

她把披肩随手往肩上一披。

vi. 投，掷，抛，扔

The young athlete throws well.

那个年轻运动员投掷得很好。

n.［C］投距，射程

My nephew lives only a stone's throw from my house.

我侄子住得离我家很近。

thumb 〔θʌm ‖ θʌm〕

n. 拇指［C］

thunder 〔ˈθʌndɚ ‖ ˈθʌndə〕

n. ❶雷，雷声［U］

After the lightning came the thunder.

闪电后接着是雷声。

❷似雷的响声，轰隆声［U］

We could hear the thunder of distant guns.

我们可以听到远处大炮的轰隆声。

❸恼怒；威吓，恐吓［C］［U］

Thursday 〔ˈθɝzdɪ ‖ ˈθɜːzdɪ〕

n. 略作 Thurs. 星期四

thus 〔ðʌs ‖ ðʌs〕

ad. ❶如此，这样，以此方式

They told her to water the flowers every morning, and she did it thus.

他们吩咐她每天早晨浇花，她照办了。

❷到如此程度

You may do thus far.

你可以做到如此程度。

❸因此，从而

He didn't work hard. Thus he was fired.

他工作不努力，因此被解雇。

ticket 〔ˈtɪkɪt ‖ ˈtɪkɪt〕

n.［C］❶票，券；车票；入场券

Admission by ticket only.

凭票入场。

❷(货物上的)标签

The ticket tells you the price of this dress.

标签告诉你这件衣服的价钱。

❸【口】(给违反交通规则者等

的）传票，罚单
Harris got a ticket for speeding yesterday.
哈里斯昨天得到一张超速驾驶罚款单。

tide 〔taɪd ‖ taɪd〕
n. ❶潮，潮汐；潮水[C][U]
The tide is in.
涨潮了。
❷浪潮[C]
❸潮流；趋势；形势[the]
We must not ignore the tide of popular opinion.
我们切不可忽视舆论的倾向。
❹【古】（现仅用于复合字）时节，季节[U]
Time and tide wait for no man.
岁月不饶人。[谚语]

tie 〔taɪ ‖ taɪ〕
[过去式]tied；[过去分词]tied
vt. ❶系，拴，捆，扎
He tied the magazines with string.
他用绳子把杂志捆起来。
❷打（结），系上
She tied the ribbon in a bow.
她把缎带系成一个蝴蝶结。
❸束缚，约束
I was tied to my job by a contract.
我因订有合同而不能离职。
vi. ❶打结
The ribbon ties well.
这条丝带打结打得很好。
❷打成平手[（＋with/for）]
The home team tied with the visitors.
主队和客队赛成平局。
n. [C]❶领带
❷联系；关系；纽带
We have established trade ties with these regions.
我们和这些地区建立了贸易关系。
❸束缚；牵累
She says the housework is a tie.
她说家务是个牵累。
❹得分相等，平手
The game ended in a tie.
这场比赛结果不分胜负。

tiger 〔ˈtaɪgɚ ‖ ˈtaɪgə〕
n. [C] ❶虎，老虎

老虎tiger

❷勇敢（或强悍）的人
The soldier was a tiger in fight.

那士兵作战勇猛。

tight 〔taɪt ‖ taɪt〕

[比]tighter;[最]tightest

a. ❶紧的,不松动的;牢固的

The lid was so tight that I couldn't open the box.

盖子太紧了,我打不开盒子。

❷拉紧的,绷紧的

He made sure that the rope was tight.

他看清楚绳子拉紧了。

❸紧身的,紧贴的

The shoes are too tight for me.

我觉得鞋子太紧。

ad. 紧,紧紧地;牢牢地

The doctor tied the bandage too tight.

医生把绷带绑得太紧。

till 〔tɪl ‖ tɪl〕

prep. ❶直到……为止

They danced till midnight.

他们跳舞跳到半夜。

❷(用于否定句)在……以前,直到……(才)

He didn't leave the office till 8 o'clock.

他直到8点才离开办公室。

conj. ❶直到……为止

The stranger waited till my master came home.

那个陌生人一直等到我主人回家。

❷(用于否定句)在……以前,直到……(才)

The struggle will not cease till the country achieves independence.

要到国家获得独立,斗争才会止息。

time 〔taɪm ‖ taɪm〕

n. ❶时间,时[U]

How time flies!

光阴似箭!

❷(办事所需)时间[U]

I have no time for novels.

我没有闲暇读小说。

❸次,回[C]

How many times have you been to France?

你到过法国几次?

❹(经历的)一段时光[C]

❺历史时期,时代[P]

Science makes progress with the times.

科学随着时代的发展而不断进步。

timetable 〔ˈtaɪmˌtebḷ ‖ ˈtaɪmteɪbl〕

n. [C] ❶(火车等的)时刻表

❷时间表;课程表

timid 〔ˈtɪmɪd ‖ ˈtɪmɪd〕

[比]timider;[最]timidest

a. 胆小的,易受惊的
He is timid by nature.
他天生胆小。

tiny 〔ˈtaɪnɪ ‖ ˈtaɪnɪ〕
[比]tinier;[最]tiniest
a. 极小的;微小的
Fleas are tiny insects.
跳蚤是极小的昆虫。

tip[1] 〔tɪp ‖ tɪp〕
n. [C] ❶顶端;尖端
He burnt the tips of his fingers.
他烧伤了指尖。
❷顶端附加的小件
Some smokers don't like cigarettes with tips.
有的烟民不喜欢抽有过滤嘴的香烟。

tip[2] 〔tɪp ‖ tɪp〕
n. 小费,赏钱[C]
I gave the doorman a tip.
我给了门房小费。

tire 〔taɪr ‖ ˈtaɪə〕
n. 轮胎;(车轮的)轮箍[C]
Tires are usually made of rubber.
轮胎通常由橡胶制成。

tired 〔taɪrd ‖ ˈtaɪəd〕
[过去式]more tired;[过去分词]most tired
a. ❶疲倦的[(+from/with)]
I was tired from having shoveling snow all day.
铲了一天的雪,我累了。
❷厌倦的;厌烦的[(+of)]
She was tired of watching television.
她看电视看得厌倦了。
❸陈腐的;破旧的
a tired car
一辆破旧的汽车

title 〔ˈtaɪtl̩ ‖ ˈtaɪtl〕
n. ❶标题,题目[C]
The title of the novel is "Sons and Lovers".
这部小说的题目是《儿子和情人》。
❷头衔;称号[C]
He was given the title of Marquis.
他被封为侯爵。
❸权利,资格;所有权[U][(+to)]
Do they have any title to the land?
他们对这土地有所有权吗?
❹(电影,电视中映出制作人员名单等的)字幕[P]

to 〔(强)tu ‖ tuː;(弱)tə ‖ tə〕,弱读在元音前读作〔tʊ ‖ tʊ〕
prep. ❶向,往,到
She lives in the house to the

T

right.
她住在右边的房子里。
❷(表示时间)直到……为止，在……之前
He wrote from morning to night.
他从早到晚写东西。
❸(表示程度，范围)到，达
He was wet to the skin.
他浑身湿透了。
❹(变)成，(变)到
The things are from bad to worse.
事情每况愈下。
❺(表示对象)对，向
She is kind to me.
她对我很友善。
❻属于，归于
The house belongs to him.
这房子是他的。
❼(表示比较，对比)比
We won the game by 5 to 3.
我们以 5 比 3 赢得了这场比赛。
❽对于，关于
It's a good thing to me.
这对我是件好事。

today 〔tə'de ‖ tə'deɪ〕
ad. ❶(在)今天
Are you going to watch the movies today?
今天你去不去看电影?
❷现今，在当代
Young people today have lots of things to do.
现在的年轻人有很多事情要做。
n. [U] ❶今天
Today is Mother's birthday.
今天是母亲的生日。
❷现今，当代
He is one of the best-known poets of today.
他是当代最负盛名的诗人之一。

toe 〔to ‖ təʊ〕
n. [C] ❶脚趾；足尖
❷(鞋，袜的)足尖部
shoes with pointed toes
尖头的鞋

together 〔tə'gɛðɚ ‖ tə'geðə〕
ad. ❶一起；共同，协力
They went to the theater together.
他们一起去看戏。
❷合起来，总共
All together, there were 15 people present.
总共有 15 人出席。
❸同时
The audience in the theatre stood up together.
剧场里的观众同时站了起来。

常用短语

together with 连同;和
He sold the house, together with the furniture.
他把房子连同家具都卖了。

toilet [ˈtɔɪlɪt ‖ ˈtɔɪlɪt]
n. ❶(有冲洗式马桶的)厕所,洗手间,盥洗室[C]
The toilet is at the end of the corridor.
盥洗室在走廊尽头。
❷梳妆,打扮[U]
She made her toilet carefully.
她仔细地梳洗了一番。

tolerable [ˈtɑlərəbl̩ ‖ ˈtɒlərəbl]
a. ❶可忍受的;可容忍的;可宽恕的
The pain is no longer tolerable.
这种疼痛让人再也无法忍受。
❷尚好的,还可以的,过得去的
My new job is tolerable.
我的新工作还说得过去。

tolerate [ˈtɑləˌret ‖ ˈtɒləˌreɪt]
[过去式]tolerated;[过去分词]tolerated
vt. 忍受;容忍,宽恕
I cannot tolerate lying.
我不容别人撒谎。

tomato [təˈmeto ‖ təˈmɑːtəʊ]
[名复]tomatoes
n. 番茄[C][U]
Tomatoes can be eaten raw.
番茄可以生吃。

tomb [tum ‖ tuːm]
n. 墓;墓碑[C]

tomorrow [təˈmɔro ‖ təˈmɒrəʊ]
ad. (在)明天
I'm leaving for New York tomorrow.
我明天动身前往纽约。
n. [U]❶明天
Tomorrow will be Sunday.
明天是星期天。
❷来日,未来
A still better tomorrow lies ahead of you.
展现在你们面前的是更加美好的未来。

常用短语

the day after tomorrow 后天

ton [tʌn ‖ tʌn]
n. ❶吨;公吨[C]
They extract 10 million tons of coal each year from underwater mines.
他们每年从水下煤矿中采掘1,000万吨煤。
❷【口】大量,许多[P][(+of)]
The movie star received tons of fans' mail.
那位影星收到了许许多多影迷

的来信。

tone 〔ton ‖ təʊn〕

n. ❶音质，音色，音调[C][U]

The teacher is speaking in a high tone.

教师正在大声说话。

❷腔调，语气[C]

He spoke in a tone of command.

他用命令的口吻说话。

❸声调，语调[C]

Mandarin Chinese has 4 tones.

汉语有 4 种声调。

tongue 〔tʌŋ ‖ tʌŋ〕

n. ❶舌，舌头[C]

a tongue depressor

压舌板，压舌片（检查口腔喉咙时用的）

❷说话能力（或方式）；口才

She has a bitter tongue.

她说话刻薄。

❸语言；方言；口语[C]

My mother tongue is Spanish.

我的母语是西班牙语。

tonight 〔tə'naɪt ‖ tə'naɪt〕

ad. 在今晚

We'll go to a concert tonight.

今晚我们去听音乐会。

n. 今晚[U]

Tonight is cold.

今晚很冷。

too 〔tu ‖ tuː〕

ad. ❶太，过分

This hat is too big for me.

这顶帽子我戴太大了。

❷【口】非常，很

She doesn't like traveling too much.

她不太喜欢旅行。

❸也；还；而且

She can speak English; she can speak French, too.

她会说英语，也会说法语。

常用短语

too… to… 太……以致不能……

The car is too expensive for me to buy.

这车太贵，我买不起。

tool 〔tul ‖ tuːl〕

n. 工具，器具，用具[C]

The gardener's tools are kept in the shed.

花匠的工具放在小屋里。

tooth 〔tuθ ‖ tuːθ〕[名复]teeth

n. [C] ❶牙齿

I brush my teeth twice a day.

我每天刷两次牙。

❷齿状物；（锯，梳，叉等的）齿

A comb has teeth.

梳子有梳齿。

❸嗜好；胃口[(+for)]

I have no tooth for candies.
我不喜欢吃糖果。

top 〔tɑp ‖ tɒp〕

n. ❶顶部；山顶；头顶[C][the][(+of)]
the top of the mountain
山顶
❷表面；上方[C][the]
the top of the page
这页的上端
❸首位，首席；上座[C][the][(+of)]
He is at the top of the class.
他在班上名列前茅。

常用短语

from top to toe 从头到脚；完完全全

topic 〔ˈtɑpɪk ‖ ˈtɒpɪk〕

n. 题目；话题；论题[C]

torch 〔tɔrtʃ ‖ tɔːtʃ〕

n. [C] ❶火炬，火把
❷【英】手电筒

torment 〔ˈtɔrmɛnt ‖ ˈtɔːment〕

[过去式]tormented；[过去分词]tormented

n. 痛苦；苦恼[C][U]
She suffered torments from her aching teeth.
她为牙痛所苦。

vt. 使痛苦，折磨；烦扰[(+with)]
Don't torment him with questions.
不要拿问题烦他了。

tortoise 〔ˈtɔrtəs ‖ ˈtɔːtəs〕

n. [C] ❶【动】陆龟；龟，乌龟
❷行动迟缓的人(或物)

torture 〔ˈtɔrtʃɚ ‖ ˈtɔːtʃə〕

[过去式]tortured；[过去分词]tortured

n. ❶拷打酷刑；拷问[U]
Many of the POWs died under torture.
许多战俘死于严刑拷打。
❷折磨，痛苦[C][U]
She suffered tortures from a toothache.
她受牙痛的折磨。

vt. ❶拷打；拷问
The police tortured him to confess his crime.
警察拷打他，逼他招供。
❷折磨；使为难[(+with/by)]
He was tortured with anxiety.
他为焦虑所苦。

total 〔ˈtotl̩ ‖ ˈtəʊtl〕

a. ❶总计的，总括的，全体的
What is the total population of Japan?
日本的总人口为多少？
❷完全的，绝对的

His plan ended in total failure.

他的计划以彻底失败告终。

n. 总数；合计[C]

Their expenses reached a total of 1,000 pounds.

他们的花费总计 1,000 英镑。

touch 〔tʌtʃ ‖ tʌtʃ〕

[过去式]touched；[过去分词]touched

vt. ❶接触，碰到

Don't touch the picture.

别碰这幅画儿。

❷触摸

She lightly touched his forehead.

她轻轻地摸了摸他的前额。

vi. 接触，碰到

They sat so close that their heads nearly touched.

他们坐得那么近，头都差不多碰到了一起。

n. ❶触，碰

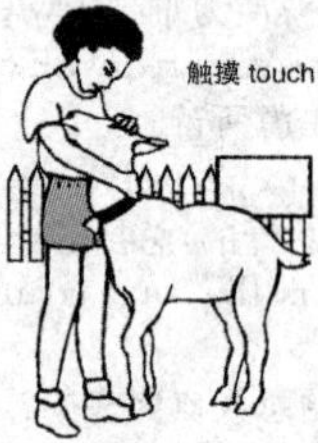

It will break at a touch.

那东西一碰就破。

❷接触，联系[U]

Let's stay in touch.

我们保持联络。

常用短语

be out of touch with 与……失去联系

keep in touch with 与……保持联络

Please keep in touch with me.

请和我保持联络。

tough 〔tʌf ‖ tʌf〕

[比]tougher；[最]toughest

a. ❶坚韧的，牢固的，折不断的

This material is as tough as leather.

这种料子像皮革般坚韧。

❷(肉等)老的，咬不动的

The steak was so tough that I couldn't eat it.

牛排太老了，我咬不动它。

❸强壮的，结实的

Donkeys are tough little animals and can carry big loads.

驴是结实的小动物，能载重负。

tour 〔tʊr ‖ tʊə〕

n. 旅行，旅游，游览[(+ around/of)][C]

I made a tour of Europe.
我到欧洲旅行了一趟。

tourist 〔ˈturɪst ‖ ˈtuərɪst〕
n. [C] ❶旅游者,观光者
❷(在国外参加)巡回比赛的运动队队员

tournament 〔ˈtɝnəmənt ‖ ˈtuənəmənt〕
n. 比赛;锦标赛;联赛[C]
He took part in a tennis tournament.
他参加了网球比赛。

towards 〔tɔrdz ‖ təˈwɔːdz〕
prep. ❶向,朝;面对
They walk towards the lake.
他们向湖那边走去。
❷将近;大约
We arrived at the hotel towards evening.
我们将近黄昏到达旅馆。
❸对于;关于
He changed his attitude towards me.
他改变了对我的态度。

towel 〔ˈtauəl ‖ ˈtauəl〕
n. 毛巾,手巾;纸巾[C]

tower 〔ˈtauɚ ‖ ˈtauə〕
n. [C]塔;塔楼;高楼
That's a television tower.
那是电视转播塔。

town 〔taun ‖ taun〕
n. ❶镇;市镇[C]
He was born in a small town 50 miles away from Chicago.
他出生在距芝加哥 50 英里的一个小镇上。
❷市区;市内商业区,中心区[U]
My husband is out of town just now.
我先生到城外去了。

toy 〔tɔɪ ‖ tɔɪ〕
n. 玩具,玩物[C]
The boy's favorite toy is a yo-yo.
这个男孩儿最心爱的玩具是溜溜球。

track 〔træk ‖ træk〕
n. ❶行踪;轨道;足迹[P]
We followed his tracks in the snow to a hut.
我们沿着他在雪地上留下的足

迹走到一间小屋旁。
❷小径,小道[C]
I followed the track through the forest.
我沿着林中小径走。
❸铁轨,轨道[C]
The track was damaged by the flood.
这段铁路线被洪水冲坏了。
❹【体】径赛运动[U]
❺跑道[C]
He runs around the track every morning.
他每天清晨绕着跑道跑步。

tractor 〔ˈtræktɚ ‖ ˈtræktə〕
n. 牵引车;拖拉机[C]

trade 〔tred ‖ treɪd〕
n. ❶贸易,交易,商业[U]
Japan does lots of trade with the United States.
日本与美国间的贸易频繁。
❷手艺;职业[C][U]
He is a blacksmith by trade.
他是个铁匠。

tradition 〔trəˈdɪʃən ‖ trəˈdɪʃən〕
n. [C][U]❶传统;传统思想
My parents did their best to keep up the family tradition.
我的父母为了保持家庭的传统竭尽全力。
❷惯例;常规
This decision represents a complete break with tradition.
这一决定完全打破了以往的惯例。
❸传说
According to the old tradition, the first American flag was made by Betsy Ross.
根据传说,第一面美国国旗是贝特西·罗斯缝制的。

traditional 〔trəˈdɪʃənl̩ ‖ trəˈdɪʃənəl〕
a. ❶传统的;惯例的;因袭的
These are the traditional food for Christmas.
这是圣诞节常吃的食物。
❷口传的,传说的

traffic 〔ˈtræfɪk ‖ ˈtræfɪk〕
n. [U] ❶交通
The bridge is open to traffic.
这座桥通车了。
❷交通行列;交通量
There is too much traffic on the road.
这条路上车辆行人太多了。

tragedy 〔'trædʒədɪ ‖ 'trædʒɪdɪ〕

n. ❶悲剧体裁[U]

Tragedy is a type of literature that involves death, suffering or disaster.

悲剧作品是文学作品的一种，内容常涉及死亡、不幸和灾难。

❷(一出)悲剧[C]

Shakespeare's *Hamlet* is one of the best-known tragedies.

莎士比亚的《哈姆雷特》是最有名的悲剧之一。

❸悲剧性事件；惨案；灾难[C][U]

The traffic accident is really a tragedy.

这次车祸真是个悲剧。

train 〔tren ‖ treɪn〕

[过去式]trained；[过去分词]trained

n. 列车，火车[C]

She came by train.

她是乘火车来的。

vt. 训练，培养

The firm trained its employees to be more efficient.

公司培训员工，使他们办事效率更高。

vi. 接受训练，锻炼[(+as/for)][+to-v]

He is training for the ministry.

他正在接受培训，准备做牧师。

traitor 〔tretɚ ‖ 'treɪtə〕

n. 叛徒；叛国者；背信弃义的人[(+to)][C]

a traitor to one's country

卖国贼

transfer 〔træn'sfɝ ‖ 'trænsfɜː〕

[过去式]transferred；[过去分词]transferred

vt. ❶搬；转换；调动[(+from/to)]

The factory will be transferred to Shanghai.

工厂要搬到上海去。

❷使换车；使转校

The teacher transferred the boy to another school.

老师将那个男孩儿转到另外一所学校。

❸转让，让渡

The man transferred his property to his nephew.

那人将财产让渡给他的侄子。

vi. ❶ 搬迁，转移；调任[(+from/to)]

He transferred to the Chicago office.

他调任到芝加哥办事处。

❷换车，转车

Transfer from the bus to that train.

从巴士换乘那班火车。
n. ❶迁移；移交；转让；转账[C][U]
He advised her transfer to a hospital.
他劝她转院。
❷转车车票；转车地点[C]
This route has many transfers.
这条路线有很多转车站。

translate〔træns'let ‖ træns'leɪt〕
[过去式]translated；[过去分词]translated
vt. ❶翻译，转译[(＋from/into)]
The novel has been translated into many languages.
这部小说已被译成多种语言。
❷(用另外的词语)解释，说明，表达
I translate his silence as a refusal.
我把他的沉默解释为拒绝。
vi. 翻译；被翻译
Many foreign expressions do not translate well into English.
许多外国用语不容易译成英语。

translation〔træns'leʃən ‖ træns'leɪʃən〕
n. ❶翻译[U]
❷译文；译本[C]

translator〔træns'letɚ ‖ træns'leɪtə〕
n. [C] ❶译者，译员，翻译；翻译家
❷翻译机

transport[1]〔træns'pɔrt ‖ træns'pɔːt〕
[过去式]transported；[过去分词]transported
vt. 运送，运输，搬运
Airplanes are used to transport passengers or freight.
飞机用来运送旅客或货物。

transport[2]〔'trænspɔrt ‖ 'trænspɔːt〕
n. ❶运输[U]
❷(军用)运输机，运输船[C]

transportation〔ˌtrænspɚ'teʃən ‖ ˌtrænspə'teɪʃən〕
n. [U] ❶运输；输送
❷【美】运输工具；交通车辆

trap〔træp ‖ træp〕
n. [C] ❶陷阱；罗网；捕捉器
The hunter set traps to catch foxes.
猎人设陷阱捕捉狐狸。
❷(陷害人的)圈套，诡计，阴谋
I knew perfectly well it was a trap.
我很清楚这是一个陷阱。

travel〔'trævḷ ‖ 'trævl〕

[过去式]travelled, traveled;
[过去分词]travelled, traveled
vi. ❶旅行
My uncle is travelling in South America.
我叔父在南美洲旅行。
❷(光,声音等)行进,传导
Light travels faster than sound.
光的速度比声音快。
❸旅行推销货物
He travels for our firm.
他为我们公司做旅行推销。
vt. ❶在……旅行,游遍
They travelled Australia from end to end.
他们游遍了澳洲。
❷经过,走过,驶过(距离)
The youngsters travel long distances to school every day.
孩子们每天走很远的路上学。
n. ❶旅行,游历[U]
We had 10 days' travel by train.
我们乘火车旅行了10天。
❷漫游;海外旅行[P]

treasure 〔ˈtrɛʒɚ ‖ ˈtreʒə〕
n. ❶金银财宝,财富[U]
It is said that the pirates buried their treasure on this island.
据说海盗把他们的金银财宝埋藏在这个岛上。
❷【口】不可多得的人才[C]
My secretary's a real treasure.
我的秘书是个难得的人才。

treat 〔trit ‖ triːt〕
[过去式]treated;[过去分词]treated
vt. ❶对待;看待,把……看做[(+as/like)]
Do not treat this serious matter as a joke.
不要把这件严肃的事情当做笑料。
❷处理;为……涂上保护层
This substance must be treated with acid.
这种材料得用酸来处理。
❸探讨;论述
The book treats some political problems.
该书论述某些政治问题。
❹医疗,治疗
The dentist is treating my teeth.
牙医正给我看牙。
❺款待,请(客)[(+to)]
He treated us to dinner.
他请我们吃晚饭。

treatment 〔ˈtritmənt ‖ ˈtriːtmənt〕
n. ❶对待;待遇[U]
The prisoners complained of

T

cruel treatment by their guards.
囚犯们抱怨看守虐待他们。
❷处理；论述[U]
I do not like his treatment of the theme in his new book.
我不喜欢他在自己新作中对这一主题的论述。
❸治疗；疗法[C][U][(＋for)]
a treatment for a cold
一个治疗感冒的方法

T

treaty ['tritɪ ‖ 'tri:tɪ]
n. ❶条约，协定[C]
The government has signed a treaty with Washington.
政府已与华盛顿签约。
❷约定，协议，契约[U]
We sold the house by private treaty.
我们私下订立协议把房子卖了。

tree [tri ‖ tri:]
n. 树；乔木；树状灌木[C]
Birds are singing in the trees.
鸟儿在树上歌唱。

tremble ['trɛbl̩ ‖ 'trembl]
[过去式]trembled；[过去分词]trembled
vi. ❶发抖；震颤[(＋with)]
Her voice trembled with anger.
她的声音因愤怒而颤抖。
❷焦虑，担忧[(＋at/for)][＋to-v]
She trembled for her daughter's safety.
她为女儿的安全而焦虑不安。
❸摇晃，摇动
The whole house trembled as the train went by.
火车开过时，整幢房子都晃动。
n. 震颤，发抖；震动[C]
Did you notice a tremble in his voice?
你是否注意到他的嗓音有点颤抖？

trend [trɛnd ‖ trend]
n. [C] ❶(海岸、河流等的)走向；延伸
❷趋势，倾向；时尚
the trend of modern living
现代生活的趋势

trial ['traɪəl ‖ 'traɪəl]
n. ❶试；试用；试验[C][U]
The trials show that smoking will do harm to people.
试验显示抽烟对人体有害。
❷考验；磨炼；棘手的事[C][(＋to)]
His blindness is a great trial to him.
眼睛看不见对他来说是非常麻烦的事。

❸审问,审判[C][U]
He was brought to trial on a charge of arson.
他因纵火罪被送法院审理。
❹尝试,努力[C]

trick 〔trɪk ‖ trɪk〕
[过去式]tricked;[过去分词]tricked
n.[C] ❶诡计;骗局;谋略;花招;奸计
He got into the castle by a trick.
他耍了个花招混进了城堡。
❷恶作剧
❸轻率愚蠢的行为
That was a rotten trick!
那样做太轻率了!
vt. ❶哄骗
They tricked me into making a mistake.
他们骗我犯错。
❷装饰,打扮[(+out/up/off)]
She tricked herself up for the banquet.
她打扮整齐去赴宴会。

trip 〔trɪp ‖ trɪp〕
n.[C]旅行;航行;行程[(+to)]
He has gone on a business trip.
他出差去了。

triumph 〔ˈtraɪəmf ‖ ˈtraɪəmf〕
n. ❶(大)胜利[C]
The football team achieved a complete triumph.
足球队大获全胜。
❷(大)成功,业绩[C]
The conquest of outer space is one of the greatest triumphs of modern science.
征服外层空间是现代科学最杰出的成就之一。
❸胜利(或成功)的喜悦,欢欣[U]
Great was his triumph on hearing this.
听到这事,他大喜过望。

trolley 〔ˈtrɑlɪ ‖ ˈtrɒlɪ〕
n.[C]【美】有轨电车(=streetcar);【英】无轨电车(=trolleybus)

troop 〔trup ‖ truːp〕
n.[C] ❶军队,部队[P]
The enemy troops withdrew.
敌军撤退了。
❷一群;大量,许多[(+of)]
The old man was surrounded by a troop of children.
那个老人被一群孩子围住了。

trouble 〔ˈtrʌbl̩ ‖ ˈtrʌbl〕
[过去式]troubled;[过去分词]troubled
n. ❶烦恼;忧虑[C][U]

Her heart was full of trouble.
她忧心忡忡。
❷困难；困境；麻烦的事[C][U]
Her son has got into trouble again.
她儿子又惹麻烦了。
❸麻烦，打扰，费事[U]
I'm sorry for the trouble I'm giving you.
给您添麻烦实在很抱歉。
❹纷争，动乱，骚乱[P]
There used to be a lot of troubles in that region.
那个地区过去发生过许多动乱。
❺故障[U][(＋with)]
What is the trouble with the car?
车出了什么毛病？
vt. ❶使烦恼；使忧虑
Losing a little money doesn't trouble me.
损失一点钱我并不在意。
❷(表示客气时用)麻烦
Could I trouble you to open the window?
麻烦你把窗子打开好吗？
❸(疾病)折磨，使疼痛
Her wound has been troubling her a lot this week.
这个星期她的伤口一直很疼。
vi. (常用于否定句和疑问句)烦恼；费心[(＋about)]
Don't trouble about that.
别为那件事费心了。

trousers 〔ˈtaʊzɚz ‖ ˈtraʊzəz〕
n. 裤子，长裤[P]
a new pair of trousers
一条新裤子

truck 〔trʌk ‖ trʌk〕
n. [C] ❶【美】卡车，载货汽车
We heard the occasional rumble of a passing truck.
我们偶尔听到卡车驶过的隆隆声。
❷【英】(铁路)敞篷货车

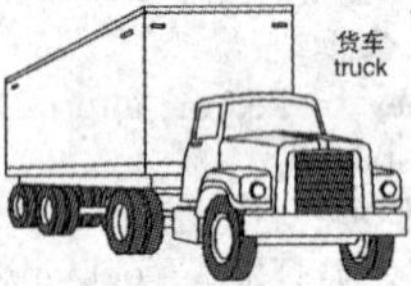

true 〔tru ‖ truː〕
[比]truer；[最]truest
a. ❶真实的，确实的
Is it true that they're getting married?
他们真要结婚了吗？
❷真的，非人造的
This is a true diamond.
这是一颗真的钻石。

❸适用的，合宜的[(+of)]
This is true of my farm.
我的农场适合这样。

truly 〔'trulɪ ‖ 'tru:lɪ〕
ad. 真实地；如实地；真正地
She loves him truly.
她真心爱着他。

trunk 〔trʌŋk ‖ trʌŋk〕
n. [C] ❶树干
The trunk of this tree is 4 meters thick.
这棵树的树干有4米粗。
❷(旅行用)大皮箱；汽车车尾的行李箱
Let me put your baggage in the trunk.
我来把你的行李放在汽车后部的行李箱内。
❸象鼻
❹躯干，身躯
The athlete has a powerful trunk.
那个运动员身躯强壮有力。

trust 〔trʌst ‖ trʌst〕
[过去式] trusted；[过去分词] trusted
n. ❶信任，信赖[U][(+in)]
I have no trust in him.
我不信任他。
❷托管，信托；管理，照顾[C][U]
Her child was left in my trust for the winter vacation.
她的孩子寒假里由我照顾。
vt. ❶信任，信赖
Why do you trust a guy like him?
你为什么要信任像他这样的家伙呢？
❷依靠，依赖
I can't trust my memory. I'd better write everything down.
我的记性靠不住，最好把什么都写下来。
❸【书】想，希望[+(that)]
I trust that your wife will soon get well.
我希望你太太能尽快痊愈。
vi. ❶信任，信赖[(+in)]
We always trust in her cautiousness.
我们对她办事谨慎一向是信赖的。
❷依赖[(+to)]
It won't do to trust to the inspiration of the moment when speaking to such a big audience.
对着这么多听众讲话，事先不准备仅靠一时的灵感是不行的。

truth 〔truθ ‖ tru:θ〕
n. ❶实话；事实；实情[the]
Neither witness told the truth.

两个见证人都没有讲实话。

❷真实性，实质[U]

I don't believe the truth of that story.

我不相信那个故事是真的。

❸真理[C]

All great truths begin as fallacies.

一切伟大的真理起初都被视为谬论。

try 〔traɪ ‖ traɪ〕

[过去式]tried；[过去分词]tried

vt. ❶试图；努力[＋to-v]

We'll try to improve our teaching methods.

我们要设法改进教学方法。

❷尝试，试行[＋v-ing]

Let's try knocking at the back door.

咱们敲后边的门试试。

❸试验，试用

Try this key.

试试这把钥匙。

vi. 试图；努力；试验；尝试

Try and eat a little.

试着吃一点吧！

n. 尝试；努力[C]

Who'd like to have a try?

谁想试试？

常用短语

try on 试穿

try out 试验

tube 〔tjub ‖ tju:b〕

n. [C] ❶管；筒

He slipped the telescope into a steel tube.

他将望远镜收进一根钢管内。

❷(装牙膏等的)软管[(＋of)]

I need a tube of toothpaste.

我需要一支牙膏。

❸【英】(有时大写)地下铁(道)[the]

She goes to work by tube.

她乘地铁上班。

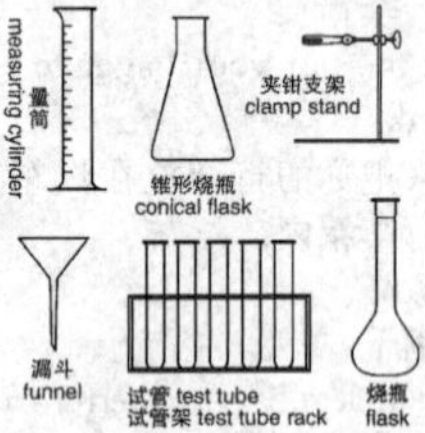

Tuesday 〔'tjuzdɪ ‖ 'tju:zdɪ〕

n. 略作 Tue. 星期二

tune 〔tun ‖ tju:n〕

n. ❶曲调；歌曲；旋律[C]

Tony wrote the words of the song and Anna wrote the tune.

托尼写歌词，安娜谱曲。

❷准确的音高，和谐的乐音[U]

The piano is out of tune.

这架钢琴走调了。

❸腔调，语气

tunnel 〔ˈtʌnl̩ ‖ ˈtʌnl〕

n. 隧道，地道[C]

Turkey 〔ˈtɝkɪ ‖ ˈtɜːkɪ〕

n. 土耳其

turn 〔tɝn ‖ tɜːn〕

[过去式]turned；[过去分词]turned

vt. ❶使转动，使旋转

He turned his head and saw a figure approaching in the darkness.

他转过头，看见在黑暗中有个人影走过来。

❷旋动，拧动

He turned the key in the lock.

他旋动插进锁里的钥匙。

❸翻，翻转

She turned a page.

她翻过一页。

❹使变得；使成为[(＋into)]

Heat turns water into vapor.

热把水变成蒸汽。

vi. ❶转动，旋转

The wheel turns when its axis moves.

轮轴动时，轮子也跟着转动。

❷旋动，拧动

The key turned in the lock.

钥匙在锁里转动了一下。

❸翻动，翻转[(＋to)]

Let's turn to page 8.

让我们翻到第 8 页。

❹变得；成为

Her face turned pale.

她脸色变得苍白。

n. [C] ❶转动，旋转

At each turn the screw goes in further.

每一次旋转都使螺丝钉更向里进。

❷转向，转弯；折回

The car made a left turn.

汽车向左转弯。

❸转角，折返点；弯曲部分

We saw a sharp turn in the road.

我们看到路上有一个急转弯。

❹(依次轮流时各自的)一次机会；轮次

Whose turn now?

该轮到谁了？

常用短语

take turns 轮流

turn into 使变成

turn off 关掉

turn on 打开;发动

Please turn on the TV.

请把电视打开。

turn out 结果是;证明是

It turned out (to be) true.

那件事结果是真的。

turtle 〔ˈtɝtḷ‖ˈtəːtl〕

n. [C]海龟;龟;甲鱼;玳瑁

T

TV 〔ˌtiˈvi‖ˌtiːˈviː〕

abbr. ＝television

twelfth 〔twlɛfθ‖twelfθ〕

a. ❶(与 the 连用)第十二的;第十二个的

❷十二分之一的

n. [C] ❶(与 the 连用)第十二(个);月的第十二日

❷十二分之一

twelve 〔twɛlv‖twelv〕

a. 十二(个,人,点,岁)的

n. 十二;十二个

twentieth 〔ˈtwɛntɪɪθ‖ˈtwentɪɪθ〕

a. ❶(与 the 连用)第二十的;第二十个的

❷二十分之一的

n. [C] ❶(与 the 连用)第二十(个);月的第二十日

❷二十分之一

twenty 〔ˈtwɛntɪ‖ˈtwentɪ〕

a. 二十的;二十个的

n. ❶二十;二十个

❷二十年代[the P]

Donna worked in Boston in the twenties.

二十年代唐娜在波士顿工作。

twice 〔twaɪs‖twaɪs〕

ad. ❶两次,两回

He comes to work twice a week.

他每周来上两次班。

❷两倍

The dining-room is twice as big as the kitchen.

餐厅是厨房的两倍大。

twin 〔twɪn‖twɪn〕

n. [C] ❶双胞胎之一

He is the younger twin of the two.

他是这对双胞胎中的弟弟。

❷孪生儿[P]

She gave birth to twins.

她生了双胞胎。

twinkle 〔ˈtwɪŋkḷ‖ˈtwɪŋkl〕

[过去式]twinkled;[过去分词] twinkled

vi. ❶(星等)闪烁;闪耀

Many stars are twinkling in the sky.

天空中有许多星星在闪耀着。

❷(眼睛)闪亮[(＋with)]

Ann's eyes twinkled with laughter.

安的双眼洋溢着笑意,闪闪发光。

n. 闪烁,闪耀

There was a twinkle in his eyes.

他的眼睛里闪烁着愉悦的光芒。

two 〔tu ‖ tuː〕

a. 二的;两个的

n. 二;两个;一对

type 〔taɪp ‖ taɪp〕

[过去式]typed;[过去分词] typed

n. [C]❶类型,型,式,样式[(＋of)]

What type of house would you prefer to live in?

你喜欢住哪一类房子?

❷典型;榜样

He is a perfect type of pedant.

他是个典型的书呆子。

vt. 用打字机打

Please type this letter for me.

请替我把这封信用打字机打出来。

vi. 打字

The young girl types well.

这个小姑娘打字打得很好。

typewriter 〔ˈtaɪpˌraɪtə ‖ ˈtaɪpˌraɪtə〕

n. 打字机[C]

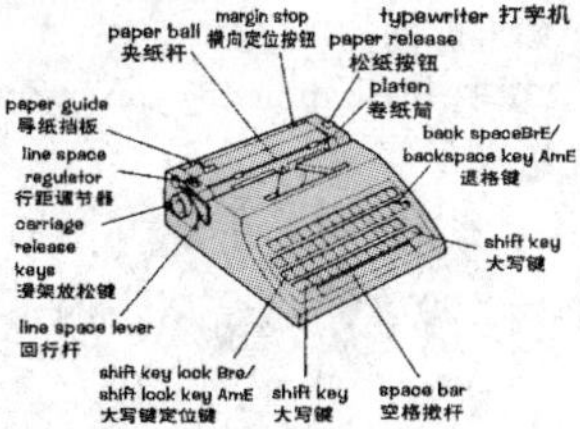

typhoon 〔taɪˈfun ‖ ˌtaɪˈfuːn〕

n. 台风[C]

飞碟UFO

U

顽童urchin

灌木丛undergrowth

ugly 〔ˈʌglɪ ‖ ˈʌglɪ〕

a. ❶丑的，难看的

ugly duckling

丑小鸭

❷邪恶的；丑恶的

umbrella 〔ʌmˈbrɛlə ‖ ʌmˈbrelə〕

n. ❶伞，雨伞

umbrella 雨伞

She was sitting under a striped umbrella.

她坐在一把条纹伞下。

❷保护伞，庇护

The new country was formed under the political umbrella of the United Nations.

这个新国家是在联合国的政治保护下创建起来的。

UN 〔ˌjuˈɛn ‖ ˌjuːˈen〕

abbr. =United Nations

n. 联合国

unable 〔ʌnˈebl̩ ‖ ʌnˈeɪbl〕

a. 不能的，不会的，不能胜任的[+to-v]

He is unable to swim.

他不会游泳。

uncertain 〔ʌnˈsɝtn̩ ‖ ʌnˈsɜːtn〕

a. ❶不明确的；含糊的；不确定的；不能断定的

The cause of the fire is still uncertain.

火灾的原因至今不明。

❷(人对……)不能确信，不确知[(+of/about)][+wh-]

He is uncertain about his future.

他对自己的前途没把握。

uncle 〔ˈʌŋkl̩ ‖ ˈʌŋkl〕

n. ❶伯父；叔父；姑父；姨丈；舅父
❷(用于对年长男子的称呼)大叔；叔叔，伯伯
Jimmy is uncle to all the kids who like to go boating with him.
那些喜欢和吉米一起乘船游玩的孩子都把他当叔叔。

uncomfortable 〔ʌnˈkʌmftəbl̩ ‖ ʌnˈkʌmftəbl〕
a. ❶不舒服的；不安的，不自在的
I feel uncomfortable with him.
和他在一起我感到不自在。
❷令人不舒服的；不方便的；令人不快的
This is an uncomfortable chair.
这把椅子坐起来不舒服。

uncommon 〔ʌnˈkɑmən ‖ ʌnˈkɒmən〕
a. 不寻常的；罕见的
That is an uncommon book.
那本书不多见。

unconscious 〔ʌnˈkɑnʃəs ‖ ʌnˈkɒnʃəs〕
a. ❶不省人事的，失去知觉的
He injured his head and was unconscious for one hour.
他伤着了头部，一个小时没有知觉。
❷不知道的，未发觉的[(+of)]
They were so quiet that he was completely unconscious of their presence.
他们非常安静，他完全不知道他们在场。
❸无意识的，不知不觉的
an unconscious error
无意识犯的错误

under 〔ˈʌndɚ ‖ ˈʌndə〕
prep. ❶在……下面，在……下方；在……里面
What are you wearing under your coat?
你外套里面穿的是什么？
❷少于；低于；未满
The truck was traveling under 50 miles per hour.
那辆卡车以每小时不到 50 英里的速度行驶着。
❸(表从属)在……的管理/统治/领导/监督之下
We work under an experienced engineer.
我们在一位经验丰富的工程师手下工作。
❹正在……之中；正受到；处于……情况之下
The bridge is under repair.
那座桥正在修理。

undergraduate 〔ˌʌndɚˈgrædʒuɪt ‖ ˌʌndəˈgrædʒuɪt〕

n. 大学生，大学肄业生[C]
（区别于 graduate 研究生）
a. 大学(或肄业)生的

underground 〔ˈʌndɚˈgraʊnd ‖ ˈʌndəgraʊnd〕
a. 地下的，地面下的
an underground passage
地下通道
n. [the]❶地面下层
❷(常大写)【英】地下铁道

understand 〔ˌʌndɚˈstænd ‖ ˌʌndəˈstænd〕
[过去式]understood；[过去分词]understood
vt. ❶理解；懂；熟谙[＋wh-]
Does he understand Japanese?
他懂日文吗？
❷据闻，获悉[＋(that)]
I understand her to be a distant relation of his.
据我了解，她是他的一位远亲。
❸认为；推断[＋(that)]
We understand that you don't approve of our idea.
据我们了解，你不赞成我们的想法。
vi. ❶理解；懂得
Now I understand.
现在我懂了。
❷熟悉[(＋about)]
He understands about diplomatic etiquette.
他熟知外交礼节。

understanding 〔ˌʌndɚˈstændɪŋ ‖ ˌʌndəˈstændɪŋ〕
n. [U] ❶理解；领会；认识
I doubt whether he had any real understanding of Shakespeare.
我怀疑他是否真正理解莎士比亚的作品。
❷理解力；判断力
The problem is beyond my understanding.
这个问题我无法理解。
❸谅解；协议；共议[(＋with)][＋that]
We came to an understanding after the argument.
争辩以后，我们达成了谅解。

underwear 〔ˈʌndɚˌwɛr ‖ ˈʌndəweə〕
n. (总称)内衣[U]

uneasy 〔ʌnˈizɪ ‖ ʌnˈi:zɪ〕
a. ❶心神不安的；担心的[(＋about)]
He was uneasy about my decision.
他对我的决定感到不安。
❷拘束的，不自在的
I feel uneasy in front of the audience.
我在观众面前感到不自在。

❸不稳定的;不宁静的
It was an uneasy alliance.
那是一个不稳定的联盟。
❹不安适的,不舒服的;不适宜的;不容易的

unemployment 〔ˌʌnɪmˈplɔɪmənt ‖ ˌʌnɪmˈplɔɪmənt〕
n. [U] ❶失业;失业状态
Millions of people were thrown into unemployment.
数百万人被迫失业。
❷失业人数
Youth unemployment is over 50%.
青年失业人数超过50%。

unequal 〔ʌnˈikwəl ‖ ʌnˈiːkwəl〕
a. 不相等的,不同的
These pencils are unequal in size.
这些铅笔长短不一样。

unexpected 〔ˌʌnɪkˈspɛktɪd ‖ ˌʌnɪkˈspektɪd〕
a. 想不到的;意外的;突然的
He died in an unexpected accident.
他死于一场事故。

unexpectedly 〔ˌʌnɪkˈspɛktɪdlɪ ‖ ʌnɪkˈspektɪdlɪ〕
ad. 未料到地,意外地
The loss was unexpectedly big.
损失大得出人意料。

unfair 〔ˌʌnˈfɛr ‖ ˌʌnˈfeə〕
a. 不公平的;不公正的,不正当的;不正直的
He was an unfair judge.
他是个不公正的法官。

unfortunate 〔ʌnˈfɔrtʃənɪt ‖ ʌnˈfɔːtʃənɪt〕
a. 不幸的,倒霉的
He was unfortunate enough to lose his parents.
他真不幸失去了双亲。

词汇拓展

unfortunately *ad.* 不幸地

unfriendly 〔ʌnˈfrɛndlɪ ‖ ʌnˈfrendlɪ〕
a. 不友好的,有敌意的
He is an unfriendly sort of fellow.
他是个不友善的人。

unhappy 〔ʌnˈhæpɪ ‖ ʌnˈhæpɪ〕
a. ❶不幸福的,不愉快的;痛苦的;悲惨的
She led an unhappy life.
她过着痛苦的生活。
❷不幸的,倒霉的
an unhappy accident
不幸的意外

词汇拓展

unhappiness *n.* 不幸

U

uniform 〔ˈjunəˌfɔrm ‖ ˈjuːnɪfɔːm〕

n. 制服;军服[C][U]

Tom looks handsome in uniform.

汤姆穿上制服很英俊。

unimportant 〔ˌʌnɪmˈpɔrtn̩t ‖ ˌʌnɪmˈpɔːtənt〕

a. 不重要的;琐碎的;无价值的

This word is unimportant.

这个字不重要。

union 〔ˈjunjən ‖ ˈjuːnjən〕

n. ❶结合;合并[U]

We are working for the union of the two countries.

我们正为这两国的合并而努力。

❷和谐;一致[U]

All the nationalities live together in perfect union.

各族人民非常和睦地生活在一起。

❸联邦,联盟[C]

❹工会;联合会,协会[C]

He was compelled to join the union as a condition of getting the job.

作为获得该工作的先决条件,他被迫加入了工会。

❺结合;结婚[C][U]

unique 〔juˈnik ‖ juːˈniːk〕

a. 唯一的,独一无二的;独特的

We had unique experience here.

我们在这里获得宝贵的经验。

unit 〔ˈjunɪt ‖ ˈjuːnɪt〕

n. [C]❶单位;单元

The hour is a unit of time.

小时是时间单位。

❷(全体中的)一个,一员

We regard husband and wife as the primary units of the family.

我们把夫妻视为家庭的基本成员。

❸(设备等的)一套,一组;装置

I'm thinking of buying a hi-fi unit.

我正在考虑买一套高保真音响设备。

unite 〔juˈnaɪt ‖ juːˈnaɪt〕

[过去式]united;[过去分词]united

vt. ❶使联合;统一;使团结

His aim is to unite his father-in-law.

他的目标是联合他岳父。

❷兼备(各种特性)

She unites common sense and

vision.

她兼具常识与见识。

❸使结婚

They were united at the church.

他们在教堂结婚。

vi. ❶联合;团结

Let us unite to fight poverty and disease.

让我们齐心协力来克服贫困和疾病。

❷联合;混合

Oil will not unite with water.

油水不相融。

United Kingdom 〔juˈnaɪtɪdˈkɪŋdəm ‖ juːˈnaɪtɪdˈkɪŋdəm〕

n. 略作 U.K. 联合王国(英国)

United Nations 〔juˈnaɪtɪdˈneʃənz ‖ juːˈnaɪtɪdˈneɪʃənz〕

n. 略作 U.N. 联合国

United States 〔juˈnaɪtɪdˈstets ‖ juːˈnaɪtɪdˈsteɪts〕(of America)

n. 略作 U.S.A. 美国

universal 〔ˌjunəˈvɝsl̩ ‖ ˌjuːnɪˈvɜːsəl〕

a. ❶全体的;普遍的;一般的

The government introduced universal secondary education years ago.

几年前,政府就倡导普及中等教育。

❷众所周知的

❸宇宙的;全世界的

Football is a universal game.

足球是一项全球性的运动。

❹万能的,通用的

This machine has a universal use in the home.

这种机器在家庭中有广泛的用途。

university 〔ˌjunəˈvɝsətɪ ‖ ˌjuːnɪˈvɜːsɪtɪ〕

n. 大学;综合性大学[C][U]

This university is composed of five colleges and one graduate school.

这所大学由五个学院和一个研究生院组成。

unjust 〔ˌʌnˈdʒʌst ‖ ˌʌnˈdʒʌst〕

a. 不公平的;不义的;不正当的

The proposal was unjust to us.

这个提议对我们不公平。

unkind 〔ˌʌnˈkaɪnd ‖ ˌʌnˈkaɪnd〕

a. 不仁慈的,不和善的,不客气的;不体谅的

He was unkind to me.

他对我很不客气。

unknown 〔ˌʌnˈnon ‖ ˌʌnˈnəʊn〕

a. 不知道的;未知的;陌生的;默默无闻的[(+to)]

The insect was unknown to

U

me.
我不知道这种昆虫。

unless 〔ən'lɛs ‖ ən'les〕
conj. 如果不，除非
I won't apologize unless she apologizes first.
除非她先道歉，否则我不道歉。

unlike 〔ˌʌn'laɪk ‖ ˌʌn'laɪk〕
a. 不同的；不相似的，相异的
The sisters are quite unlike.
这姐妹俩一点儿都不像。
prep. 不像，和……不同
Unlike him, his son is tall.
他的儿子很高，一点儿不像他。

unlucky 〔ʌn'lʌkɪ ‖ ʌn'lʌkɪ〕
a. ❶不幸的；倒霉的
It's an unlucky day today.
今天真倒霉。
❷不祥的；不顺利的；不凑巧的
Thirteen is an unlucky number.
13 是不吉利的数字。

unnatural 〔ʌn'nætʃərəl ‖ ʌn'nætʃərəl〕
a. 不自然的，造作的
He died an unnatural death.
他死于非命。

unnecessary 〔ʌn'nɛsəˌsɛrɪ ‖ ʌn'nesəsərɪ〕
a. 不需要的；不必要的；多余的
It is an unnecessary book.
这本书是多余的。

unpleasant 〔ʌn'plɛzn̩t ‖ ʌn'pleznt〕
a. 使人不愉快的；不中意的；讨厌的
He is an unpleasant fellow.
他是个让人讨厌的家伙。

until 〔ən'tɪl ‖ ən'tɪl〕
prep. ❶直到……时候，到……为止
Will this fish keep until tomorrow?
这条鱼能搁到明天吗？
❷(用于否定句)在……之前，直到……(才)
She didn't go to bed until 11 o'clock.
她直到 11 点才上床睡觉。
conj. ❶直到……时候，到……为止
He worked in Hong Kong until his father found him a job in Canada.
在他父亲给他在加拿大找到差事前，他一直在香港工作。
❷(用于否定句)在……以前，直到……才
She didn't go to bed until her daughter came back.
她一直等到女儿回来才去睡觉。

unusual 〔ʌn'juʒuəl ‖ ʌn'juːʒuəl〕

a. 不平常的；稀有的；奇特的
It's unusual for her to get angry.
她会生气真稀奇。

unwilling 〔ʌnˈwɪlɪŋ ‖ ʌnˈwɪlɪŋ〕
a. 不愿意的；不情愿的；厌恶的 [+to-v]
He gave an unwilling smile.
他勉强笑了一下。

up 〔ʌp ‖ ʌp〕
ad. ❶向上，往上；向楼上
They hung the map up.
他们把地图挂起来。
❷在上面；在楼上
She lives two floors up.
她住在再往上两层。
❸(价格，水平等)上升，上扬
Prices for consumer goods are going up.
消费品价格在上涨。
❹(姿态)直立地；起床；起来
Please stand up!
请起立！
❺在北方；向北方；向前；靠近
The man came up to me.
那个人向我走来。
❻彻底地，完全地
Cork the bottle up.
把瓶子加塞封紧。
prep. ❶向……上，往……上
❷在……之上
Her room is up those stairs.
她的房间在楼上。
❸向……的上游；沿着
She walked up the path.
她沿着小路走。

upon 〔əˈpɑn ‖ əˈpɒn〕
prep. ❶在……上面
He laid a hand upon my shoulder.
他把一只手放在我的肩上。
❷在……后；立即
I will give you a phone upon my arriving there.
我一到那儿就给你打电话。
❸根据；依靠
We acted upon his instructions.
我们根据他的指示办事。
❹(走)上……，(爬)上……
He climbed upon his horse.
他爬上马背。

upper 〔ˈʌpɚ ‖ ˈʌpə〕
a. ❶(地点，位置等)较高的；上面的；上首的
He has a scar on his upper lip.
他的上唇有一道疤痕。
❷上游的；内地的；北部的
the upper reaches of the Mississippi River
密西西比河上游
❸(地位，等级)较高的；上层的；上流的

This part of town is where the upper class live.
镇上这个地区是上层阶级的人住的。

upset 〔ˌʌpˈsɛt ‖ ˌʌpˈset〕
a. 心烦的，苦恼的；难过的；失望的[(+about)]

upside 〔ˈʌpˌsaɪd ‖ ˈʌpsaɪd〕
n. 上部；上面；上方
He turned the table upside down.
他把桌子反转过来。

常用短语

upside down 乱七八糟；颠倒

upstairs 〔ˌʌpˈstɛrz ‖ ˌʌpˈsteəz〕
ad. 在楼上；往楼上
He went upstairs.
他上楼了。

up-to-date 〔ˈʌptəˈdet ‖ ˈʌptəˈdeɪt〕
a. ❶最新的；包含最新信息的
an up-to-date report
有关最新情况的报告
❷时新的；新式的；现代的
an up-to-date factory
一座现代化的工厂

upward 〔ˈʌpwɚd ‖ ˈʌpwəd〕
a. 向上的；升高的
He would steal upward glances at the clock.
他不时偷偷往上看钟。
ad. ❶向上；在上面
The bird flew upward.
鸟儿向上飞去。
❷以上；超过
Children of 12 years and upward must pay full fare.
12岁以上的儿童必须付全费。

urban 〔ˈɝbən ‖ ˈɜːbən〕
a. 城市的；居住在城市的
urban life
城市生活

urge 〔ɝdʒ ‖ ɜːdʒ〕
[过去式] urged；[过去分词] urged
vt. ❶催促；力劝；激励；怂恿
They urged us to go at once.
他们催促我们马上去。
❷极力主张；强烈要求[(+on)][+that]
My friends urged that I (should) apply for the job.
朋友们极力劝我申请那份工作。
❸推进；驱策
We urged the school team on with loud cheers.
我们大声助威，激励校队拼搏。
vi. 极力主张；强烈要求
The citizens urged for the construction of a new hospital.

市民们强烈要求建造一个新医院。

n. 强烈的欲望；冲动；迫切的要求[C][the]

The vacation is coming and I have an urge to travel.

假期快到了，我很想外出旅行。

urgent 〔ˈɝdʒənt ‖ ˈɜːdʒənt〕

a. 紧急的，急迫的

It's urgent to let him know the truth.

告诉他真相是刻不容缓的。

词汇拓展

urgency *n.* 紧急

us 〔ʌs ‖ ʌs〕

pron. (we 的宾格)我们

They met us at the station.

他们在车站接我们。

usage 〔ˈjusɪdʒ ‖ ˈjuːzɪdʒ〕

n. ❶使用，用法；处理，对待[U][(+of)]

❷习惯，习俗[C][U]

❸【文】惯用法；语法[C][U]

use 〔ˈjuz ‖ juːz〕

[过去式]used；[过去分词]used

vt. ❶用，使用

May I use your pen?

我用一下你的笔可以吗？

❷发挥；行使

He promised to use his influence.

他答应运用他的影响力。

❸利用(他人，时间，机遇等)

They used him to shock the others.

他们利用他来吓唬别人。

vi. (现仅用于 used to do 结构)过去惯常，以前习惯于

We used to grow peanuts.

我们过去是种花生的。

n. ❶用，使用；利用[U][(+of)]

He makes good use of his time.

他能充分利用时间。

❷使用权；使用能力[U][(+of)]

He gave me the use of his bike.

他让我使用他的自行车。

❸用途，功能[C][U]

❹效用；益处；价值[U]

What's the use of worrying?

担心有什么用呢？

❺用法[U]

常用短语

in use 在使用中

The TV set is still in use.

那部电视机还在使用。

make use of 利用

Make good use of this opportunity.

U

好好利用这次机会。

put to use 用;利用

They put it to practical use.

他们把它加以实际运用。

used[1] 〔just ‖ juːst〕

a. 习惯于[(+to)]

I am used to walking to school.

我习惯走路上学。

used[2] 〔juzd ‖ juːzd〕

a. 旧的;用旧了的

My younger brother bought a used car.

我弟弟买了一部旧车。

useful 〔ˈjusfəl ‖ ˈjuːsfəl〕

a. 有用的;有益的;有帮助的[(+to/for/in)]

She gave us some useful information.

她给了我们一些很有用的信息。

useless 〔ˈjusləs ‖ ˈjuːsləs〕

a. 无用的;无价值的;无效的;无益的

usual 〔ˈjuʒʊəl ‖ ˈjuːʒʊəl〕

a. 通常的,平常的;惯常的,司空见惯的

Today he came home later than usual.

今天他回家比平时迟。

usually 〔ˈjuʒʊəlɪ ‖ ˈjuːʒʊəlɪ〕

ad. 通常地;惯常地

He usually goes out on Saturday night.

他星期六晚上经常出去。

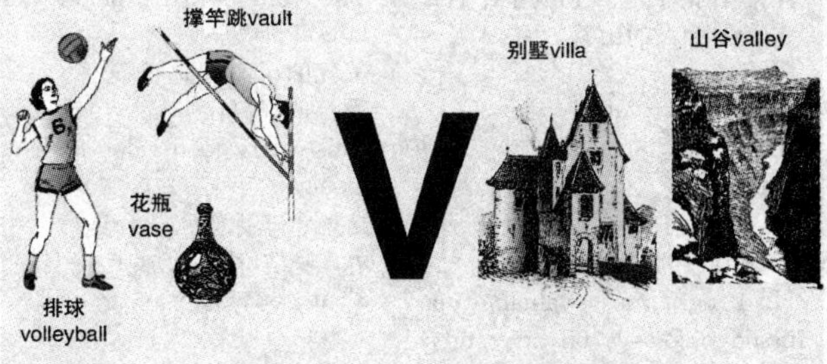

vacation 〔veˈkeʃən ‖ veɪˈkeɪʃən〕

n. 休假；假期；休庭期；休假日 [C][U]

School is closed for the summer and children are on vacation.

学校夏天关闭，孩子们放假。

vacuum 〔ˈvækjuəm ‖ ˈvækjuəm〕

n. 真空[C]

a vacuum cleaner

吸尘器

vague 〔veg ‖ veɪg〕

a. ❶(形状等)模糊不清的，朦胧的

I saw a vague figure in the dark.

我在黑暗中看到一个模糊的人影。

❷(想法等)不明确的；暧昧的；含糊的

a vague answer

含糊的回答

vain 〔ven ‖ veɪn〕

a. ❶爱虚荣的，自负的，炫耀的

She is vain and extravagant.

她既爱虚荣又奢侈。

❷徒然的，无益的

They made vain attempts to reach the mountaintop.

他们几次徒然尝试想攀登山顶。

常用短语

in vain 徒劳

He tried, but in vain.

他试过了，但是徒劳。

valley 〔ˈvælɪ ‖ ˈvælɪ〕

n. [C] ❶山谷；溪谷

The road gradually widened until we found ourselves in a large valley.

路渐渐宽了起来，最后我们走进了一个大的山谷。
❷流域
the Yangtze valley
长江流域

valuable 〔ˈvæljuəbḷ ‖ ˈvæljʊəbl〕
a. ❶值钱的，贵重的
He bought me a valuable diamond ring as a birthday present.
他给我买了一只贵重的钻戒作生日礼物。
❷有用的，有价值的[(＋for/to)]
This experience is valuable to me.
这一经历对我很有用。
n. 贵重物品，财产[P]
Guests may deposit their valuables in the hotel safe.
旅客可将贵重物品存放在旅馆的保险柜中。

value 〔ˈvælju ‖ ˈvælju:〕
[过去式]valued；[过去分词]valued
n. ❶重要性，益处[U]
This dictionary is of little value to you.
这本词典对你没有什么帮助。
❷价值；价格[C][U]
The value of the dollar may fall.
美元的币值可能下降。
❸等值；等价物[U]
This car is good value for your money.
这辆汽车你买得很合算。
vt. ❶估价，评价[(＋at)]
That watch was valued at $100.
那只表估计值100美元。
❷尊重；重视，珍视
My father values honesty beyond all things.
我父亲把诚实看得比什么都重要。

vanish 〔ˈvænɪʃ ‖ ˈvænɪʃ〕
[过去式]vanished；[过去分词]vanished
vi. ❶突然不见；消失
When I turned around, she had vanished.
我转过身，她已不见了。
❷消逝；绝迹
Many species have now vanished from the earth.
许多物种已在地球上绝迹了。

vapo(u)r 〔ˈvepɚ ‖ ˈveɪpə〕
n. ❶水汽；雾气；蒸汽；烟雾[C][U]
A cloud is a mass of vapor in

the sky.
云是天空中的一团水汽。
❷无实质之物；幻想[C]
What amazing vapors a lonely man may get into his head!
一个寂寞的人脑子里会生成多么令人惊异的幻想啊！

variety 〔vəˈraɪətɪ ‖ vəˈraɪətɪ〕
n. ❶多样化，变化[U]
What other ways do you know to add variety?
你知道其他增加变化的方法吗？
❷种种[(+of)]
He has a variety of interests.
他有多种爱好。
❸种类[C]
Hospitals deal with diseases of every variety.
医院诊治各种各样的疾病。

常用短语

a variety of 种种

various 〔ˈvɛrɪəs ‖ ˈveərɪəs〕
a. ❶不同的；各种各样的，形形色色的
Everyone arrived late at the party for various reasons.
由于种种原因，每个人赴会都迟到了。
❷好几个的；许多的
Wheat is grown in various parts of the country.
全国许多地方都种小麦。

vary 〔ˈvɛrɪ ‖ ˈveərɪ〕
[过去式]varied；[过去分词] varied
vt. ❶使不同；变更；修改
He never varied his habits.
他从未改变过自己的习惯。
❷使多样化
Teachers should vary their lessons to make them more interesting.
为了增加趣味，教师应该使自己的课多样化。
vi. 变化；呈多样化
That sort of thing varies from person to person.
那种事因人而异。

vase 〔ves ‖ veɪs〕
n. 花瓶；(装饰用的)瓶[C]

vast 〔væst ‖ vɑːst〕
a. ❶广阔的，浩瀚的，广大的
It is a vast desert.

那是一片辽阔的沙漠。

❷大量的,巨额的

A billion dollars is a vast amount of money.

10 亿美元是一笔巨款。

❸【口】非常的,莫大的

That will make a vast difference.

那将会有天壤之别。

vegetable 〔ˈvɛdʒətəbḷ ‖ ˈvedʒtəbl〕

n. [C]❶蔬菜;青菜

蔬菜 vegetable

We grow a lot of different vegetables.

我们种植多种不同的蔬菜。

❷植物人

The freshmen always seem like vegetables.

新生看起来总像植物人。

a. 蔬菜的

The doctor put me on a vegetable diet.

医生嘱我吃素食。

vehicle 〔ˈviɪkḷ ‖ ˈviːɪkl〕

n. [C] ❶运载工具;车辆

❷传播媒介;工具,手段[(+for/of)]

a vehicle for moral teaching

道德教化的媒介

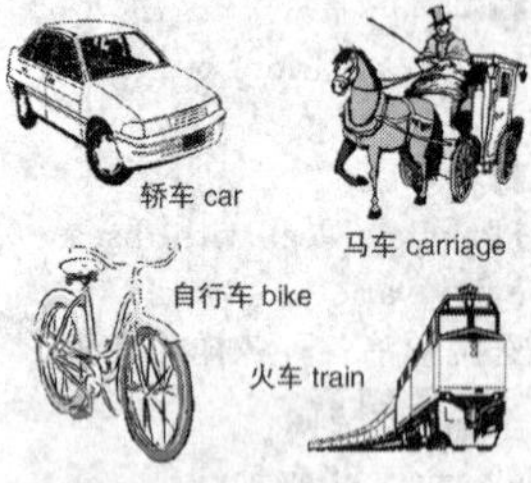

车辆 vehicle

veil 〔vel ‖ veɪl〕

n. [C] ❶面纱,面罩

The bride's face was covered in a white veil.

新娘的脸上蒙着白色的面纱。

❷帷幕;遮蔽物[(+of)]

There was a veil of mist over the mountains.

山上覆盖着一层薄雾。
❸托词；幌子[the][(+of)]
They did evil under the veil of patriotism.
他们在爱国主义的幌子下作恶。

venture 〔ˈvɛntʃɚ ‖ ˈventʃə〕
[过去式]ventured；[过去分词]ventured
n. [C] ❶冒险；冒险事业，投机活动
They were the astronauts on the first venture to the moon.
他们是首次登月球探险的太空人。
❷投机活动；企业
He has started a joint venture in Singapore.
他已在新加坡办起一家合资公司。
vt. ❶使冒险；冒……之险；拿……冒险
They ventured their lives in exploring the desert.
他们冒着生命危险去沙漠探险。
❷以……作赌注[(+on)]
He ventured large sums of money on speculative stocks.
他将大笔的钱拿去做股票投机。
❸大胆提出(或说出)；敢于[+to-v][+that]
I venture that you are wrong.
我冒昧说一句，你错了。
vi. 冒险；大胆行事[(+on/upon)]
He ventured upon an enterprise.
他大胆地开始了他的企业。

verb 〔vɝb ‖ vɜːb〕
n.【文】动词[C]

version 〔ˈvɝʒən ‖ ˈvɜːʃən〕
n. [C]❶译文；译本[(+of)]
the German version of the novel
这部小说的德文译本
❷(某人或从某角度对事物的)一种描述，说法[(+of)]
This is her version of the affair.
这是她对这件事的说明。

very 〔ˈvɛrɪ ‖ ˈverɪ〕
ad. ❶非常，很
He walked very fast.
他走得非常快。
❷(用于形容词最高级或 first, last, opposite, own 等之前)真正地，极其
This is the very best novel I've read lately.
这是我最近读过的最好的小说。

❸(用于否定句)(不)太……,(不)怎样……;决(非)
That game was not very exciting.
那场比赛并不怎么精彩刺激。
a. ❶正是;恰好是
She died in the very room.
她就是在这个房间里逝世的。
❷仅仅;甚至
She shuddered at the very thought of a snake.
一想到蛇她就惊恐万状。
❸完全的,十足的
What he said turned out to be the very reverse of the truth.
结果发现他所说的与事实完全相反。

vessel ['vɛsḷ ‖ 'vesl]
n.[C] ❶船,舰
❷容器,器皿
Cups, basins, pots, bottles, casks, etc., are vessels that hold liquids.
杯、盆、罐、瓶、桶等都是盛液体的容器。
❸血管,脉管

vibrate ['vaɪbret ‖ 'vaɪbreɪt]
[过去式]vibrated;[过去分词]vibrated
vi. ❶颤动;振动;震动
The bridge vibrated under a heavy truck.
桥因重载卡车经过而颤动。
❷(情感上)被撼动;感应,共鸣

victim ['vɪktɪm ‖ 'vɪktɪm]
n.[C] ❶牺牲者,遇难者[(+of)]
The victims of the explosion were buried last week.
爆炸事故的罹难者于上周举行了葬礼。
❷受害者,受骗者,受灾者[(+of)]
They are the victims of the civil war.
他们是内战的受害者。
❸(祭神的)牺牲品,祭品

victory ['vɪktərɪ ‖ 'vɪktərɪ]
n. 胜利;战胜;成功[C][U]
The basketball team had a string of victories last season.
这个篮球队在上一个赛季中赢得了一连串的胜利。

view [vju ‖ vjuː]
n. ❶视力;视野[U]
Victory is in view.
胜利在望。
❷观看;眺望[(+of)]
There's a fine view of the lake from our hotel window.
从我们旅馆的窗口可以看到湖的美丽风光。

❸景色;风景画,风景照片[C]
❹看法,观点[C][+(that)][(+about/on)]
May I have your views on the question?
可以让我知道您对这个问题的看法吗?
She tried writing out her views.
她试着把自己的想法写下来。

viewpoint [ˈvjuˌpɔɪnt ‖ ˈvjuːpɔɪnt]
n. 观察位置,视角;观点,见解[C]
A heavy rain is good from the viewpoint of farmers.
从农民的立场来看,下场大雨是好事。

village [ˈvɪlɪdʒ ‖ ˈvɪlɪdʒ]
n. ❶村庄,村[C]
They lived in a remote mountain village.
他们住在一个偏僻的山村。
❷村民[the]
The whole village turned out to watch the parade.
全村的人都出来观看游行。

vinegar [ˈvɪnɪgɚ ‖ ˈvɪnɪgə]
n. 醋[U]
wine vinegar
葡萄酒醋

violence [ˈvaɪələns ‖ ˈvaɪələns]
n. [U] ❶暴力,暴力行为
The dictator ruled with violence.
独裁者实施暴政。
❷激烈,猛烈
The wind blew with great violence.
风异常猛烈地吹着。
❸强力,猛劲
He flung the door open with violence.
他猛然将门打开。

violin [ˌvaɪəˈlɪn ‖ ˌvaɪəˈlɪn]
n. [C] ❶小提琴
❷小提琴演奏者,小提琴手

virgin [ˈvɝdʒɪn ‖ ˈvɜːdʒɪn]
n. [C]❶处女,未婚女子
❷(大写)圣母马利亚[the]

virtual [ˈvɝtʃuəl ‖ ˈvɜːtʃuəl]
a. 事实上的,实际上的,实质上的;虚拟的

virtue [ˈvɝtʃu ‖ ˈvɜːtʃuː]
n. ❶ 善,德[U]
He is a man of great virtue.
他是一个品德高尚的人。
❷美德,德行[C]
Kindness is but one of his virtues.
善良仅是他的美德之一。
❸贞操[U]
❹优点,长处[C][U]

The car has its drawbacks and it has its virtues.
这辆汽车有其短处，也有其长处。

visible ['vɪzəbḷ ‖ 'vɪzəbl]
a. ❶可看见的[(+to)]
These tiny creatures are hardly visible to the naked eyes.
这些微小的生物肉眼几乎看不见。
❷显而易见的，(公众人物)引人注目的
She showed no visible nervousness.
她没有表现出明显的紧张。
❸常在公众场合(或报刊，电视上)露面的
Mr. Brown is a highly visible politician.
布朗先生是一位经常公开露面的政客。

vision ['vɪʒən ‖ 'vɪʒən]
n. ❶视力；视觉[U]
People wear glasses to improve their vision.
人们戴眼镜以改善视力。
❷看见；所见事物[C][U]
The vision of the table loaded with food made our mouths water.
看见桌上堆满了食物使我们垂涎欲滴。
❸洞察力，眼光[U]
He is a man of great vision.
他是位有远见的人。

visit ['vɪzɪt ‖ 'vɪzɪt]
[过去式] visited; [过去分词] visited
vt. ❶参观；拜访；探望
This afternoon we're going to visit a friend in hospital.
今天下午我们将去探望一位住院的朋友。
❷视察
The Prime Minister visited several factories in our city.
首相视察了我市几个工厂。
vi. ❶参观；访问
He is visiting in New York.
他现在人在纽约。
❷【美】暂住[(+with)]
Amy will come down and visit with you for a couple of days.
艾米会来你这儿做客住上几天。
n. [C] ❶参观；访问；探望
I paid a visit to my former teacher of English.
我拜访了我以前的英语老师。
❷暂住，逗留
He met his future father-in-law during his visit to Boston.

他在波士顿小住期间遇见了他未来的岳父。

常用短语

pay/make a visit to 参观;访问

visitor 〔ˈvɪzɪtɚ ‖ ˈvɪzɪtə〕

n. [C] ❶访问者;留住客;探病者

Mary was a frequent visitor to our house.

玛丽过去是我们家的常客。

❷观光者;参观者

There are many visitors to the White House every year.

每年参观白宫的游客很多。

visual 〔ˈvɪʒuəl ‖ ˈvɪʒuəl〕

a. 视力的;视觉的;看得见的,可被看见的;视觉的

visual objects

眼睛看得见的东西

vitamin 〔ˈvaɪtəmɪn ‖ ˈvaɪtəmɪn〕

n. 维生素[P]

vivid 〔ˈvɪvɪd ‖ ˈvɪvɪd〕

a. ❶(色彩,光线等)鲜艳的;鲜明的;强烈的

The color of her dress is vivid.

她衣服的颜色很鲜艳。

❷生动的;逼真的;清晰的

I have a vivid memory of her face.

我清楚地记得她的脸。

vocabulary 〔vəˈkæbjəˌlɛrɪ ‖ vəˈkæbjʊlərɪ〕

n. 词汇;语汇;用字范围[C][U]

Wide reading will increase your vocabulary.

博览群书会增加你的词汇量。

vocation 〔voˈkeʃən ‖ vəʊˈkeɪʃən〕

n. 行业,职业[C]

voice 〔vɔɪs ‖ vɔɪs〕

n. ❶声音;嗓子[C][U]

His son talked of his trip to Hong Kong in a cheerful voice.

他儿子兴高采烈地谈了他的香港之行。

❷表达的意见,发言权[U][(+in)]

I have little voice in the matter.

我对此事没有多少发言权。

❸【文】语态

volcano 〔vɑlˈkeno ‖ vɒlˈkeɪnəʊ〕

n. 火山[C]

volleyball 〔ˈvɑlɪˌbɔl ‖ ˈvɒlɪbɔːl〕

n. 排球;排球运动

play volleyball

打排球

volume 〔ˈvɑljəm ‖ ˈvɒljuːm〕

n. ❶卷,册[C]

That encyclopedia is in 20 volumes.

那套百科全书有20卷。

❷体积；容积[U]
The volume of this container is 1,000 cubic feet.
该容器的容积是 1,000 立方英尺。
❸(生产，交易等的)量；额[C][U]
The volume of business with Japan has increased.
与日本的贸易额增加了。
❹音量[U]

voluntary [ˈvɑlənˌtɛrɪ ‖ ˈvɒləntərɪ]
a. 自愿的，志愿的

volunteer [ˌvɑlənˈtɪr ‖ ˈvɒləntɪə]
n. [C] ❶自愿参加者，志愿者，义工
Any volunteers?
有自告奋勇的吗?
❷志愿兵，义勇兵

vote [vot ‖ vəʊt]
[过去式]voted；[过去分词]voted
n. ❶选举，投票，表决[C]
The matter will be decided by vote.
此事将投票表决。
❷票，选票[C][(+for/against)]
There were 16 votes in favor of my suggestion, and 15 against.
16 票赞成我的建议，15 票反对。
❸选举权，投票权[the]
In that country, people get the vote at the age of 18.
在那个国家，人们年满 18 岁获得选举权。
vi. 投票；表决；选举[(+for/against/on)][+to-v]
As we are not unanimous for this matter, let's vote on it.
因为我们在这件事上无法取得同意，我们表决吧。
vt. ❶投票决定；投票同意；选举；表决
They voted her their headmistress.
他们选她做校长。
❷公议，一致认为
The party was voted a great success.
大家一致认为聚会很成功。

voyage [ˈvɔɪ·ɪdʒ ‖ ˈvɔɪɪdʒ]
n. [C] ❶航海，航行，乘船旅游
The voyage from America to France used to take two months.
从美国到法国的航行过去要花两个月时间。
❷航空，空中旅行；太空旅行

W

鲸鱼
whale

结婚
wedding

除草weed

W

摔跤wrestling

wage 〔wedʒ ‖ weɪdʒ〕
n. 薪水；报酬［P］
His wages are 300 dollars a week.
他的工资为每周 300 美元。

waist 〔west ‖ weɪst〕
n.［C］❶腰，腰部
She tied an apron around her waist.
她将围裙系在腰间。
❷(衣服的)腰身部分
The dress needs taking in a bit at the waist.
这件连衫裙腰身需要改小一些。
❸背心；紧身胸衣；衬衫；小孩的内衣

wait 〔wet ‖ weɪt〕
［过去式］waited；［过去分词］waited
vi. ❶等，等待［(＋for)］［＋to-v］
Dodge is waiting to have a word with you.
道奇正等着和你说话。
❷延缓处理；耽搁
That matter can wait.
那件事可以暂时搁置一下。
❸(常用进行时)已准备好，已就绪
Your dinner is waiting.
你的晚餐已经做好了。
vt. ❶等待(机会等)
He held her hand and waited the answer.
他握着她的手等待回答。
❷【口】(为……)延后(用餐等)［(＋for)］
Don't wait supper for me.
别等我吃晚饭。

waiter 〔'wetɚ ‖ weɪtə〕
n. (男)侍者，服务生［C］
The waiter came to take their

W

order.
男侍来请他们点菜。

waitress 〔ˈwetrɪs ‖ ˈweɪtrɪs〕
n. 女服务生，女侍应生[C]

wake 〔wek ‖ weɪk〕
[过去式]waked, woke; [过去分词]waked, woken
vi. 醒来；醒着[(+up)]
I woke up at 6 this morning.
今天早晨我 6 点钟醒来。
vt. 唤醒，弄醒[(+up)]
Please wake me up at 7 : 00.
请于 7 点钟叫醒我。

walk 〔wɔk ‖ wɔːk〕
[过去式]walked; [过去分词]walked
vi. 走；散步
He likes walking.
他喜欢步行。
vt. ❶走过，走遍；沿……走
I heard him walking the floor.
我听见他在地板上踱步。
❷陪……走；帮助(某人)走
The mother walked the child out of the room.
母亲带着孩子走出了房间。
❸遛(狗等)
❹推着……走；挪动
He walked his bike up the hill.
他推着自行车上的山。
n. ❶走；步行；散步[C]
She used to take a walk after supper.
她过去常在晚饭后散步。
❷步行距离
The bank is a 10 minutes' walk from here.
银行从这里走过去 10 分钟就到了。
❸步法，步行姿态[U]
I knew her by her walk.
我从走路的姿势看出是她。

wall 〔wɔl ‖ wɔːl〕
n. 墙，壁；围墙；城墙[C]

wallet 〔ˈwɑlɪt ‖ ˈwɒlɪt〕
n. [C] ❶皮夹子，钱包
❷(皮制的)公事包；旅行袋

wander 〔ˈwɑndɚ ‖ ˈwɒndə〕
[过去式] wandered; [过去分词]wandered
vi. ❶漫游；闲逛；流浪；徘徊
He wandered in the streets.
他在街上闲逛。
❷离开正道；离题[(+ from/off)]
During the storm the ship wandered from its course.
船在风暴中偏离了航道。
❸(精神)错乱；(思想)混乱；出神，开小差
My attention wandered.
我走了神。

vt. 漫游于，徘徊于
The poet wanted to wander those countries on his own.
诗人想独自漫游那些国家。

want 〔wɑnt ‖ wɒnt〕
［过去式］wanted；［过去分词］wanted
vt. ❶要，想要
I don't want my daughter taken out after dark.
我不愿有人在天黑以后带我女儿外出。
❷想见；要求（某人）来；想用（某人）
You're wanted on the phone.
有你的电话。
❸缉拿，追捕
The robber is wanted by the police.
警方在通缉那个强盗。
❹需要［＋v-ing］
This wants washing.
这个需要洗了。
vi. ❶缺乏，缺少；需要［（＋for）］
You shall want for nothing.
你不会缺任何东西。
❷生活困苦，贫困
The opera star wanted in her later years.
那位歌剧明星晚年生活困苦。
n. ［U］❶缺乏，不足［（＋of）］
He did not get the promotion for want of judgement.
他因缺乏判断力而未获提升。
❷匮乏，贫困
❸需要
The house is in want of repair.
这座房子需要修理。

war 〔wɔr ‖ wɔː〕
n. ［C］［U］❶战争
❷斗争；竞赛；对抗，冲突
The mayor is confident the war against crime will be won.
市长确信对犯罪活动的斗争必定胜利。

warm 〔wɔrm ‖ wɔːm〕
［比］warmer；［最］warmest
a. ❶温暖的，暖和的
The day was warm and cloudless.
天气温暖而晴朗。
❷保暖的；使暖的
❸热情的；衷心的
Aunt Sue is a very warm person.
苏阿姨是个极为热诚的人。

warn 〔wɔrn ‖ wɔːn〕
［过去式］warned；［过去分词］warned
vt. ❶警告；告诫；提醒［（＋of/against）］

W

He warned me against going outside alone at night.
他提醒我晚上不要单独出去。
❷预先通知[(+that)]
The weather station warned that a hurricane was coming.
气象台预报飓风即将来临。

warning ['wɔrnɪŋ‖'wɔːnɪŋ]
n. 警告；告诫；警报[C][U]
I gave him a warning.
我给了他一个警告。

was [wɑz‖wɒz]
(is 或 am 的过去式)
It was rainy yesterday.
昨天是雨天。

wash [wɑʃ‖wɒʃ]
[过去式]washed；[过去分词] washed
vt. ❶洗，洗涤
She washed her face and hands, then went downstairs.
她洗了脸和手之后走下楼去。
❷洗掉[(+off/away)]
They washed those marks off the wall.
他们把墙上的那些印记洗掉了。
❸洗刷(罪过)
He is trying to wash away his sins.
他正试图洗刷他的罪过。
vi. ❶洗手；洗脸；洗澡；洗衣
He likes to wash in cold water.
他喜欢用冷水洗澡。
❷耐洗
This cloth washes well.
这种布很耐洗。
❸冲击，拍打；溅泼[(+against/over)]
Huge waves washed over the deck of the ship.
巨浪从船甲板上打了过去。

Washington ['wɑʃɪŋtən‖wɒʃɪŋtən]
n. ❶美国华盛顿州；美国首都华盛顿
❷美国第一任总统华盛顿

waste [west‖weɪst]
[过去式]wasted；[过去分词] wasted
vt. ❶浪费；滥用；未充分利用[(+on)]
Don't waste your time and energy on trifles.
别把你的时间和精力浪费在琐事上。
❷使荒芜；使荒废
The drought wasted the land.
旱灾使田地荒芜。
n. ❶浪费；滥用[U][(+of)]
Doing such a job is a waste of his talents.

做这种工作是在浪费他的才能。

❷废(弃)物;废料[U];排泄物

A lot of poisonous waste from the chemical works polluted the river.

化工厂的许多有毒废料污染了这条河。

❸荒地,荒野[P]

Few animals can exist in the frozen wastes of the Arctic.

几乎没有动物能在北极洲冰封的荒芜地区生存。

watch [wɑtʃ ‖ wɒtʃ]

[过去式]watched;[过去分词]watched

n. ❶表[C]

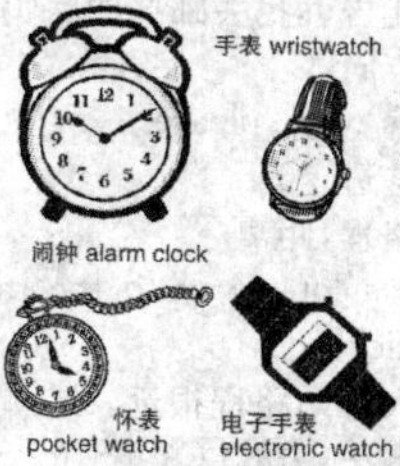

❷看守,监视;警戒,注意[U]

The would-be murderer was kept under close watch.

那个意欲行凶的人被置于严密监视下。

❸守卫,看守,值班人[C]

He is on watch.

他在值班。

vt. ❶观看;注视;留神观察

I watched him put on his coat.

我看着他穿上衣服。

❷小心,留意;提防[+(that)][+wh-]

Watch that the milk doesn't boil over.

小心别让牛奶溢出来。

❸守卫,看守

❹看护,监视

They had her watched by detectives.

他们把她置于侦探的监视之下。

vi. ❶注视,观看

I seldom play chess, but I like to watch.

我很少下棋,但是喜欢看。

❷等待,留心[(+for)]

He watched for his chance to propose to her.

他在等待时机向她求婚。

❸当心,注意

We must watch for fires.

我们一定要当心火灾。

water [ˈwɔtɚ ‖ ˈwɔːtə]

n. ❶水[U]

Fish live in water.

鱼生活在水中。
❷(江,湖,海等的)水体;大片的水[P]
Those plants can grow only in deep waters.
那些植物只能在深水中生长。
❸(国家的)海域,领海[P]
The ship was in European waters.
船在欧洲水域航行。

waterfall [ˈwɔtɚ͵fɔl ‖ ˈwɔːtəfɔːl]
n. 瀑布[C]

wave [wev ‖ weɪv]
[过去式]waved;[过去分词]waved
n. [C]❶波,波浪
❷(手之)挥动,挥手示意
He gave me a wave.
他朝我挥手。
❸浪潮;(情绪的)高涨;(活动等的)高潮[(+of)]
A wave of anger swept over him.
他心头涌起一股怒潮。
vt. ❶对……挥(手,旗等)
He waved the servant out of his room.
他挥手叫仆人离开房间。
❷向……挥手示意;挥手表示(致敬,告别等)
Martin waved us goodbye.
马丁向我们挥手告别。
vi. ❶挥手(或旗等)示意
She waved at him.
她朝他挥手。
❷起伏;摇动;飘扬
The flags were waving in the wind.
旗帜在风中飘扬。
❸(头发等)呈波形;卷曲
Her hair waves naturally.
她的头发自然卷曲。

wax [wæks ‖ wæks]
n. 蜡;蜂蜡;石蜡;蜡状物[U]

way [we ‖ weɪ]
n. ❶路,通路,道路[C]
Can you show me the way to the Post Office?
你能告诉我去邮局的路吗?
❷方向[C]
This way, please.
请这边走。
❸路程,距离
It's a long way to the railroad station.
到火车站路程很远。
❹方法,方式[C][(+to-v)]
Scientists are trying to find ways to prevent disease.
科学家们正试图找到防止疾病的方法。
❺风俗,习惯;风度;作风[C]

Don't mind his teasing. It's just his way.
不要介意他的嘲笑，他就是这么个人。

常用短语

by way of **经由**
He went to America by way of Hawaii.
他经由夏威夷去美国。

by the way **顺便说说**
By the way, have you seen my umbrella anywhere?
顺便问一下，你在什么地方见过我的伞吗？

in a way **在某种程度上**
In a way he is right.
某种程度上说，他是对的。

in the way **妨碍的**
Don't stand in my way.
别妨碍我。

we 〔wi ‖ wiː〕
pron. ❶（主格）我们
We are glad to see you.
我们很高兴见到你。
❷（包括自身在内的泛指）人们
We have lots of rain in June.
在 6 月雨量很大。

weak 〔wik ‖ wiːk〕
［比］weaker；［最］weakest
a. ❶弱的，虚弱的；衰弱的
She is still weak after her long illness.
久病之后她仍很虚弱。
❷软弱的，懦弱的；优柔寡断的
He is a man of weak character.
他这个人性格软弱。
❸（能力等）弱的，差的［（＋at/in）］
He was weak in mathematics, but good at English.
他数学差，但英语好。

weakness 〔ˈwiknɪs ‖ ˈwiːknɪs〕
n. ❶虚弱；软弱；薄弱［U］
❷弱点；缺点［U］

wealth 〔wɛlθ ‖ welθ〕
n. ❶财富；财产；资源；富有［U］
It was a period of wealth and prosperity.
那是一个富有和繁荣的时期。
❷丰富，大量［（＋of）］
The dictionary gives us a wealth of phrases and sentences to illustrate meaning.
这本词典给了我们许多说明字义的短语和句子。

wealthy 〔ˈwɛlθɪ ‖ welθɪ〕
［比］wealthier；［最］wealthiest
a. 富的；富裕的；丰富的
He is a wealthy businessman.
他是个富有的商人。

wear 〔wɛr ‖ weə〕
［过去式］wore；［过去分词］

worn

vt. ❶穿着;戴着;佩戴着;涂抹(香水,化妆品)

wear perfume / makeup / cologne

涂抹香水/化妆品/古龙水

❷(习惯性地)戴着(假发,眼镜等)

wear glasses / a wig

戴眼镜/假发

❸面露;面带;面有……色

He was wearing a pleasant smile.

他一直面露愉快的微笑。

❹(将胡须,头发)留成……的样子;保持……的样子

He wears his hair long.

他留着长发。

vi. ❶磨损;穿破;变旧;用坏

I like this shirt, but the neck has worn.

我喜欢这件衬衫,但是领子已旧了。

❷耐久;耐穿;耐磨

That cloth will wear for years and years.

那种布料可以穿好多年。

weather 〔ˈwɛðɚ ‖ ˈweðə〕

n. 天气[U]

Whether we will go picnicking tomorrow depends on the weather.

明天我们是否去野餐取决于天气好坏。

weave 〔wiv ‖ wiːv〕

[过去式] wove; [过去分词] woven

vt. ❶织;编,编制

weave thread into cloth

把线织成布

❷编排;编造

weave a story

编故事

❸(蜘蛛等)结(网)

web 〔wɛb ‖ web〕

n. 蜘蛛网;网状物;网状组织[C]

web site

(互联网)网址

wedding 〔ˈwɛdɪŋ ‖ ˈwedɪŋ〕

n. [C] ❶结婚典礼

The wedding will take place in October.

婚礼将于10月举行。

❷结婚纪念日

A golden wedding is the fiftieth anniversary of a marriage.

金婚是结婚50周年纪念日。

Wednesday 〔ˈwɛnzdɪ ‖ ˈwenzdɪ〕

n. 略作 Wed. 星期三

week 〔wik ‖ wiːk〕

n. [C] ❶周，一星期
She goes to the cinema once a week.
她每星期去看一次电影。
❷工作日，上课日，普通日
The five-day week is now usual in institutions of higher learning.
每周上5天课在高等学府已很普遍。

weekday 〔ˈwikˌde ‖ ˈwiːkdeɪ〕
n. 平日；工作日[C]

weekend 〔ˈwikˈɛnd ‖ ˌwiːkˈend〕
n. [C] ❶周末；周末的休假
He works at/on weekends.
他周末工作。
❷(大学等的)周末聚会
a. 周末的；周末用的
My daughter has got a weekend job.
我女儿找到了一份周末的工作。

weekly 〔ˈwiklɪ ‖ ˈwiːklɪ〕
a. 每周的；一周一次的；周刊的；周报的
weekly wages
周薪
ad. 每周；每周一次
She wrote to her mother weekly.
她每周给她母亲写一封信。
n. 周刊；周报[C]

weep 〔wip ‖ wiːp〕
[过去式] wept；[过去分词] wept
vi. ❶哭泣，流泪[(+over/for)]
The girl wept over her sad fate.
那个女孩为自己悲惨的命运而哭泣。

❷悲叹，哀悼[(+over/for)]
We all wept in silence for the deceased.
我们都默默为死者哀悼。
vt. 流(泪)；哭泣
The little girl wept herself to sleep.
小女孩哭着哭着就入睡了。

weigh 〔we ‖ weɪ〕
[过去式] weighed；[过去分词] weighed
vt. ❶称……的重量，掂估……的分量
He weighed the parcel by hand.
他用手估量那个包裹的重量。
❷考虑；权衡

They weighed the advantages and disadvantages before making the decision.
他们权衡利弊之后才作出决定。
vi. ❶有……重量；称起来
How much do you weigh?
你体重多少？
❷有分量，有重要性，有影响
Her suggestion weighed heavily in this decision.
她的建议对作出这一决定起了重要作用。

weight 〔wet ‖ weɪt〕
n. ❶重，重量；体重[C][U]
What is your weight?
你体重多少？
❷砝码[C]
❸(精神的)压力；重担；负担[C][(+on/off)]
That's quite a weight off my mind.
那真叫我如释重负。
❹价值；重要性；势力；影响[U]
Our boss's opinions seem to carry very little weight at home.
我们老板的意见在家里似乎没有什么权威。

welcome 〔ˈwɛlkəm ‖ ˈwelkəm〕
[过去式]welcomed；[过去分词]welcomed
int. 欢迎(光临)
Hello, Sarah! Welcome back to London!
你好，萨拉！欢迎回到伦敦来！
vt. ❶欢迎
The mayor welcomed the visiting guests at the airport.
市长到机场欢迎来宾。
❷欣然接受
She didn't welcome the suggestion.
她不接受这项建议。
a. ❶受欢迎的
She was a welcome visitor.
她是个受欢迎的来宾。
❷被允许的，可随意使用的[(+to)][+to-v]
You know you are welcome to stay.
你知道，我们欢迎你住下。
n. 欢迎，款待；欢迎辞[C]
He received a cordial welcome at Cambridge.
他在剑桥受到了热诚的欢迎。

welfare 〔ˈwɛlˌfɛr ‖ ˈwelfeə〕
n. [U] ❶福利；幸福；健康安乐
She works hard for the welfare of the poor.
她为了穷人的福利而辛勤工作。

❷【美】社会救济(制度)
They are living on welfare now.
他们现在靠社会救济生活。

well[1]〔wɛl ‖ wel〕
[比]better;[最]best
ad. ❶很好地;满意地;成功地
Do the boys eat well at school?
孩子们在学校吃得好吗?
❷充分地,彻底地
Think well before you act.
请三思而后行。
❸相当地,颇,很
Her son is well past forty.
她儿子已四十好几岁了。

常用短语

well off 富裕的
as well 也;同样地;还不如

int. ❶(表示惊异,怀疑)哟,啊,哎呀
Well, I didn't think to see you here!
哎呀,没想到会在这儿见到你!
❷(表示同意,让步等)嗯,好吧
Well, perhaps that's true.
嗯,也许那是真的。
❸(表示规劝,责备等)嗳,好啦
Well, you shouldn't get angry about such a trifle.
嗳,你不应该为这么一点儿小事生气。
❹(用以继续原来的话题或引入新的话题)这个;喔;唔

a. ❶健康的,健全的,安好的
I'm not well; my head aches.
我不舒服,头痛。
❷好的,令人满意的
I knew that all was well with her.
我知道她一切顺心如意。

well[2]〔wɛl ‖ wel〕
n. [C] ❶井,水井;油井;气井
❷来源,源泉
An encyclopedia is a well of knowledge.
百科全书是知识的源泉。

well-known〔ˈwɛlˈnon ‖ ˈwelˈnəun〕
a. ❶出名的,众所周知的[(+for/as)]
She is well-known for her work with the poor.
她因为帮助穷人而闻名。
❷熟知的

were〔wɝ ‖ wɜː〕
(are的过去式)
We were lucky.
我们很幸运。

west〔wɛst ‖ west〕
n. 西;西方[the]
Libya lies to the west of Egypt.
利比亚位于埃及以西。

W

W

a. ❶西的，西方的；西部的
He has been to most of West Europe.
西欧大部分地方他都去过。
❷在西方的；向西的；朝西的
❸(风)由西吹来的
There was a west wind blowing.
当时正刮着西风。
ad. 向西方；在西方；自西方
I drove west along the road.
我沿路向西驶去。

western 〔ˈwɛstɚn ‖ ˈwestən〕
a. ❶西的；西方的；西部的
a western country
西方国家
❷朝西的；向西的

wet 〔wɛt ‖ wet〕
[比]wetter；[最]wettest
a. ❶湿的，潮湿的
The ground was still wet from last night's storm.
昨夜暴风雨后，地上还是湿的。
❷雨天的，下雨的，多雨的
What a wet day!
这多雨的天气！
n. 下雨(天气)[the]
We went through the wet to the flower show.
我们冒雨前去参观花展。

whale 〔hwel ‖ hweɪl〕
n. 鲸

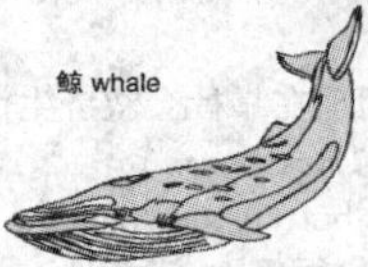

what 〔hwɑt ‖ hwɒt〕
pron. ❶(用作疑问代词)什么
What did you say?
你说什么？
❷(用于感叹句)多少
What she must have paid for her diamonds!
她买那些钻石首饰一定花了不少钱！
❸(用作关系代词)所……的事物(或人)
We must decide what to do next.
我们必须决定下一步做什么。
a. ❶(表示疑问)什么
What day is it today?
今天星期几？
❷(表示感叹)多么，何等
What a good heart you have!
你的心肠真好！
int. (表示惊讶，气愤等)什么

whatever 〔hwɑtˈɛvɚ ‖ wɒtˈevə〕
n. ❶任何……的事物；无论什么；凡是……的东西

I will do whatever I can to help you.
任何能帮得上忙的，我都会尽力而为。
❷不管什么
Whatever happens, I won't change my mind.
不管发生什么我都不会改变主意。
❸【口】究竟什么
Whatever has happened?
究竟发生了什么事？
a. ❶任何……的；凡是……的
You may write on whatever subject you like.
你可以写任何你喜欢的题目。
❷不管什么样的，无论怎么的
Whatever weather it is, we will go.
不管天气怎样，我们还是要去。
❸(用在与 no, any 连用的名词之后)一点……都(不)，什么都(不)；毫不(＝at all)
There is no doubt whatever about it.
对于那事，我毫无异议。

wheat 〔hwit ‖ wiːt〕
n. 小麦[U]

wheel 〔hwil ‖ wiːl〕
n. ❶轮子，车轮[C]
❷(汽车的)方向盘；船的(舵轮)[the]
Let me take the wheel.
我来开车。

when 〔hwɛn ‖ wen〕
ad. ❶(用作疑问副词)什么时候，何时
I'd like to know when they'll let him out.
我想知道他们什么时候放他。
❷(用作关系副词，引导关系从句)当……时
There were times when I didn't know what to do.
有些时候我不知道该怎么办才好。
conj. ❶当……时
It was snowing when he arrived at the constructive site.
他到达工地时，正在下雪。
❷既然，考虑到
How can he get the promotion when his boss dislikes him?
既然上司不喜欢他，那他怎么会获得提升呢？
❸虽然，然而
I had only 15 dollars about me when the book I wanted cost 20.
我身上只带了 15 美元，可是我想买的那本书定价 20 美元。
❹在那时，然后

W

pron. 什么时候,那时
Since when has she taught here?
她从什么时候开始在这儿教书的?

whenever 〔hwɛn'ɛvɚ ‖ wen'evə〕
ad. ❶无论什么时候
❷【口】究竟什么时候

where 〔hwɛr ‖ weə〕
ad. ❶(用作疑问副词)在哪里;往哪里;从哪里;在哪一点上
The driver asked me where I wanted to go.
司机问我想去哪里。
❷(用作关系副词,引导关系从句)在那里;往那里
That's where we differ.
那是我们的分歧所在。
conj. 在……处;到……的地方;……的地方
I'll meet him where I first met you.
我将在初次见你的地方与他会面。
pron. 哪里,何处
Where does he come from?
他是哪里人?

wherever 〔hwɛr'ɛvɚ ‖ weər'evə〕
ad. ❶无论什么地方;不管去任何地方
You may sit down wherever you like.
随便你坐哪儿都可以。
❷【口】(用作疑问副词)究竟在哪里;究竟到哪里
Wherever did I put my glasses?
我究竟把眼镜放到哪儿了?

whether 〔'hwɛðɚ ‖ weðə〕
conj. ❶(引导名词从句)是否
Ask him whether he can come or not.
问问他是否能来。
❷(与 or 连用,引导状语从句)不管是……(或是)
We'll go on with the work, whether we can find the necessary tools or not.
不管我们能否找到所需的工具,我们都要把这件工作做下去。

which 〔hwɪtʃ ‖ wɪtʃ〕
pron. ❶(用作疑问代词)哪一个,哪一些
Which is my seat?
哪个座位是我的?
❷(用作关系代词)那一个,那一些
He also had a gun with which to defend himself.
他还有一把自卫用的枪。
a. ❶(用作疑问形容词)哪一

个,哪一些
Which university did you go to, Oxford or Cambridge?
你上过哪所大学? 牛津还是剑桥?
❷(用作关系形容词)这一个,这些
The doctor told him to give up smoking, which advice he took.
医生嘱他戒烟,他接受了这一忠告。

while 〔hwaɪl ‖ waɪl〕
n. 一会儿,一段时间
I'll be back in a while.
我一会儿就回来。
conj. ❶当……的时候,和……同时
She listened closely while he read the letter.
他读信时,她听得很仔细。
❷而,然而
I like tea while she likes coffee.
我喜欢喝茶,而她喜欢喝咖啡。
❸虽然,尽管
While I like the color of the hat, I do not like its shape.
虽然我喜欢这顶帽子的颜色,但我不喜欢它的形状。

whip 〔hwɪp ‖ wɪp〕
[过去式]whipped;[过去分词]whipped
vt. 鞭笞,抽打
These boys are whipping tops.
这些男孩子正在抽陀螺。
n. [C] ❶鞭子
The old man seldom used his whip on his horse.
老人很少用鞭子抽他的马。
❷抽打;一挥;一击

whirl 〔hwɜːl ‖ wɜːl〕
[过去式]whirled;[过去分词]whirled
vi. ❶旋转,回旋
The electric fan blades whirled in the hot room.
电扇的扇叶在闷热的房内旋转着。
❷急驶;飞跑
The car whirled down the street.
汽车在街道上疾驰而过。
❸头晕眼花,感到昏乱
The strong medicine made my head whirl.
这种烈性药使我头晕眼花。
vt. ❶使旋转;使突然转向
The wind whirled the dead leaves about.
风把枯叶吹得团团转。
❷飞快地带走;卷走
We were whirled away in a hel-

icopter.
直升机迅速把我们运走。
n. [C] ❶旋转,回旋[(+of)]
The colorful whirl of the dancers was beautiful to watch.
舞蹈者多彩多姿的旋转令人赏心悦目。
❷(一阵)头晕;(一阵)昏乱
His thoughts are in a whirl.
他的思想乱作一团。

whiskey ['hwɪskɪ ‖ 'wɪskɪ]
n. ❶威士忌酒[U]
❷一杯威士忌酒[C]
Two whiskeys, please.
请来两杯威士忌。

whisper ['hwɪspɚ ‖ 'wɪspə]
[过去式]whispered;[过去分词]whispered
vi. ❶低语,耳语;私语
She is whispering to him.
她正对他窃窃私语。
❷(风,树叶等)飒飒作响
The wind was whispering in the trees.
风在树林中飒飒作响。
vt. 低声说出;私下告诉
"She is coming," he whispered.
"她来了,"他低声地说。
n. [C] ❶耳语,私语
They debated it in whispers.
他们低声辩论。
❷飒飒声;潺潺声
❸传闻,流言[(+about)][+that]
I've heard a whisper that he has cancer.
我听到他得了癌症的传闻。

whistle ['hwɪsl̩ ‖ 'wɪsl]
n. ❶口哨;警笛;汽笛;哨子[C]
The referee blew his whistle, and the game stopped.
裁判吹响哨子,比赛停止。
❷哨音;笛声[C]

white [hwaɪt ‖ waɪt]
[比]whiter;[最]whitest
a. ❶白色的
❷苍白的
She turned white with rage.
她气得脸色发白。
❸白种人的
n. ❶白色[U]
❷白种人[C]
That restaurant used to serve whites only.
那家餐厅过去只接待白人。

who [hu ‖ huː]
pron. ❶(用作疑问代词)谁,什么人
Did Mary tell you who that girl's father is?
玛丽有没有告诉你那个女孩的

父亲是谁?

❷(用作限定性关系代词)……的人

The girl who spoke is my best friend.

那个讲话的女孩是我最好的朋友。

❸(用作非限定关系代词)他;她;他们;她们

I went to the movies with Mary, who I think you once met.

我与玛丽一起去看电影,我想你见过她。

whoever 〔hu'ɛvɚ ‖ huː'evə〕

pron. ❶无论谁

Whoever comes to see me will be welcomed.

无论谁来看我,我都欢迎。

❷到底是谁

Whoever did such a thing?

到底谁干了这种事?

whole 〔hol ‖ həul〕

a. ❶全部的,全体的,所有的,完全的

I'm deeply sorry about the whole business.

对整个事情我深感遗憾。

❷整个的;完整的;无缺的,无损的

He was surprised to find himself whole after the car accident.

他很惊讶自己在车祸中毫发未伤。

❸整整的

He spent two whole years writing the novel.

他花了整整两年时间写那本小说。

n. 全部,全体[the][(+of)]

The whole of Spain was jubilant.

西班牙举国欢腾。

常用短语

as a whole 作为一个整体;整个看来

We must consider these matters as a whole.

我们必须从整体的角度来考虑这些问题。

on the whole 总的看来;基本上;大体上

Englishmen are, on the whole, conservative.

总的来说,英国人是保守的。

whom 〔hum ‖ huːm〕

pron. (who 的宾格,用在正式的讲话及书面语中)

❶(用作疑问代词)谁,什么人

I know who you are and whom you represent.

我知道你是谁并代表谁。

W

❷(用作限定性关系代词)……的人
I'll give my vote to the man in whom I have faith.
我将把我的选票投给我所相信的人。
❸(用作非限定关系代词)他,她;他们,她们
My new neighbor, whom I introduced to you the other day, had a heart attack last night.
前日我介绍你认识的我那位新邻居昨晚心脏病发作了。

whose 〔huz ‖ huːz〕
(who 或 which 的所有格)
pron. ❶(用作疑问代词)谁的
Whose books are these?
这些书是谁的?
❷(用作关系代词)那个人的,那些人的;他(她)们;他(她)们的
Chopin, whose works are world-famous, composed some of his music in this room.
肖邦的音乐作品举世闻名,其中的一部分就是在这间屋子里创作的。
❸(用作关系代词)它的;它们的
The word, whose meaning escapes me, probably derives from Latin.
那个词可能源自拉丁文,其意思我想不起来了。

why 〔hwaɪ ‖ waɪ〕
ad. ❶(用作疑问副词)为什么
Why should you be so interested in my affairs?
你为何对我的事这么感兴趣?
❷(用作关系副词)为什么
These are the reasons why we do it.
这些就是我们为什么要做这件事的理由。

wide 〔waɪd ‖ waɪd〕
[比]wider;[最]widest
a. ❶宽阔的;宽松的
They came to a wide river.
他们来到了一条宽阔的河边。
❷宽度为……的,……宽的
The lake is about 6 miles wide.
这个湖约 6 英里宽。
❸广阔的;广泛的
He has a wide knowledge of French history.
他具有广博的法国历史知识。
❹张大的,张得很开的;开得很大的
ad. ❶张得(或开得)很大地;充分地
She opened the door wide so that the room was lighter.
她把门开大以使屋内明亮一些。

❷远离(目标)地,偏离地

❸广阔地;广泛地

I've searched far and wide for the book and I still can't find it.

我到处寻找该书,结果仍然没能找到。

widely 〔'waɪdlɪ ‖ 'waɪdlɪ〕

ad. ❶范围广地;广泛地

Jews are widely scattered over Europe.

犹太人散布在欧洲各处。

❷远;大大地

His account is widely different from the fact.

他的报告和事实大有出入。

widow 〔'wɪdo ‖ 'wɪdəʊ〕

n. 寡妇[C]

width 〔wɪdθ ‖ wɪdθ〕

n. 宽度;阔度;宽阔[C][U]

The road has a width of 20 feet. = The road is 20 feet in width.

这条路有 20 英尺宽。

wife 〔waɪf ‖ waɪf〕

n. 妻子,太太,夫人;已婚妇女[C]

The officials came to the party with their wives.

官员们携带妻子参加宴会。

〔反义〕husband 丈夫

wild 〔waɪld ‖ waɪld〕

a. ❶野的;野生的,未被人驯养的,自然生长的

Those are wild roses.

那些是野玫瑰。

❷荒凉的,无人烟的

We traveled through wild, mountainous country.

我们穿越了荒凉而多山的地区。

❸难驾驭的;任性的,无法无天的;粗野的

She is afraid of his wild looks.

她害怕他那粗野的神情。

❹猛烈的,狂风暴雨的

On a wild night our regiment took the fort by surprise.

在一个狂风暴雨之夜,我团出其不意地攻占了那个要塞。

❺疯狂的,狂怒的

词汇拓展

wildly *ad.* 狂暴地

wilderness *n.* 荒野

will 〔wɪl ‖ wɪl〕

[过去式] would

v. aux. ❶(表示单纯的将来)将,会

He will be home at 6:00.

他 6 点回家。

❷(表示意志,意愿)愿,要

You will come, won't you?

W

你会来的，是不是？

❸(表示经常性，习惯性)经常，惯于，总是

These things will happen.

这种事总是要发生的。

❹(Will you…？的句型)

(要求，劝诱)帮忙做……好吗？要不要……

Will you open the window?

请打开窗子好吗？

Will you / Won't you have another cup of coffee?

要不要再来杯咖啡？

[Would you…？的用法比较委婉客气]

❺(表示猜测)可能，大概

The teacher will be over 50.

老师的年龄大概超过 50 岁了吧。

> 在条件句中不用 will 或 shall 表示将来时间，而用一般时
>
> If it is fine tomorrow, I will go.
>
> 如果明天天气好的话我就去。
>
> **用法工具箱**

n. ❶意志，毅力；自制力[C][U]

Jim has a strong will.

吉姆是个意志坚强的人。

❷心愿；目的；意愿[+to-v]

He had a strong will to beat his opponent.

他有击败对手的强烈欲望。

❸决心；意图

She had no will of her own.

她这人没有主见。

❹遗嘱[C]

The dying woman prepared a will.

那位濒死的妇人准备了一份遗嘱。

willing ['wɪlɪŋ‖'wɪlɪŋ]

a. ❶愿意的，乐意的[+to-v][+that]

They are willing to come.

他们愿意来。

❷心甘情愿的，积极肯做的

We received willing help.

我们得到了志愿的援助。

win [wɪn‖wɪn]

[过去式]won；[过去分词]won

vt. ❶在……中获胜(或成功)

Their team has won the game.

他们队赢了这场比赛。

❷赢得，获得，夺得

His modesty won him praises.

他的谦虚为他赢得了赞扬。

vi. 获胜,成功
I won purely by chance.
我完全是侥幸赢的。

wind 〔wɪnd ‖ wɪnd〕
n. ❶风[C][U]
The north wind is blowing hard.
北风劲吹。
❷呼吸[U]
She paused for wind after climbing those stairs.
爬了那几级楼梯后,她停下来喘口气。

window 〔ˈwɪndo ‖ ˈwɪndəʊ〕
n. [C] ❶窗,窗户;(商店)橱窗
She sat in the window, staring into the distance.
她坐在窗旁,凝视着远方。
❷窗玻璃
Nick was scolded for breaking the window.
尼克因打破窗户玻璃而挨骂。
❸【计算机】窗口,视见区

windy 〔ˈwɪndɪ ‖ ˈwɪndɪ〕
[比]windier;[最]windiest
a. 刮风的;多风的;风大的
a windy day
刮风的天气

wine 〔waɪn ‖ waɪn〕
n. 葡萄酒;水果酒;酒[C][U]
May I help you to another glass of wine?
让我来给你再斟杯酒好吗?

wing 〔wɪŋ ‖ wɪŋ〕
n. [C] ❶翅膀
He aimed his gun at the eagle spreading its wings.
他的枪瞄准那只展开翅膀的老鹰。
❷机翼

winner 〔ˈwɪnɚ ‖ ˈwɪnə〕
n. 获胜者,优胜者[C]
Who was the winner?
谁是获胜者?

winter 〔ˈwɪntɚ ‖ ˈwɪntə〕
n. 冬,冬季;冷天[C][U]
We have passed the last few winters in the south.
近几年冬天我们都是在南方度过的。

wipe 〔waɪp ‖ waɪp〕
[过去式]wiped;[过去分词]wiped
vt. ❶揩,擦;揩干;擦净
wipe one's eyes
擦干眼泪
❷擦去;去除;消灭
You'd better wipe the thought from your mind.
你还是打消那个念头吧。
vi. 擦;抹,揩
The paint won't wipe off easily.

这油漆不容易擦掉。

wire 〔waɪr ‖ ˈwaɪə〕

n. ❶金属线，金属丝[C][U]

steel wire

钢丝

❷电缆，电线；电话线[C][U]

His wire is busy just now.

他的电话现在占线。

❸【口】电报[C]

I sent a wire to my mother this morning.

今天上午我给母亲拍了电报。

wireless 〔ˈwaɪrlɪs ‖ ˈwaɪəlɪs〕

n. ❶【主英】无线电；无线电收音机[C]

❷无线电报；无线电话[U]

wisdom 〔ˈwɪzdəm ‖ ˈwɪzdəm〕

n. ❶智慧，才智，明智[U]

I would question the wisdom of borrowing such a large sum of money.

我怀疑借这么一大笔钱是否明智。

❷知识，学问，常识[U]

the collected wisdom of many centuries

许多世纪积累下来的知识

❸贤人

wise 〔waɪz ‖ waɪz〕

a. ❶有智慧的；聪明的

The wisdom of the masses exceeds that of the wisest individual.

三个臭皮匠，赛过诸葛亮。

❷英明的；明智的[+to-v]

You are wise not to join the club.

你不加入俱乐部是明智的。

❸博学的，有见识的

wish 〔wɪʃ ‖ wɪʃ〕

[过去式]wished；[过去分词]wished

vt. ❶但愿[+(that)]

I wish (that) I had never met her.

我要是没遇见过她就好了。

❷想要；希望，渴望[+to-v]

We wish to visit the new museum very much.

我们很想去参观新博物馆。

❸祝，祝愿（某人好运、幸福等）；向……道（早安等）

I wish you a happy birthday.

祝你生日快乐。

vi. 希望，想要

We have everything we can wish for.

我们希望得到的东西都有了。

n. [C] ❶希望，愿望[(+for)][+to-v][+(that)]

Her wish to become a doctor has come true.

她想当医生的愿望实现了。
❷心愿，想要的东西
She has got her wish at last.
她终于如愿以偿。
❸祝福，祈愿[P]
Please send her my good wishes when you write to her.
你给她写信时，请代我向她致意。

with 〔wɪð ‖ wɪð〕
prep. ❶与……在一起，偕同，和……，跟
She lives with her son.
她和儿子住在一起。
❷带着……；有……的
The girl with long hair is my classmate.
长头发的女孩是我同学。
❸以（手段，材料），用（工具）
My American friend is learning to eat with chopsticks.
我的一位美国朋友在学着用筷子吃饭。
❹表伴随的状态
I slept with the windows open.
我开着窗子睡的觉。
❺在……一边，赞成
I agree with you.
我赞同你的意见。
I am with you.
我站在你这边。
❻表方式
He swam across the river with difficulty.
他好不容易才游过河。
He can read French with ease.
他能轻松地读法文。
❼跟……（分手）
I parted with her at the entrance.
我在入口处和她分手。
❽由于，因为
He was absent with a cold.
他因感冒而缺席。

withdraw 〔wɪðˈdrɔ ‖ wɪðˈdrɔː〕
[过去式]withdrew；[过去分词]withdrawn
vt. ❶抽回；拉开；移开
He withdrew his hands from the stove.
他从火炉边缩回手。
❷取消；撤回；撤销
He withdrew his statement.
他撤回了他的声明。
vi. 撤退；离开；退出[(＋from)]
She withdrew from the room.
她退出了房间。

within 〔wɪðˈɪn ‖ wɪðˈɪn〕
prep. ❶在……范围内；不超过
They finished the house within half a year.
他们在半年内盖好了这幢房

屋。
❷在……里面，在……内部
He kept within doors all day yesterday.
他昨天一天都没出门。

without〔wɪð'aʊt ‖ wɪð'aʊt〕
prep. ❶无，没有，不
He entered without knocking at the door.
他没敲门就进来了。
He went out without a hat.
他没有戴帽子就出去了。
❷在……外面，在……外部
He lives in a cottage 3 miles without the town.
他住在城外 3 英里远的一所村舍里。
❸假如没有
Without air, we could not live.
没有空气我们就不能活。

witness〔'wɪtnɪs ‖ 'wɪtnɪs〕
[过去式] witnessed; [过去分词] witnessed
n. ❶目击者；见证人 [C][(+of/to)]
I was a witness to the argument.
我是那场争论的见证人。
❷【律】证人；证物；连署人[C]
He was called as a defense witness.
他被传唤作被告的证人。
❸证词[U]
She was punished for giving false witness.
她因作伪证受到惩处。
❹证据，证明[C][(+to)]
vt. ❶目击
I witnessed the traffic accident.
我目睹了那次交通事故。
❷作……的证人；连署
The two servants witnessed Mr. Smith's will.
两个仆人在史密斯先生的遗嘱上签名作证。
❸是……的发生地点
The year 1849 witnessed a great war in Hungary.
1849 年匈牙利发生了一场大战。

wolf〔wulf ‖ wulf〕[名复] wolves
n. [C] ❶狼
Wolves kill sheep and sometimes even attack men.
狼吃羊，有时候甚至袭击人。
❷【口】色狼，色鬼

狼
wolf

W

woman 〔ˈwʊmən ‖ ˈwʊmən〕
[名复]women
n. ❶成年女子,妇女,女人[C]
Ask the women to stay home.
叫女人们待在家里。
❷女性[U]
Woman lives longer than man in general.
女性通常比男性长寿。

wonder 〔ˈwʌndɚ ‖ ˈwʌndə〕
[过去式]wondered;[过去分词]wondered
vi. 觉得奇怪;不明白[(+at)][(+to-v)]
I wonder at her rudeness.
我对她的粗鲁感到惊讶。
vt. ❶想知道[+wh-]
I wonder whether you like her.
我不知道你是否喜欢她。
❷对……感到奇怪[+(that)]
We wonder that the little boy is a university student.
我们很惊奇这个小男孩儿是大学生。
n. ❶惊奇;惊异;惊叹[U]
There was a look of wonder in his eyes.
他眼中露出惊奇的神色。
❷奇迹;奇观;奇事[C]
It is a wonder that he remained alive after dropping from the roof of a ten-storied building.
他从一幢10层楼的楼顶上摔下来还活着,真是奇迹。

wonderful 〔ˈwʌndɚfəl ‖ ˈwʌndəfəl〕
a. ❶【口】极好的;精彩的
It's wonderful.
好极了。
❷惊人的;奇妙的;非同寻常的
He told me a wonderful story.
他给我讲了个奇妙的故事。

wood 〔wʊd ‖ wʊd〕
n. ❶木头;木材;木柴[U]
❷森林,树林[C]
It is lovely walking in the woods.
在树林中散步很愉快。

wool 〔wʊl ‖ wʊl〕
n. [U]❶羊毛
❷毛线;毛织品
Many people wear wool in winter.
冬天许多人穿毛料衣服。

word 〔wɝd ‖ wɜːd〕
n. ❶字,单词[C]
❷(简短的)几句话
He threw a word in now and again.
他不时插一两句话。
❸话,谈话;言辞;歌词[P]
I cannot remember the words of

the song.
我忘了那首歌的歌词。
❹消息，音讯；传说[U]
He sent word to us that he would not be able to come.
他带信来，说他来不了。

work 〔wɚk ‖ wɜːk〕
[过去式]worked，[过去分词]worked
n. ❶工作；劳动；作业；事[U]
It takes a lot of work to dig a deep well.
挖一口深井很费事。
❷职业，业务[U]
❸(待做的)工作；功课[U]
I have to bring my work home today.
今天我得把工作带回家做。
❹成果，产品；工艺品，针线活[U]
This bamboo basket is my own work.
这只竹篮是我自己编的。
❺著作，作品[P]
the works of Shakespeare
莎士比亚的作品
vi. ❶工作，劳动，干活
She works in a restaurant.
她在一家饭店工作。
❷(机器等)运转，活动
The machine won't work.
机器不转了。
❸起作用；行得通
Your suggestion works well.
你的建议很有效。
vt. 开动；操作
Please tell me how to work the machine.
请告诉我如何操纵这台机器。

worker 〔ˈwɚkɚ ‖ ˈwɜːkə〕
n. [C] ❶工人，劳工，劳动者
How many workers are there on the farm?
农场上有多少工人？
❷工作者；人员
She is a social worker.
她是一个社会福利工作者。
❸【昆】职虫(如工蜂，工蚁等)
The workers have little pollen baskets on their legs.
工蜂脚上有装花粉的小“篮子”。

workman 〔ˈwɚkmən ‖ ˈwɜːkmən〕
n. 工匠，技工；工人[C]

world 〔wɚld ‖ wɜːld〕
n. ❶世界；地球；宇宙[the]
The blind people live in a dark world.
盲人生活在黑暗的世界里。
❷(指一群生物)世界[the]
the animal world

动物世界

❸领域[the]

He is a big figure in the business world.

他在商界是个有声望的人物。

❹人，众人[the]

His suicide shocked the world.

他的自杀震惊了世人。

worldwide 〔ˈwɝldwaɪd ‖ ˈwɜːldwaɪd〕

a. 世界范围的，遍及全球的

ad. 在世界各地；在全世界

worm 〔wɝm ‖ wɜːm〕

n. [C] ❶虫，蠕虫；蛀虫；寄生虫；幼虫

All the apples had worms in them.

这些苹果里都有蛀虫。

❷可怜虫；小人物；懦夫

You're no worm, and you're a man; so get up, lad, and fight.

你不是懦夫，你是一个男子汉；小伙子，爬起来，去搏斗。

worry 〔ˈwɝɪ ‖ ˈwʌrɪ〕

[过去式]worried；[过去分词]worried

vt. ❶使担心，使发愁

Nothing worries me.

我没有什么可担心的。

❷担心，发愁[＋wh-][＋(that)]

The teacher worried that these problems might be too hard for her students.

老师担心这些题目会对学生太难。

❸使不安宁；骚扰；折磨

For God's sake, don't worry me.

看在上帝的分上，别使我不得安宁。

vi. 忧虑，担心[(＋about/over)]

Don't worry about the matter, and take it easy.

别担心那件事，轻松一点儿。

n. ❶烦恼；焦虑；担心[U]

❷令人发愁的事(或人)[C]

Mother's illness was always a great worry to me.

母亲的病一直是我非常担心的事。

worse 〔wɝs ‖ wɜːs〕

a. ❶(bad 的比较级)更坏的，更差的，更恶化的

To make matters worse, I locked my keys in the car.

更糟的是，我把钥匙锁在车里了。

❷(ill 的比较级)(病情)更重的

My cold is getting worse.

我的感冒更重了。

W

worst 〔wɜ˞st ‖ wɜːst〕

(bad,ill 的最高级)

a. ❶最坏的;最差的

Of all the boys I know, Jack is the worst.

在我认识的小孩儿中,杰克最坏。

❷最不利的;最痛苦的;错误最多的;效能最低的

This is the worst composition ever written by my students.

我的学生所写的作文中这是错误最多的一篇。

worth 〔wɜ˞θ ‖ wɜːθ〕

a. ❶有(……的)价值,值……

This necklace is worth 1,000 US dollars.

这条项链值 1,000 美元。

❷值得(做……)

That article is not worth reading.

那篇文章不值得一读。

n. [U] ❶价值

This research project is of great worth.

这个研究项目很有价值。

❷值一定金额的数量

He keeps in the safe $3 million worth of diamonds.

他在保险箱里放着值 300 万美元的钻石。

worthy 〔ˈwɜ˞ðɪ ‖ ˈwɜːðɪ〕

[比]worthier;[最]worthiest

a. ❶有价值的;可尊敬的;相称的;值得注意的

She is willing to donate money to a worthy cause.

她愿为高尚的事业捐款。

❷值得的,配得上的,足以……的[(+of)][+to-v]

She is worthy to receive such honor.

她应该得到此荣誉。

would 〔wʊd ‖ wʊd〕

v. aux. ❶(will 的过去时,表示过去将来时)将

She said she would come.

她说过她会来的。

❷(表示意志)愿,要;偏要

I told her to stop nagging, but she just wouldn't listen.

我叫她别再唠叨,可她就是不听。

❸(表示过去的习惯)总是,总会,总要

He would sit silent for hours.

他常常接连好几个小时默默地坐着。

❹(表示虚拟,假设,条件等)要,将要;会,就会

If he had been there, he would have helped you.

假如他那时在场,他一定会帮助你的。

wound 〔wund ‖ wuːnd〕

n. [C] ❶创伤,伤;伤口;伤疤

He had a bullet wound in his chest.

他胸部有枪伤。

❷(对感情,名誉等的)伤害,损害,创伤

That was a wound to the child's pride.

那是对孩子自尊心的伤害。

wrist 〔rɪst ‖ rɪst〕

n. 腕;腕关节[C]

write 〔raɪt ‖ raɪt〕

[过去式] wrote; [过去分词] written

vt. ❶写下,书写

I've written only one page.

我只写了一页。

❷写(书等),编写(乐曲等)

He wrote lots of poems in his life.

他一生中写了许多诗。

❸写信给;写信说[+ to][+ that]

She wrote to Ellis that his father was not well.

她写信给埃利斯,告诉他他父亲身体欠佳。

vi. ❶写;写字

This pen writes well.

这支笔写起来很流畅。

❷写信[(+to)]

She writes to her parents once a week.

她每周给父母写一封信。

writer 〔'raɪtɚ ‖ 'raɪtə〕

n. 作者;作家;记者;撰稿人[C]

He is one of the President's speech writers.

他是总统演讲的撰稿人之一。

writing 〔'raɪtɪŋ ‖ 'raɪtɪŋ〕

n. ❶书写;写作;书面形式[U]

Put your ideas in writing.

把你的想法写下来。

❷书法;笔迹[U]

Your writing is hard to read.

你的笔迹很难辨认。

❸著作;文学作品[P]

She has read all the writings of Shakespeare.

她读过莎士比亚的全部著作。

常用短语

writing-case 文具盒

wrong 〔rɔŋ ‖ rɒŋ〕

[比] more wrong; [最] most wrong

a. ❶错误的;不对的

I took the wrong way.

我走错了路。

❷不道德的;犯罪的;邪恶的

W

[＋to-v]
It is wrong of you to bully the child.
你不该欺负那个孩子。
❸不正常的;出毛病的;不健全的[(＋with)]
What's wrong with the machine?
这台机器出了什么毛病?
ad. 错误地
He guessed wrong.
他猜错了。
n. ❶错误[U]
It is not always easy to know the difference between right and wrong.
分辨是非并不总是很容易的。
❷不道德;违法,犯罪[U]
❸坏事,不道德行为;不法行为[C]
The man has committed many wrongs.
那个人干了许多坏事。

wrongful 〔'rɔŋfl ‖ rɒŋfəl〕
a. ❶恶劣的;不公允的;不义的
❷违法的;非法的;不正当的

圣诞节Xmas

X

X光片 X-ray

Xmas 〔ˈkrɪsməs ‖ ˈkrɪsməs〕
n. 圣诞节(=Christmas)

x-ray 〔ˈɛksˈre ‖ ˈeksreɪ〕
n. [C] ❶X 射线,X 光[P]
❷X 光照片

Y

牦牛yak

Y

长江Yangtze River

Yangtse River

n. 【地质】长江

yard[1] 〔jɑrd ‖ jɑːd〕

n. 码(英美长度单位,＝3 英尺)[C]

One yard is nearly a meter in length.

一码约等于一米长。

yard[2] 〔jɑrd ‖ jɑːd〕

n. [C] ❶ 院子;天井;庭院

She raises chickens in the yard.

她在院子里养鸡。

❷【美】后院

后院
gard

yawn 〔jɔn ‖ jɔːn〕

[过去式]yawned;[过去分词]yawned

n. 呵欠[C]

The baby gave a big yawn.

这个婴儿打了个大呵欠。

vi. 打呵欠

He is yawning again.

他又打呵欠了。

打哈欠
yawning

year 〔jɪr ‖ jɪə〕

n. [C] ❶年,一年

We haven't seen him this year.

我们今年没见过他。

❷年纪,岁数;老年[P]

Though advanced in years, he

has a keen sense of hearing.
他虽然上了年纪，但听觉十分灵敏。

yearbook 〔'jɪrˌbuk ‖ 'jɪəbuk〕
n. 年鉴；年报；年刊[C]

yell 〔jɛl ‖ jel〕
[过去式]yelled；[过去分词]yelled
vi. ❶叫喊；吼叫(声)
He yelled with pain.
他痛得直叫。
❷(拉拉队等)齐声呐喊
n. 叫喊；吼叫[C]
I heard a yell inside.
我听到里面一声喊叫。

yellow 〔'jɛlol ‖ 'jeləʊ〕
[比]yellower；[最]yellowest
a. ❶黄色的
❷黄皮肤的；黄色人种的
The Chinese belong to the yellow race.
中国人属于黄种人。
n. ❶黄色；黄色颜料(或染料)[C][U]
Yellow is my favorite color.
黄色是我最喜欢的颜色。
❷蛋黄[C][U]
❸黄种人[C]

yes 〔jɛs ‖ jes〕
ad. ❶是，是的
"Is this your pen?"
"这是你的钢笔吗？"
"Yes, it is."
"是的。"
❷(表示疑问或鼓励对方进一步讲述)是吗，真的吗
"Dad said he would buy you a car."
"爸爸说他要买一辆汽车给你。"
"Yes?"
"真的？"
❸(征求对方意见)是不是
❹(回答呼唤)嗳，是，在这儿
"Frank!"
"弗兰克！"
"Yes, Mother."
"在这儿呢，妈。"
n. [C]肯定的回答，同意
She nodded yes.
她点头同意。

yesterday 〔'jɛstɚdɪ ‖ 'jestədɪ〕
ad. 昨天
It seems as if that had happened only yesterday.
那件事仿佛是昨天刚发生似的。
n. ❶昨天[U]
Yesterday was my birthday.
昨天是我的生日。
❷过去的日子，往昔[P]
Recalling cheerful yesterdays

Y

cheered the lady.
回忆欢乐的往昔使这位女士感到欣慰。

yet 〔jet ‖ jet〕
ad. ❶(用于否定句)还(没)
The moon has not risen yet.
月亮还没有升起。
❷(用于疑问句)现在,已经
Has he finished the work yet?
那工作他做完了没有?
❸总有一天,终必
He will suffer for fun yet.
他总有一天会因贪玩吃苦头。
❹(与比较级连用)更,益发
I have a yet harder task.
我还有更艰巨的任务。
❺依然,还
The poor girl loves him yet.
那个可怜的姑娘还爱着他。
conj. 可是,却,然而
I don't know him, yet I can get his help.
我不认识他,但我会得到他的帮助。

you 〔(强)ju ‖ ju:;(弱)jʊ ‖ jə〕
pron. ❶(主格)你;你们
You two clean the hall.
你们两个人打扫大厅。
❷(主格)你,任何人
You can never predict what would happen next.
谁也无法预料接着会发生什么事。
❸(宾格)你;你们
Thank you for your help.
谢谢你帮忙。

young 〔jʌŋ ‖ jʌŋ〕
[比]younger;[最]youngest
a. ❶年轻的;相对年轻的;幼小的;青春时期的
My sister is too young to go to school.
我妹妹还未到上学年龄。
❷像青年的,朝气蓬勃的
He is old in age yet young in spirit.
他虽年老,但朝气蓬勃。
❸初期的,开始不久的
The young nation is faced with many difficulties.
那个新建立的国家面临着许多困难。
n. ❶青年们[the]
Generally speaking, the old are more conservative than the young.
一般而言,老年人比年轻人更保守。
❷崽,雏
The swallow is showing its young how to fly.
老燕正在教雏燕学飞。

Y

your 〔jur ‖ jɔː〕

pron. ❶(you 的所有格)你的；你们的

I think your suggestion will work.

我看你的建议能行得通。

❷(泛指)一个人的，任何人的

❸【口】(含贬义)你(们)所说的，你(们)那种，所谓的

So that is your effective remedy, right?

原来那就是你们所谓的有效药物，是吗？

yours 〔jurz ‖ jɔːz〕

pron. (you 的名词性物主代词)

❶你的(东西)；你们的(东西)

This is our room, and that's yours.

这是我们的房间，那是你们的。

❷尊函

❸你(们)的家属

❹(用作信尾签名前之敬语)

Yours sincerely

你真挚的

yourself 〔ˈjurˈsɛlf ‖ jɔːˈself〕

pron. ❶(your 的反身代词)你自己

Don't tire yourself too much.

别太累着自己。

❷(加强语气)你亲自，你本人

Do it yourself.

你自己干吧。

youth 〔juθ ‖ juːθ〕

n. ❶青春时代，青少年时期[U]

I spent my youth in the country.

我在乡间度过了青少年时代。

❷(男)青年，小伙子[C]

There are groups of youths playing basketball over there.

那里，一群群小伙子正在打篮球。

❸年轻；朝气；青春[U]

My youth has gone.

我的青春已不复存在。

Z

Z

zebra 〔zibrə ‖ ˈziːbrə〕
n. 【动】斑马[C]

zero 〔zɪro ‖ ˈzɪərəʊ〕
n. ❶零；零号[C]
❷(刻度表上的)零点，零位；(气温的)零摄氏度[U]

zone 〔zon ‖ zəʊn〕
n. [C] ❶地带；地区
I'd like to see Europe as a nuclear-free zone.
我希望欧洲成为无核区。
❷带；气候带；动植物分布带
Most of the world's wheat is grown in the north temperate zone.
世界上大部分小麦种植在北温带。
❸区；邮区；(电话等的)分区；时区

zoo 〔zu ‖ zuː〕
n. 动物园[C]

附录一

不规则动词表

Infinitive 不定式	Past Tense 过去式	Past Participle 过去分词
abide	abode, abided	abode, abided
alight	alighted	alighted
arise	arose	arisen
awake	awoke, awaked	awoken, awaked
be (am, is, are)	was, were	been
bear	bore	borne, born
beat	beat	beat, beaten
become	became	become
befall	befell	befallen
beget	begot	begotten, begot
begin	began	begun
behold	beheld	beheld
bend	bent	bent
bereave	bereaved, bereft	bereaved, bereft
beseech	besought, beseeched	besought, beseeched
beset	beset	beset
bespeak	bespoke	bespoken
bespread	bespread	bespread
bestrew	bestrewed	bestrewn, bestrewed
bestride	bestrode	bestridden
bet	bet, betted	bet, betted
betake	betook	betaken
bid	bade, bid	bidden, bid

Infinitive 不定式	Past Tense 过去式	Past Participle 过去分词
bide	bode, bided	bided
bind	bound	bound
bite	bit	bitten, bit
bleed	bled	bled
blend	blended, blent	blended, blent
bless	blessed, blest	blessed, blest
blow	blew	blown
break	broke	broken
breed	bred	bred
bring	brought	brought
broadcast	broadcast, broadcasted	broadcast, broadcasted
browbeat	browbeat	browbeaten
build	built	built
burn	burnt, burned	burnt, burned
burst	burst	burst
buy	bought	bought
cast	cast	cast
catch	caught	caught
chide	chid, chided	chid, chidden, chided(美)
choose	chose	chosen
cleave	cleft, clove	cleft, cloven
cling	clung	clung
clothe	clothed, clad(美)	clothed, clad(美)
come	came	come

cost	cost	cost
creep	crept	crept
crow	crowed, crew	crowed
cut	cut	cut
deal	dealt	dealt
dig	dug	dug
dispread	dispread	dispread
dive	dived, dove(美)	dived
do	did	done
draw	drew	drawn
dream	dreamed, dreamt	dreamed, dreamt
drink	drank	drunk
drive	drove	driven
dwell	dwelt, dwelled	dwelt, dwelled
eat	ate	eaten
fall	fell	fallen
feed	fed	fed
feel	felt	felt
fight	fought	fought
find	found	found
flee	fled	fled
fling	flung	flung
fly	flew	flown
forbear	forbore	forborne
forbid	forbade, forbad	forbidden
forecast	forecast, forecasted	forecast, forecasted
foreknow	foreknew	foreknown
foresee	foresaw	foreseen
foreshow	foreshowed	foreshown
foretell	foretold	foretold
forget	forgot	forgotten, forgot
forgive	forgave	forgiven
forsake	forsook	forsaken

forswear	forswore	forsworn
freeze	froze	frozen
gainsay	gainsaid	gainsaid
get	got	got, gotten(美)
gild	gilded, gilt	gilded, gilt
give	gave	given
go	went	gone
grind	ground	ground
grow	grew	grown
hamstring	hamstrung, hamstringed	hamstrung, hamstringed
hang[1]	hung	hung
hang[2]	hanged	hanged
have(has)	had	had
hear	heard	heard
heave[1]	heaved	heaved
heave[2]	hove	hove
hew	hewed	hewed, hewn
hide	hid	hidden
hit	hit	hit
hold	held	held
hurt	hurt	hurt
inlay	inlaid	inlaid
keep	kept	kept
kneel	knelt, kneeled(美)	knelt, kneeled(美)
knit	knit, knitted	knit, knitted
know	knew	known
lade	laded	laded, laden
lay	laid	laid
lead	led	led
lean	leant, leaned(美)	leant, leaned(美)
leap	leapt, leaped(美)	leapt, leaped(美)
learn	learned, learnt	learned, learnt

leave	left	left
lend	lent	lent
let	let	let
lie[1]	lay	lain
lie[2]	lied	lied
light	lit, lighted	lit, lighted
lose	lost	lost
make	made	made
mean	meant	meant
meet	met	met
melt	melted	melted, molten
misdeal	misdealt	misdealt
misgive	misgave	misgiven
mislay	mislaid	mislaid
mislead	misled	misled
misspell	misspelt, misspelled	misspelt, misspelled
misspend	misspent	misspent
mistake	mistook	mistaken
misunderstand	misunderstood	misunderstood
mow	mowed	mowed, mown
outbid	outbid, outbade(美)	outbid, outbidden(美)
outbreed	outbred	outbred
outdo	outdid	outdone
outgrow	outgrew	outgrown
outlay	outlaid	outlaid
outride	outrode	outridden
outrun	outran	outrun
outsell	outsold	outsold
outshine	outshone	outshone
outshoot	outshot	outshot
outsit	outsat	outsat
outspend	outspent	outspent
outspread	outspread	outspread
outwear	outwore	outworn
overbid	overbid	overbidden, overbid
overbuy	overbought	overbought
overcast	overcast	overcast
overcome	overcame	overcome
overdo	overdid	overdone
overdraw	overdrew	overdrawn
overdrive	overdrove	overdriven
overeat	overate	overeaten
overfeed	overfed	overfed
overfly	overflew	overflown
overgrow	overgrew	overgrown
overhang	overhung	overhung
overhear	overheard	overheard
overlap	overlapped	overlapped
overlay	overlaid	overlaid
overleap	overleapt, overleaped	overleapt, overleaped
overlie	overlay	overlain
overpay	overpaid	overpaid
override	overrode	overridden
overrun	overran	overrun
oversee	oversaw	overseen
overset	overset	overset
overshoot	overshot	overshot
oversleep	overslept	overslept
overspend	overspent	overspent
overspread	overspread	overspread
overtake	overtook	overtaken
overthrow	overthrew	overthrown
overwind	overwound	overwound
overwrite	overwrote	overwritten

partake	partook	partaken
pay	paid	paid
precast	precast	precast
prove	proved	proved, proven
put	put	put
quit	quit, quitted	quit, quitted
read	read[red]	read[red]
rebuild	rebuilt	rebuilt
recast	recast	recast
redo	redid	redone
reeve	reeved, rove	reeved, rove
relay	relaid	relaid
remake	remade	remade
rend	rent	rent
repay	repaid	repaid
reset	reset	reset
retell	retold	retold
rewrite	rewrote	rewritten
rid	rid, ridded	rid, ridded
ride	rode	ridden
ring[1]	rang	rung
ring[2]	ringed	ringed
rise	rose	risen
rive	rived	riven, rived
run	ran	run
saw	sawed	sawn, sawed(美)
say	said	said
see	saw	seen
seek	sought	sought
sell	sold	sold
send	sent	sent
set	set	set
sew	sewed	sewn, sewed(美)

shake	shook	shaken
shave	shaved	shaved, shaven
shear	sheared	sheared, shorn
shed	shed	shed
shine	shone	shone
shoe	shod, shoed	shod, shoed
shoot	shot	shot
show	showed	shown, showed(美)
shred	shredded, shred	shredded, shred
shrink	shrank, shrunk	shrunk, shrunken
shrive	shrove, shrived	shriven, shrived
shut	shut	shut
sing	sang	sung
sink	sank, sunk(美)	sunk, sunken(美)
sit	sat	sat
slay	slew	slain
sleep	slept	slept
slide	slid	slid
sling	slung	slung
slink	slunk	slunk
slit	slit	slit
smell	smelt, smelled(美)	smelt, smelled(美)
smite	smote	smitten, smote(美)
sow	sowed	sown, sowed
speak	spoke	spoken
speed	sped, speeded(美)	sped, speeded(美)

spell	spelt, spelled	spelt, spelled
spend	spent	spent
spill	spilled, spilt	spilled, spilt
spin	spun	spun
spit	spat, spit(美)	spat, spit(美)
split	split	split
spoil	spoiled, spoilt	spoiled, spoilt
spread	spread	spread
spring	sprang, sprung(美)	sprung
stand	stood	stood
stave	staved, stove	staved, stove
steal	stole	stolen
stick	stuck	stuck
sting	stung	stung
stink	stank, stunk	stunk
strew	strewed	strewn, strewed
stride	strode	stridden
strike	struck	struck, stricken
string	strung	strung
strive	strove, strived(美)	striven, strived
swear	swore	sworn
sweat	sweat, sweated	sweat, sweated
sweep	swept	swept
swell	swelled	swollen, swelled
swim	swam	swum
swing	swung	swung
take	took	taken
teach	taught	taught
tear	tore	torn
tell	told	told
think	thought	thought
thrive	throve, thrived	thriven, thrived
throw	threw	thrown
thrust	thrust	thrust
tread	trod	trodden, trod
unbend	unbent	unbent
unbind	unbound	unbound
unbuild	unbuilt	unbuilt
underbid	underbid	underbidden, underbid
underbuy	underbought	underbought
undercut	undercut	undercut
underfeed	underfed	underfed
undergo	underwent	undergone
underlay	underlaid	underlaid
underlet	underlet	underlet
underlie	underlay	underlain
underpay	underpaid	underpaid
undersell	undersold	undersold
undershoot	undershot	undershot
understand	understood	understood
undertake	undertook	undertaken
underwrite	underwrote	underwritten
undo	undid	undone
undraw	undrew	undrawn
unfreeze	unfroze	unfrozen
ungird	ungirded, ungirt	ungirded, ungirt
unhang	unhung	unhung
unknit	unknitted, unknit	unknitted, unknit
unlade	unladed	unladed, unladen
unlay	unlaid	unlaid

unlearn	unlearnt, unlearned	unlearnt, unlearned
unmake	unmade	unmade
unreeve	unrove, unreeved	unrove, unreeved
unsay	unsaid	unsaid
unset	unset	unset
unsling	unslung	unslung
unstick	unstuck	unstuck
unstring	unstrung	unstrung
unswear	unswore	unsworn
unteach	untaught	untaught
unthink	unthought	unthought
untread	untrod	untrodden, untrod
unweave	unwove	unwoven
unwind	unwound	unwound
upbuild	upbuilt	upbuilt
uphold	upheld	upheld
uppercut	uppercut	uppercut

uprise	uprose	uprisen
upset	upset	upset
upsweep	upswept	upswept
upswing	upswung	upswung
wake	waked, woke	waked, woken
waylay	waylaid	waylaid
wear	wore	worn
weave[1]	wove	woven
weave[2]	weaved	weaved
wed	wedded, wed	wedded, wed
weep	wept	wept
wet	wet, wetted	wet, wetted
win	won	won
wind[1]	winded	winded
wind[2]	wound	wound
withdraw	withdrew	withdrawn
withhold	withheld	withheld
withstand	withstood	withstood
wring	wrung	wrung
write	wrote	written

附录二

数字的读法

Ⅰ Cardinals 基数词

68	sixty-eight
100	a[one]hundred
102	a[one]hundred(and)two
746	seven hundred (and) forty-six
1,000	a[one]thousand [a 只用于一个数字的开头,后面有百位数时要用 one thousand]
1,100	one thousand,one hundred [两处均不用 a]
5,647	five thousand,six hundred and forty-seven
10,000	ten thousand
100,000	a[one]hundred thousand
1,000,000	a[one]million
100,000,000	a[one]hundred million
563,032,406	five hundred and sixty-three million, thirty-two thousand, four hundred and six [and 只放在“百”与后面的数之间]
十亿	[英]a[one]thousand million
	[美]a[one]billion
百亿	[英]ten thousand million
	[美]ten billion
千亿	[英]one hundred thousand million
	[美]one hundred billion
万亿(兆)	[英]one billion
	[美]one trillion

Ⅱ Fractions 分数

1/2	a[one]half

附录

1/3	a[one]third
1/4	a quarter[one fourth]
1/5	a[one]fifth
2/3	two thirds
9/10	nine tenths
12¾	twelve and three quarters
10%	ten per cent
5‰	five per mill

Ⅲ Decimals 小数

0.7	nought[zero]point seven; point seven
0.02	point nought two
356.409	three hundred and fifty-six point four nought nine
$28.3\dot{7}$	twenty-eight point three seven, seven recurring
0.5%	decimal five percent

(注：读门牌、电话、账号等，把数字一个个分开说。0 常读作[əʊ]，而在测定计量时说 zero，如 Room 306 读作 Room three o six；-11.4℃读作 eleven point four degrees below zero Centigrade)

Ⅳ Mathematic Forms 数学式

9+3=12	Nine plus three equals twelve.
8+2=10	Eight and two are ten.
7+0=7	Seven and nought is equal to seven.
20+14+56=90	Twenty, fourteen and fifty-six added together are [make]ninety.
13−5=8	Thirteen minus five equals [is equal to]eight.
3−2=1	Two from three leaves one.
1×1=1	One multiplied by one equals one; Once one is one.
2×5=10	Twice five is ten.
6×0=0	Six multiplied by nought equals nought.
7×8=56	Seven times eight is fifty-six.
20÷5=4	Twenty divided by five makes [is equal to]four.
24÷3=8	Three into twenty-four goes eight times.
1∶3=3∶9	One is to three as three is to nine; The ratio of one to three equals the ratio of three to nine.

a^2	a square; a squared
x^3	x cube; x cubed; cube x
$a^2+3b=8$	a squared and three times b makes eight.
$\sqrt{120}$	The square [second] root of one hundred and twenty.
$\sqrt[3]{309}$	The cube [third] root of three hundred and nine.

V Year 年份(表示在某年或某年代用介词 in)

206 B. C.	two o[əʊ] six B. C. [ˌbiːˈsiː]
770	seven seventy, seven seven o[əʊ], seven hundred and seventy
1900	nineteen hundred
19—	nineteen something
1905	nineteen o[əʊ] five
1992	nineteen ninety-two
2000	two thousand
2001	two thousand and one
1990's [1990s]	nineteen nineties (20 世纪 90 年代)

(注:年、月、日的写法与读法:Dec. 31(st), 1918 读作 December thirty-first [the thirty-first of December] nineteen eighteen. 在"某日"前用 on;在年份与日期之间用逗号)

附录三

附录

学校里的常用语言

教学用具

bookends	书夹
blackboard	黑板
lecture platform	讲台
magnifier	放大镜
pointer	教鞭
wall map; hanging chart	挂图
pencil box	铅笔盒
eraser	橡皮
ruler	尺
triangle	三角板
compass	圆规
pencil sharpener	卷笔刀
pin; office pin	大头针
paper clip	曲别针
clip	书钉;回形针
paste	糨糊
correction fluid	修改液
glue	胶水
wastebasket	废纸篓
ball pen	圆珠笔
fountain pen	钢笔
ink	墨水
eraser	黑板擦
Chinese writing brush	毛笔
chalk	粉笔
wax crayon	蜡笔
protractor	量角器
globe	地球仪
tack	图钉
lantern slide	幻灯片
stapler	订书机
staples	订书钉

课 程

required(compulsory)course	必修课
minor course	副课
political course; politics	政治课
Chinese	语文
Russian	俄语
arithmetic	算术
trigonometry(trig.)	三角学
plane (solid, analytical) geometry	平面(立体,解析)几何
history	历史
composition	作文
spoken language	口语
music	音乐
biology	生物学
major course	主课
basic course	基础课
physical education; PE	体育
English	英语
mathematics; maths	数学
algebra	代数

geometry 几何
physics 物理
chemistry 化学
geography 地理
politics 政治
arts 美术
drawing 图画
zoology 动物学

学校生活

学生生活

student body card; student's identity card 学生证
school-fee 学费
a "three-good" student 三好学生
holidays 假期
summer vacation 暑假
winter vacation 寒假
summer camp 夏令营
sports meeting; athletic meeting 运动会
school band 学校乐队
recreational activities; recreation 文娱活动
after-school activities 校外活动
English Evening 英语晚会
military training 军训
gate 校门
school paper 校报
school uniform 校服
school doctor 校医
school bus 校车
record of formal schooling 学历
physical examination 体格检查
dormitory 学生宿舍
electric lamp 电灯
to cut class 旷课
clothes-hanger 吊衣架
graduate 毕业生
duty roster; rota 值日表
clinic 医务室
newspaper 报纸
wall newspaper 墙报
class book 班级点名册
diary 日记本
exercise book 练习册
birthday card 生日卡
post card 明信片
New Year's Eve entertainment 除夕晚会
to enter a higher school 升学
to repeat the year's work 留级
to miss a class 缺课
bookshelf 书架
to make up a missed lesson 补课
voluntary labour 义务劳动
the anniversary of the founding of a school 校庆
school badge 校徽
school regulations 校规
dining-room 食堂
classroom building 教学楼
lab 实验室

附录

language lab 语言实验室
library 图书馆
reading-room 阅览室
music room 音乐室
gymnasium 体育室，健身房
conference room 会议室
auditorium 礼堂
broadcasting room 广播室
honour roll 光荣榜
complaint box 意见箱
parking place 停车场
bicycle shed 自行车棚
schedule; school timetable 课程表
to have four classes/ periods 上 4 节课
to have a PE (physical education) class 有 1 节体育课
to study by oneself in scheduled time (free time) 自习
open class 公开课

学校组织机构及人员

committee on school affairs 校务委员会
president (大学)校长
dean 系主任
Youth League general branch 团总支
Secretary of League general branch 团总支书记
Secretary of League sub-branch 团支部书记
The Students' Union; Student Council 学生会
Chairman of the Students' Union 学生会主席
The Young Pioneers Committee 少先队委
Supervisor of the Young Pioneers 少先队辅导员
Captain 大队长
Section Leader 中队长
to visit a class 听课
Squad Leader 小队长
head teacher; class adviser 班主任
president of class 班主席
class committee 班委
monitor; class monitor 班长
vice-monitor 副班长
Student in charge of studies 学习委员
Student in charge of propaganda work 宣传委员
Student in charge of recreational activities 文娱委员
Student in charge of general affairs 生活委员
Student in charge of physical education 体育委员
group leader 小组长
Student in charge of English study 英语课代表
student on duty 值日生

作息时间表

A. M.（上午）

6:00	Getting up	起床
6:20-6:40	Morning exercises	早操
6:50-7:20	Breakfast	早饭
7:30-8:00	Morning reading	早读
8:00	First bell	预备铃
8:10-8:55	1st period	第一节
9:05-9:50	2nd period	第二节
9:50-10:10	Setting-up exercises	健身(课间)操
10:10-10:55	3rd period	第三节
11:05-11:50	4th period	第四节
12:00	Lunch	午饭

P. M.（下午）

12:00-2:00	Noon rest	午休
2:30-3:15	5th period	第五节
3:25-4:10	6th period	第六节
4:20-5:50	Sports and Recreational Activities	文体活动
6:00	Supper	晚饭
7:30-9:00	Self-study	自习
9:15	Going to bed	就寝
9:30	Lights out	熄灯

考试与测验

test; quiz	测验
exam; examination	考试
entrance exam	入学考试
end-of-the-unit exam	单元考试
mid-term exam	期中考试
open-book exam	开卷考试
graduation exam	毕业考试
final exam; final	期末考试
fail	不及格
pass	及格;通过
reciting	背诵
writing from memory	默写
written examination	笔试
oral examination	口试
dictation	听写
multiple-choice test	选择题
make-up examination	补考
marks	分数
grading	打分数
report card	成绩单
A(excellent)	优
B(superior)	良
C(average)	中
D(fail)	劣

附录

各类学校名称

kindergarten 幼儿园
primary (elementary) school 小学
junior (senior) high school 初(高)中
middle school 中学
experimental middle school 实验中学
agricultural middle school 农业中学
college 学院、专科学校
institute 大学、学院
university 大学
spare-time college 业余大学
institute of foreign languages 外语学院
normal university; teachers' university 师范大学
university of science and engineering 理工科大学
institute for nationalities 民族学院
teachers' college 师范学院
physical culture institute 体育学院
medical college 医学院
college of economics 经济学院
secondary professional training school 中等专科学校
dancing school 舞蹈学校
health school 卫生学校
adult school 成人学校
school for kindergarten teachers 幼儿师范学校
normal school 师范学校
commercial school 商业学校
attached school 附属学校
evening (night) school 夜校